Polar
Vortex

DENISE DORRANCE

Polar Vortex

A FAMILY MEMOIR

THE EXPERIMENT

NEW YORK

Mother's Day 1968

IN MEMORY OF MY MOM

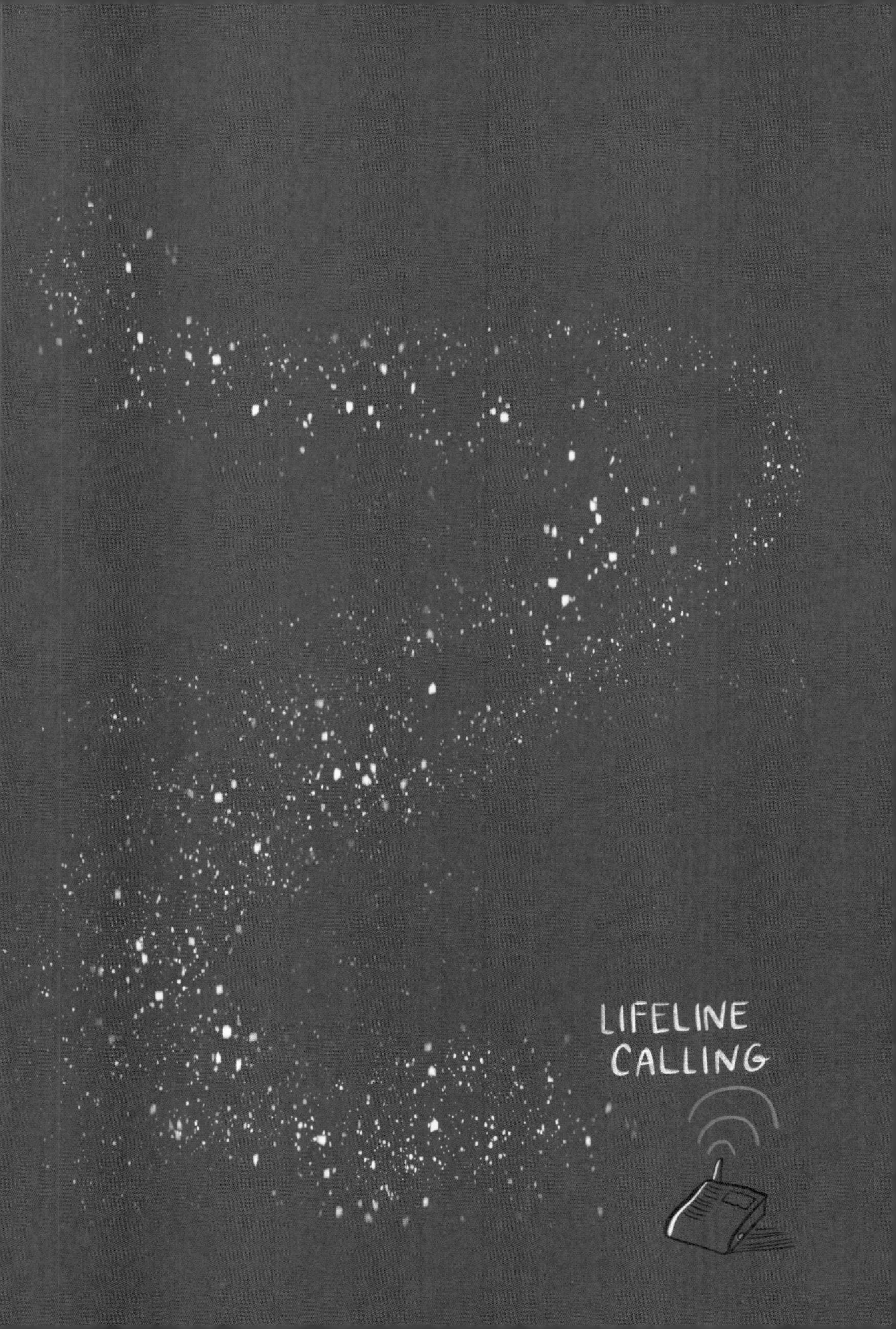
LIFELINE
CALLING

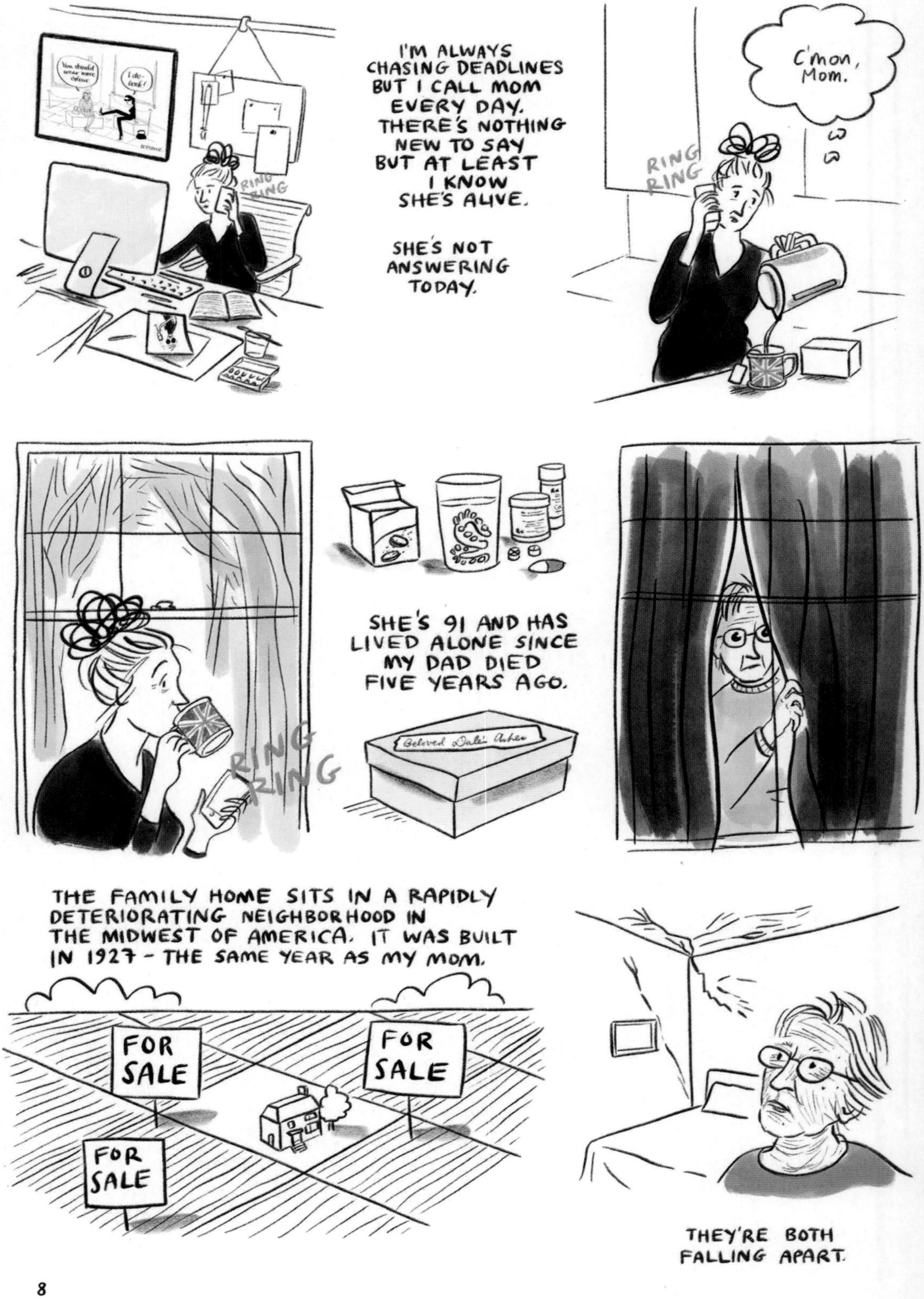
RING RING
I'M ALWAYS CHASING DEADLINES BUT I CALL MOM EVERY DAY. THERE'S NOTHING NEW TO SAY BUT AT LEAST I KNOW SHE'S ALIVE.
SHE'S NOT ANSWERING TODAY.
RING RING
C'mon, Mom.
RING RING
SHE'S 91 AND HAS LIVED ALONE SINCE MY DAD DIED FIVE YEARS AGO.
Beloved Dale's Ashes
THE FAMILY HOME SITS IN A RAPIDLY DETERIORATING NEIGHBORHOOD IN THE MIDWEST OF AMERICA. IT WAS BUILT IN 1927 - THE SAME YEAR AS MY MOM.
FOR SALE
FOR SALE
FOR SALE
THEY'RE BOTH FALLING APART.

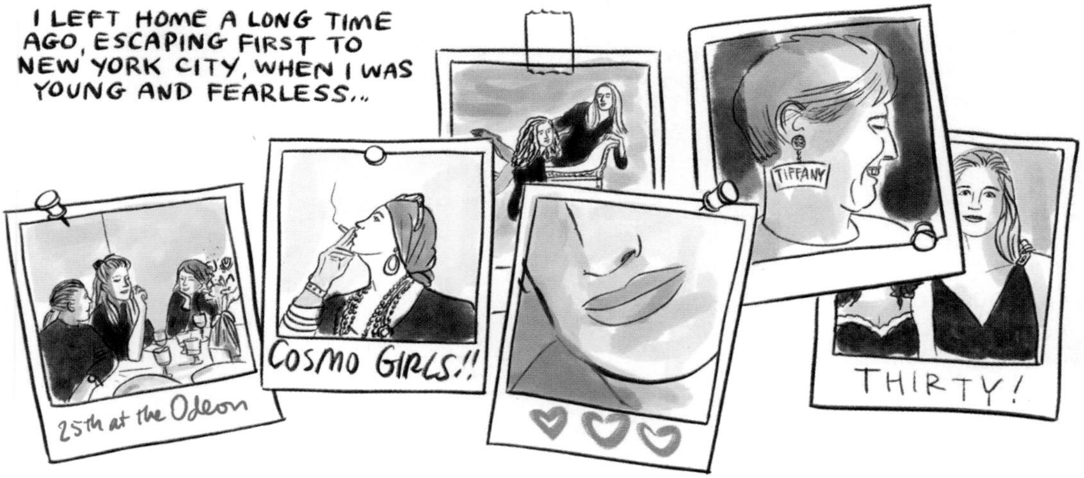
I LEFT HOME A LONG TIME AGO, ESCAPING FIRST TO NEW YORK CITY, WHEN I WAS YOUNG AND FEARLESS...
25th at the Odeon
COSMO GIRLS!!
TIFFANY
THIRTY!

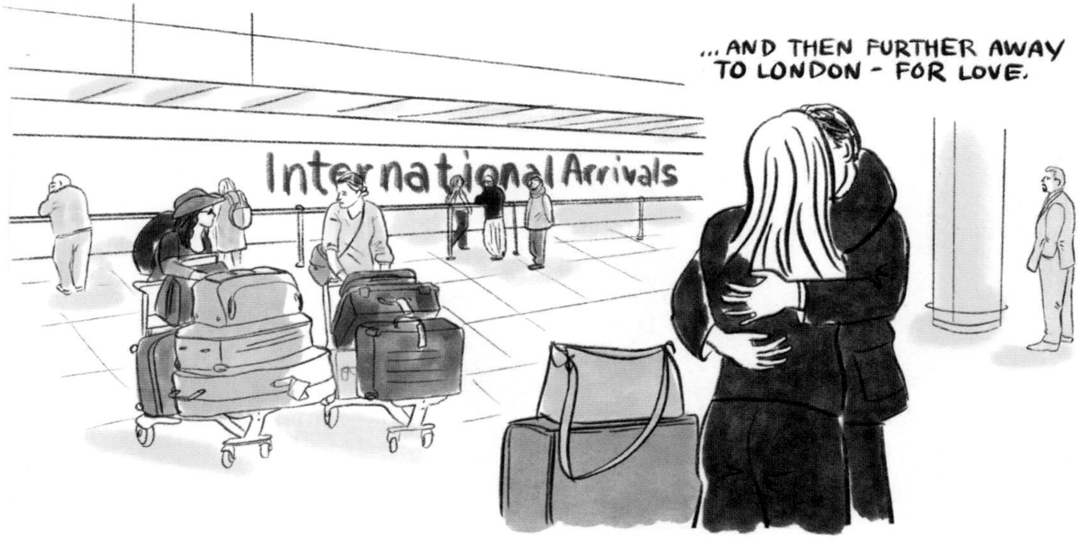
International Arrivals
...AND THEN FURTHER AWAY TO LONDON - FOR LOVE.

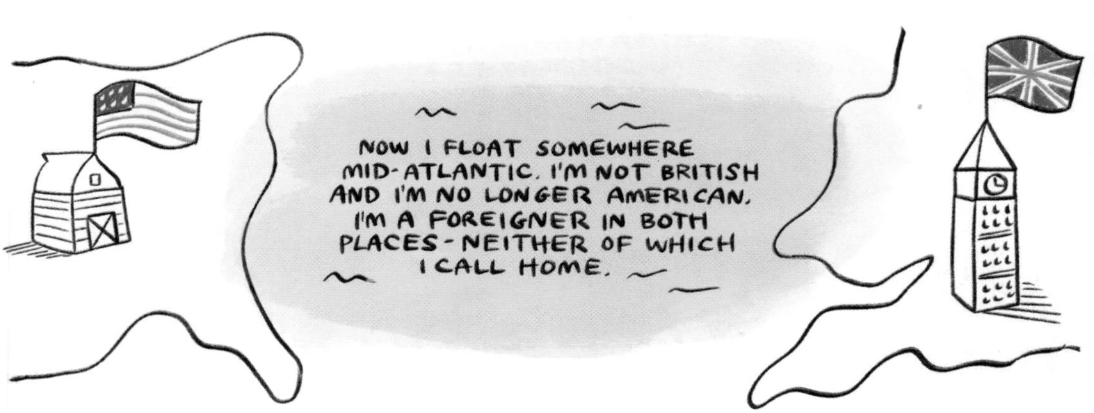
NOW I FLOAT SOMEWHERE MID-ATLANTIC. I'M NOT BRITISH AND I'M NO LONGER AMERICAN. I'M A FOREIGNER IN BOTH PLACES - NEITHER OF WHICH I CALL HOME.

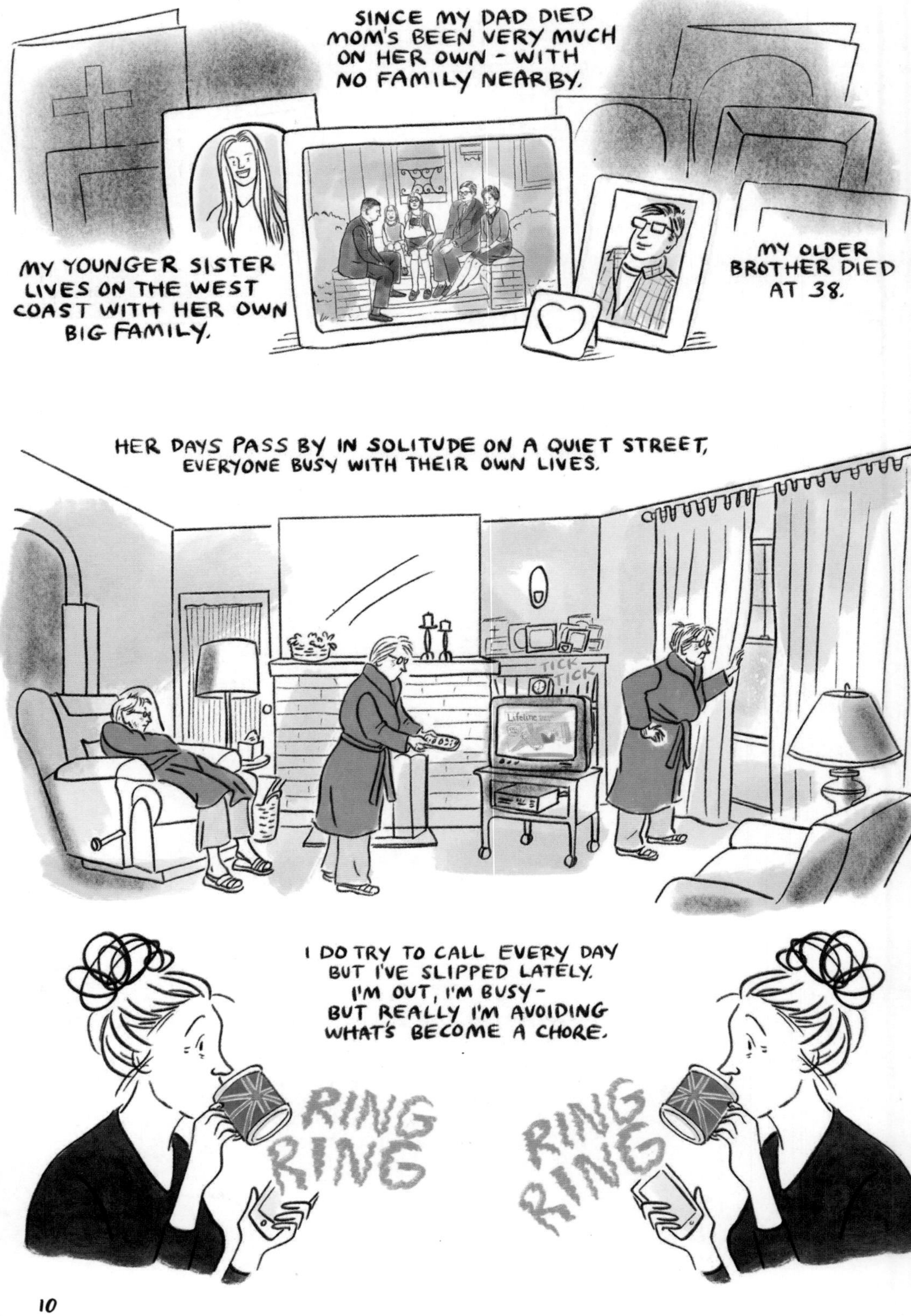
SINCE MY DAD DIED MOM'S BEEN VERY MUCH ON HER OWN - WITH NO FAMILY NEARBY.
MY YOUNGER SISTER LIVES ON THE WEST COAST WITH HER OWN BIG FAMILY.
MY OLDER BROTHER DIED AT 38.
HER DAYS PASS BY IN SOLITUDE ON A QUIET STREET, EVERYONE BUSY WITH THEIR OWN LIVES.
TICK TICK
Lifeline
I DO TRY TO CALL EVERY DAY BUT I'VE SLIPPED LATELY. I'M OUT, I'M BUSY - BUT REALLY I'M AVOIDING WHAT'S BECOME A CHORE.
RING RING
RING RING

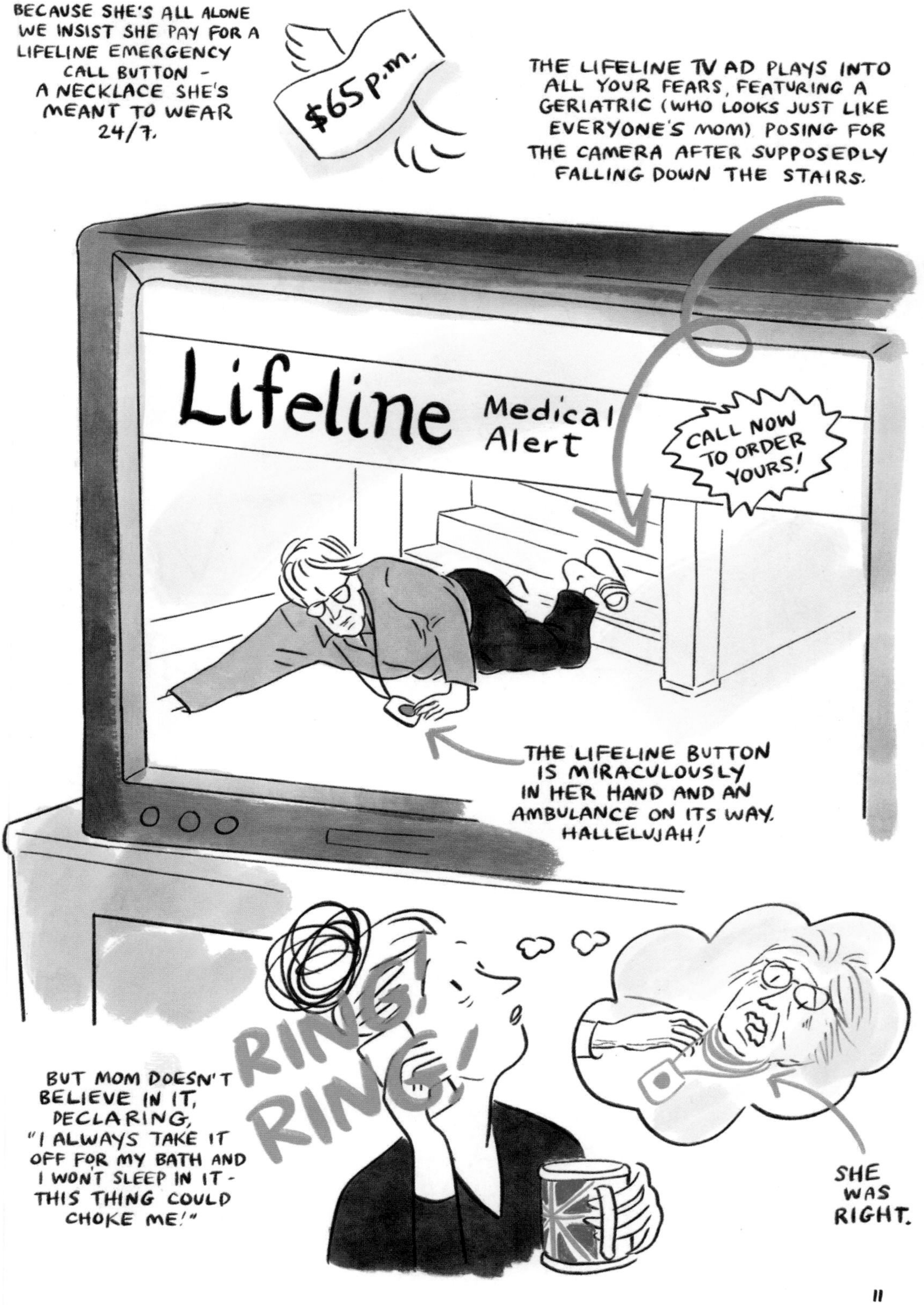
BECAUSE SHE'S ALL ALONE WE INSIST SHE PAY FOR A LIFELINE EMERGENCY CALL BUTTON - A NECKLACE SHE'S MEANT TO WEAR 24/7.
$65 p.m.
THE LIFELINE TV AD PLAYS INTO ALL YOUR FEARS, FEATURING A GERIATRIC (WHO LOOKS JUST LIKE EVERYONE'S MOM) POSING FOR THE CAMERA AFTER SUPPOSEDLY FALLING DOWN THE STAIRS.
Lifeline
Medical Alert
CALL NOW TO ORDER YOURS!
THE LIFELINE BUTTON IS MIRACULOUSLY IN HER HAND AND AN AMBULANCE ON ITS WAY. HALLELUJAH!
BUT MOM DOESN'T BELIEVE IN IT, DECLARING, "I ALWAYS TAKE IT OFF FOR MY BATH AND I WON'T SLEEP IN IT - THIS THING COULD CHOKE ME!"
RING! RING!
SHE WAS RIGHT.

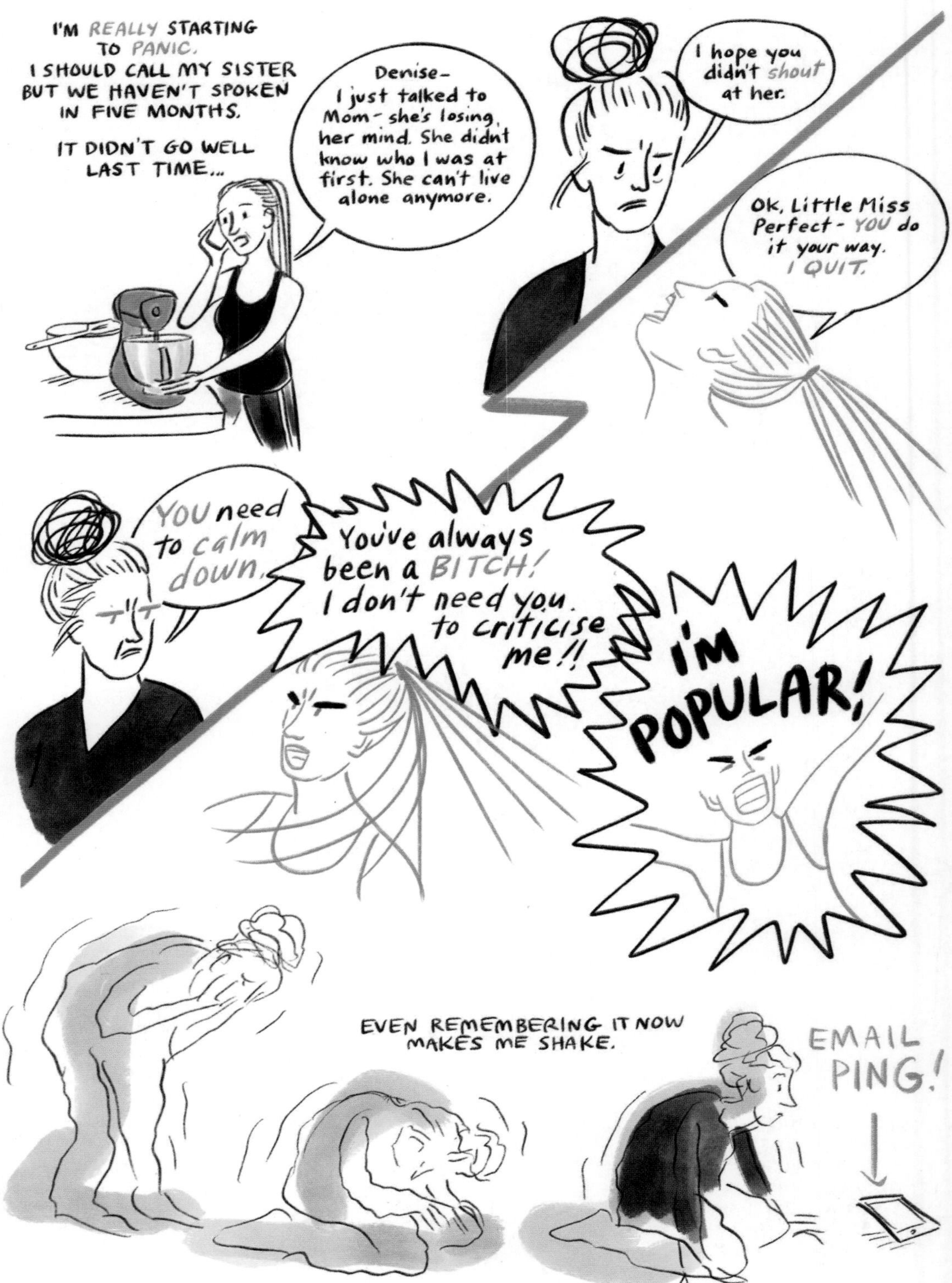
I'M REALLY STARTING TO PANIC.
I SHOULD CALL MY SISTER BUT WE HAVEN'T SPOKEN IN FIVE MONTHS.
IT DIDN'T GO WELL LAST TIME...
Denise- I just talked to Mom- she's losing her mind. She didn't know who I was at first. She can't live alone anymore.
I hope you didn't shout at her.
Ok, Little Miss Perfect - YOU do it your way. I QUIT.
YOU need to calm down.
You've always been a BITCH! I don't need you to criticise me!!
I'M POPULAR!
EVEN REMEMBERING IT NOW MAKES ME SHAKE.
EMAIL PING!

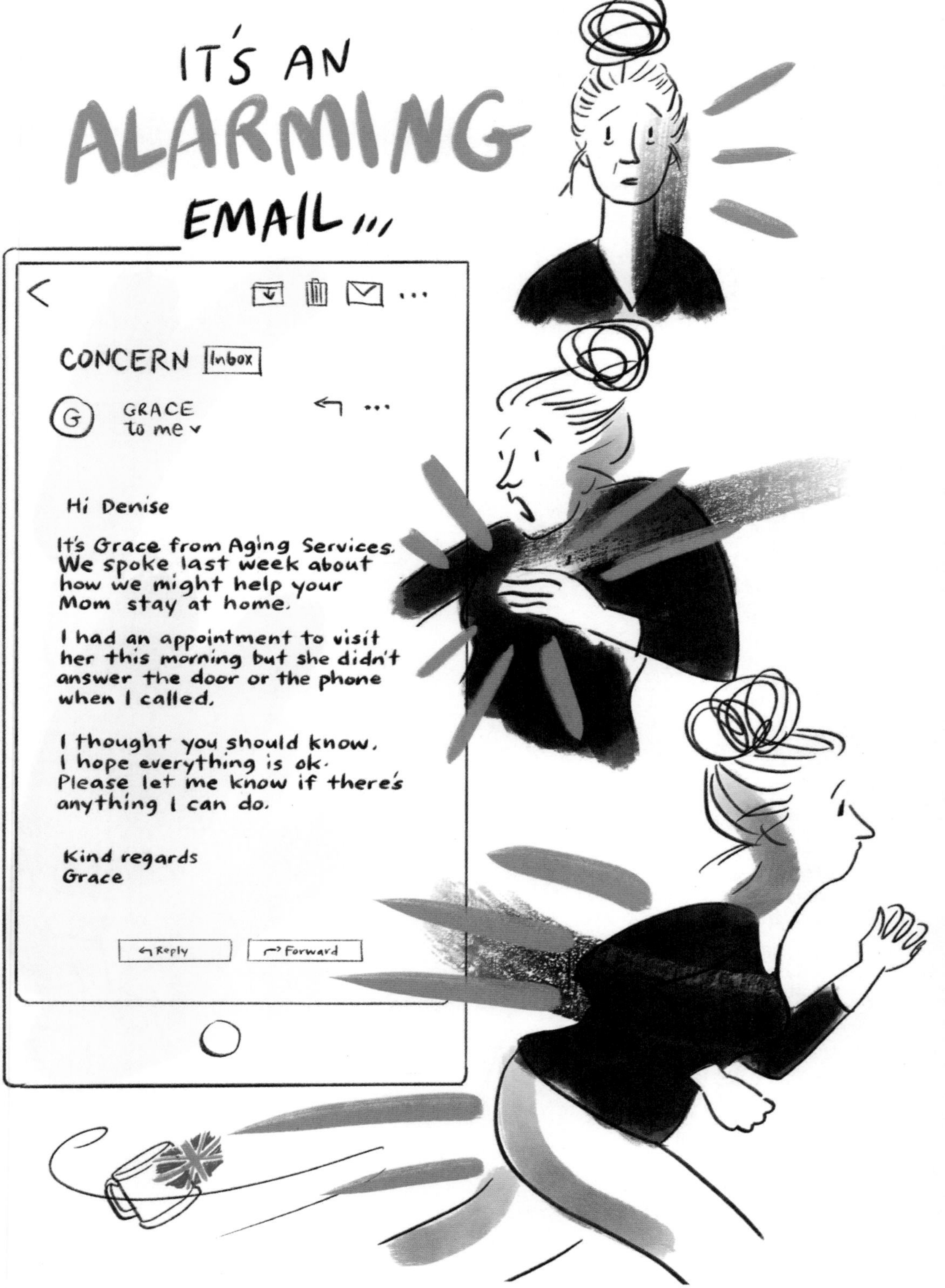
IT'S AN ALARMING EMAIL...
CONCERN Inbox
GRACE
to me
Hi Denise
It's Grace from Aging Services. We spoke last week about how we might help your Mom stay at home.
I had an appointment to visit her this morning but she didn't answer the door or the phone when I called.
I thought you should know. I hope everything is ok. Please let me know if there's anything I can do.
Kind regards
Grace
Reply
Forward

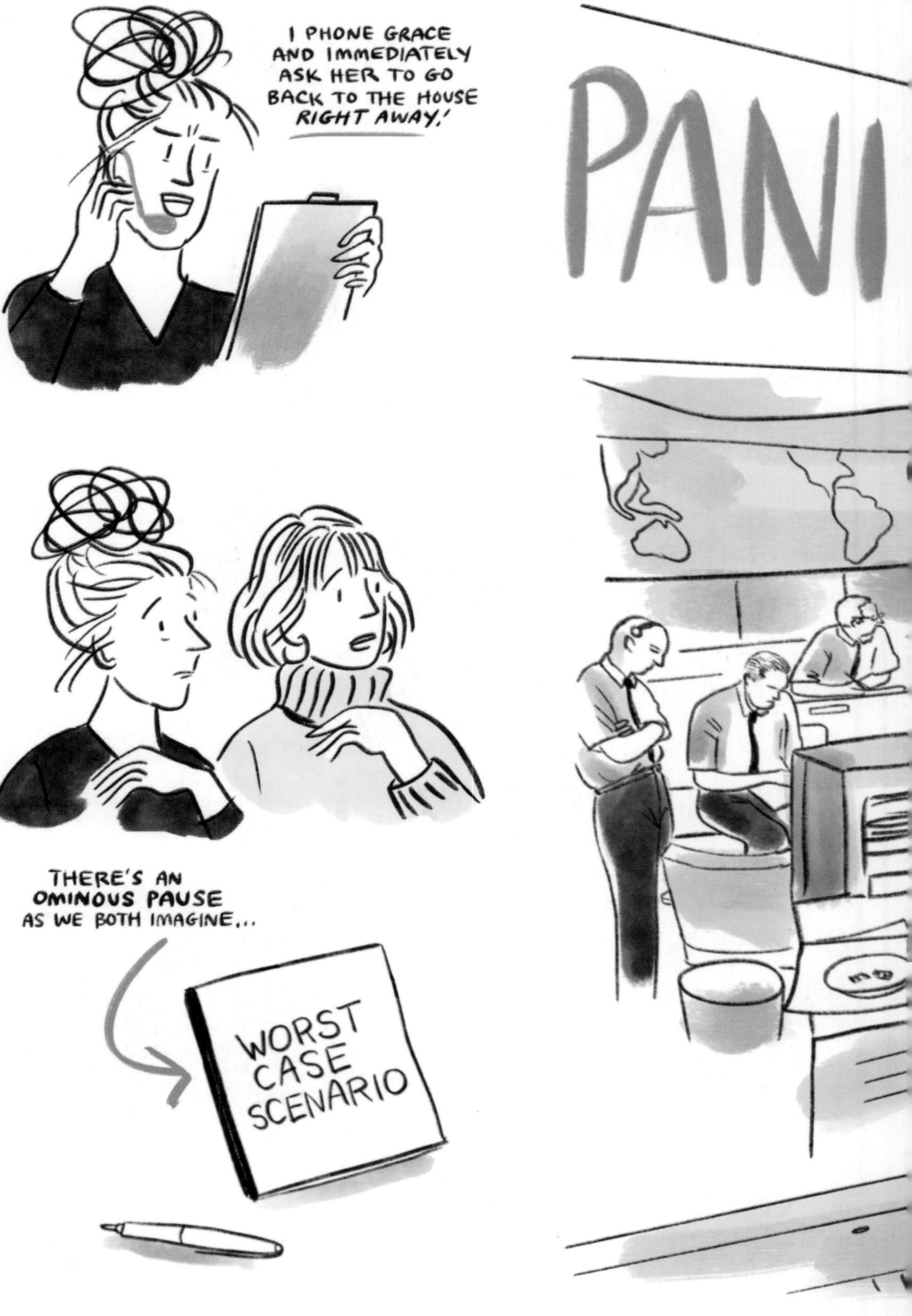
I PHONE GRACE AND IMMEDIATELY ASK HER TO GO BACK TO THE HOUSE *RIGHT AWAY!*
THERE'S AN OMINOUS PAUSE AS WE BOTH IMAGINE...
WORST CASE SCENARIO
PANI

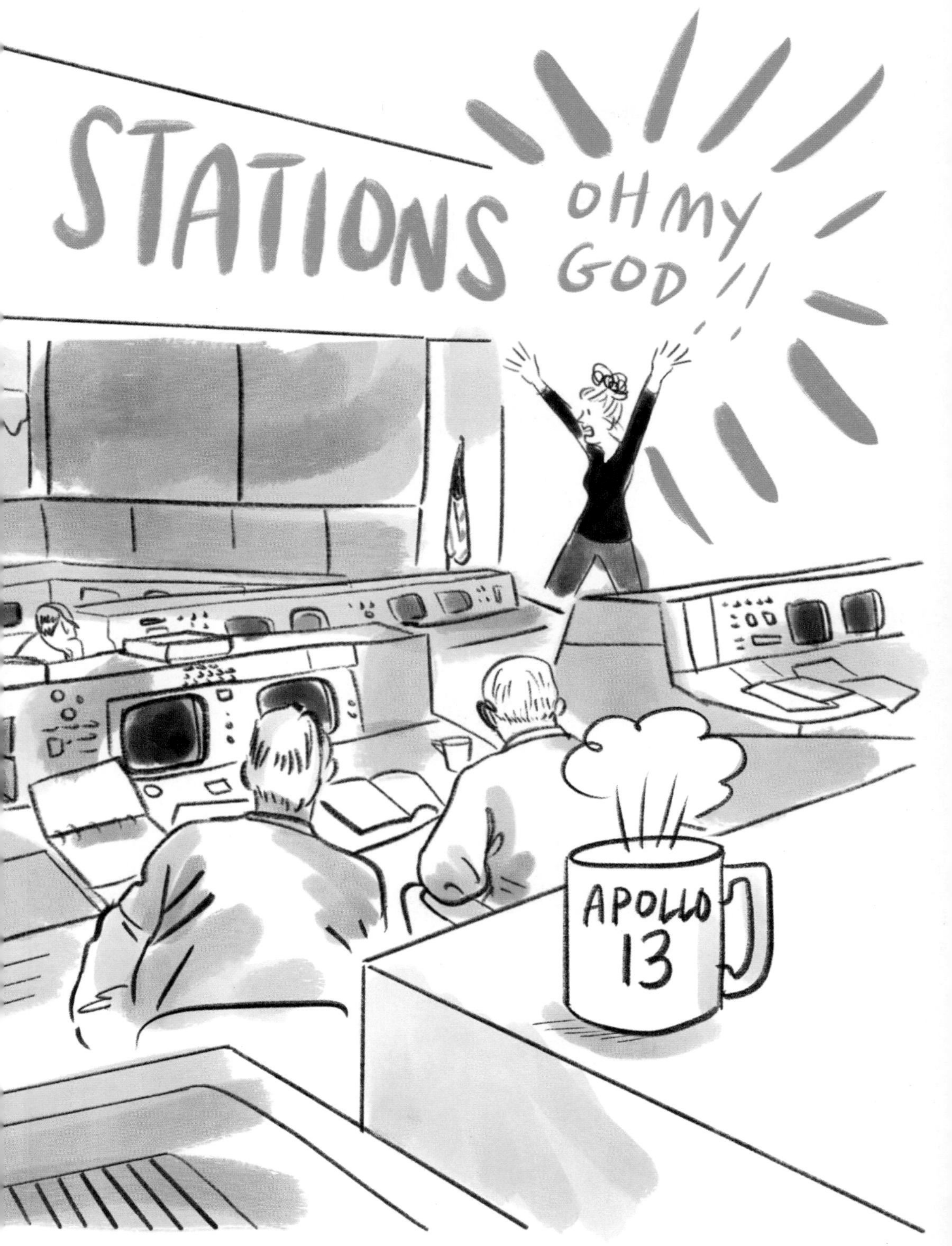
STATIONS
OH MY GOD
APOLLO 13

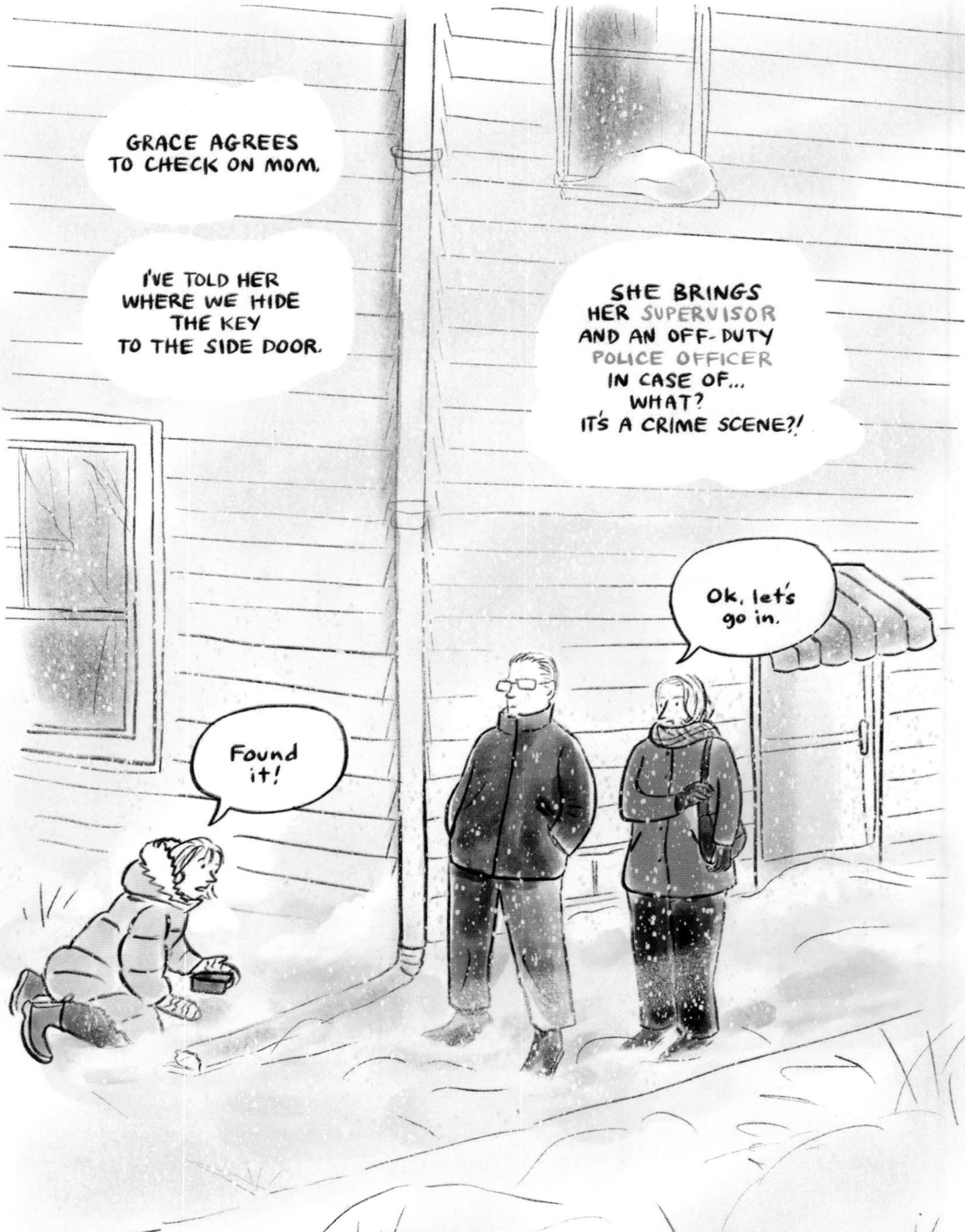
GRACE AGREES TO CHECK ON MOM.
I'VE TOLD HER WHERE WE HIDE THE KEY TO THE SIDE DOOR.
SHE BRINGS HER SUPERVISOR AND AN OFF-DUTY POLICE OFFICER IN CASE OF... WHAT? IT'S A CRIME SCENE?!
Ok, let's go in.
Found it!

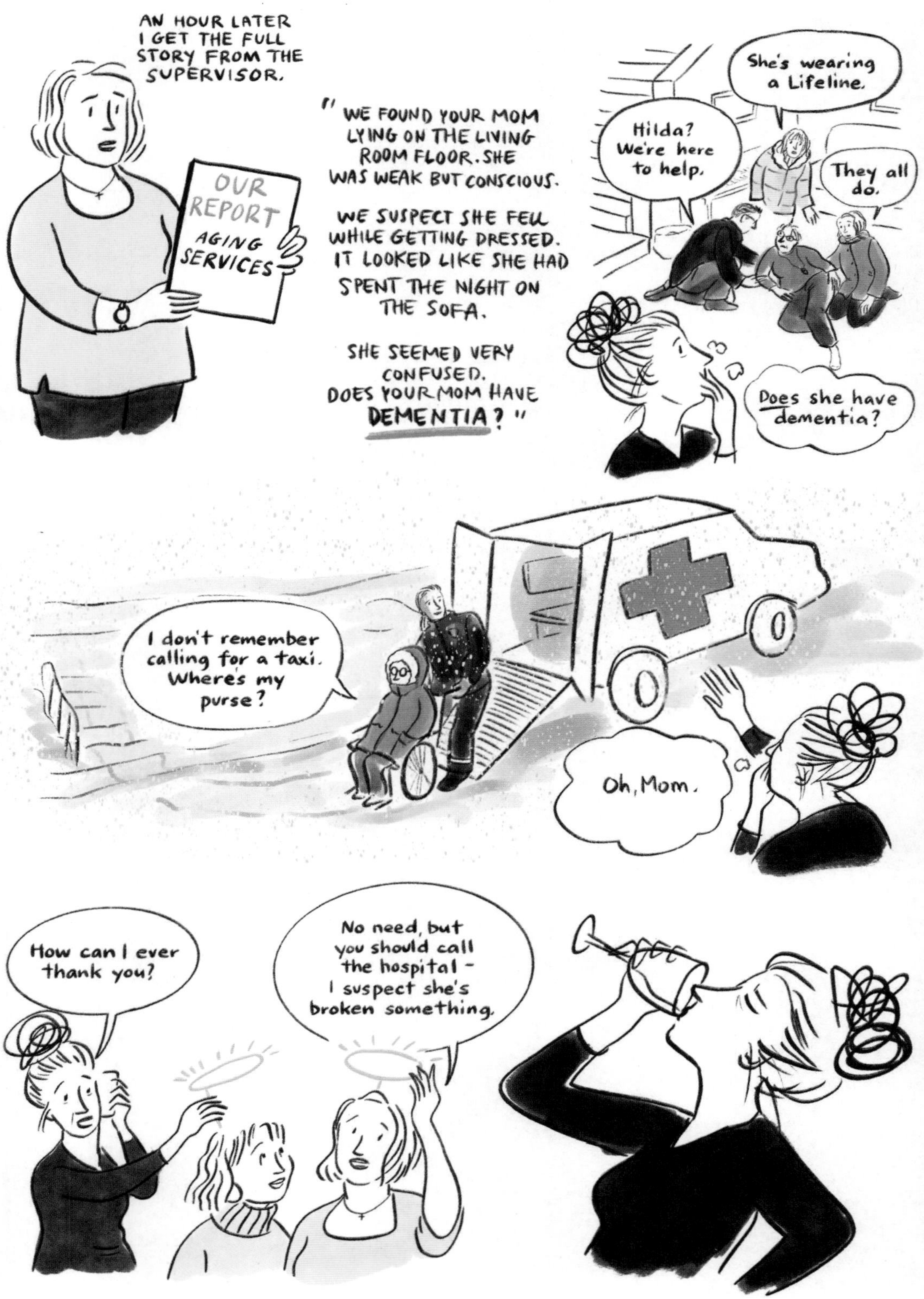

AN HOUR LATER I GET THE FULL STORY FROM THE SUPERVISOR.
OUR REPORT
AGING SERVICES
"WE FOUND YOUR MOM LYING ON THE LIVING ROOM FLOOR. SHE WAS WEAK BUT CONSCIOUS.
WE SUSPECT SHE FELL WHILE GETTING DRESSED. IT LOOKED LIKE SHE HAD SPENT THE NIGHT ON THE SOFA.
SHE SEEMED VERY CONFUSED. DOES YOUR MOM HAVE DEMENTIA?"
She's wearing a Lifeline.
Hilda? We're here to help.
They all do.
Does she have dementia?
I don't remember calling for a taxi. Where's my purse?
Oh, Mom.
How can I ever thank you?
No need, but you should call the hospital - I suspect she's broken something.

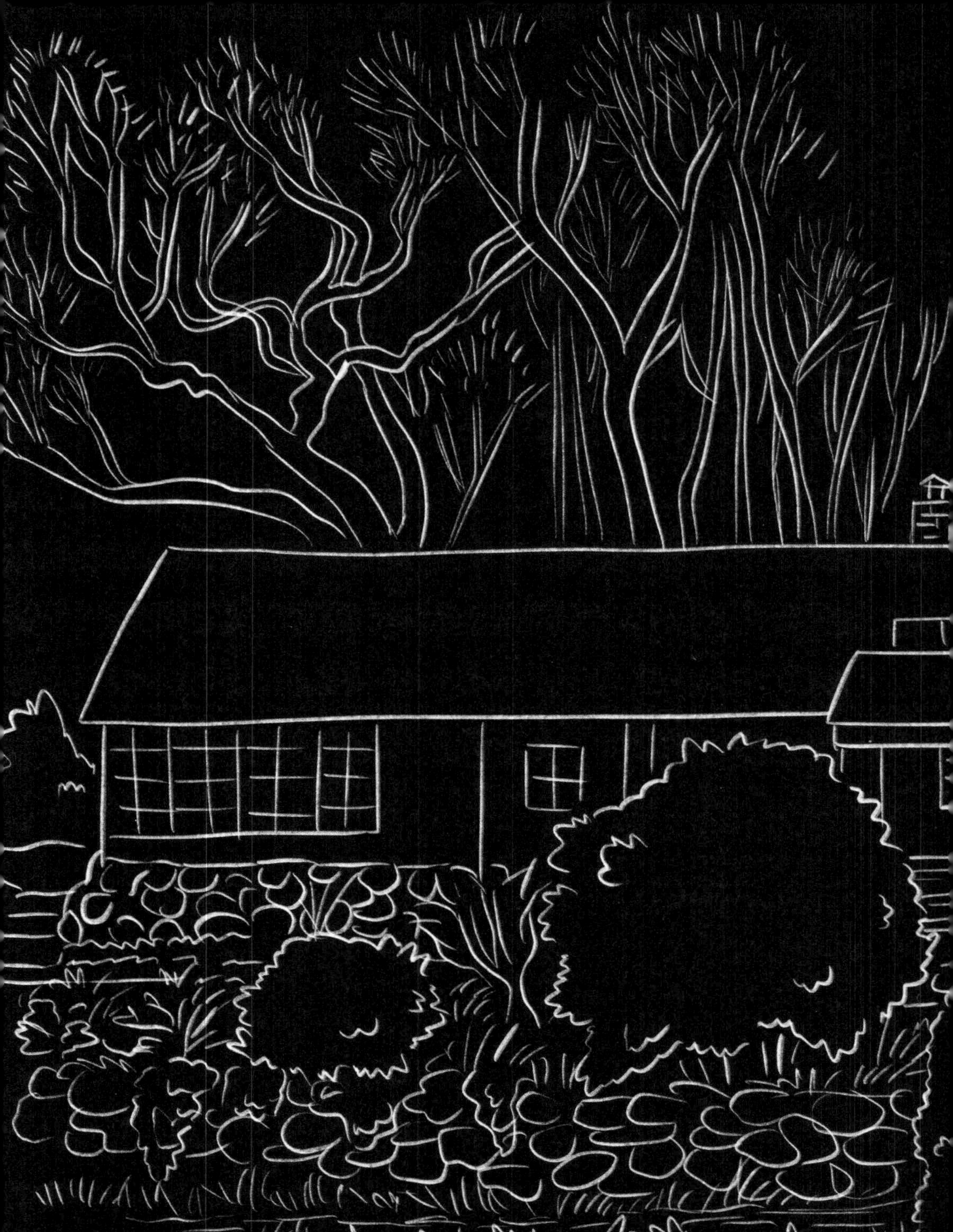

THE HOSPITAL IS STILL ADMITTING MOM—THEY
TELL ME TO CALL BACK IN A COUPLE OF HOURS.

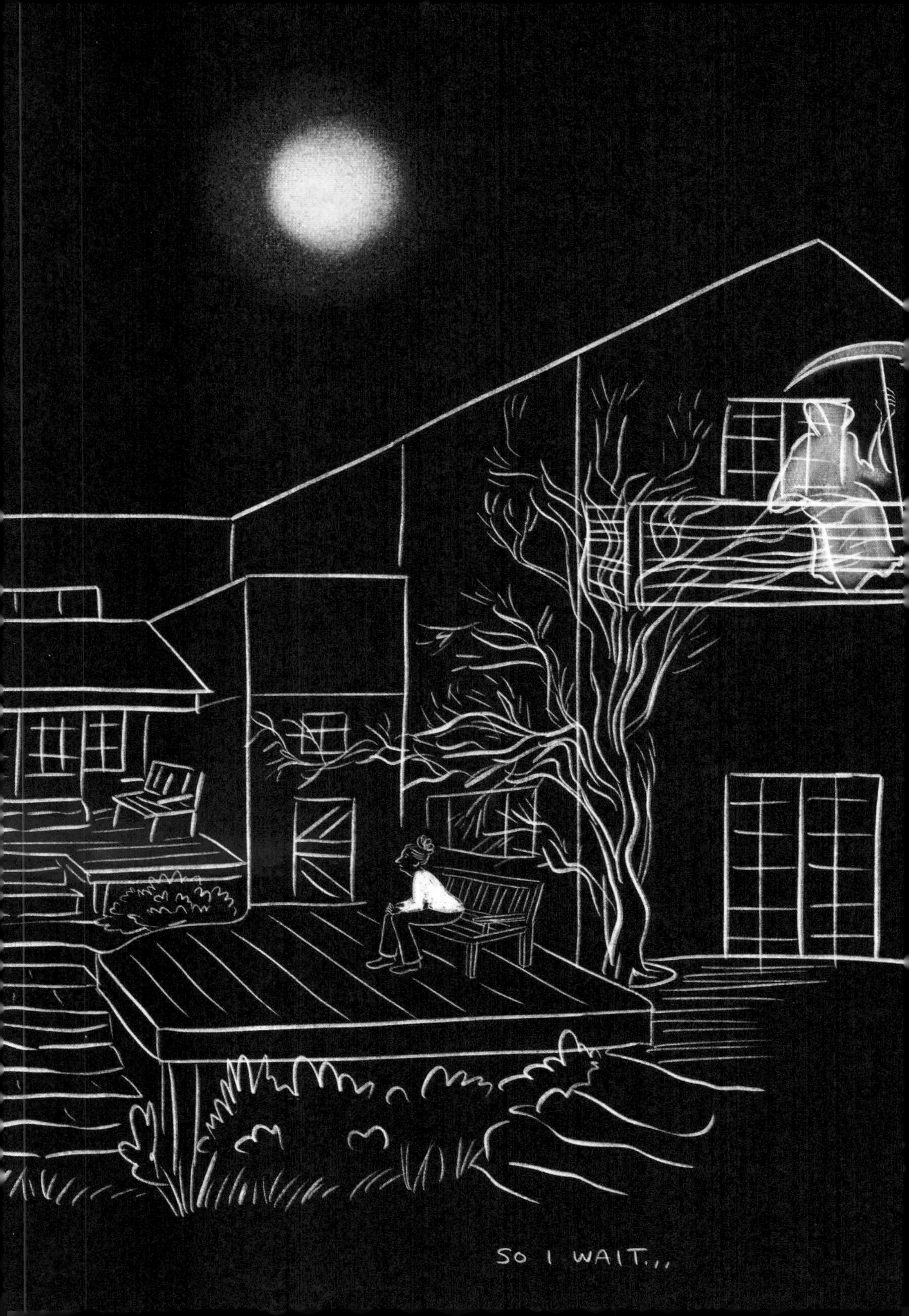
SO I WAIT...

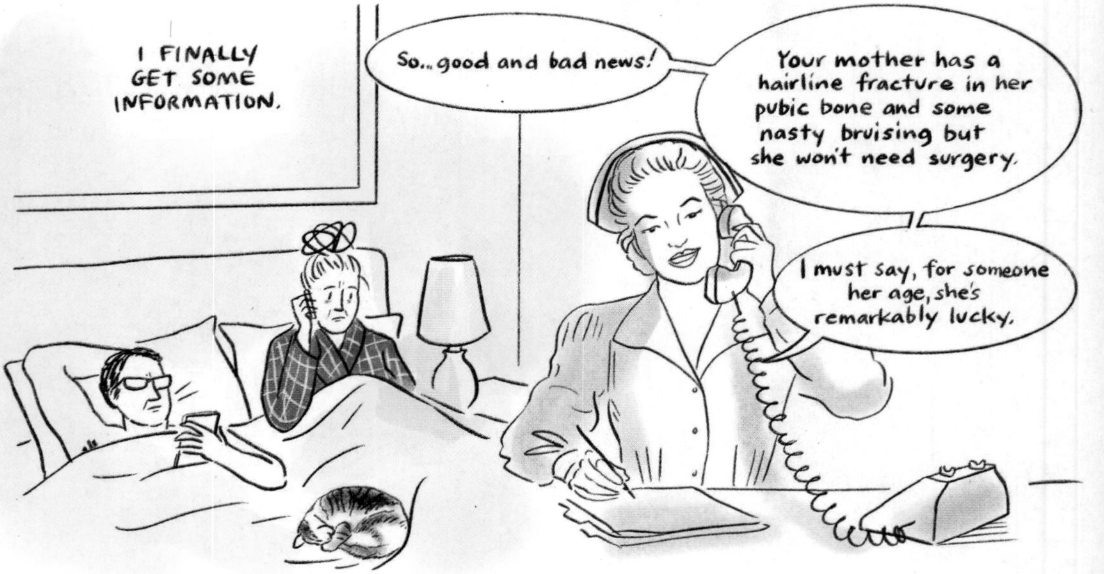
I FINALLY GET SOME INFORMATION.
So... good and bad news!
Your mother has a hairline fracture in her pubic bone and some nasty bruising but she won't need surgery.
I must say, for someone her age, she's remarkably lucky.

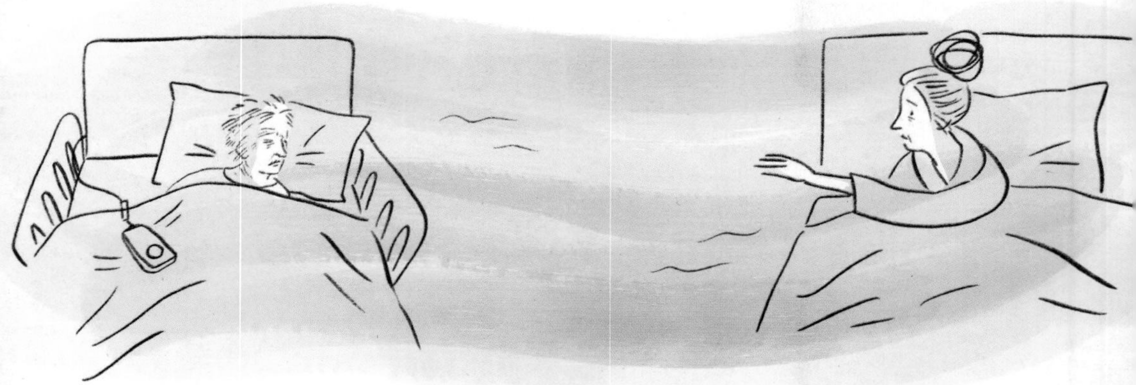

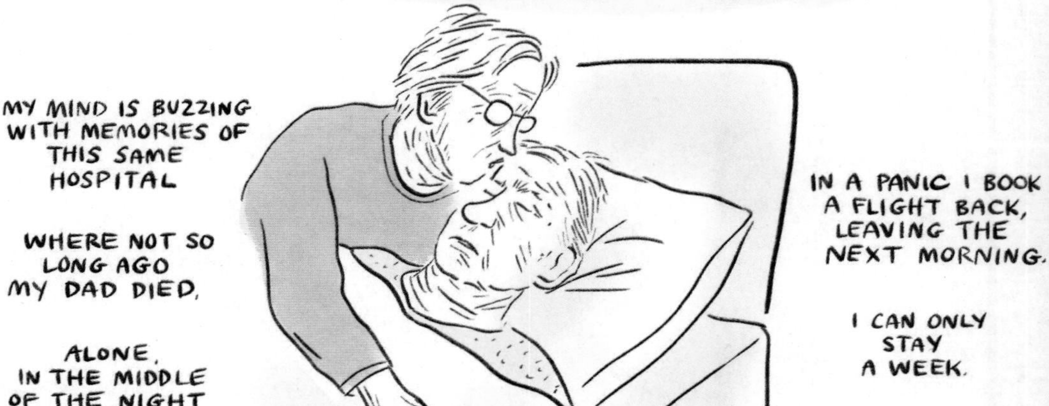
MY MIND IS BUZZING WITH MEMORIES OF THIS SAME HOSPITAL
WHERE NOT SO LONG AGO MY DAD DIED,
ALONE, IN THE MIDDLE OF THE NIGHT FROM A HEART ATTACK.
IN A PANIC I BOOK A FLIGHT BACK, LEAVING THE NEXT MORNING.
I CAN ONLY STAY A WEEK.

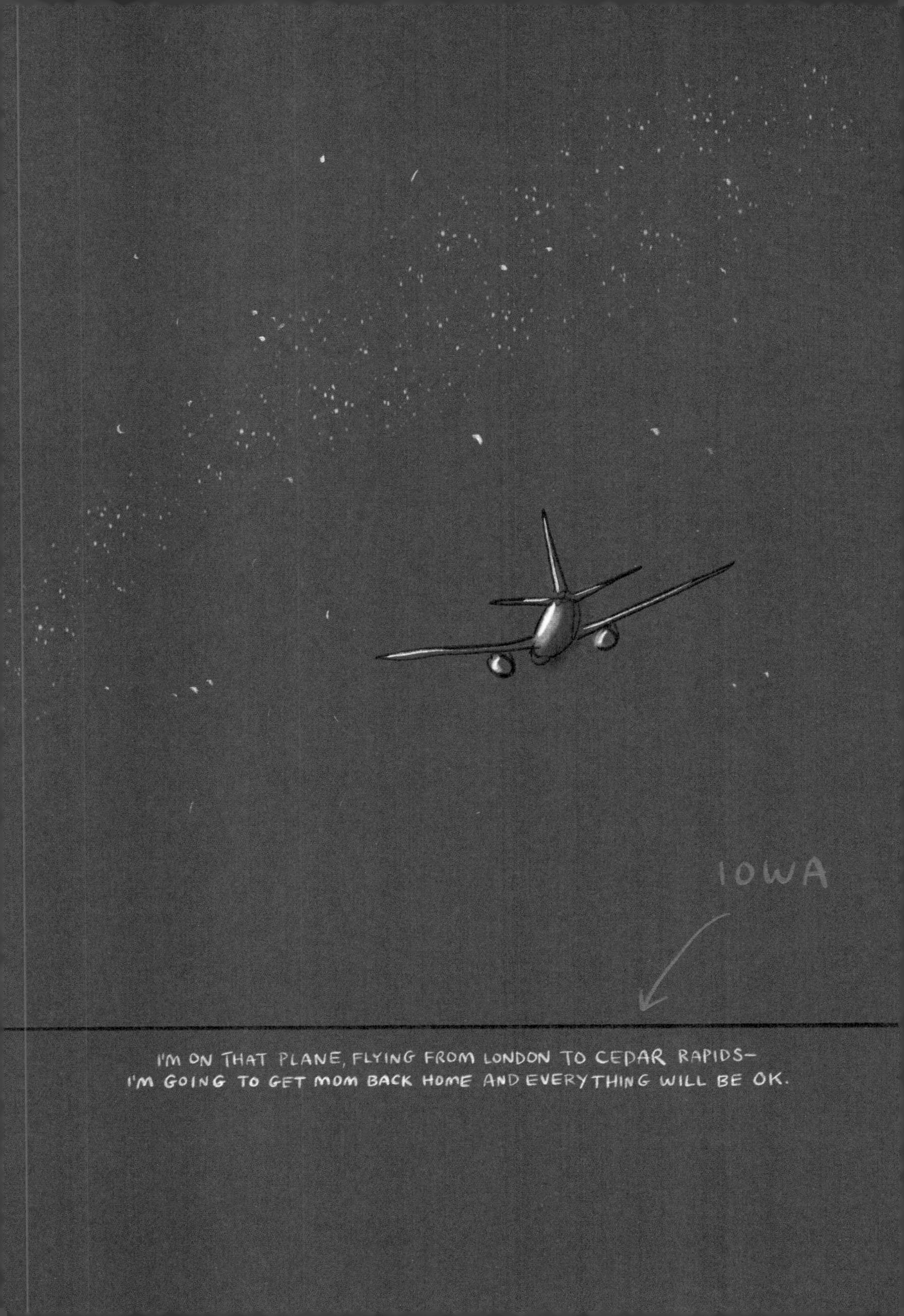
IOWA
I'M ON THAT PLANE, FLYING FROM LONDON TO CEDAR RAPIDS—
I'M GOING TO GET MOM BACK HOME AND EVERYTHING WILL BE OK.

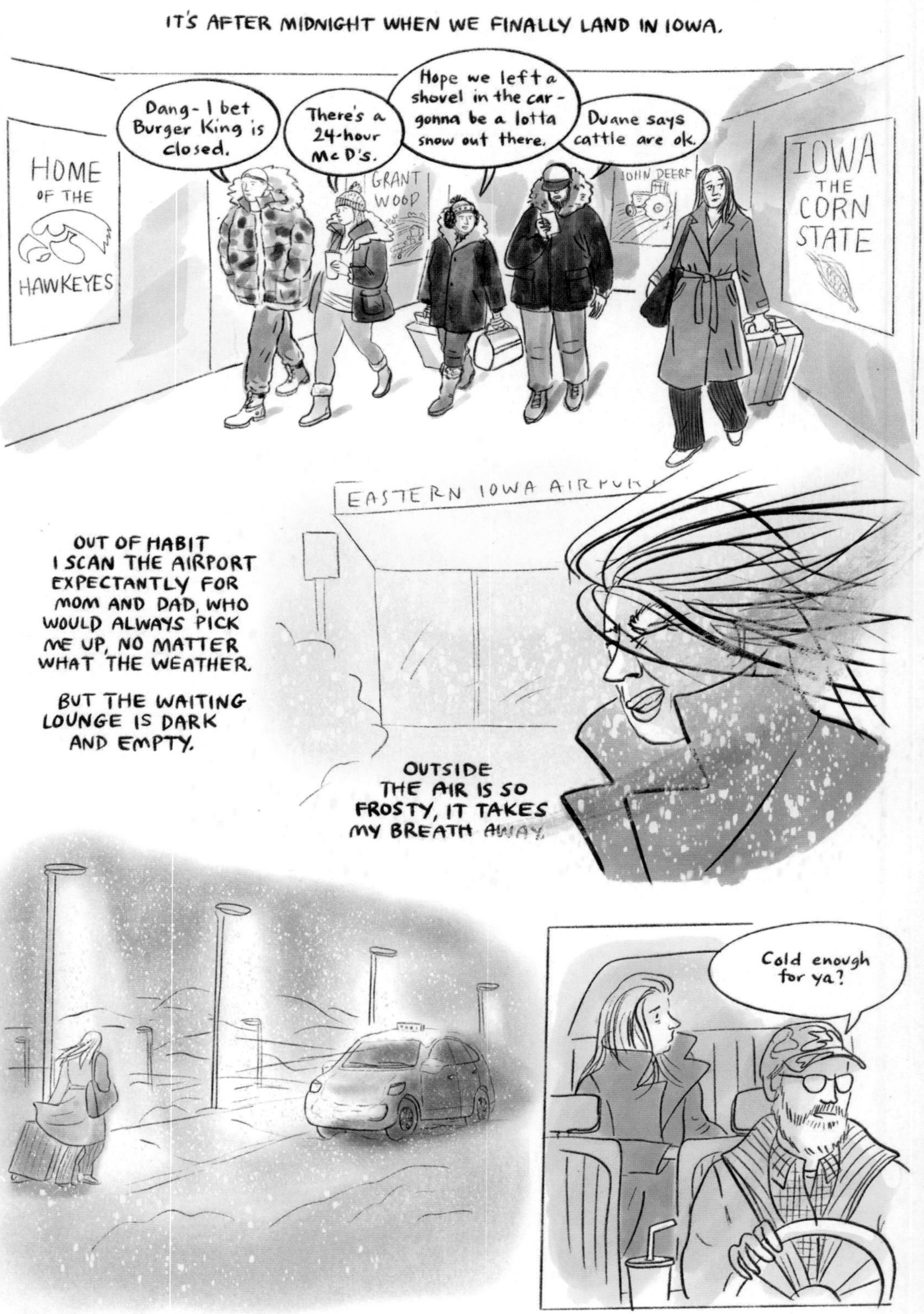
IT'S AFTER MIDNIGHT WHEN WE FINALLY LAND IN IOWA.
Dang- I bet Burger King is closed.
There's a 24-hour McD's.
Hope we left a shovel in the car- gonna be a lotta snow out there.
Duane says cattle are ok.
HOME OF THE HAWKEYES
GRANT WOOD
JOHN DEERE
IOWA THE CORN STATE
EASTERN IOWA AIRPORT
OUT OF HABIT I SCAN THE AIRPORT EXPECTANTLY FOR MOM AND DAD, WHO WOULD ALWAYS PICK ME UP, NO MATTER WHAT THE WEATHER.
BUT THE WAITING LOUNGE IS DARK AND EMPTY.
OUTSIDE THE AIR IS SO FROSTY, IT TAKES MY BREATH AWAY.
TAXI
Cold enough for ya?

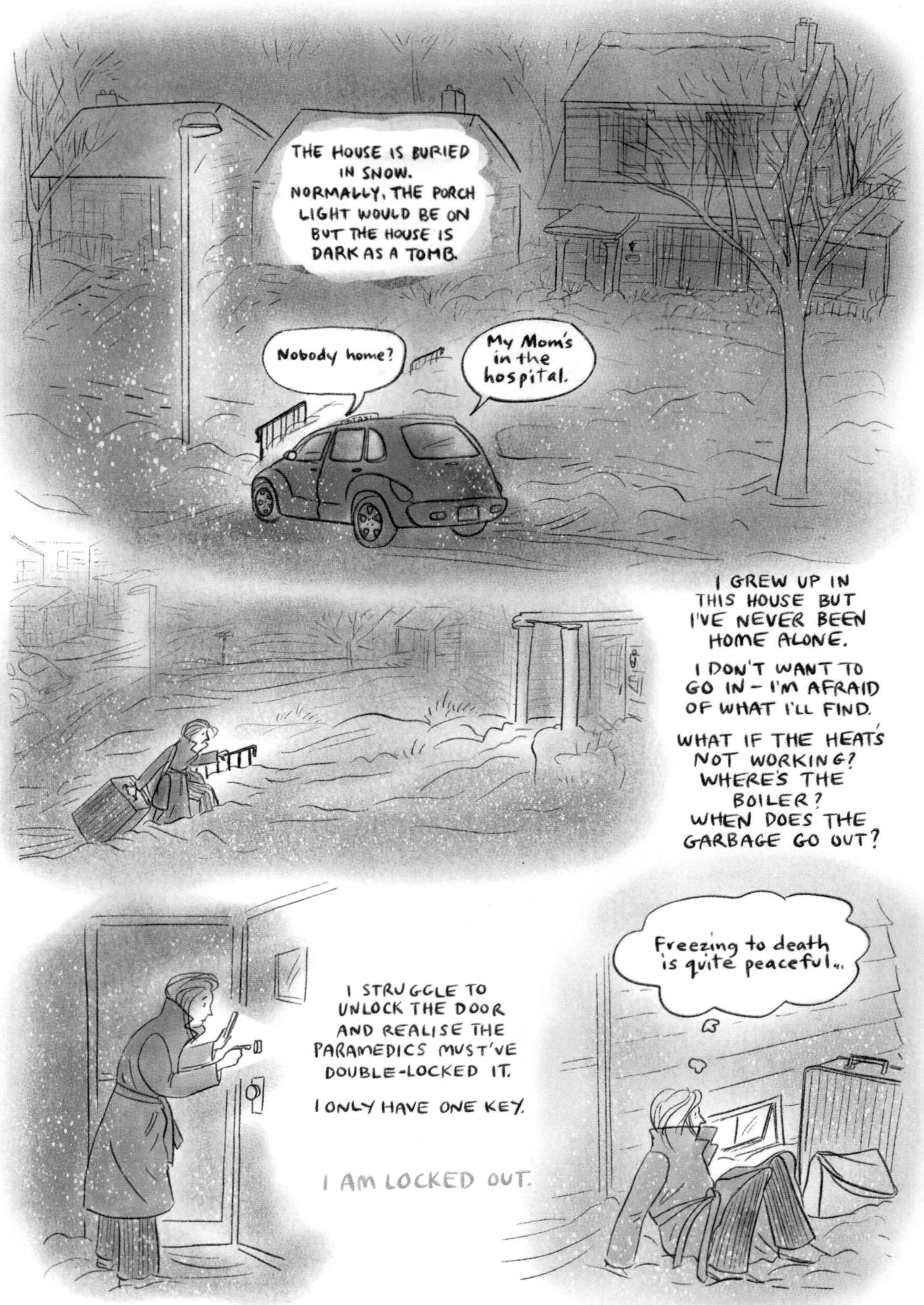
THE HOUSE IS BURIED IN SNOW. NORMALLY, THE PORCH LIGHT WOULD BE ON BUT THE HOUSE IS DARK AS A TOMB.
Nobody home?
My Mom's in the hospital.
TAXI
I GREW UP IN THIS HOUSE BUT I'VE NEVER BEEN HOME ALONE.
I DON'T WANT TO GO IN - I'M AFRAID OF WHAT I'LL FIND.
WHAT IF THE HEAT'S NOT WORKING? WHERE'S THE BOILER? WHEN DOES THE GARBAGE GO OUT?
I STRUGGLE TO UNLOCK THE DOOR AND REALISE THE PARAMEDICS MUST'VE DOUBLE-LOCKED IT.
I ONLY HAVE ONE KEY.
I AM LOCKED OUT.
Freezing to death is quite peaceful..

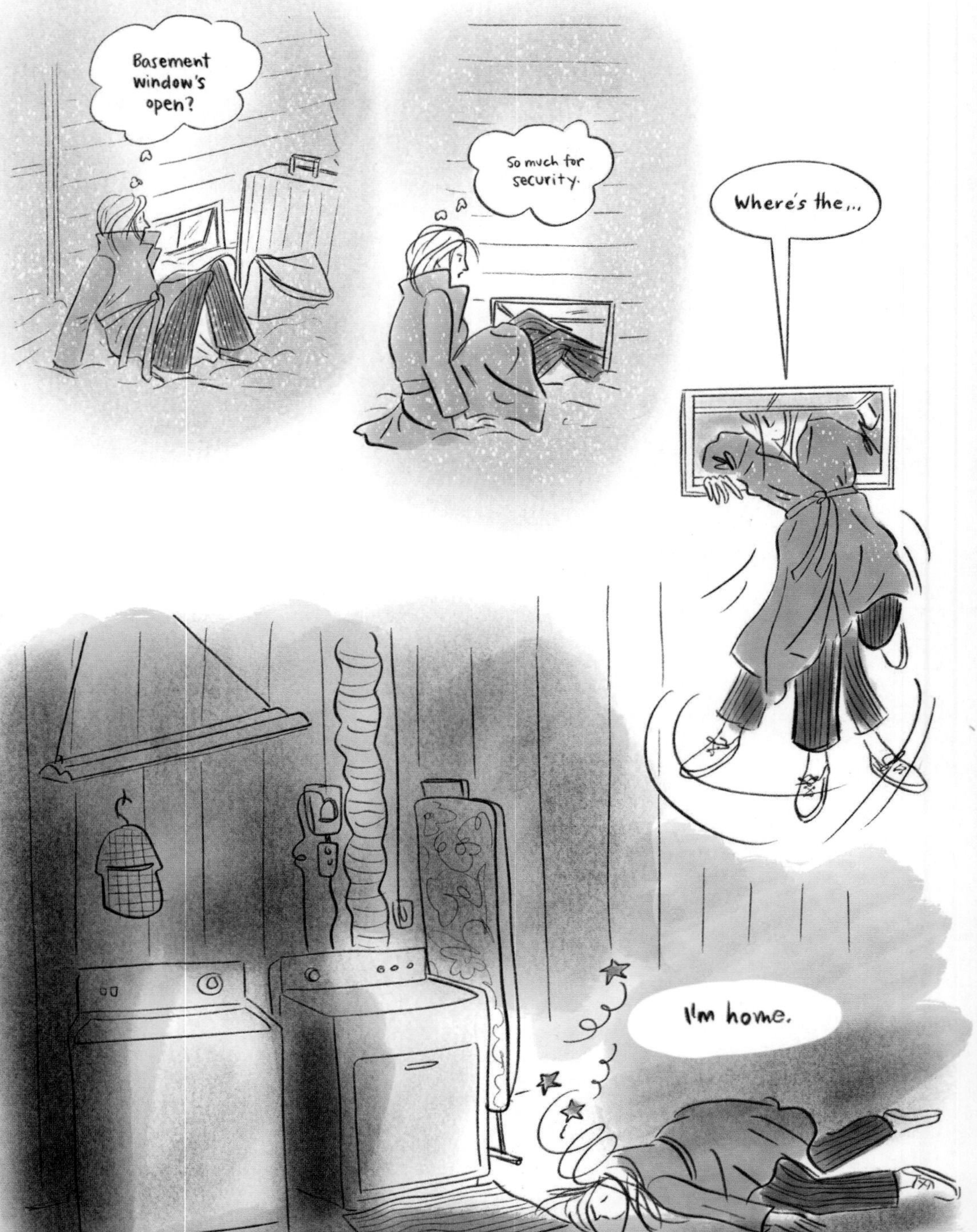
Basement window's open?
So much for security.
Where's the...
I'm home.

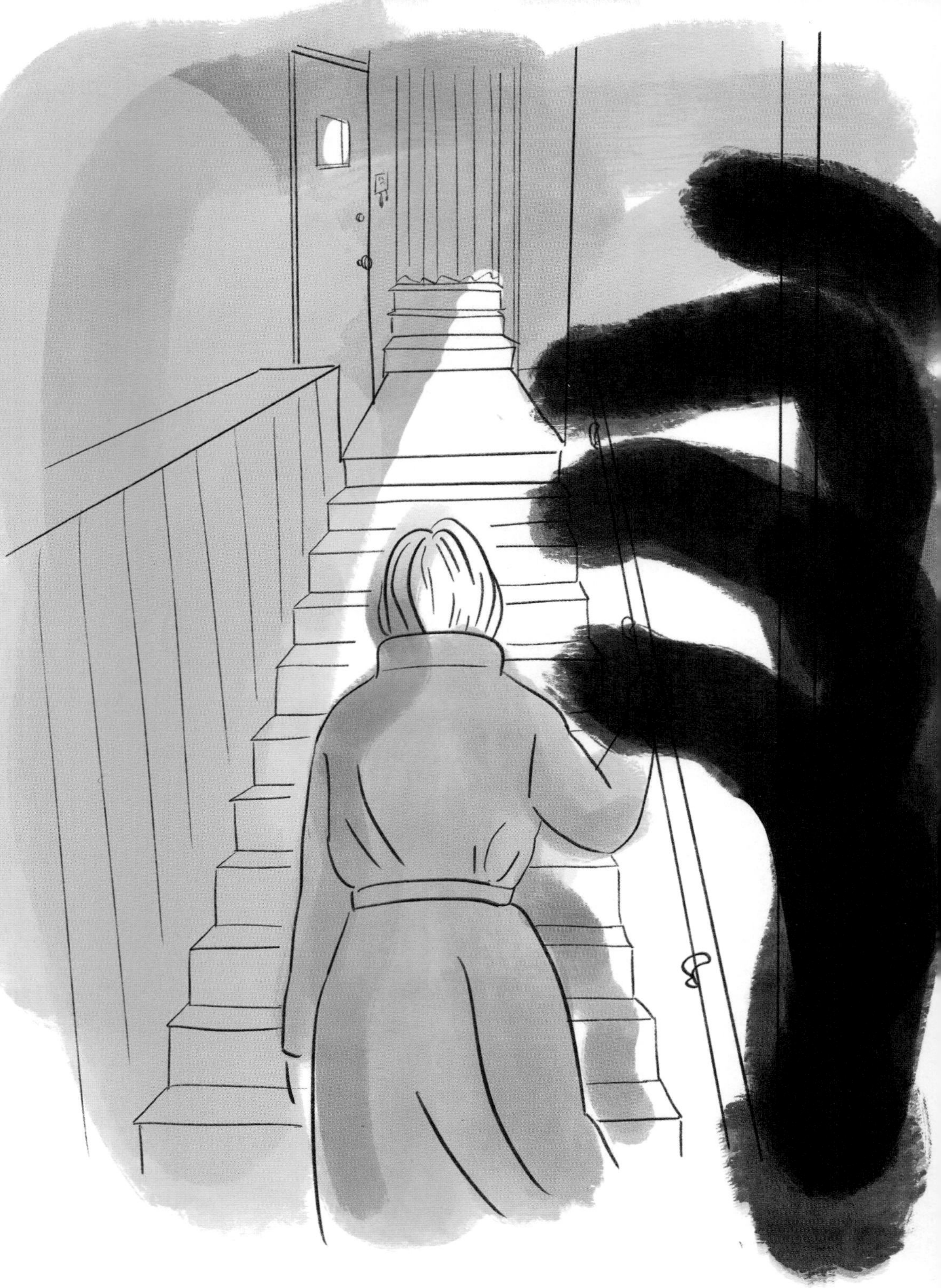

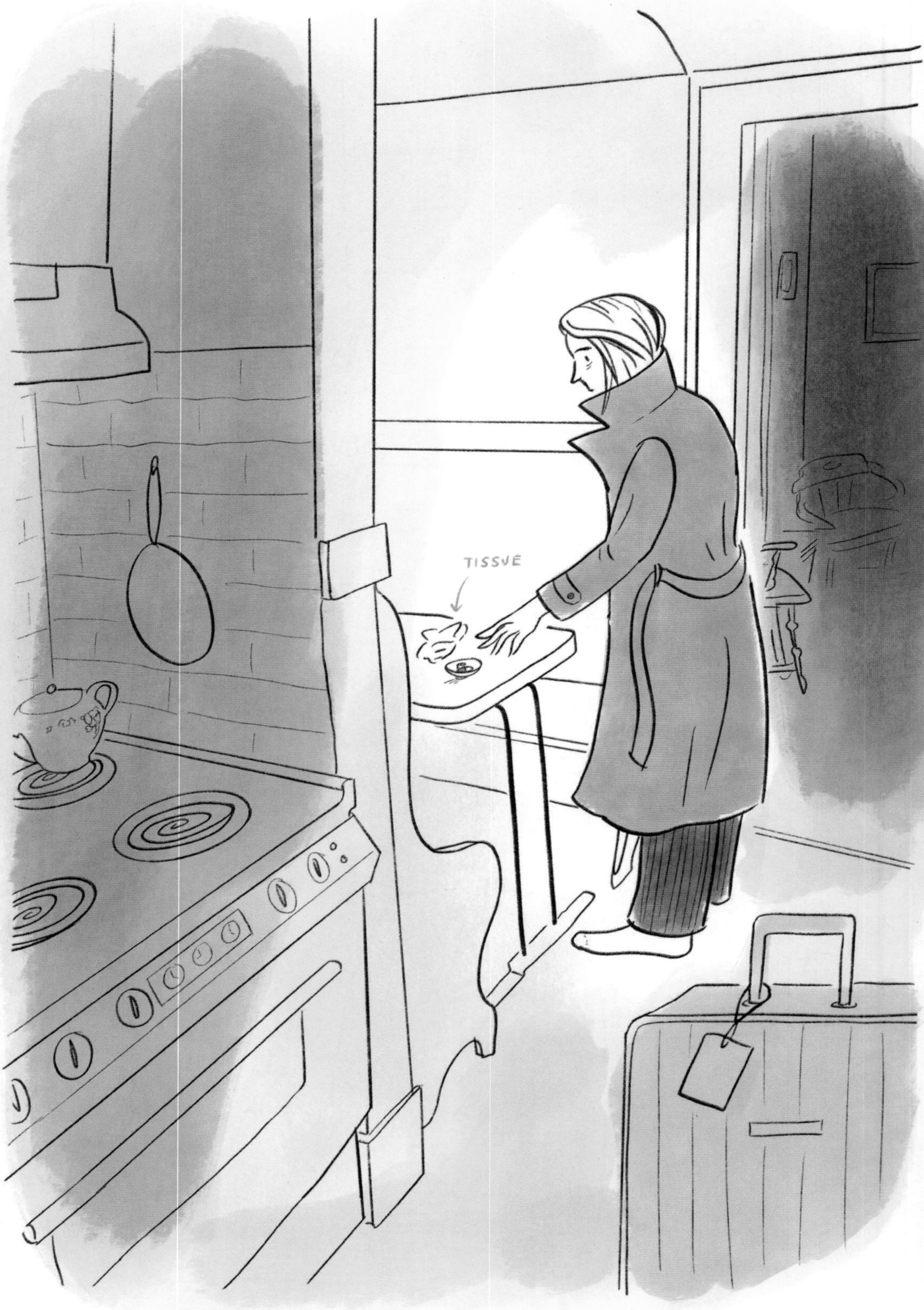
TISSUE

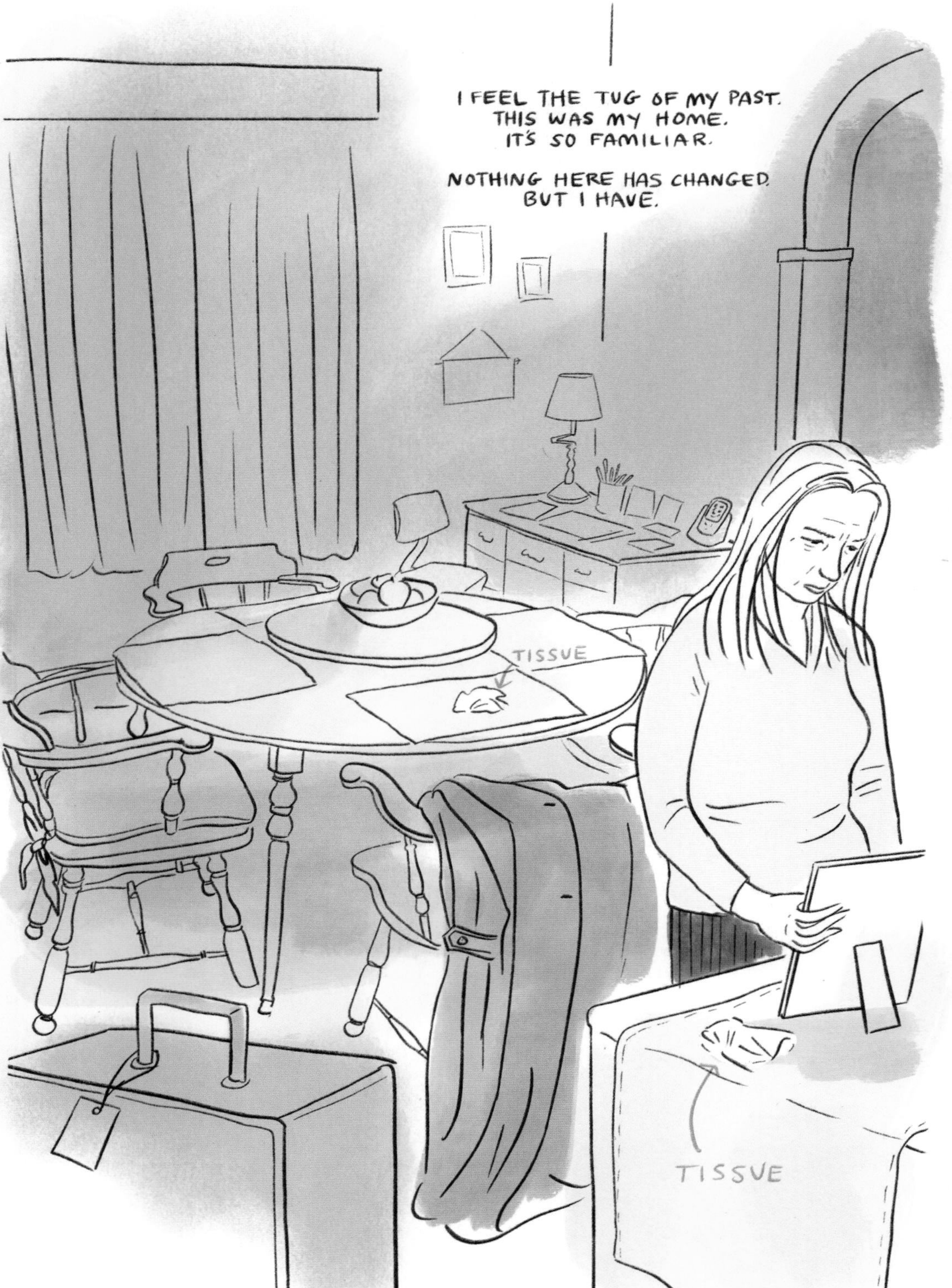
I FEEL THE TUG OF MY PAST.
THIS WAS MY HOME.
IT'S SO FAMILIAR.
NOTHING HERE HAS CHANGED.
BUT I HAVE.
TISSUE
TISSUE

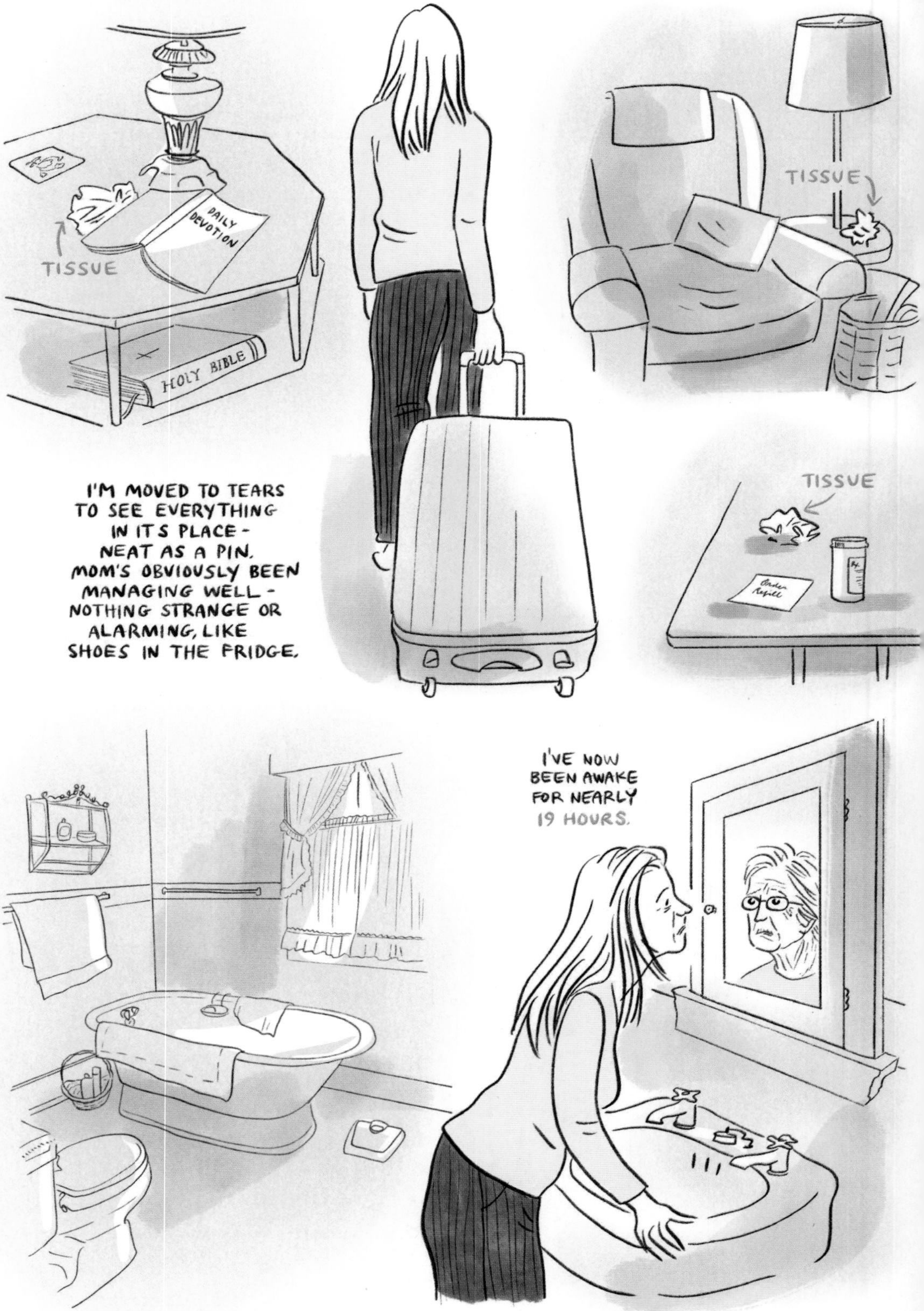
DAILY DEVOTION
TISSUE
HOLY BIBLE
TISSUE
I'M MOVED TO TEARS TO SEE EVERYTHING IN ITS PLACE - NEAT AS A PIN. MOM'S OBVIOUSLY BEEN MANAGING WELL - NOTHING STRANGE OR ALARMING, LIKE SHOES IN THE FRIDGE.
TISSUE
Order Refill
I'VE NOW BEEN AWAKE FOR NEARLY 19 HOURS.

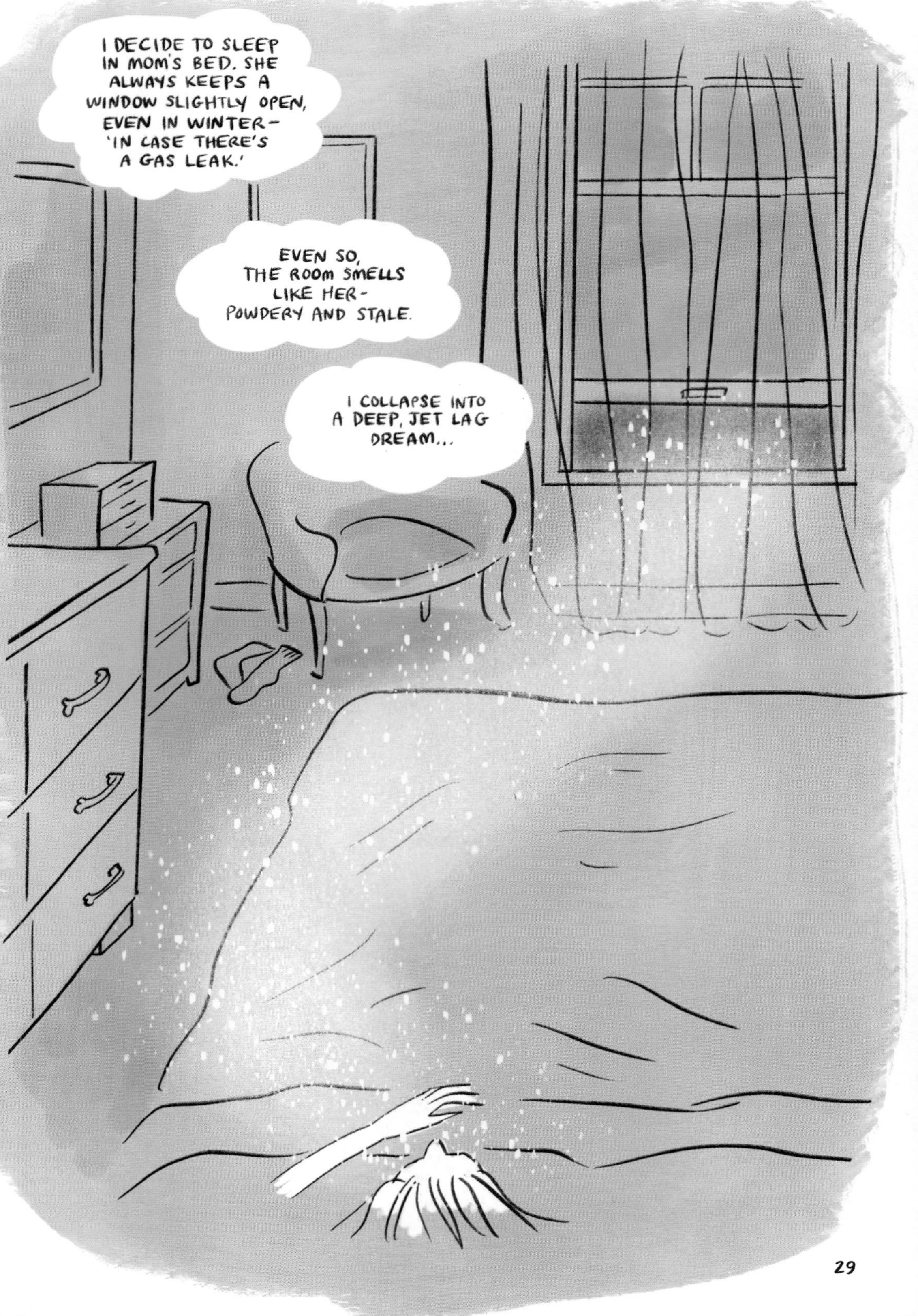
I DECIDE TO SLEEP IN MOM'S BED. SHE ALWAYS KEEPS A WINDOW SLIGHTLY OPEN, EVEN IN WINTER— 'IN CASE THERE'S A GAS LEAK.'
EVEN SO, THE ROOM SMELLS LIKE HER— POWDERY AND STALE.
I COLLAPSE INTO A DEEP, JET LAG DREAM...

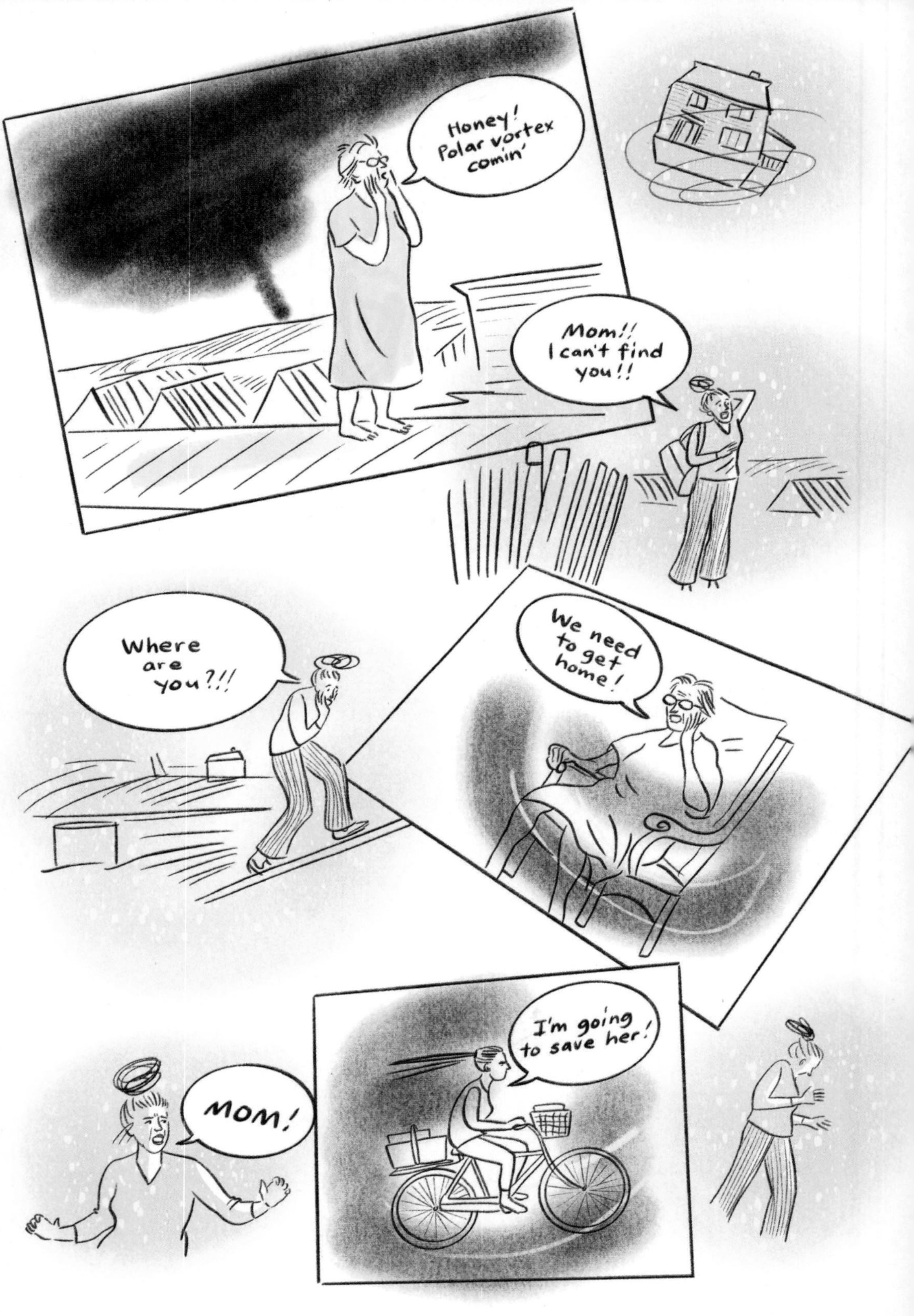
Honey! Polar vortex comin'
Mom!! I can't find you!!
Where are you?!!
We need to get home!
MOM!
I'm going to save her!

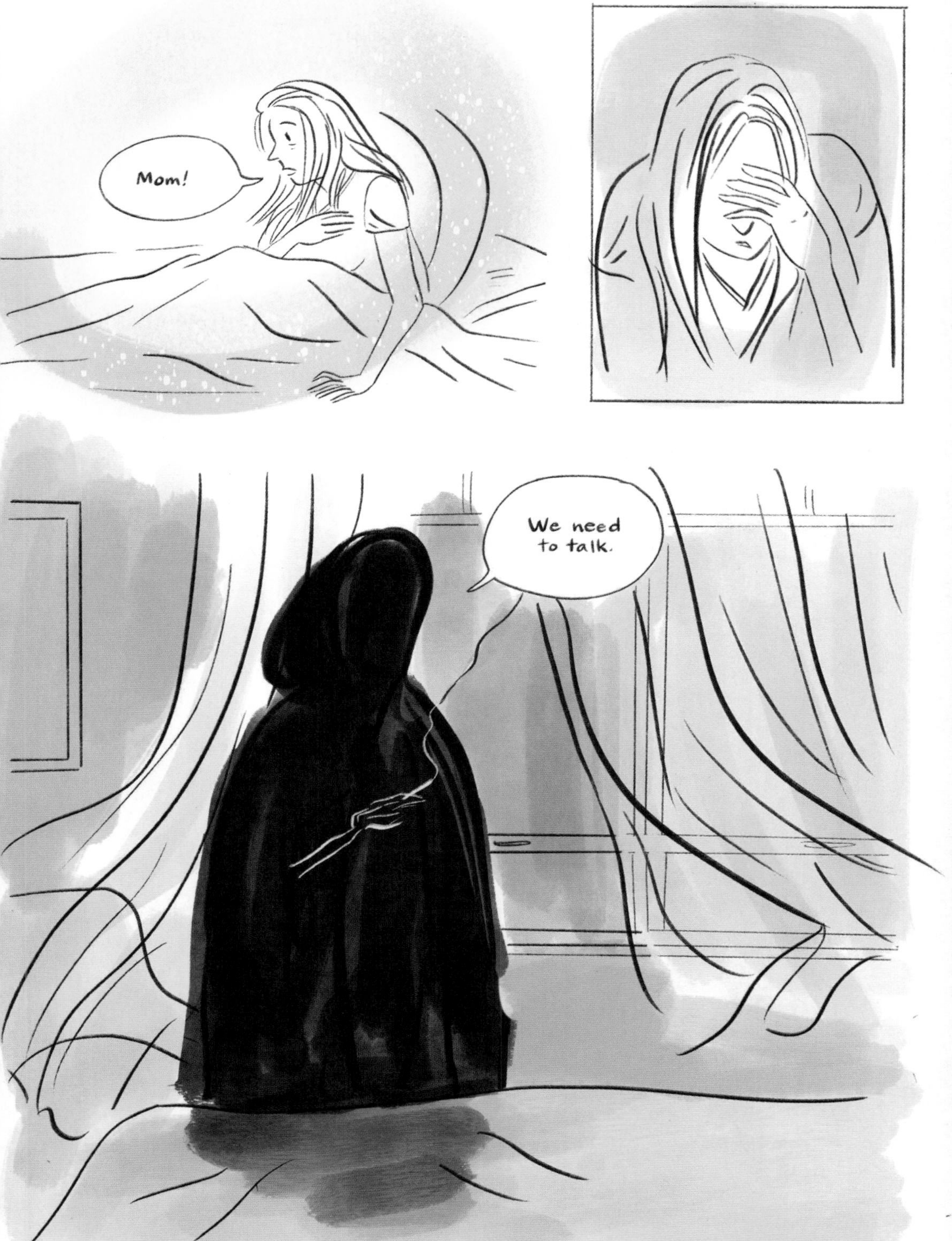
Mom!
We need to talk.

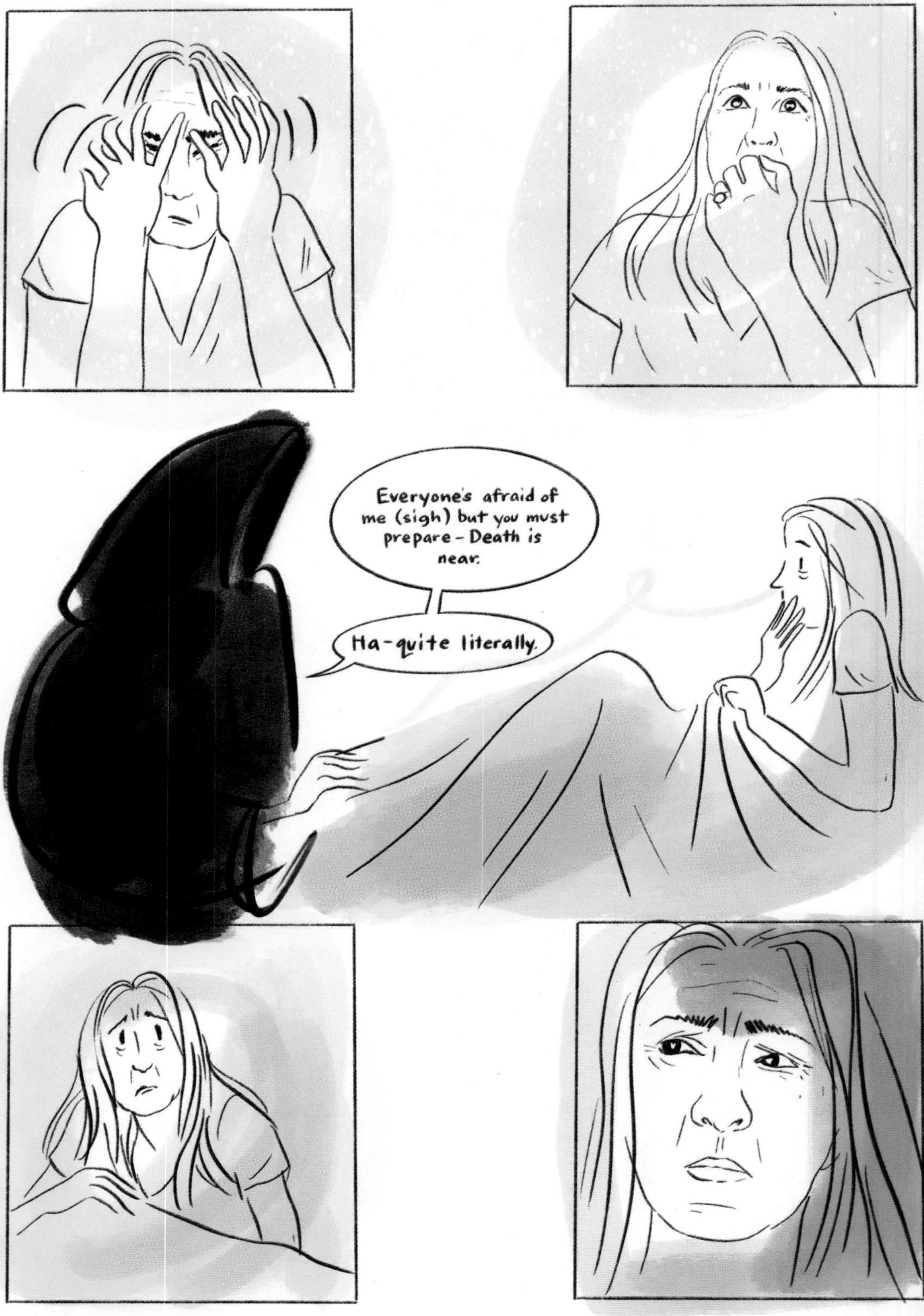
Everyone's afraid of me (sigh) but you must prepare - Death is near.
Ha - quite literally.

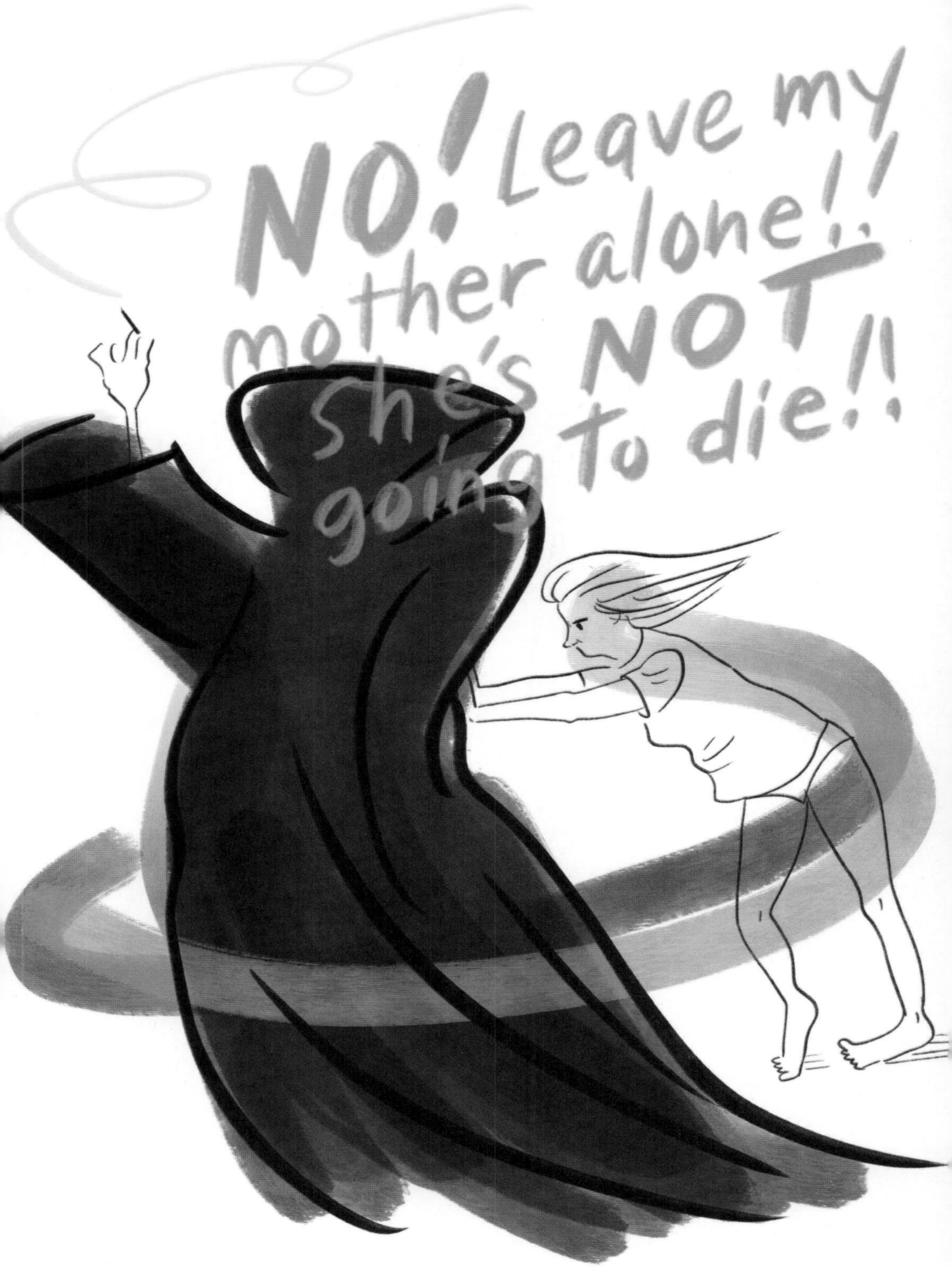
NO! Leave my mother alone!! She's NOT going to die!!

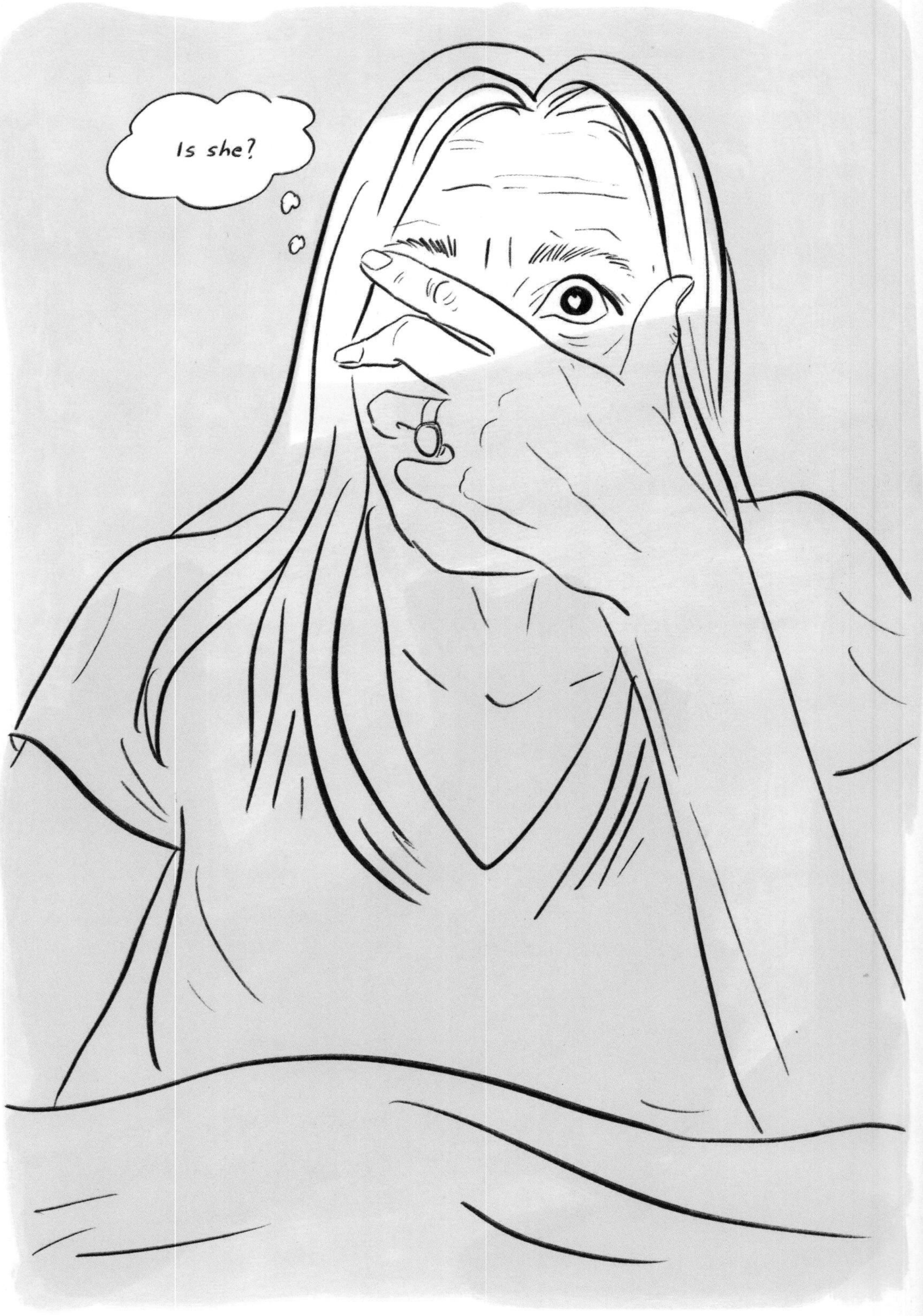
Is she?

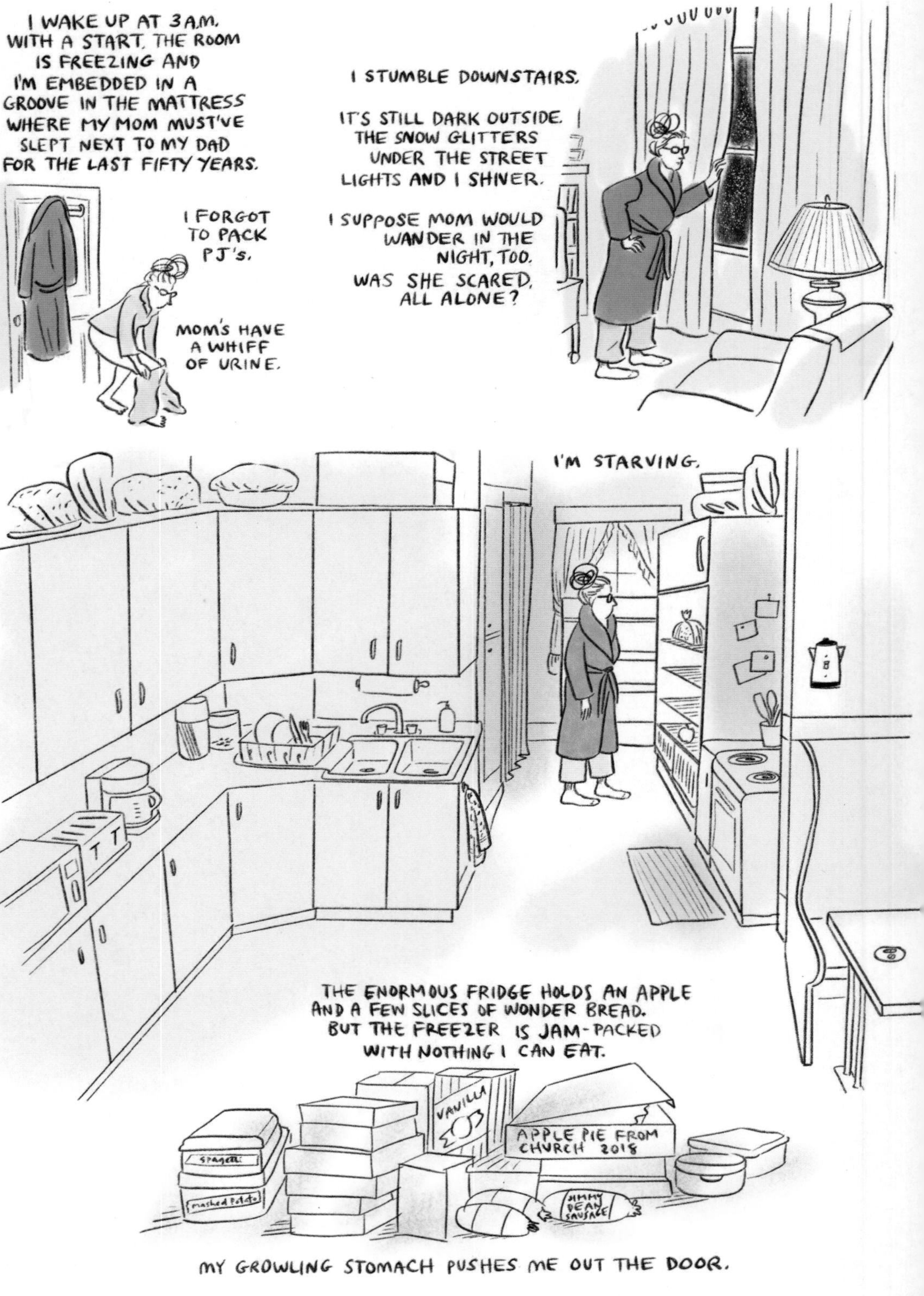
I WAKE UP AT 3A.M. WITH A START. THE ROOM IS FREEZING AND I'M EMBEDDED IN A GROOVE IN THE MATTRESS WHERE MY MOM MUST'VE SLEPT NEXT TO MY DAD FOR THE LAST FIFTY YEARS.
I FORGOT TO PACK PJ's.
MOM'S HAVE A WHIFF OF URINE.
I STUMBLE DOWNSTAIRS.
IT'S STILL DARK OUTSIDE. THE SNOW GLITTERS UNDER THE STREET LIGHTS AND I SHIVER.
I SUPPOSE MOM WOULD WANDER IN THE NIGHT, TOO.
WAS SHE SCARED, ALL ALONE?
I'M STARVING.
THE ENORMOUS FRIDGE HOLDS AN APPLE AND A FEW SLICES OF WONDER BREAD. BUT THE FREEZER IS JAM-PACKED WITH NOTHING I CAN EAT.
VANILLA
APPLE PIE FROM CHURCH 2018
mashed Potato
JIMMY DEAN SAUSAGE
MY GROWLING STOMACH PUSHES ME OUT THE DOOR.

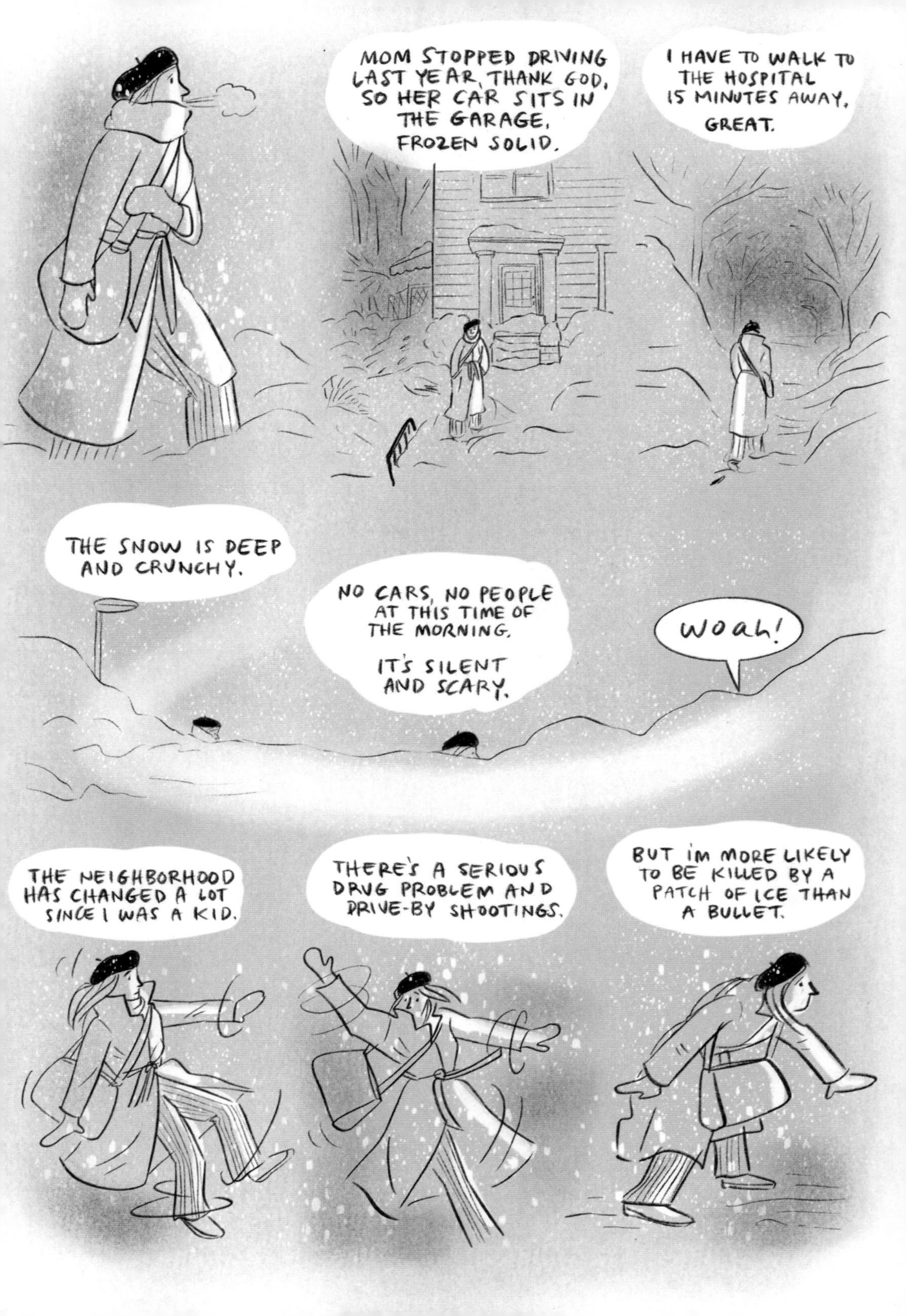
MOM STOPPED DRIVING LAST YEAR, THANK GOD, SO HER CAR SITS IN THE GARAGE, FROZEN SOLID.
I HAVE TO WALK TO THE HOSPITAL 15 MINUTES AWAY.
GREAT.
THE SNOW IS DEEP AND CRUNCHY.
NO CARS, NO PEOPLE AT THIS TIME OF THE MORNING.
IT'S SILENT AND SCARY.
Woah!
THE NEIGHBORHOOD HAS CHANGED A LOT SINCE I WAS A KID.
THERE'S A SERIOUS DRUG PROBLEM AND DRIVE-BY SHOOTINGS.
BUT I'M MORE LIKELY TO BE KILLED BY A PATCH OF ICE THAN A BULLET.

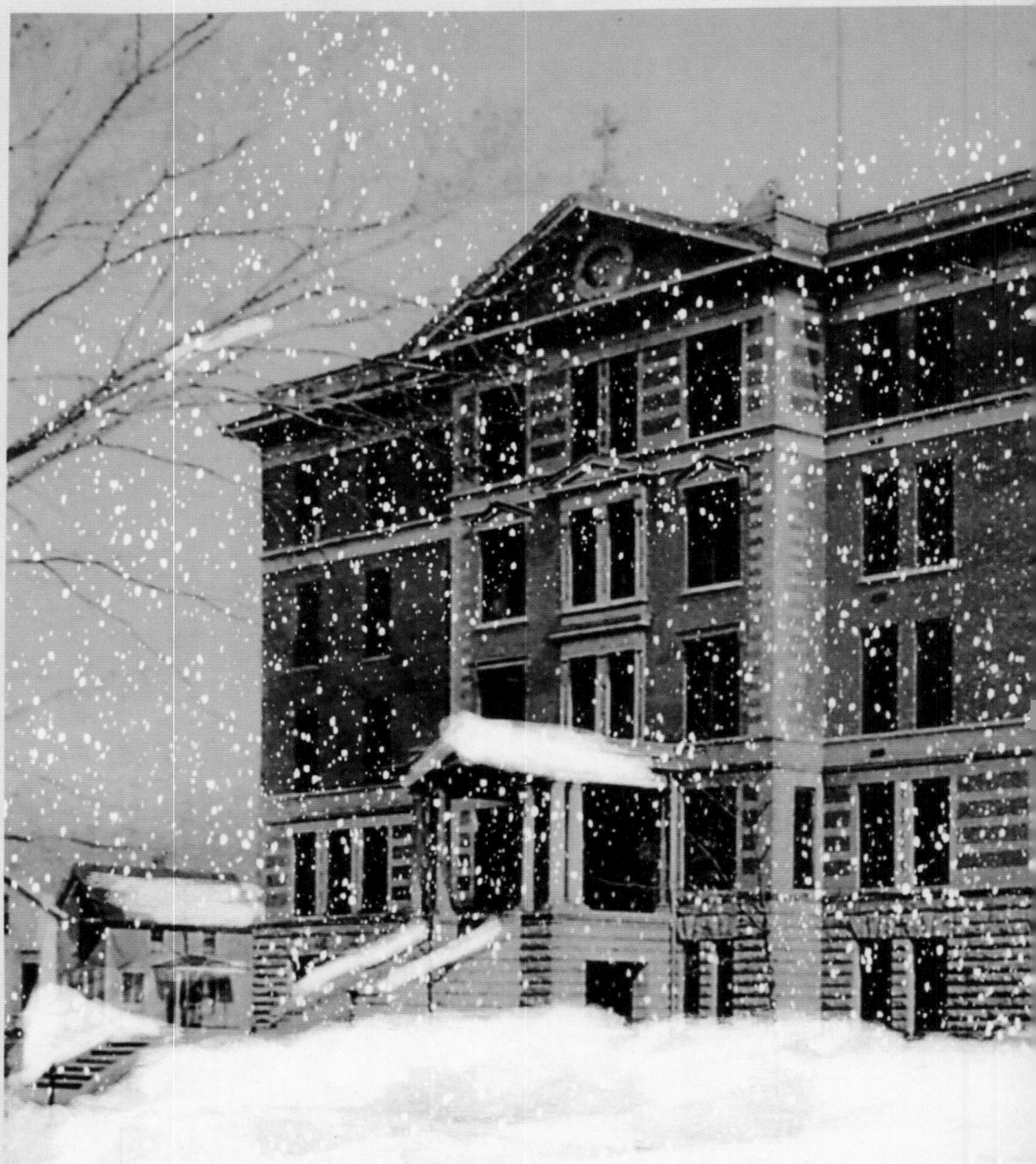

Hospital, Ced

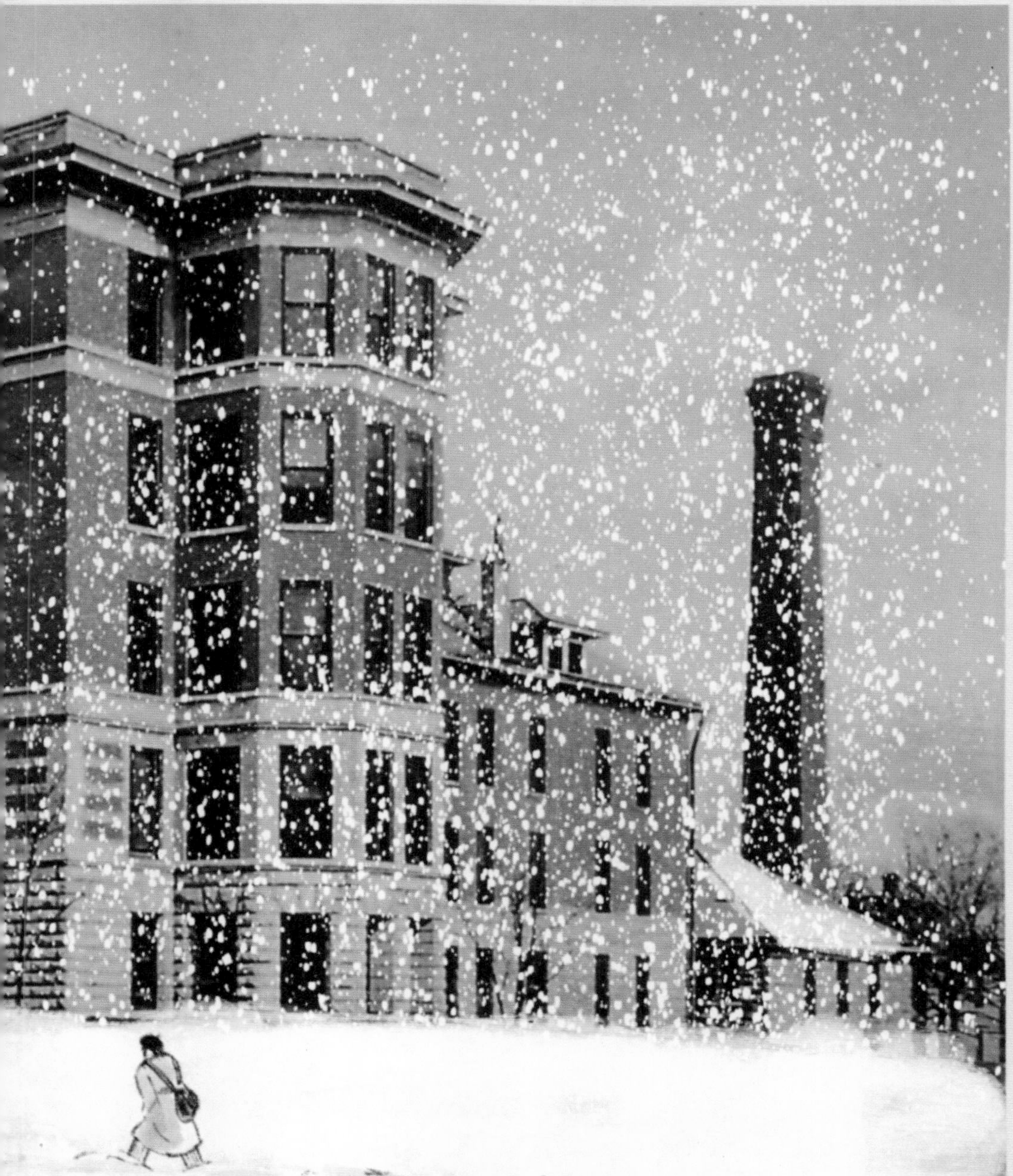

apids, Iowa.

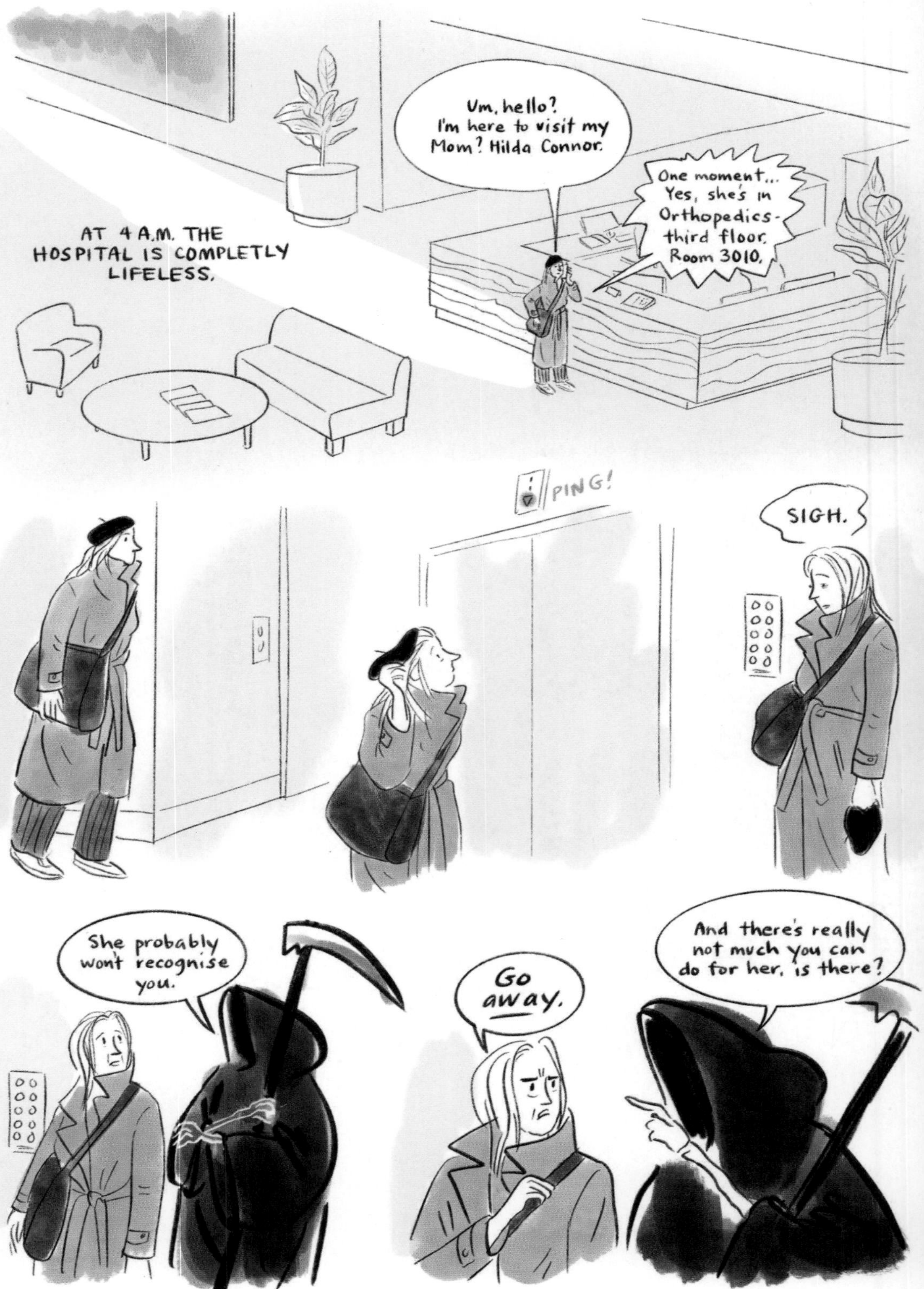
AT 4 A.M. THE HOSPITAL IS COMPLETLY LIFELESS.
Um, hello? I'm here to visit my Mom? Hilda Connor.
One moment... Yes, she's in Orthopedics-third floor. Room 3010.
PING!
SIGH.
She probably won't recognise you.
Go away.
And there's really not much you can do for her, is there?

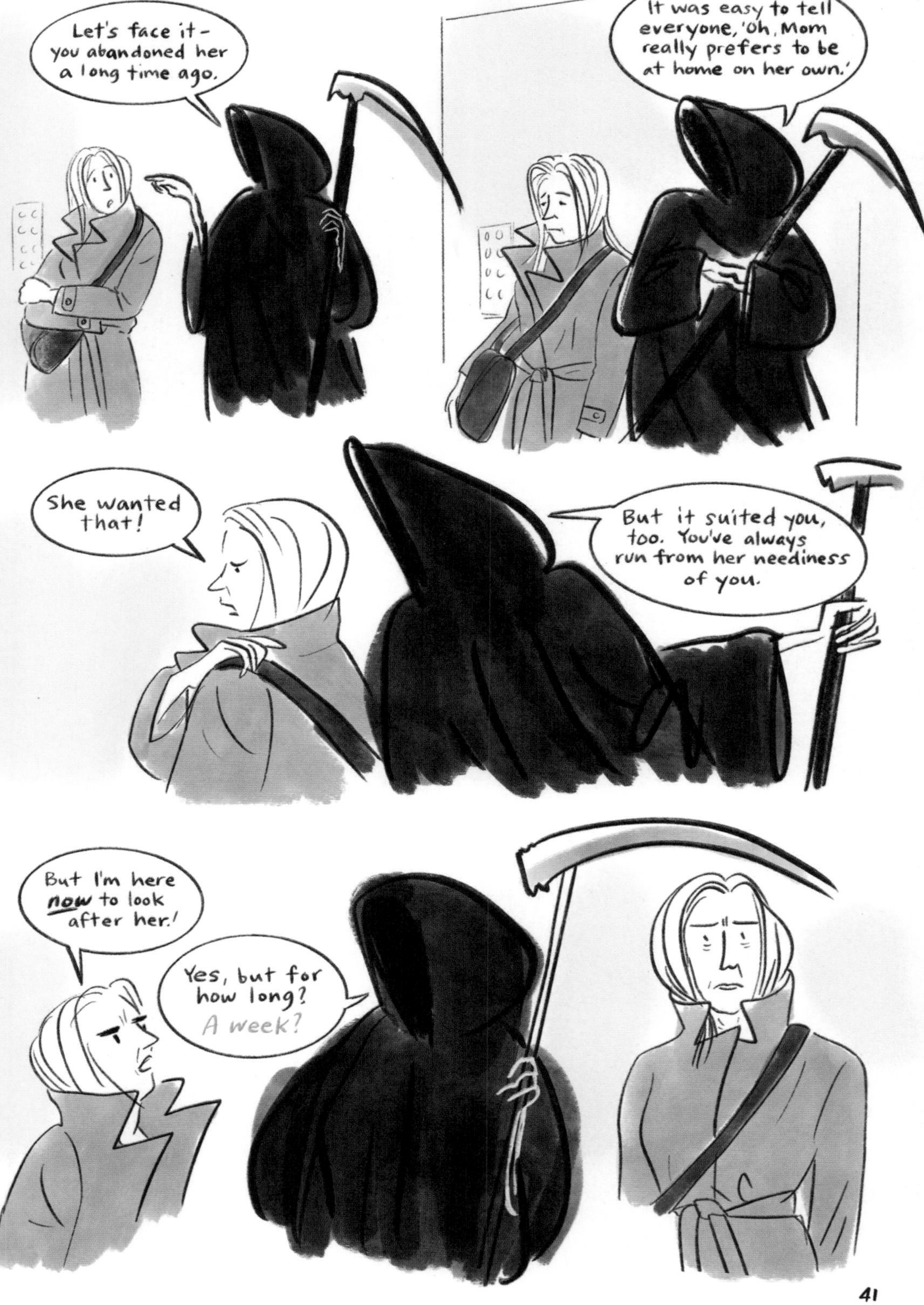
Let's face it - you abandoned her a long time ago.
It was easy to tell everyone, 'Oh, Mom really prefers to be at home on her own.'
She wanted that!
But it suited you, too. You've always run from her neediness of you.
But I'm here now to look after her!
Yes, but for how long? A week?

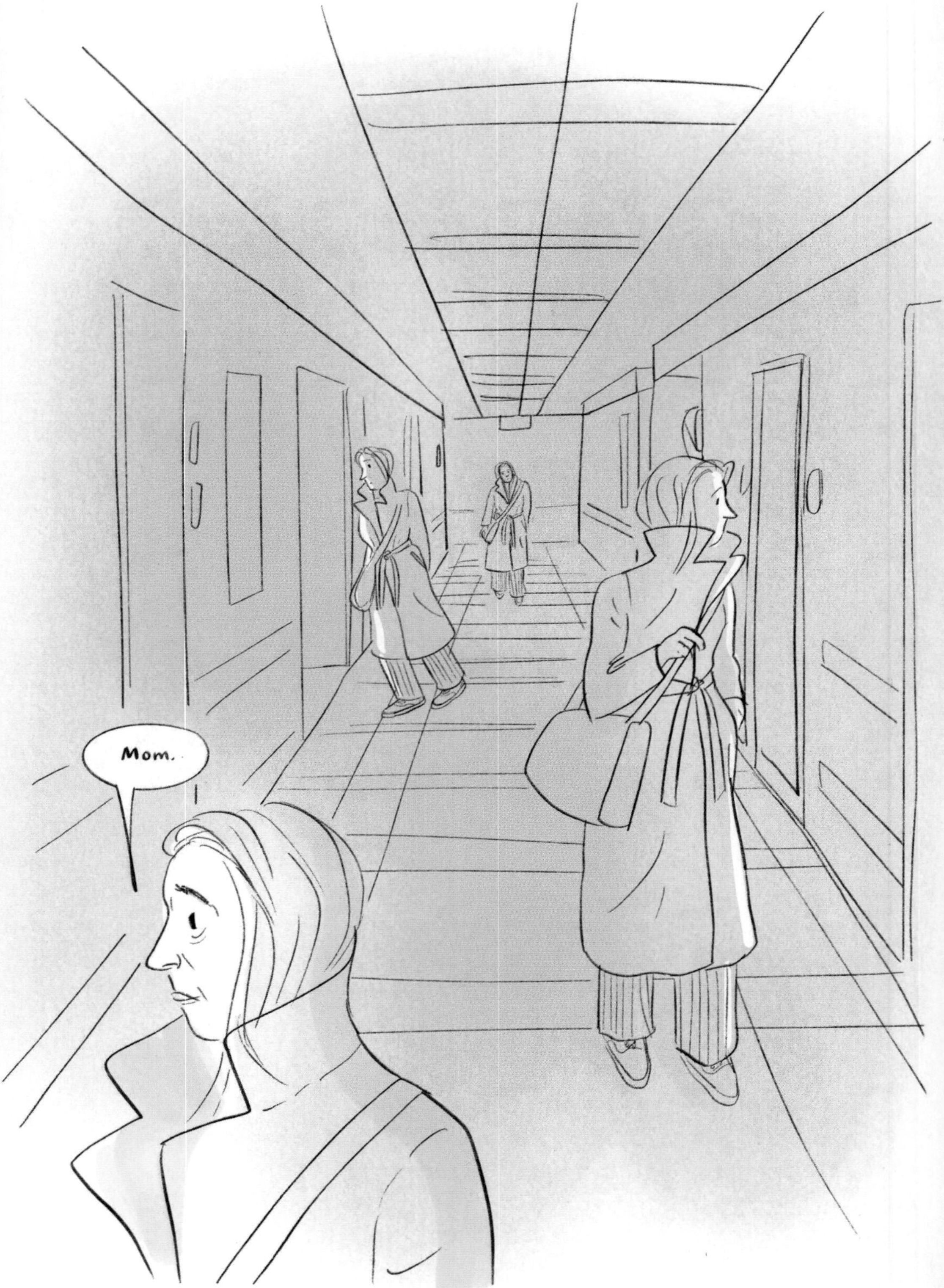
Mom.

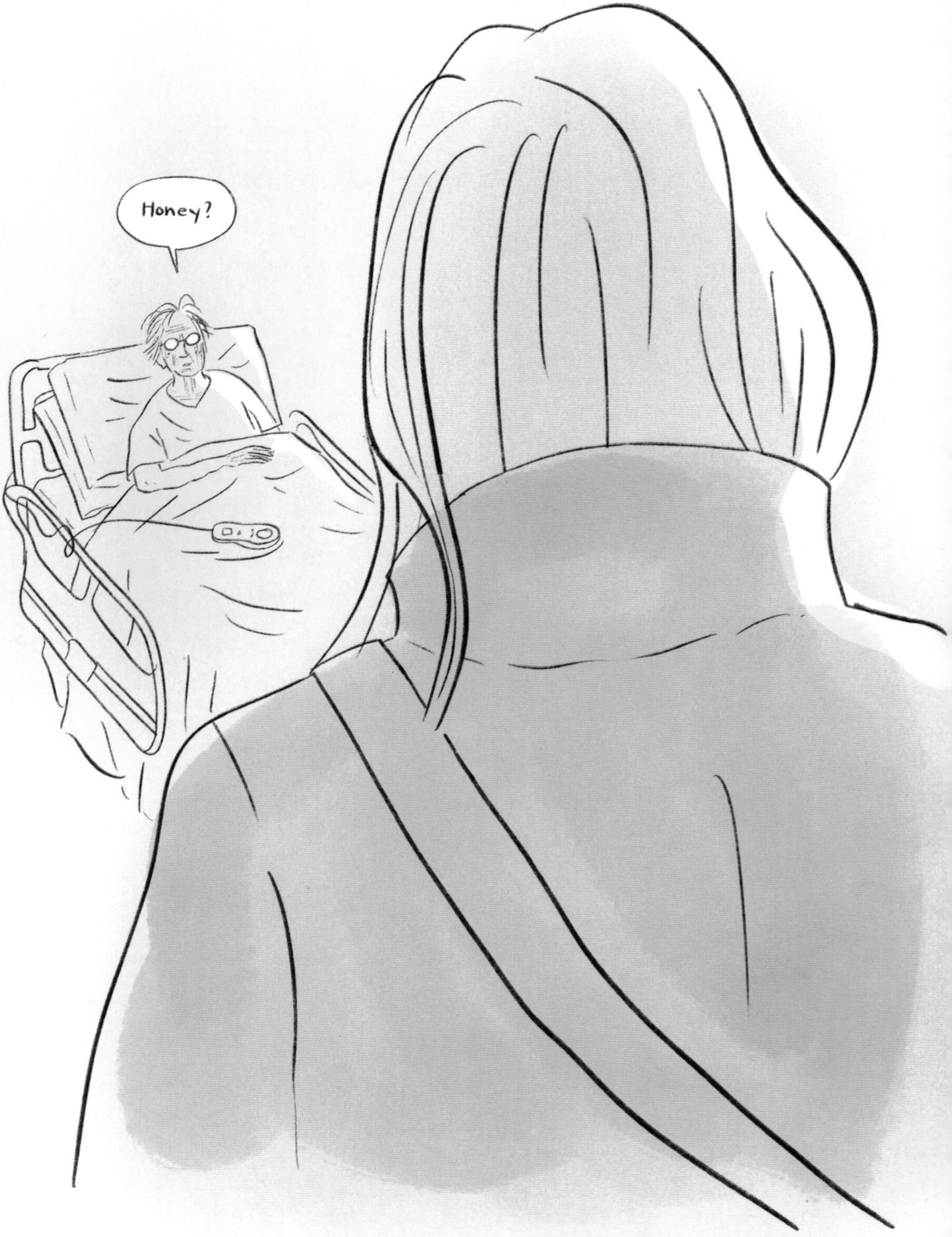
Honey?

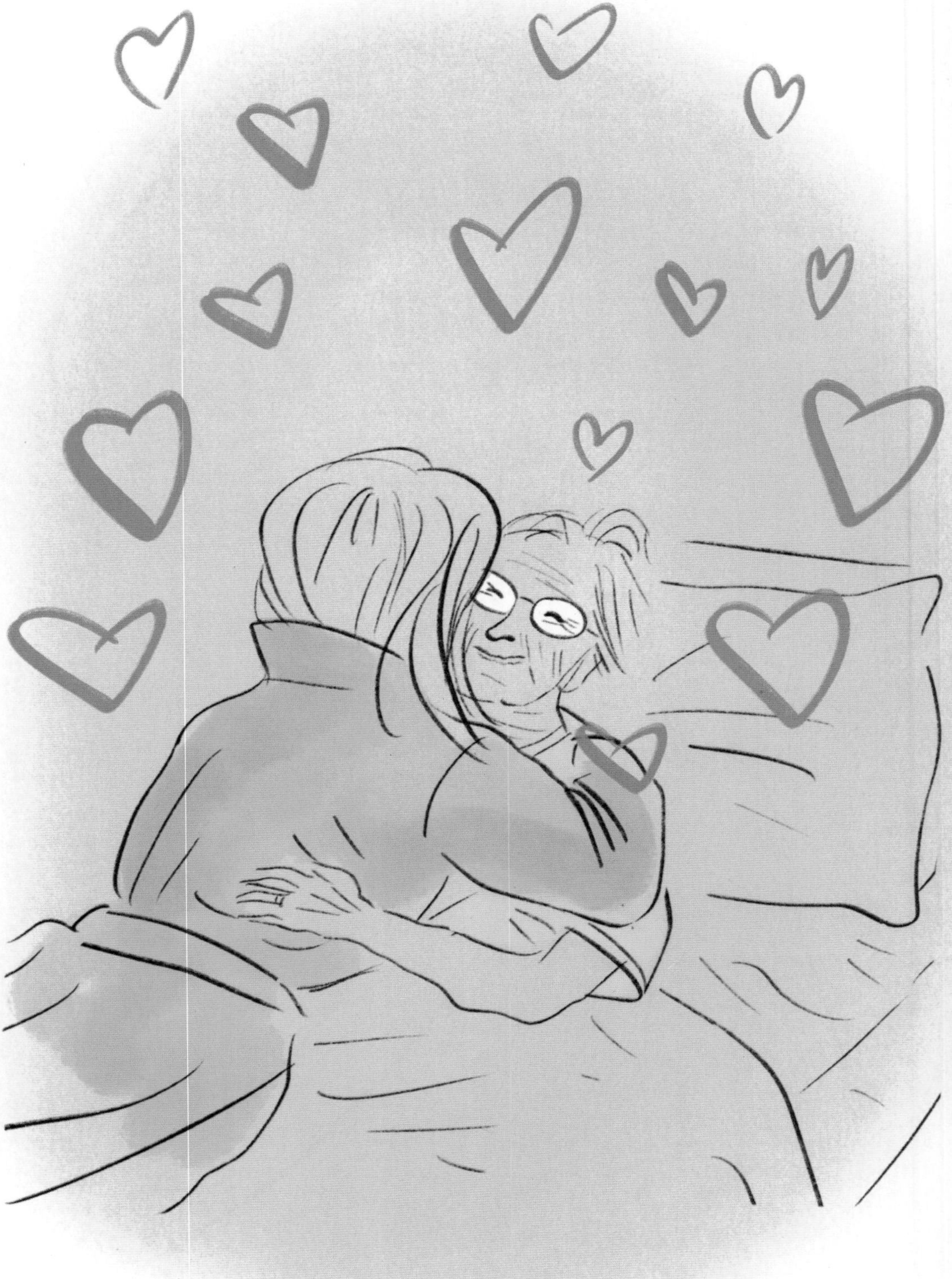

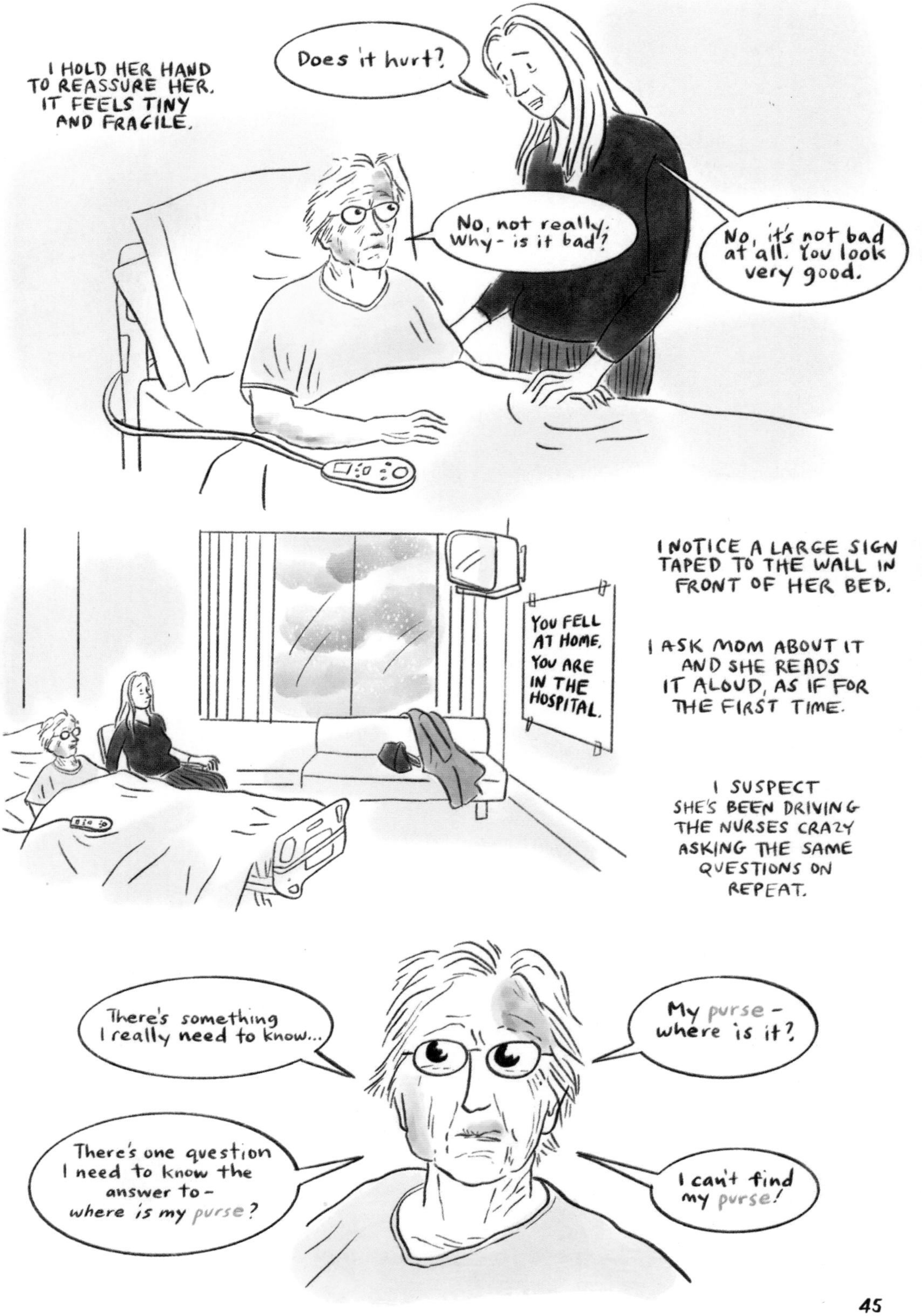
I HOLD HER HAND TO REASSURE HER. IT FEELS TINY AND FRAGILE.
Does it hurt?
No, not really. Why - is it bad?
No, it's not bad at all. You look very good.
I NOTICE A LARGE SIGN TAPED TO THE WALL IN FRONT OF HER BED.
YOU FELL AT HOME. YOU ARE IN THE HOSPITAL.
I ASK MOM ABOUT IT AND SHE READS IT ALOUD, AS IF FOR THE FIRST TIME.
I SUSPECT SHE'S BEEN DRIVING THE NURSES CRAZY ASKING THE SAME QUESTIONS ON REPEAT.
There's something I really need to know...
My purse - where is it?
There's one question I need to know the answer to - where is my purse?
I can't find my purse!

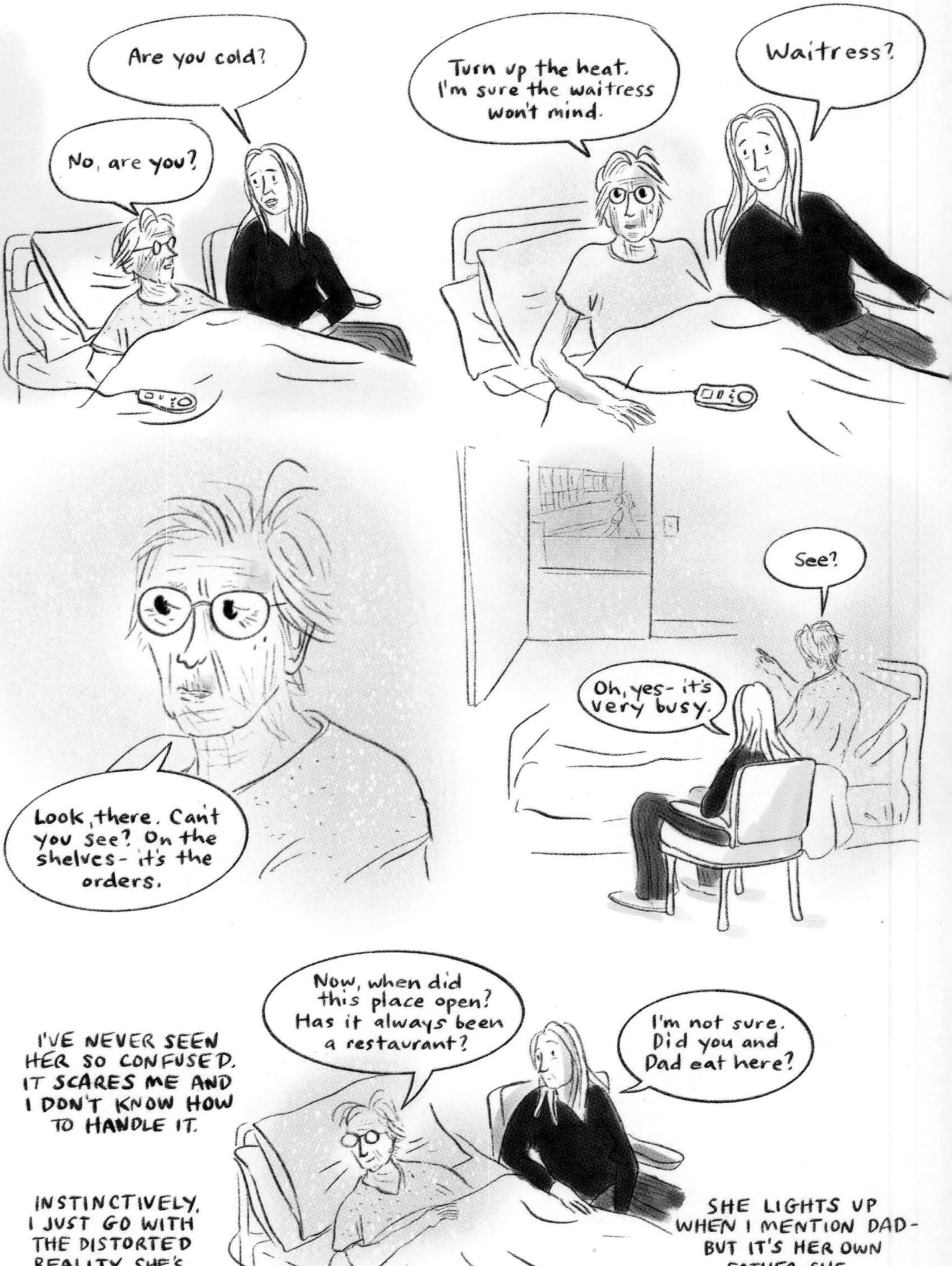

Are you cold?
No, are you?
Turn up the heat. I'm sure the waitress won't mind.
Waitress?
Look, there. Can't you see? On the shelves- it's the orders.
See?
Oh, yes- it's very busy.
I'VE NEVER SEEN HER SO CONFUSED. IT SCARES ME AND I DON'T KNOW HOW TO HANDLE IT.
Now, when did this place open? Has it always been a restaurant?
I'm not sure. Did you and Dad eat here?
INSTINCTIVELY, I JUST GO WITH THE DISTORTED REALITY SHE'S LOST IN.
SHE LIGHTS UP WHEN I MENTION DAD- BUT IT'S HER OWN FATHER SHE REMEMBERS...

SHE SOUNDS CRAZY, TALKING ABOUT FILLING UP AT THE GAS STATION WITH HER MOM AND DAD- AND THE NICE MAN IN THE BROWN SUIT.

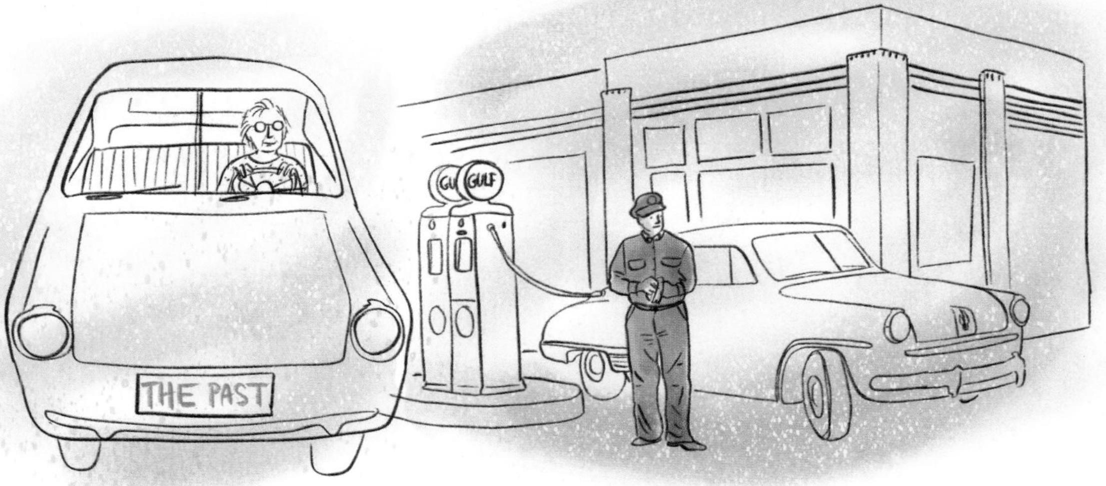

GULF
THE PAST

BUT BIZARRELY, SHE SOUNDS HAPPY, GIGGLING EVEN.

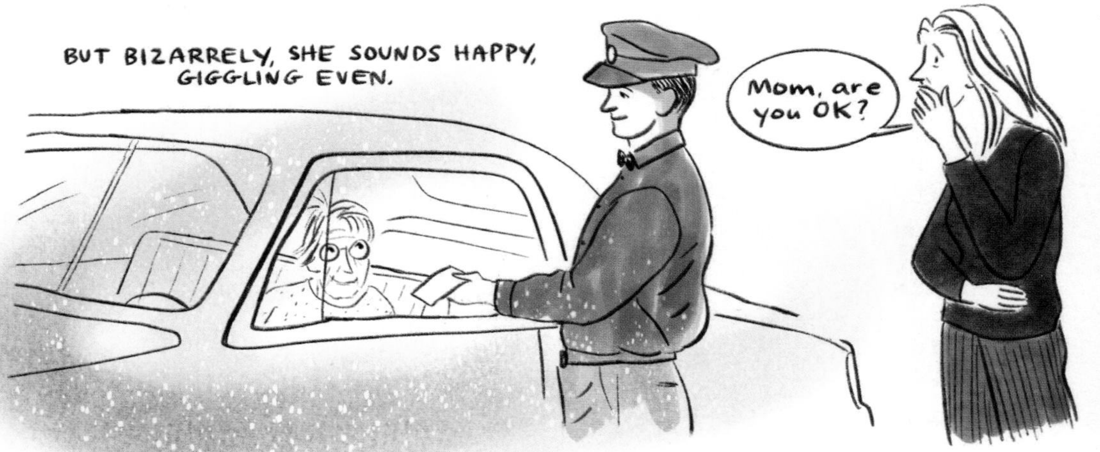

Mom, are you OK?

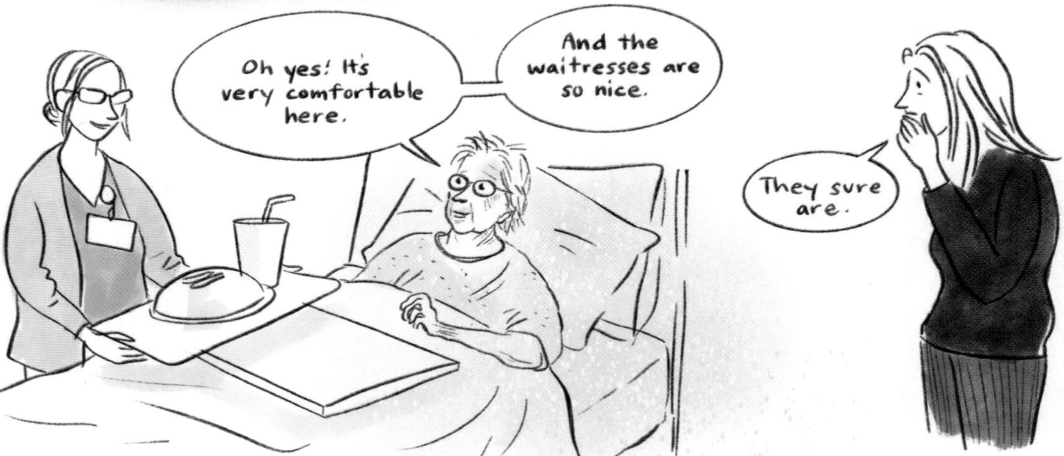

Oh yes! It's very comfortable here.
And the waitresses are so nice.
They sure are.

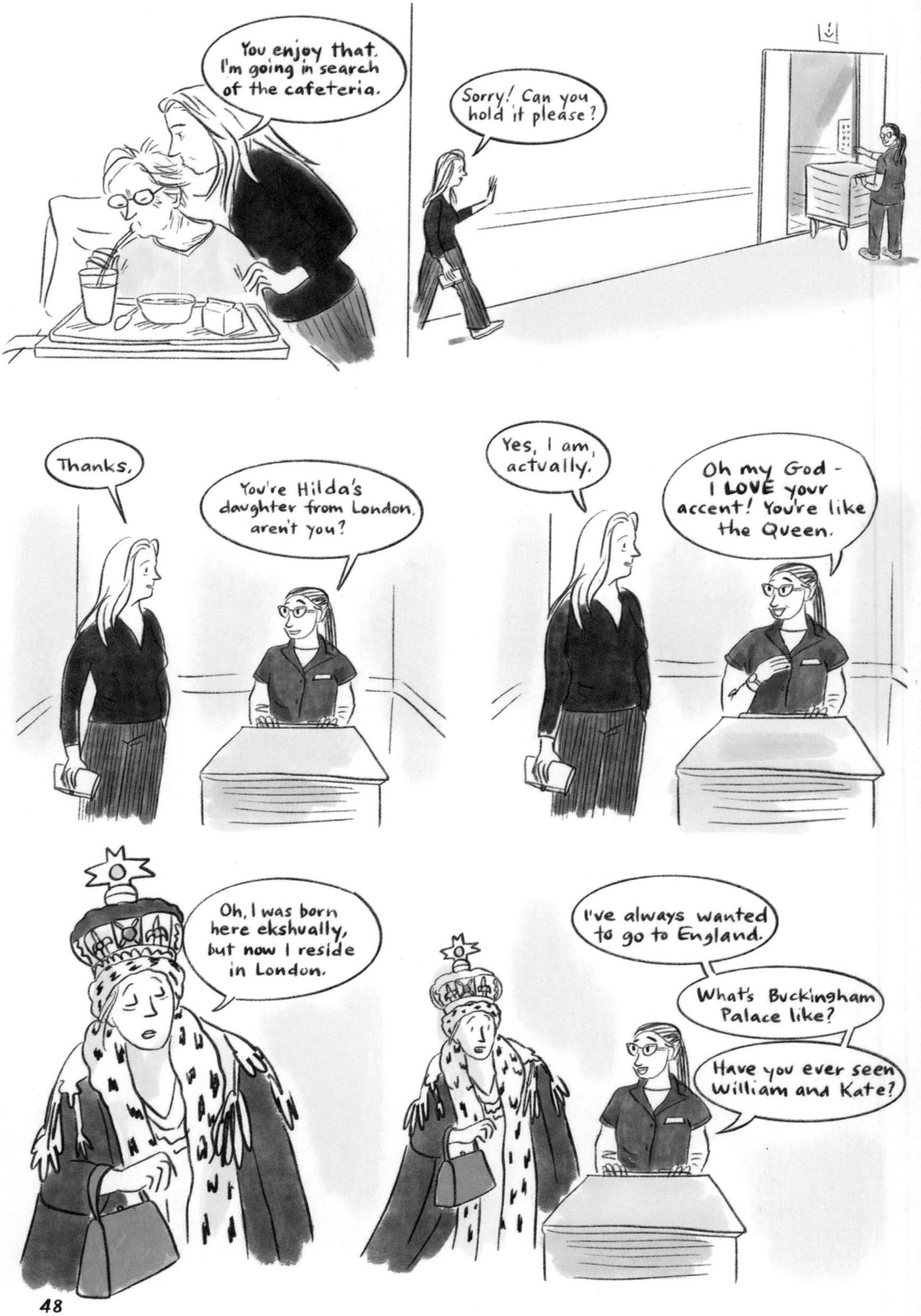
You enjoy that. I'm going in search of the cafeteria.
Sorry! Can you hold it please?
Thanks.
You're Hilda's daughter from London, aren't you?
Yes, I am, actually.
Oh my God - I **LOVE** your accent! You're like the Queen.
Oh, I was born here ekshually, but now I reside in London.
I've always wanted to go to England.
What's Buckingham Palace like?
Have you ever seen William and Kate?

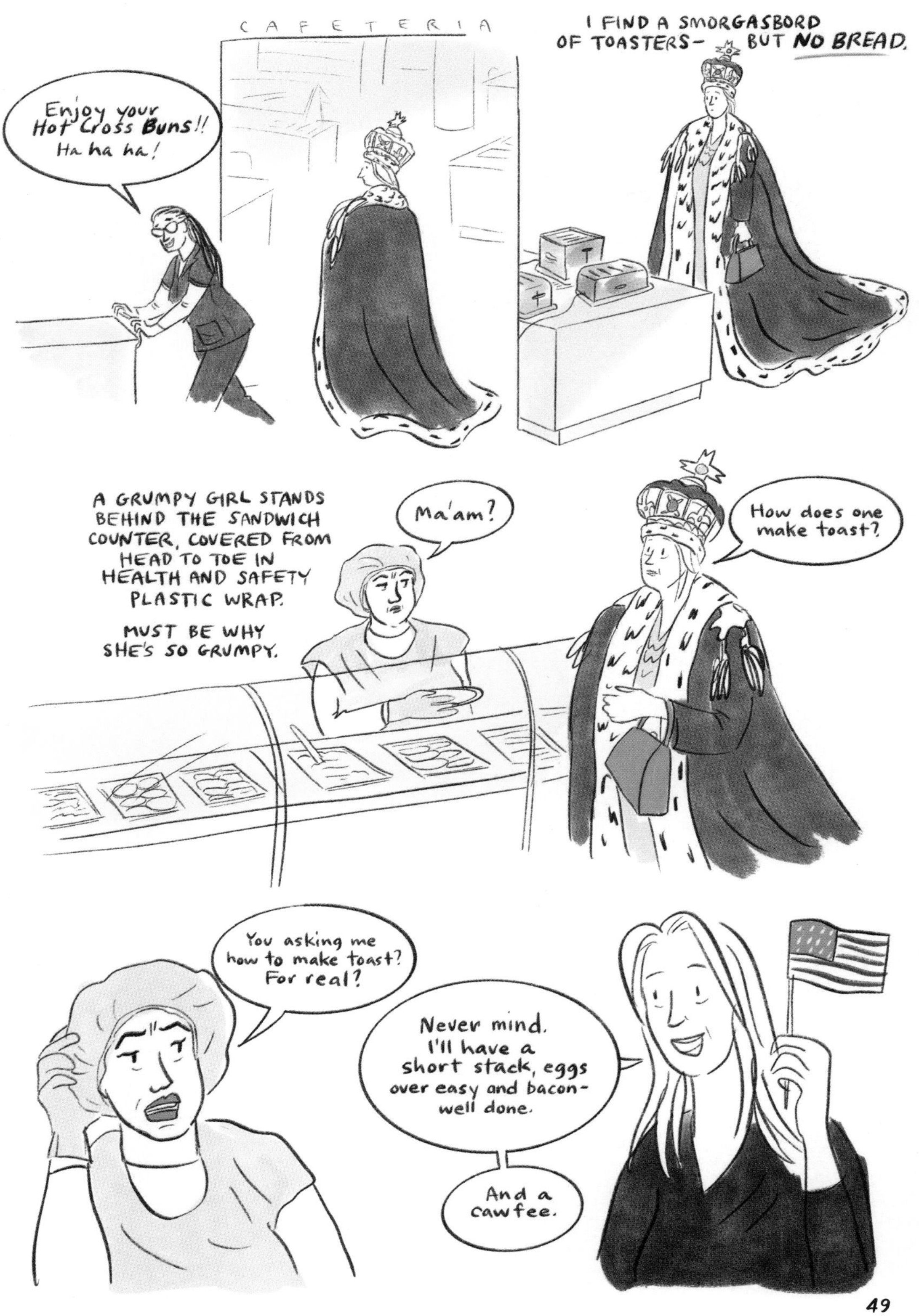
CAFETERIA
Enjoy your Hot Cross Buns!! Ha ha ha!
I FIND A SMORGASBORD OF TOASTERS- BUT NO BREAD.
A GRUMPY GIRL STANDS BEHIND THE SANDWICH COUNTER, COVERED FROM HEAD TO TOE IN HEALTH AND SAFETY PLASTIC WRAP.
MUST BE WHY SHE'S SO GRUMPY.
Ma'am?
How does one make toast?
You asking me how to make toast? For real?
Never mind. I'll have a short stack, eggs over easy and bacon- well done.
And a cawfee.

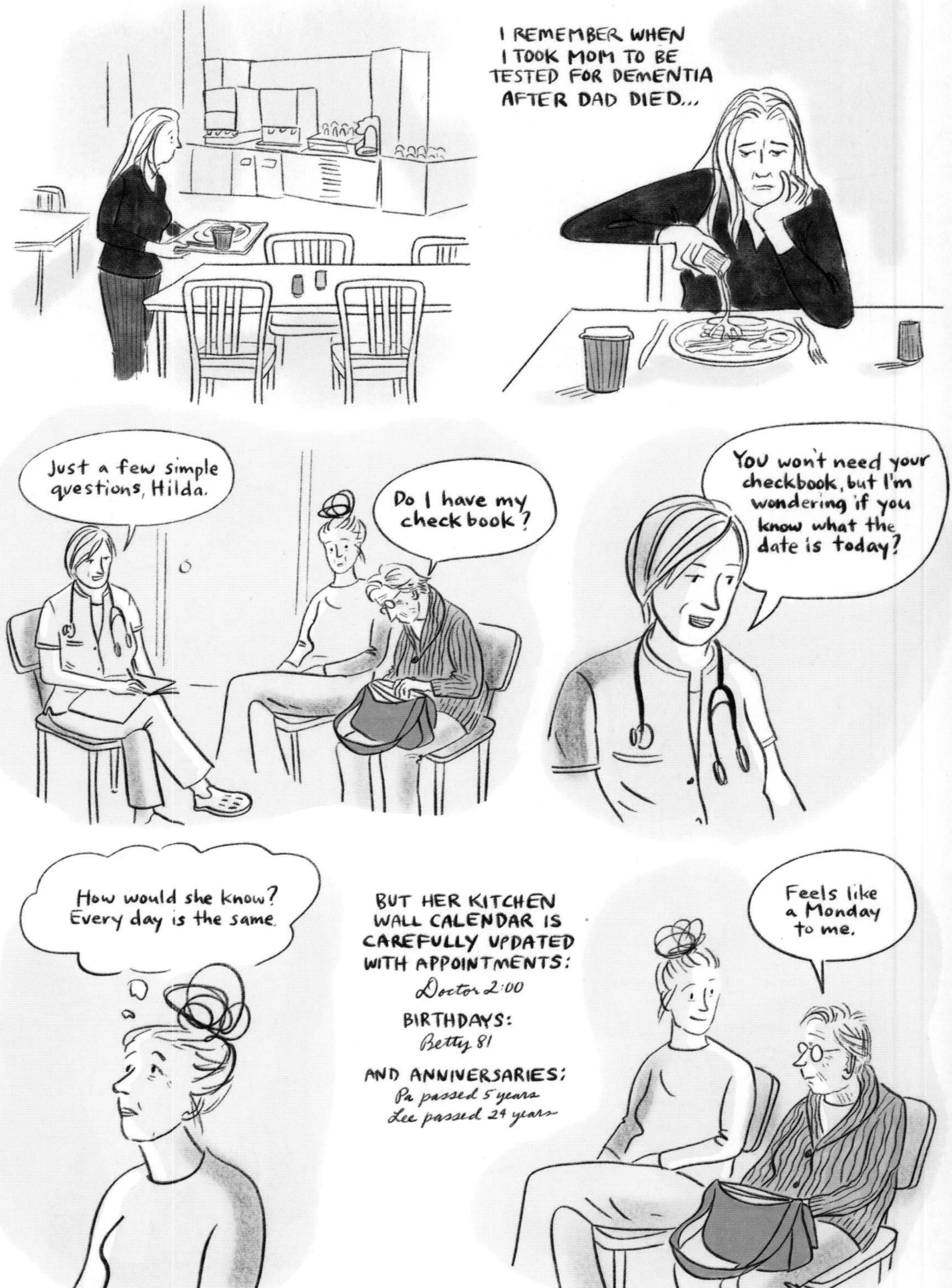
I REMEMBER WHEN I TOOK MOM TO BE TESTED FOR DEMENTIA AFTER DAD DIED...
Just a few simple questions, Hilda.
Do I have my check book?
You won't need your checkbook, but I'm wondering if you know what the date is today?
How would she know? Every day is the same.
BUT HER KITCHEN WALL CALENDAR IS CAREFULLY UPDATED WITH APPOINTMENTS:
Doctor 2:00
BIRTHDAYS:
Betty 81
AND ANNIVERSARIES:
Pa passed 5 years
Lee passed 24 years
Feels like a Monday to me.

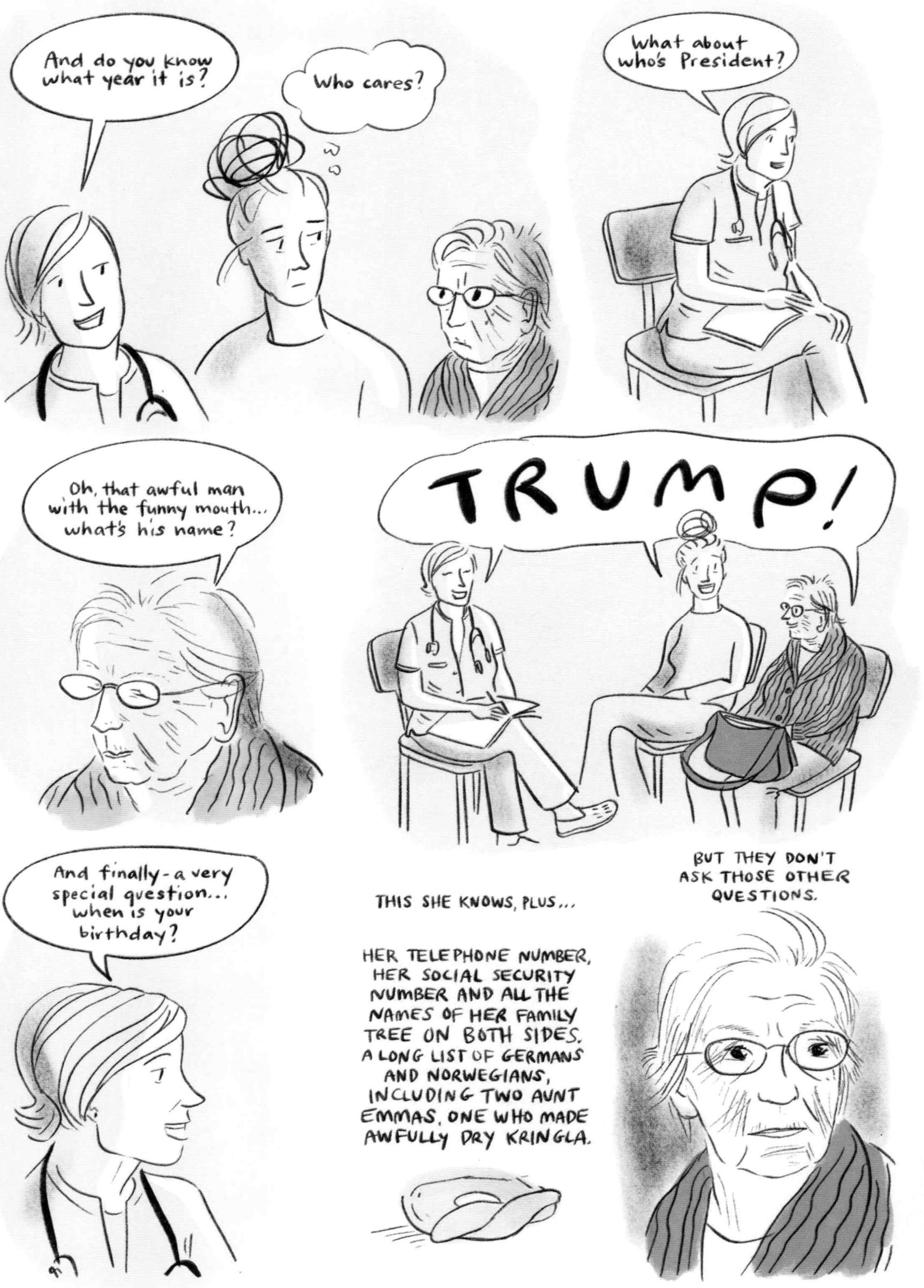
And do you know what year it is?
Who cares?
What about who's President?
Oh, that awful man with the funny mouth... what's his name?
TRUMP!
And finally - a very special question... when is your birthday?
THIS SHE KNOWS, PLUS...
HER TELEPHONE NUMBER, HER SOCIAL SECURITY NUMBER AND ALL THE NAMES OF HER FAMILY TREE ON BOTH SIDES. A LONG LIST OF GERMANS AND NORWEGIANS, INCLUDING TWO AUNT EMMAS, ONE WHO MADE AWFULLY DRY KRINGLA.
BUT THEY DON'T ASK THOSE OTHER QUESTIONS.

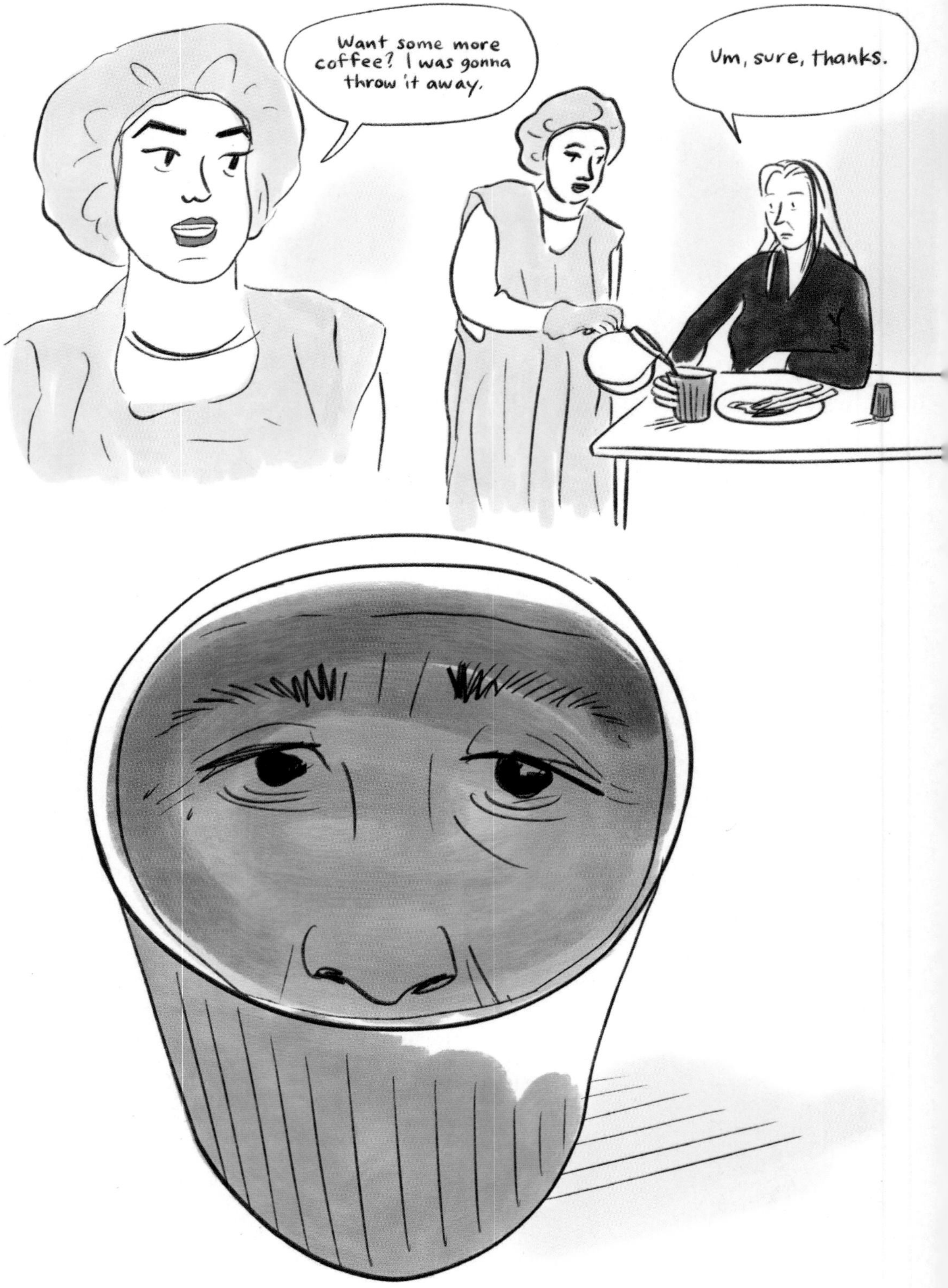
Want some more coffee? I was gonna throw it away.
Um, sure, thanks.

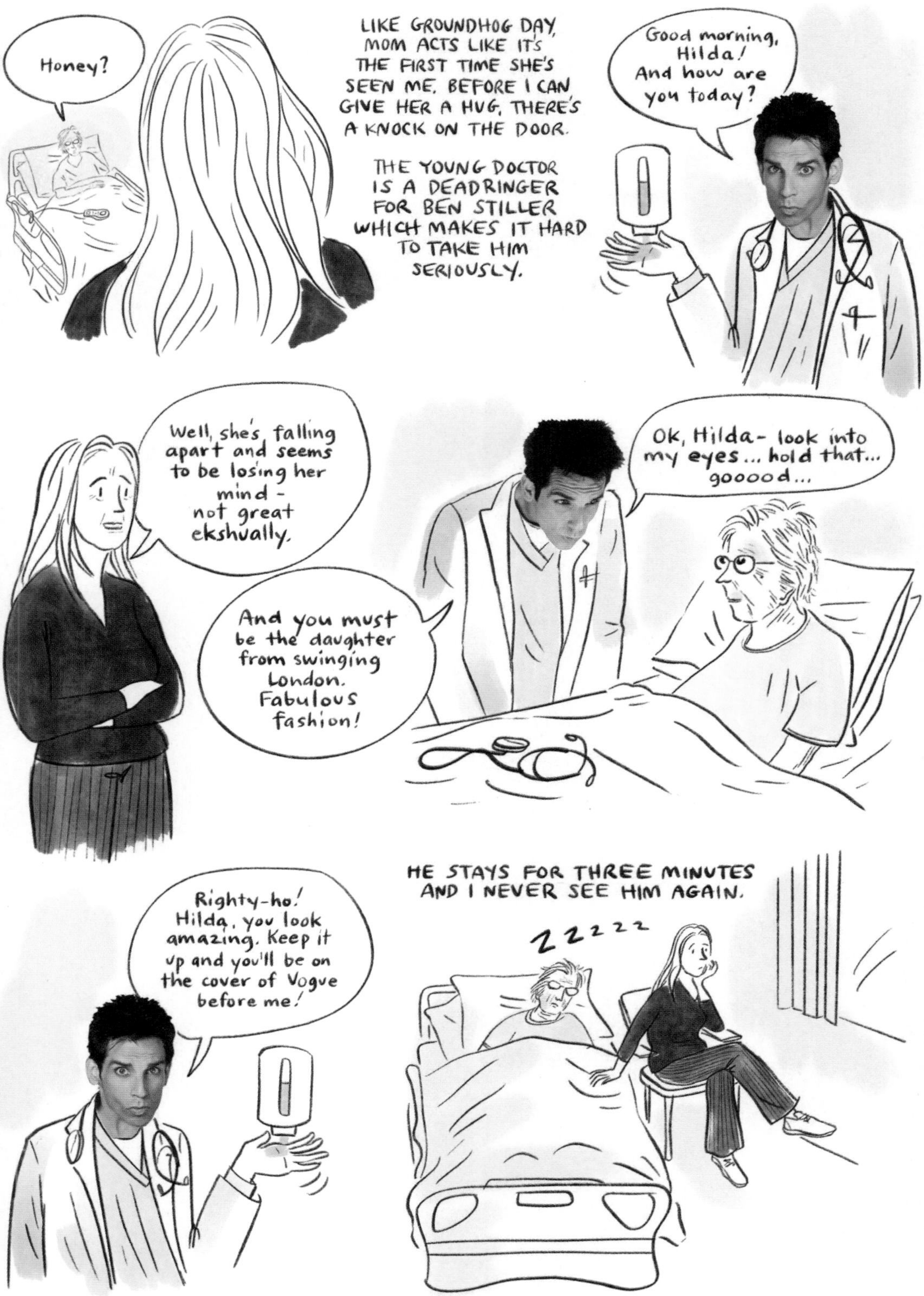
Honey?
LIKE GROUNDHOG DAY, MOM ACTS LIKE IT'S THE FIRST TIME SHE'S SEEN ME. BEFORE I CAN GIVE HER A HUG, THERE'S A KNOCK ON THE DOOR.
THE YOUNG DOCTOR IS A DEADRINGER FOR BEN STILLER WHICH MAKES IT HARD TO TAKE HIM SERIOUSLY.
Good morning, Hilda! And how are you today?
Well, she's falling apart and seems to be losing her mind - not great ekshvally.
Ok, Hilda- look into my eyes... hold that... gooood...
And you must be the daughter from swinging London. Fabulous fashion!
Righty-ho! Hilda, you look amazing. Keep it up and you'll be on the cover of Vogue before me!
HE STAYS FOR THREE MINUTES AND I NEVER SEE HIM AGAIN.
ZZZZZ

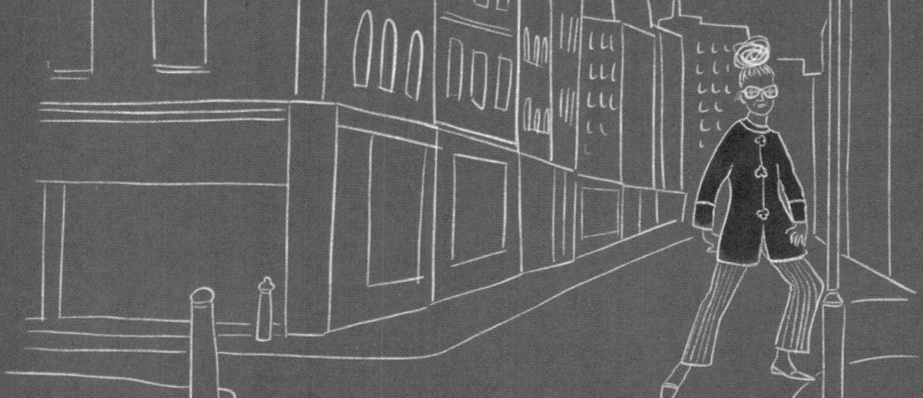
CARNABY ST.

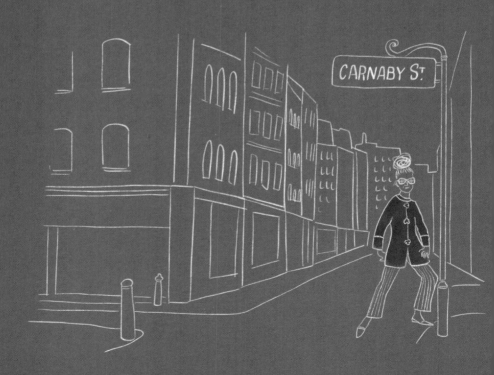

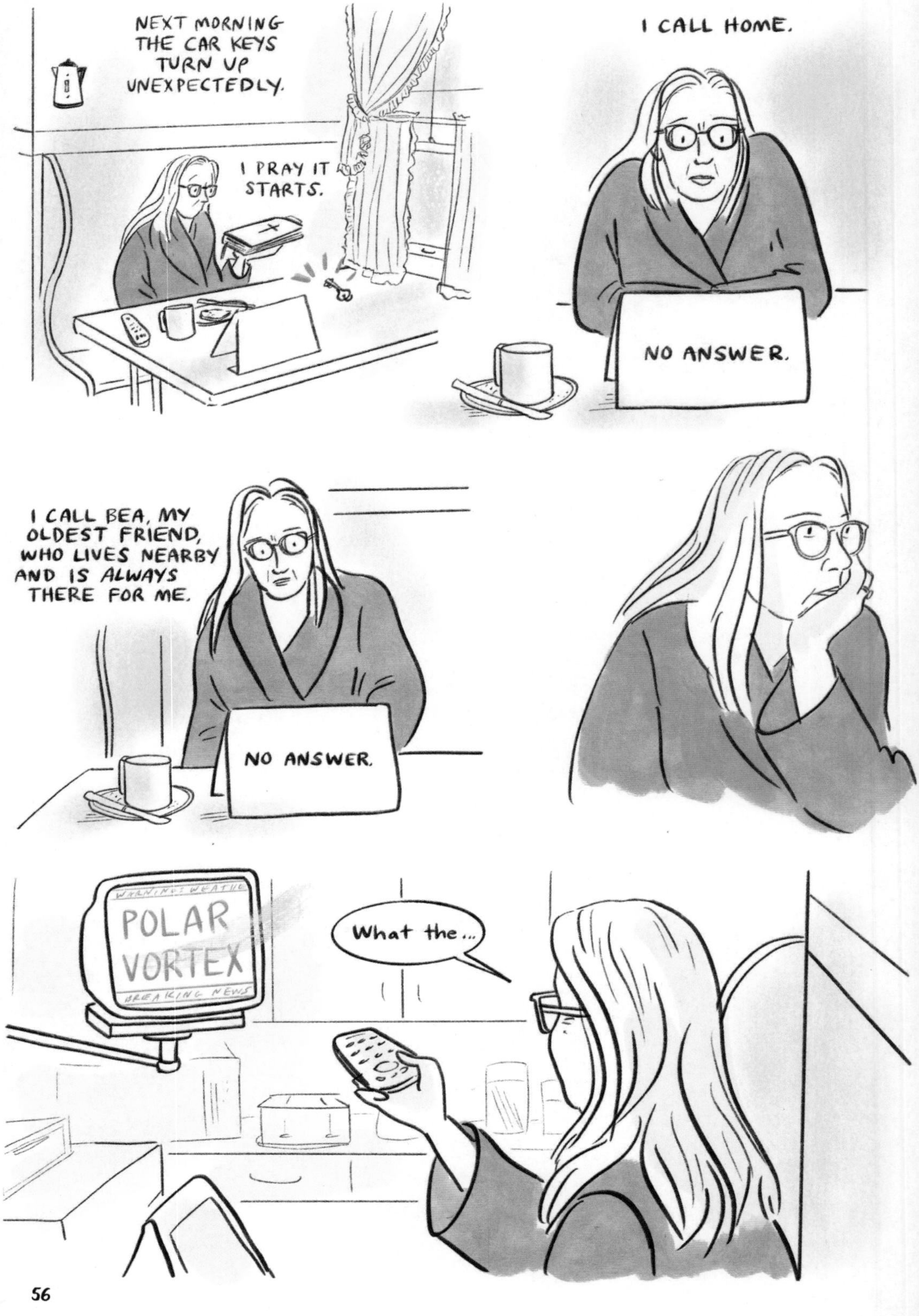
NEXT MORNING THE CAR KEYS TURN UP UNEXPECTEDLY.
I PRAY IT STARTS.
I CALL HOME.
NO ANSWER.
I CALL BEA, MY OLDEST FRIEND, WHO LIVES NEARBY AND IS *ALWAYS* THERE FOR ME.
NO ANSWER.
POLAR VORTEX
What the...

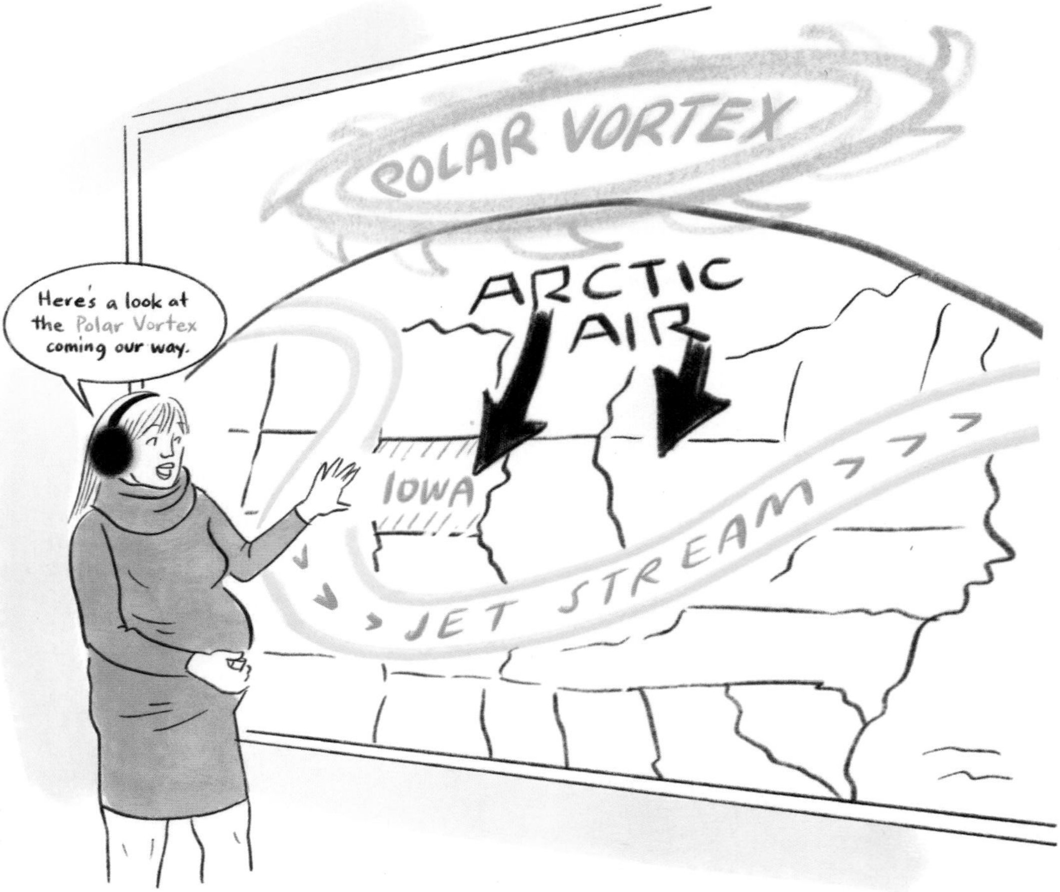
POLAR VORTEX
ARCTIC AIR
IOWA
JET STREAM
Here's a look at the Polar Vortex coming our way.

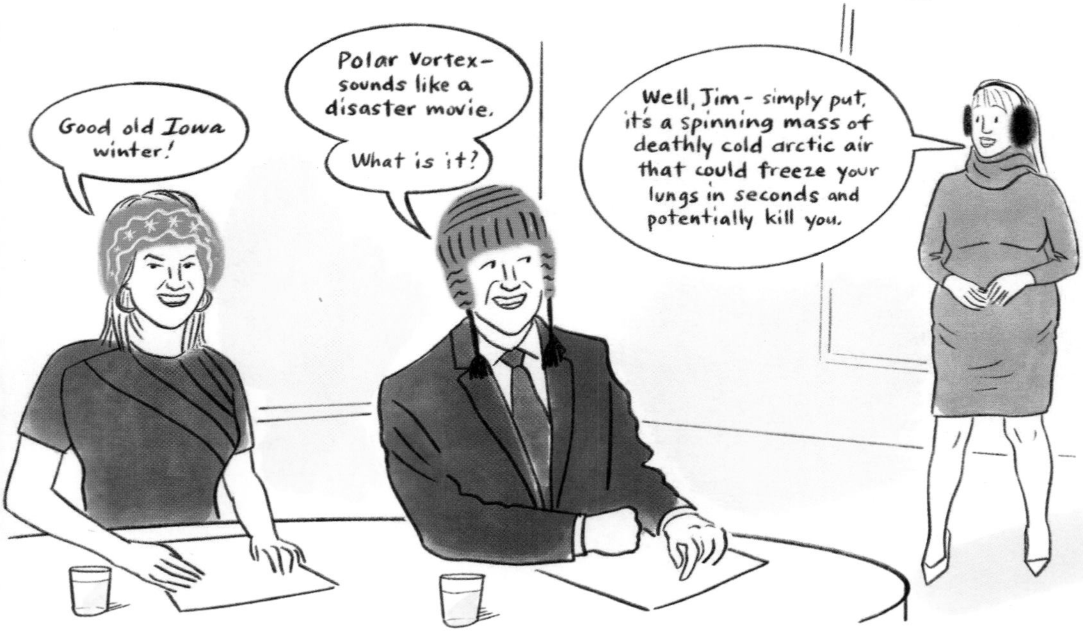
Good old Iowa winter!
Polar Vortex- sounds like a disaster movie.
What is it?
Well, Jim - simply put, it's a spinning mass of deathly cold arctic air that could freeze your lungs in seconds and potentially kill you.

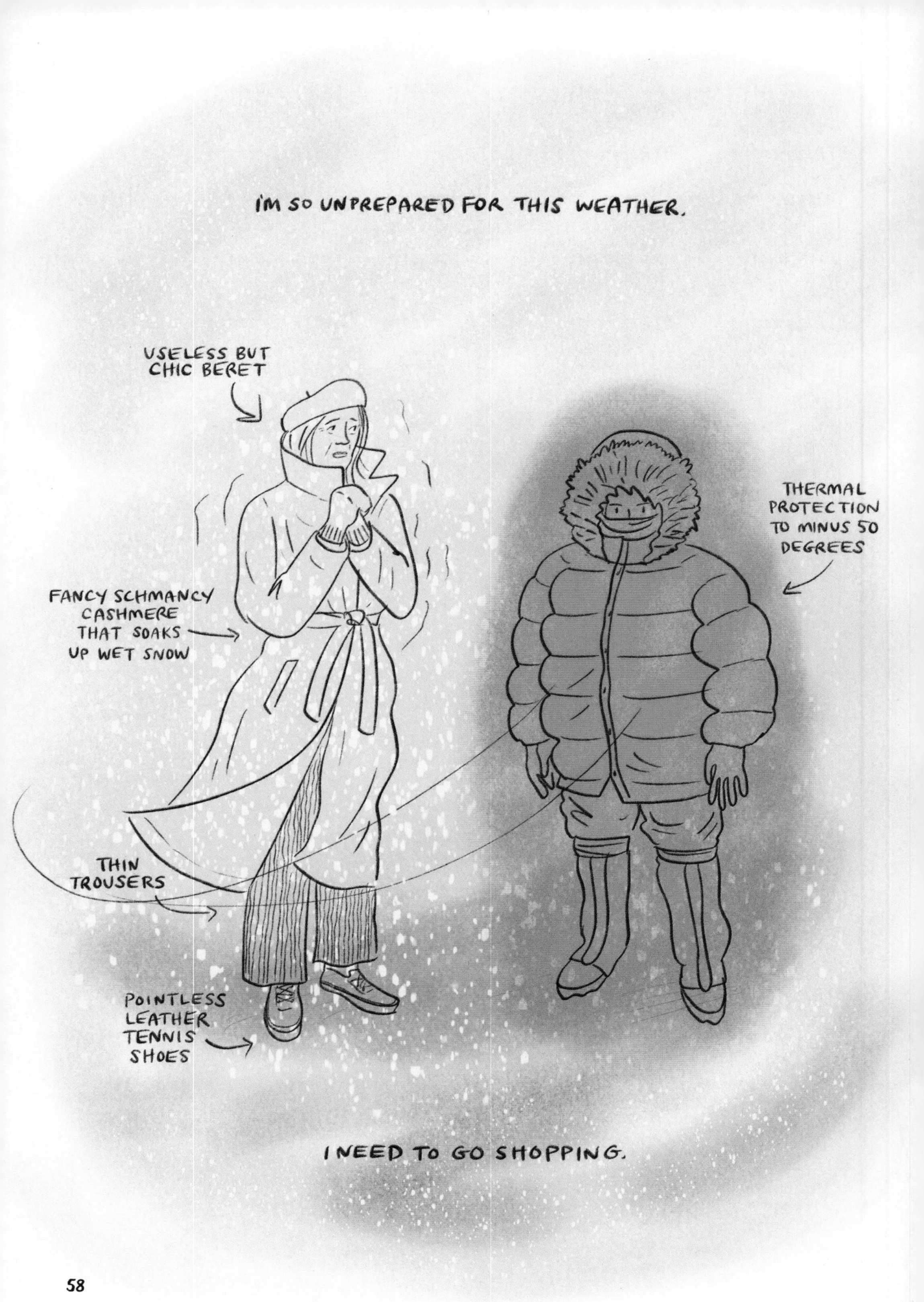
I'M SO UNPREPARED FOR THIS WEATHER.
USELESS BUT CHIC BERET
FANCY SCHMANCY CASHMERE THAT SOAKS UP WET SNOW
THIN TROUSERS
POINTLESS LEATHER TENNIS SHOES
THERMAL PROTECTION TO MINUS 50 DEGREES
I NEED TO GO SHOPPING.

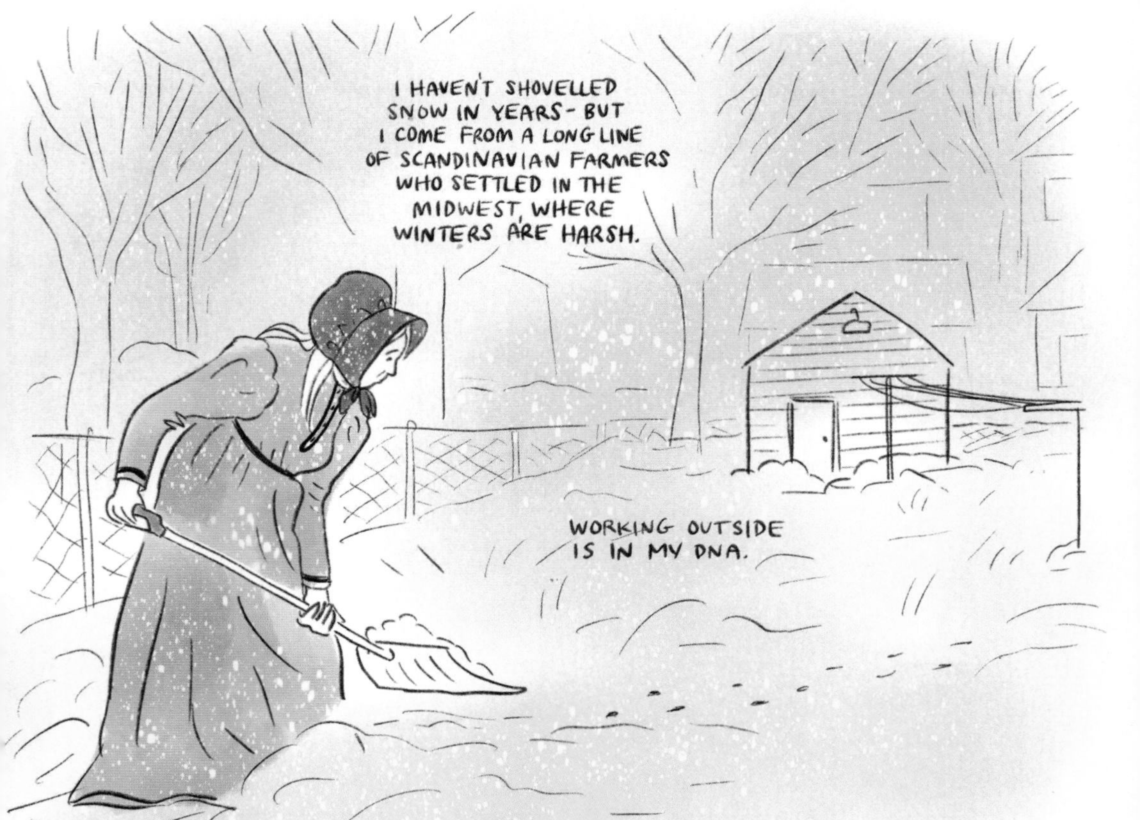
I HAVEN'T SHOVELLED SNOW IN YEARS- BUT I COME FROM A LONG LINE OF SCANDINAVIAN FARMERS WHO SETTLED IN THE MIDWEST, WHERE WINTERS ARE HARSH.
WORKING OUTSIDE IS IN MY DNA.

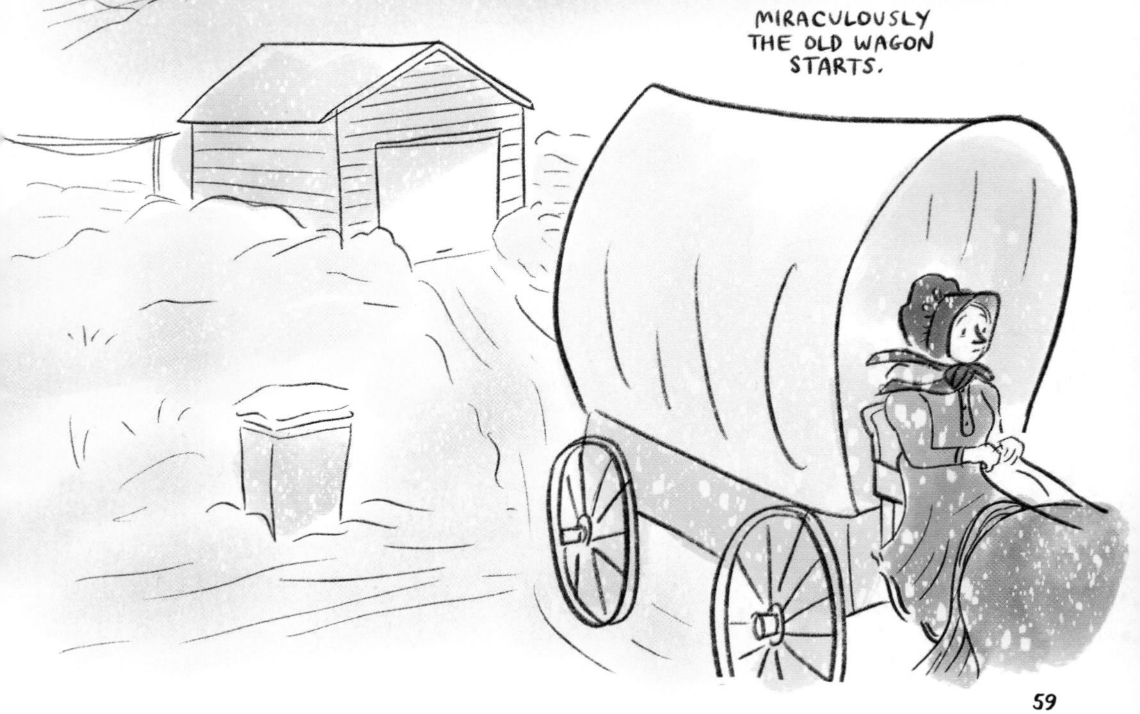
MIRACULOUSLY THE OLD WAGON STARTS.

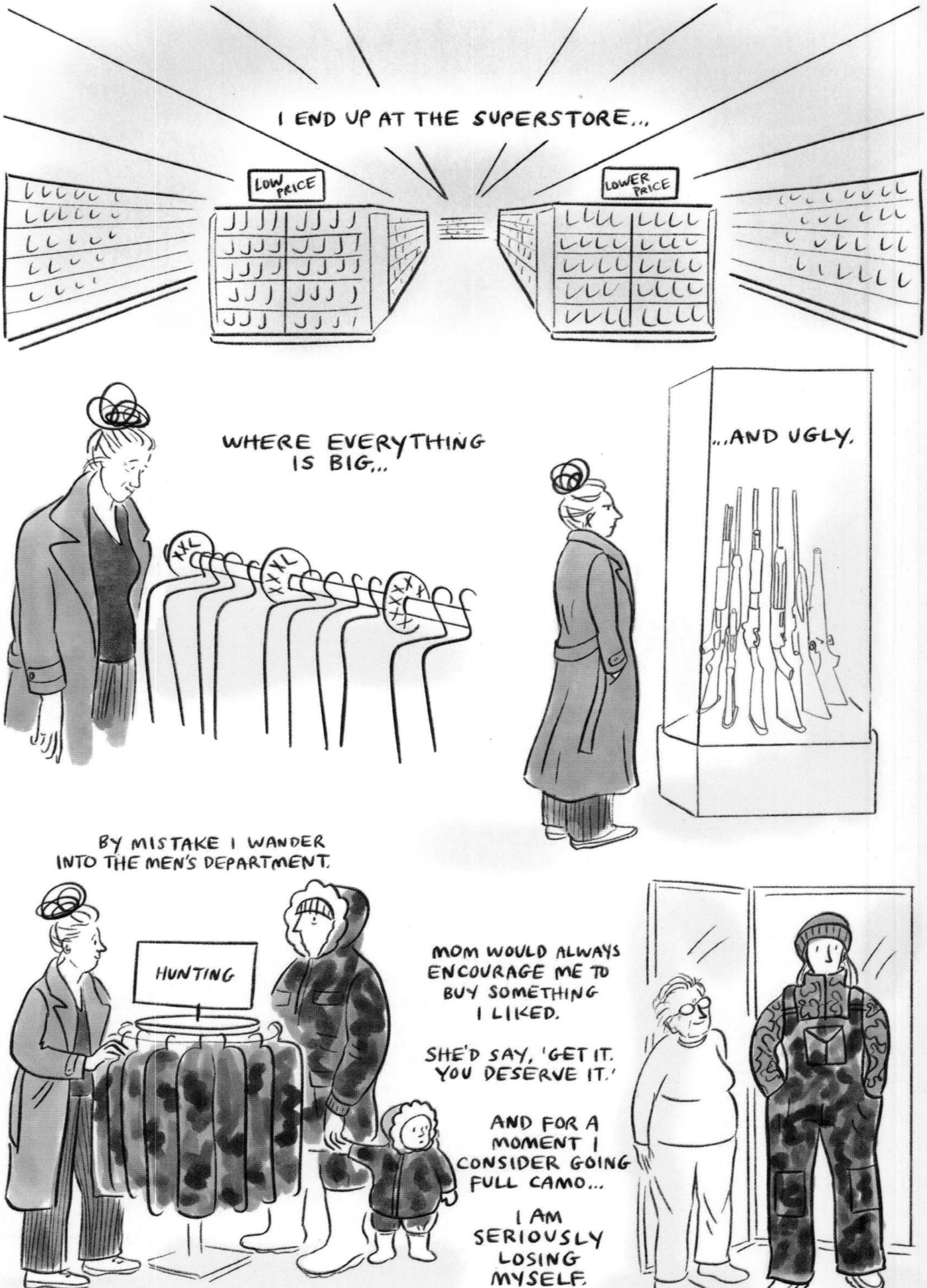
I END UP AT THE SUPERSTORE...
LOW PRICE
LOWER PRICE
WHERE EVERYTHING IS BIG...
XXL
XXXL
XXXXL
...AND UGLY.
BY MISTAKE I WANDER INTO THE MEN'S DEPARTMENT.
HUNTING
MOM WOULD ALWAYS ENCOURAGE ME TO BUY SOMETHING I LIKED.
SHE'D SAY, 'GET IT. YOU DESERVE IT.'
AND FOR A MOMENT I CONSIDER GOING FULL CAMO...
I AM SERIOUSLY LOSING MYSELF.

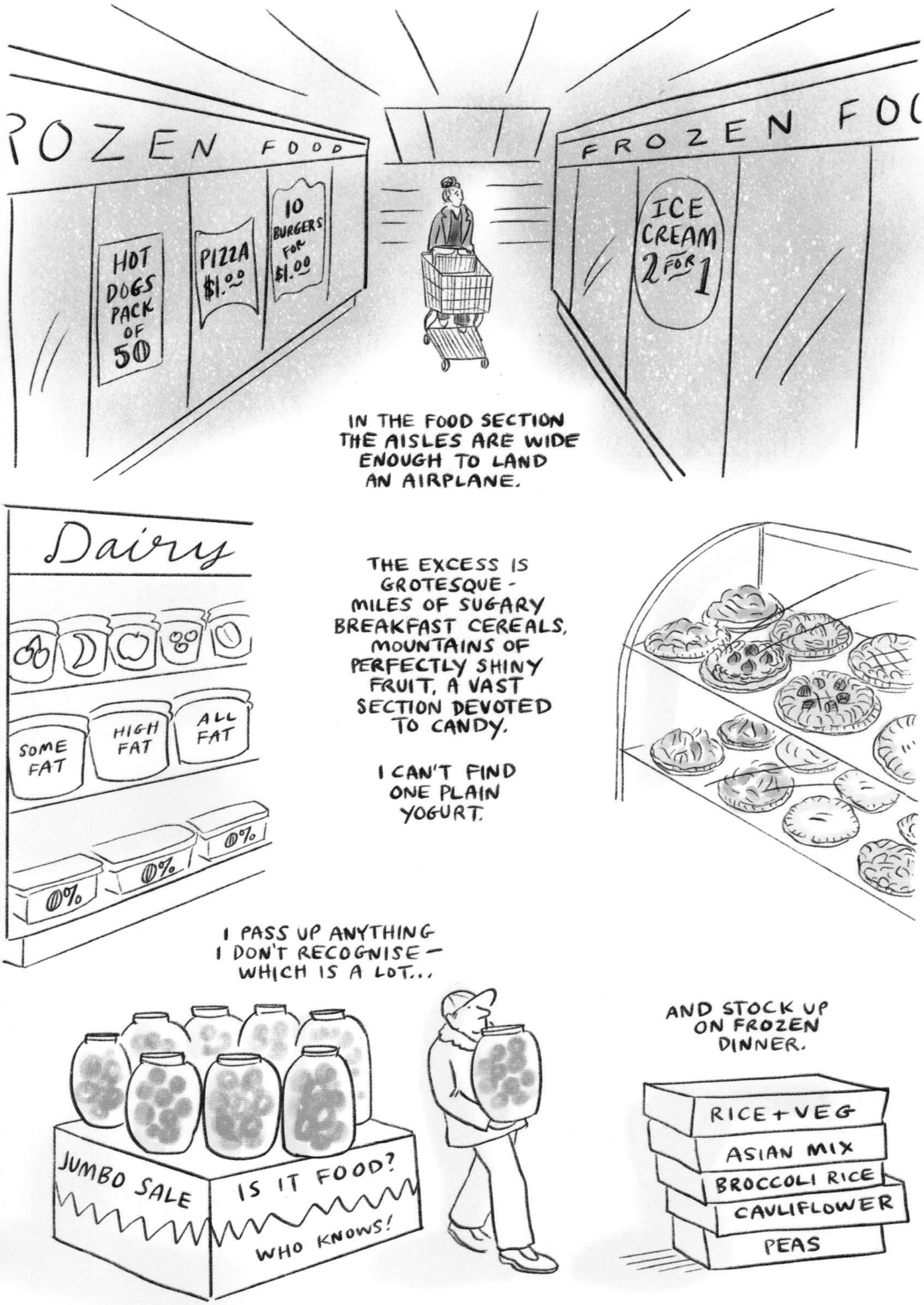

FROZEN FOOD
HOT DOGS PACK OF 50
PIZZA $1.00
10 BURGERS FOR $1.00
FROZEN FOO
ICE CREAM 2 FOR 1
IN THE FOOD SECTION THE AISLES ARE WIDE ENOUGH TO LAND AN AIRPLANE.
Dairy
SOME FAT
HIGH FAT
ALL FAT
0%
0%
0%
THE EXCESS IS GROTESQUE - MILES OF SUGARY BREAKFAST CEREALS, MOUNTAINS OF PERFECTLY SHINY FRUIT, A VAST SECTION DEVOTED TO CANDY.
I CAN'T FIND ONE PLAIN YOGURT.
I PASS UP ANYTHING I DON'T RECOGNISE - WHICH IS A LOT...
JUMBO SALE
IS IT FOOD?
WHO KNOWS!
AND STOCK UP ON FROZEN DINNER.
RICE + VEG
ASIAN MIX
BROCCOLI RICE
CAULIFLOWER
PEAS

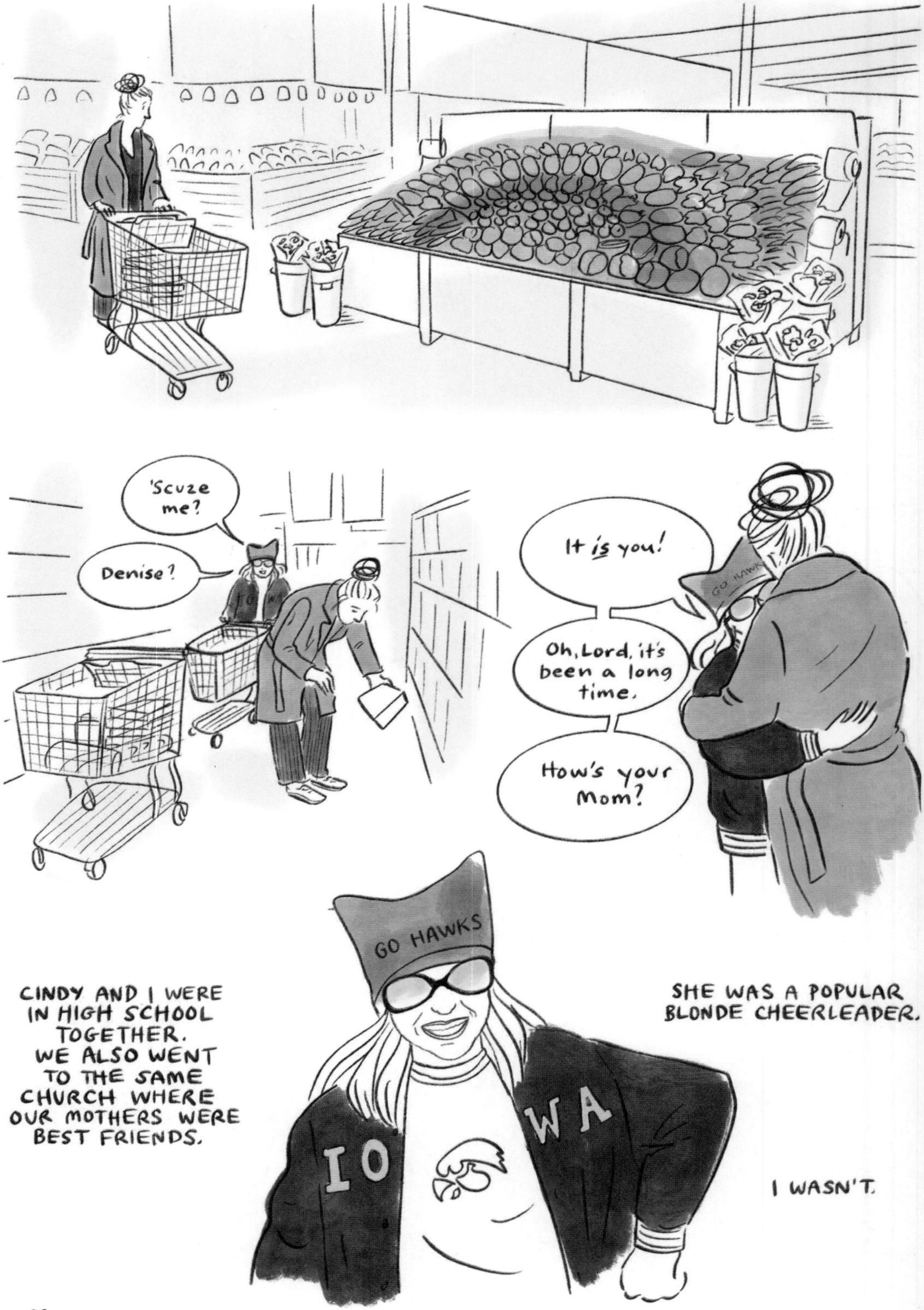
'Scuze me?
Denise?
It is you!
Oh, Lord, it's been a long time.
How's your Mom?
GO HAWKS
CINDY AND I WERE IN HIGH SCHOOL TOGETHER. WE ALSO WENT TO THE SAME CHURCH WHERE OUR MOTHERS WERE BEST FRIENDS.
GO HAWKS
IOWA
SHE WAS A POPULAR BLONDE CHEERLEADER.
I WASN'T.

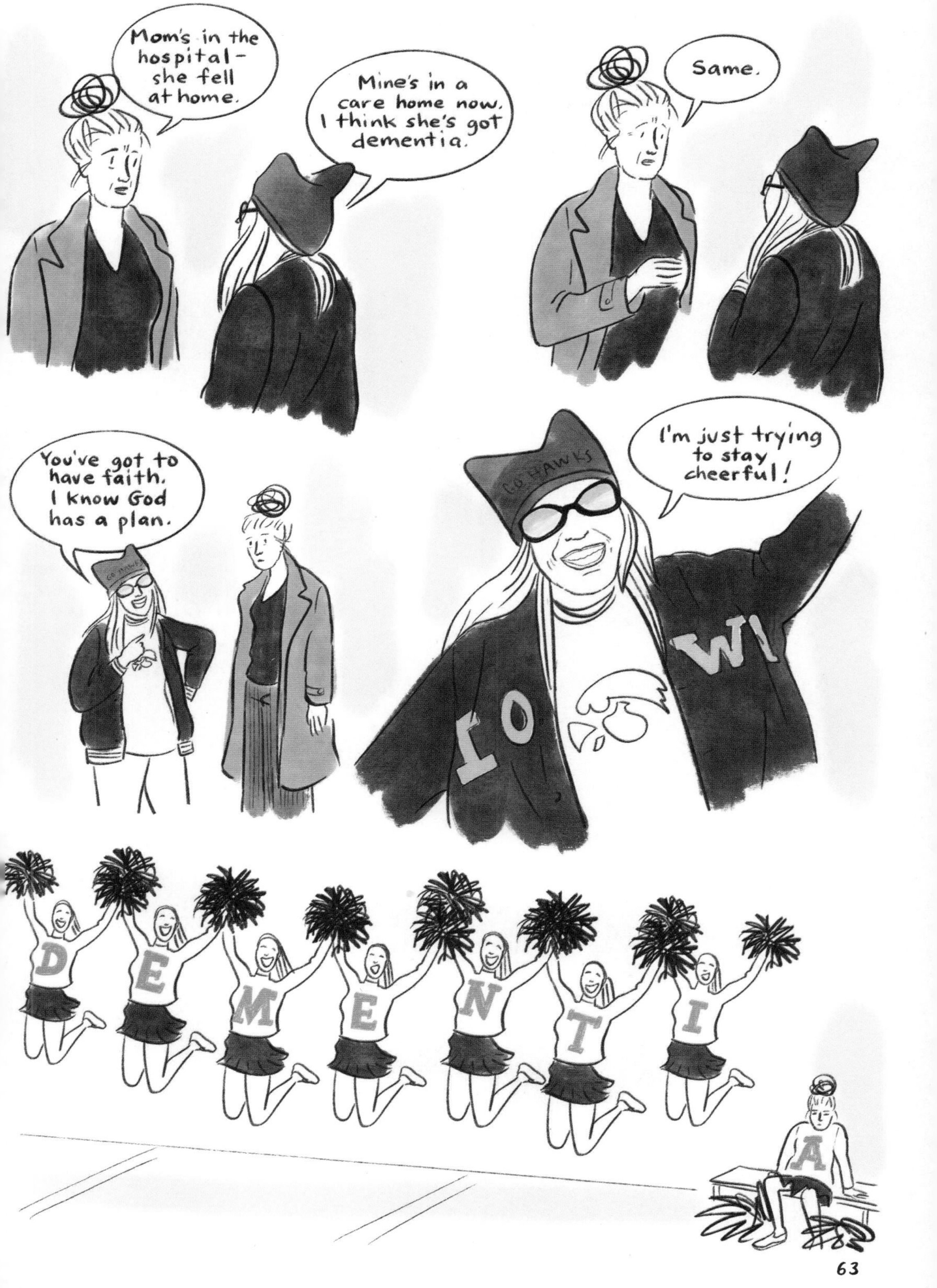
Mom's in the hospital- she fell at home.
Mine's in a care home now. I think she's got dementia.
Same.
You've got to have faith. I know God has a plan.
I'm just trying to stay cheerful!
GO HAWKS
IOWA
D E M E N T I
A

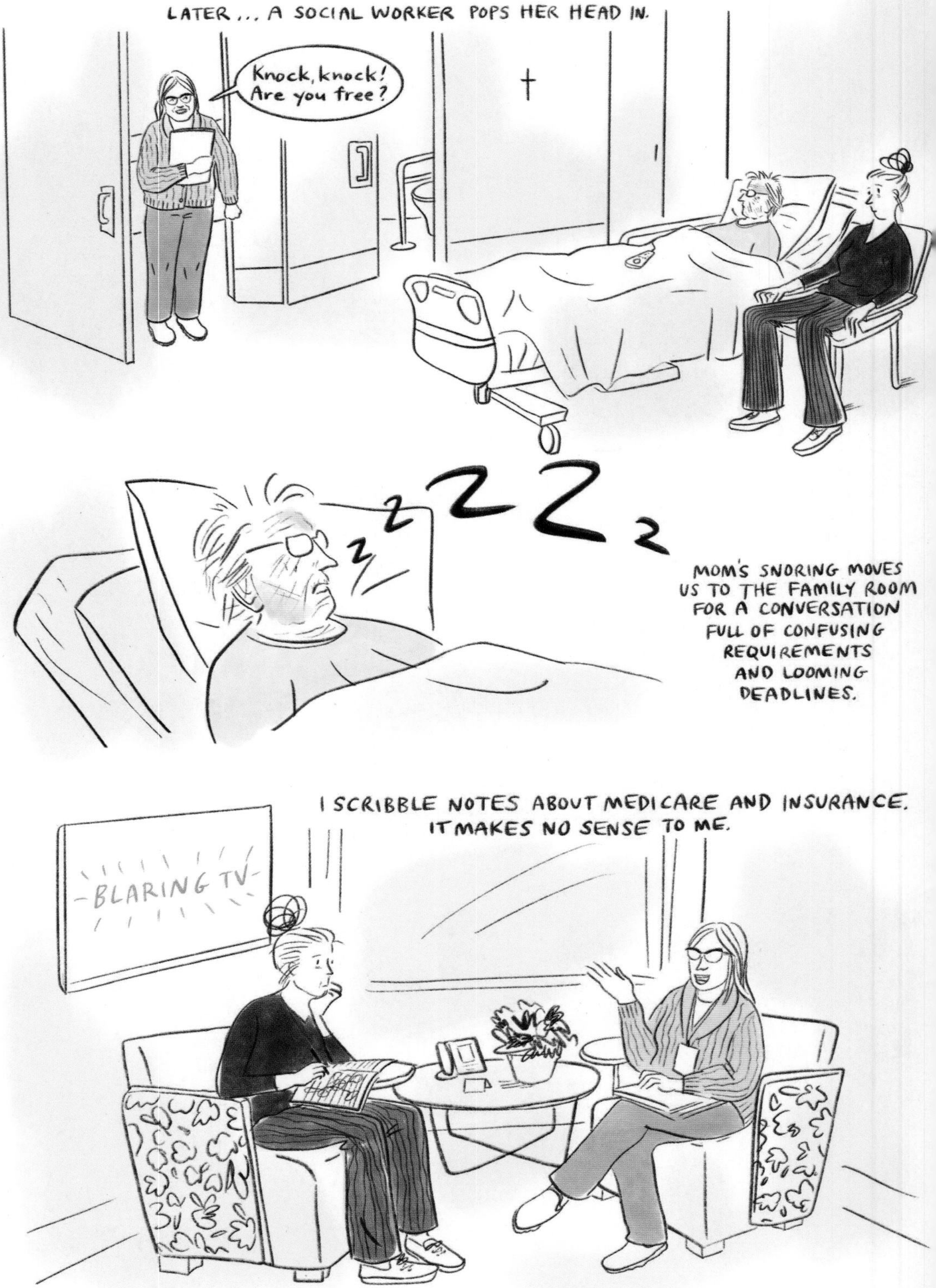
LATER... A SOCIAL WORKER POPS HER HEAD IN.
Knock, knock! Are you free?
ZZZZZ
MOM'S SNORING MOVES US TO THE FAMILY ROOM FOR A CONVERSATION FULL OF CONFUSING REQUIREMENTS AND LOOMING DEADLINES.
I SCRIBBLE NOTES ABOUT MEDICARE AND INSURANCE. IT MAKES NO SENSE TO ME.
BLARING TV

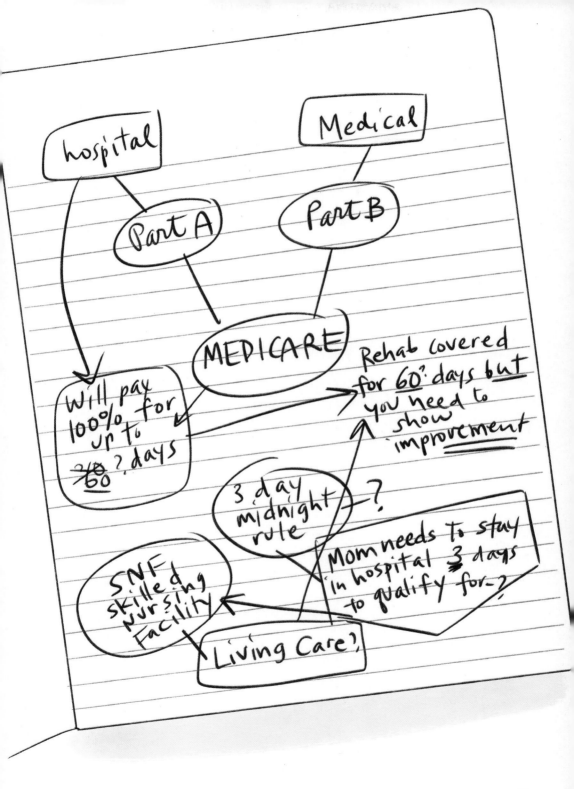

hospital

Medical

Part A

Part B

MEDICARE

Will pay 100% for up to 2̶0̶ ? days 60

Rehab covered for 60? days but you need to show improvement

3 day midnight rule — ?

Mom needs to stay in hospital 3 days to qualify for ?

SNF skilled nursing facility

Living Care?

THE LONG AND SHORT OF IT IS THAT MOM'S PRIVATE HEALTH INSURANCE

WILL ONLY PAY FOR HER TO BE IN THE HOSPITAL

FOR THREE MORE DAYS!

AFTER THREE DAYS SHE WILL BE MOVED TO LIVING CARE

A REHAB CENTER JUST FIVE MINUTES AWAY.

INSURANCE WILL CONTINUE TO COVER HER,

BUT ONLY AS LONG AS HER HEALTH KEEPS IMPROVING.

OTHERWISE...

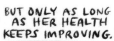

THE INSURANCE PIT

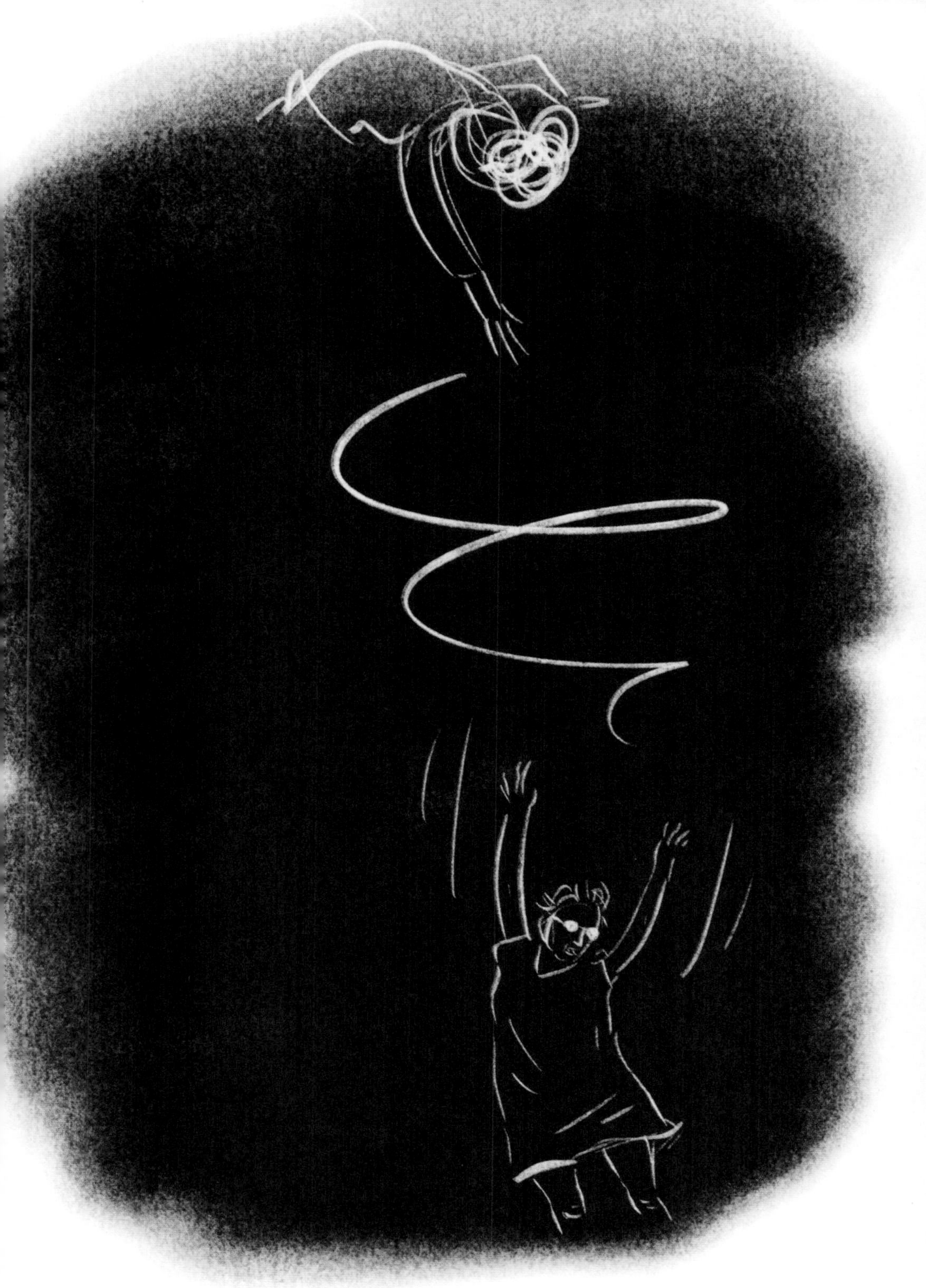

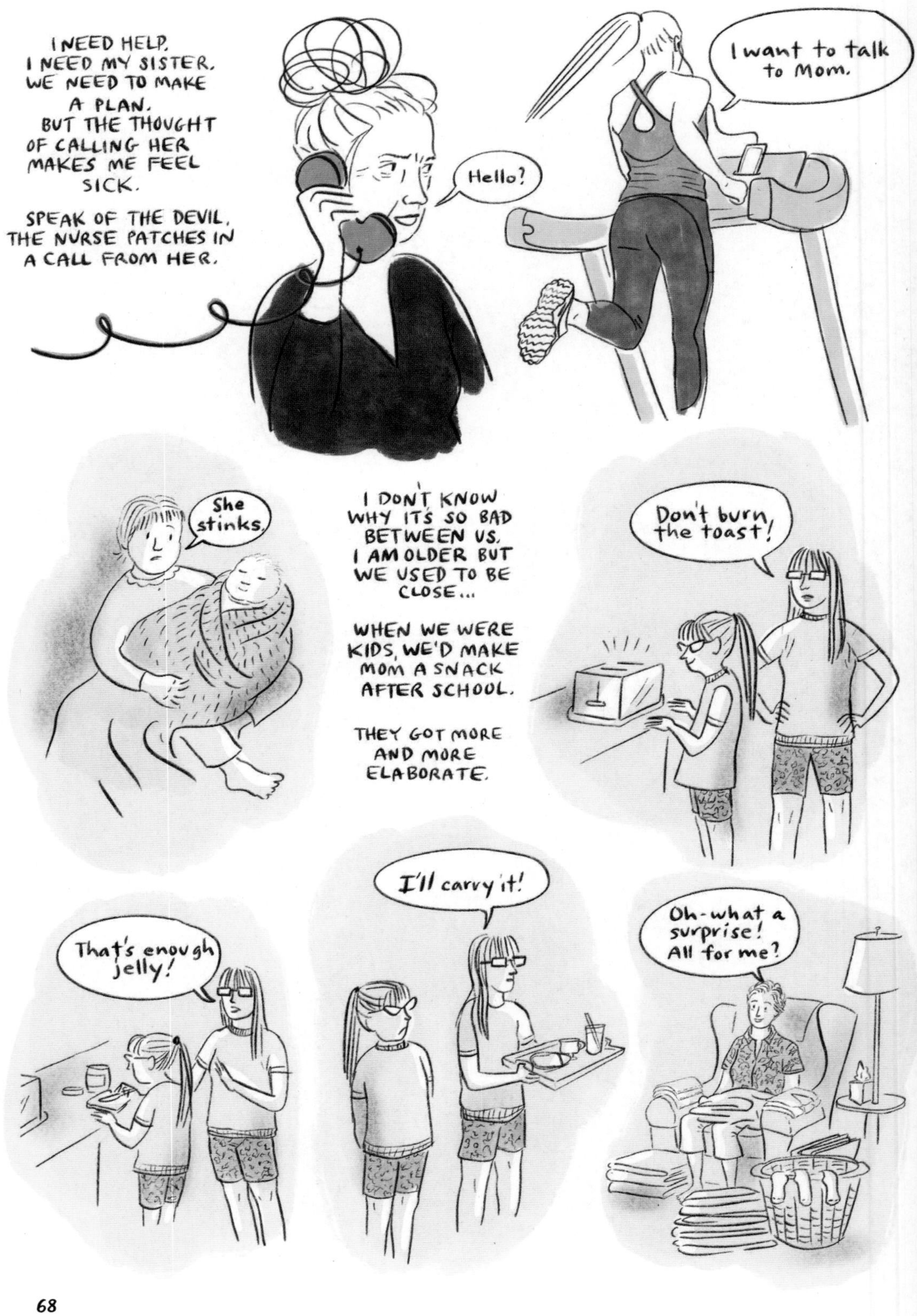

I NEED HELP. I NEED MY SISTER. WE NEED TO MAKE A PLAN. BUT THE THOUGHT OF CALLING HER MAKES ME FEEL SICK.
SPEAK OF THE DEVIL, THE NURSE PATCHES IN A CALL FROM HER.
Hello?
I want to talk to Mom.
She stinks.
I DON'T KNOW WHY IT'S SO BAD BETWEEN US. I AM OLDER BUT WE USED TO BE CLOSE...
WHEN WE WERE KIDS, WE'D MAKE MOM A SNACK AFTER SCHOOL.
THEY GOT MORE AND MORE ELABORATE.
Don't burn the toast!
That's enough jelly!
I'll carry it!
Oh-what a surprise! All for me?

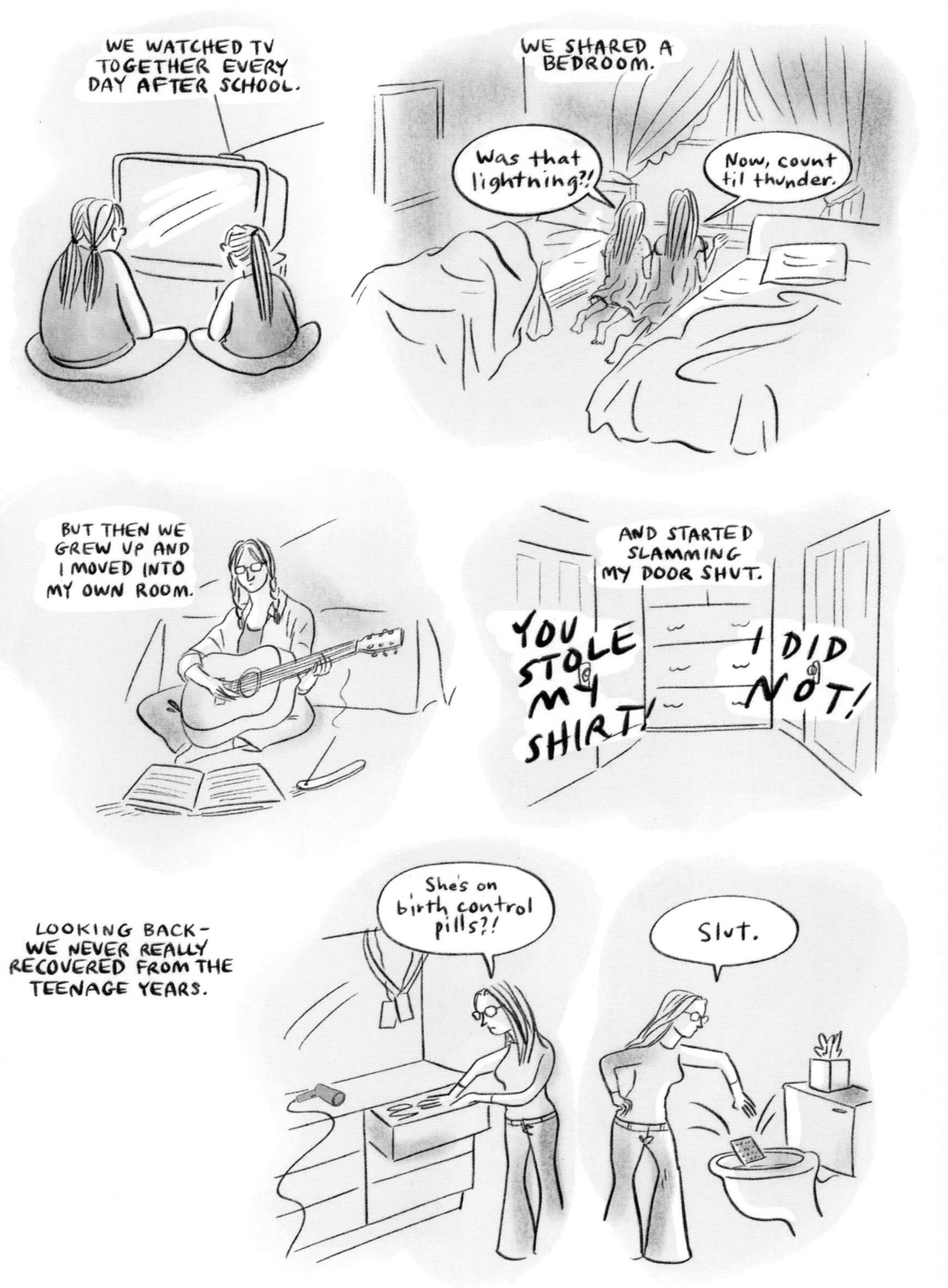

WE WATCHED TV TOGETHER EVERY DAY AFTER SCHOOL.
WE SHARED A BEDROOM.
Was that lightning?!
Now, count til thunder.
BUT THEN WE GREW UP AND I MOVED INTO MY OWN ROOM.
AND STARTED SLAMMING MY DOOR SHUT.
YOU STOLE MY SHIRT!
I DID NOT!
LOOKING BACK- WE NEVER REALLY RECOVERED FROM THE TEENAGE YEARS.
She's on birth control pills?!
Slut.

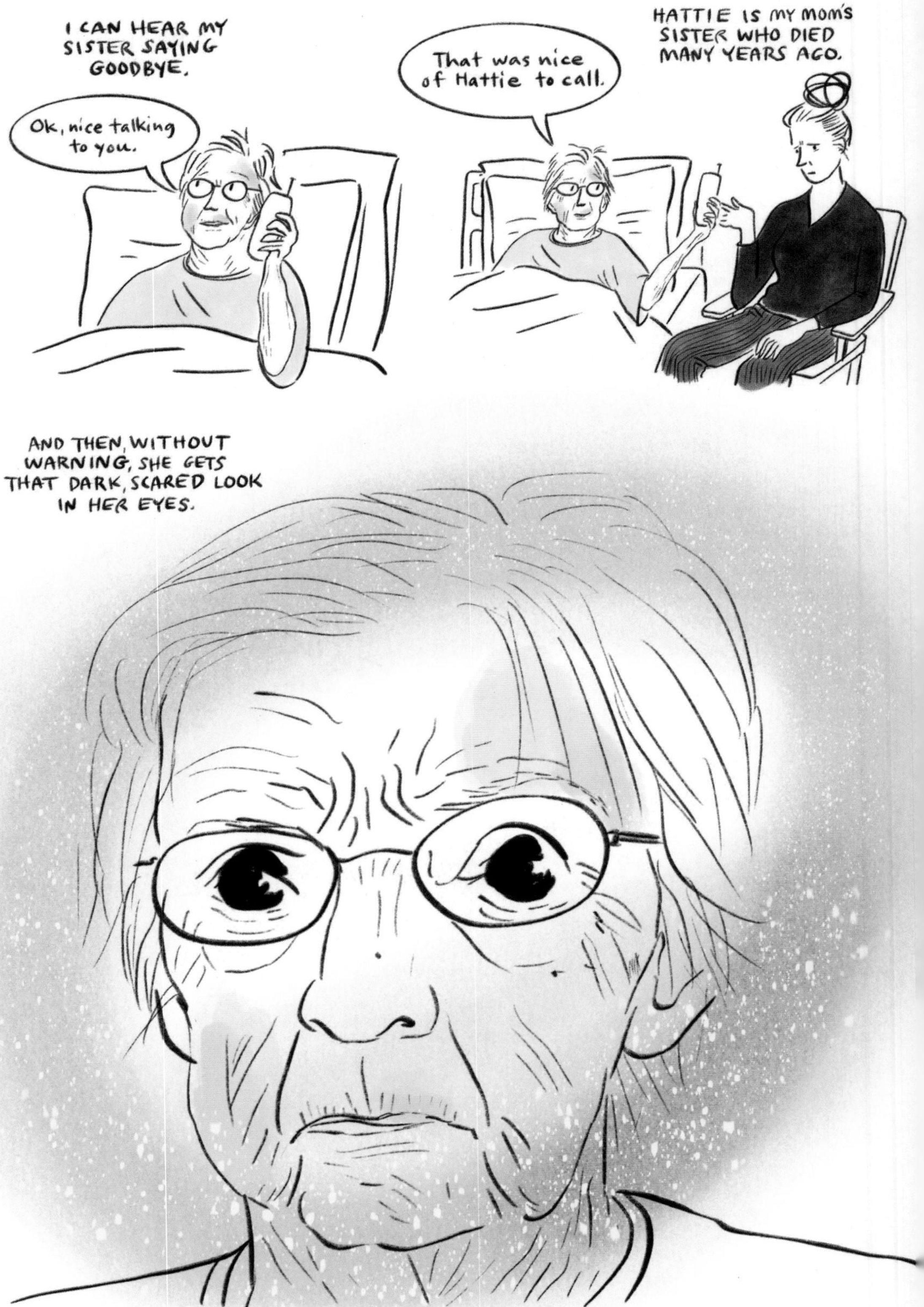
I CAN HEAR MY SISTER SAYING GOODBYE.
Ok, nice talking to you.
That was nice of Hattie to call.
HATTIE IS MY MOM'S SISTER WHO DIED MANY YEARS AGO.
AND THEN, WITHOUT WARNING, SHE GETS THAT DARK, SCARED LOOK IN HER EYES.

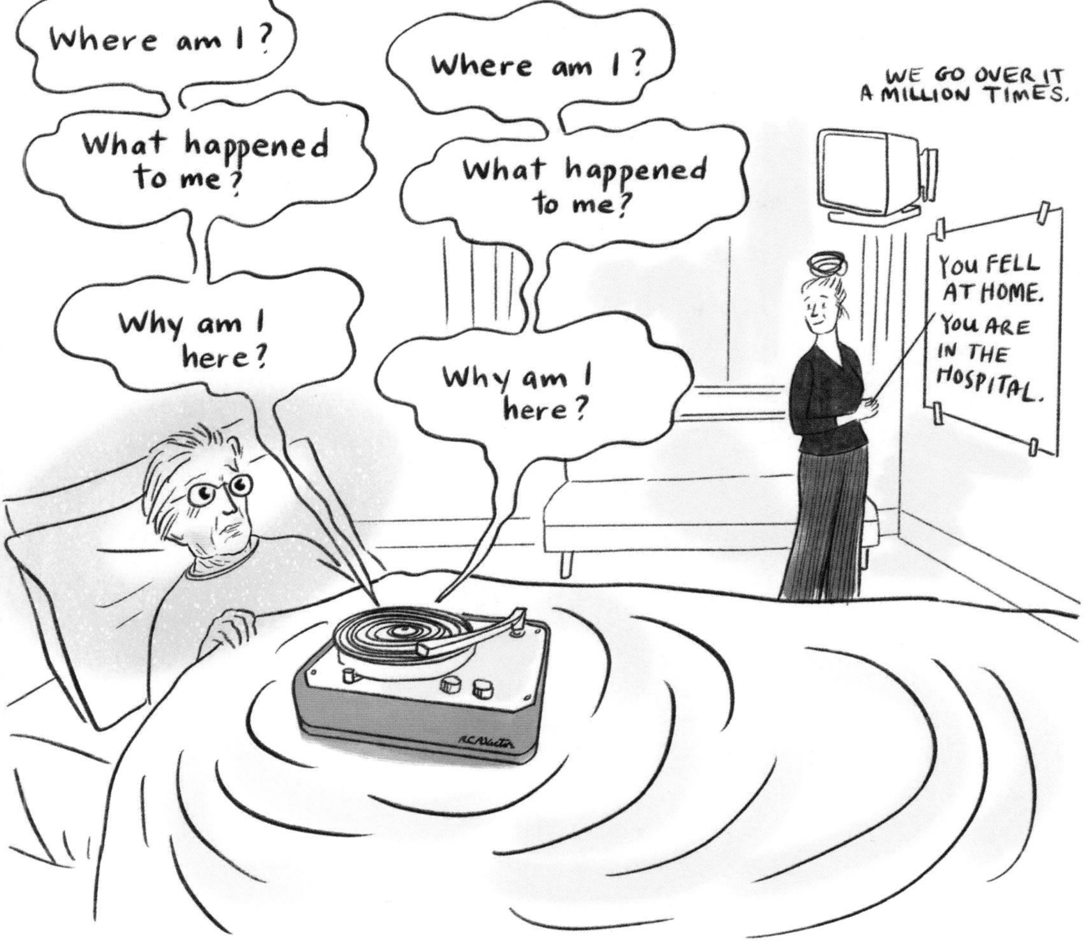
Where am I?
What happened to me?
Why am I here?
Where am I?
What happened to me?
Why am I here?
WE GO OVER IT A MILLION TIMES.
YOU FELL AT HOME. YOU ARE IN THE HOSPITAL.

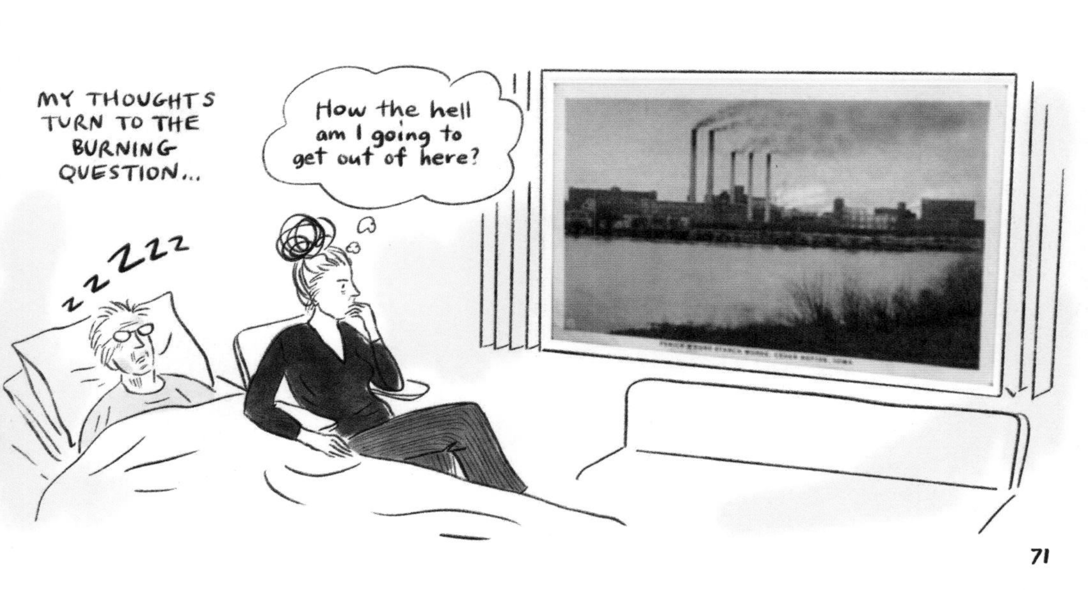
MY THOUGHTS TURN TO THE BURNING QUESTION...
How the hell am I going to get out of here?
zzZZZ

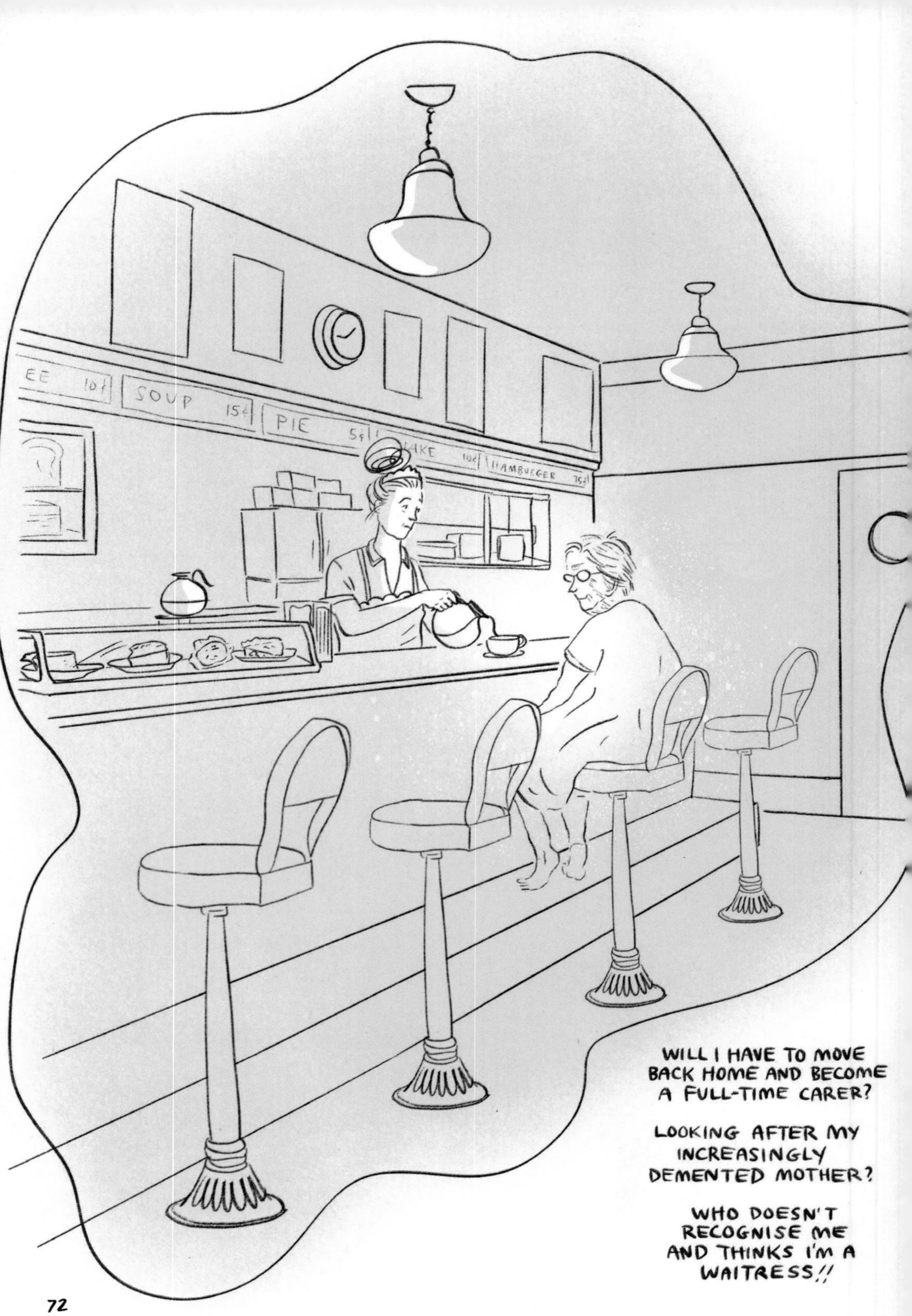
SOUP
PIE
WILL I HAVE TO MOVE BACK HOME AND BECOME A FULL-TIME CARER?
LOOKING AFTER MY INCREASINGLY DEMENTED MOTHER?
WHO DOESN'T RECOGNISE ME AND THINKS I'M A WAITRESS!!

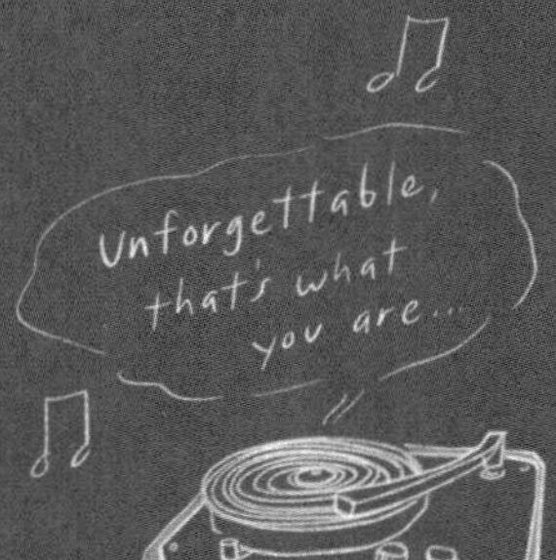
Unforgettable,
that's what
you are...

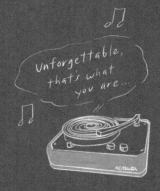

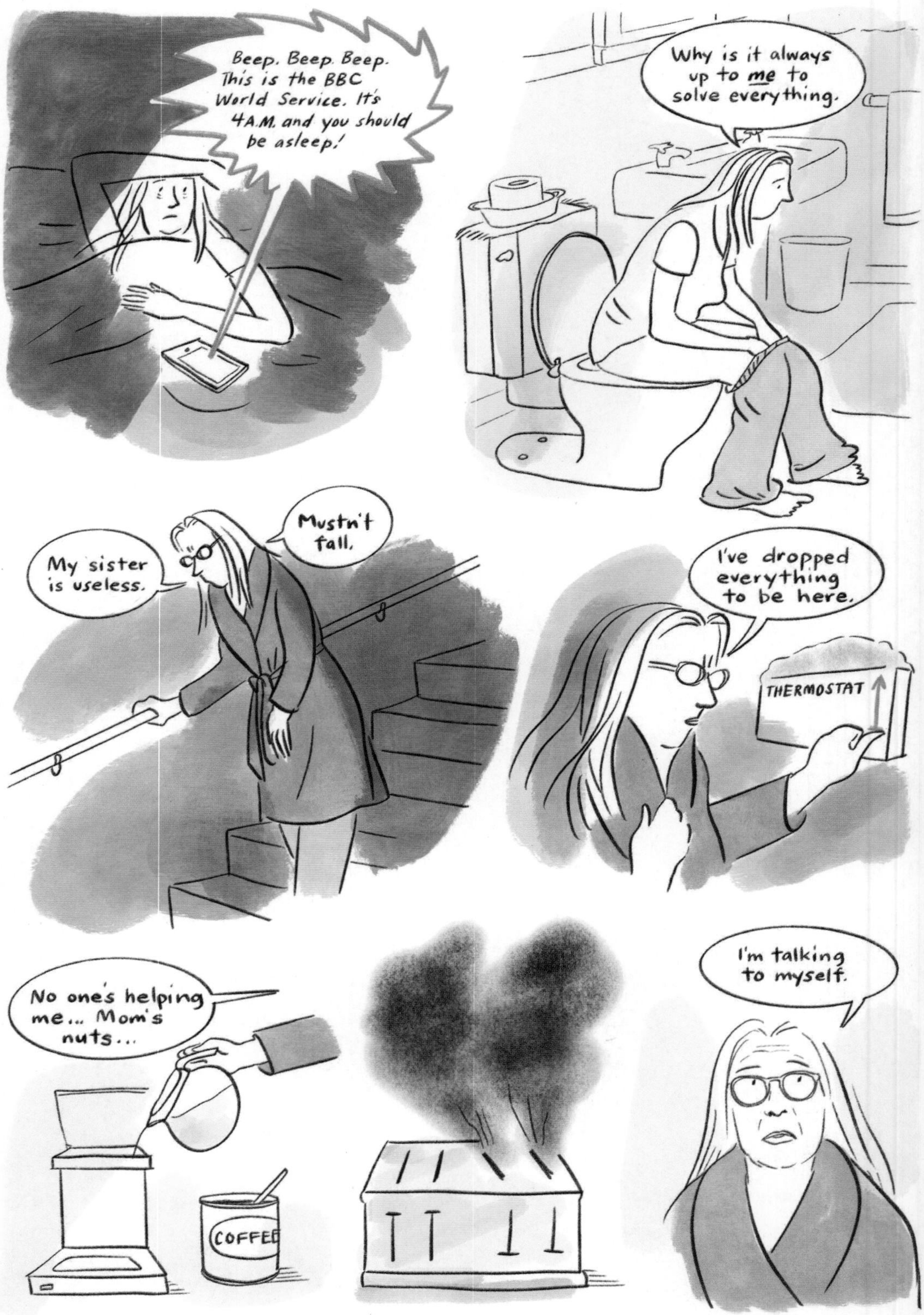
Beep. Beep. Beep. This is the BBC World Service. It's 4 A.M. and you should be asleep!
Why is it always up to me to solve everything.
My sister is useless.
Mustn't fall.
I've dropped everything to be here.
THERMOSTAT
No one's helping me... Mom's nuts...
COFFEE
I'm talking to myself.

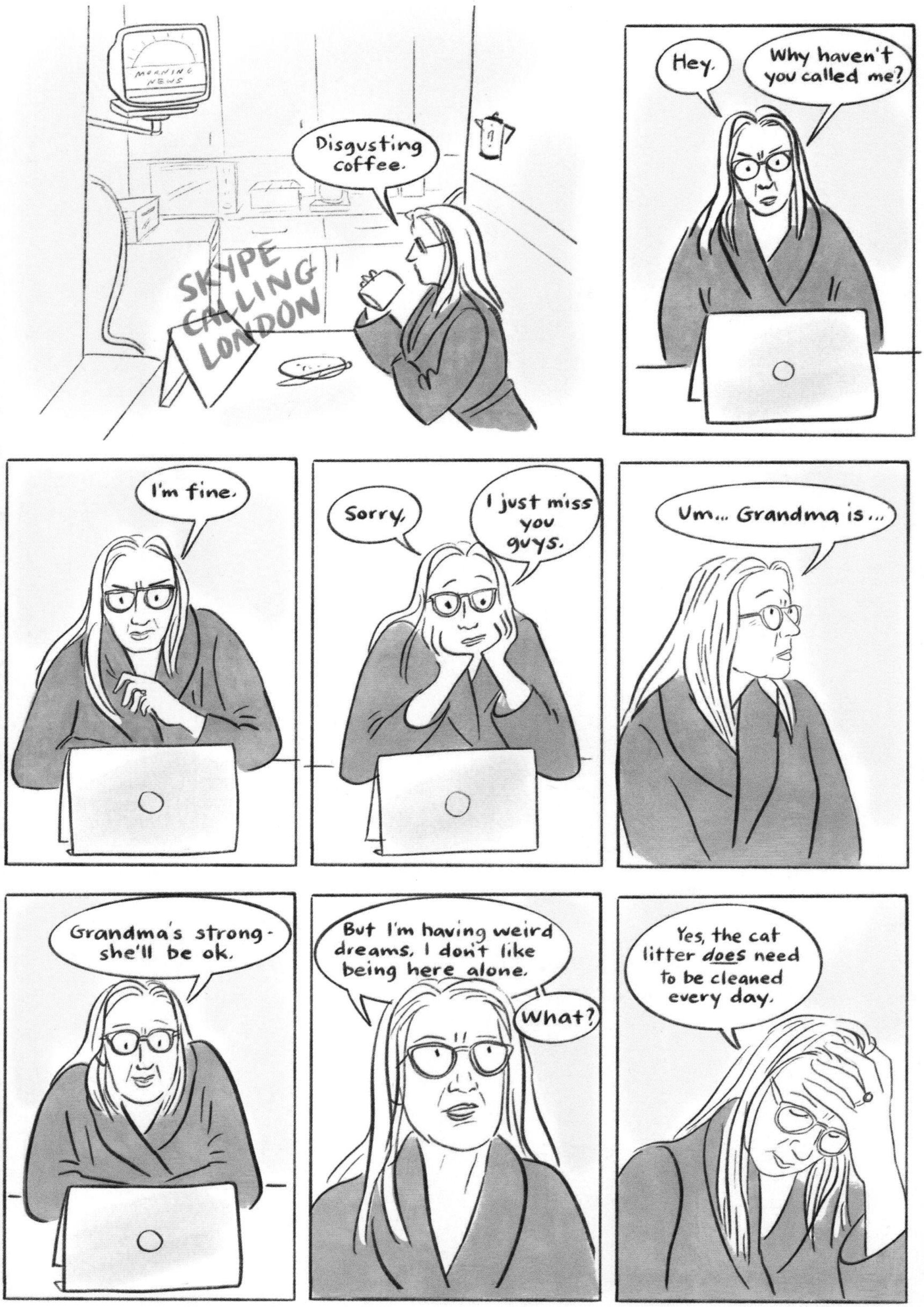
MORNING NEWS
Disgusting coffee.
SKYPE CALLING LONDON
Hey.
Why haven't you called me?
I'm fine.
Sorry,
I just miss you guys.
Um... Grandma is...
Grandma's strong - she'll be ok.
But I'm having weird dreams. I don't like being here alone.
What?
Yes, the cat litter *does* need to be cleaned every day.

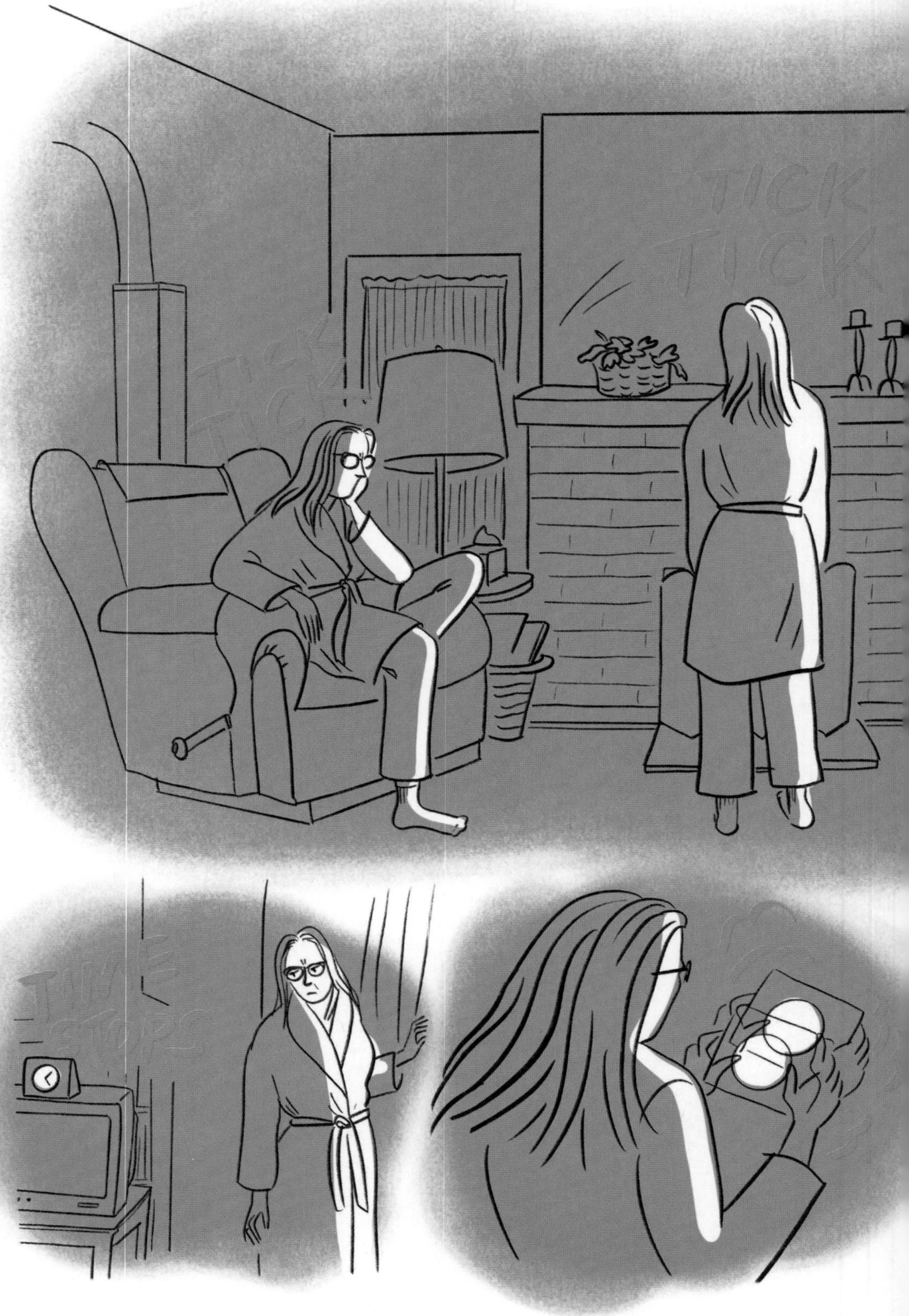
TICK
TICK
TICK
TICK
TIME
STOPS

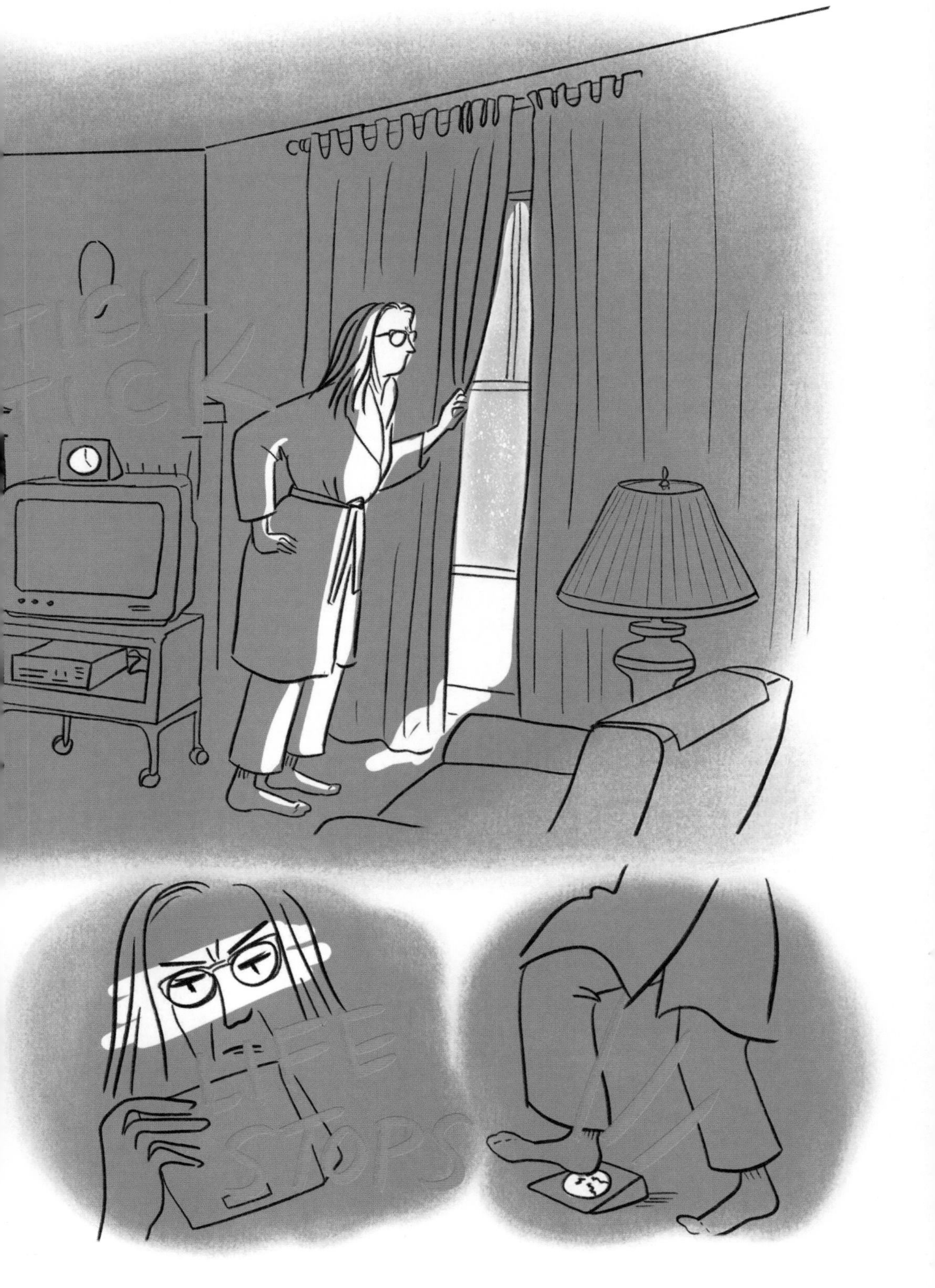

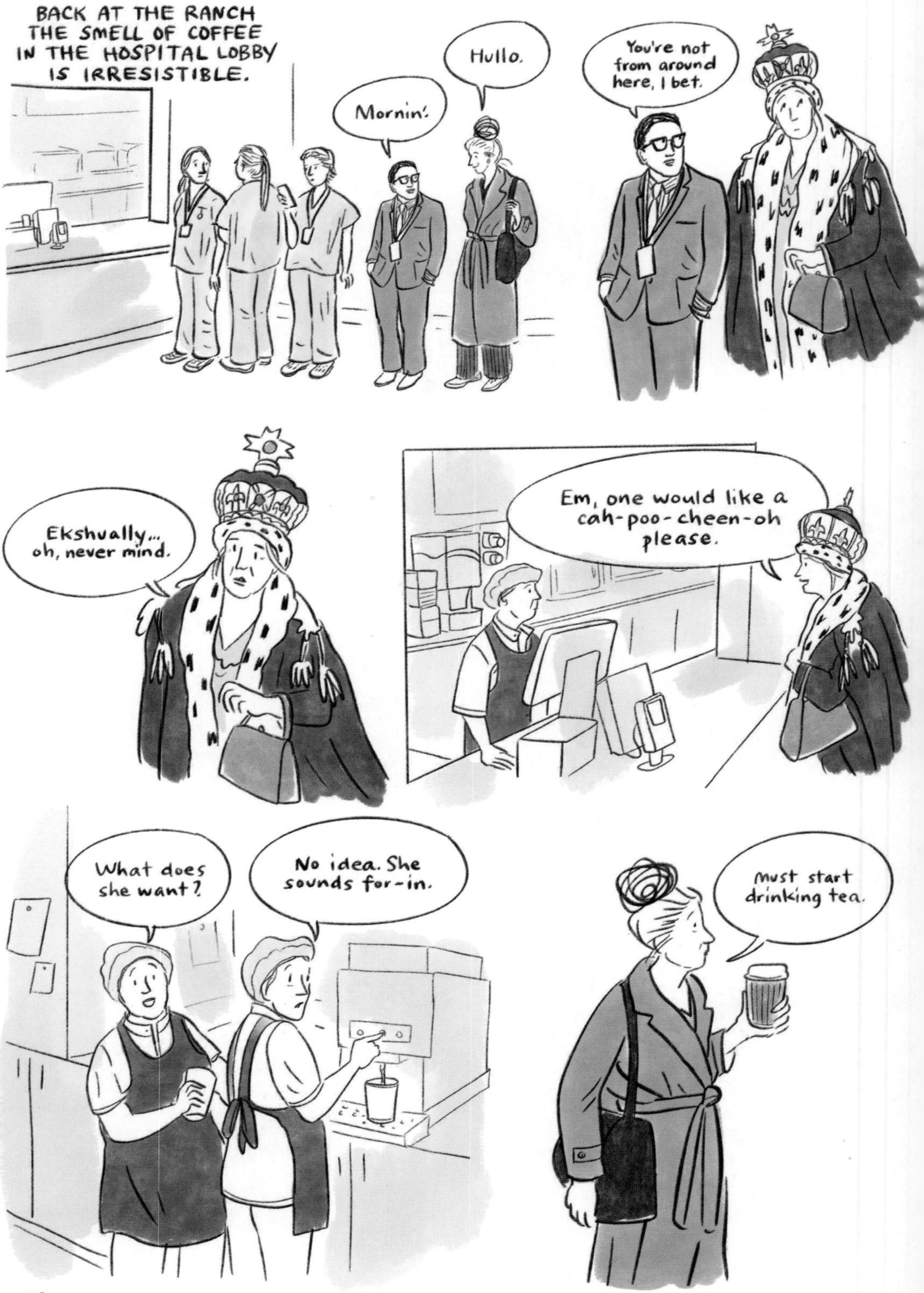
BACK AT THE RANCH THE SMELL OF COFFEE IN THE HOSPITAL LOBBY IS IRRESISTIBLE.
Mornin'.
Hullo.
You're not from around here, I bet.
Ekshually... oh, never mind.
Em, one would like a cah-poo-cheen-oh please.
What does she want?
No idea. She sounds for-in.
Must start drinking tea.

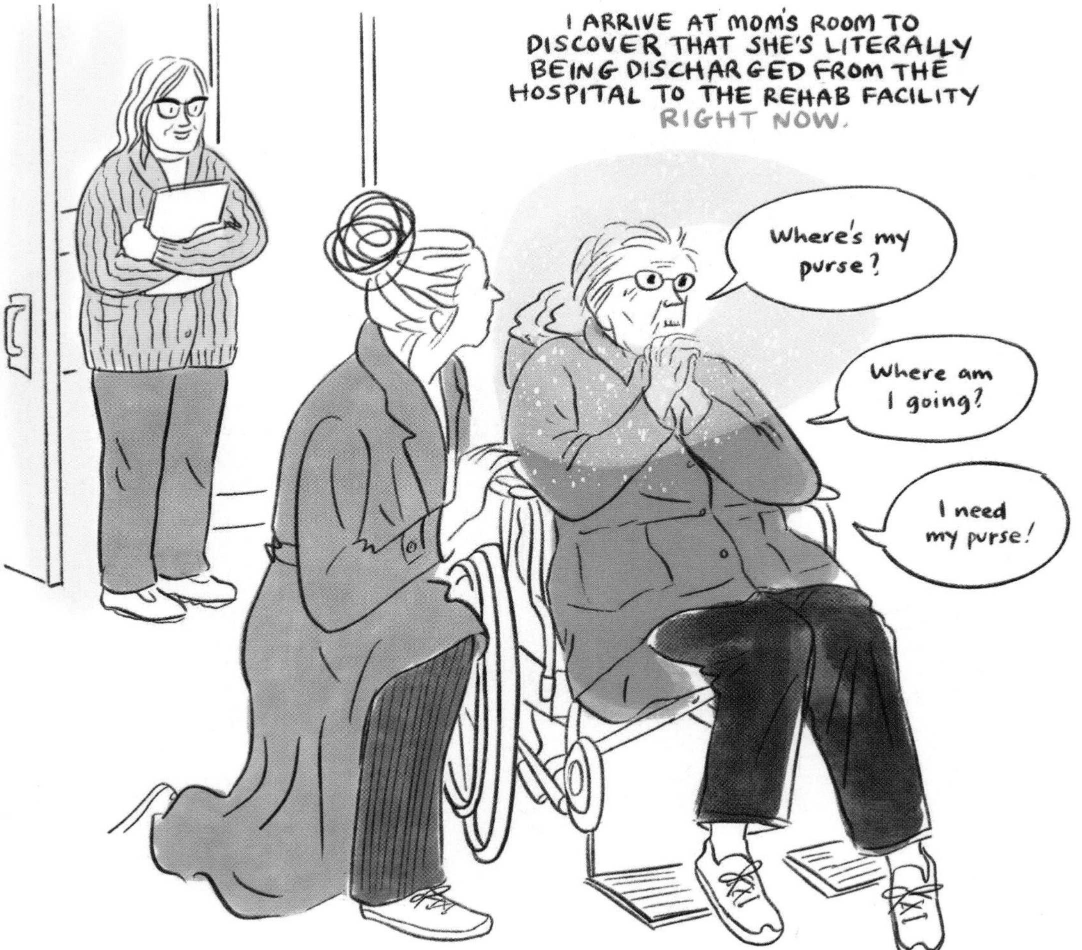
I ARRIVE AT MOM'S ROOM TO DISCOVER THAT SHE'S LITERALLY BEING DISCHARGED FROM THE HOSPITAL TO THE REHAB FACILITY RIGHT NOW.
Where's my purse?
Where am I going?
I need my purse!

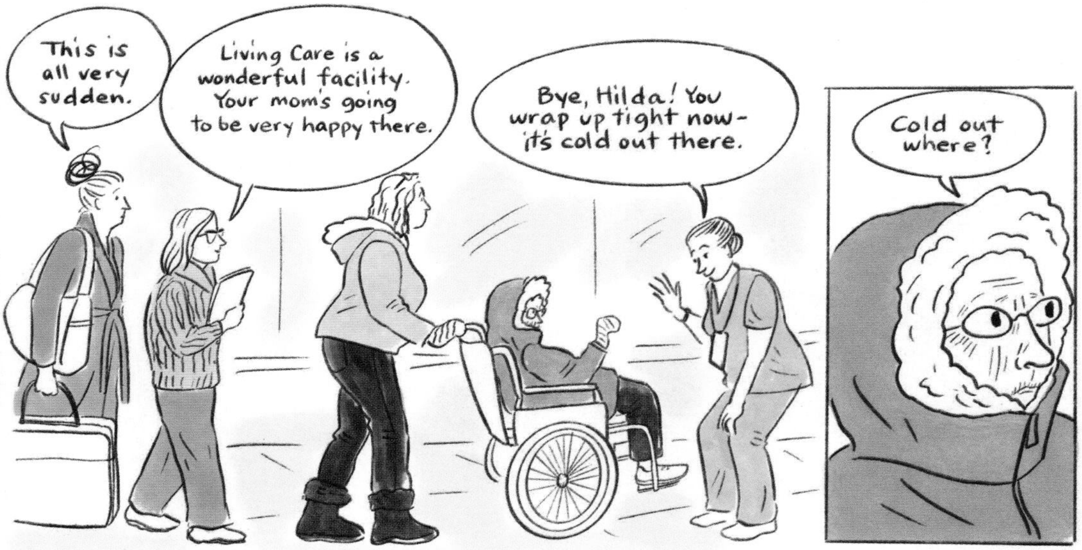
This is all very sudden.
Living Care is a wonderful facility. Your mom's going to be very happy there.
Bye, Hilda! You wrap up tight now - it's cold out there.
Cold out where?

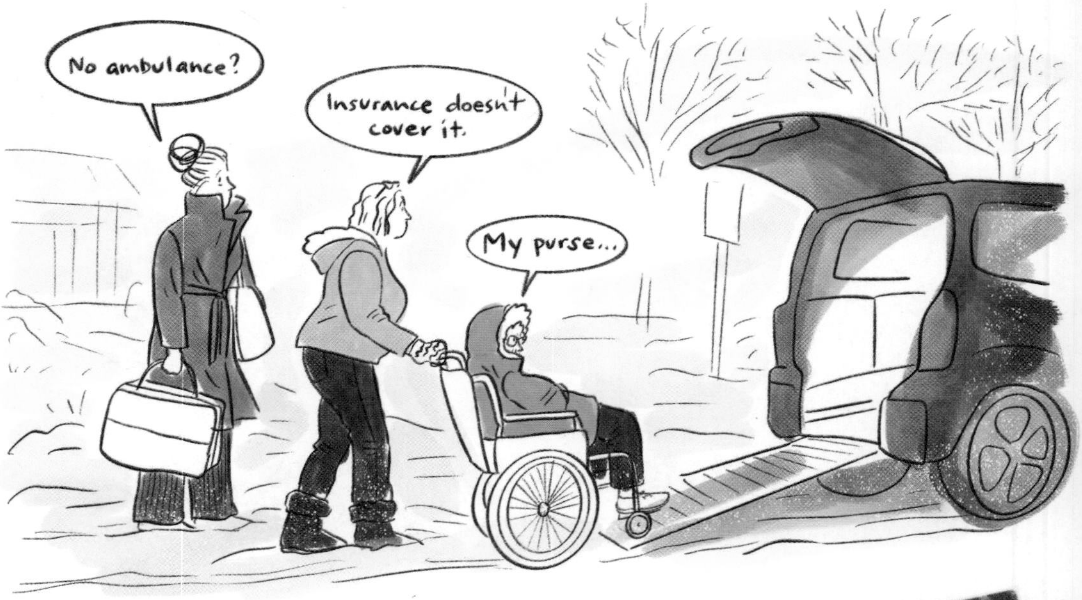
No ambulance?
Insurance doesn't cover it.
My purse...

AS WE DRIVE THROUGH DOWNTOWN
I POINT OUT THE LANDMARKS
MOM SHOULD RECOGNISE-

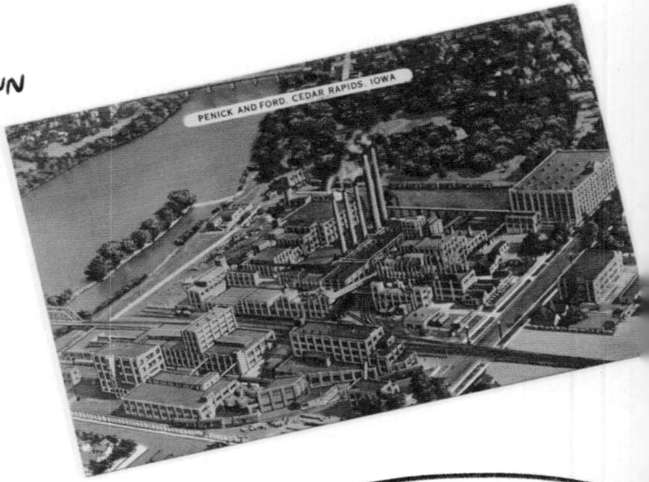
PENICK AND FORD, CEDAR RAPIDS, IOWA

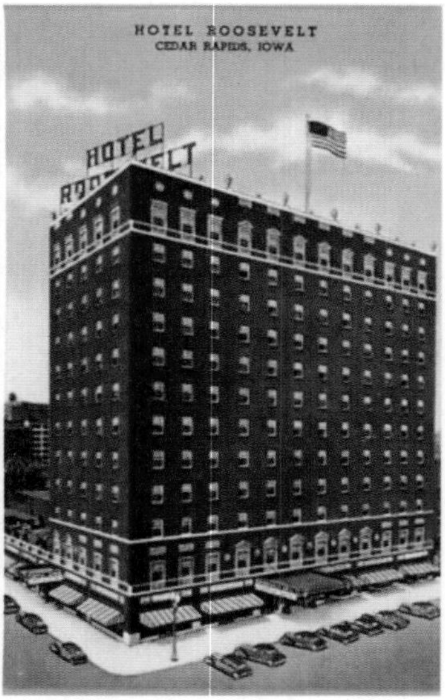
HOTEL ROOSEVELT
CEDAR RAPIDS, IOWA
HOTEL

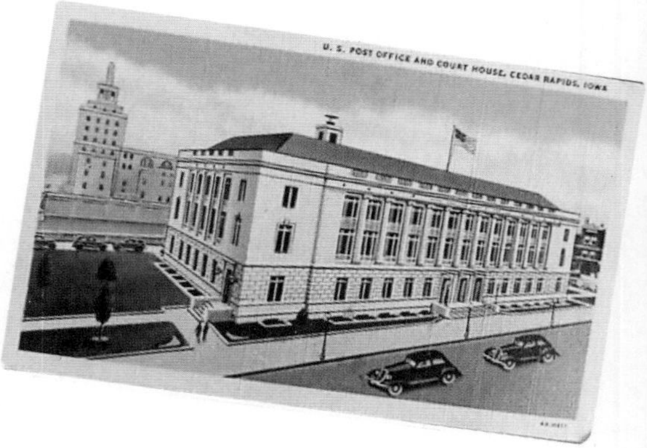
U. S. POST OFFICE AND COURT HOUSE, CEDAR RAPIDS, IOWA

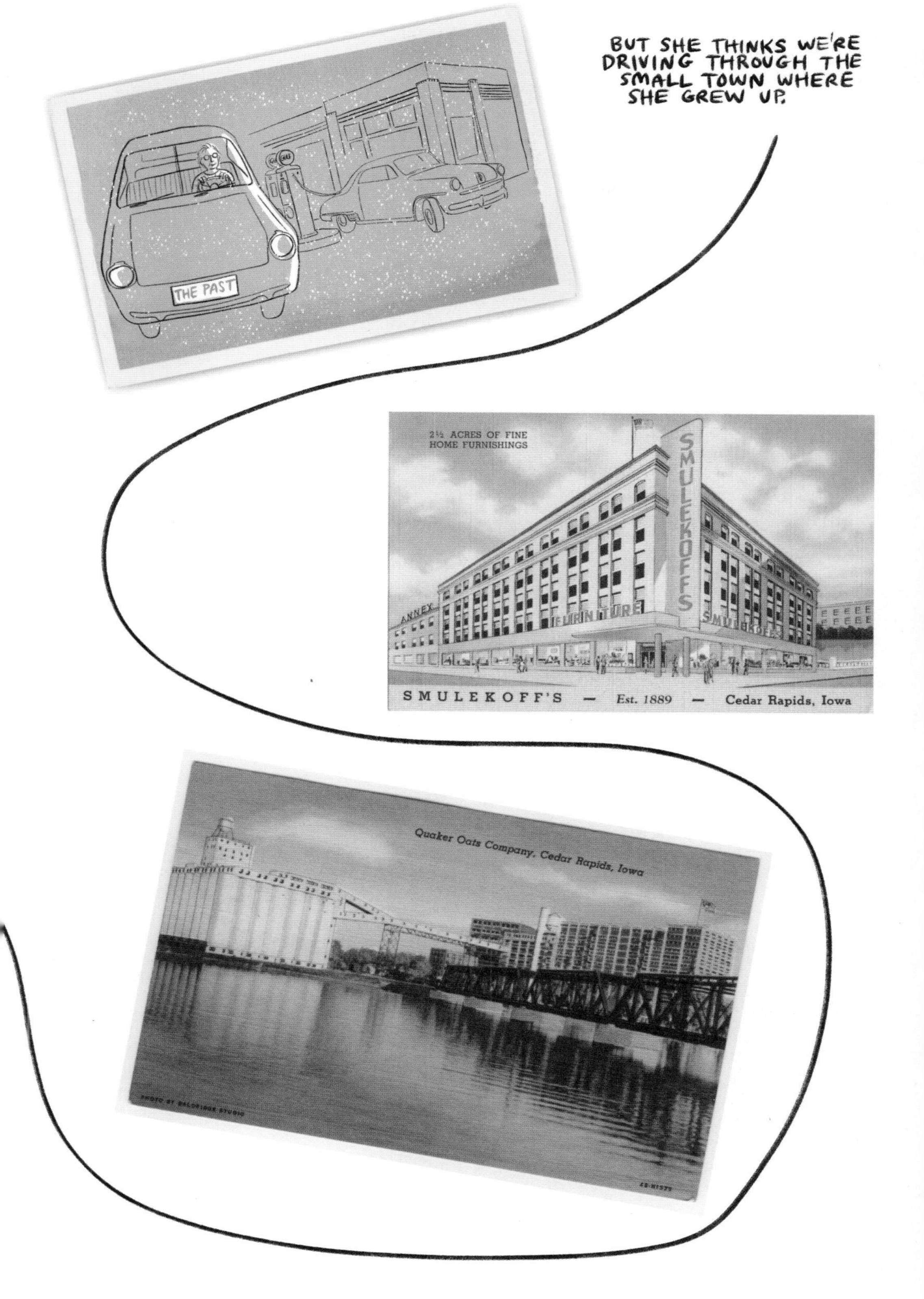
BUT SHE THINKS WE'RE DRIVING THROUGH THE SMALL TOWN WHERE SHE GREW UP.
THE PAST
2½ ACRES OF FINE HOME FURNISHINGS
SMULEKOFFS
ANNEX
FURNITURE
SMULEKOFFS
SMULEKOFF'S — Est. 1889 — Cedar Rapids, Iowa
Quaker Oats Company, Cedar Rapids, Iowa

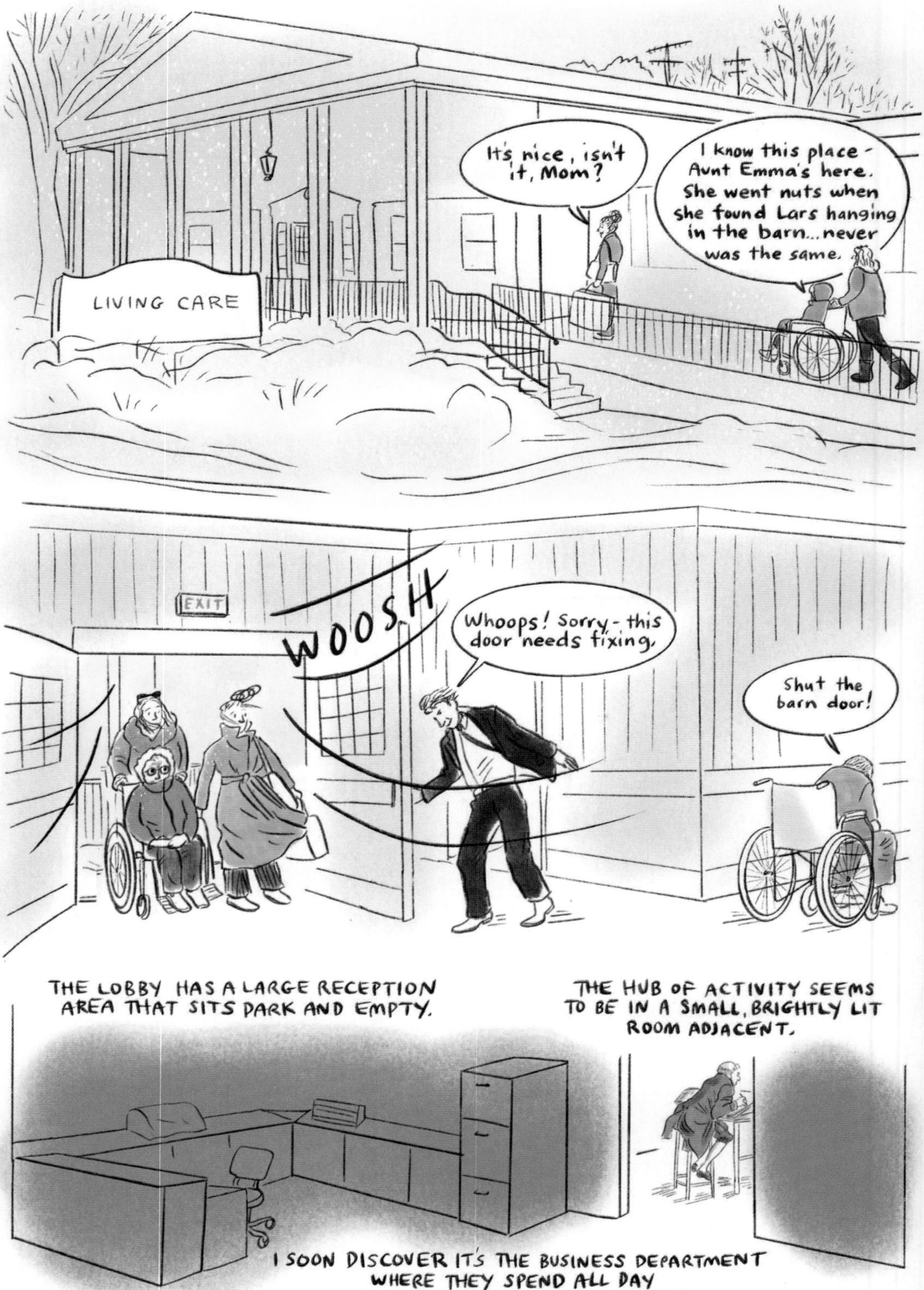
It's nice, isn't it, Mom?
I know this place - Aunt Emma's here. She went nuts when she found Lars hanging in the barn... never was the same.
LIVING CARE
EXIT
WOOSH
Whoops! Sorry - this door needs fixing.
Shut the barn door!
THE LOBBY HAS A LARGE RECEPTION AREA THAT SITS DARK AND EMPTY.
THE HUB OF ACTIVITY SEEMS TO BE IN A SMALL, BRIGHTLY LIT ROOM ADJACENT.
I SOON DISCOVER IT'S THE BUSINESS DEPARTMENT WHERE THEY SPEND ALL DAY CRANKING OUT INSURANCE FORMS.

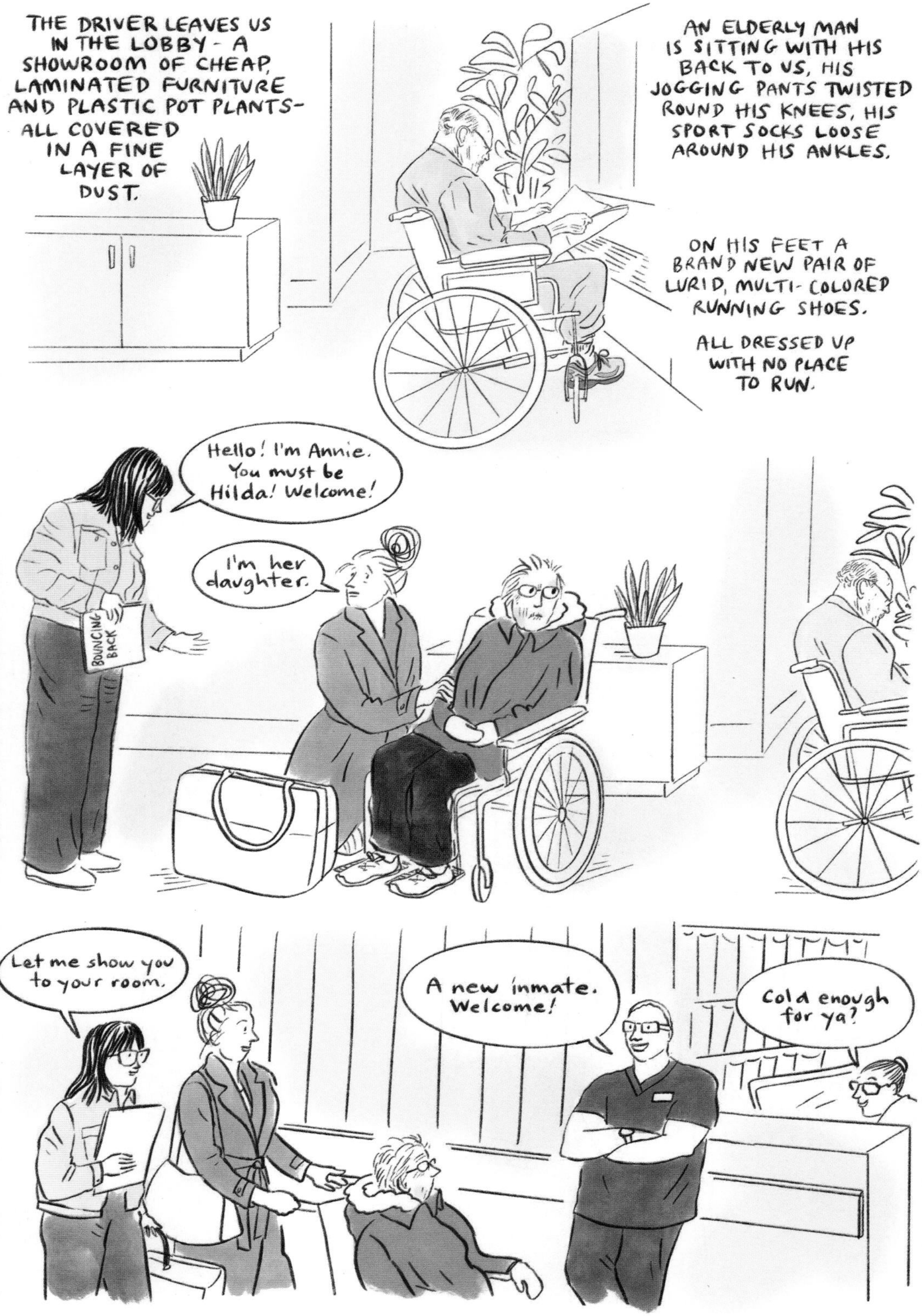
THE DRIVER LEAVES US IN THE LOBBY - A SHOWROOM OF CHEAP, LAMINATED FURNITURE AND PLASTIC POT PLANTS- ALL COVERED IN A FINE LAYER OF DUST.
AN ELDERLY MAN IS SITTING WITH HIS BACK TO US, HIS JOGGING PANTS TWISTED ROUND HIS KNEES, HIS SPORT SOCKS LOOSE AROUND HIS ANKLES.
ON HIS FEET A BRAND NEW PAIR OF LURID, MULTI-COLORED RUNNING SHOES.
ALL DRESSED UP WITH NO PLACE TO RUN.
Hello! I'm Annie. You must be Hilda! Welcome!
I'm her daughter.
BOUNCING BACK
Let me show you to your room.
A new inmate. Welcome!
Cold enough for ya?

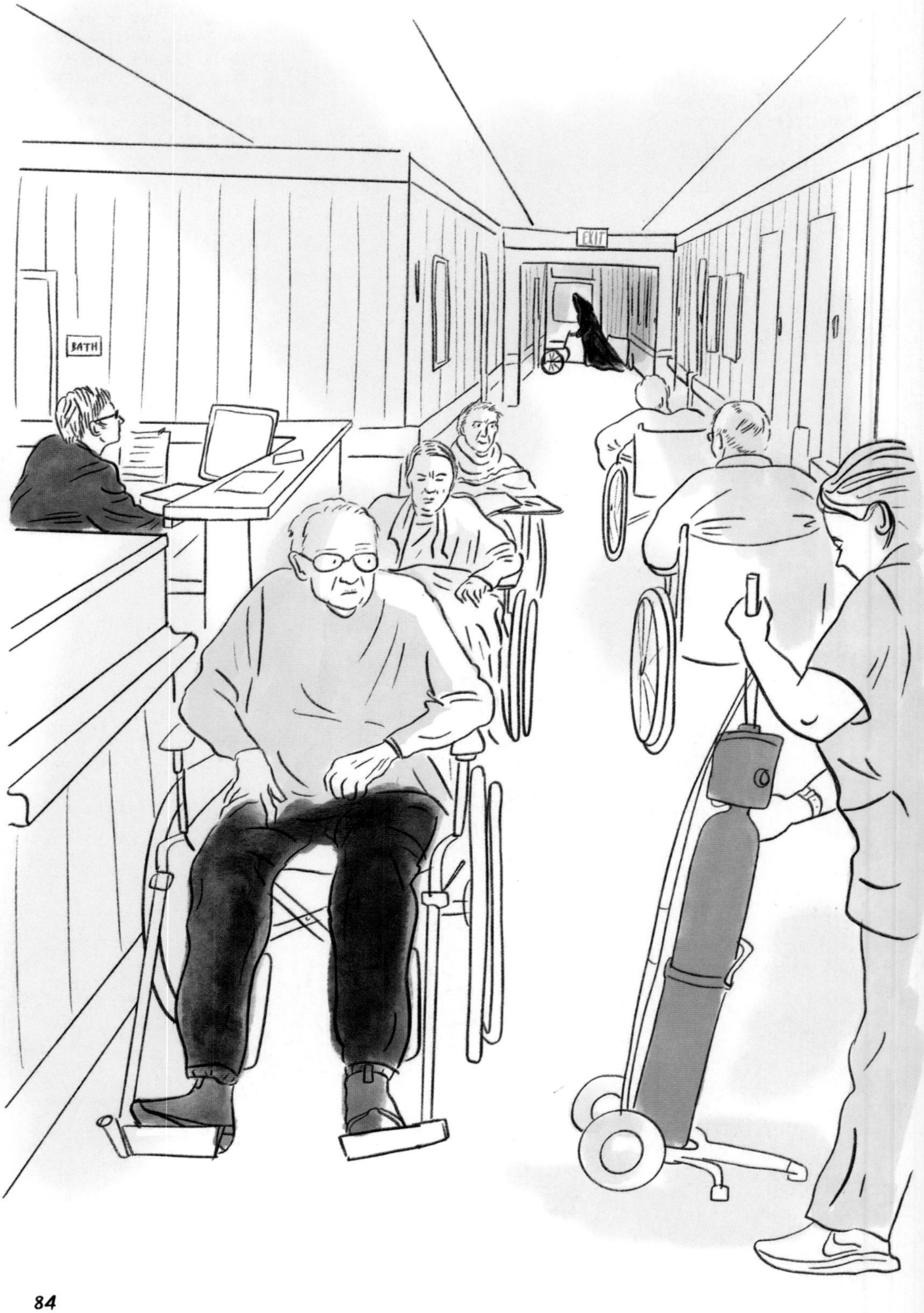
BATH
EXIT

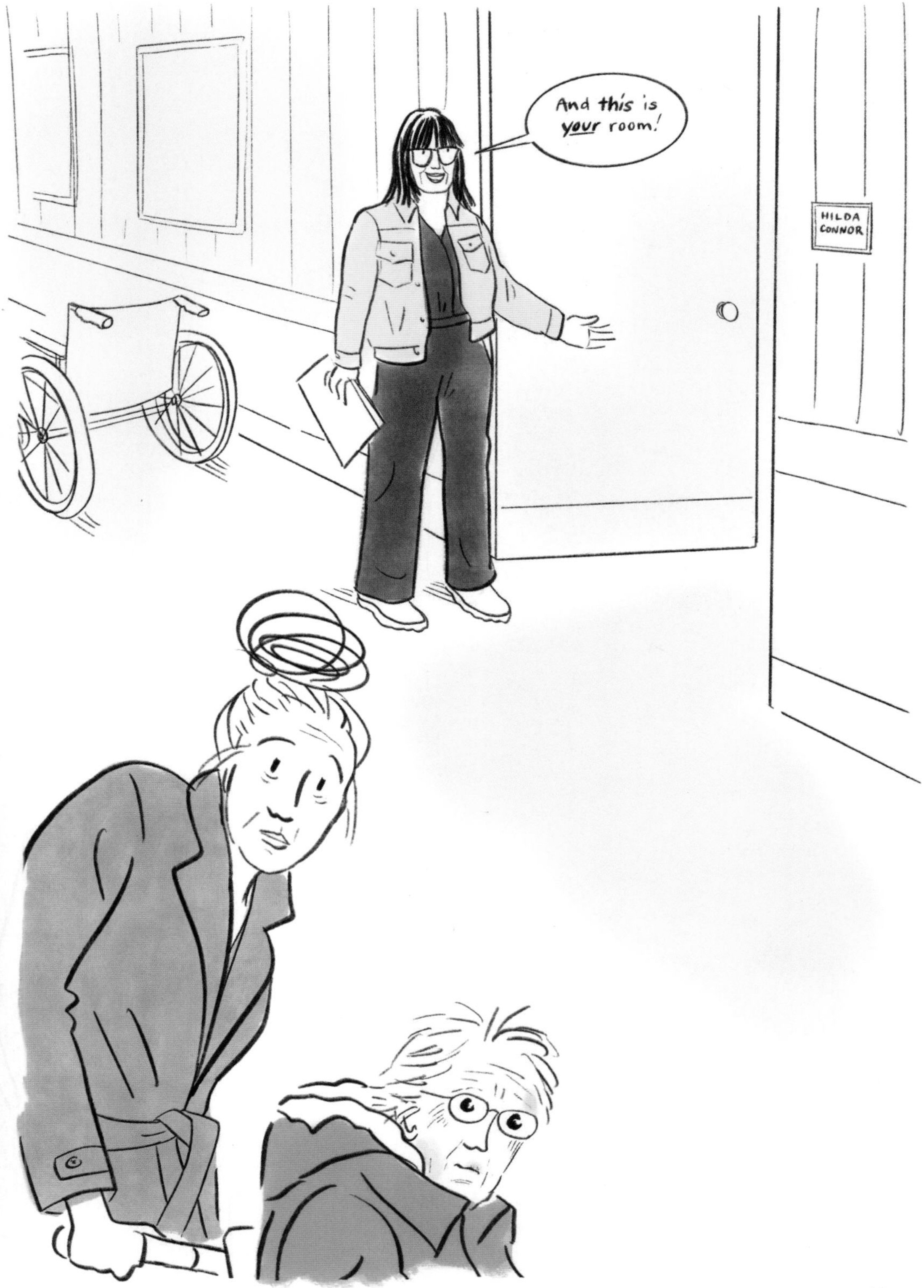
And this is your room!
HILDA CONNOR

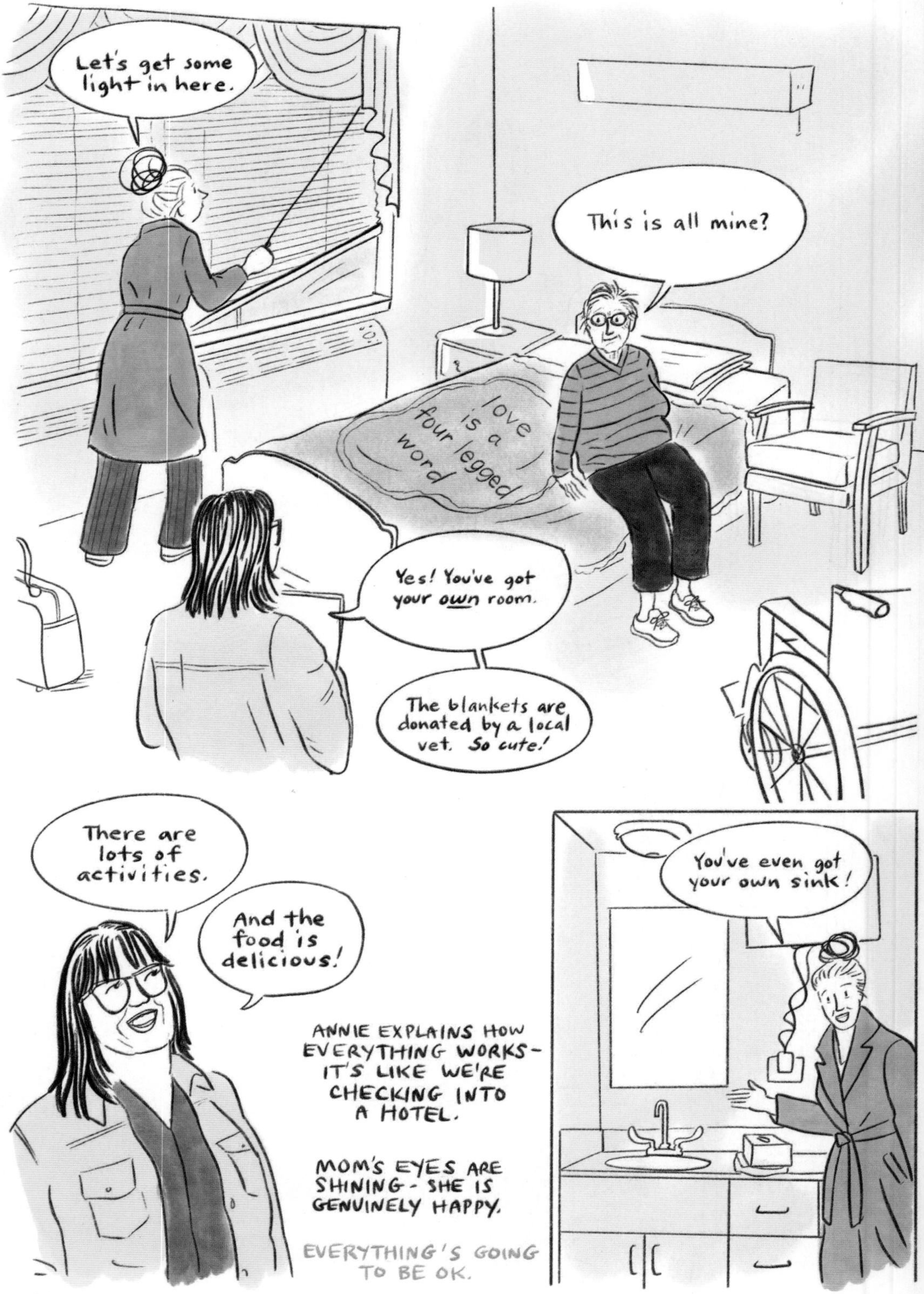
Let's get some light in here.
This is all mine?
love is a four legged word
Yes! You've got your own room.
The blankets are donated by a local vet. So cute!
There are lots of activities.
And the food is delicious!
ANNIE EXPLAINS HOW EVERYTHING WORKS - IT'S LIKE WE'RE CHECKING INTO A HOTEL.
MOM'S EYES ARE SHINING - SHE IS GENUINELY HAPPY.
EVERYTHING'S GOING TO BE OK.
You've even got your own sink!

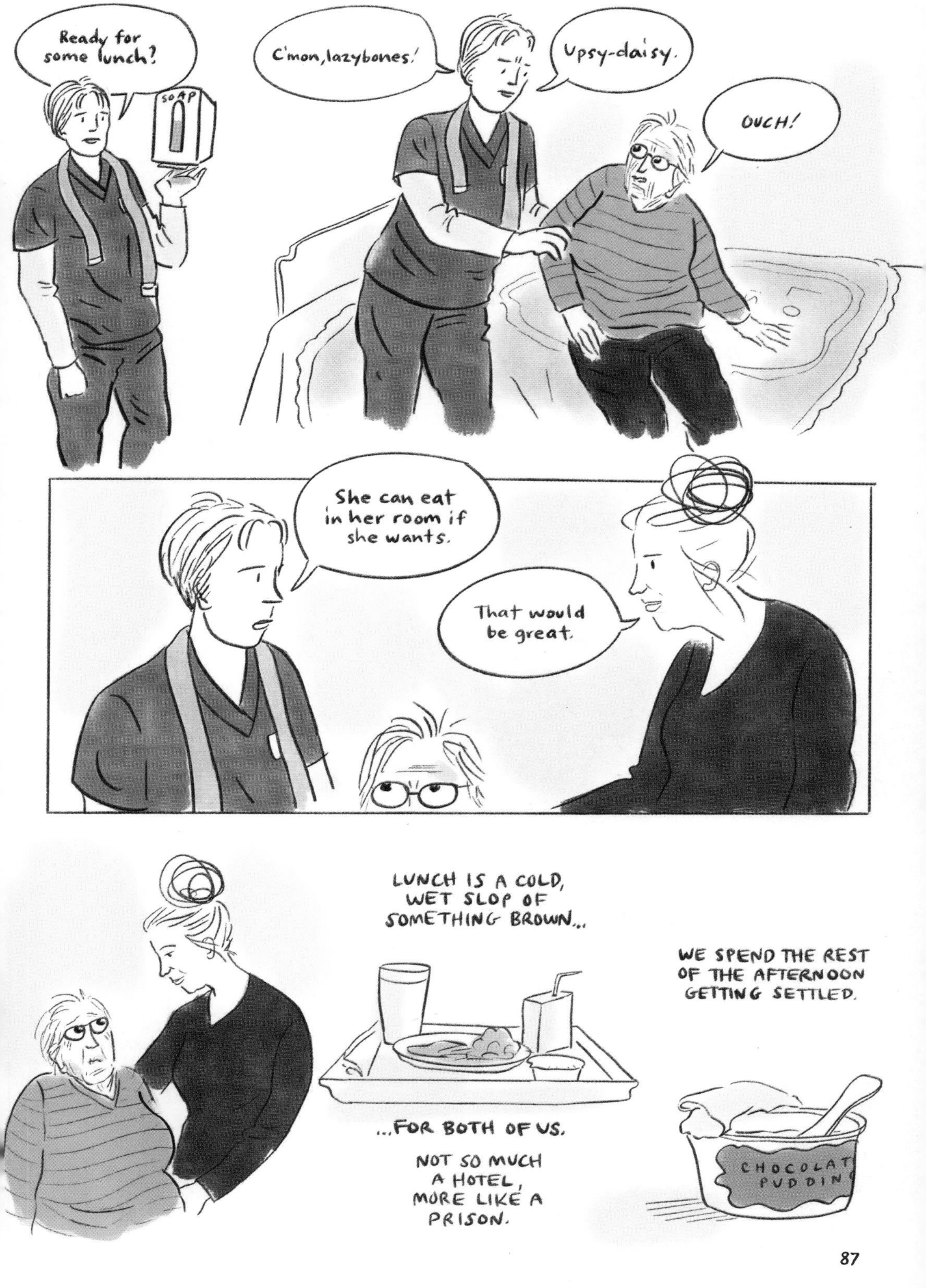
Ready for some lunch?
SOAP
C'mon, lazybones!
Upsy-daisy.
OUCH!
She can eat in her room if she wants.
That would be great.
LUNCH IS A COLD, WET SLOP OF SOMETHING BROWN...
...FOR BOTH OF US.
NOT SO MUCH A HOTEL, MORE LIKE A PRISON.
WE SPEND THE REST OF THE AFTERNOON GETTING SETTLED.

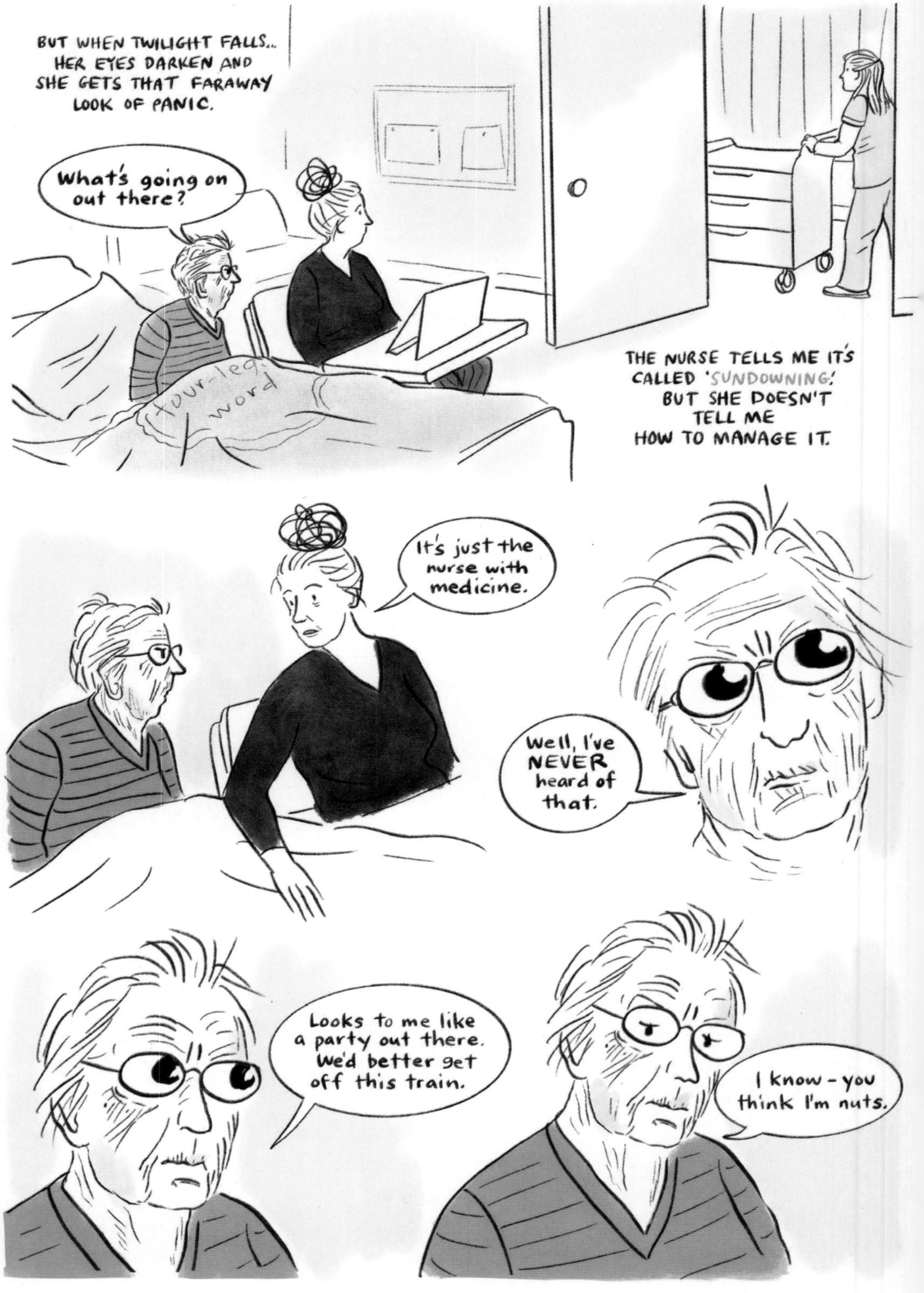
BUT WHEN TWILIGHT FALLS.. HER EYES DARKEN AND SHE GETS THAT FARAWAY LOOK OF PANIC.
What's going on out there?
four-leg word
THE NURSE TELLS ME IT'S CALLED 'SUNDOWNING.' BUT SHE DOESN'T TELL ME HOW TO MANAGE IT.
It's just the nurse with medicine.
Well, I've NEVER heard of that.
Looks to me like a party out there. We'd better get off this train.
I know - you think I'm nuts.

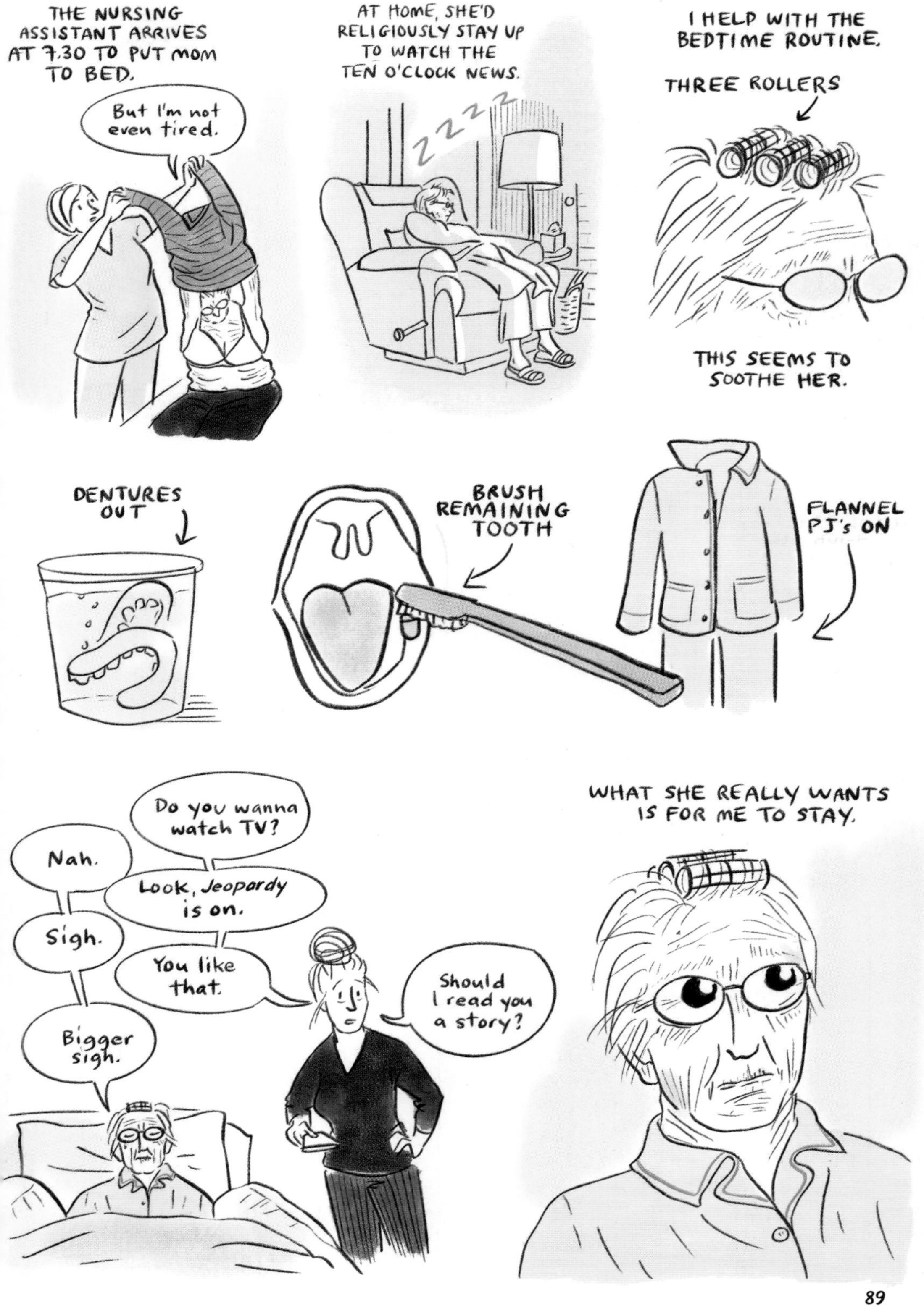
THE NURSING ASSISTANT ARRIVES AT 7.30 TO PUT MOM TO BED.
But I'm not even tired.
AT HOME, SHE'D RELIGIOUSLY STAY UP TO WATCH THE TEN O'CLOCK NEWS.
ZZZZZ
I HELP WITH THE BEDTIME ROUTINE.
THREE ROLLERS
THIS SEEMS TO SOOTHE HER.
DENTURES OUT
BRUSH REMAINING TOOTH
FLANNEL PJ's ON
Do you wanna watch TV?
Nah.
Look, Jeopardy is on.
Sigh.
You like that.
Bigger sigh.
Should I read you a story?
WHAT SHE REALLY WANTS IS FOR ME TO STAY.

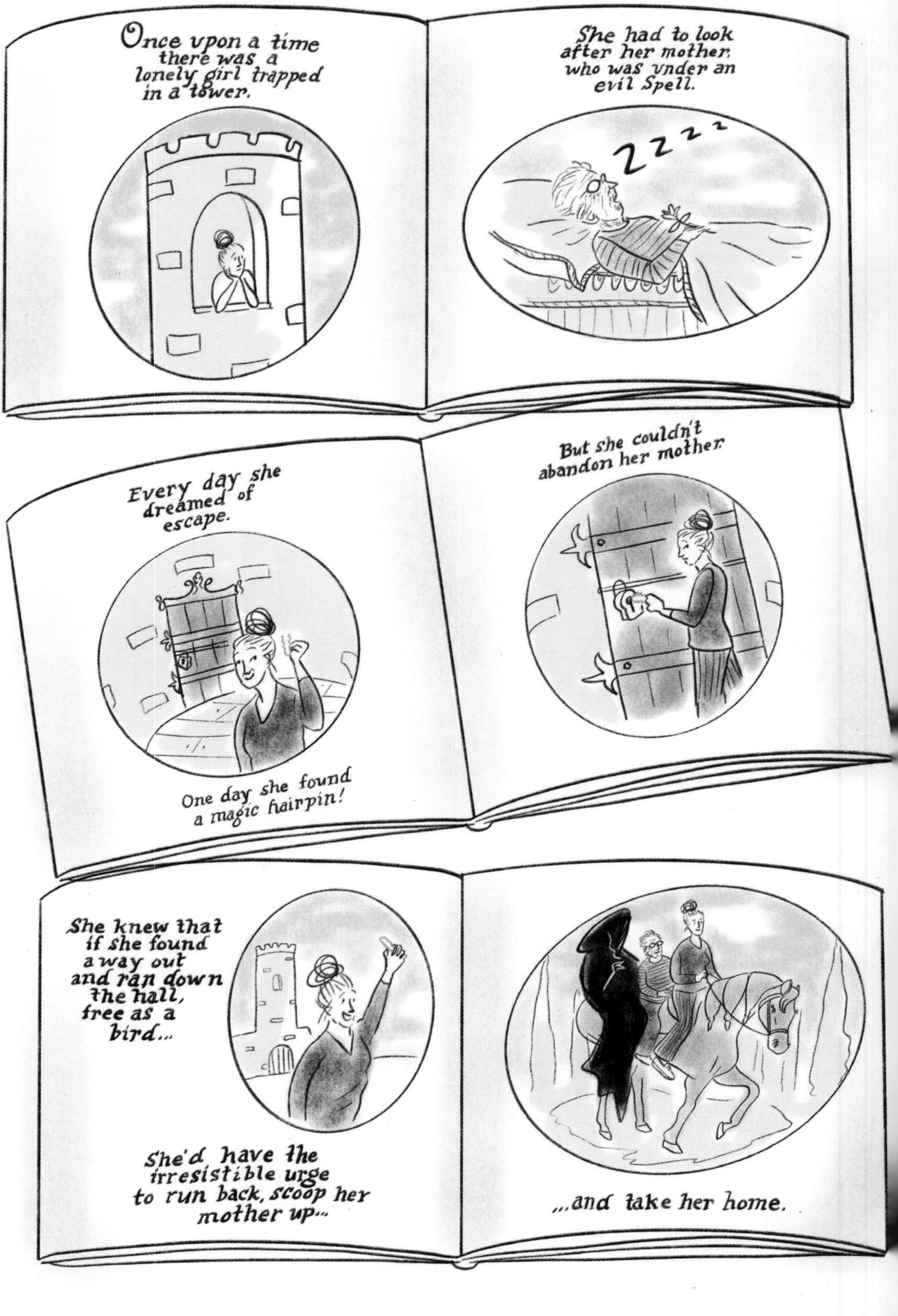

Once upon a time there was a lonely girl trapped in a tower.
She had to look after her mother, who was under an evil Spell.
Z Z Z Z
Every day she dreamed of escape.
One day she found a magic hairpin!
But she couldn't abandon her mother.
She knew that if she found a way out and ran down the hall, free as a bird...
She'd have the irresistible urge to run back, scoop her mother up...
...and take her home.

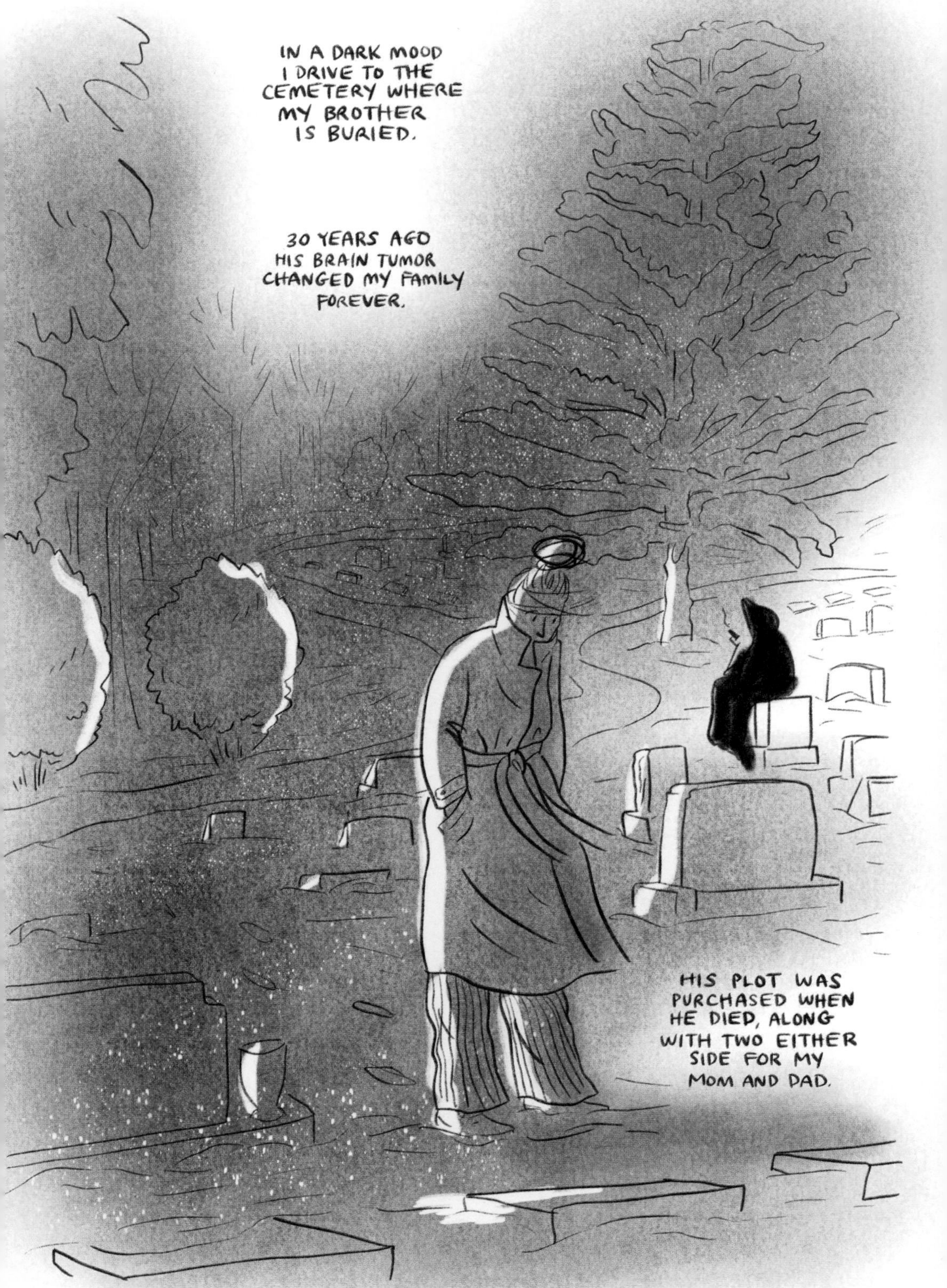
IN A DARK MOOD I DRIVE TO THE CEMETERY WHERE MY BROTHER IS BURIED.
30 YEARS AGO HIS BRAIN TUMOR CHANGED MY FAMILY FOREVER.
HIS PLOT WAS PURCHASED WHEN HE DIED, ALONG WITH TWO EITHER SIDE FOR MY MOM AND DAD.

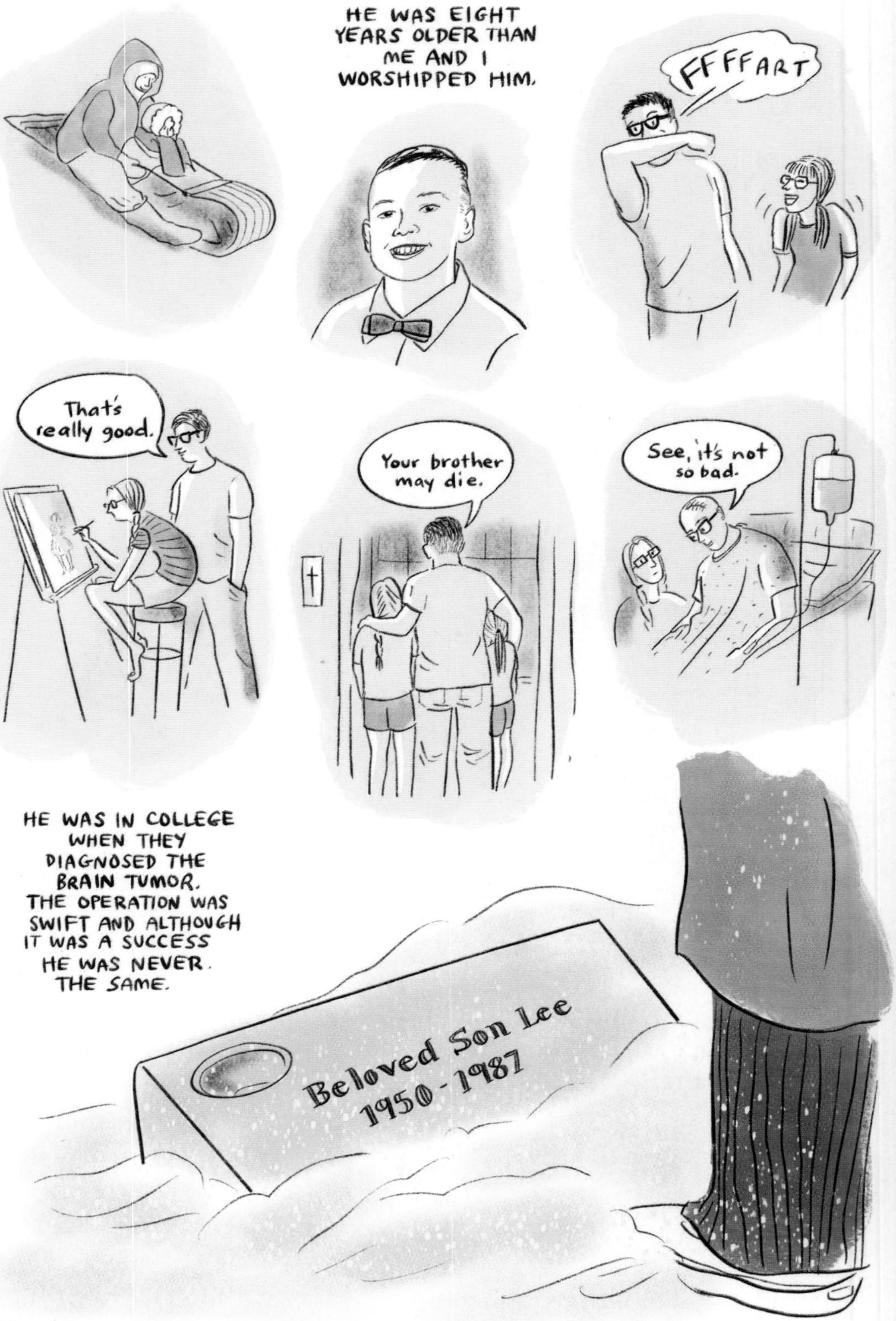
HE WAS EIGHT YEARS OLDER THAN ME AND I WORSHIPPED HIM.
FFFFART
That's really good.
Your brother may die.
See, it's not so bad.
HE WAS IN COLLEGE WHEN THEY DIAGNOSED THE BRAIN TUMOR. THE OPERATION WAS SWIFT AND ALTHOUGH IT WAS A SUCCESS HE WAS NEVER THE SAME.
Beloved Son Lee
1950 - 1987

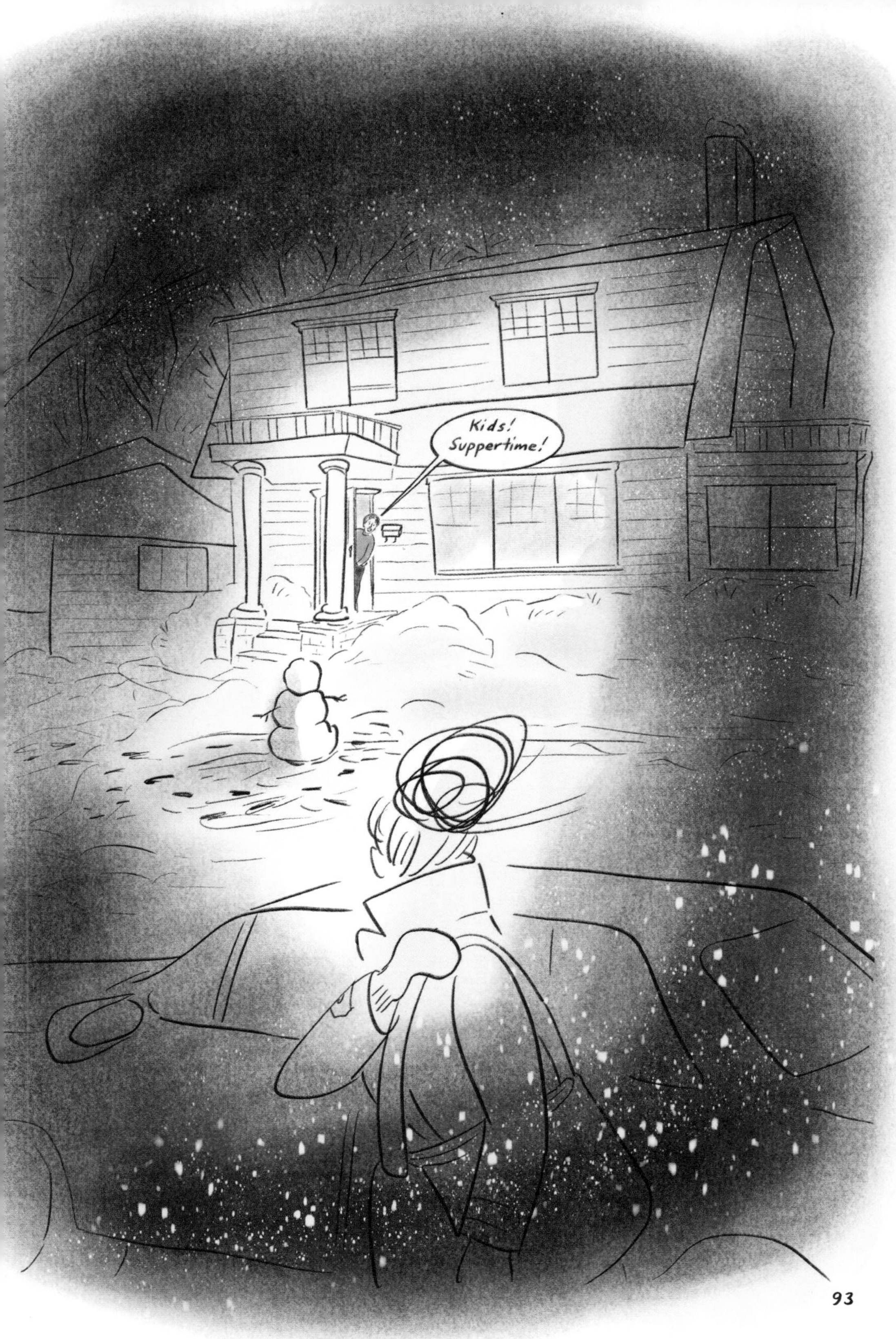
Kids! Suppertime!

THE BASEMENT STILL SCARES ME, ITS DARK CORNERS FILLED WITH THE SPIDERY COBWEBS AND MONSTERS I FEARED AS I CHILD.

BUT I HAVE TO DO LAUNDRY.

I HOPE I SURVIVE IT.

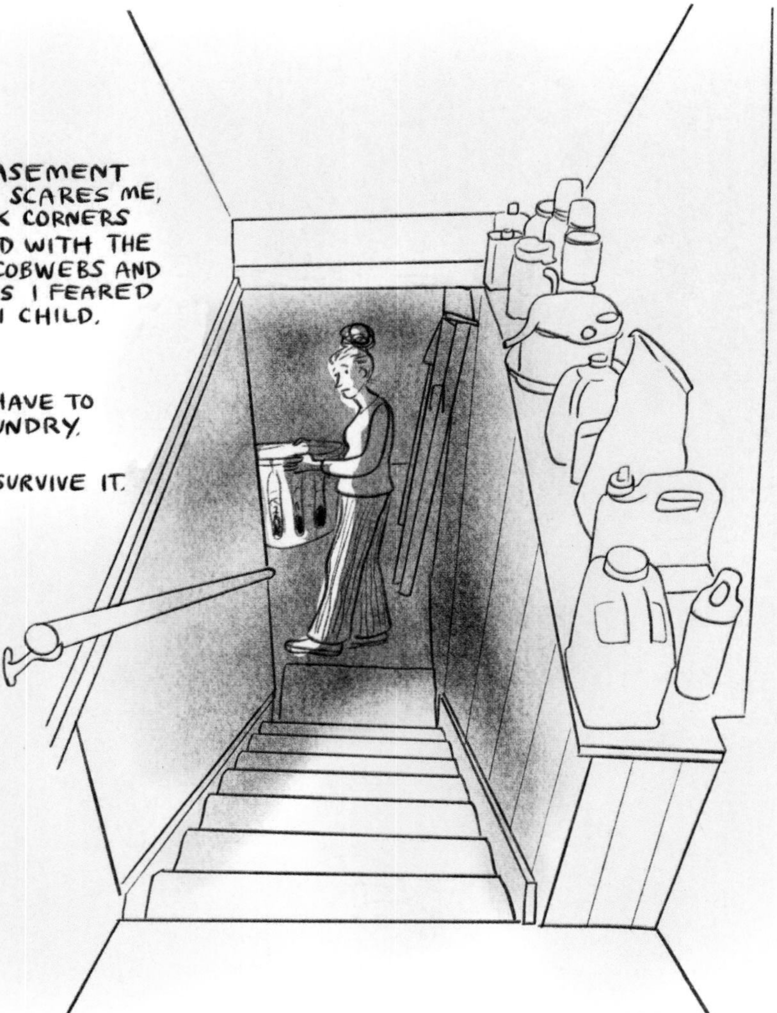

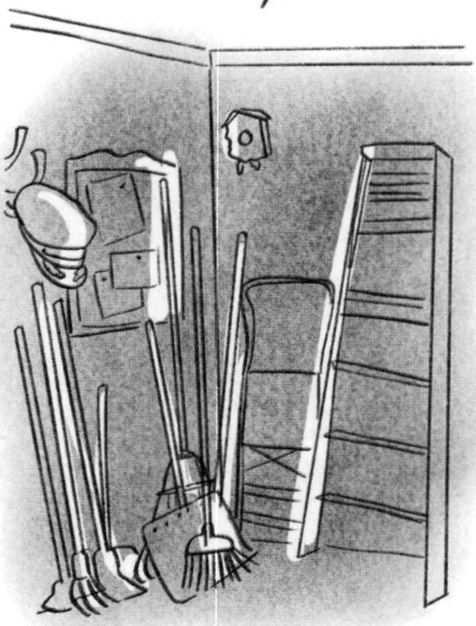

OVER THE YEARS IT'S BECOME A GRAVEYARD DEDICATED TO CONSUMPTION.

WHY SAVE ANYTHING? YOU DIE AND LEAVE A HOUSE FULL OF CRAP FOR SOMEONE ELSE TO DEAL WITH.

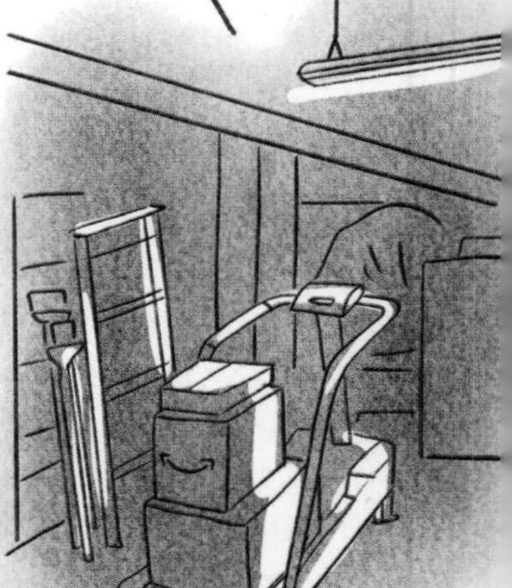

MY DAD'S WORKSHOP
IS IN THE CORNER,
STUFFED TO THE GILLS
WITH HIS TOOLS,
WHICH USED TO BE
STORED CAREFULLY
BUT ARE NOW
JUMBLED AND RUSTING.

ONE SHELF HOLDS AN
ODD COLLECTION
OF OBJECTS, ALMOST
A SHRINE TO HIS PAST.

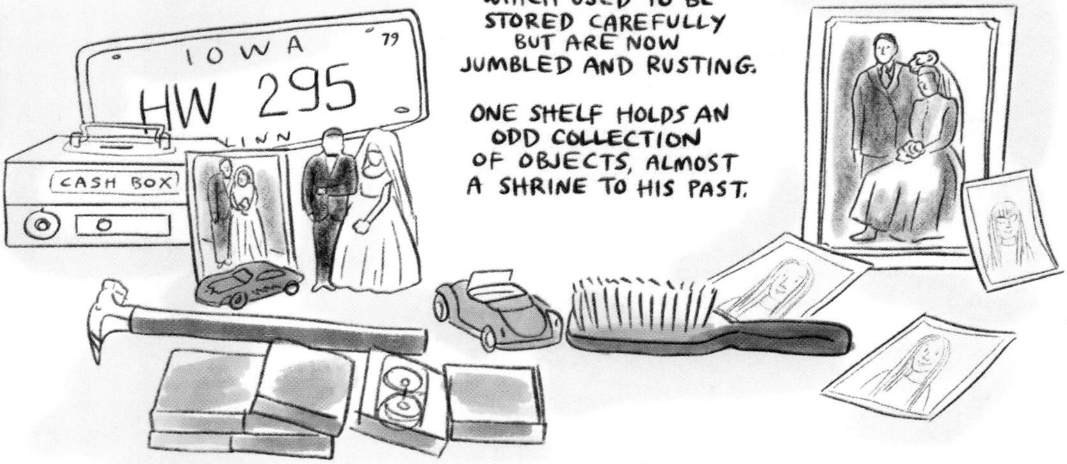
IOWA 79
HW 295
LINN
CASH BOX

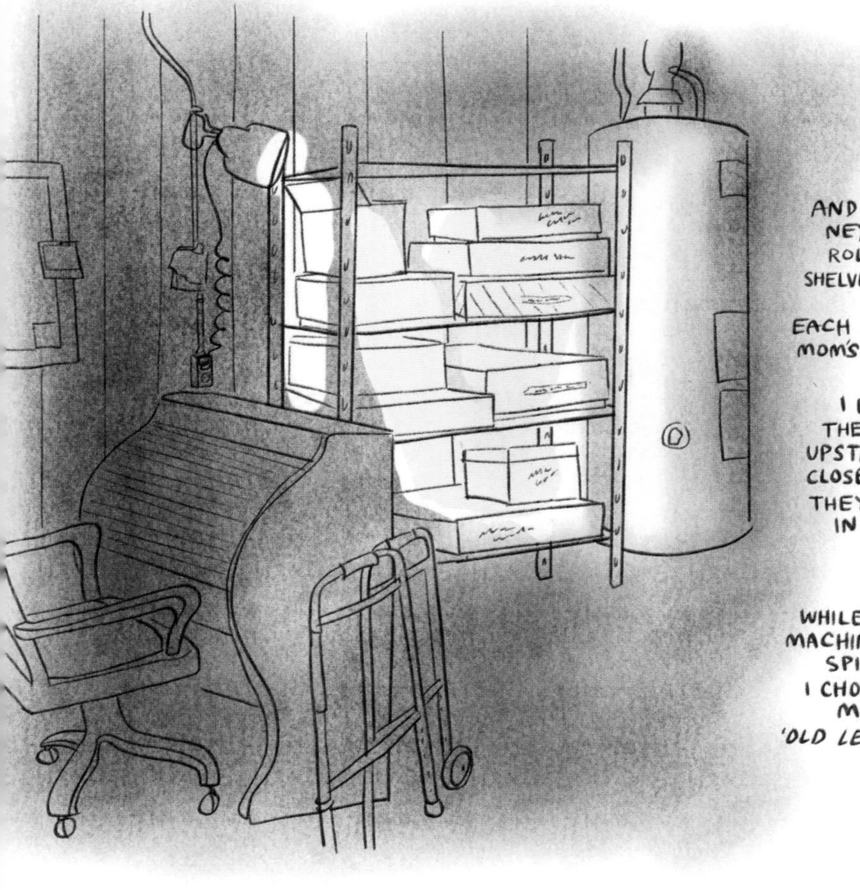

AND THEN I SPY,
NEXT TO DAD'S
ROLLTOP DESK,
SHELVES FILLED WITH
BOXES –
EACH IS LABELLED IN
MOM'S HANDWRITING.

I REMEMBER
THESE USED TO BE
UPSTAIRS IN THE
CLOSET – WHY ARE
THEY DOWN HERE,
IN THE DAMP?

WHILE THE WASHING
MACHINE GOES INTO
SPIN CYCLE
I CHOOSE A BOX
MARKED
'OLD LETTERS + CARDS.'

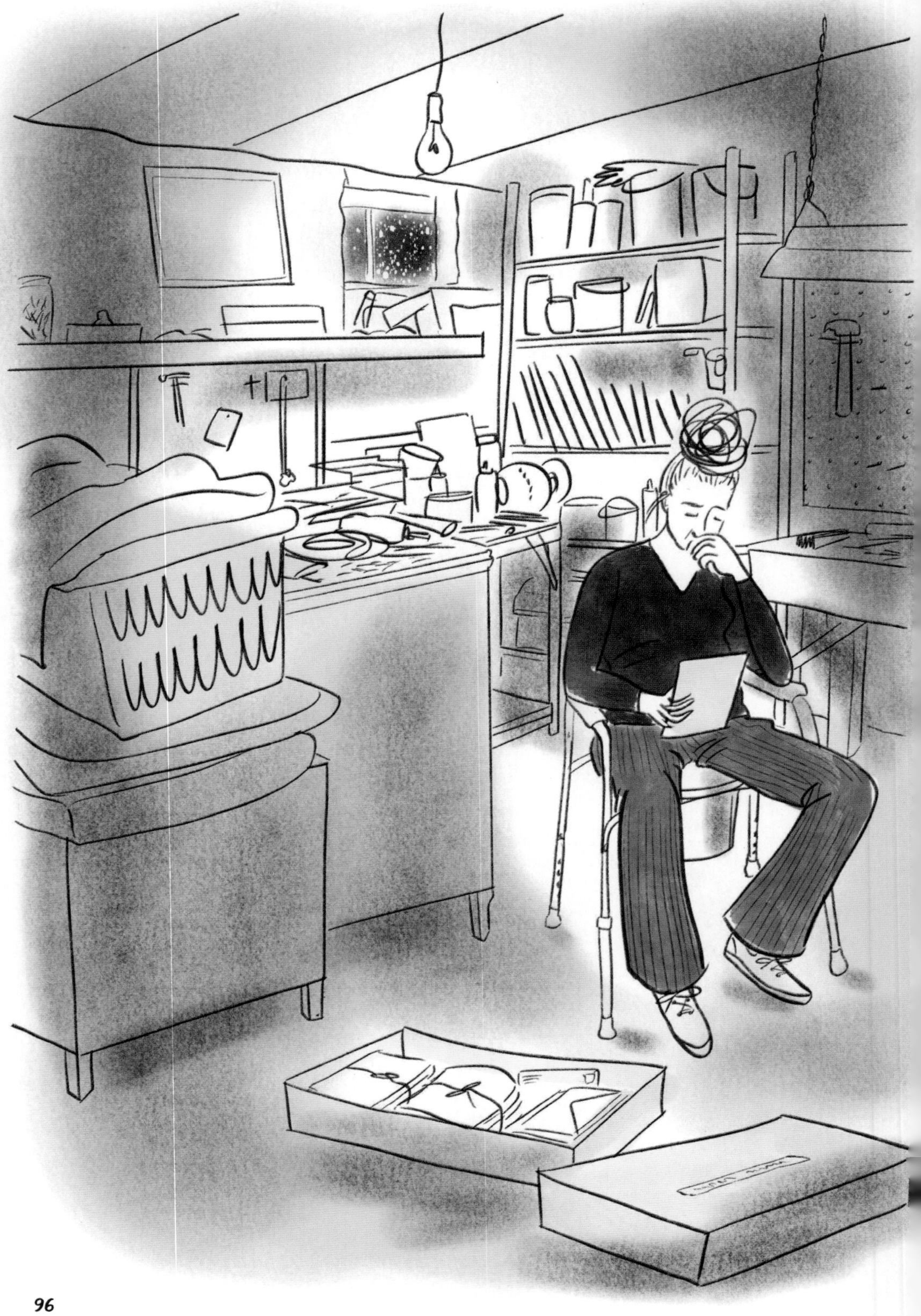

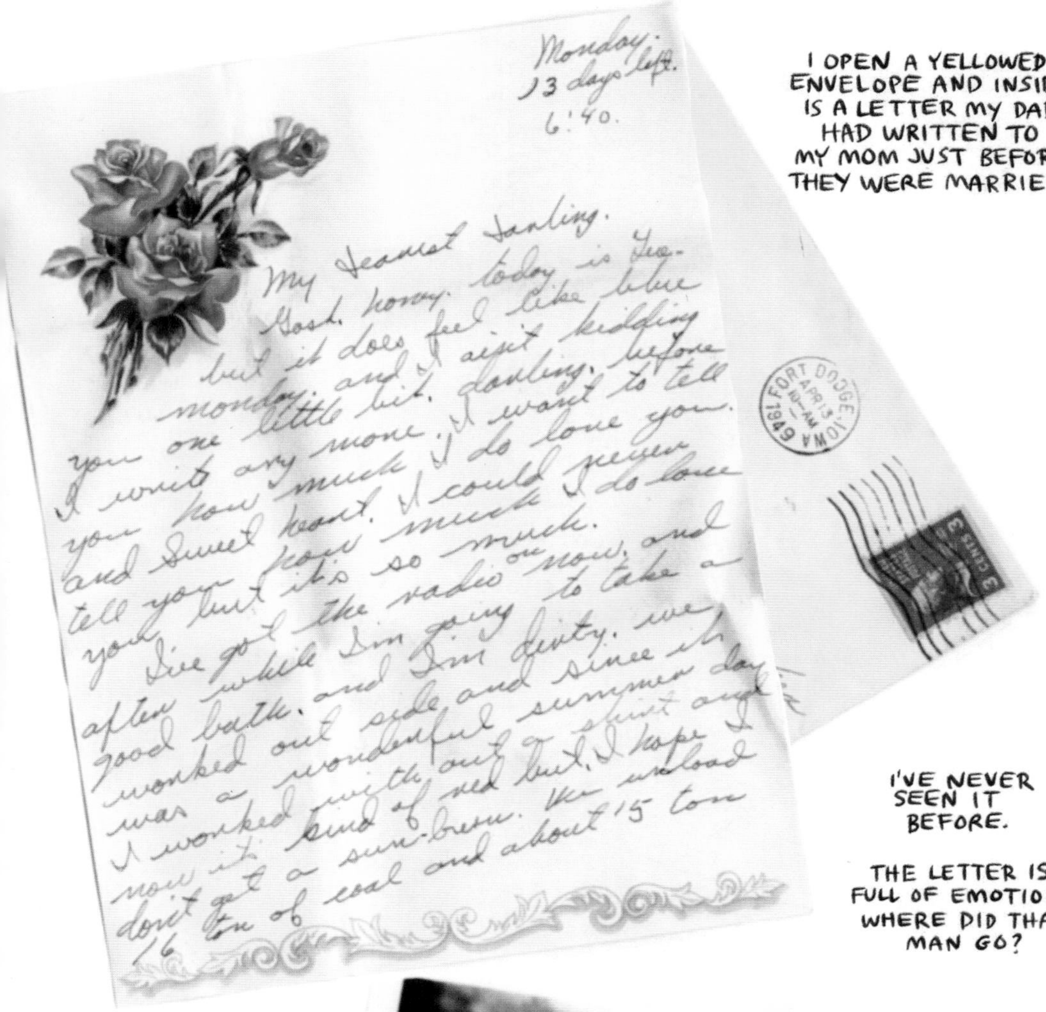
Monday.
13 days left.
6:40.

My dearest darling.
Gosh, honey, today is Tue-
but it does feel like blue
monday, and I ain't kidding
you one little bit, darling, before
I write any more, I want to tell
you how much I do love you.
and Sweet heart, I could never
tell you how much I do love
you, but it's so much.
I've got the radio on now, and
after while I'm going to take a
good bath, and I'm dirty. we
worked out side, and since it
was a wonderful summer day
I worked with out a shirt and
now it's kind of red but, I hope I
don't get a sun-burn. We unload
16 ton of coal and about 15 ton

FORT DODGE, IOWA
APR 13
1946

I OPEN A YELLOWED ENVELOPE AND INSIDE IS A LETTER MY DAD HAD WRITTEN TO MY MOM JUST BEFORE THEY WERE MARRIED.

I'VE NEVER SEEN IT BEFORE.

THE LETTER IS FULL OF EMOTION. WHERE DID THAT MAN GO?

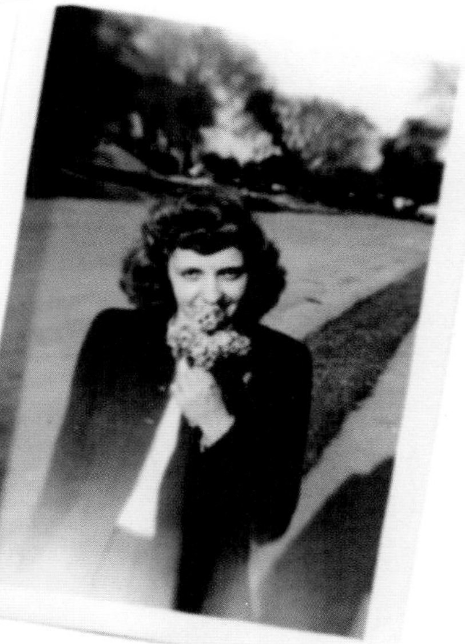

THE FAMILY LEGEND IS THAT MY PARENTS' MARRIAGE BEGAN WITH A BLIND DATE.

MY DAD TURNED UP WITH A HUGE BANDAGE OVER ONE EYE.

MOM CLAIMS SHE MARRIED HIM BECAUSE SHE FELT SORRY FOR HIM.

TURNS OUT HE WAS RECOVERING FROM BONE CANCER SURGERY, WHICH LATER LEFT A DEEP DENT BETWEEN HIS EYES.

HE NEVER WANTED TO TALK ABOUT IT. HE WAS A MAN OF FEW WORDS.

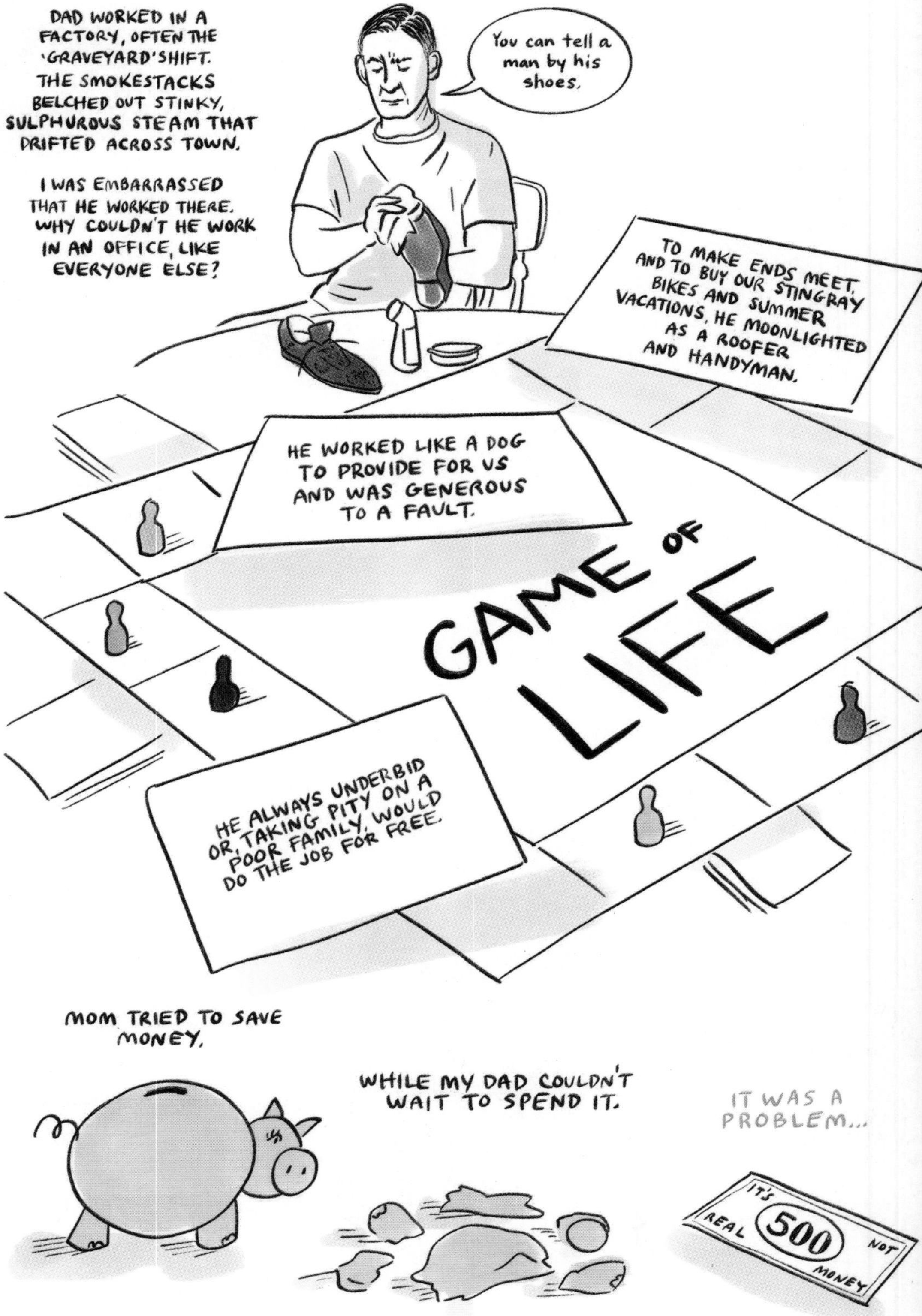

DAD WORKED IN A FACTORY, OFTEN THE 'GRAVEYARD' SHIFT. THE SMOKESTACKS BELCHED OUT STINKY, SULPHUROUS STEAM THAT DRIFTED ACROSS TOWN.
I WAS EMBARRASSED THAT HE WORKED THERE. WHY COULDN'T HE WORK IN AN OFFICE, LIKE EVERYONE ELSE?
You can tell a man by his shoes.
TO MAKE ENDS MEET, AND TO BUY OUR STINGRAY BIKES AND SUMMER VACATIONS, HE MOONLIGHTED AS A ROOFER AND HANDYMAN.
HE WORKED LIKE A DOG TO PROVIDE FOR US AND WAS GENEROUS TO A FAULT.
GAME OF LIFE
HE ALWAYS UNDERBID OR, TAKING PITY ON A POOR FAMILY, WOULD DO THE JOB FOR FREE.
MOM TRIED TO SAVE MONEY,
WHILE MY DAD COULDN'T WAIT TO SPEND IT.
IT WAS A PROBLEM...
IT'S REAL 500 NOT MONEY

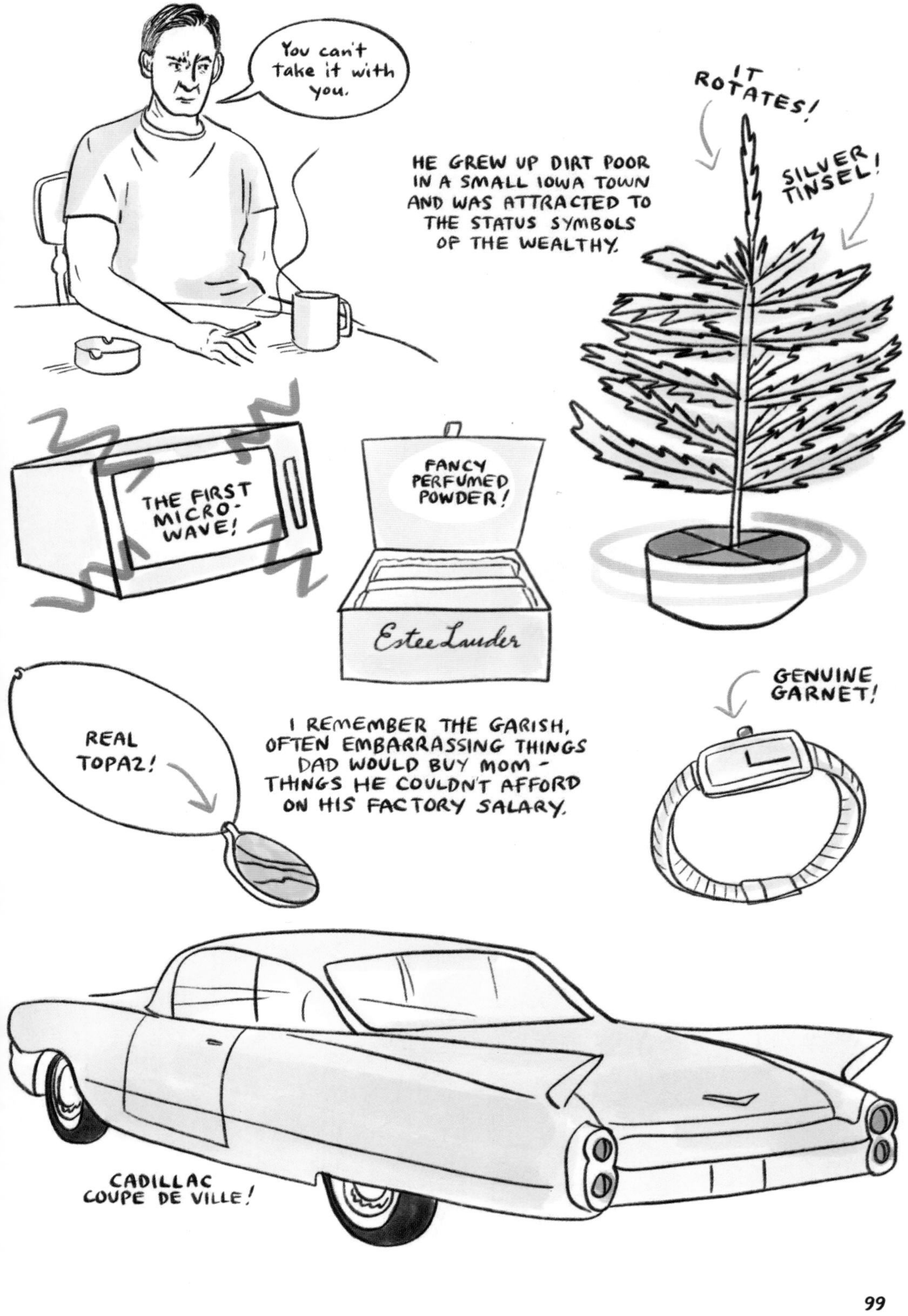
You can't take it with you.
HE GREW UP DIRT POOR IN A SMALL IOWA TOWN AND WAS ATTRACTED TO THE STATUS SYMBOLS OF THE WEALTHY.
IT ROTATES!
SILVER TINSEL!
THE FIRST MICRO-WAVE!
FANCY PERFUMED POWDER!
Estee Lauder
REAL TOPAZ!
I REMEMBER THE GARISH, OFTEN EMBARRASSING THINGS DAD WOULD BUY MOM - THINGS HE COULDN'T AFFORD ON HIS FACTORY SALARY.
GENUINE GARNET!
CADILLAC COUPE DE VILLE!

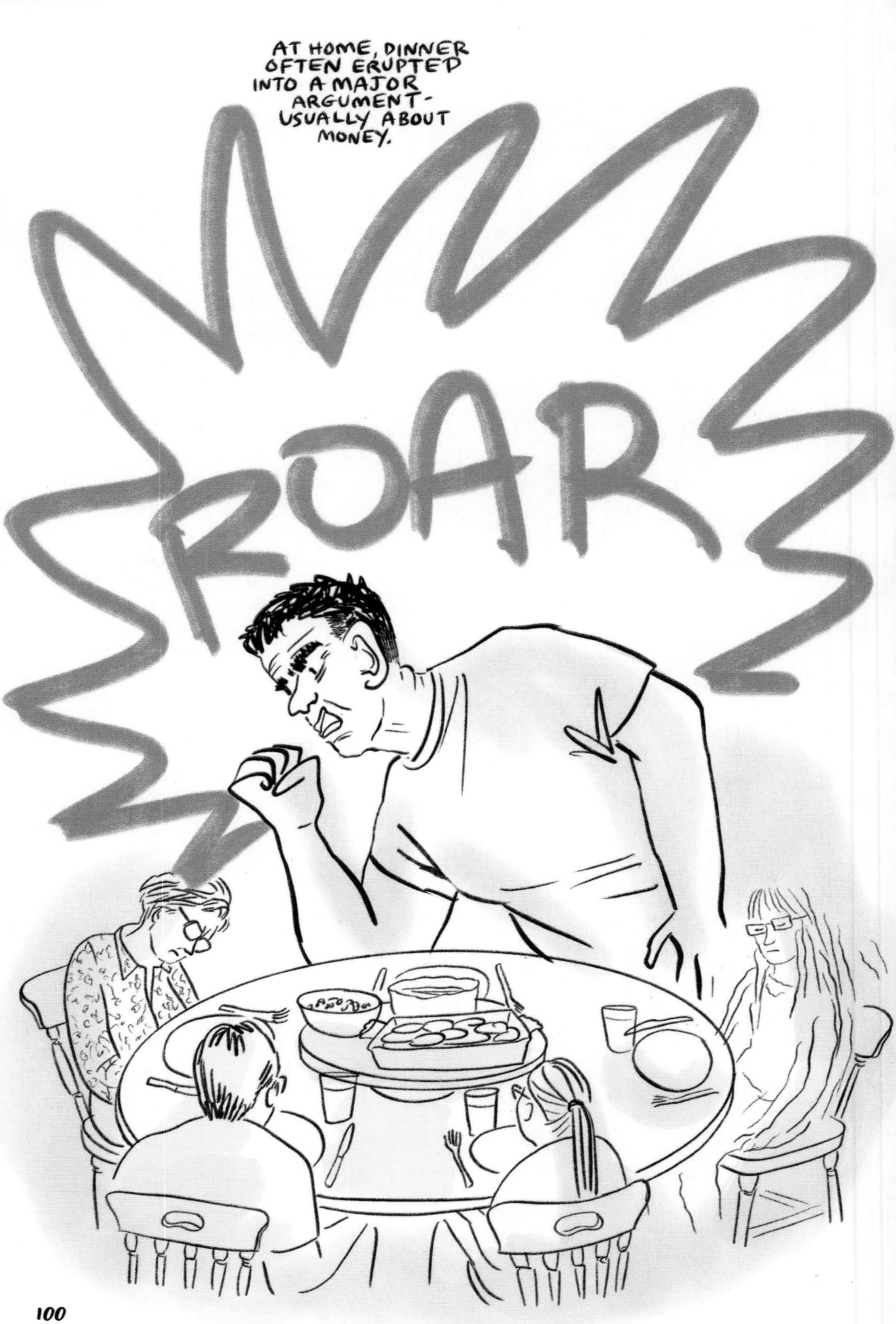
AT HOME, DINNER OFTEN ERUPTED INTO A MAJOR ARGUMENT- USUALLY ABOUT MONEY.
ROAR

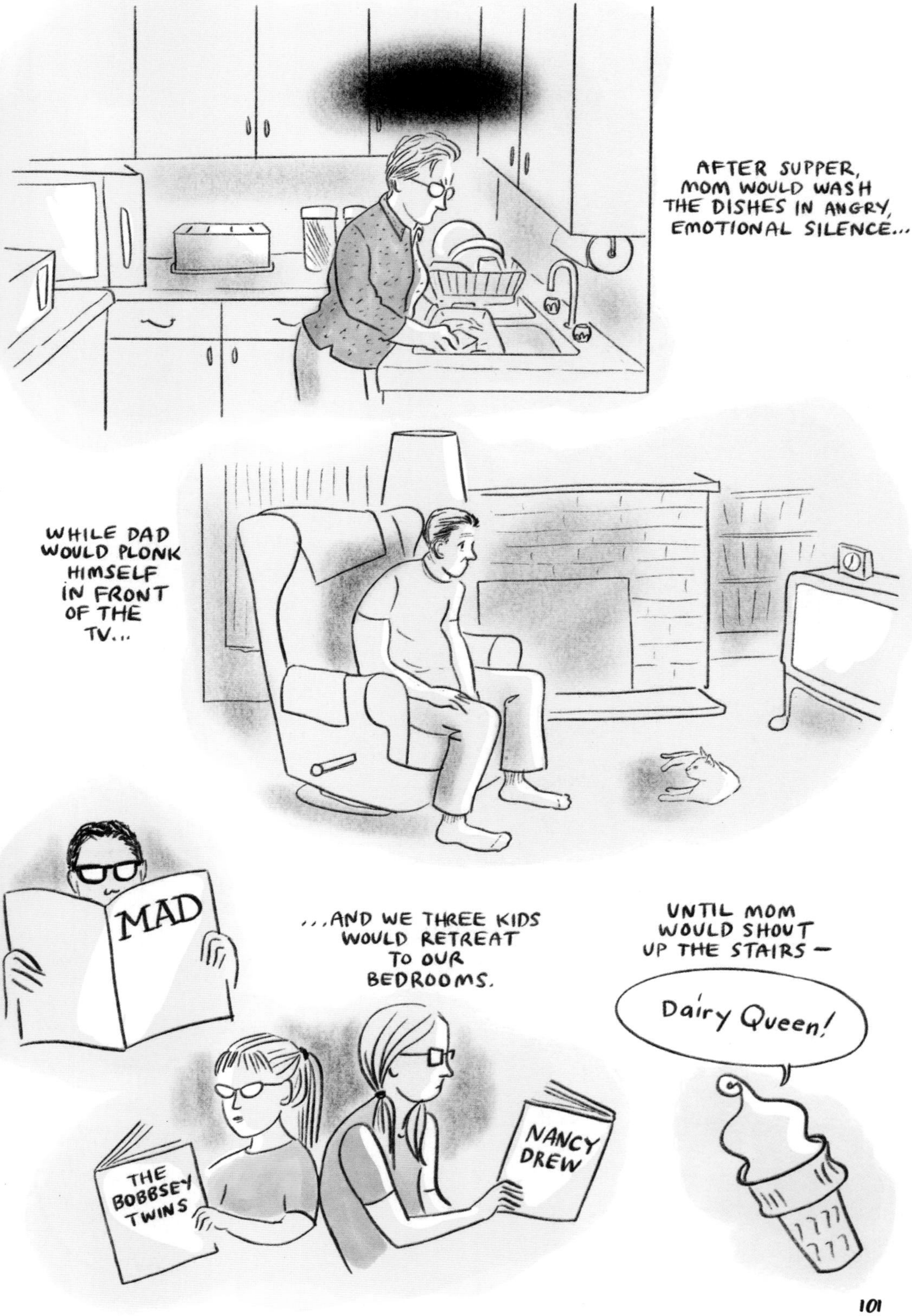
AFTER SUPPER, MOM WOULD WASH THE DISHES IN ANGRY, EMOTIONAL SILENCE...
WHILE DAD WOULD PLONK HIMSELF IN FRONT OF THE TV...
MAD
...AND WE THREE KIDS WOULD RETREAT TO OUR BEDROOMS.
THE BOBBSEY TWINS
NANCY DREW
UNTIL MOM WOULD SHOUT UP THE STAIRS —
Dairy Queen!

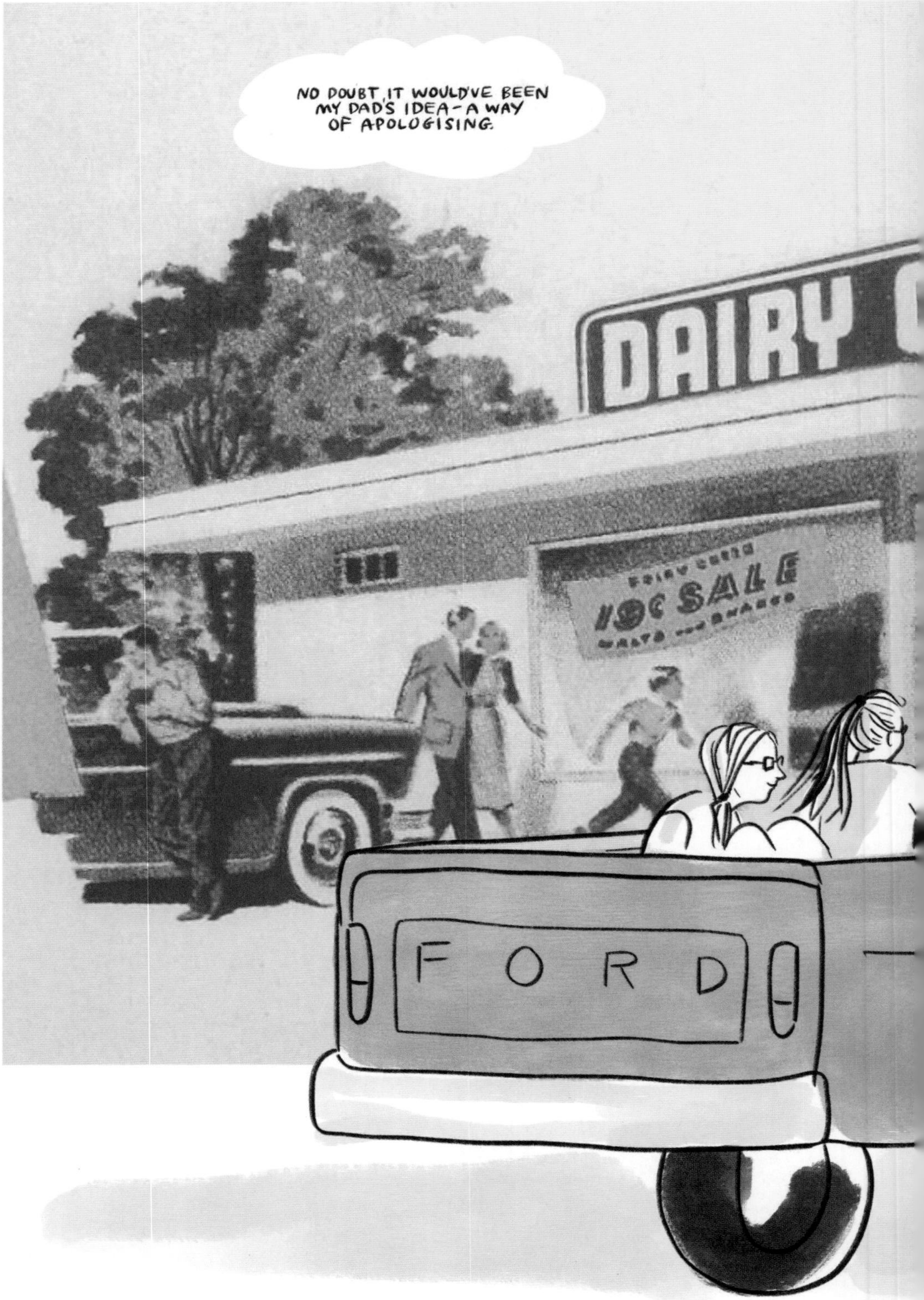
NO DOUBT, IT WOULD'VE BEEN MY DAD'S IDEA - A WAY OF APOLOGISING.
DAIRY
SALE
FORD

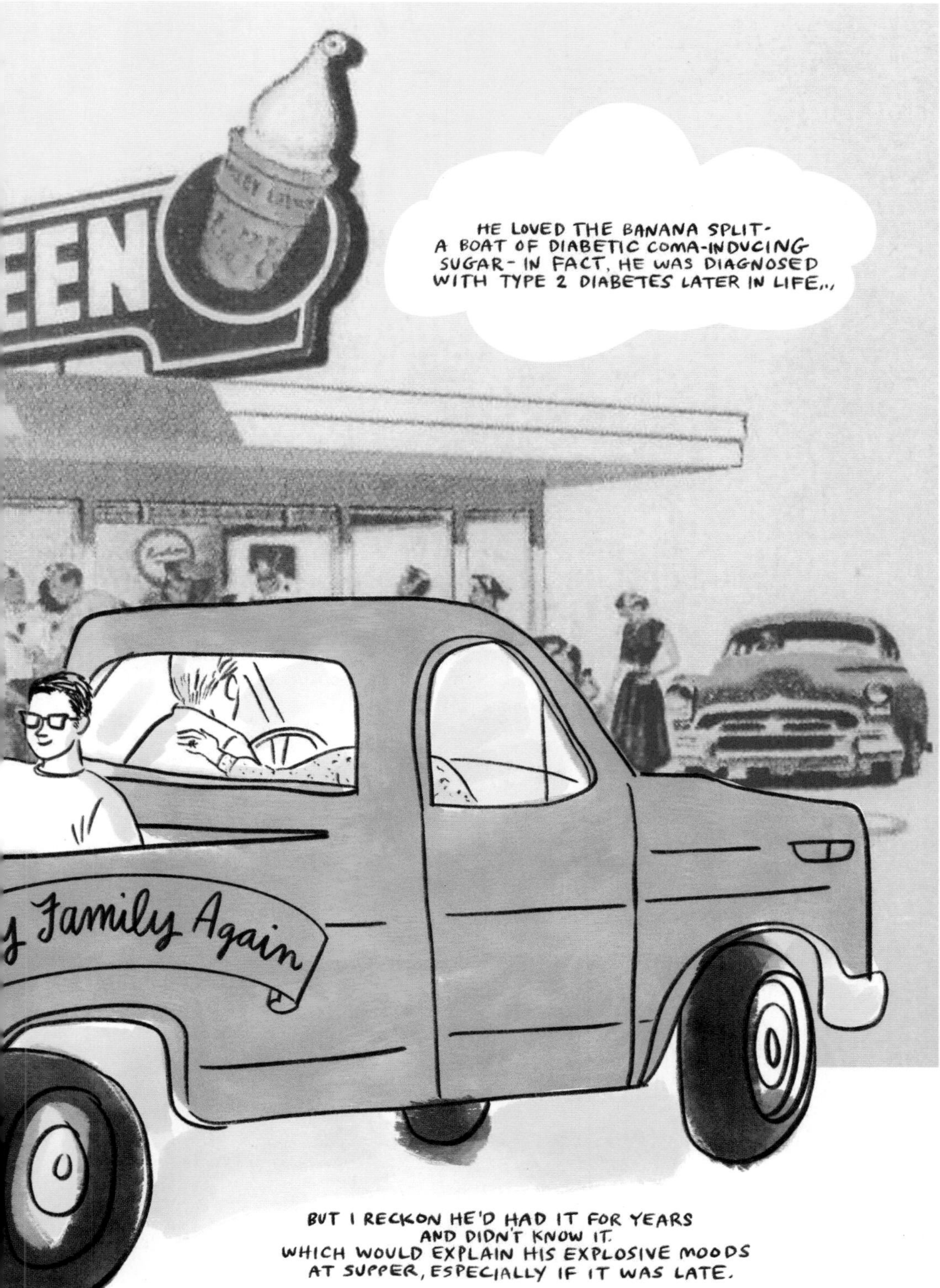
HE LOVED THE BANANA SPLIT- A BOAT OF DIABETIC COMA-INDUCING SUGAR- IN FACT, HE WAS DIAGNOSED WITH TYPE 2 DIABETES LATER IN LIFE...
EEN
y Family Again
BUT I RECKON HE'D HAD IT FOR YEARS AND DIDN'T KNOW IT. WHICH WOULD EXPLAIN HIS EXPLOSIVE MOODS AT SUPPER, ESPECIALLY IF IT WAS LATE.

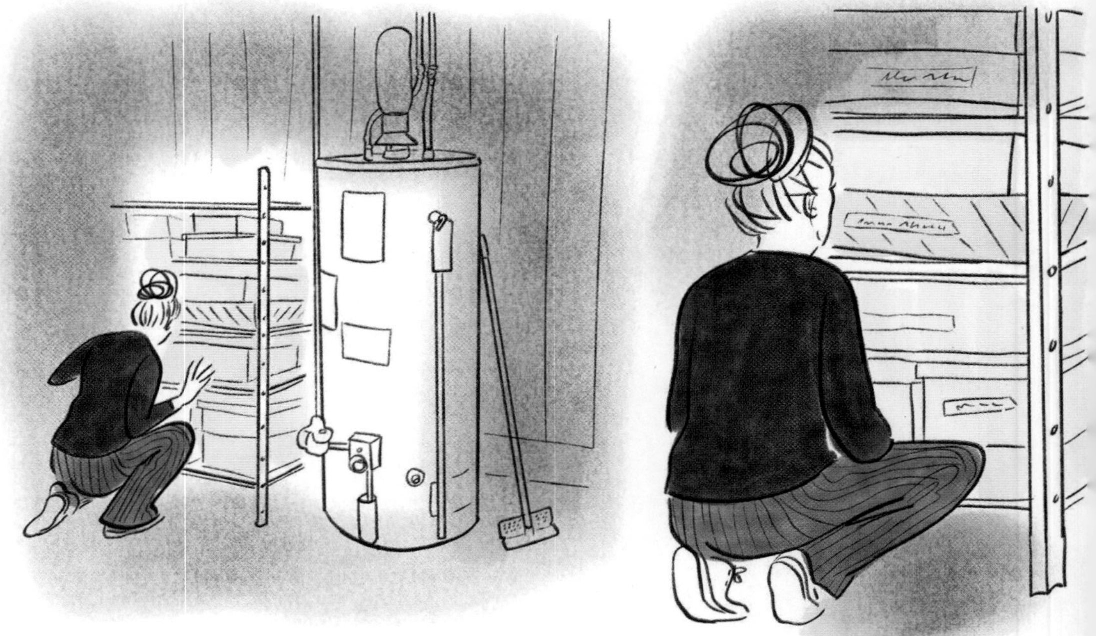

THERE'S A HUGE PILE OF BOXES TO GO THROUGH BUT I AM ALREADY EMOTIONALLY DRAINED BY THE MEMORIES.

I TAKE A BOX LABELLED *'BABY BIRTHDAY CARDS'* AND PUT IT BACK IN MOM'S BEDROOM CLOSET.

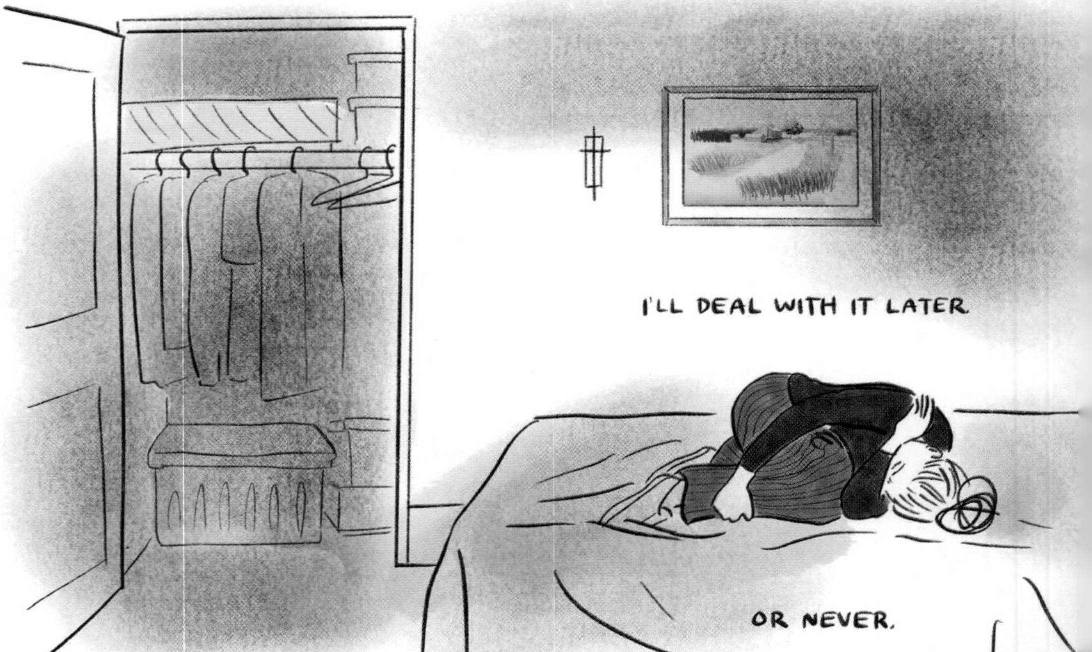
I'LL DEAL WITH IT LATER.
OR NEVER.

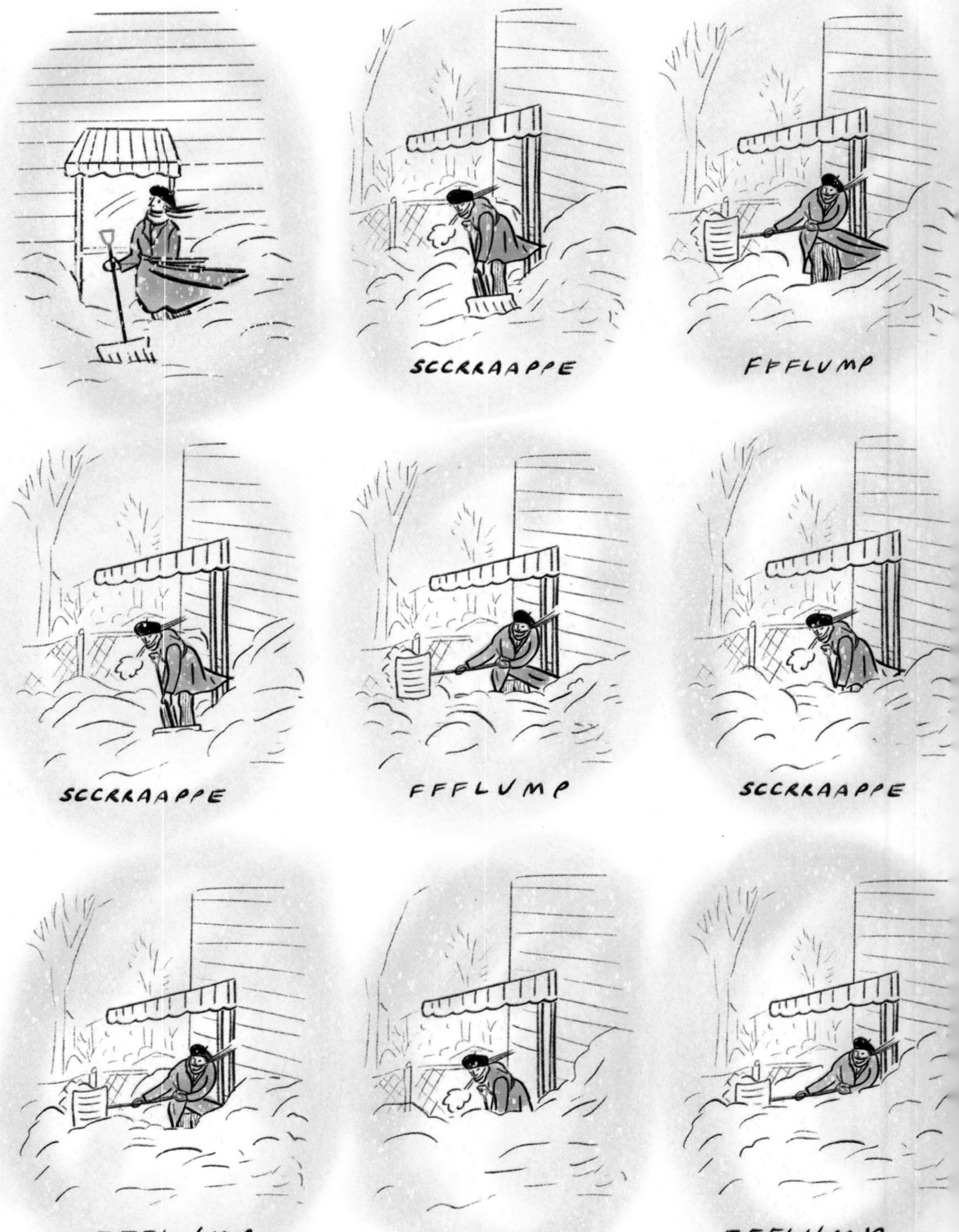
SCCRRAAPPE
FFFLUMP
SCCRRAAPPE
FFFLUMP
SCCRRAAPPE
FFFLUMP
SCCRRAAPPE
FFFLUMP

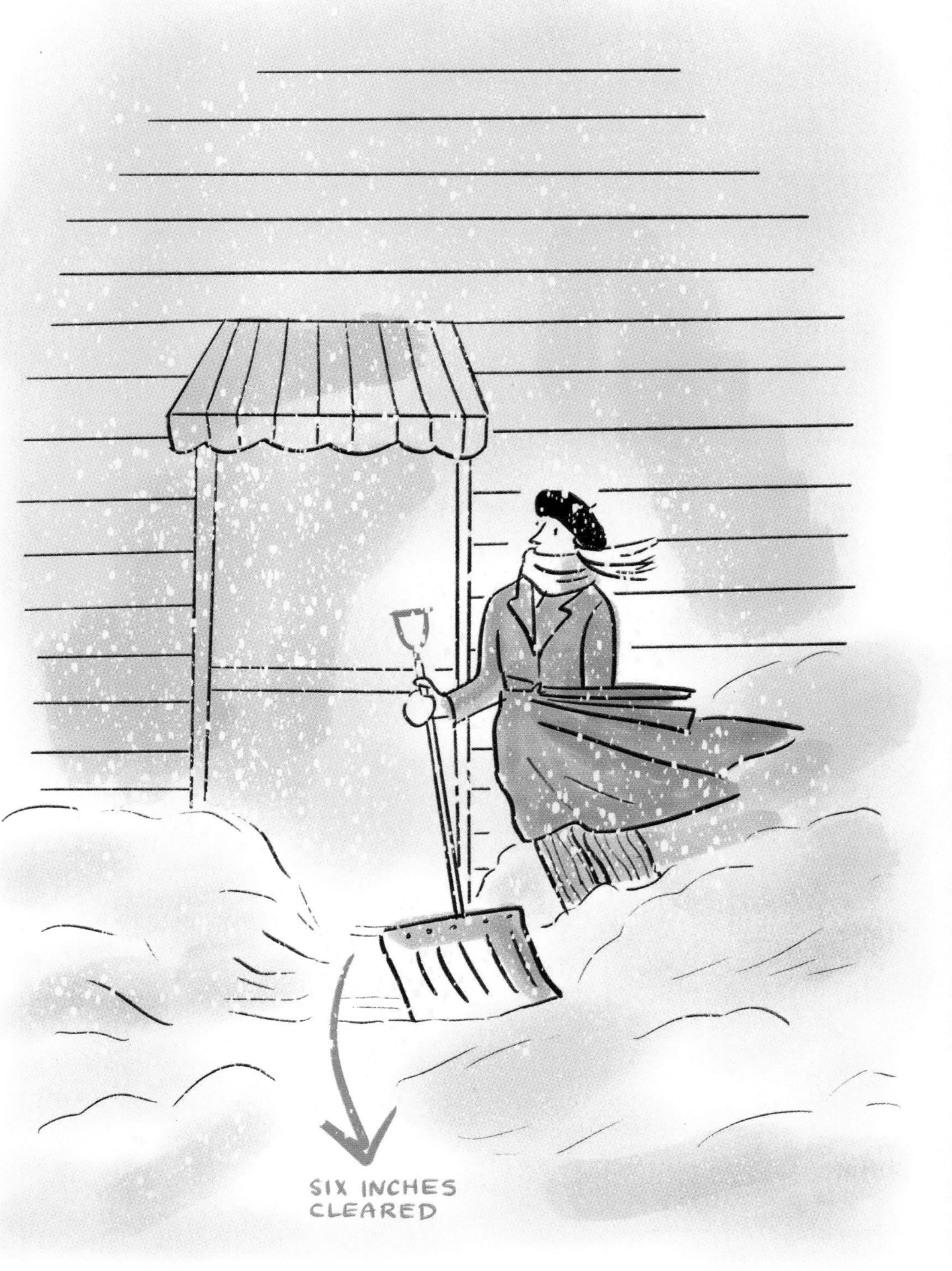
SIX INCHES
CLEARED

THE NEXT MORNING IS SUNNY AND FREEZING COLD.
I RUSH TO ARRIVE EARLY AND FIND MOM ALREADY IN THE DINING ROOM.

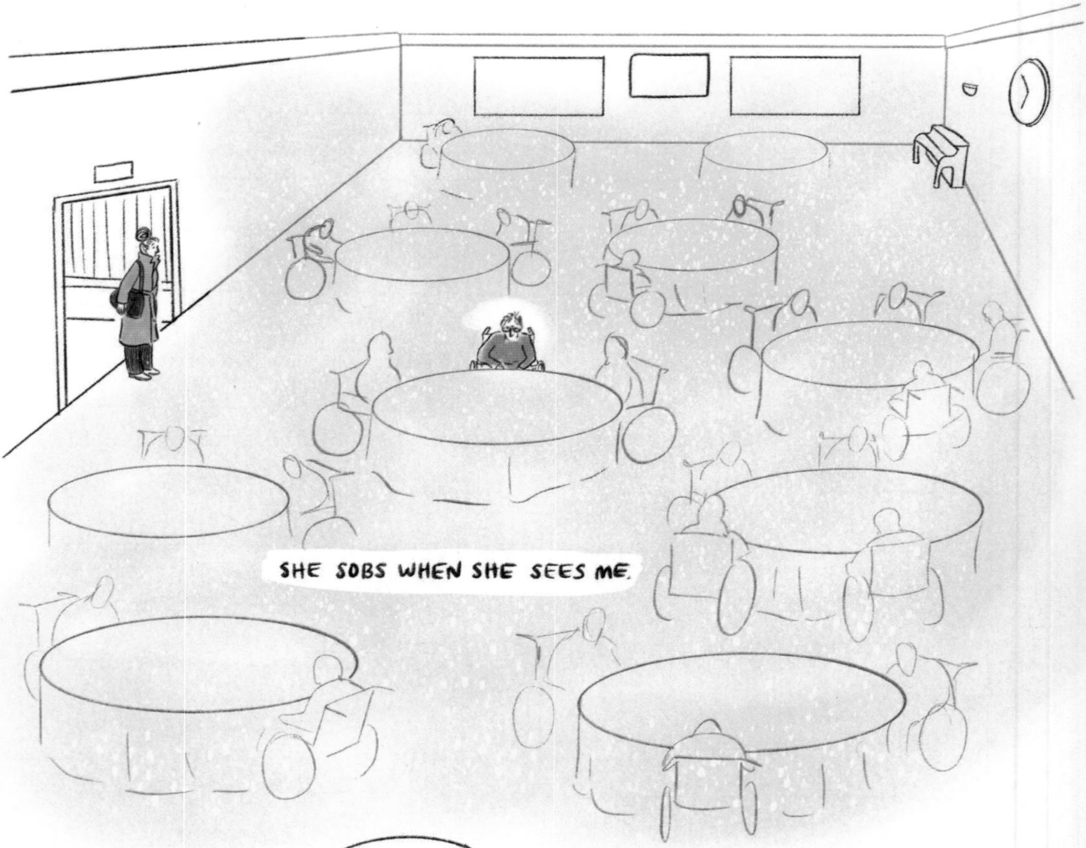
SHE SOBS WHEN SHE SEES ME.

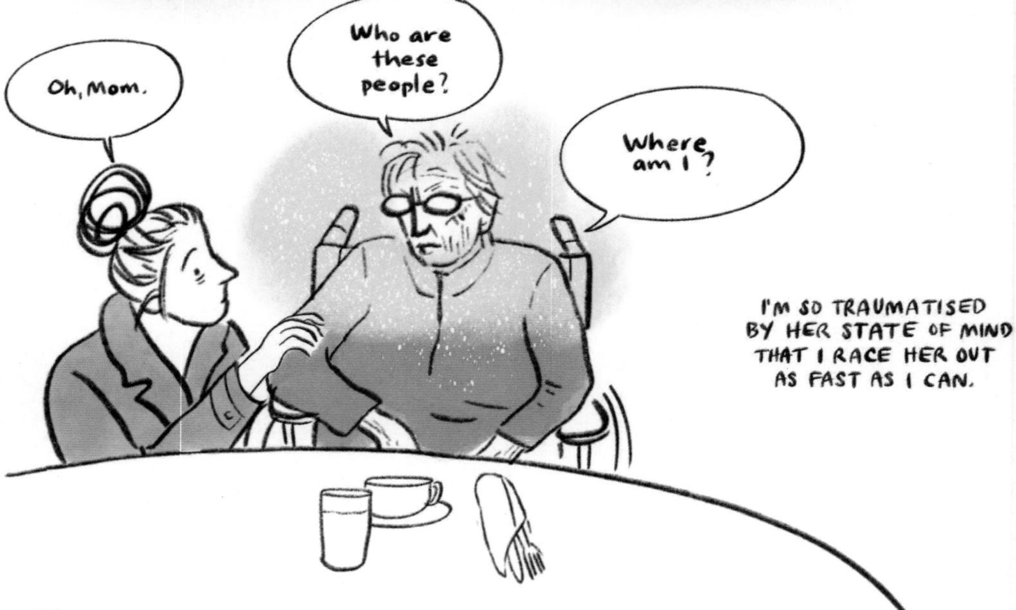
Oh, Mom.
Who are these people?
Where am I?
I'M SO TRAUMATISED BY HER STATE OF MIND THAT I RACE HER OUT AS FAST AS I CAN.

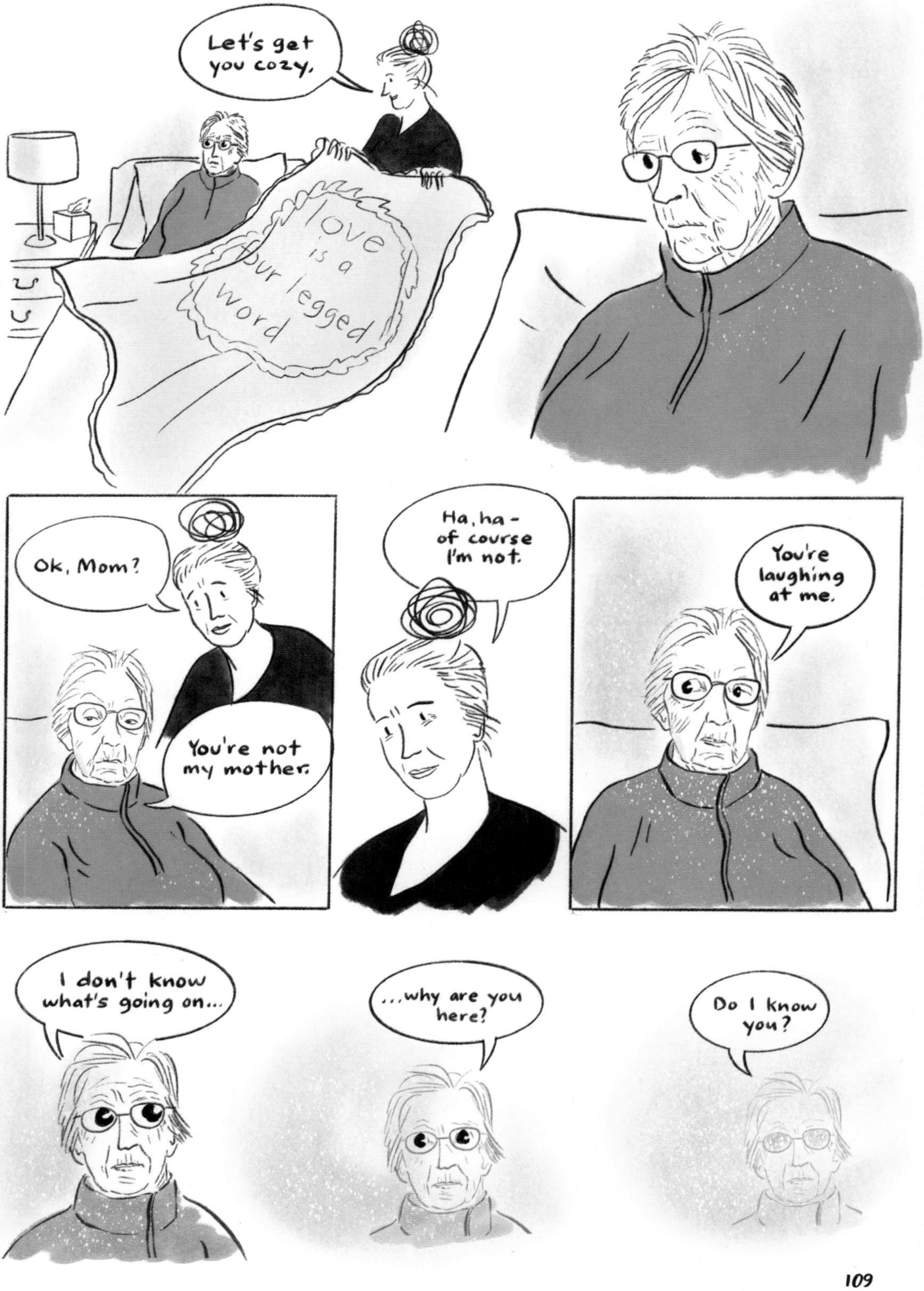
Let's get you cozy,
love is a four legged word
Ok, Mom?
You're not my mother.
Ha, ha - of course I'm not.
You're laughing at me.
I don't know what's going on...
...why are you here?
Do I know you?

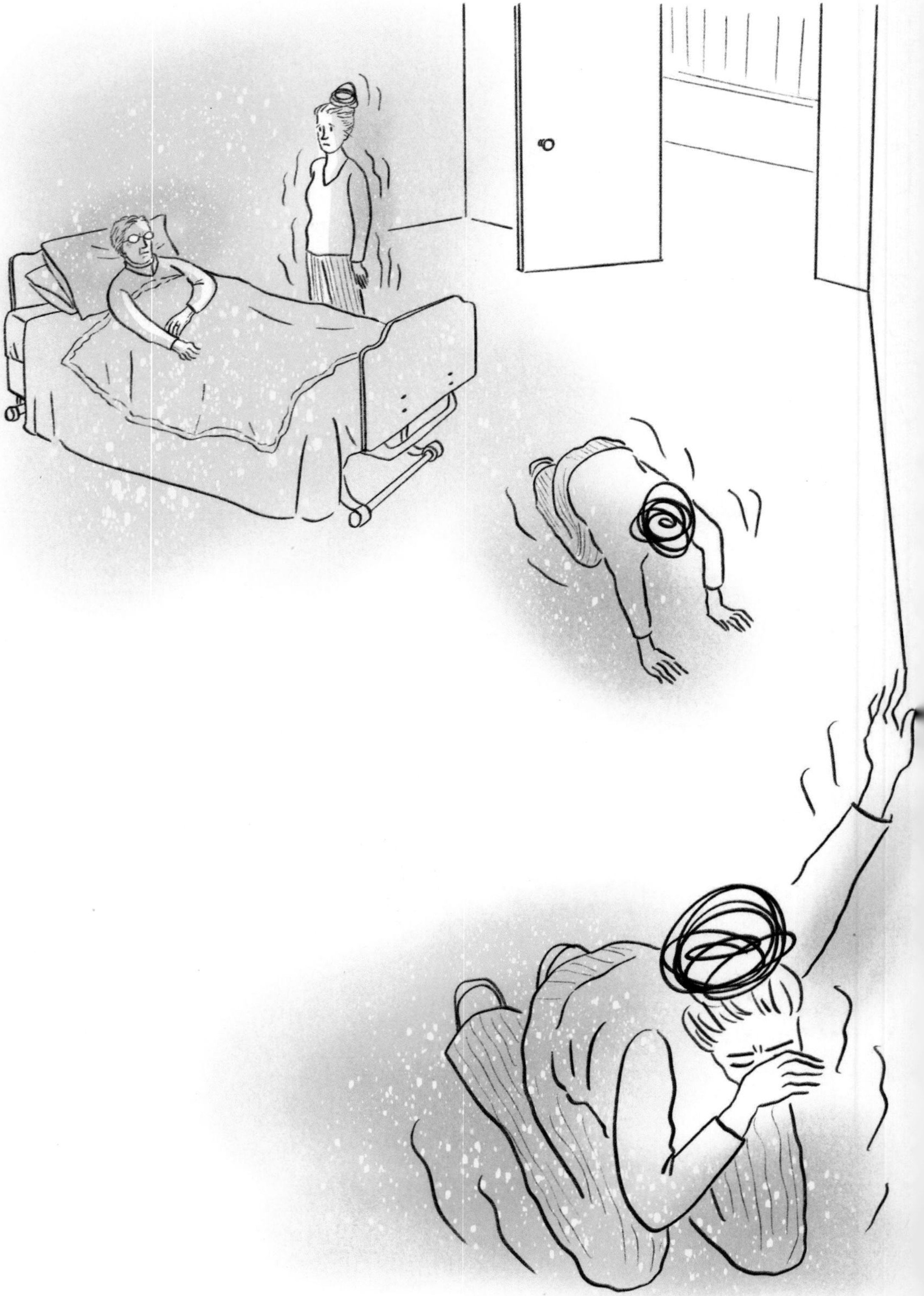

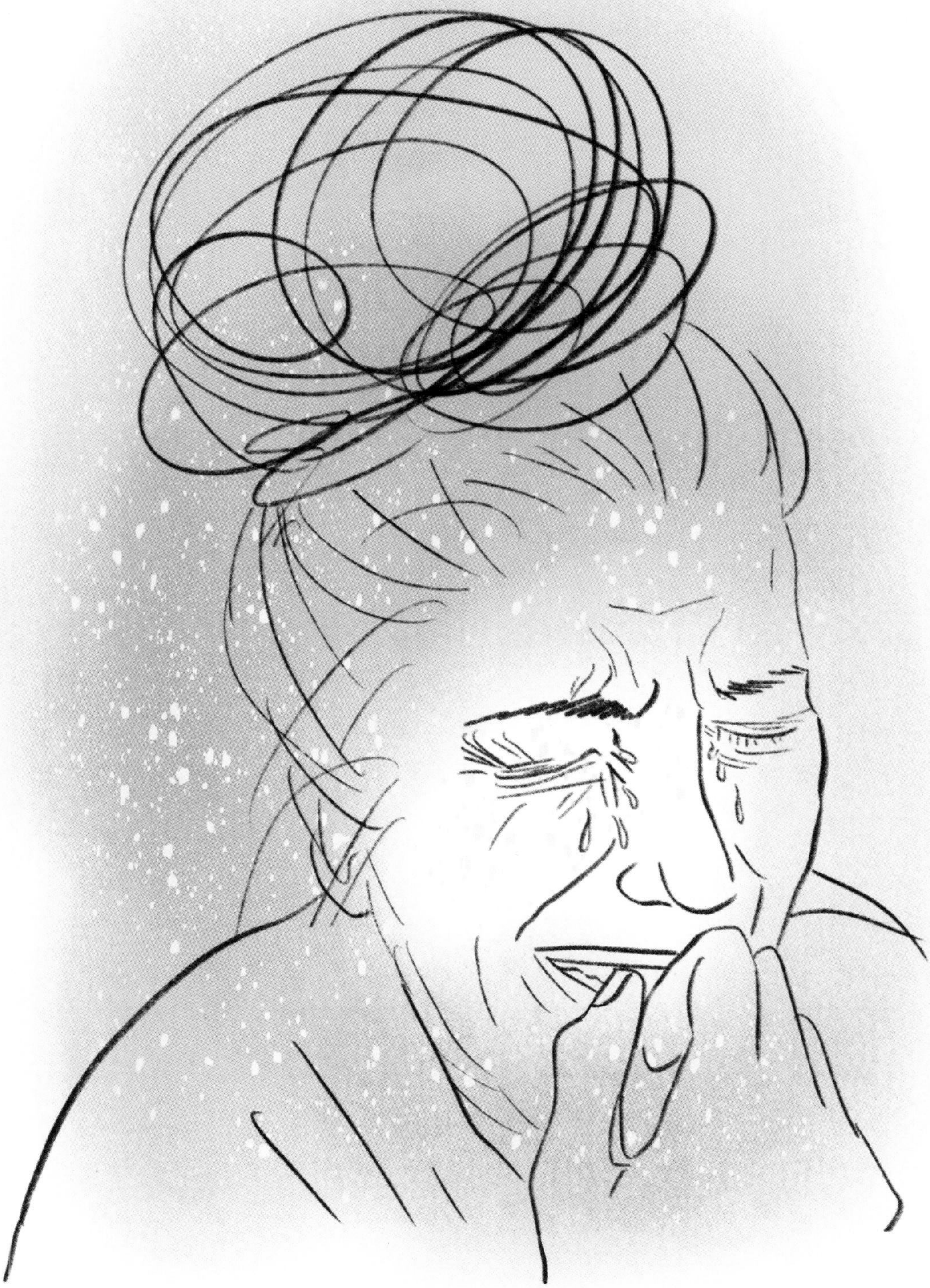

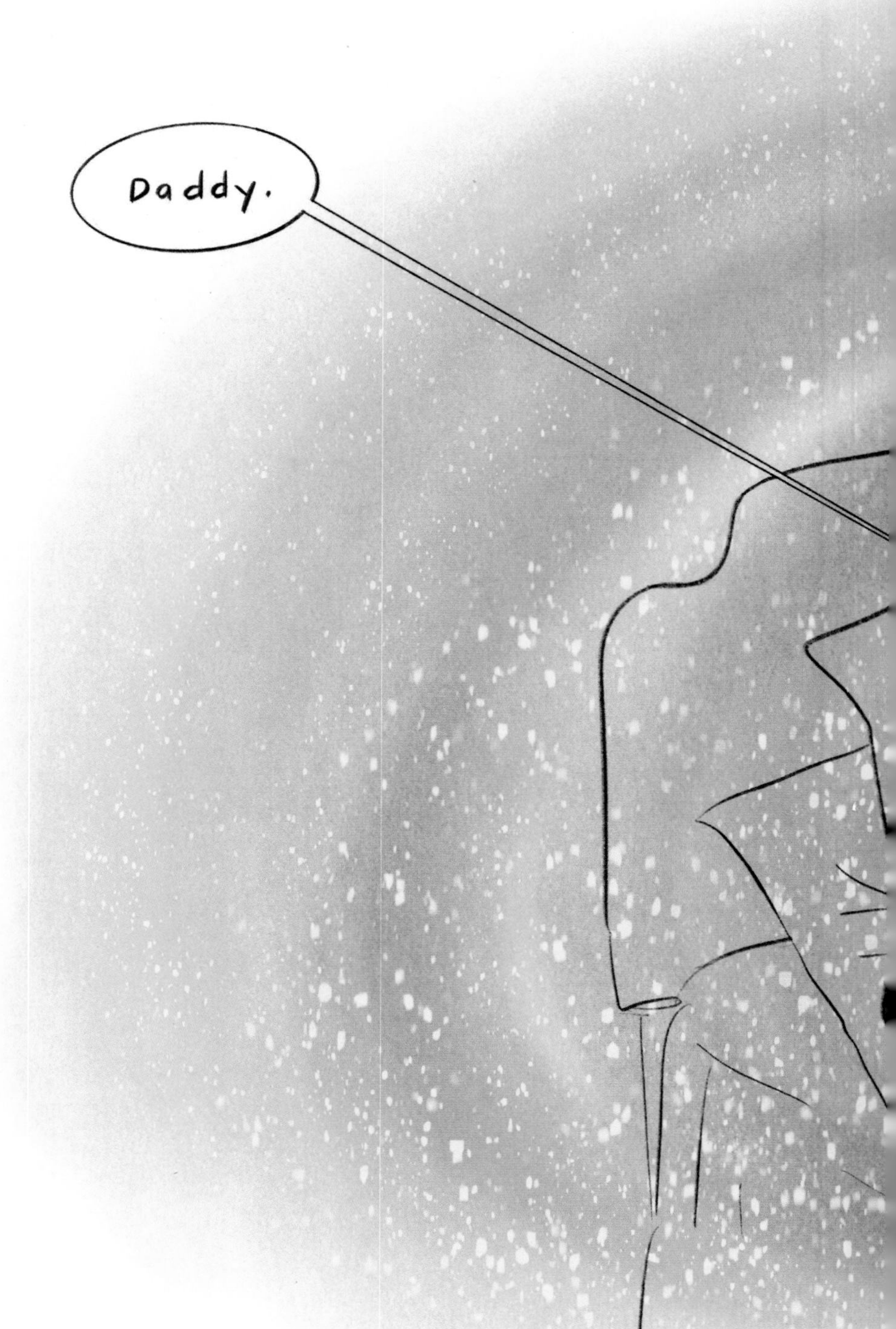
Daddy.

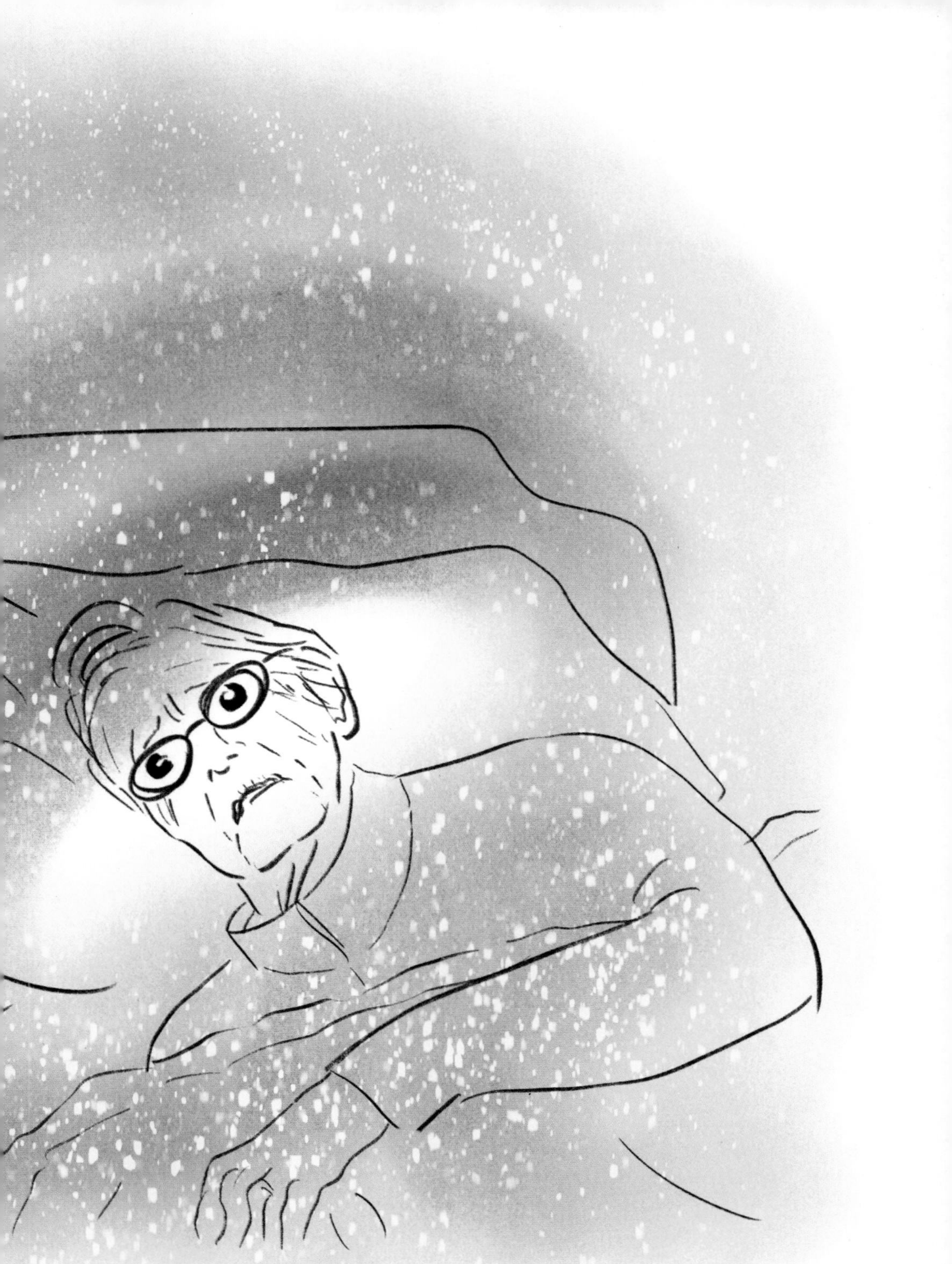

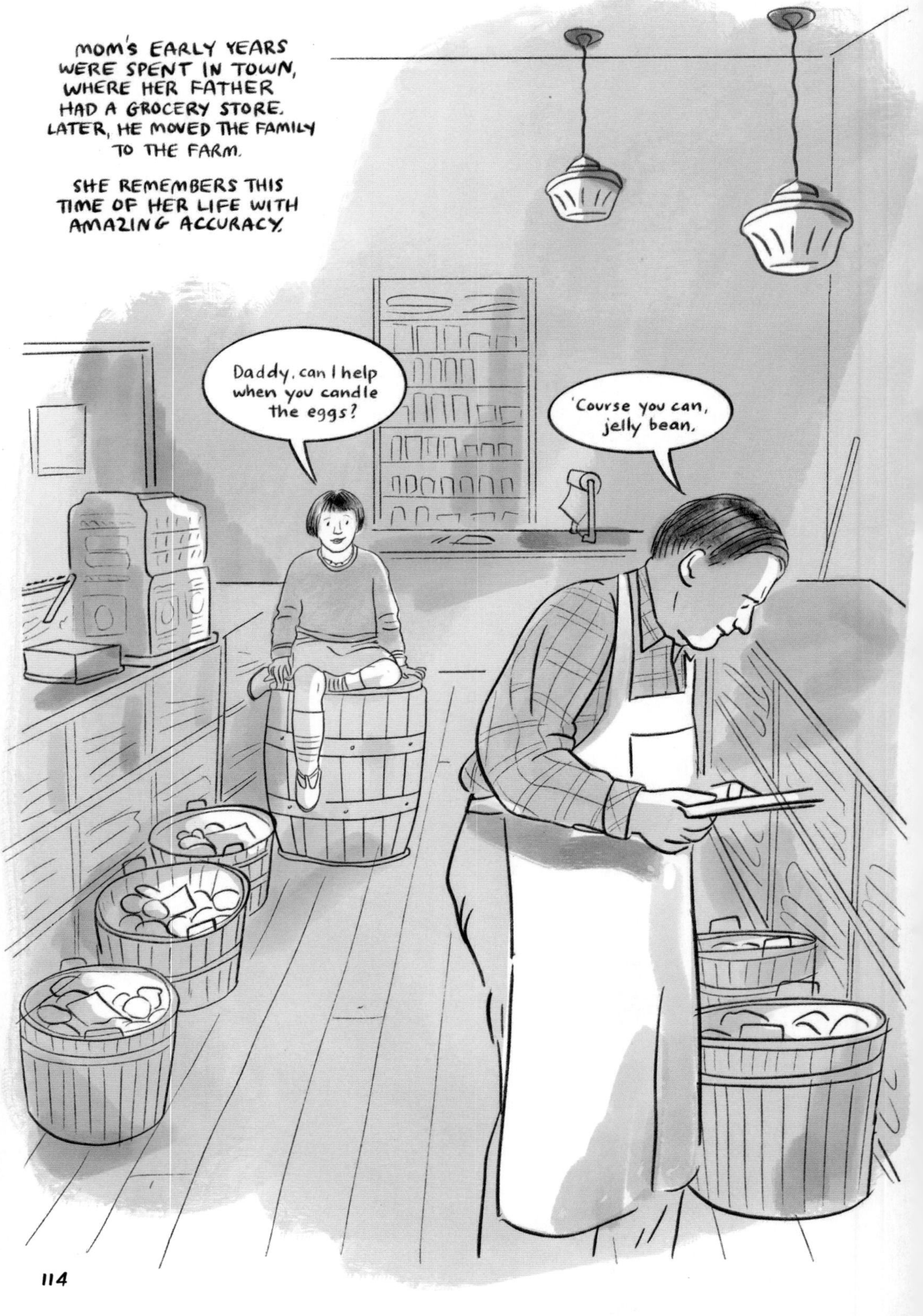
MOM'S EARLY YEARS WERE SPENT IN TOWN, WHERE HER FATHER HAD A GROCERY STORE. LATER, HE MOVED THE FAMILY TO THE FARM.
SHE REMEMBERS THIS TIME OF HER LIFE WITH AMAZING ACCURACY.
Daddy, can I help when you candle the eggs?
'Course you can, jelly bean.

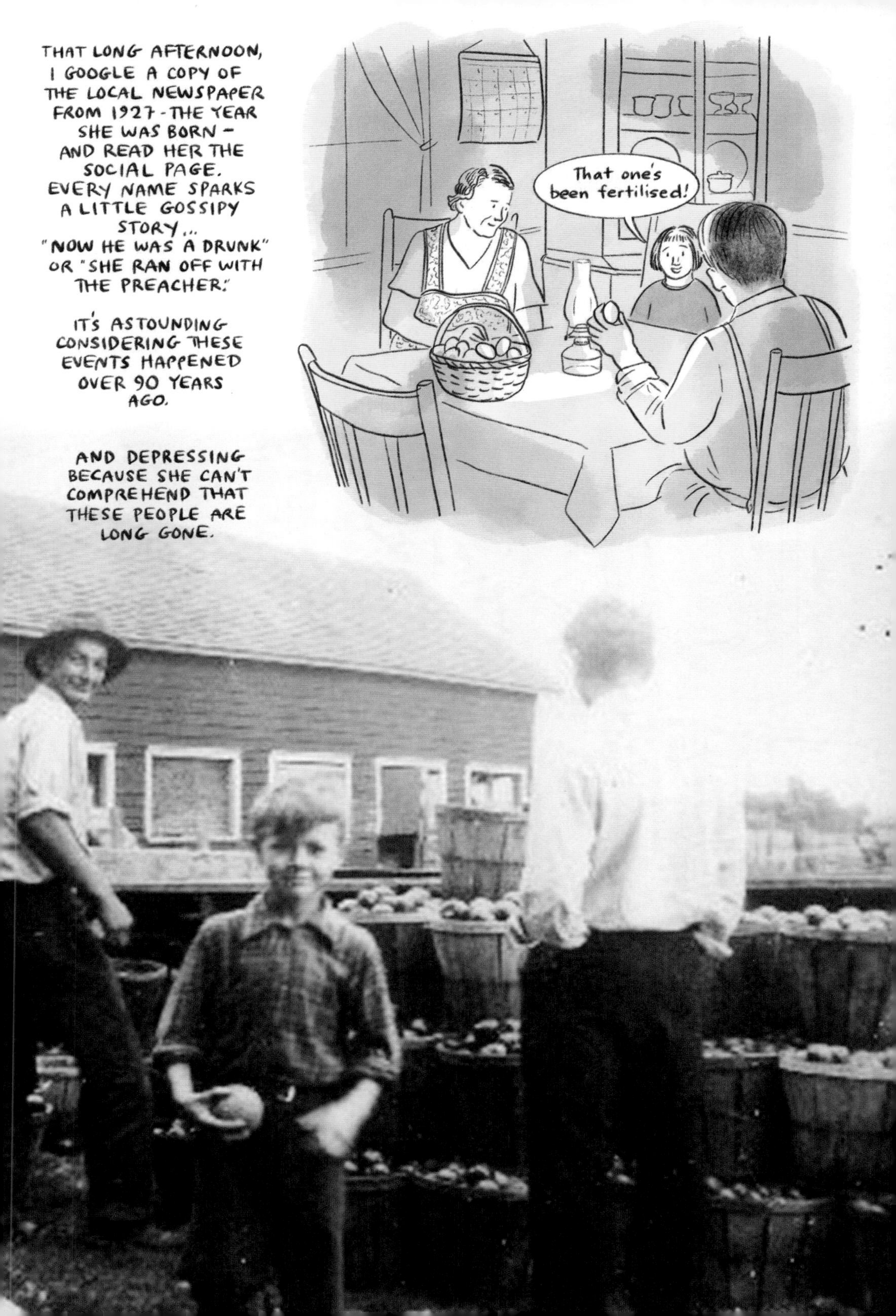
THAT LONG AFTERNOON, I GOOGLE A COPY OF THE LOCAL NEWSPAPER FROM 1927 - THE YEAR SHE WAS BORN - AND READ HER THE SOCIAL PAGE. EVERY NAME SPARKS A LITTLE GOSSIPY STORY... "NOW HE WAS A DRUNK" OR "SHE RAN OFF WITH THE PREACHER."
That one's been fertilised!
IT'S ASTOUNDING CONSIDERING THESE EVENTS HAPPENED OVER 90 YEARS AGO.
AND DEPRESSING BECAUSE SHE CAN'T COMPREHEND THAT THESE PEOPLE ARE LONG GONE.

AND SO THE INSURANCE TARGETS BEGIN...

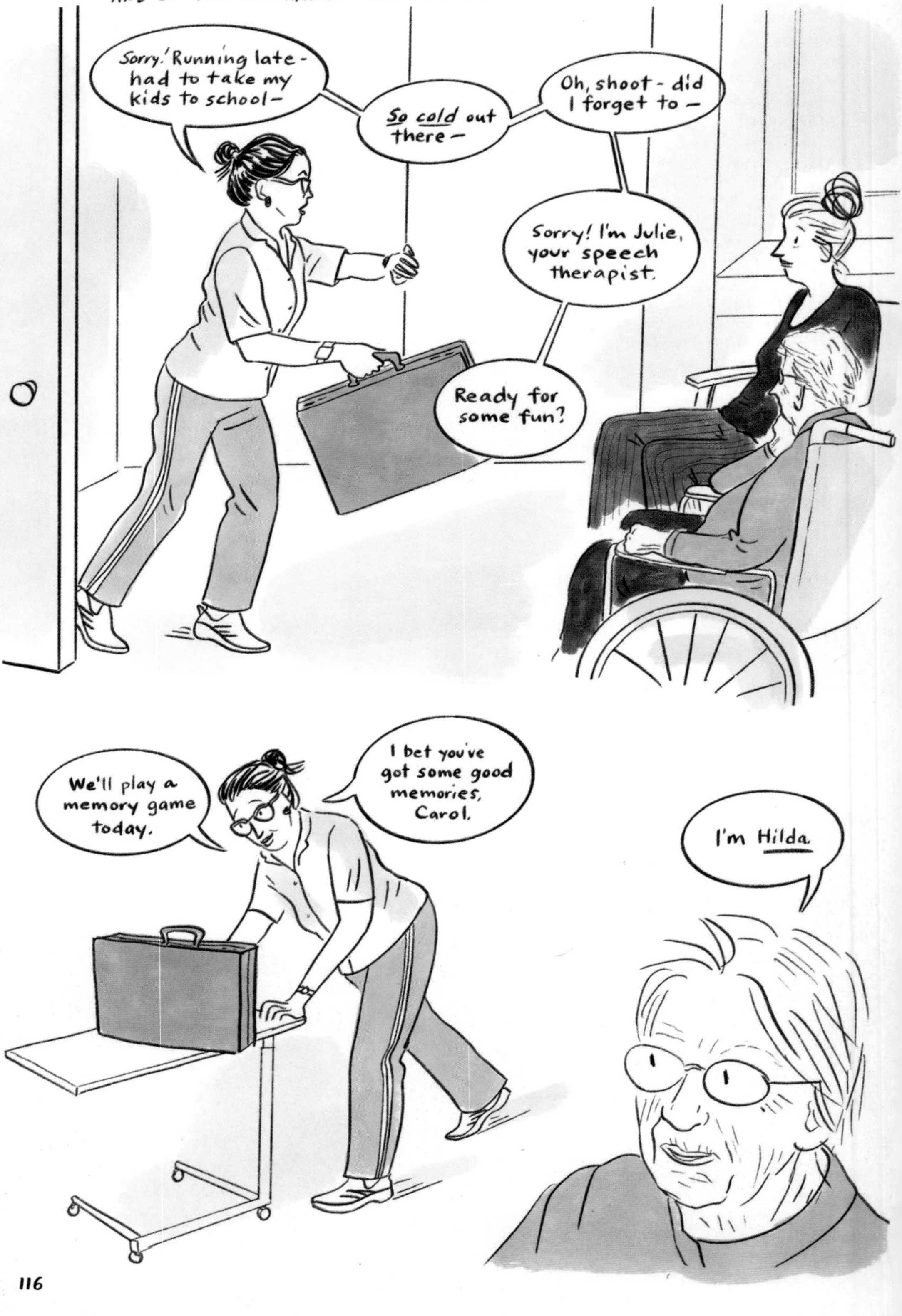

Sorry! Running late - had to take my kids to school -
So cold out there -
Oh, shoot - did I forget to -
Sorry! I'm Julie, your speech therapist.
Ready for some fun?
We'll play a memory game today.
I bet you've got some good memories, Carol.
I'm Hilda.

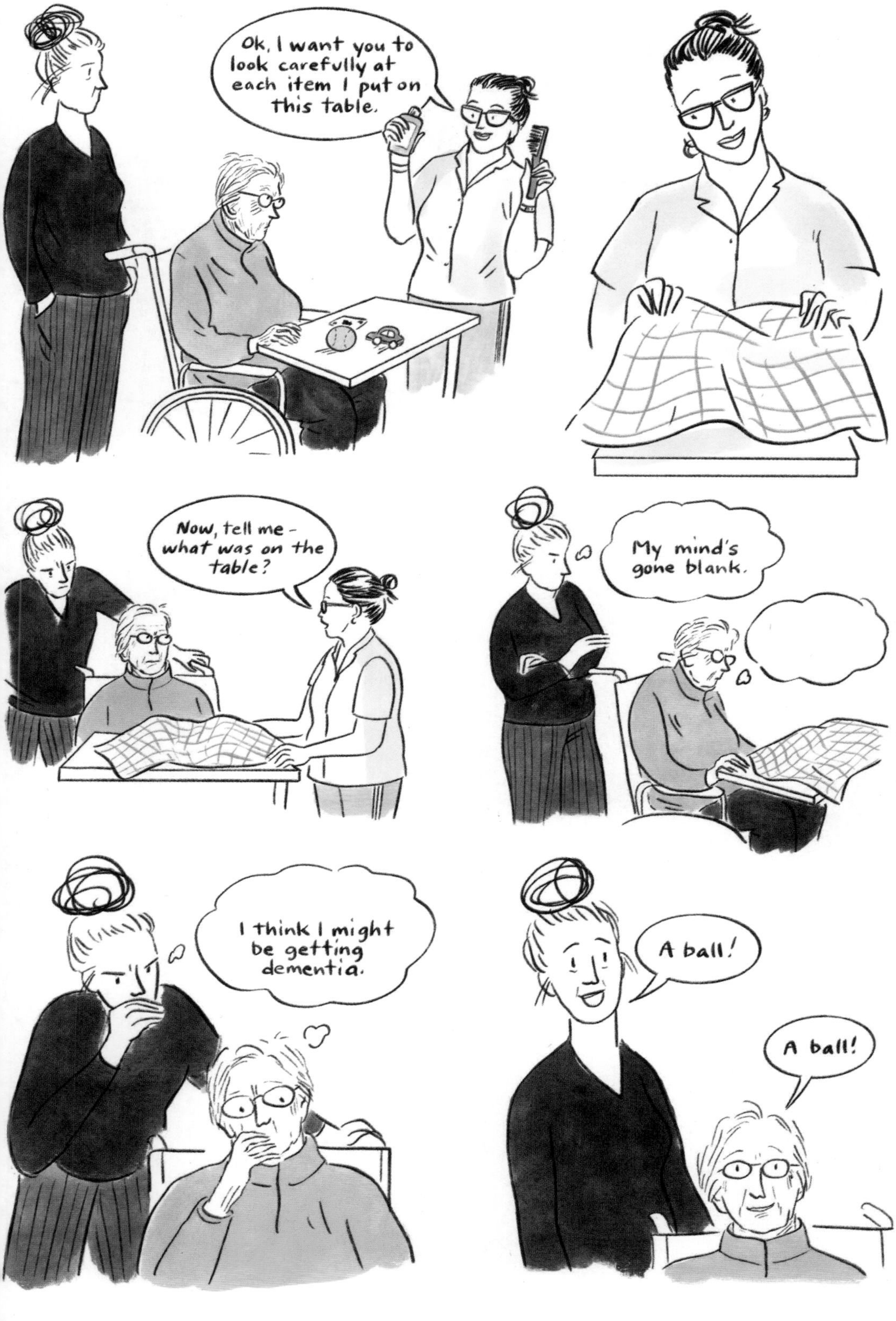
Ok, I want you to look carefully at each item I put on this table.
Now, tell me - what was on the table?
My mind's gone blank.
I think I might be getting dementia.
A ball!
A ball!

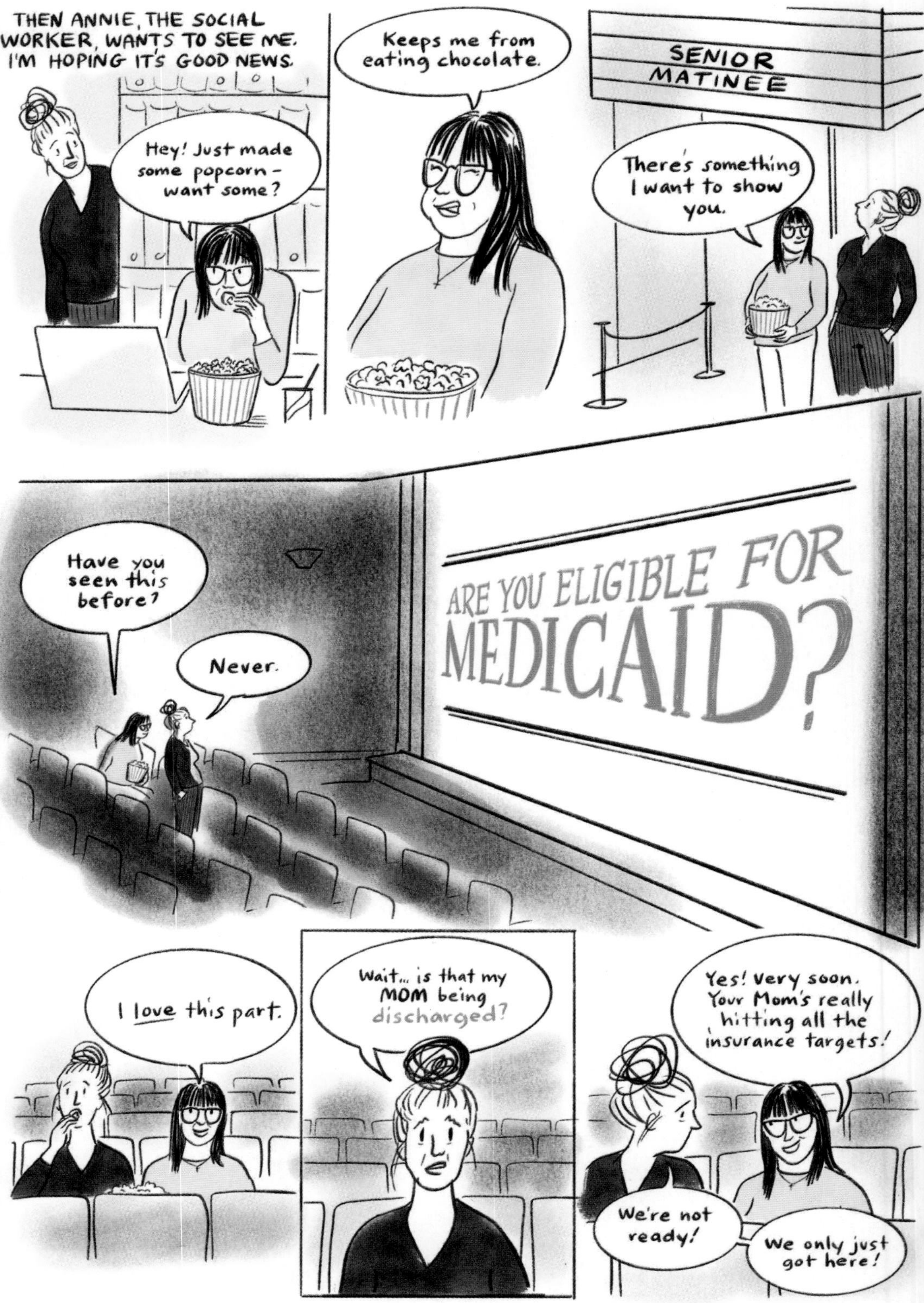
THEN ANNIE, THE SOCIAL WORKER, WANTS TO SEE ME. I'M HOPING IT'S GOOD NEWS.
Hey! Just made some popcorn - want some?
Keeps me from eating chocolate.
SENIOR MATINEE
There's something I want to show you.
Have you seen this before?
Never.
ARE YOU ELIGIBLE FOR MEDICAID?
I love this part.
Wait... is that my MOM being discharged?
Yes! Very soon. Your Mom's really hitting all the insurance targets!
We're not ready!
We only just got here!

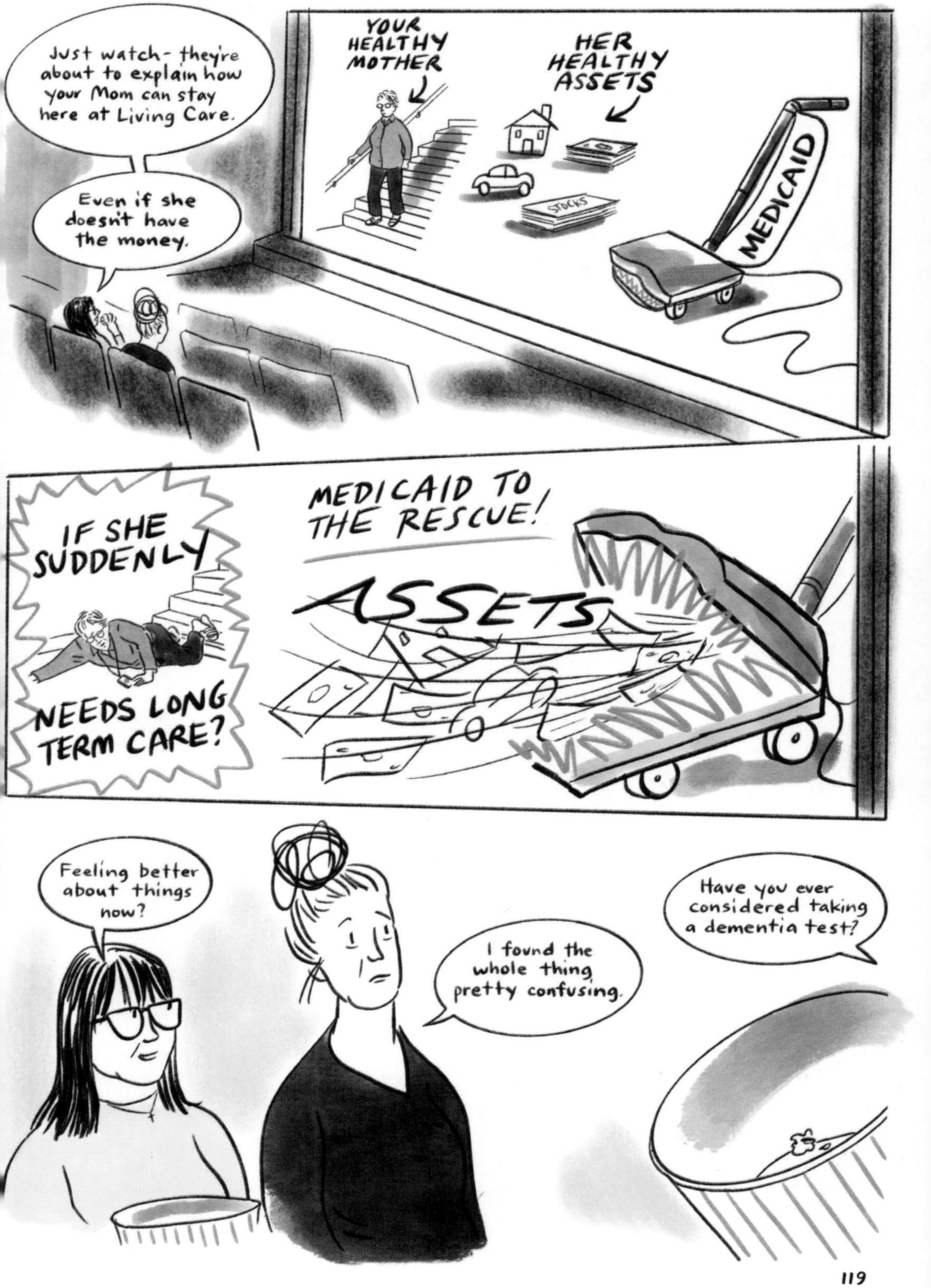

Just watch- they're about to explain how your Mom can stay here at Living Care.
Even if she doesn't have the money.
YOUR HEALTHY MOTHER
HER HEALTHY ASSETS
STOCKS
MEDICAID
IF SHE SUDDENLY
NEEDS LONG TERM CARE?
MEDICAID TO THE RESCUE!
ASSETS
Feeling better about things now?
I found the whole thing pretty confusing.
Have you ever considered taking a dementia test?

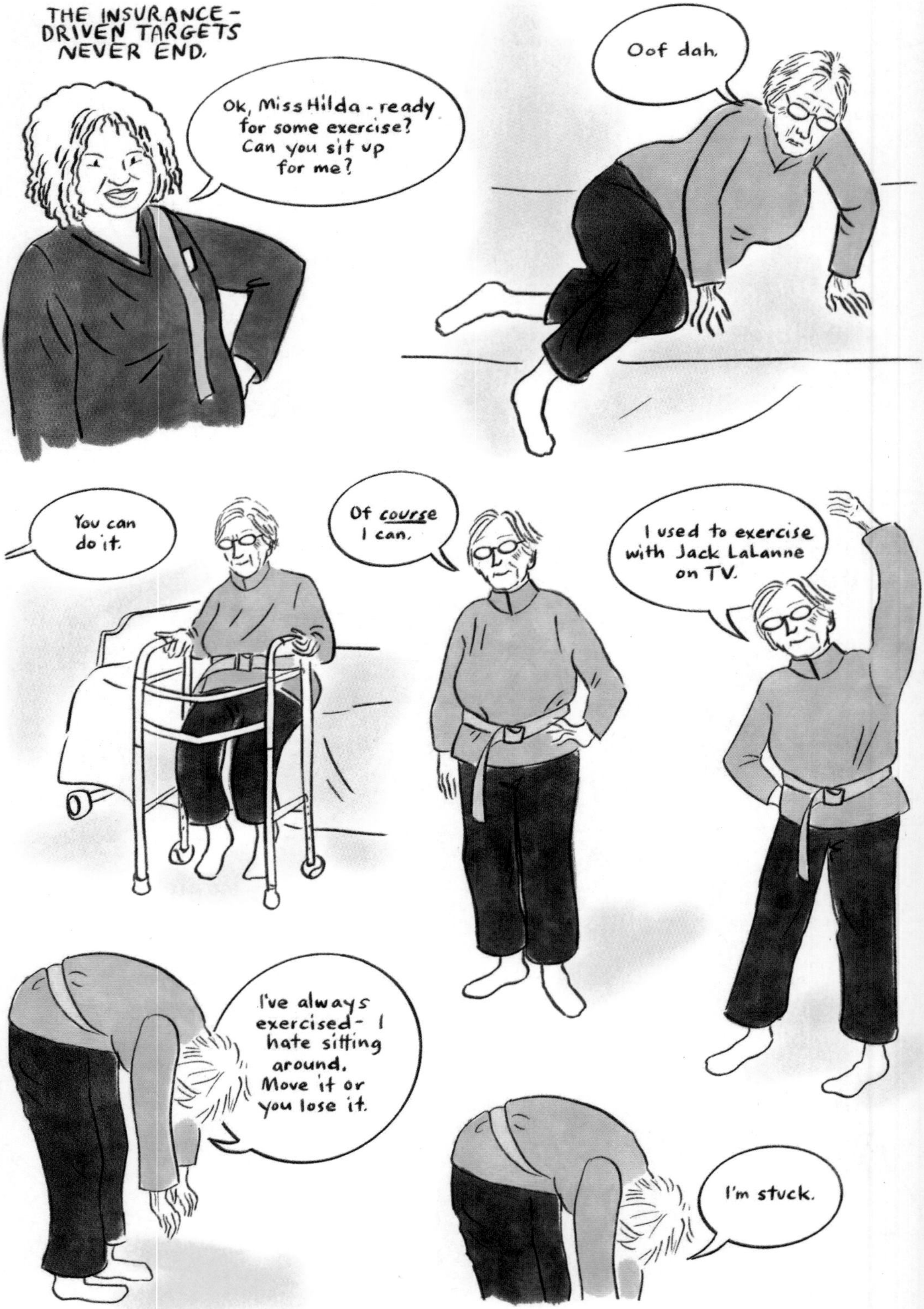
THE INSURANCE-DRIVEN TARGETS NEVER END.
Ok, Miss Hilda - ready for some exercise? Can you sit up for me?
Oof dah.
You can do it.
Of course I can.
I used to exercise with Jack LaLanne on TV.
I've always exercised - I hate sitting around. Move it or you lose it.
I'm stuck.

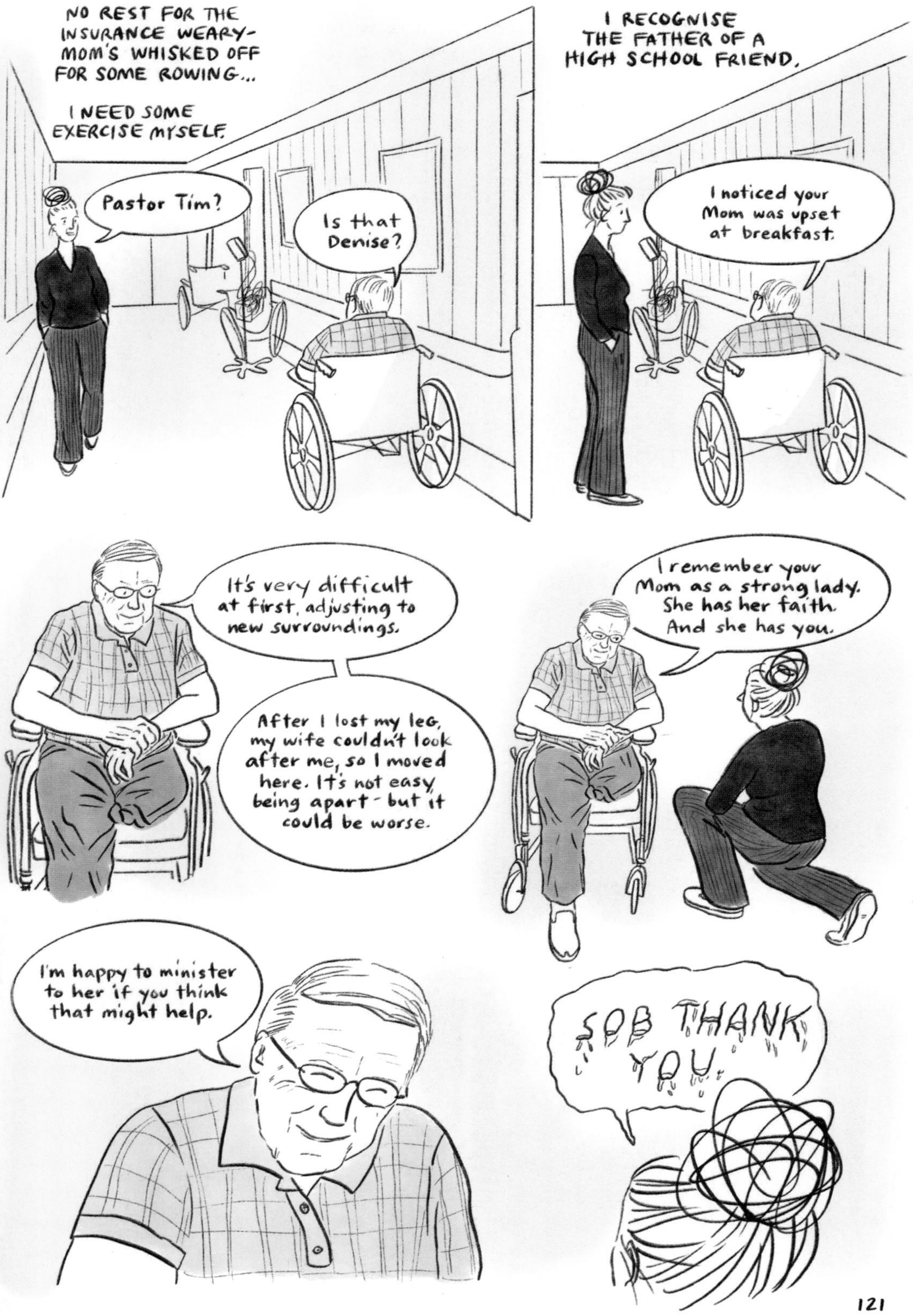
NO REST FOR THE INSURANCE WEARY- MOM'S WHISKED OFF FOR SOME ROWING...
I NEED SOME EXERCISE MYSELF.
Pastor Tim?
Is that Denise?
I RECOGNISE THE FATHER OF A HIGH SCHOOL FRIEND.
I noticed your Mom was upset at breakfast.
It's very difficult at first, adjusting to new surroundings.
After I lost my leg, my wife couldn't look after me, so I moved here. It's not easy being apart - but it could be worse.
I remember your Mom as a strong lady. She has her faith. And she has you.
I'm happy to minister to her if you think that might help.
SOB THANK YOU.

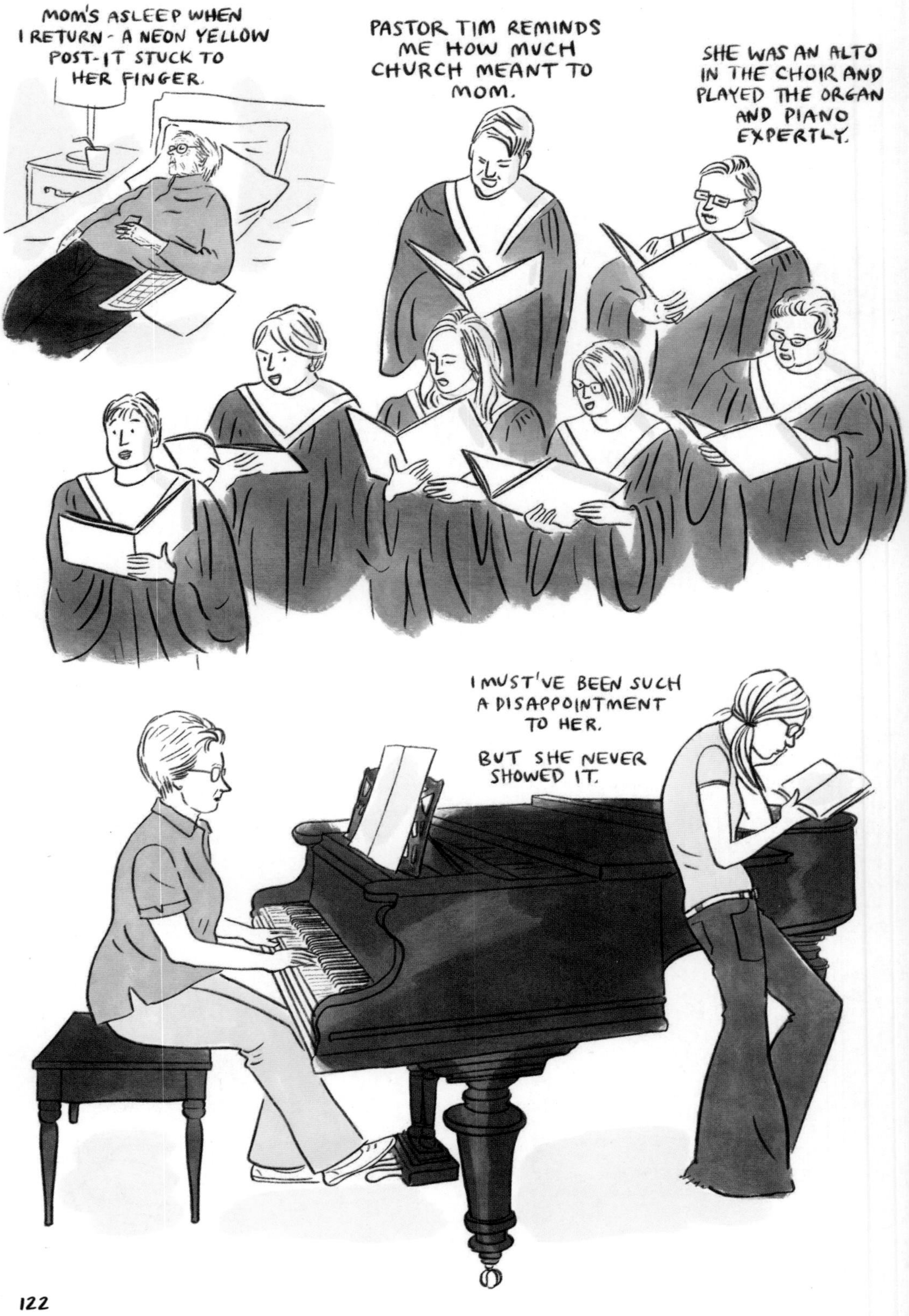
MOM'S ASLEEP WHEN I RETURN - A NEON YELLOW POST-IT STUCK TO HER FINGER.
PASTOR TIM REMINDS ME HOW MUCH CHURCH MEANT TO MOM.
SHE WAS AN ALTO IN THE CHOIR AND PLAYED THE ORGAN AND PIANO EXPERTLY.
I MUST'VE BEEN SUCH A DISAPPOINTMENT TO HER.
BUT SHE NEVER SHOWED IT.

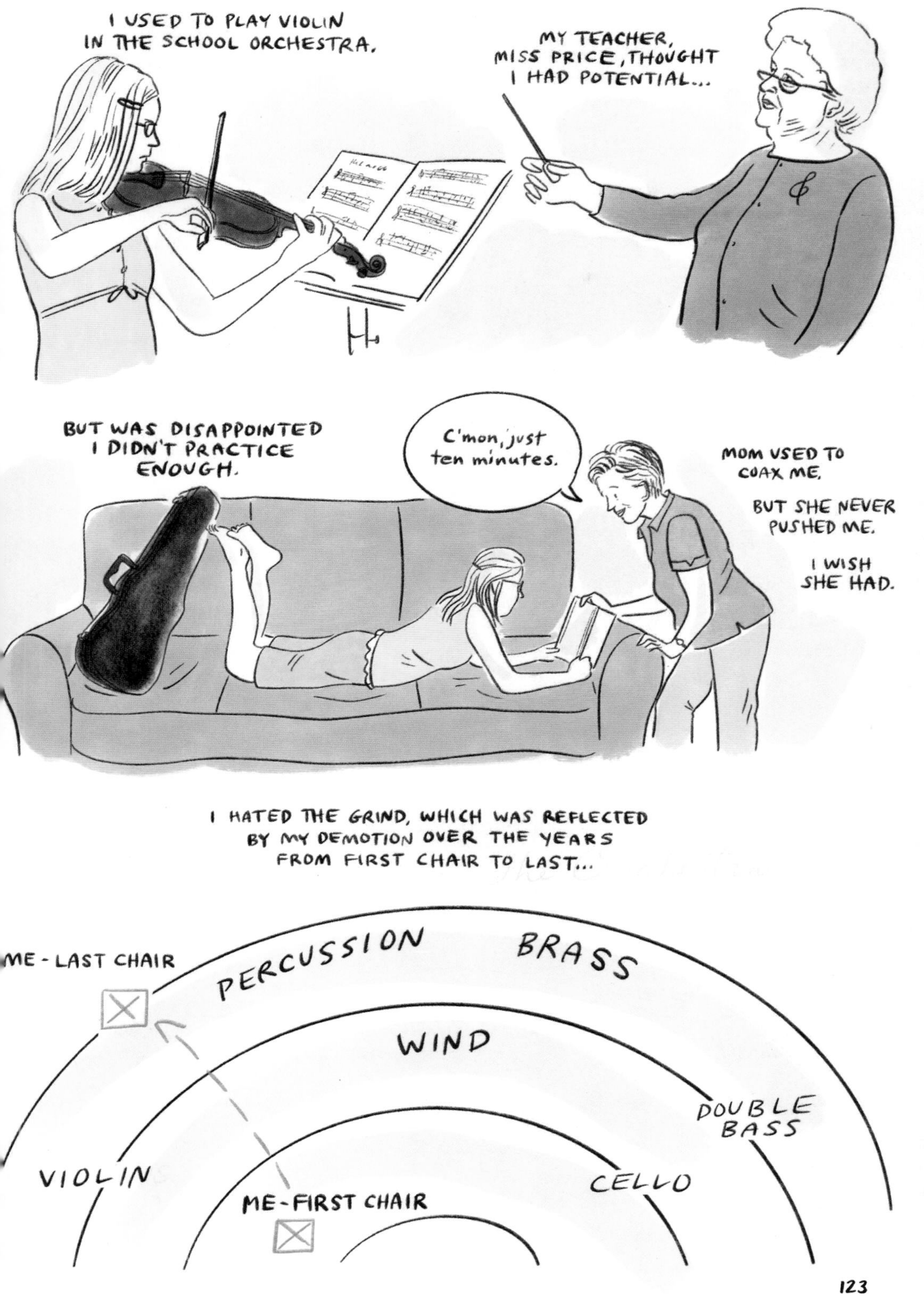
I USED TO PLAY VIOLIN IN THE SCHOOL ORCHESTRA.
MY TEACHER, MISS PRICE, THOUGHT I HAD POTENTIAL...
BUT WAS DISAPPOINTED I DIDN'T PRACTICE ENOUGH.
C'mon, just ten minutes.
MOM USED TO COAX ME.
BUT SHE NEVER PUSHED ME.
I WISH SHE HAD.
I HATED THE GRIND, WHICH WAS REFLECTED BY MY DEMOTION OVER THE YEARS FROM FIRST CHAIR TO LAST...
ME - LAST CHAIR
PERCUSSION
BRASS
WIND
DOUBLE BASS
VIOLIN
CELLO
ME-FIRST CHAIR

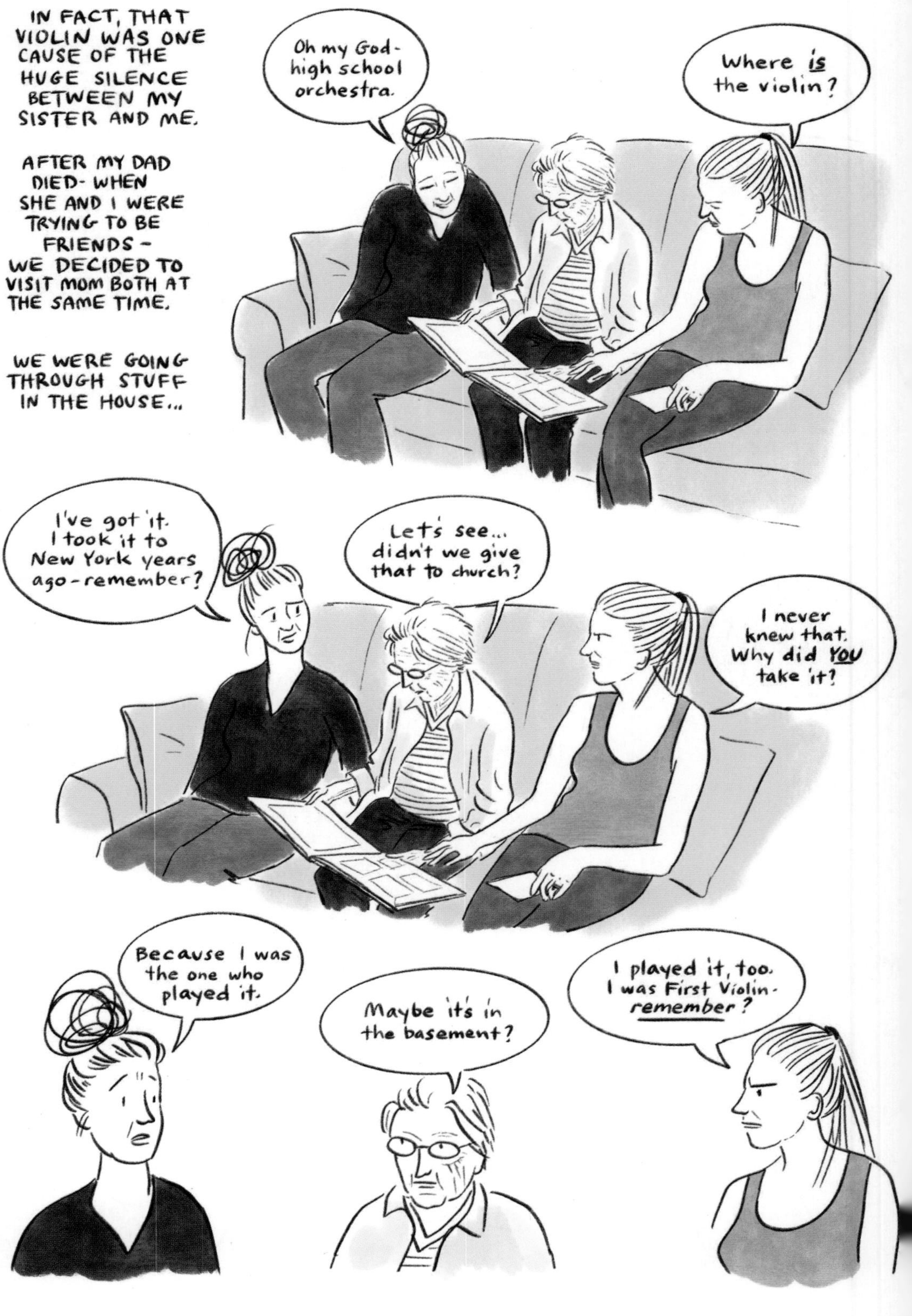
IN FACT, THAT VIOLIN WAS ONE CAUSE OF THE HUGE SILENCE BETWEEN MY SISTER AND ME.
AFTER MY DAD DIED- WHEN SHE AND I WERE TRYING TO BE FRIENDS - WE DECIDED TO VISIT MOM BOTH AT THE SAME TIME.
WE WERE GOING THROUGH STUFF IN THE HOUSE...
Oh my God- high school orchestra.
Where is the violin?
I've got it. I took it to New York years ago-remember?
Let's see... didn't we give that to church?
I never knew that. Why did YOU take it?
Because I was the one who played it.
Maybe it's in the basement?
I played it, too. I was First Violin- remember?

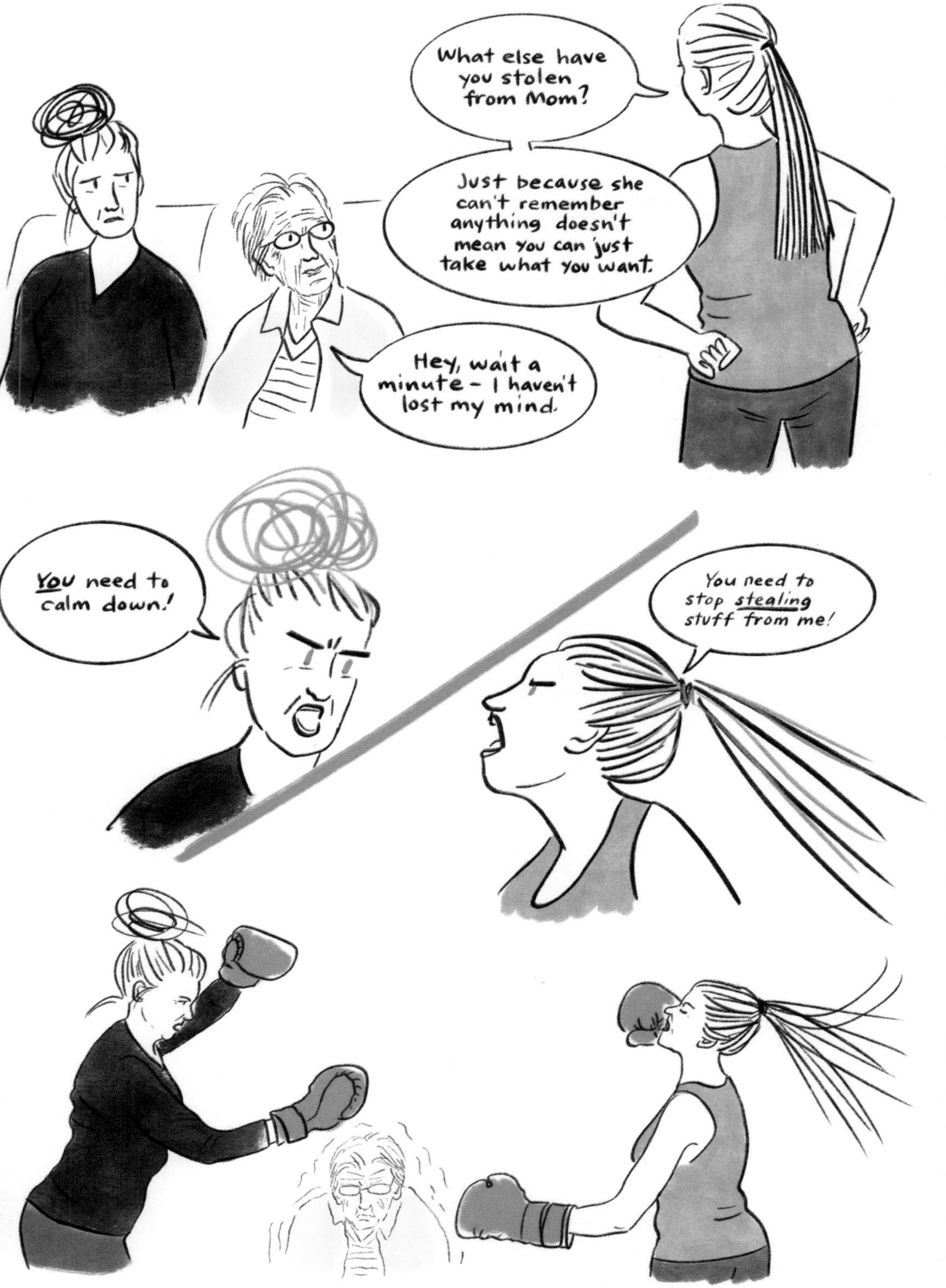
What else have you stolen from Mom?
Just because she can't remember anything doesn't mean you can just take what you want.
Hey, wait a minute – I haven't lost my mind.
YOU need to calm down!
You need to stop stealing stuff from me!
THERE ARE TIMES I'M GLAD MOM CAN'T REMEMBER.

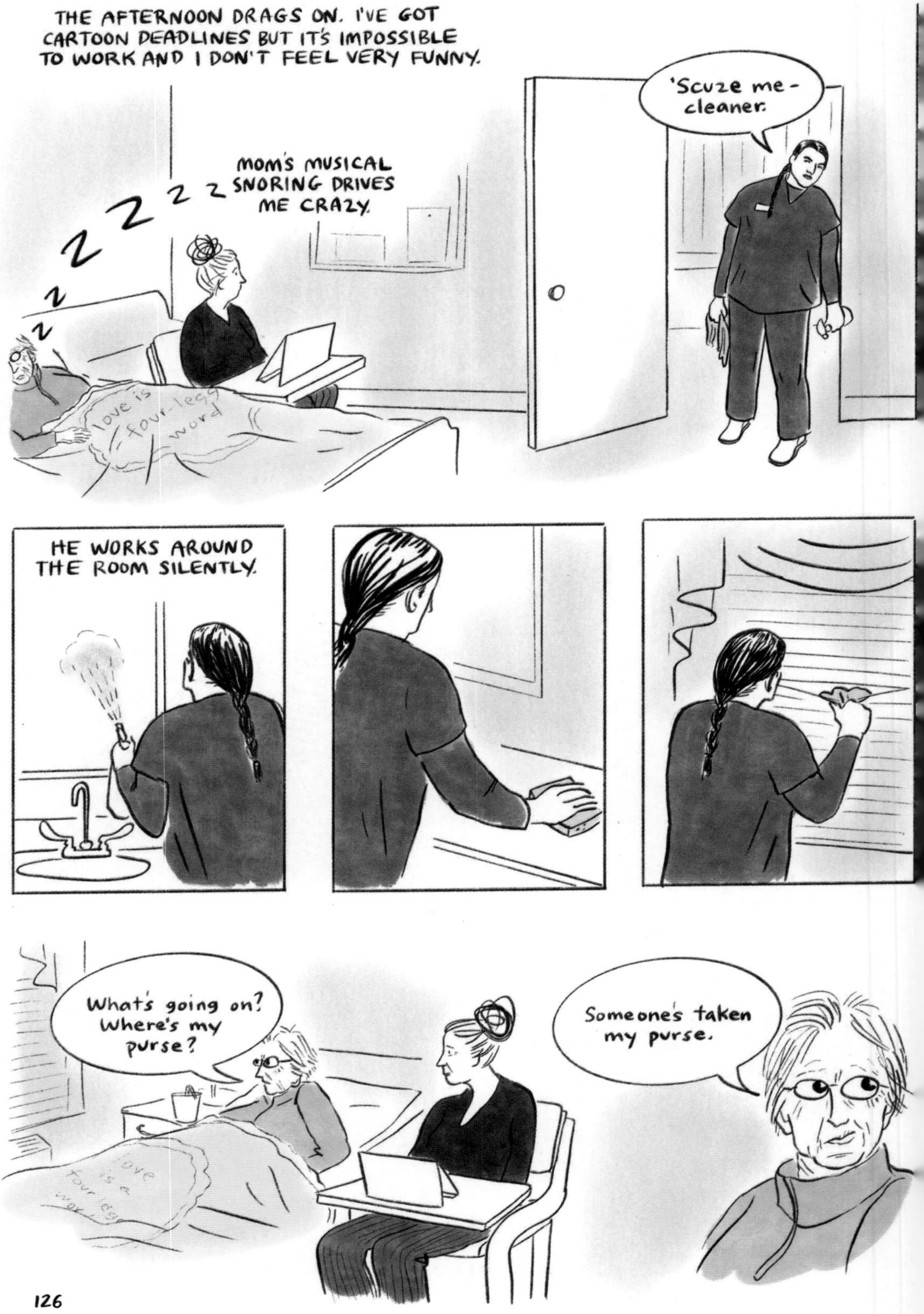
THE AFTERNOON DRAGS ON. I'VE GOT CARTOON DEADLINES BUT IT'S IMPOSSIBLE TO WORK AND I DON'T FEEL VERY FUNNY.
Z Z Z Z Z Z Z
MOM'S MUSICAL SNORING DRIVES ME CRAZY.
'Scuze me - cleaner.
HE WORKS AROUND THE ROOM SILENTLY.
What's going on? Where's my purse?
Someone's taken my purse.

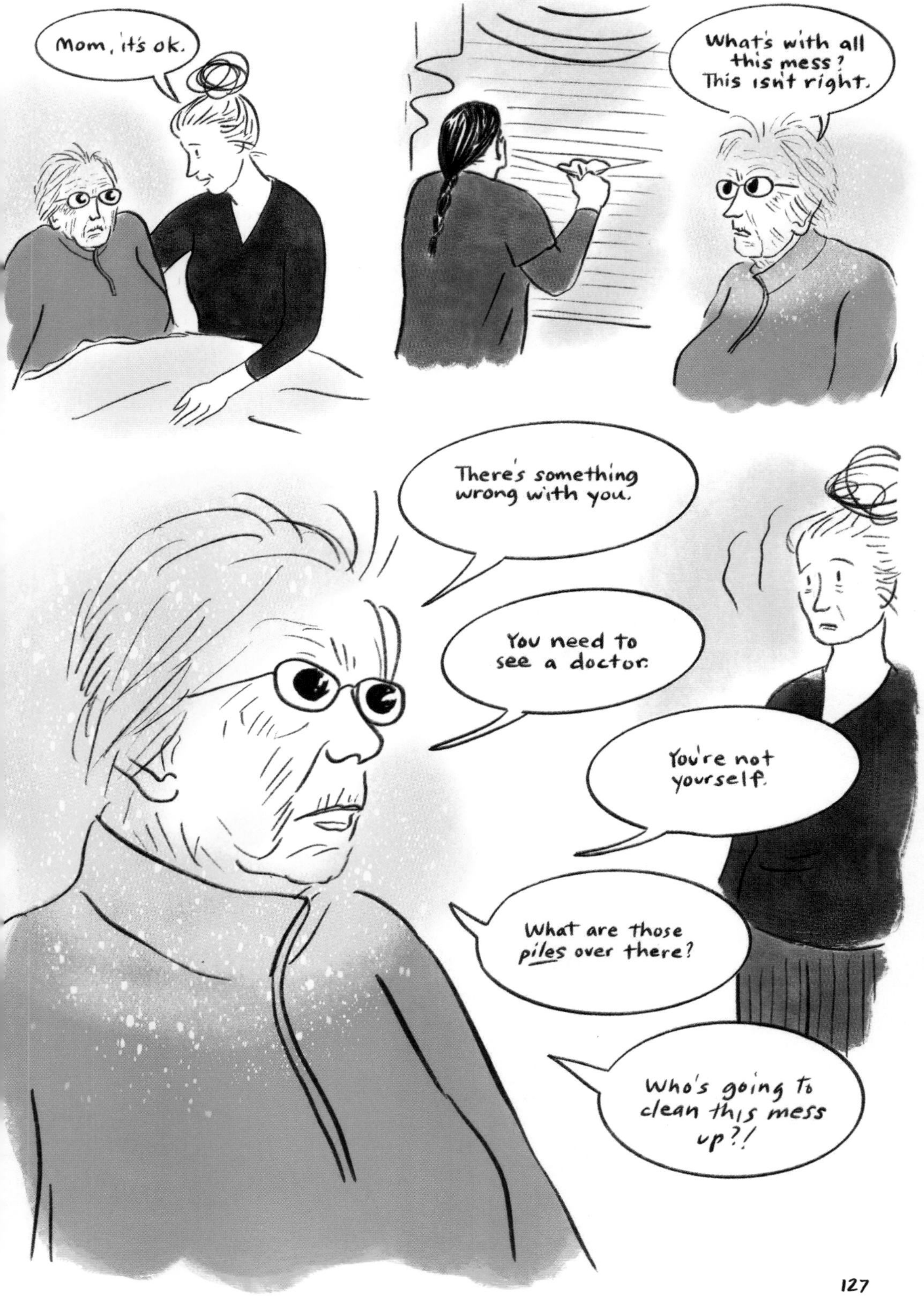
Mom, it's ok.
What's with all this mess? This isn't right.
There's something wrong with you.
You need to see a doctor.
You're not yourself.
What are those piles over there?
Who's going to clean this mess up?!

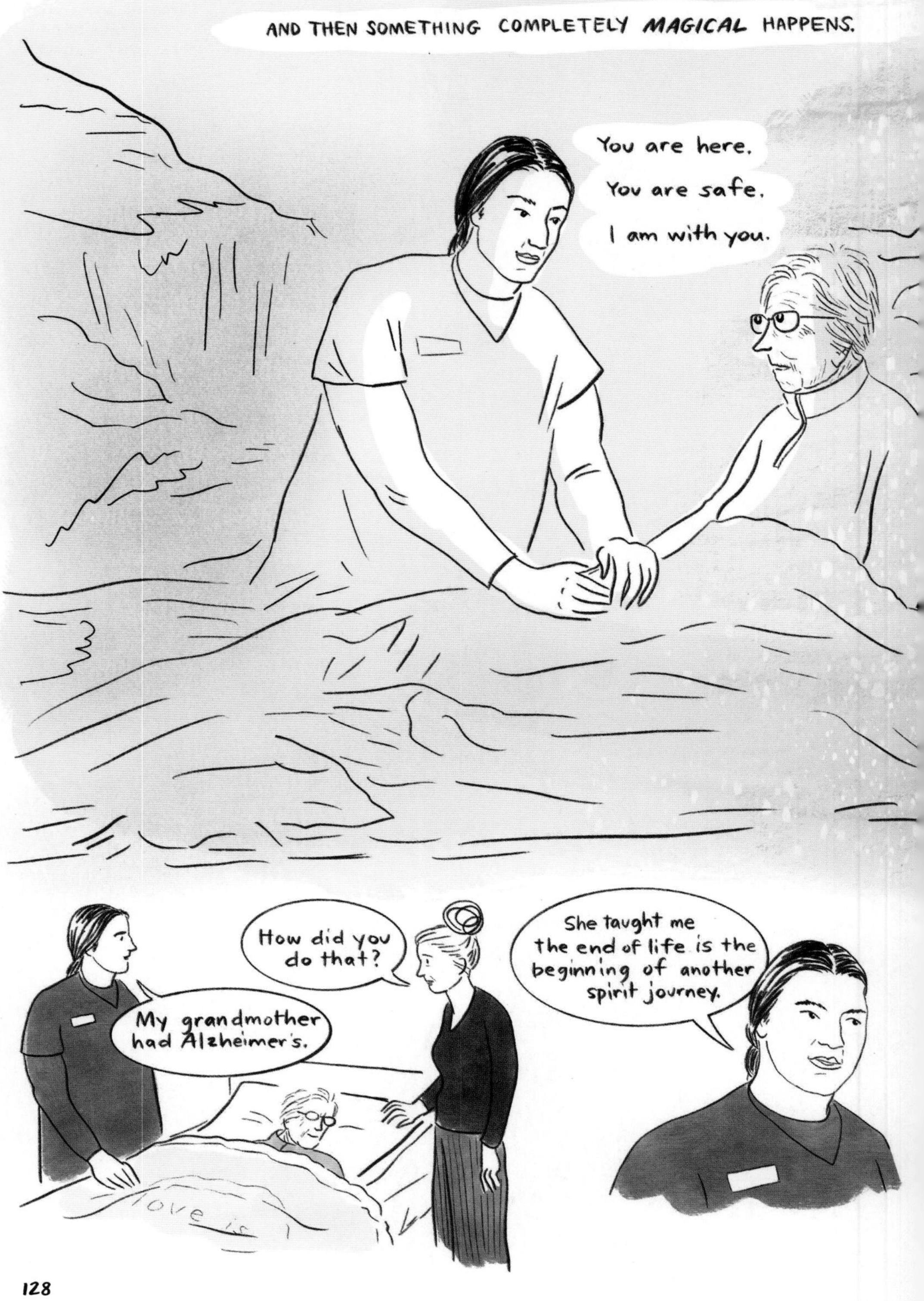
AND THEN SOMETHING COMPLETELY MAGICAL HAPPENS.
You are here.
You are safe.
I am with you.
How did you do that?
My grandmother had Alzheimer's.
She taught me the end of life is the beginning of another spirit journey.
love is

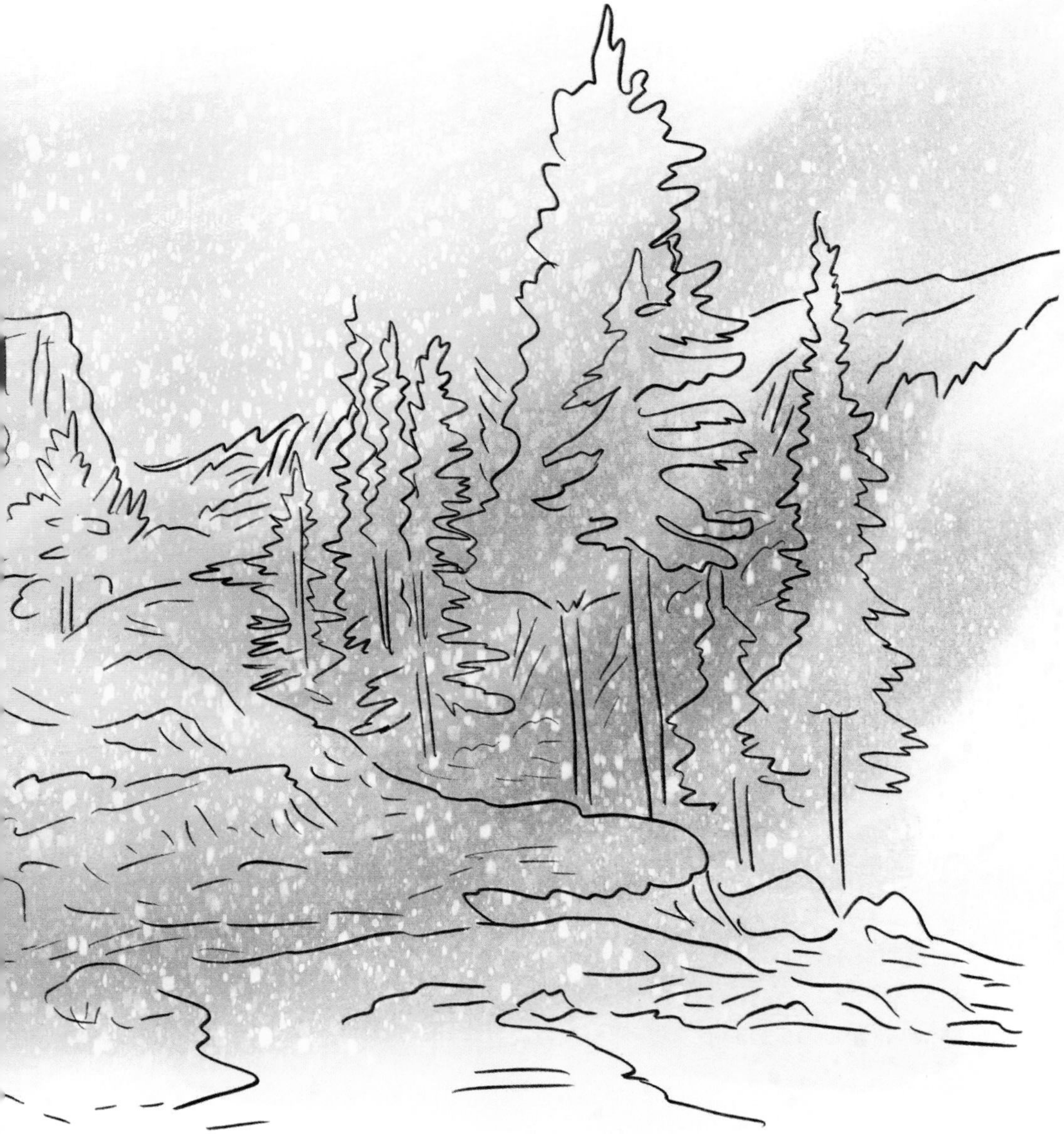

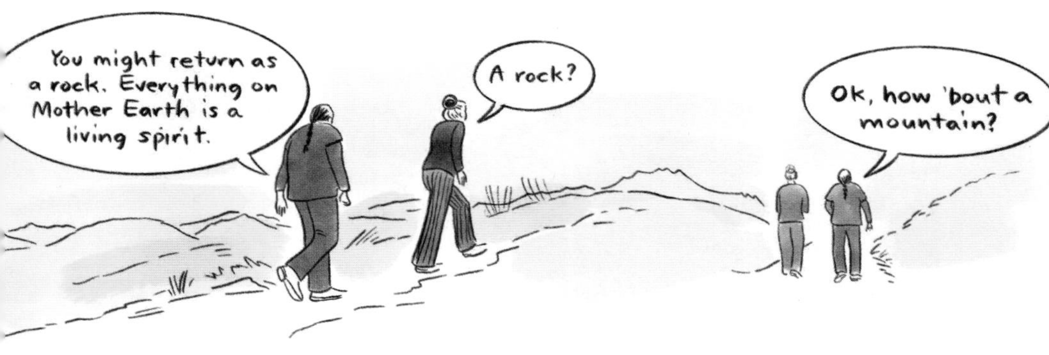
You might return as a rock. Everything on Mother Earth is a living spirit.
A rock?
Ok, how 'bout a mountain?

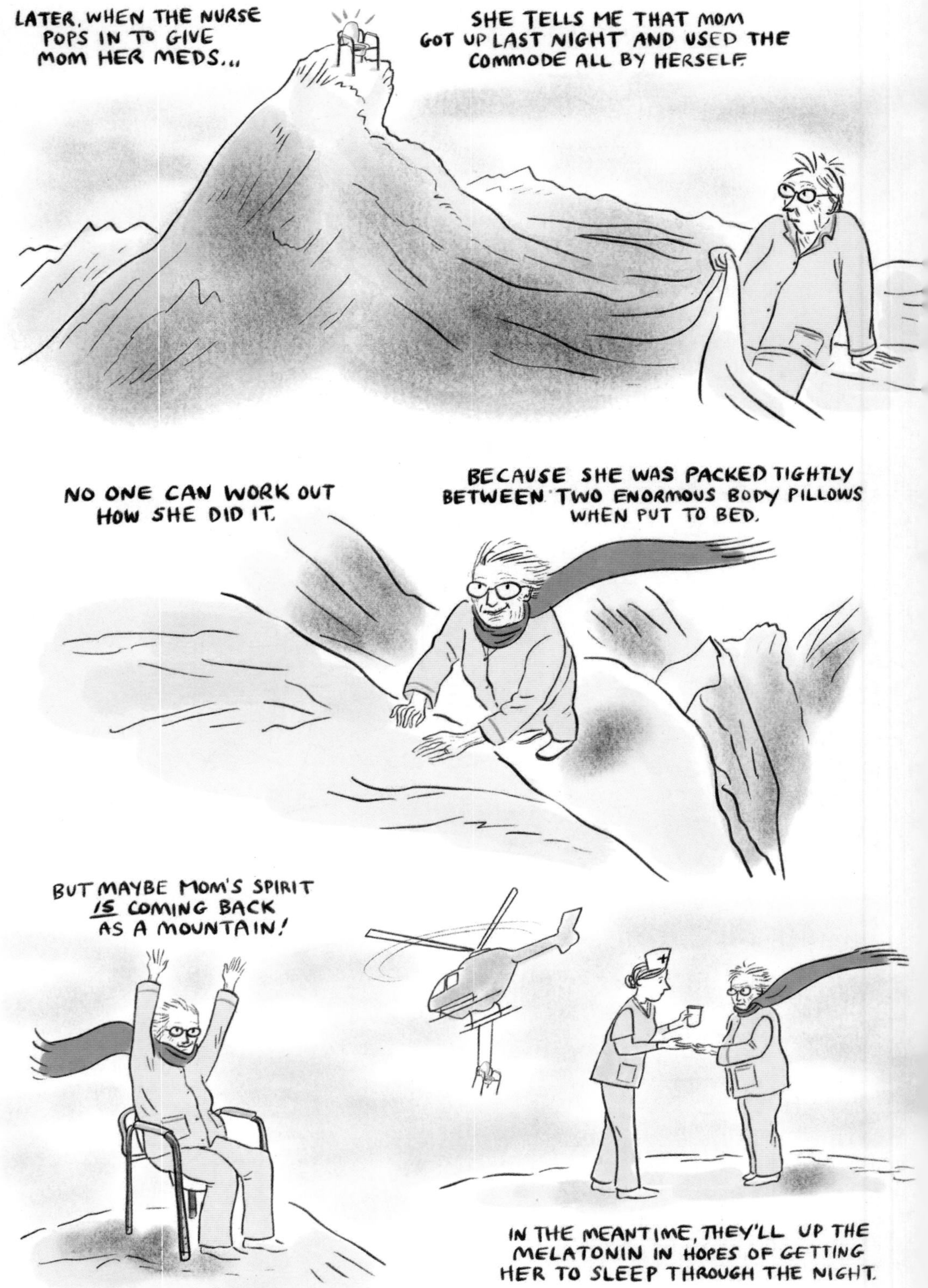
LATER, WHEN THE NURSE POPS IN TO GIVE MOM HER MEDS...
SHE TELLS ME THAT MOM GOT UP LAST NIGHT AND USED THE COMMODE ALL BY HERSELF.
NO ONE CAN WORK OUT HOW SHE DID IT.
BECAUSE SHE WAS PACKED TIGHTLY BETWEEN TWO ENORMOUS BODY PILLOWS WHEN PUT TO BED.
BUT MAYBE MOM'S SPIRIT IS COMING BACK AS A MOUNTAIN!
IN THE MEANTIME, THEY'LL UP THE MELATONIN IN HOPES OF GETTING HER TO SLEEP THROUGH THE NIGHT.

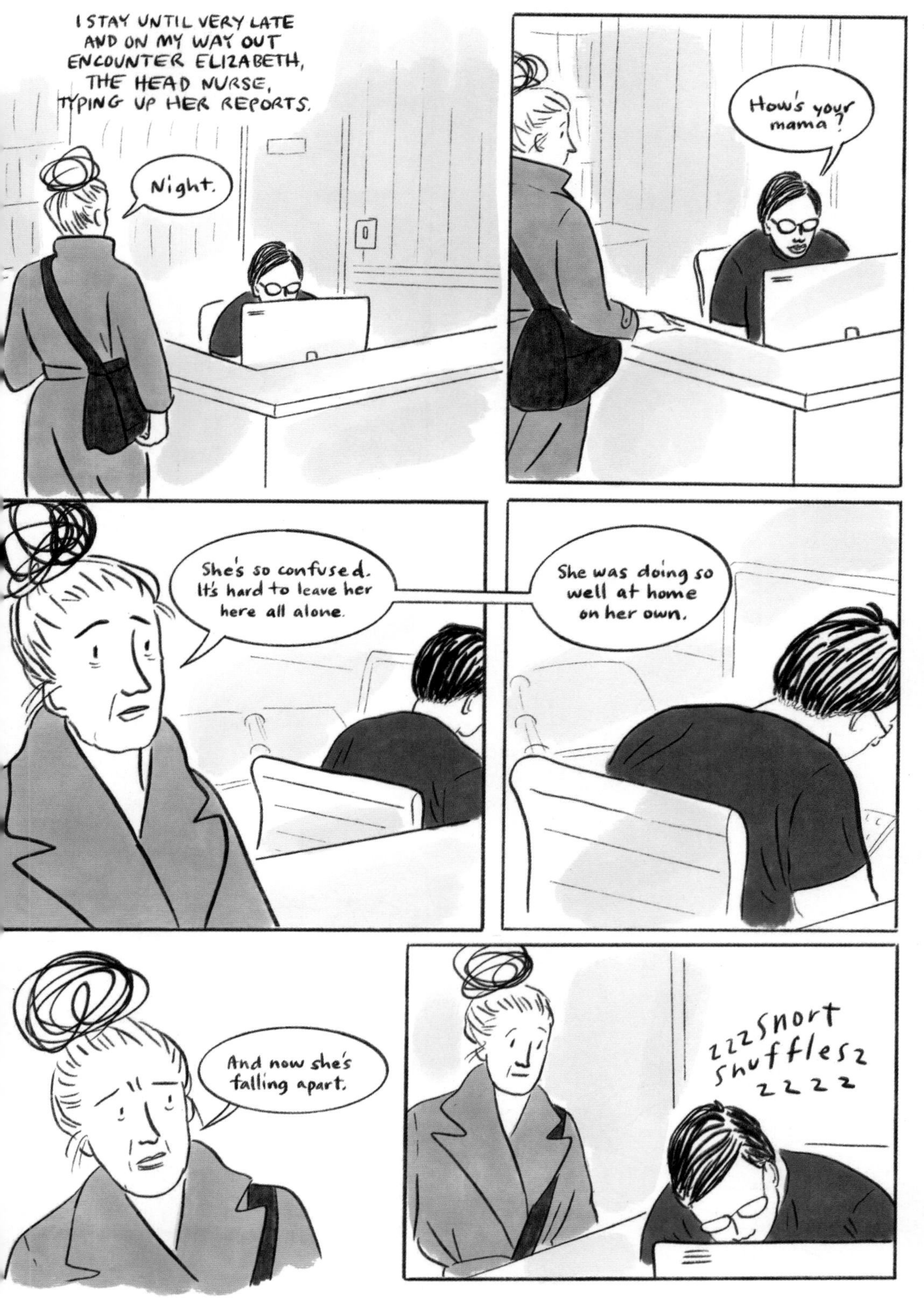
I STAY UNTIL VERY LATE AND ON MY WAY OUT ENCOUNTER ELIZABETH, THE HEAD NURSE, TYPING UP HER REPORTS.
Night.
How's your mama?
She's so confused. It's hard to leave her here all alone.
She was doing so well at home on her own.
And now she's falling apart.
zzzsnort shufflesz zzzz

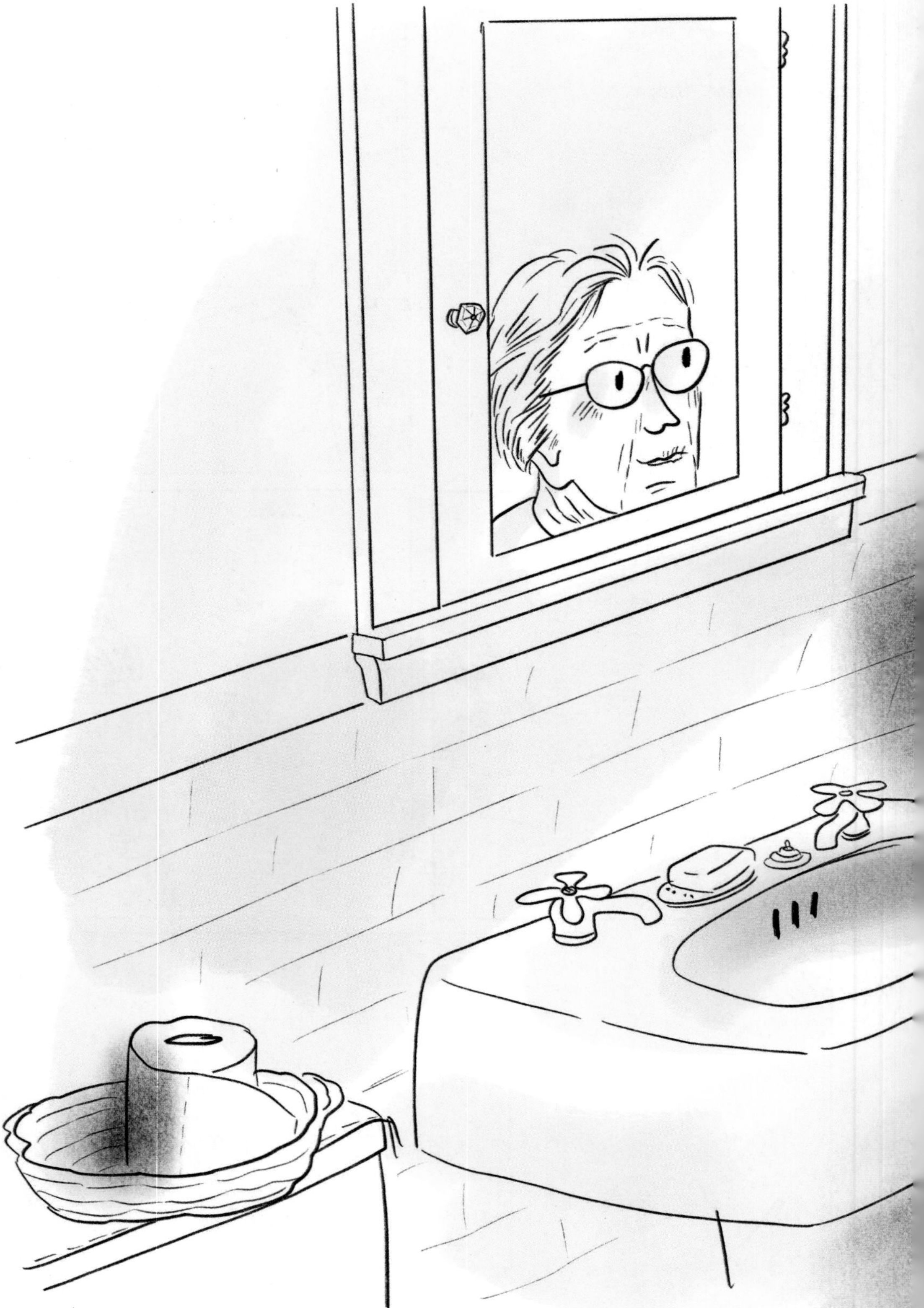

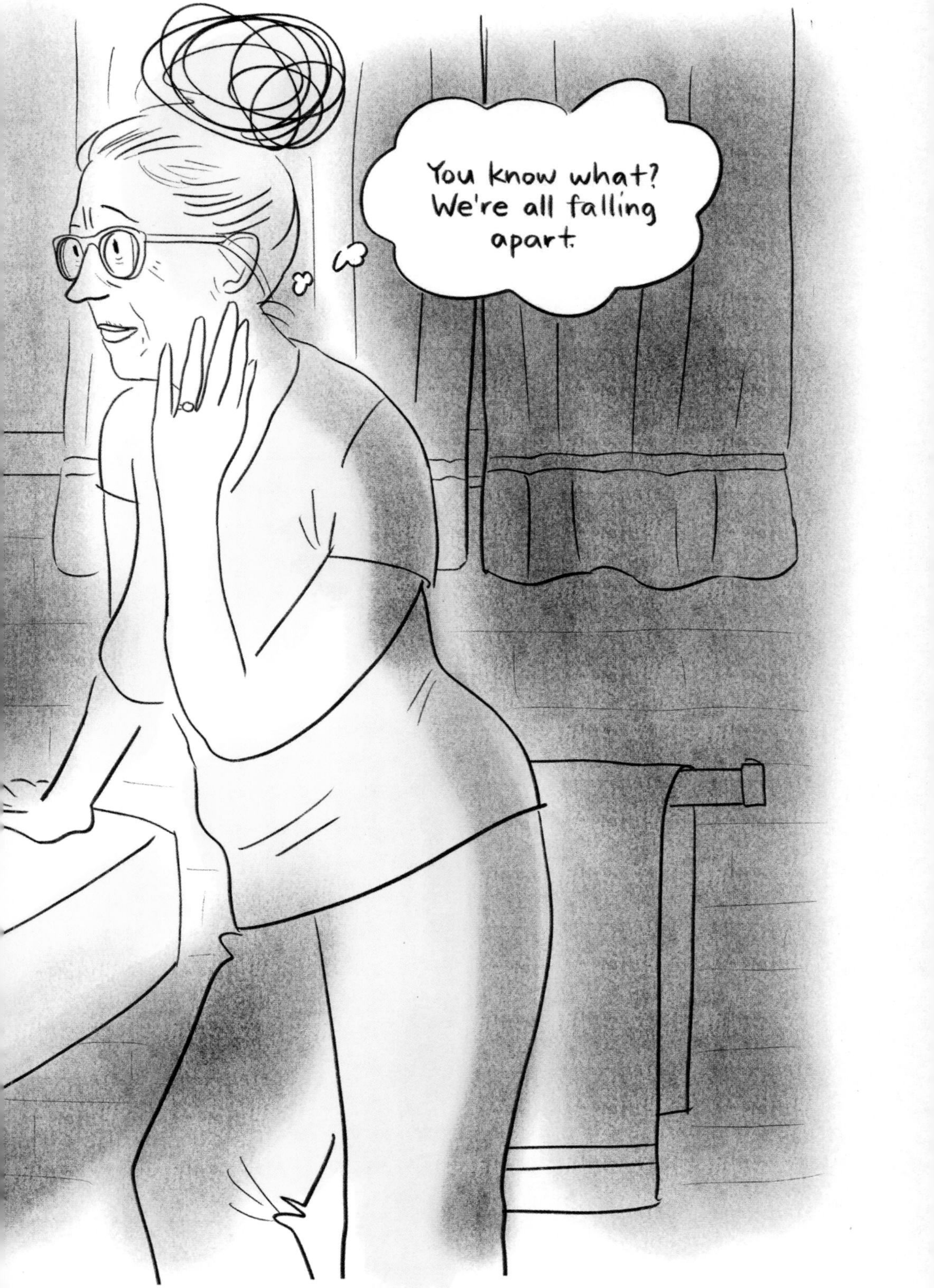
You know what? We're all falling apart.

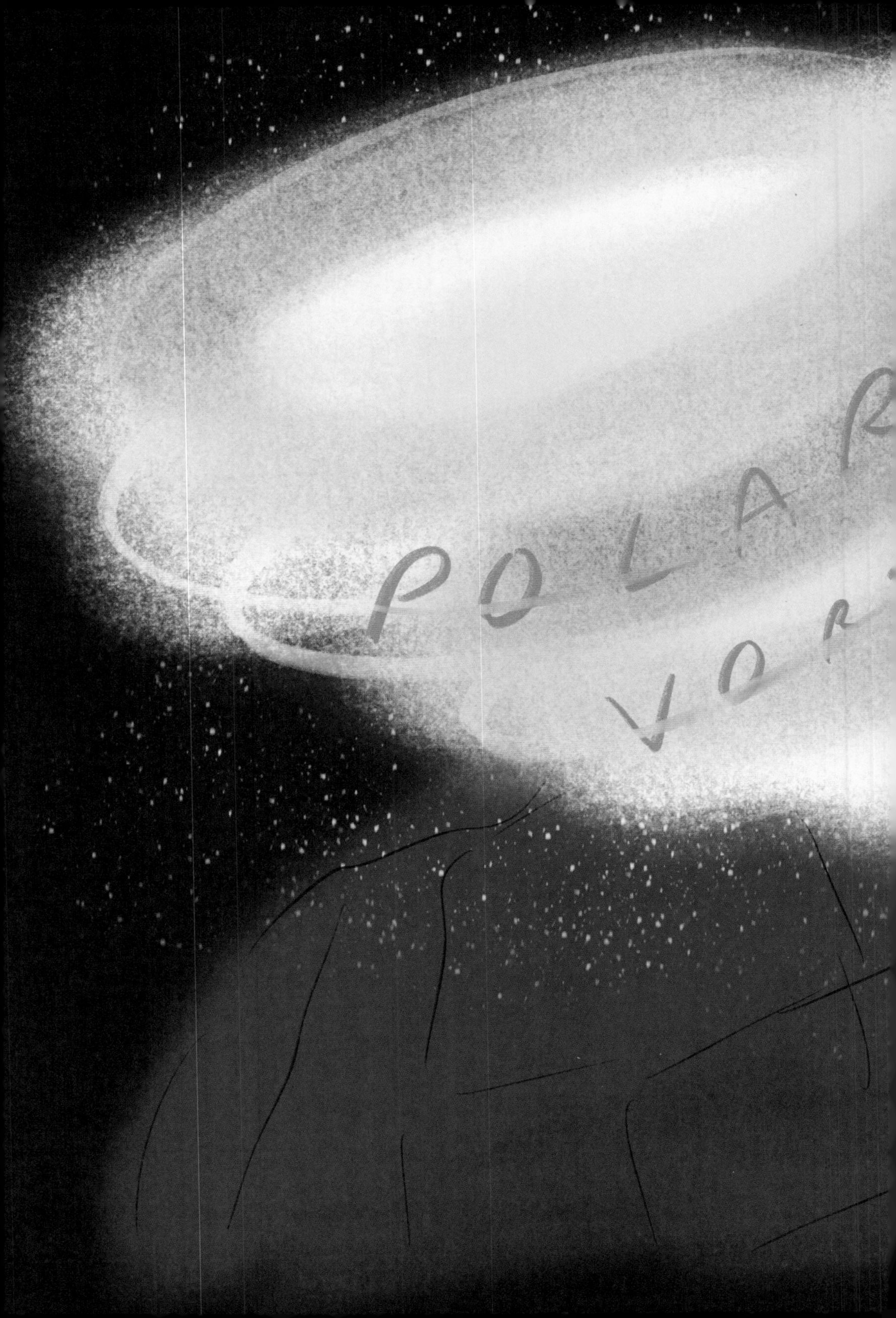
POLAR
VOR

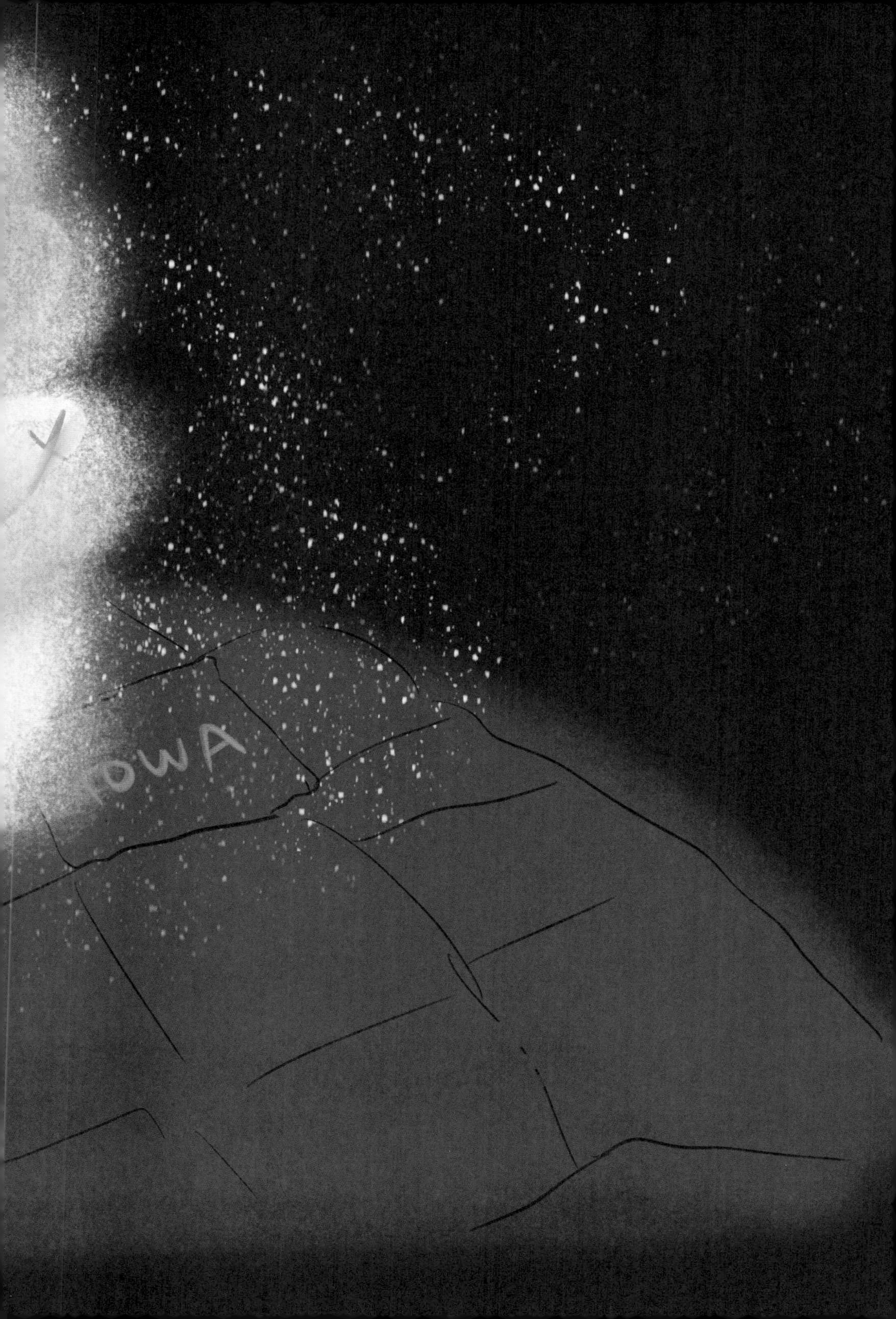
IOWA

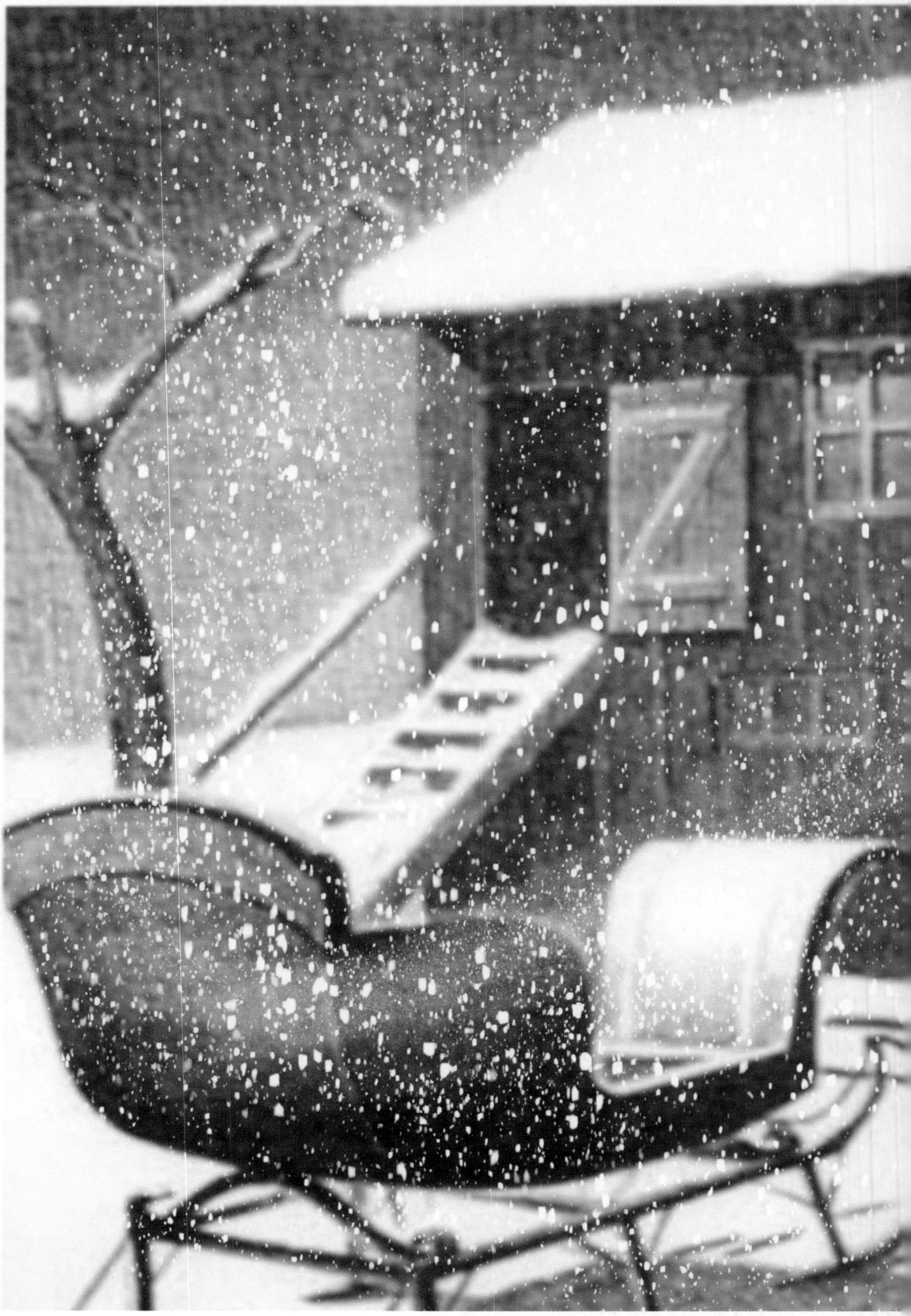

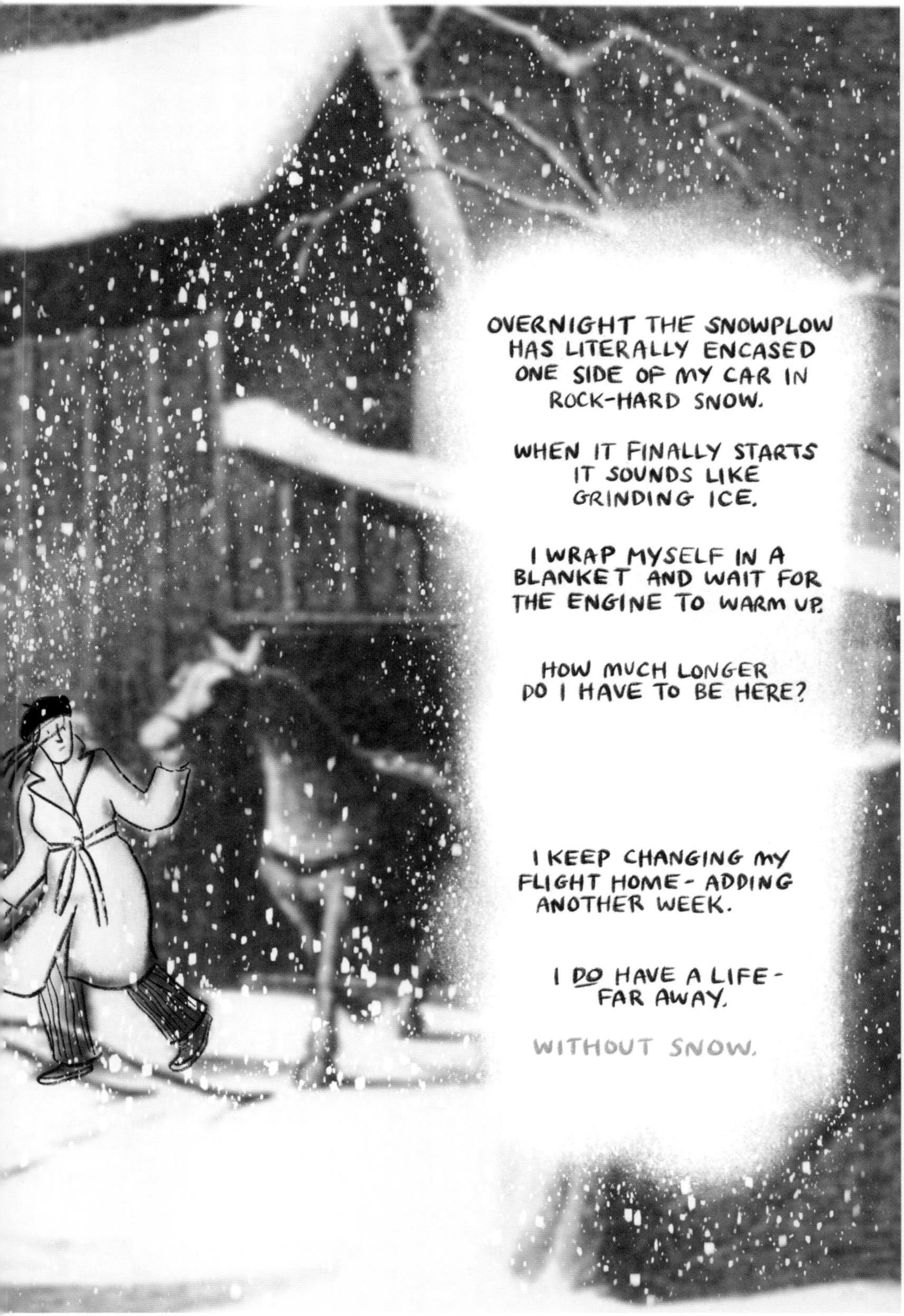
OVERNIGHT THE SNOWPLOW HAS LITERALLY ENCASED ONE SIDE OF MY CAR IN ROCK-HARD SNOW.
WHEN IT FINALLY STARTS IT SOUNDS LIKE GRINDING ICE.
I WRAP MYSELF IN A BLANKET AND WAIT FOR THE ENGINE TO WARM UP.
HOW MUCH LONGER DO I HAVE TO BE HERE?
I KEEP CHANGING MY FLIGHT HOME- ADDING ANOTHER WEEK.
I DO HAVE A LIFE- FAR AWAY.
WITHOUT SNOW.

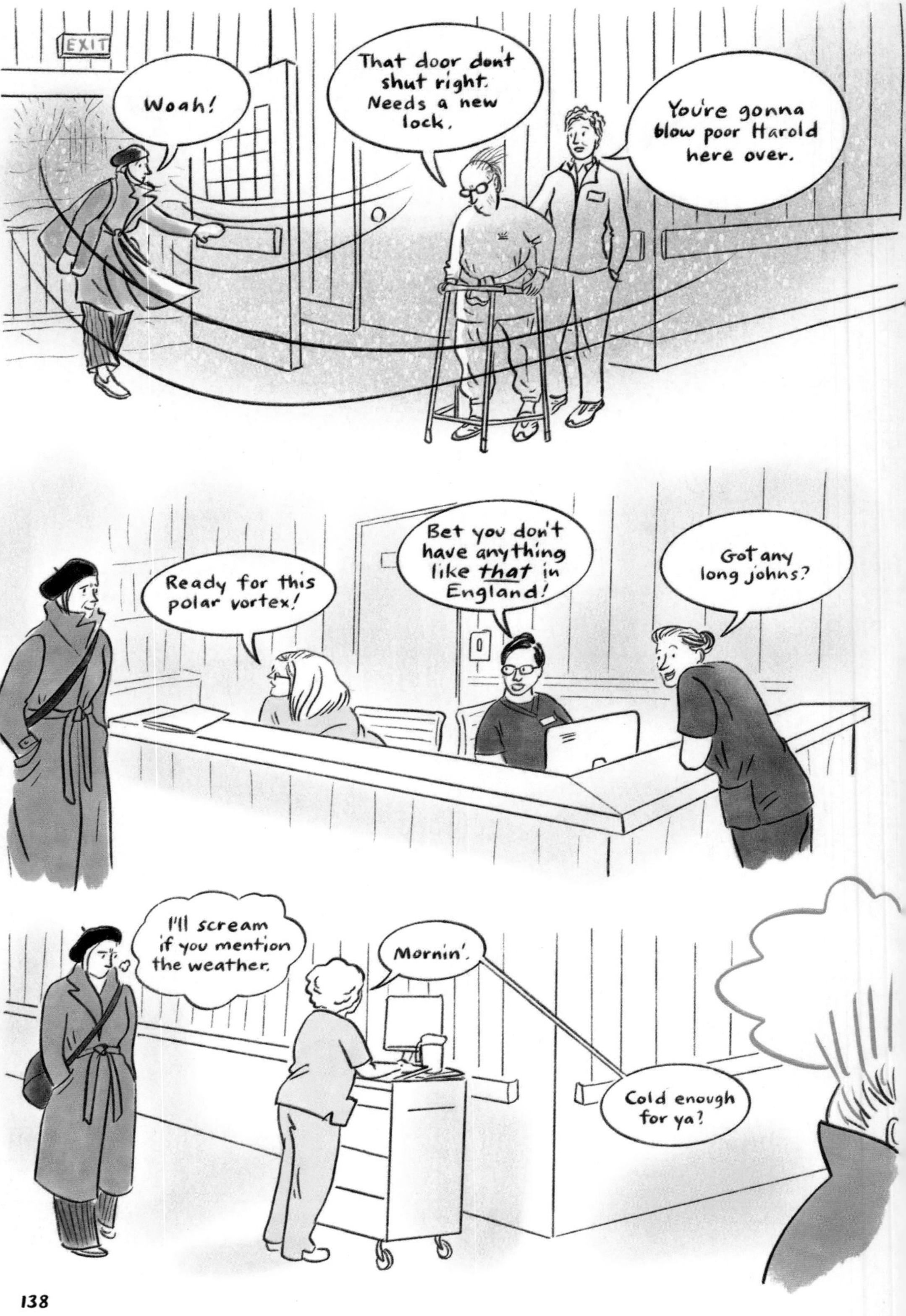
EXIT
Woah!
That door don't shut right. Needs a new lock.
You're gonna blow poor Harold here over.
Ready for this polar vortex!
Bet you don't have anything like that in England!
Got any long johns?
I'll scream if you mention the weather.
Mornin'.
Cold enough for ya?

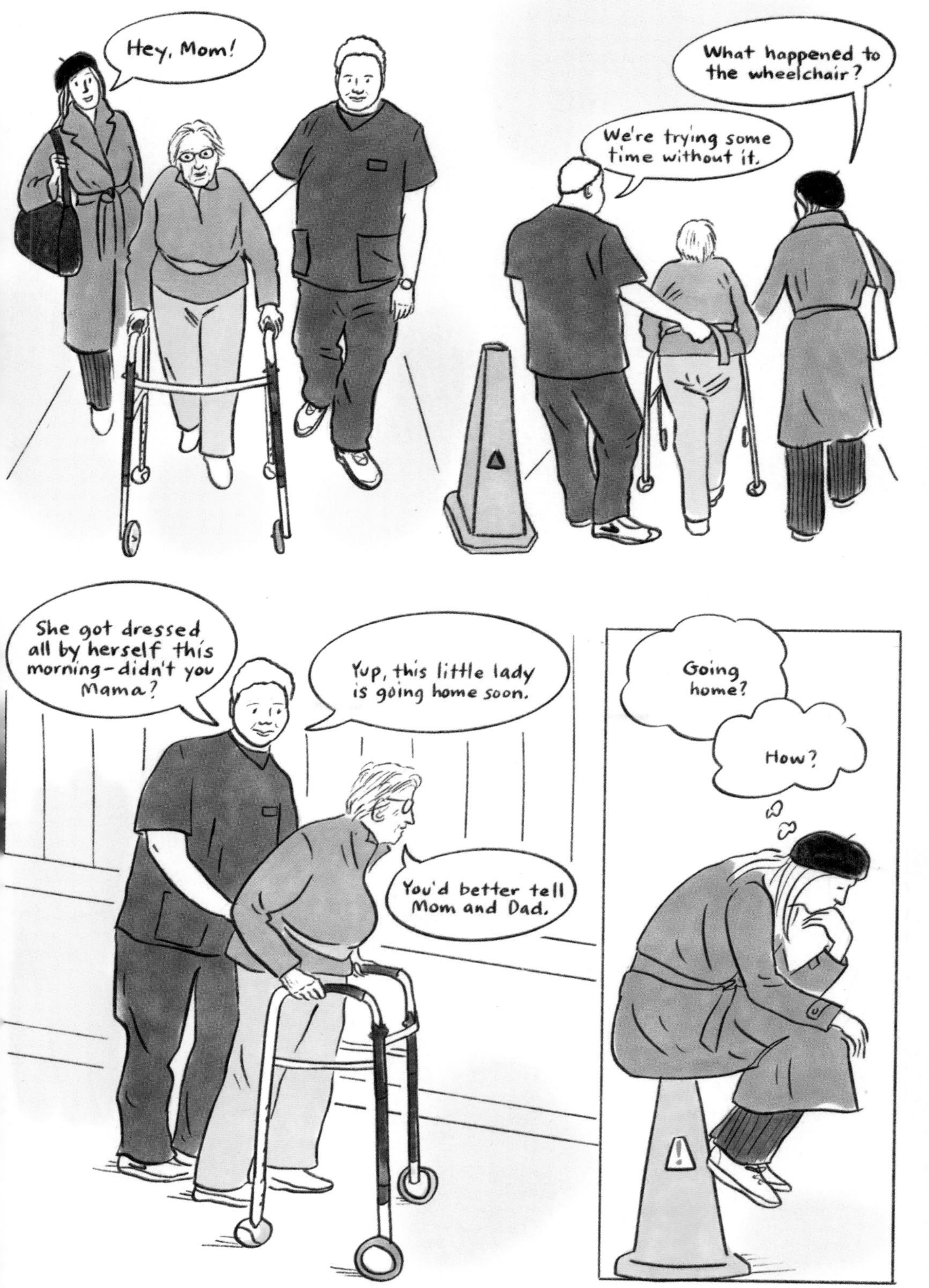
Hey, Mom!
What happened to the wheelchair?
We're trying some time without it.
She got dressed all by herself this morning - didn't you Mama?
Yup, this little lady is going home soon.
You'd better tell Mom and Dad.
Going home?
How?

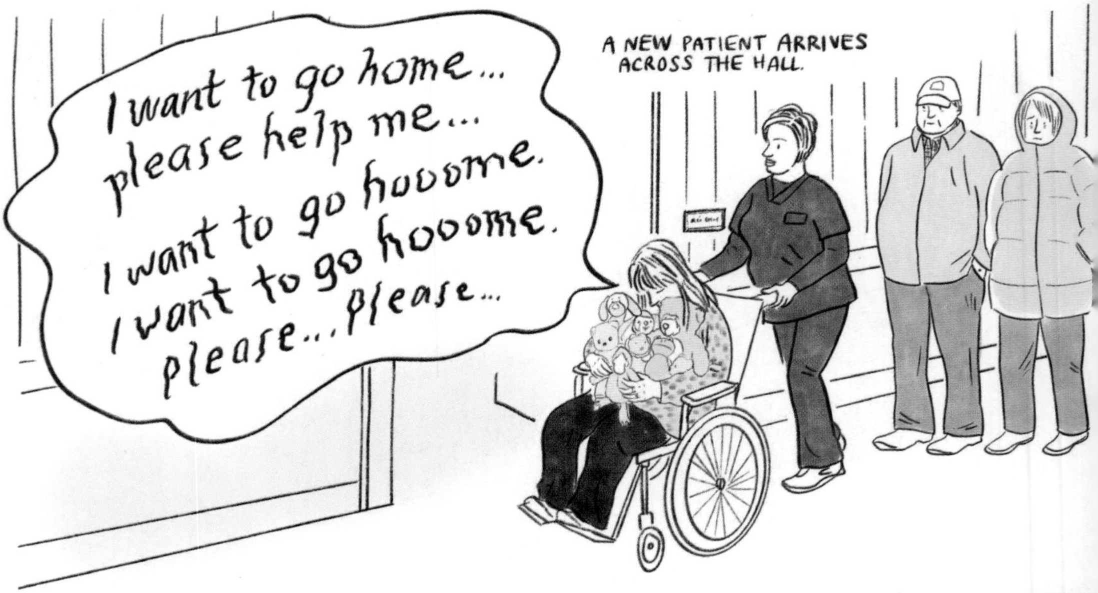
A NEW PATIENT ARRIVES ACROSS THE HALL.
I want to go home... please help me... I want to go hooome. I want to go hooome. please... please...

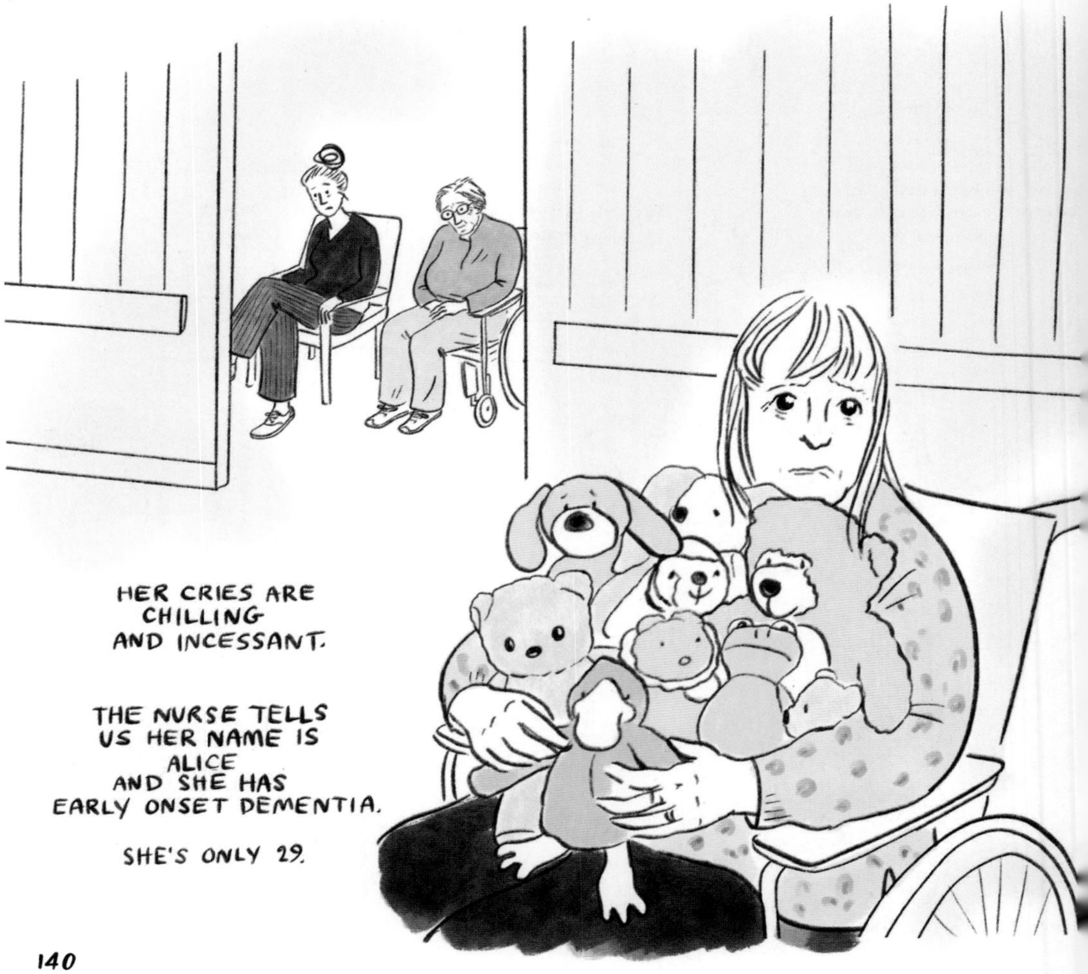
HER CRIES ARE CHILLING AND INCESSANT.
THE NURSE TELLS US HER NAME IS ALICE AND SHE HAS EARLY ONSET DEMENTIA.
SHE'S ONLY 29.

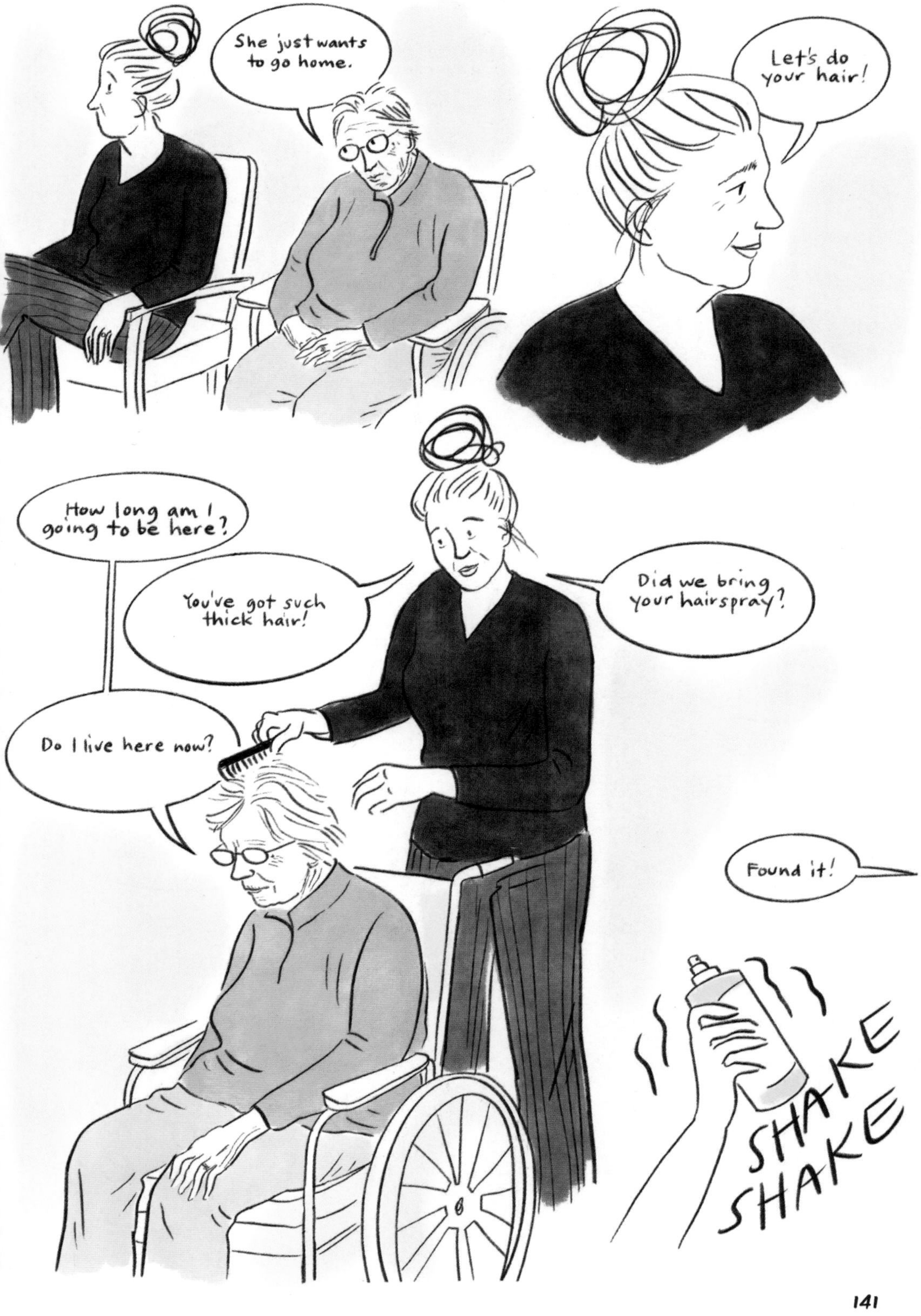
She just wants to go home.
Let's do your hair!
How long am I going to be here?
You've got such thick hair!
Did we bring your hairspray?
Do I live here now?
Found it!
SHAKE
SHAKE

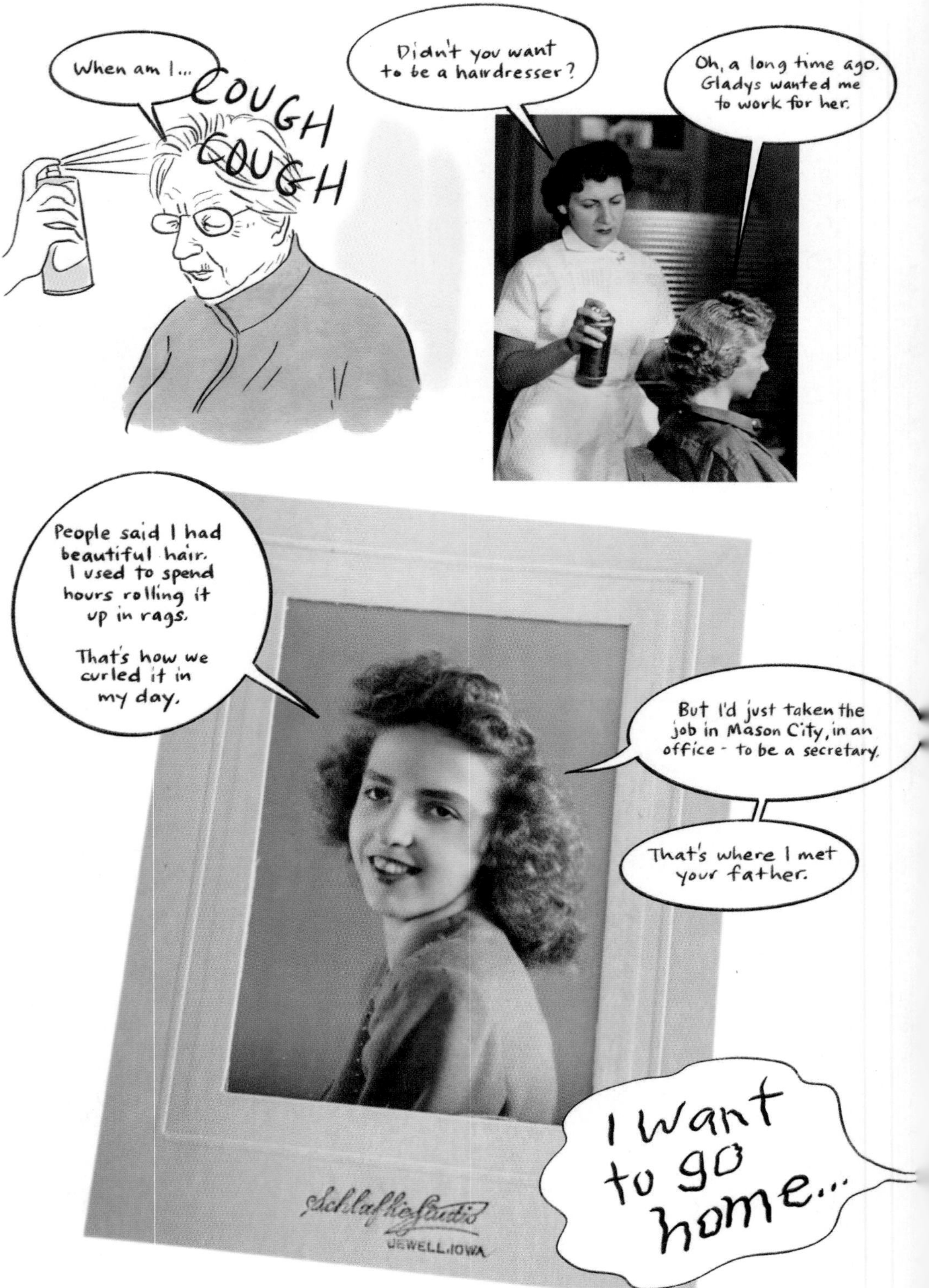
When am I...
COUGH
COUGH
Didn't you want to be a hairdresser?
Oh, a long time ago. Gladys wanted me to work for her.
People said I had beautiful hair. I used to spend hours rolling it up in rags.
That's how we curled it in my day.
But I'd just taken the job in Mason City, in an office - to be a secretary.
That's where I met your father.
I want to go home...
Schlafke Studio
JEWELL, IOWA

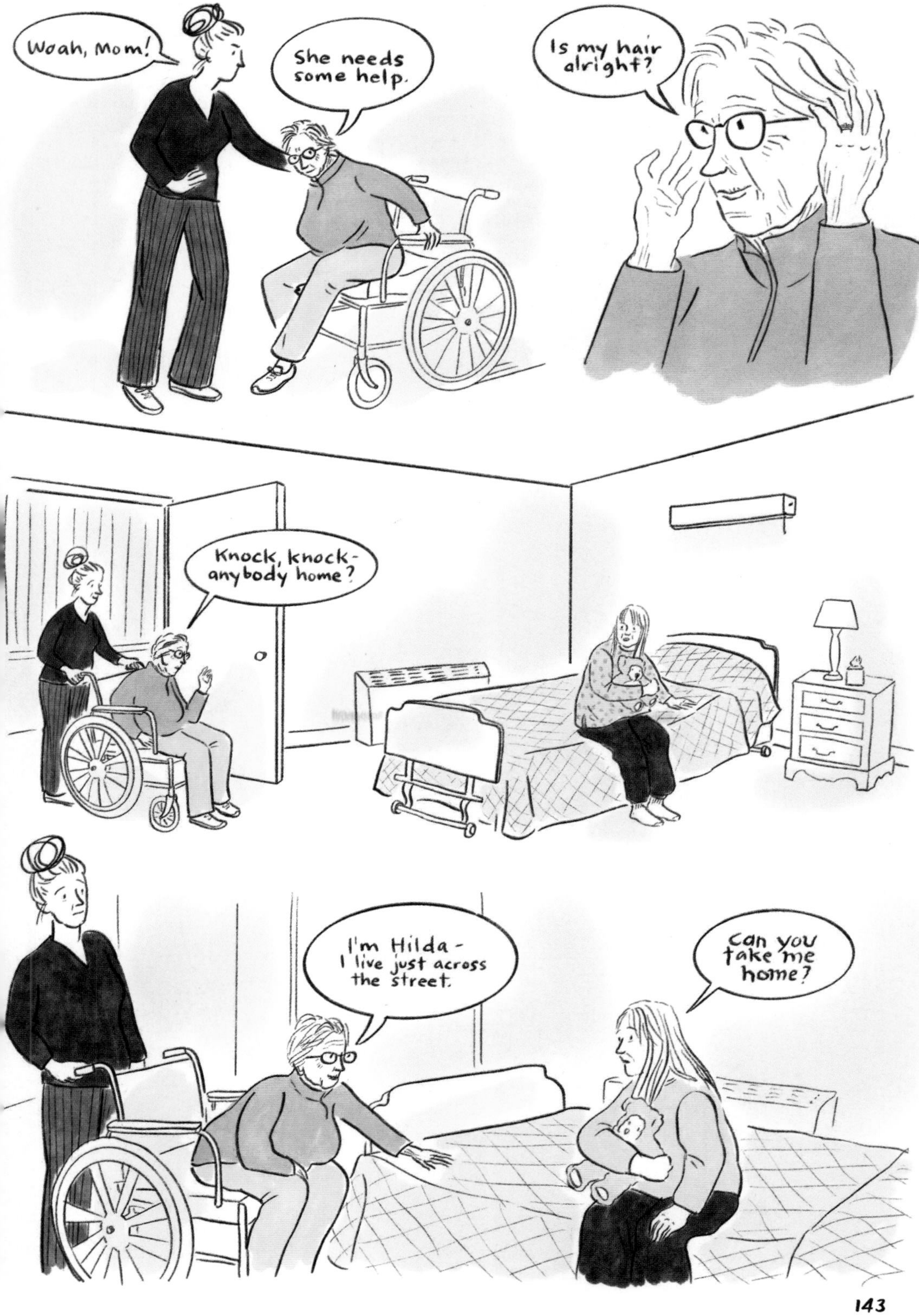

Woah, Mom!
She needs some help.
Is my hair alright?
Knock, knock- anybody home?
I'm Hilda - I live just across the street.
Can you take me home?

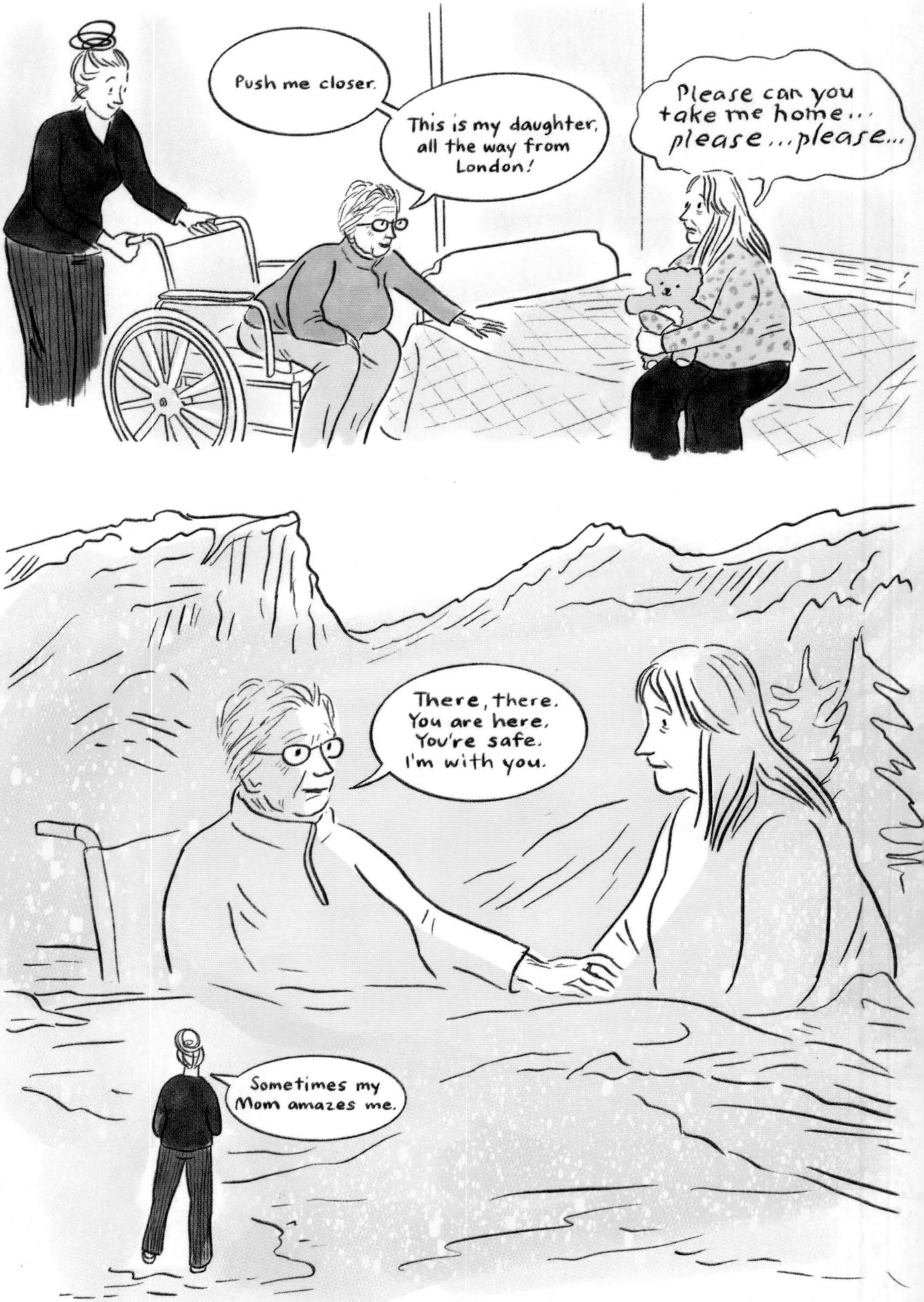
Push me closer.
This is my daughter, all the way from London!
Please can you take me home... please...please...
There, there. You are here. You're safe. I'm with you.
Sometimes my Mom amazes me.

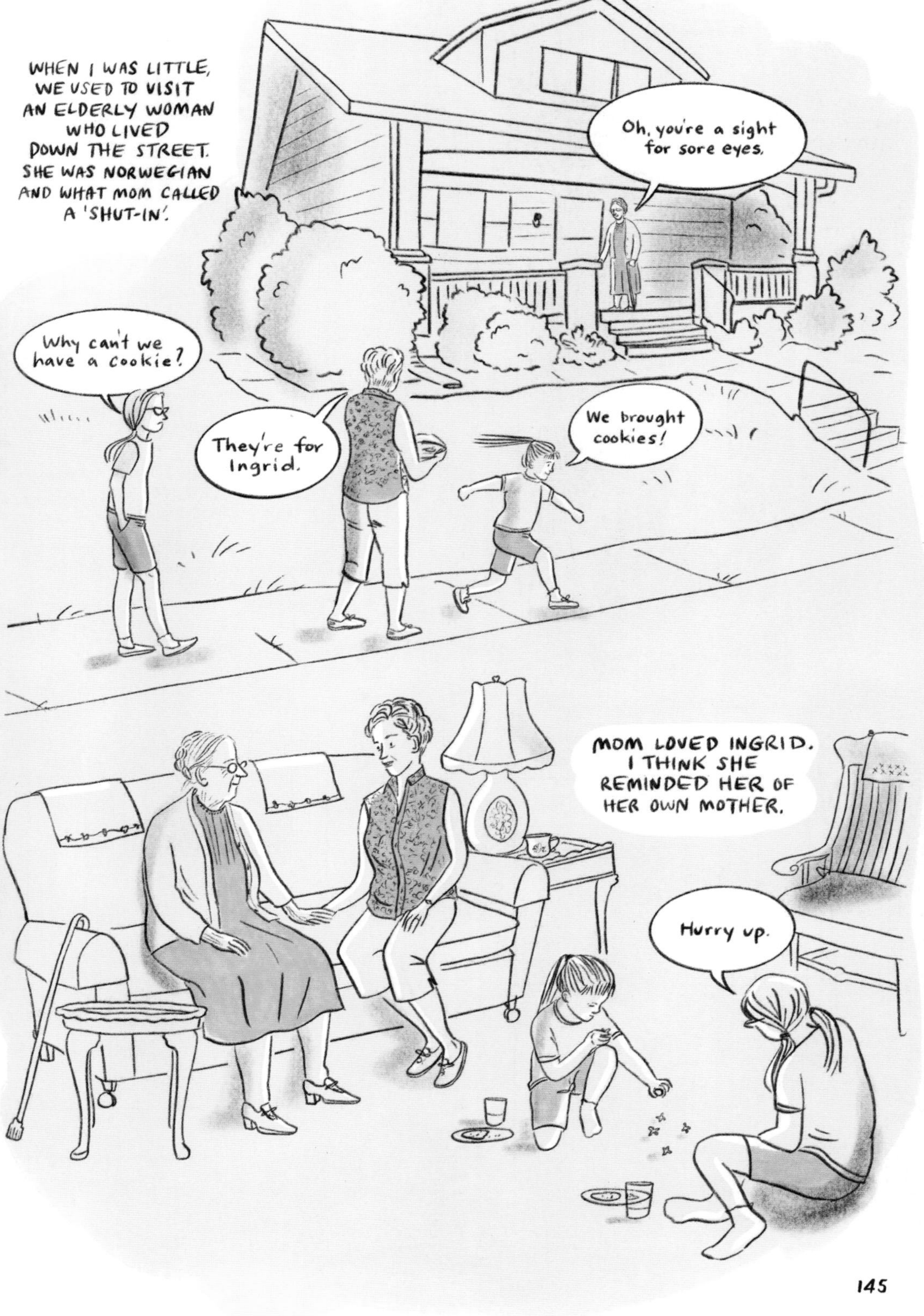
WHEN I WAS LITTLE, WE USED TO VISIT AN ELDERLY WOMAN WHO LIVED DOWN THE STREET. SHE WAS NORWEGIAN AND WHAT MOM CALLED A 'SHUT-IN'.
Oh, you're a sight for sore eyes.
Why can't we have a cookie?
They're for Ingrid.
We brought cookies!
MOM LOVED INGRID. I THINK SHE REMINDED HER OF HER OWN MOTHER.
Hurry up.

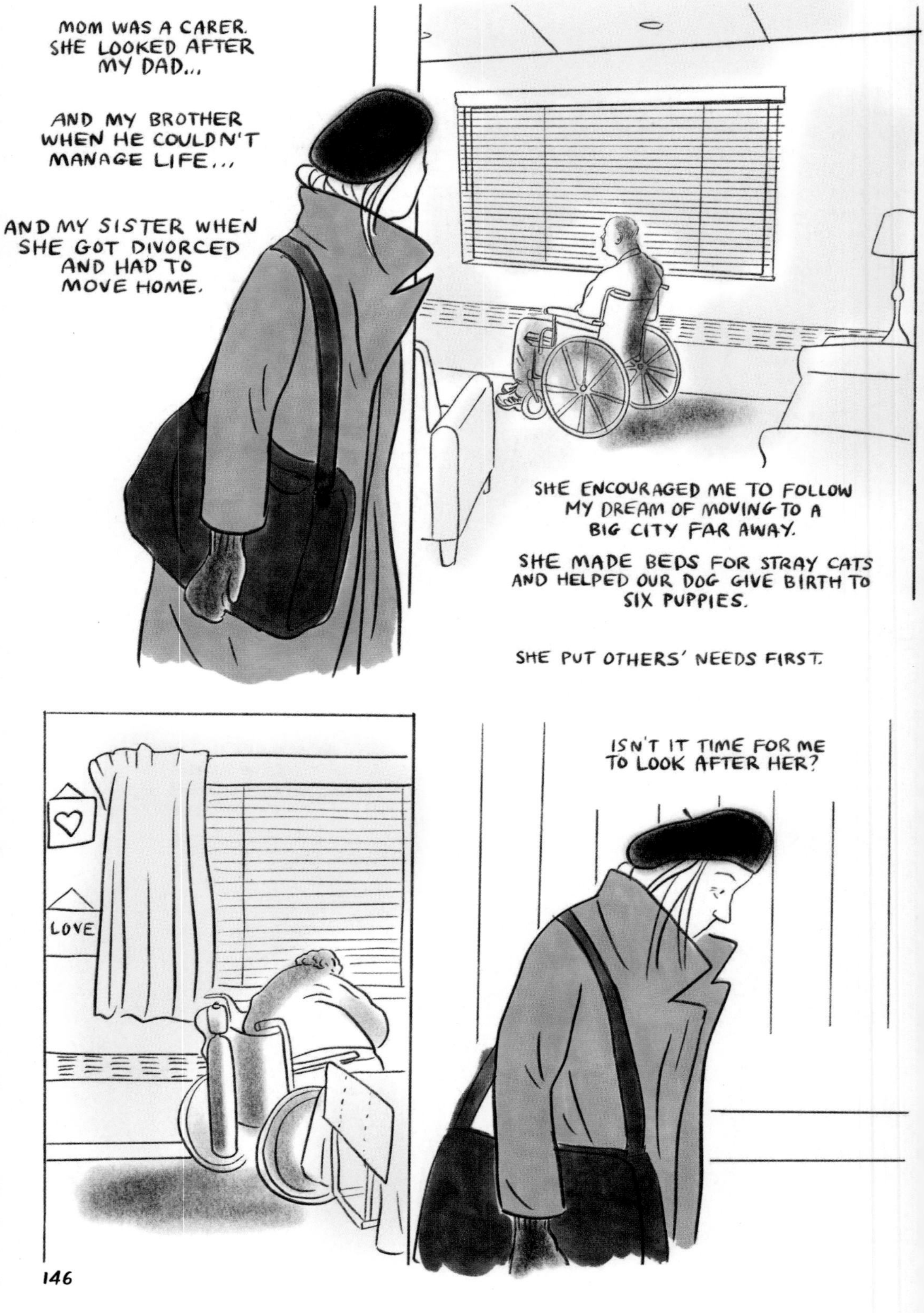
MOM WAS A CARER. SHE LOOKED AFTER MY DAD...
AND MY BROTHER WHEN HE COULDN'T MANAGE LIFE...
AND MY SISTER WHEN SHE GOT DIVORCED AND HAD TO MOVE HOME.
SHE ENCOURAGED ME TO FOLLOW MY DREAM OF MOVING TO A BIG CITY FAR AWAY.
SHE MADE BEDS FOR STRAY CATS AND HELPED OUR DOG GIVE BIRTH TO SIX PUPPIES.
SHE PUT OTHERS' NEEDS FIRST.
LOVE
ISN'T IT TIME FOR ME TO LOOK AFTER HER?

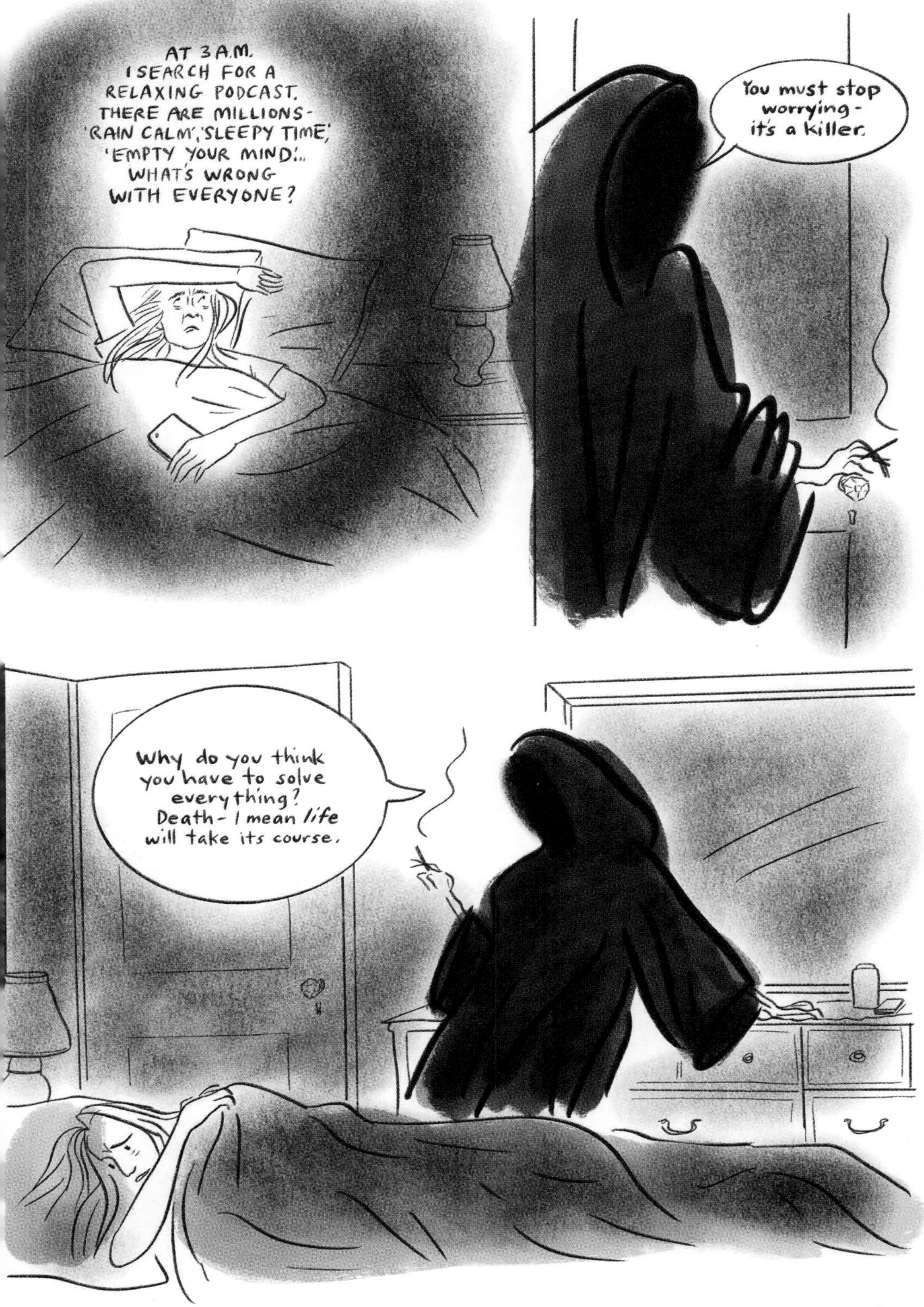
AT 3 A.M. I SEARCH FOR A RELAXING PODCAST. THERE ARE MILLIONS - 'RAIN CALM', 'SLEEPY TIME', 'EMPTY YOUR MIND'... WHAT'S WRONG WITH EVERYONE?
You must stop worrying - it's a killer.
Why do you think you have to solve everything? Death - I mean *life* will take its course.

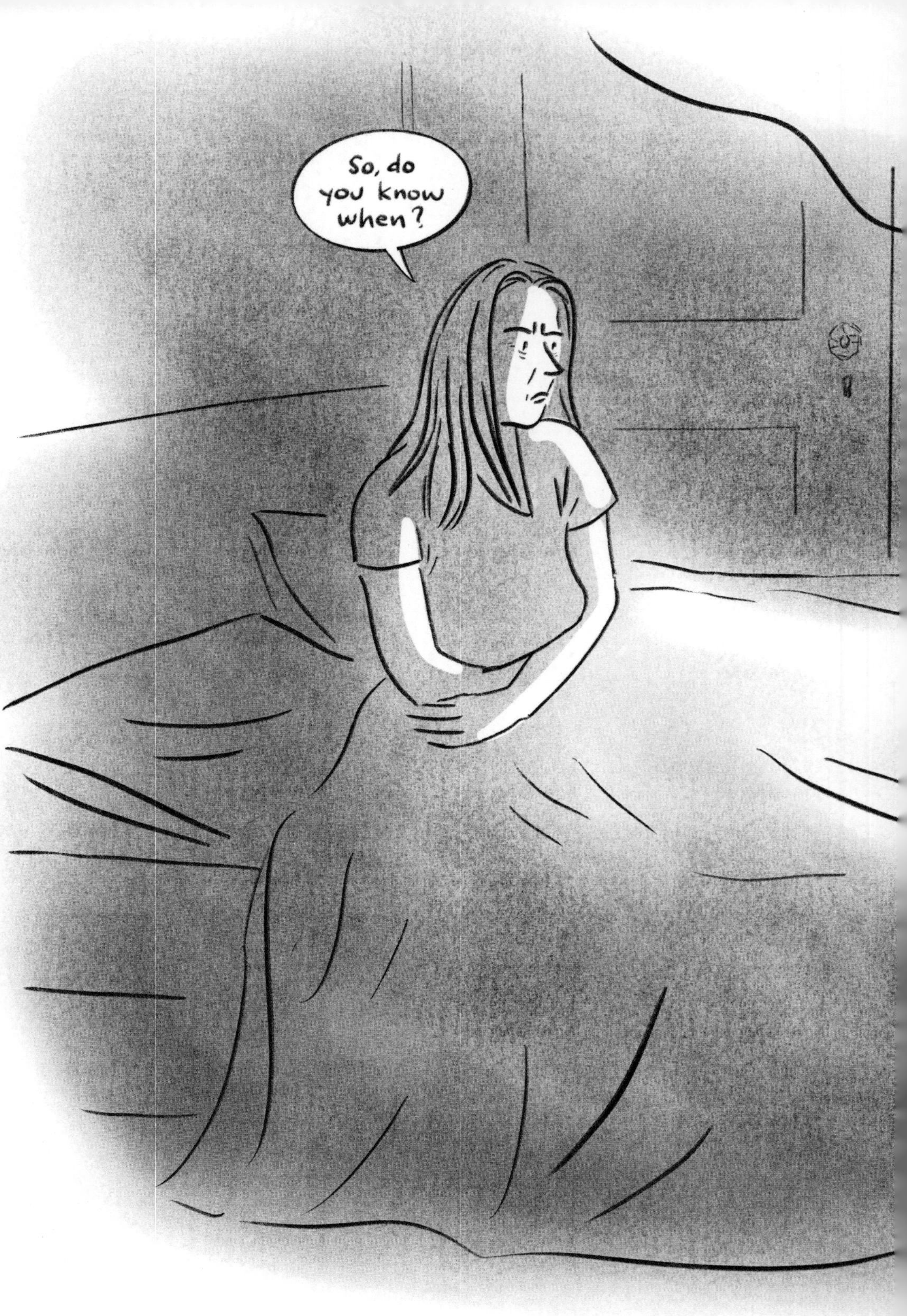
So, do you know when?

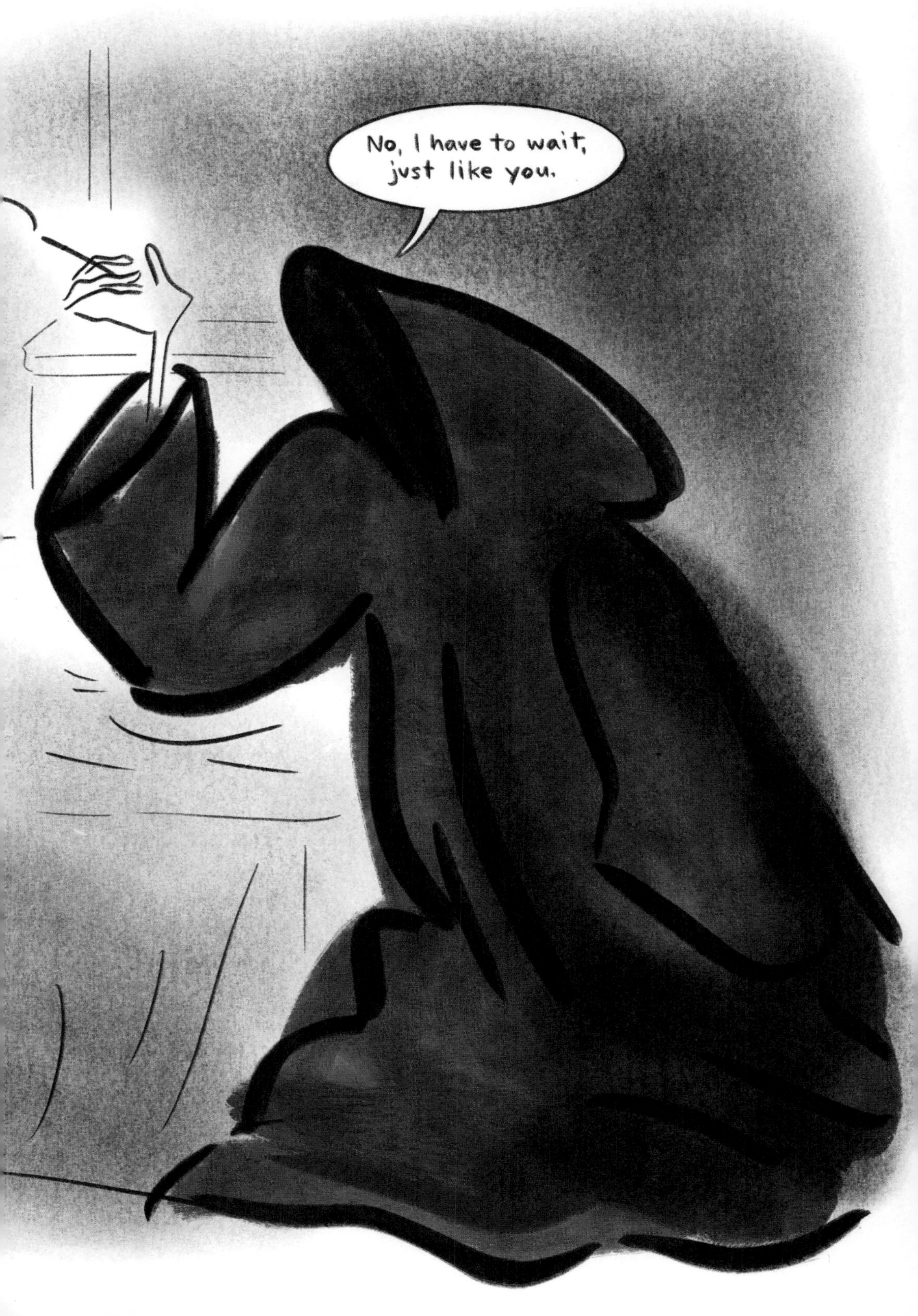
No, I have to wait, just like you.

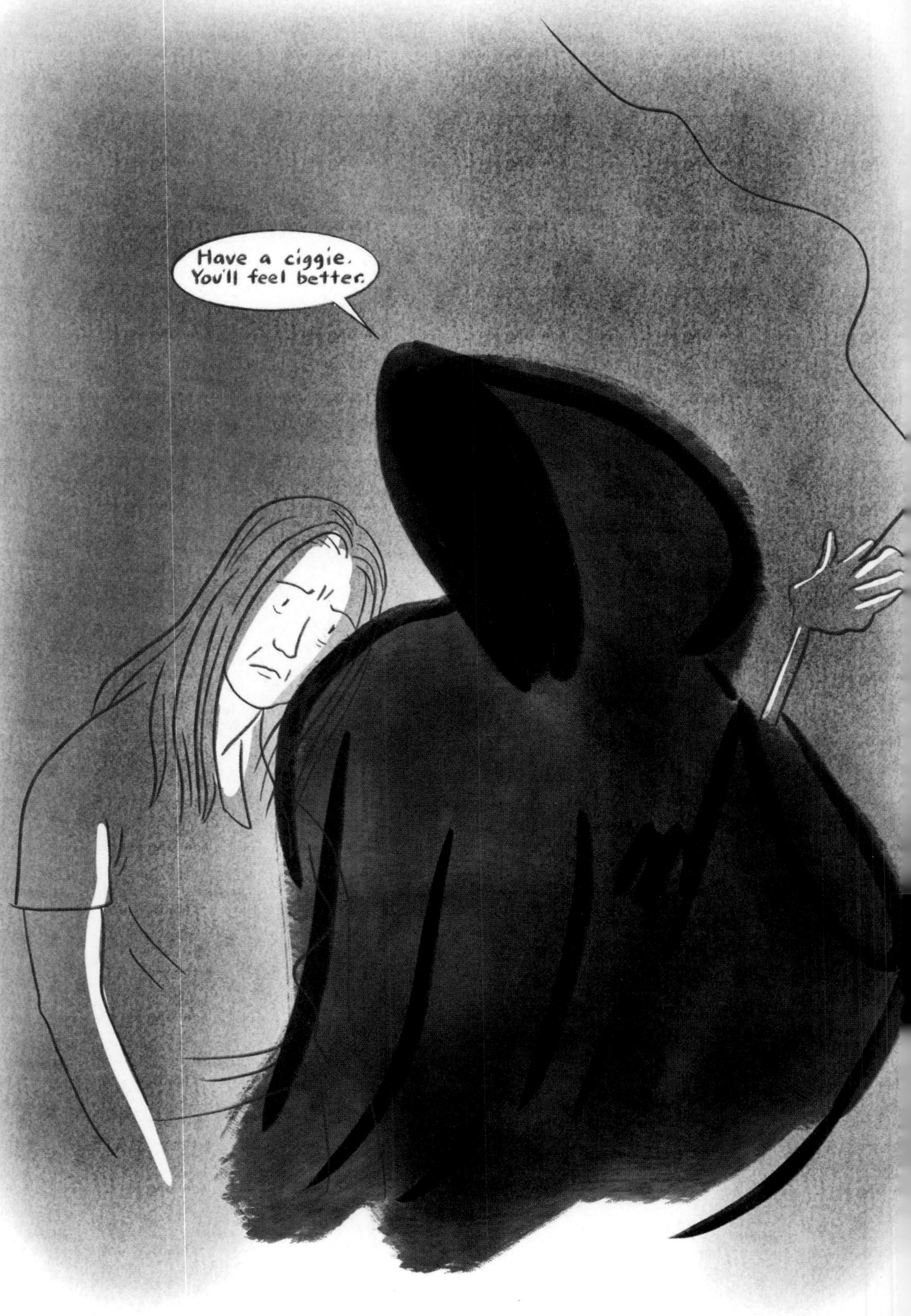
Have a ciggie. You'll feel better.

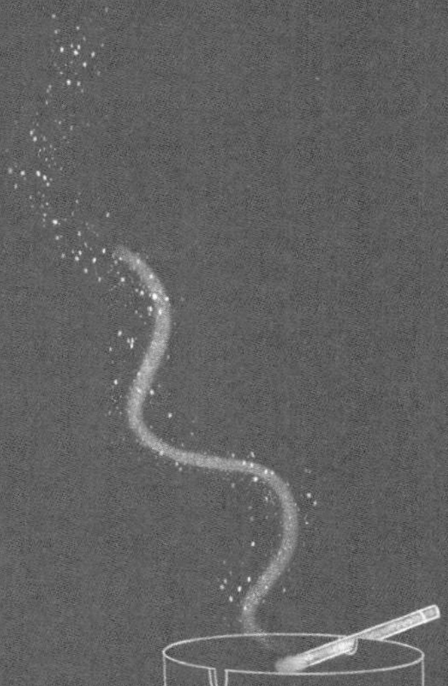

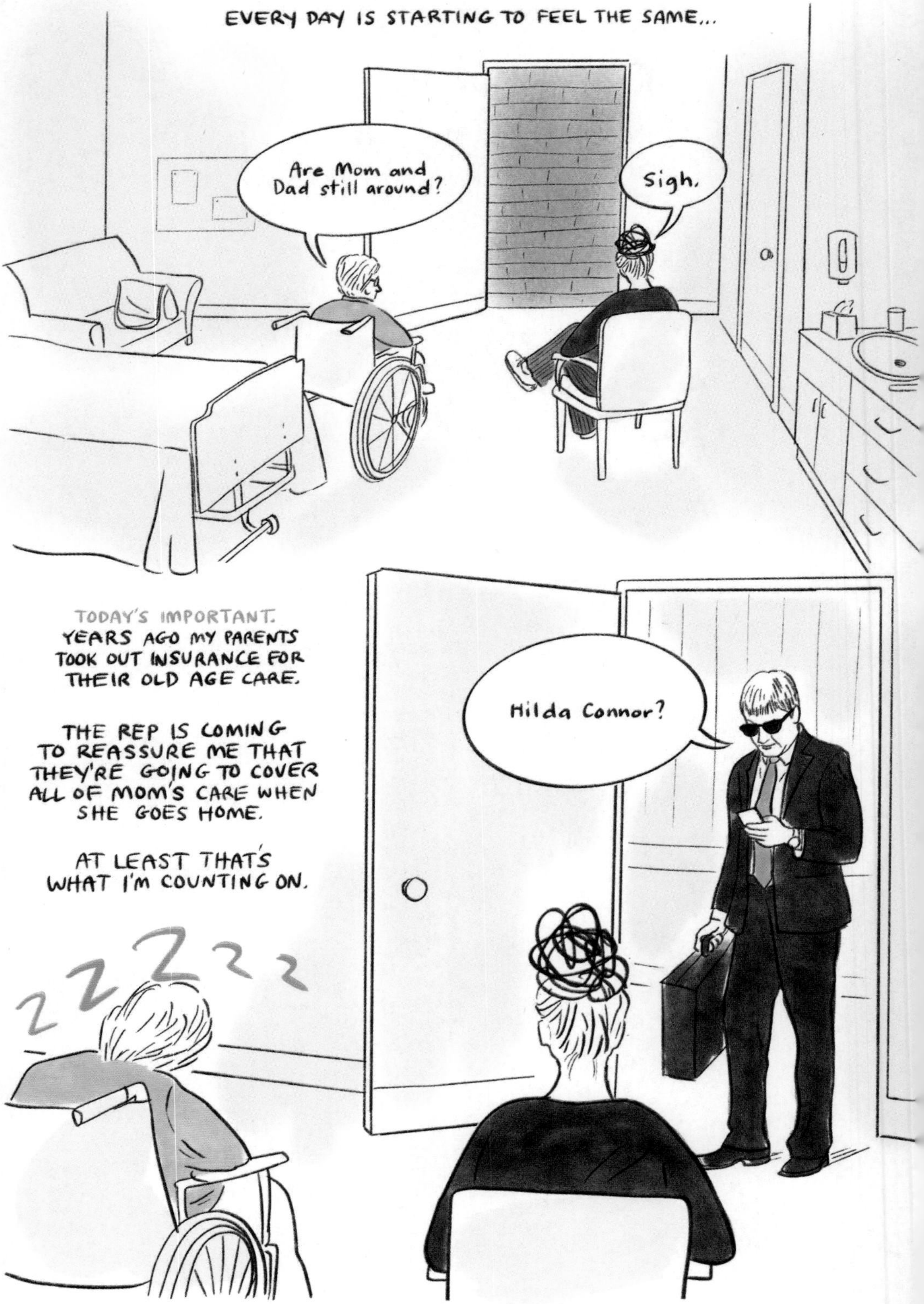
EVERY DAY IS STARTING TO FEEL THE SAME...
Are Mom and Dad still around?
Sigh.
TODAY'S IMPORTANT. YEARS AGO MY PARENTS TOOK OUT INSURANCE FOR THEIR OLD AGE CARE.
THE REP IS COMING TO REASSURE ME THAT THEY'RE GOING TO COVER ALL OF MOM'S CARE WHEN SHE GOES HOME.
AT LEAST THAT'S WHAT I'M COUNTING ON.
Hilda Connor?
ZZZZZZ

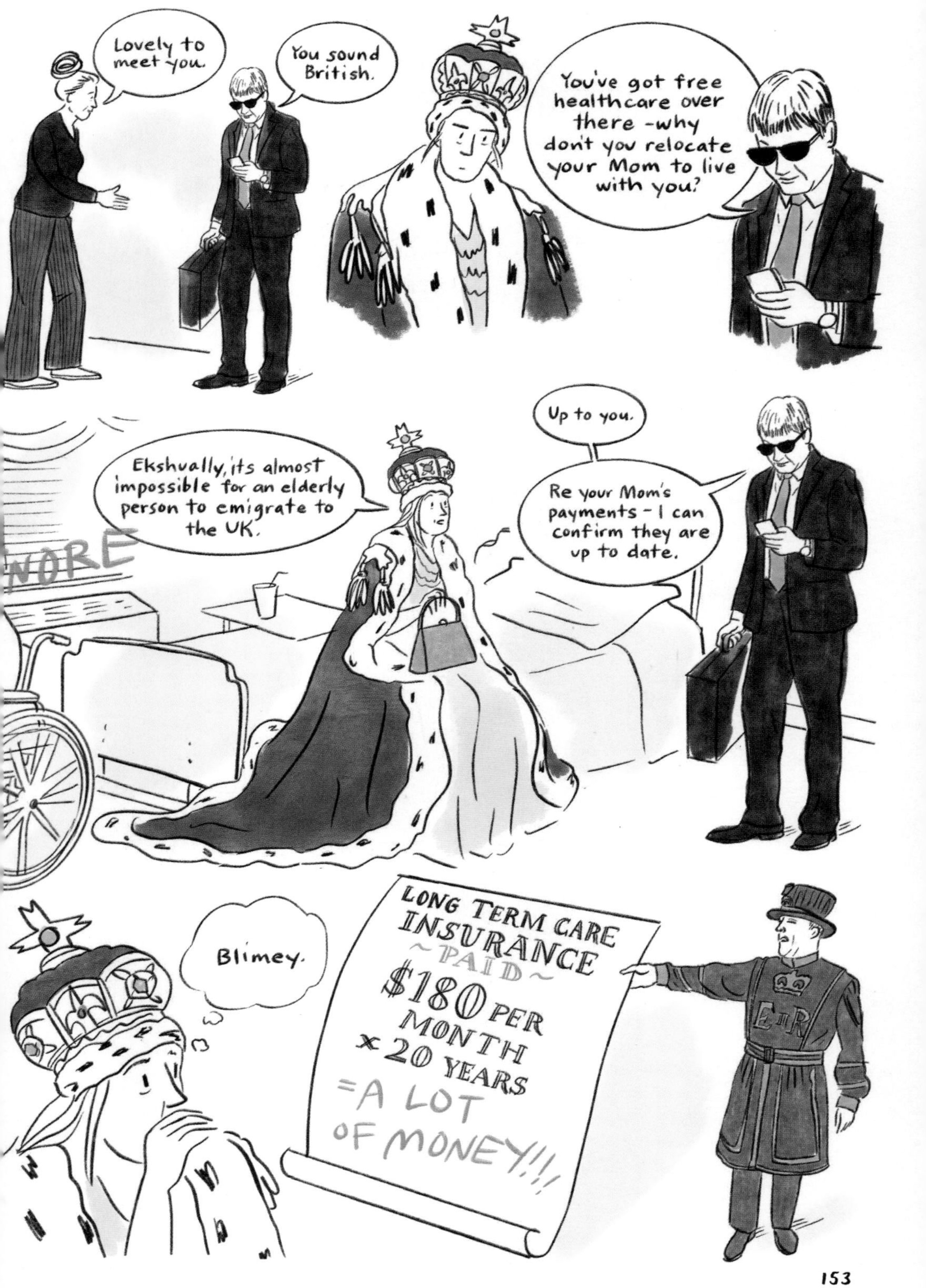
Lovely to meet you.
You sound British.
You've got free healthcare over there -why don't you relocate your Mom to live with you?
Ekshually, its almost impossible for an elderly person to emigrate to the UK.
NORE
Up to you.
Re your Mom's payments - I can confirm they are up to date.
Blimey.
LONG TERM CARE INSURANCE
~PAID~
$180 PER MONTH
x 20 YEARS
=A LOT OF MONEY!!!
EIIR

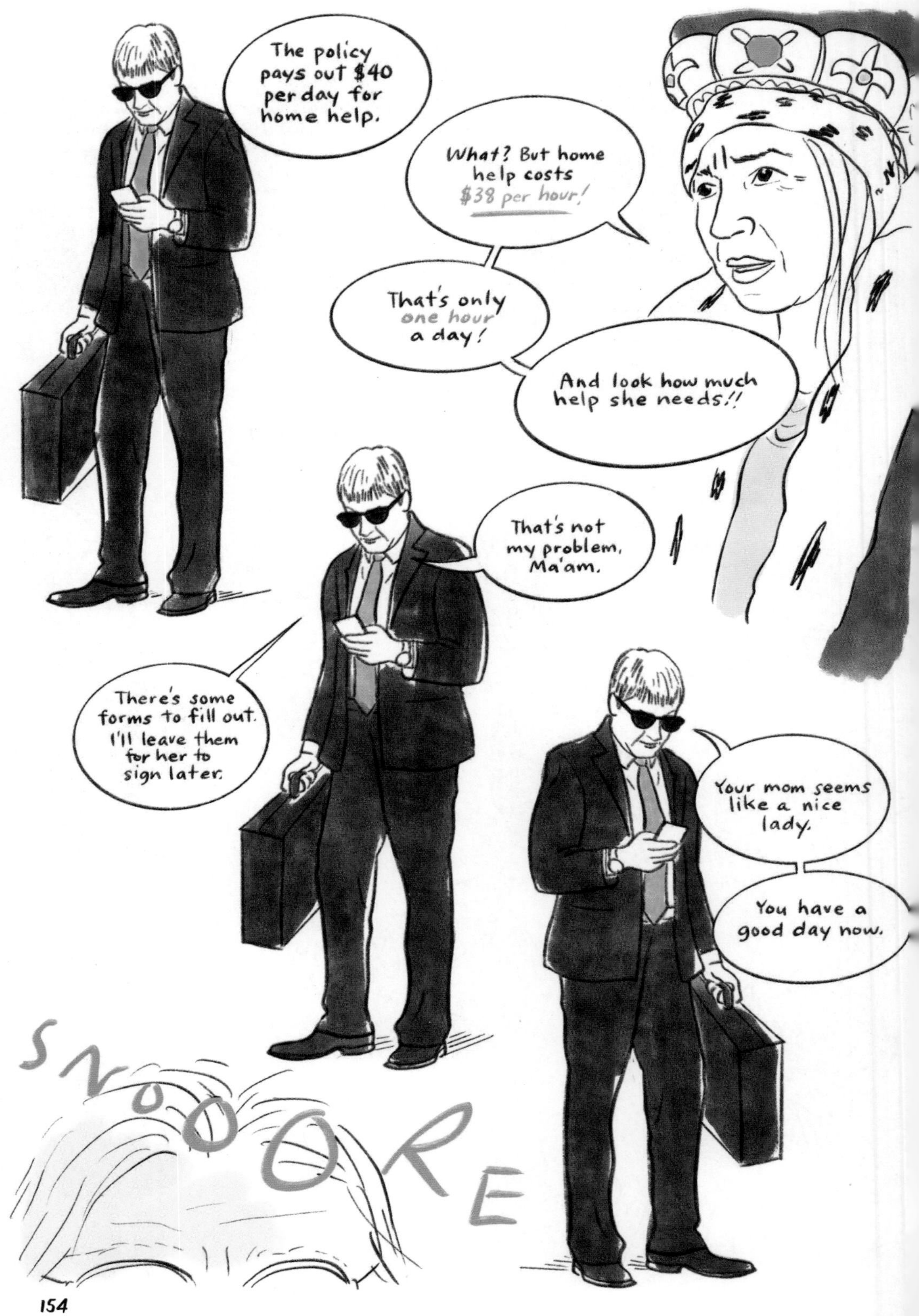
The policy pays out $40 per day for home help.
What? But home help costs $38 per hour!
That's only one hour a day!
And look how much help she needs!!
That's not my problem, Ma'am.
There's some forms to fill out. I'll leave them for her to sign later.
Your mom seems like a nice lady.
You have a good day now.
SNOOORE

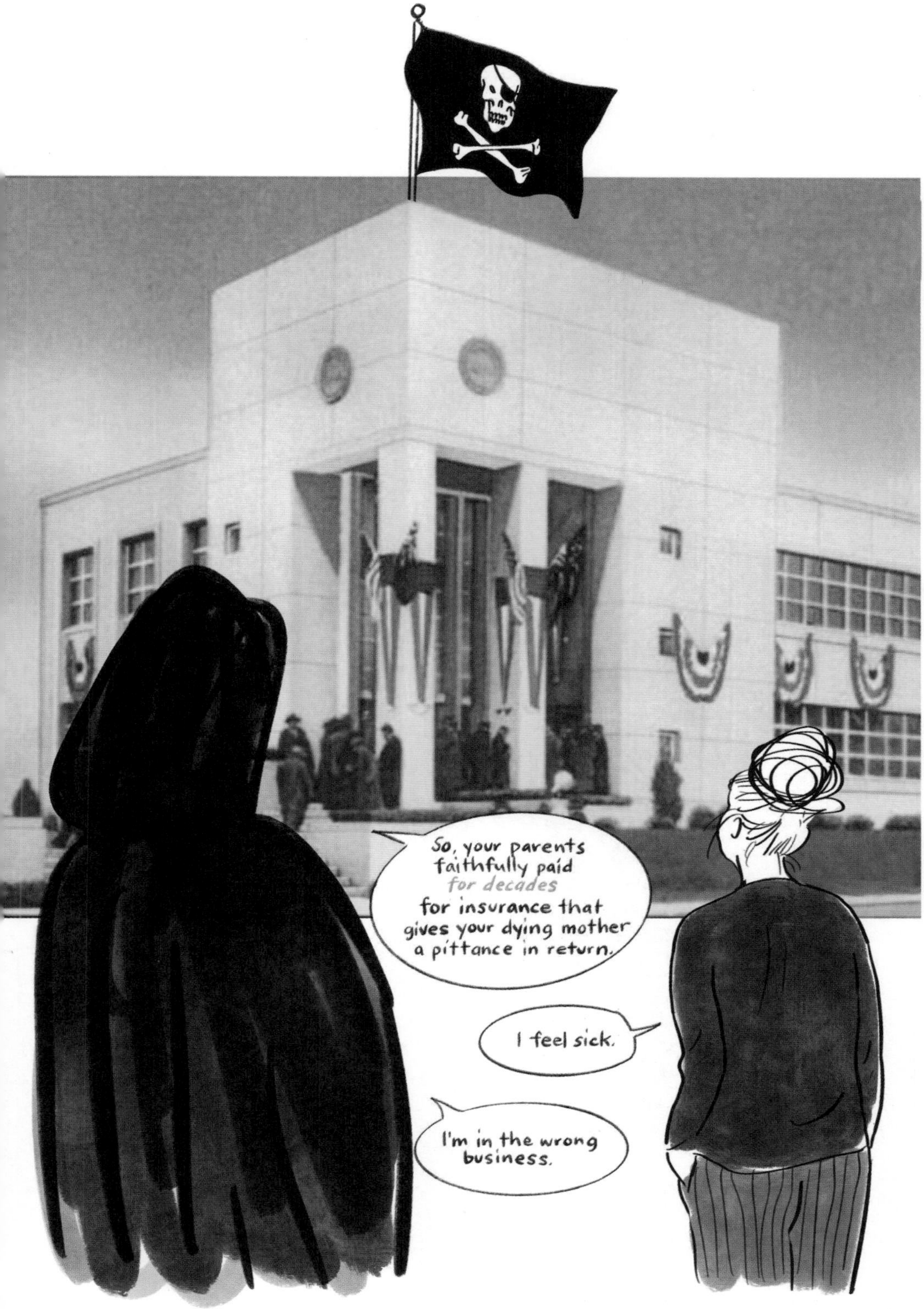
So, your parents faithfully paid for decades for insurance that gives your dying mother a pittance in return.
I feel sick.
I'm in the wrong business.

SO THAT'S THE DEAL...
WE SIGN UP FOR MEDICAID AND HAND OVER
EVERY SINGLE ASSET, LEAVING MOM TO LIVE HERE
UNTIL SHE DIES... ALONE.

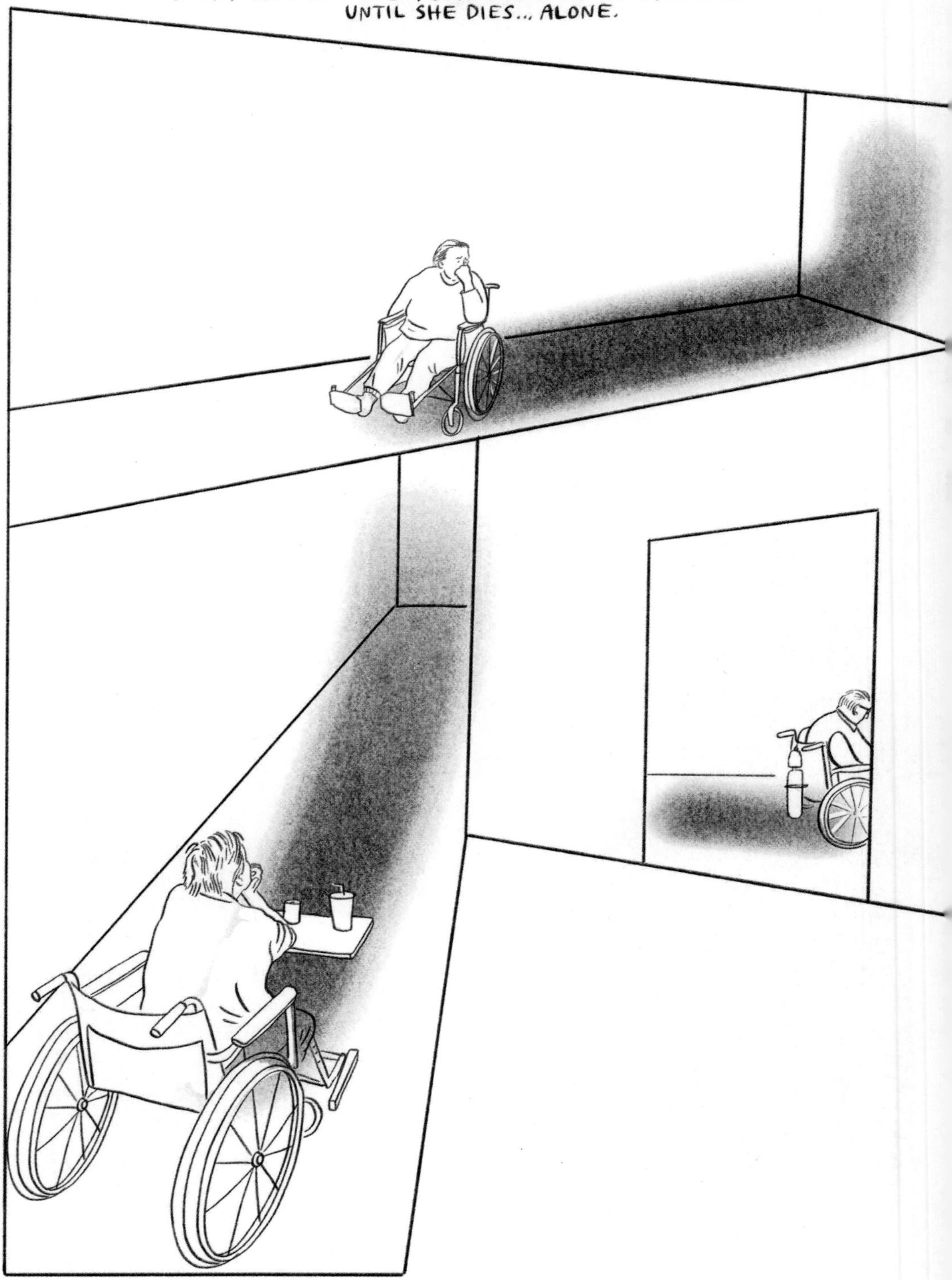

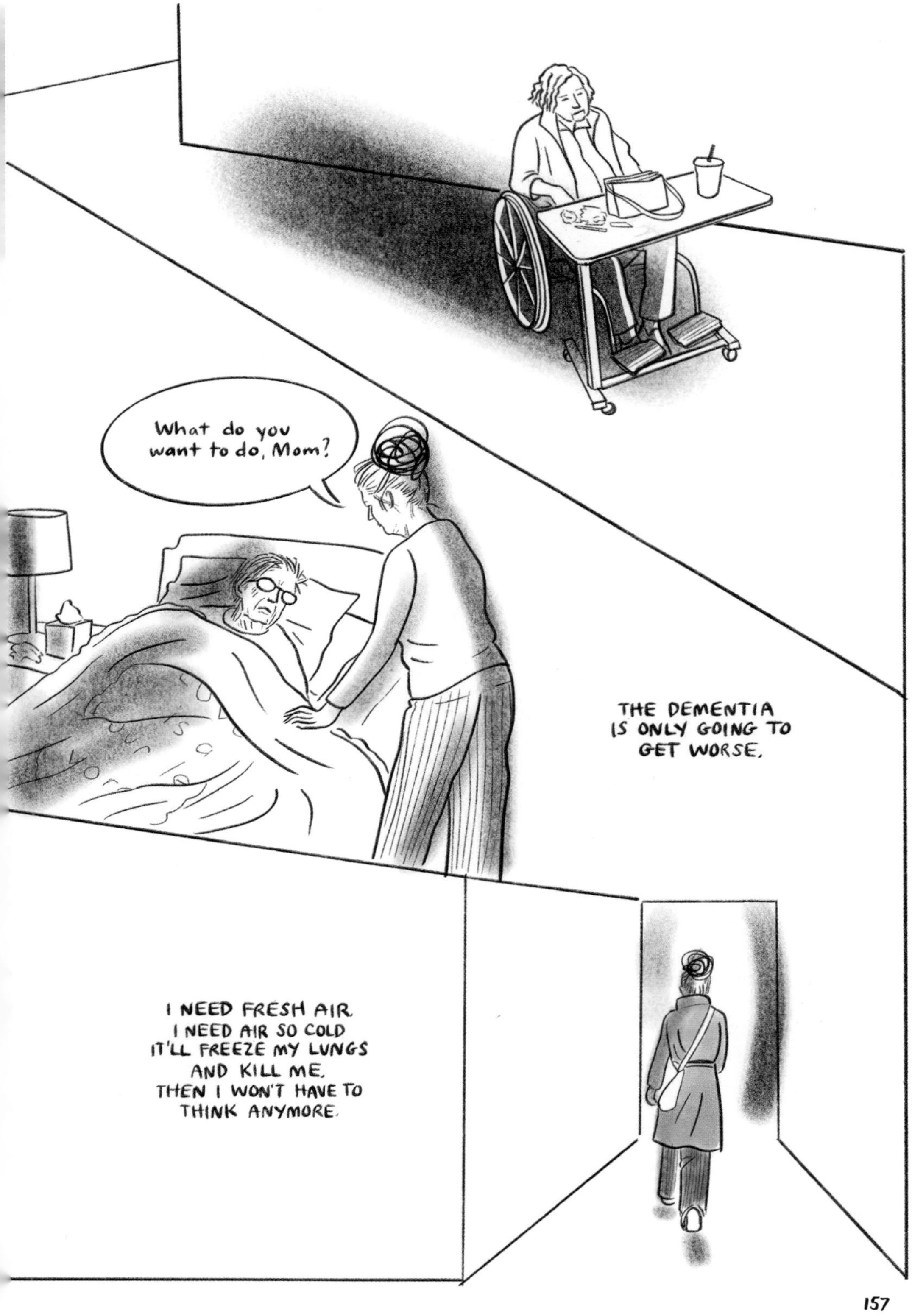

What do you want to do, Mom?
THE DEMENTIA IS ONLY GOING TO GET WORSE.
I NEED FRESH AIR. I NEED AIR SO COLD IT'LL FREEZE MY LUNGS AND KILL ME. THEN I WON'T HAVE TO THINK ANYMORE.

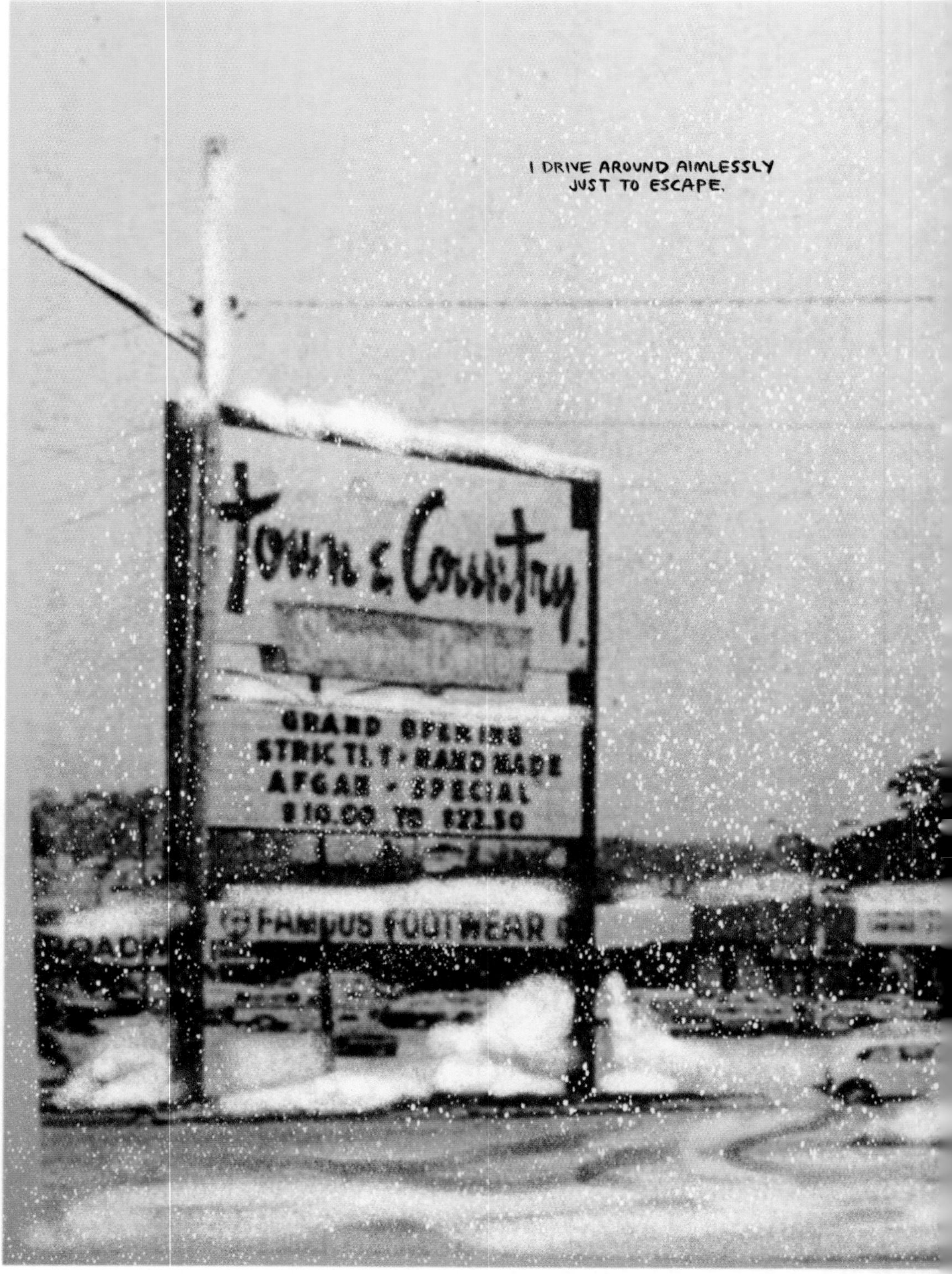
I DRIVE AROUND AIMLESSLY
JUST TO ESCAPE.
Town & Country
GRAND OPENING
STRICTLY HAND MADE
AFGAN SPECIAL
$10.00 TO $22.50
FAMOUS FOOTWEAR

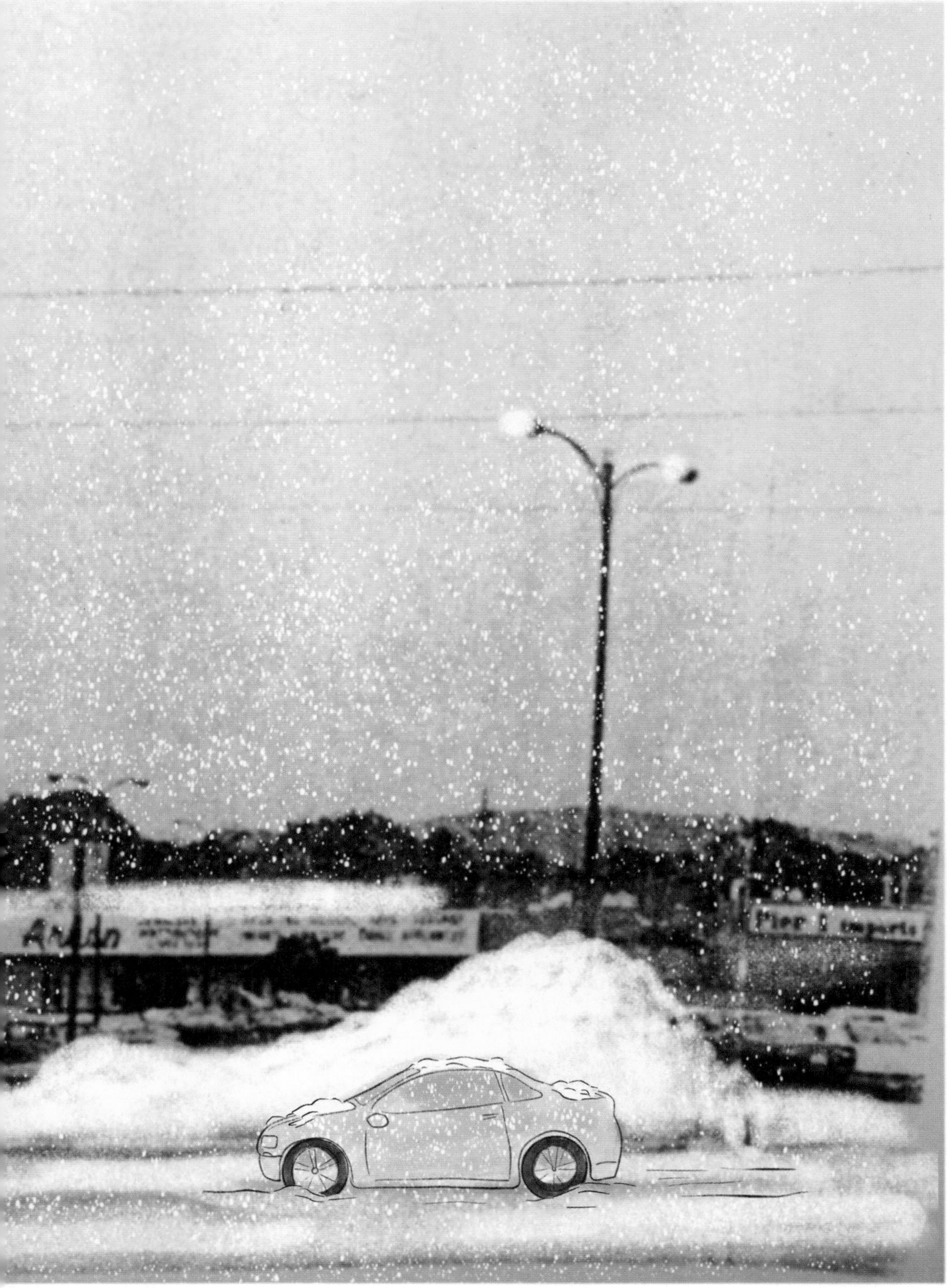

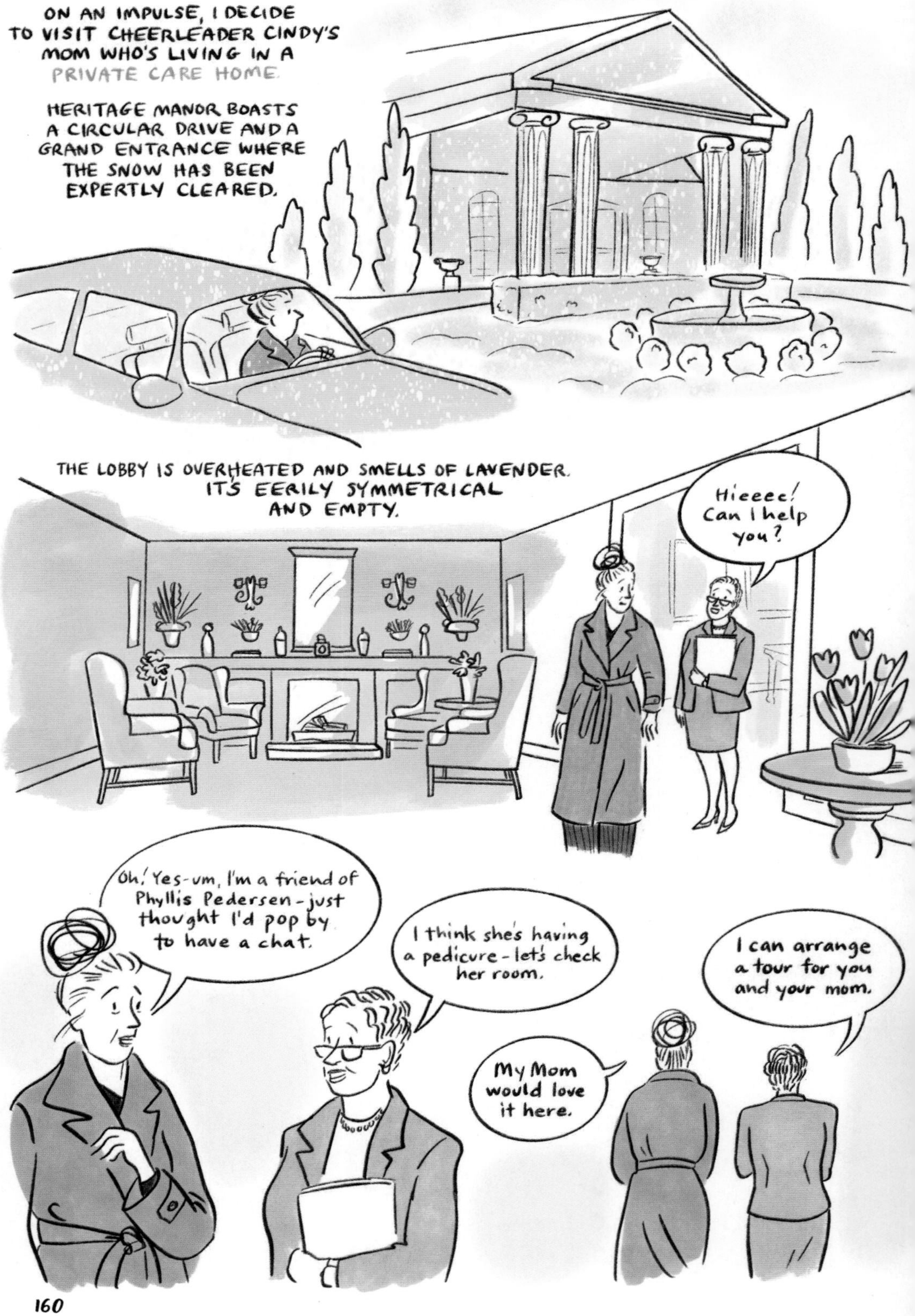

ON AN IMPULSE, I DECIDE TO VISIT CHEERLEADER CINDY'S MOM WHO'S LIVING IN A PRIVATE CARE HOME.
HERITAGE MANOR BOASTS A CIRCULAR DRIVE AND A GRAND ENTRANCE WHERE THE SNOW HAS BEEN EXPERTLY CLEARED.
THE LOBBY IS OVERHEATED AND SMELLS OF LAVENDER. IT'S EERILY SYMMETRICAL AND EMPTY.
Hieeee! Can I help you?
Oh! Yes-um, I'm a friend of Phyllis Pedersen-just thought I'd pop by to have a chat.
I think she's having a pedicure-let's check her room.
My Mom would love it here.
I can arrange a tour for you and your mom.

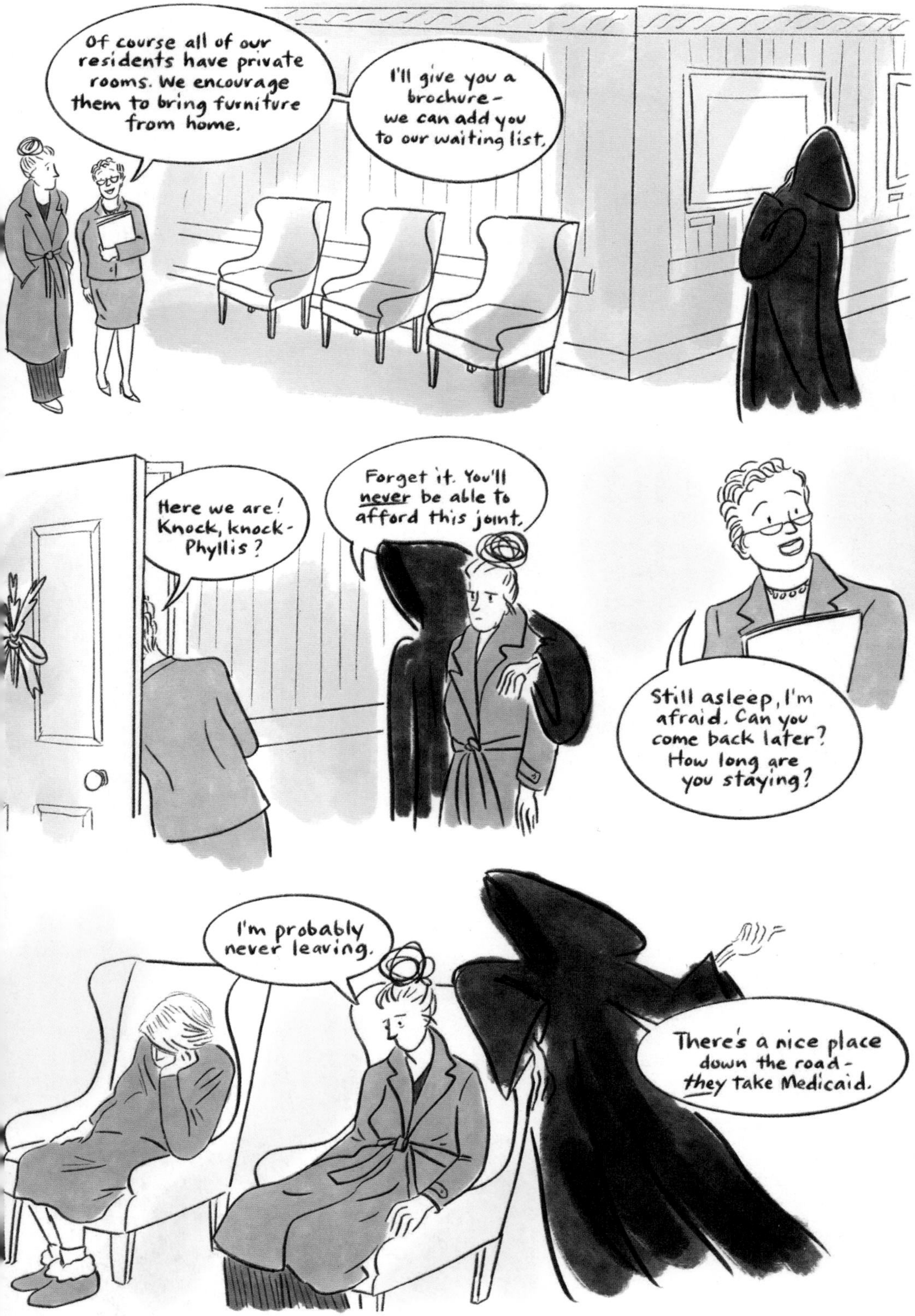
Of course all of our residents have private rooms. We encourage them to bring furniture from home.
I'll give you a brochure - we can add you to our waiting list.
Here we are! Knock, knock - Phyllis?
Forget it. You'll never be able to afford this joint.
Still asleep, I'm afraid. Can you come back later? How long are you staying?
I'm probably never leaving.
There's a nice place down the road - they take Medicaid.

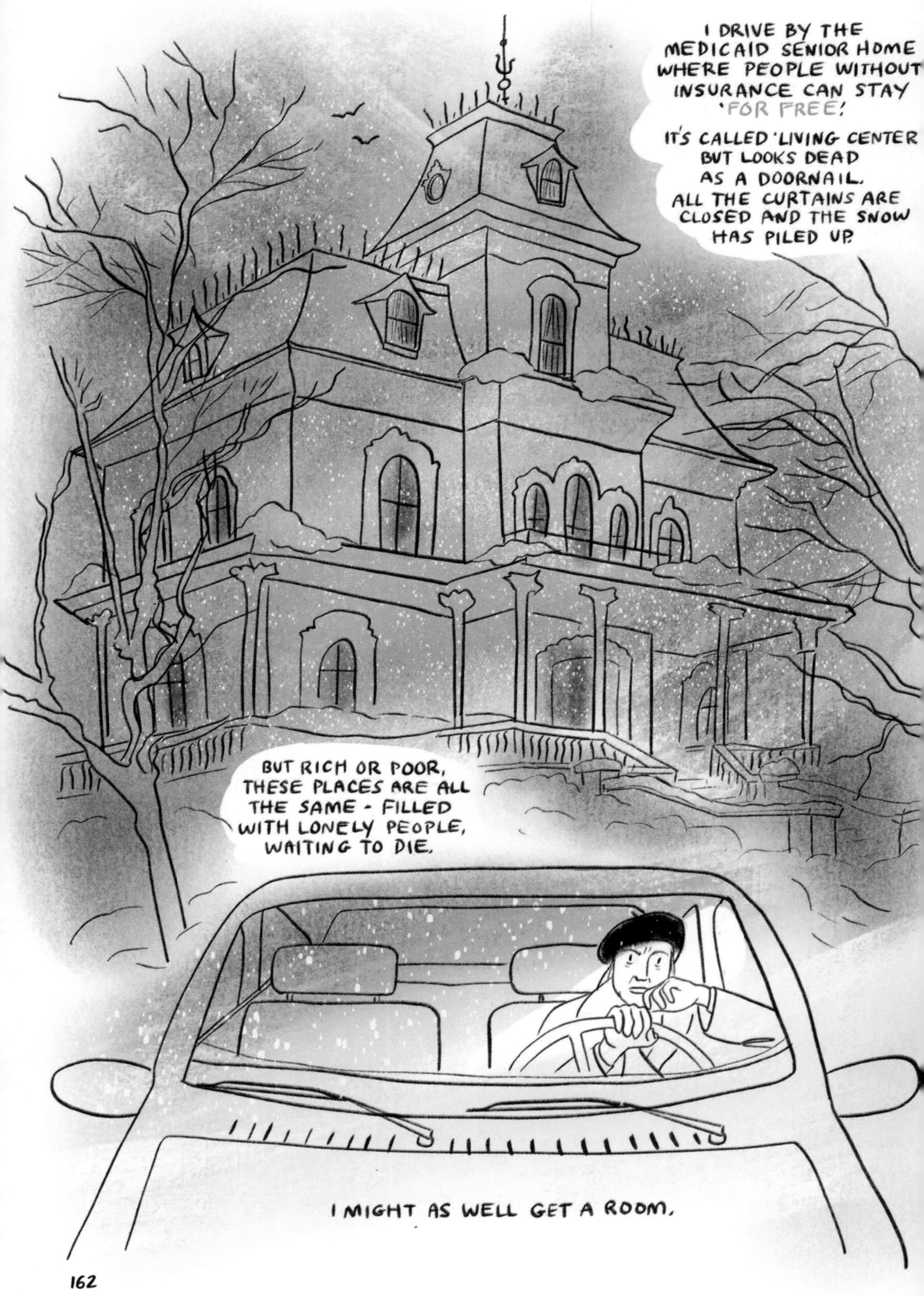
I DRIVE BY THE MEDICAID SENIOR HOME WHERE PEOPLE WITHOUT INSURANCE CAN STAY 'FOR FREE.'
IT'S CALLED 'LIVING CENTER' BUT LOOKS DEAD AS A DOORNAIL. ALL THE CURTAINS ARE CLOSED AND THE SNOW HAS PILED UP.
BUT RICH OR POOR, THESE PLACES ARE ALL THE SAME - FILLED WITH LONELY PEOPLE, WAITING TO DIE.
I MIGHT AS WELL GET A ROOM.

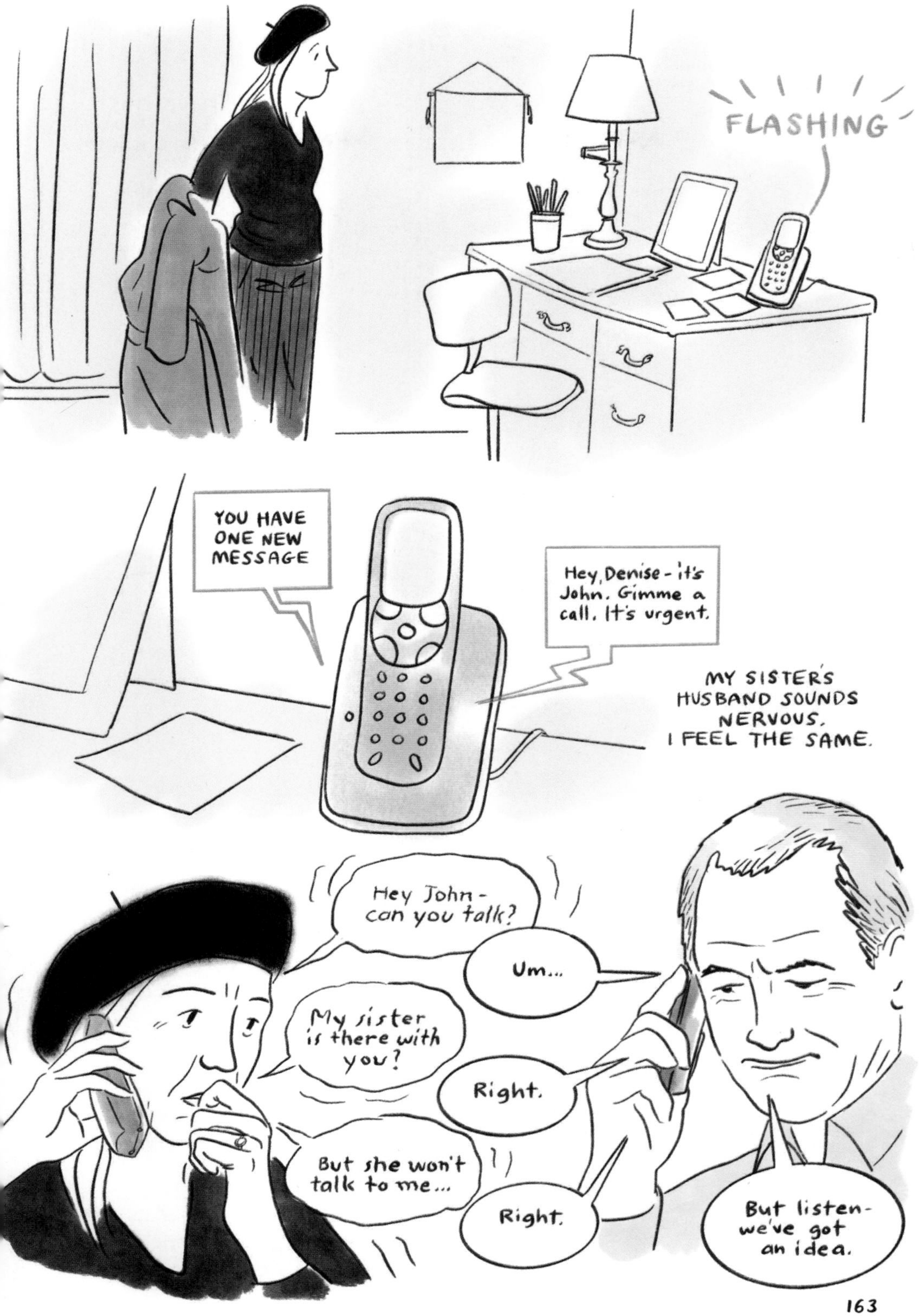
FLASHING
YOU HAVE ONE NEW MESSAGE
Hey, Denise - it's John. Gimme a call. It's urgent.
MY SISTER'S HUSBAND SOUNDS NERVOUS.
I FEEL THE SAME.
Hey John - can you talk?
Um...
My sister is there with you?
Right.
But she won't talk to me...
Right.
But listen - we've got an idea.

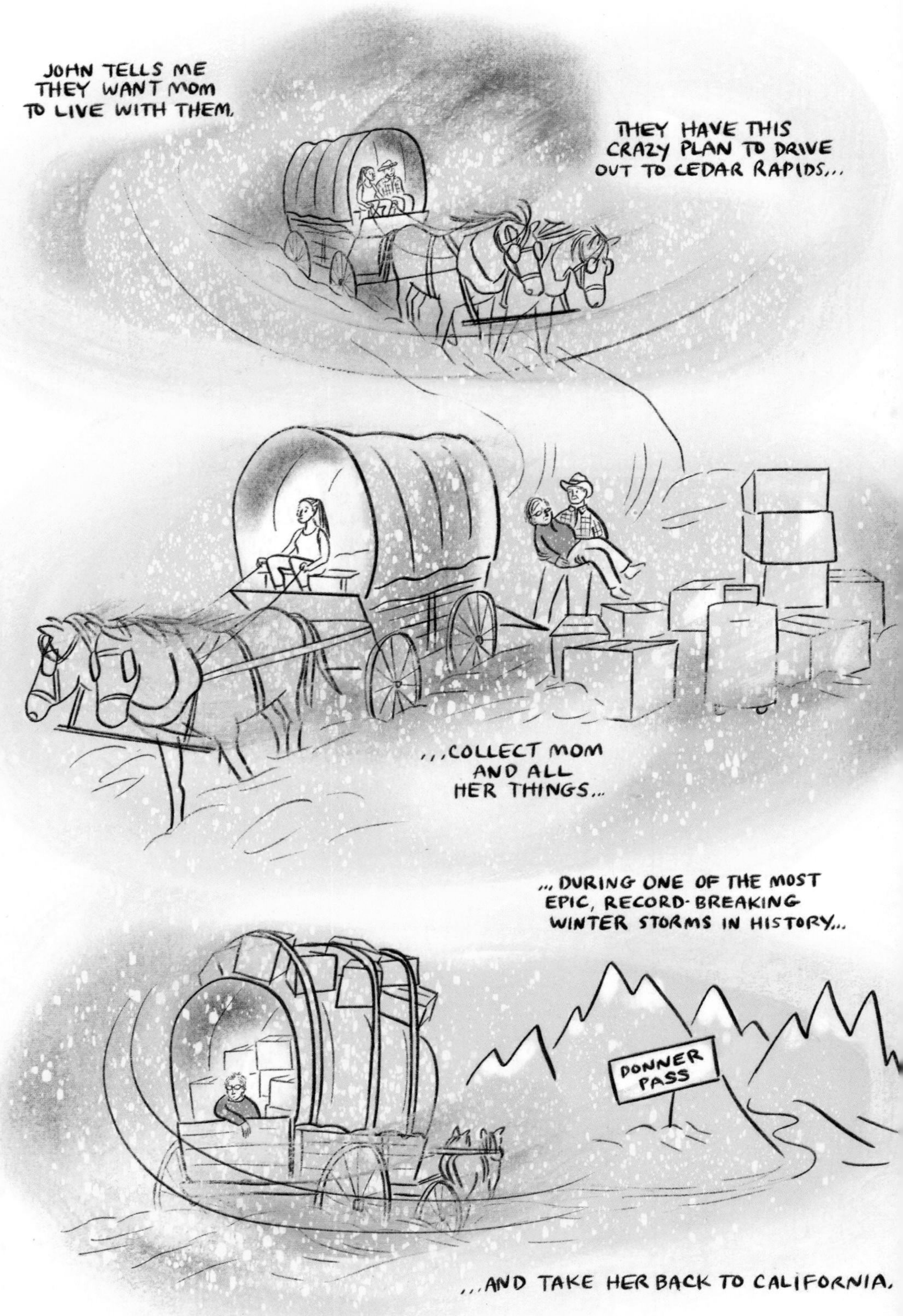
JOHN TELLS ME THEY WANT MOM TO LIVE WITH THEM.
THEY HAVE THIS CRAZY PLAN TO DRIVE OUT TO CEDAR RAPIDS...
...COLLECT MOM AND ALL HER THINGS...
...DURING ONE OF THE MOST EPIC, RECORD-BREAKING WINTER STORMS IN HISTORY...
DONNER PASS
...AND TAKE HER BACK TO CALIFORNIA.

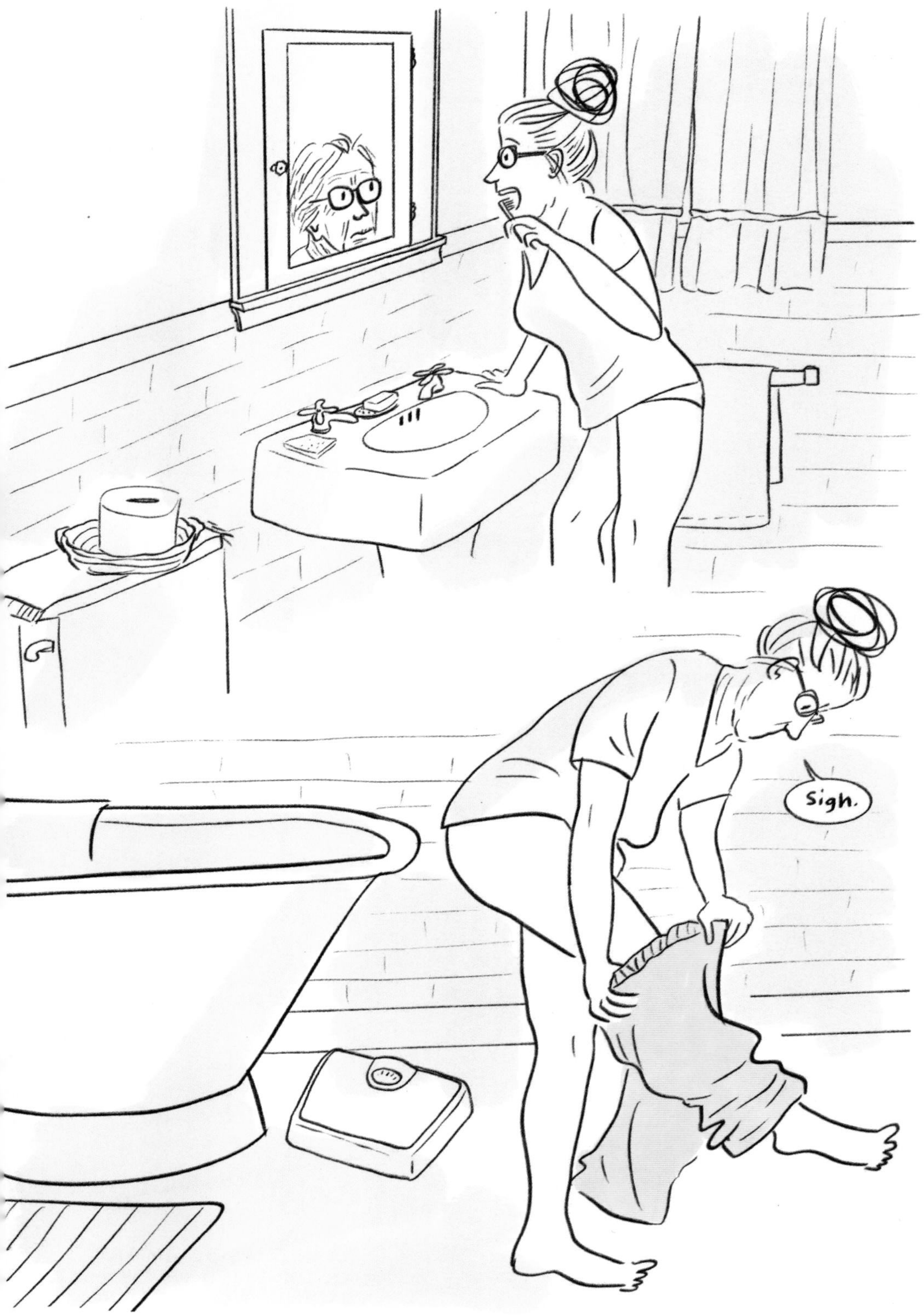
Sigh.

AS IF AN ALARM'S GONE OFF, I WAKE UP AT 3 A.M. IN A SWEAT.

Might as well open it.

THE BOX REVEALS THREE FIRMLY TIED BUNDLES OF CARDS— ONE FOR EACH OF US KIDS.

WELCOME!

Baby Dear!

TUCKED INSIDE A CARD FOR THE BIRTH OF MY SISTER I FIND A LETTER...

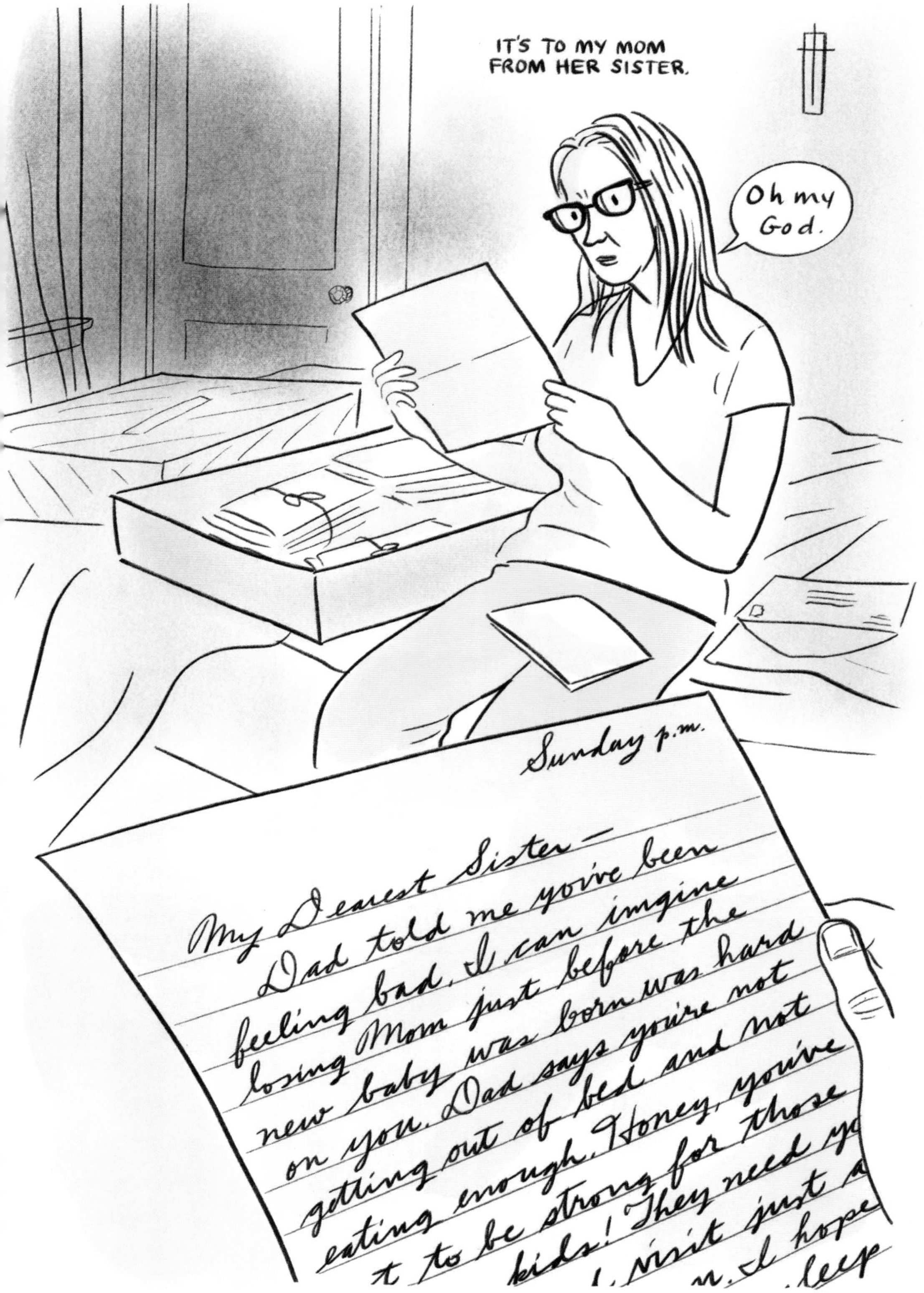
IT'S TO MY MOM FROM HER SISTER.
Oh my God.
Sunday p.m.
My Dearest Sister—
Dad told me you've been
feeling bad. I can imgine
losing Mom just before the
new baby was born was hard
on you. Dad says you're not
getting out of bed and not
eating enough. Honey, you've
to be strong for those
kids! They need
visit just
I hope

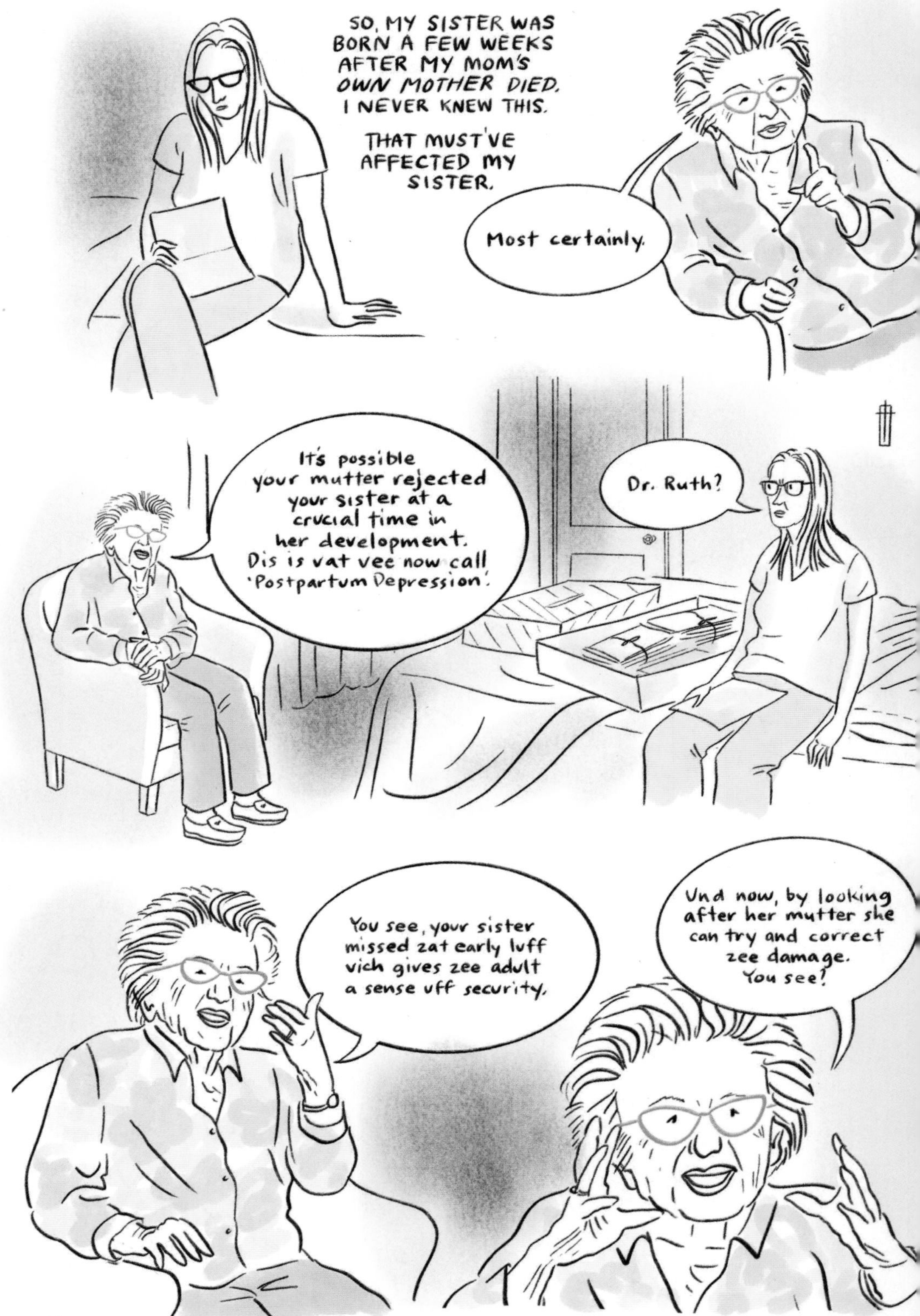
SO, MY SISTER WAS BORN A FEW WEEKS AFTER MY MOM'S *OWN MOTHER DIED.* I NEVER KNEW THIS.
THAT MUST'VE AFFECTED MY SISTER.
Most certainly.
It's possible your mutter rejected your sister at a crucial time in her development. Dis is vat vee now call 'Postpartum Depression'.
Dr. Ruth?
You see, your sister missed zat early luff vich gives zee adult a sense uff security.
Und now, by looking after her mutter she can try and correct zee damage. You see?

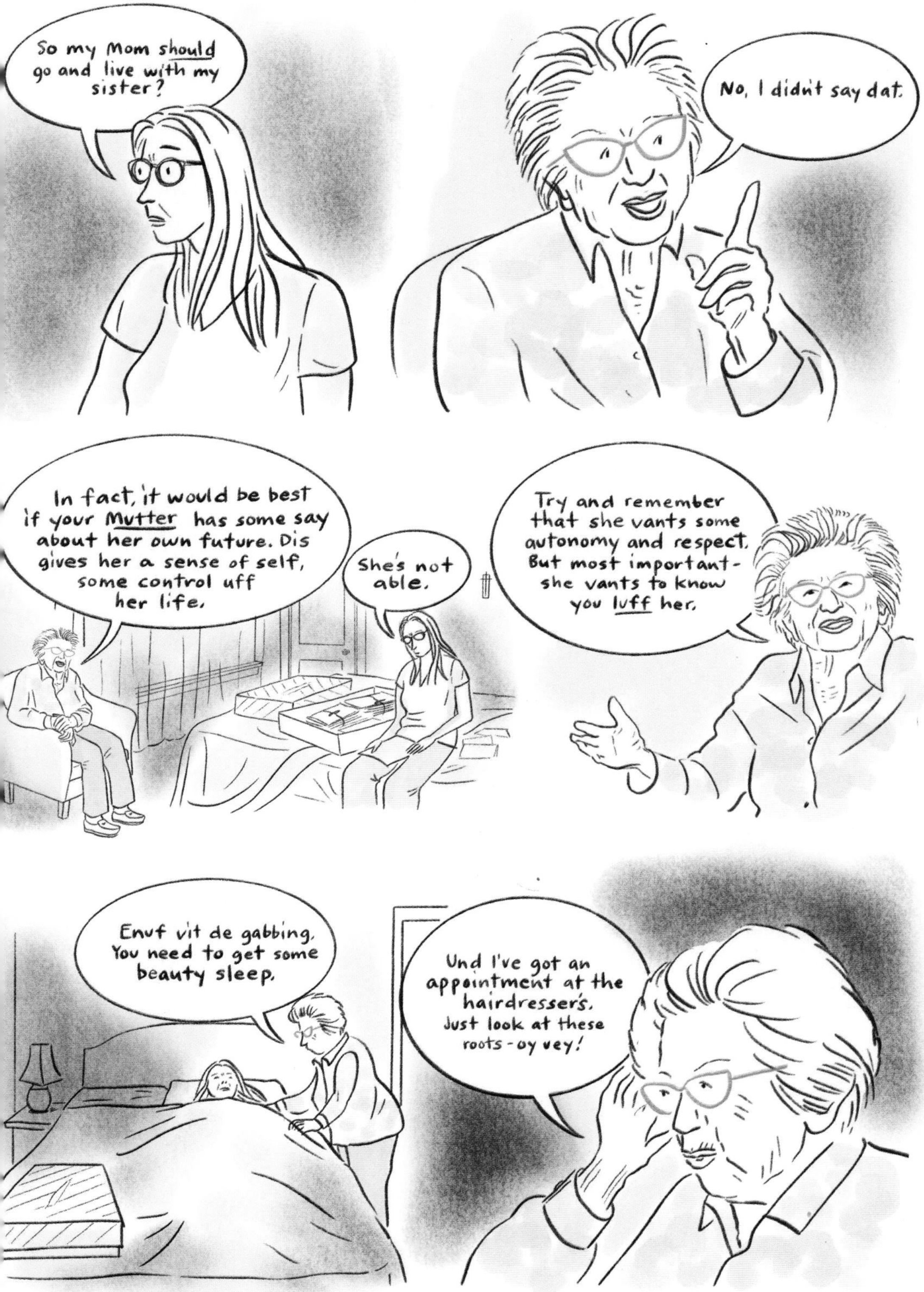
So my Mom should go and live with my sister?
No, I didn't say dat.
In fact, it would be best if your Mutter has some say about her own future. Dis gives her a sense of self, some control uff her life.
She's not able.
Try and remember that she vants some autonomy and respect. But most important- she vants to know you luff her.
Enuf vit de gabbing. You need to get some beauty sleep.
Und I've got an appointment at the hairdresser's. Just look at these roots - oy vey!

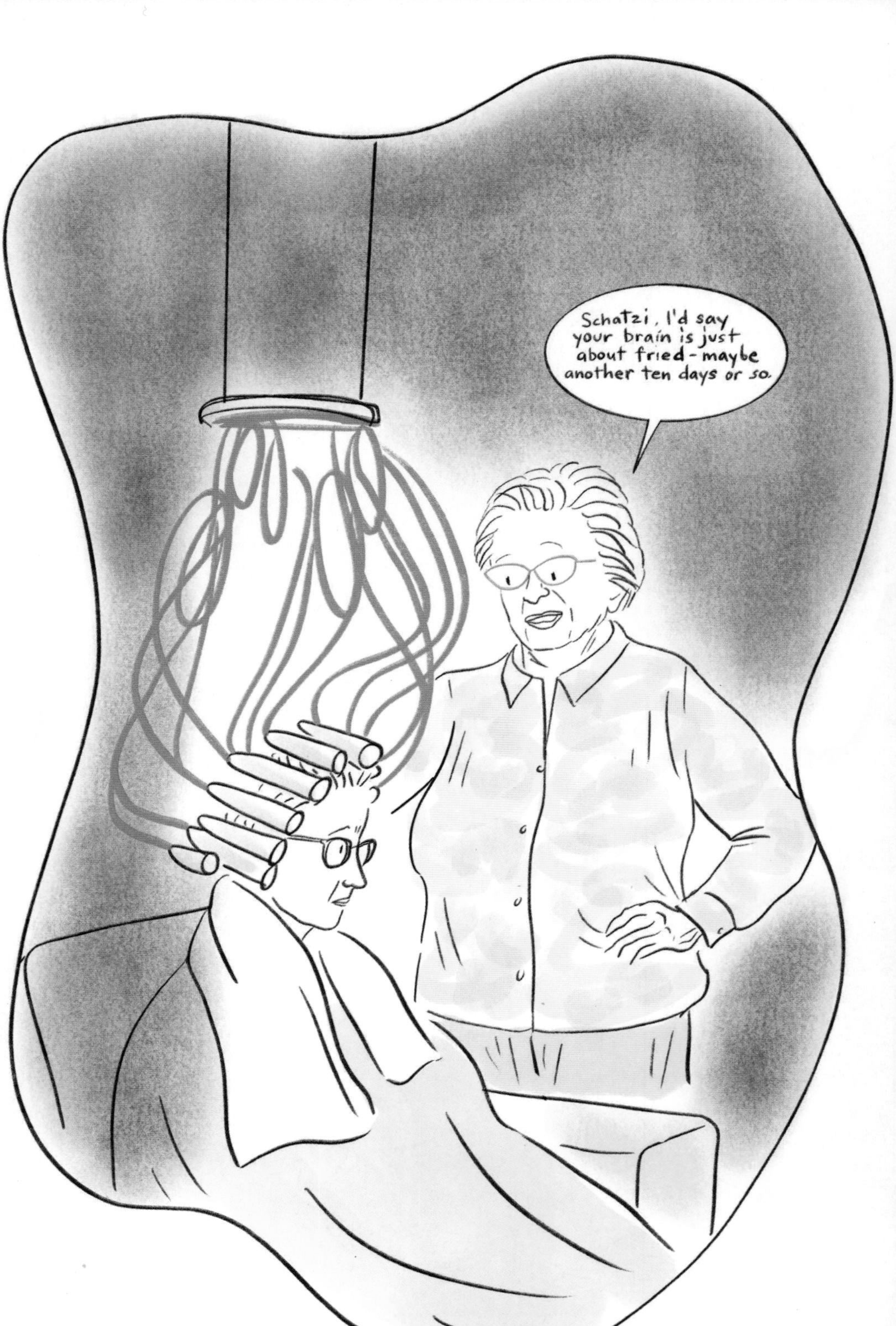
Schatzi, I'd say your brain is just about fried - maybe another ten days or so.

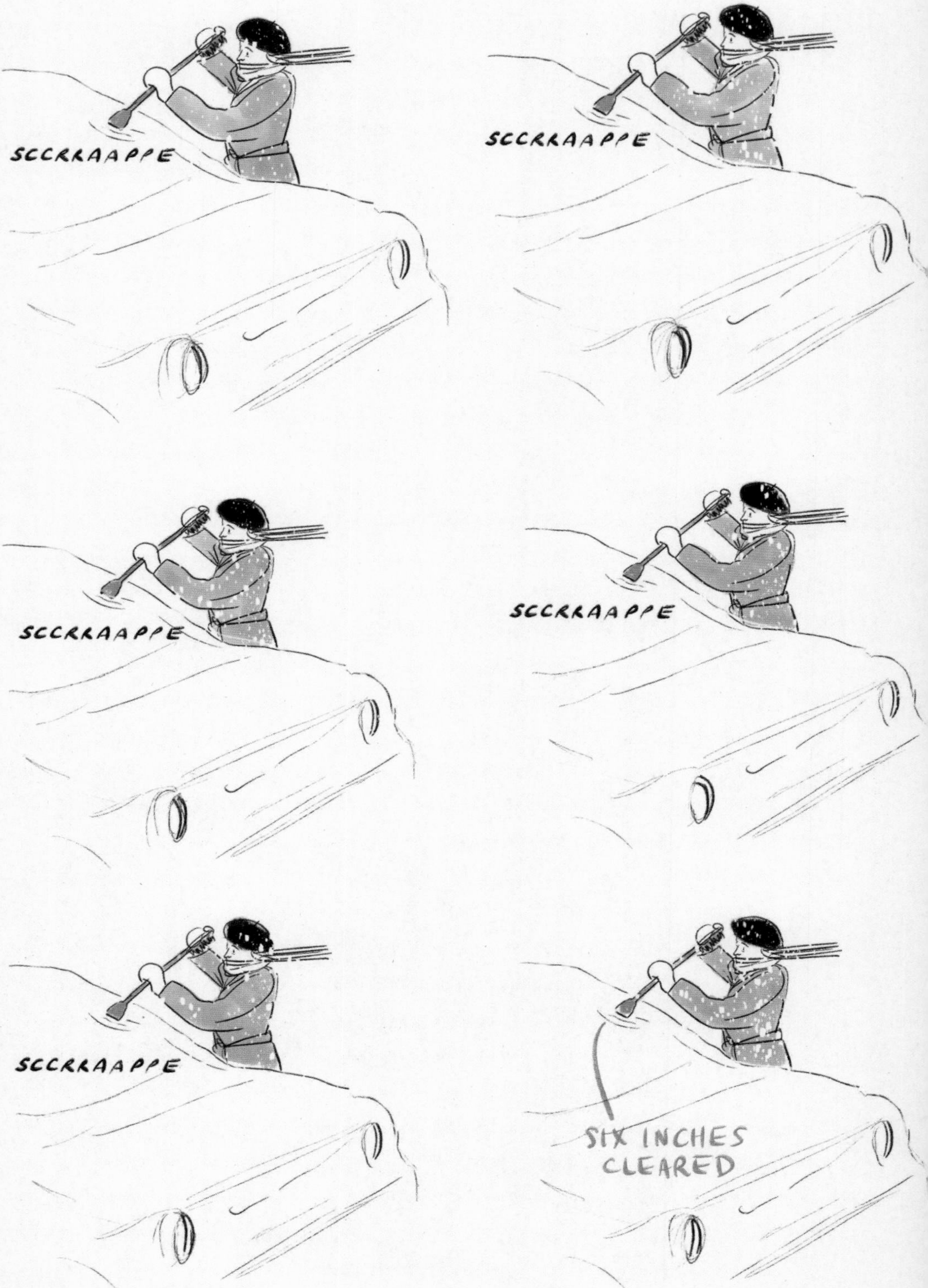
SCCRRAAPPE
SCCRRAAPPE
SCCRRAAPPE
SCCRRAAPPE
SCCRRAAPPE
SIX INCHES CLEARED

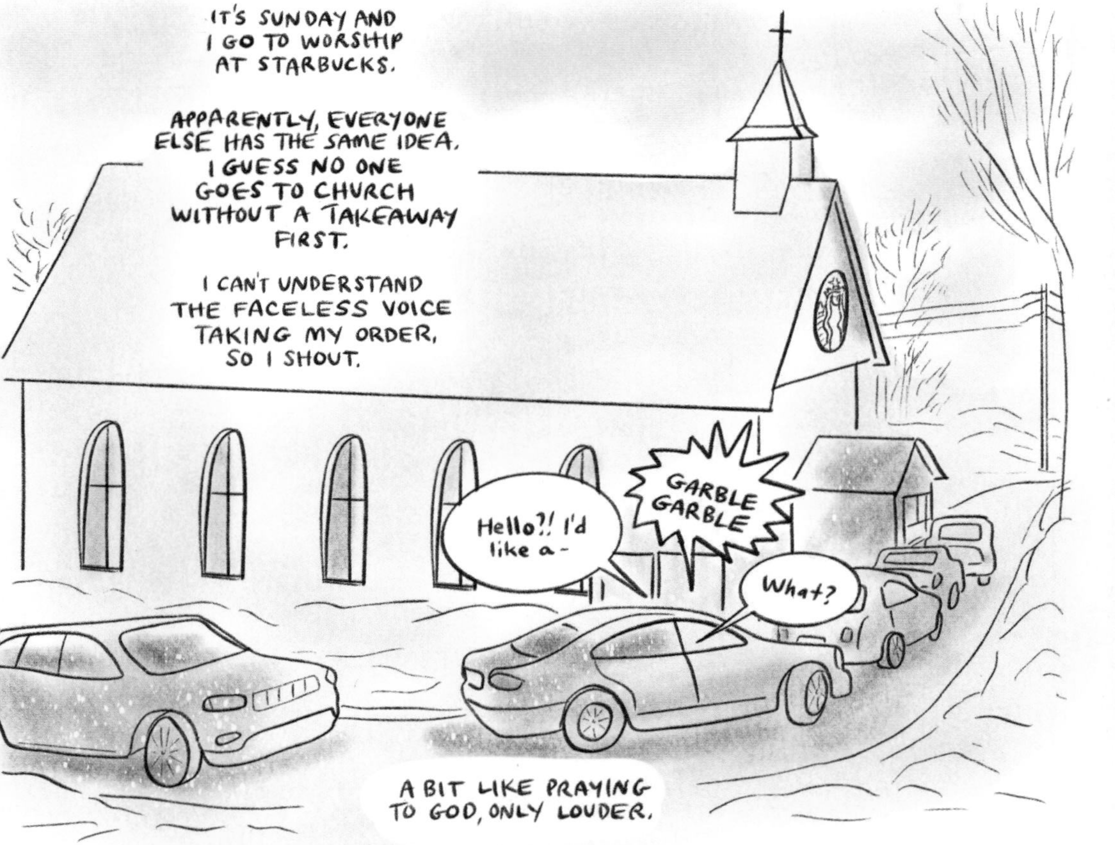
IT'S SUNDAY AND I GO TO WORSHIP AT STARBUCKS.
APPARENTLY, EVERYONE ELSE HAS THE SAME IDEA. I GUESS NO ONE GOES TO CHURCH WITHOUT A TAKEAWAY FIRST.
I CAN'T UNDERSTAND THE FACELESS VOICE TAKING MY ORDER, SO I SHOUT.
Hello?! I'd like a -
GARBLE GARBLE
What?
A BIT LIKE PRAYING TO GOD, ONLY LOUDER.

MY ORDER SIZES, AND THE FREQUENCY WITH WHICH I EAT IN THE CAR, ARE INCREASING THE LONGER I STAY HERE.

I'M GOING TO NEED A McDONALD'S SUPERSIZE FOR LUNCH.

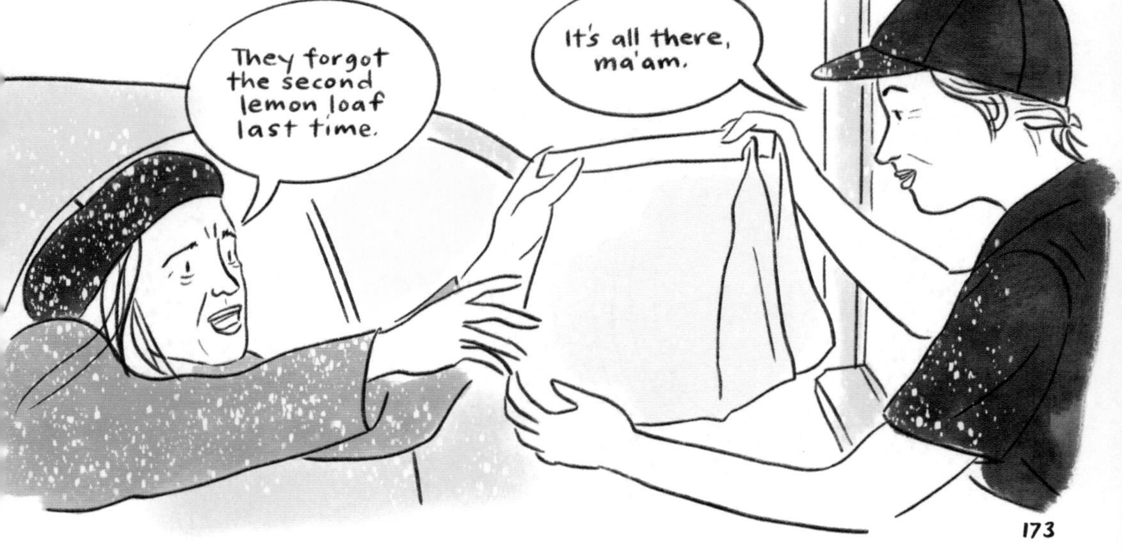
They forgot the second lemon loaf last time.
It's all there, ma'am.

I FIND MOM SITTING IN HER DARK ROOM, SNORING.
IT MAKES ME CRY.

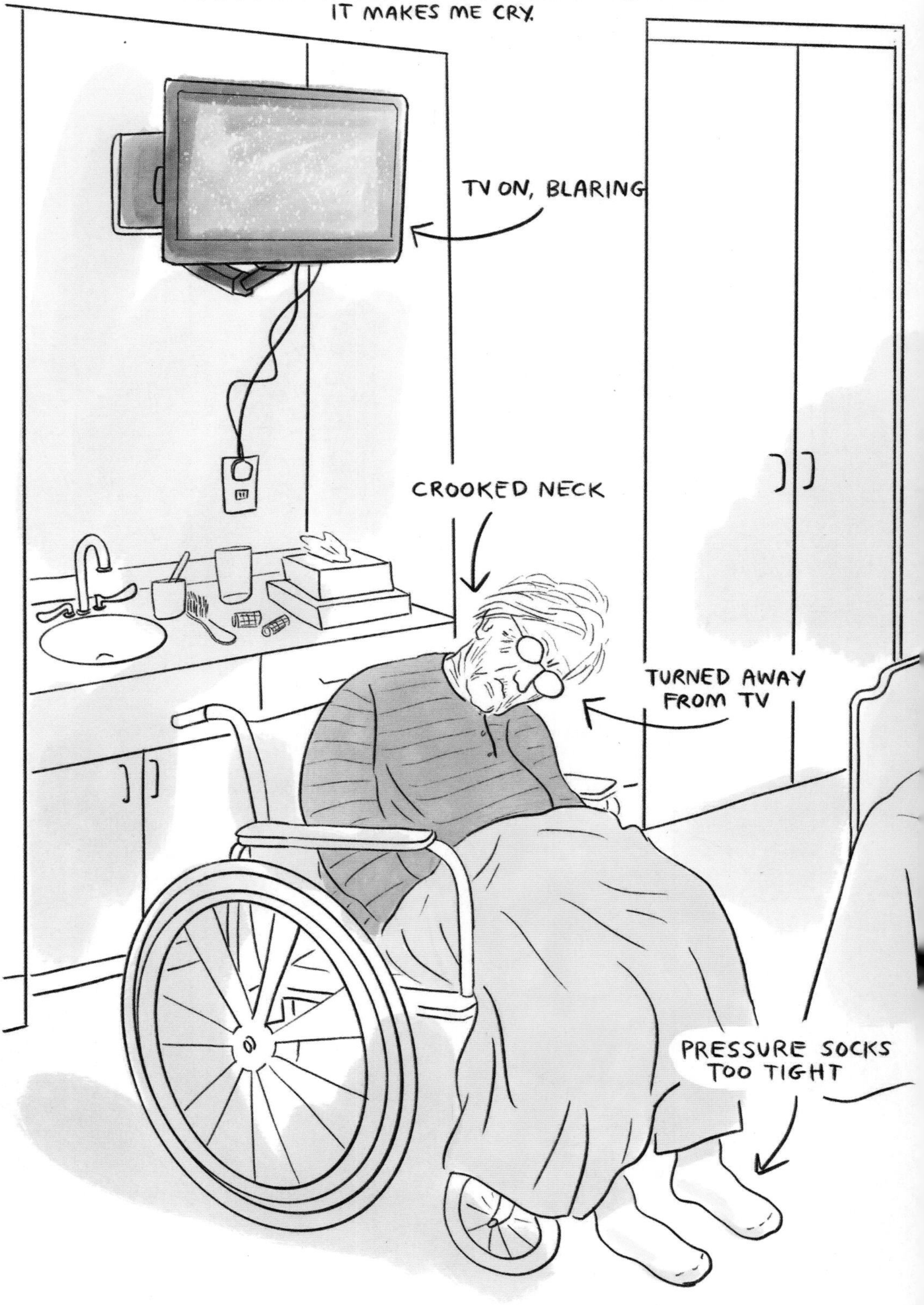
TV ON, BLARING
CROOKED NECK
TURNED AWAY FROM TV
PRESSURE SOCKS TOO TIGHT

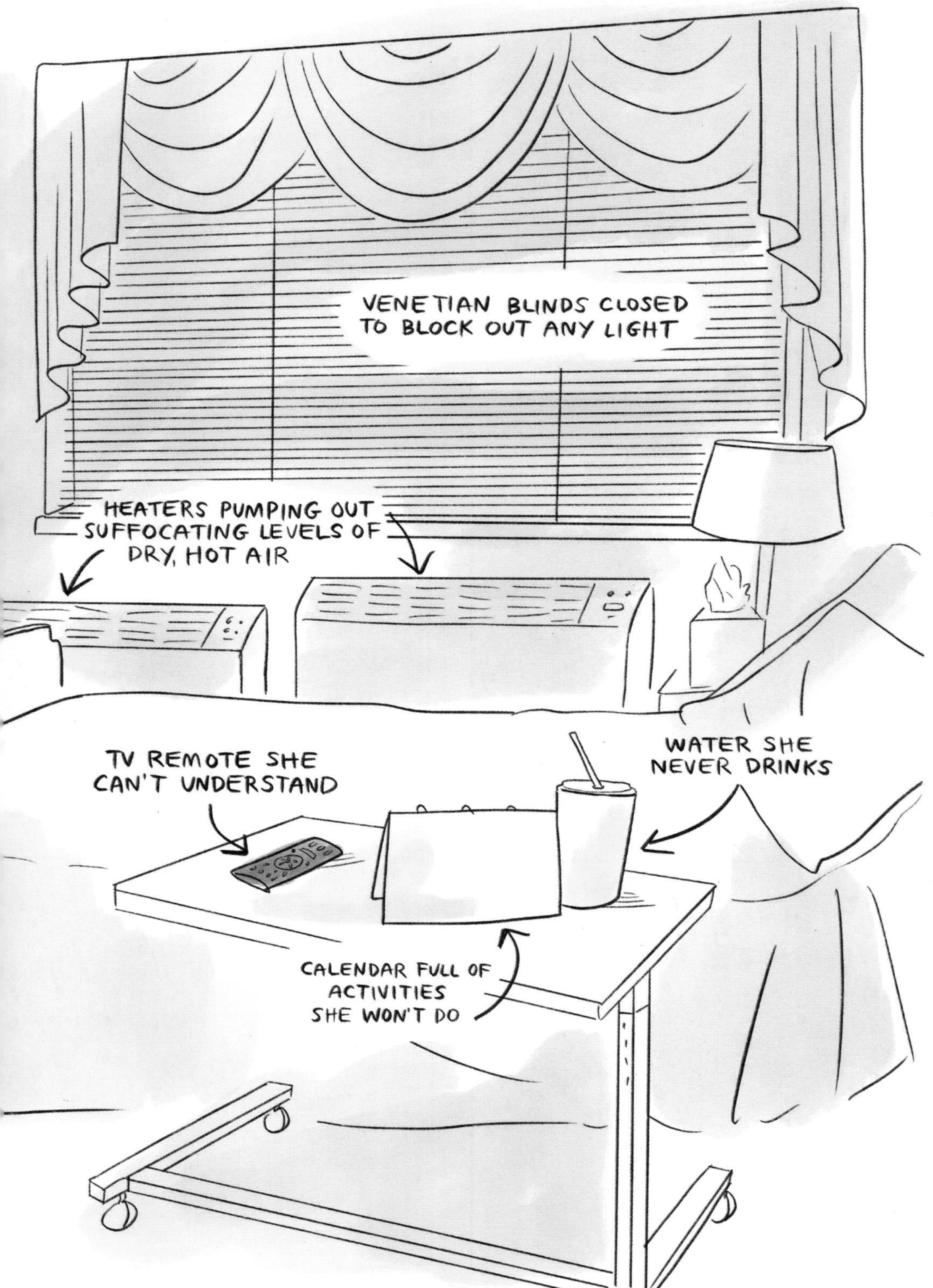
VENETIAN BLINDS CLOSED TO BLOCK OUT ANY LIGHT
HEATERS PUMPING OUT SUFFOCATING LEVELS OF DRY, HOT AIR
TV REMOTE SHE CAN'T UNDERSTAND
WATER SHE NEVER DRINKS
CALENDAR FULL OF ACTIVITIES SHE WON'T DO

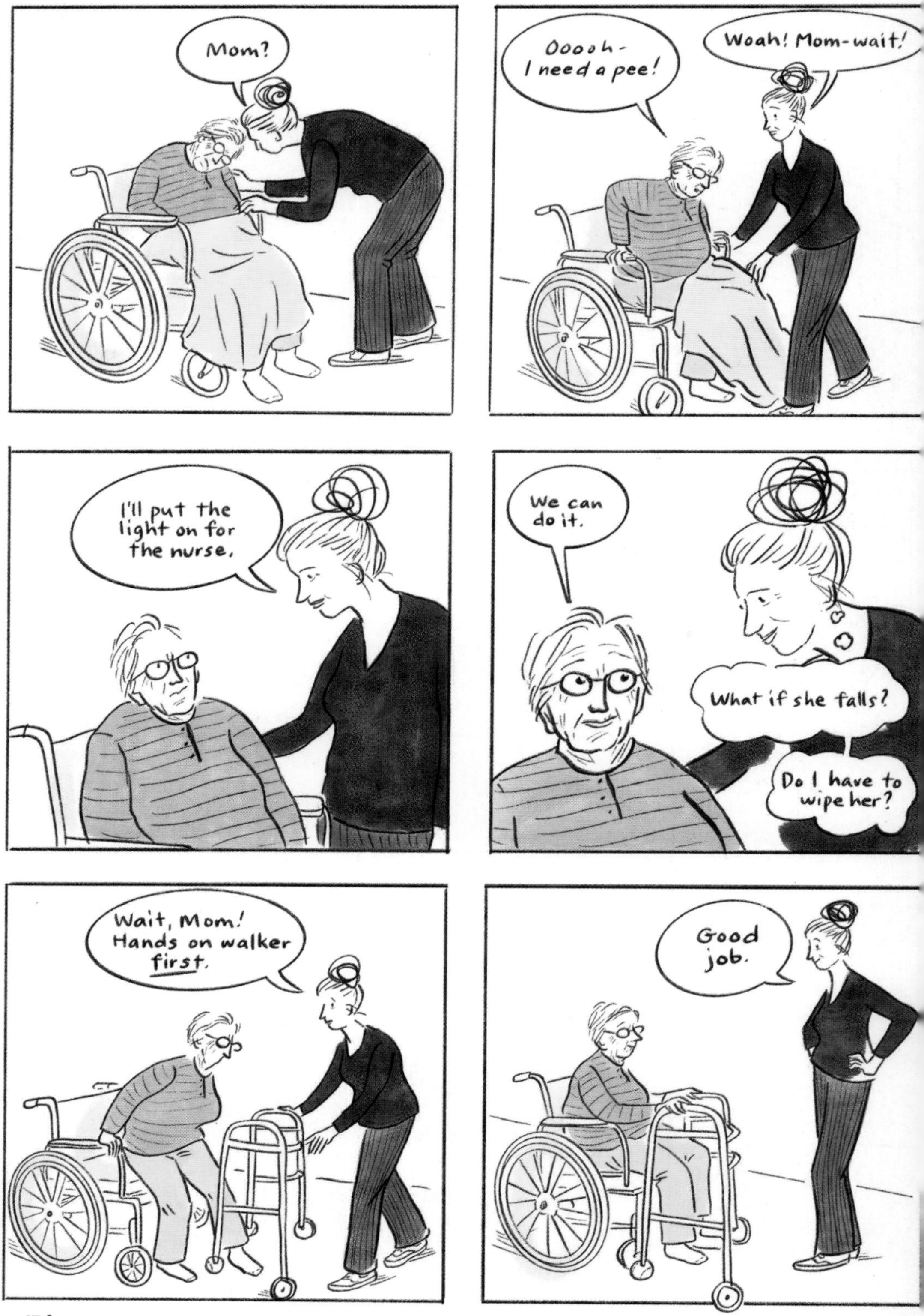
Mom?
Ooooh-
I need a pee!
Woah! Mom-wait!
I'll put the light on for the nurse.
We can do it.
What if she falls?
Do I have to wipe her?
Wait, Mom! Hands on walker first.
Good job.

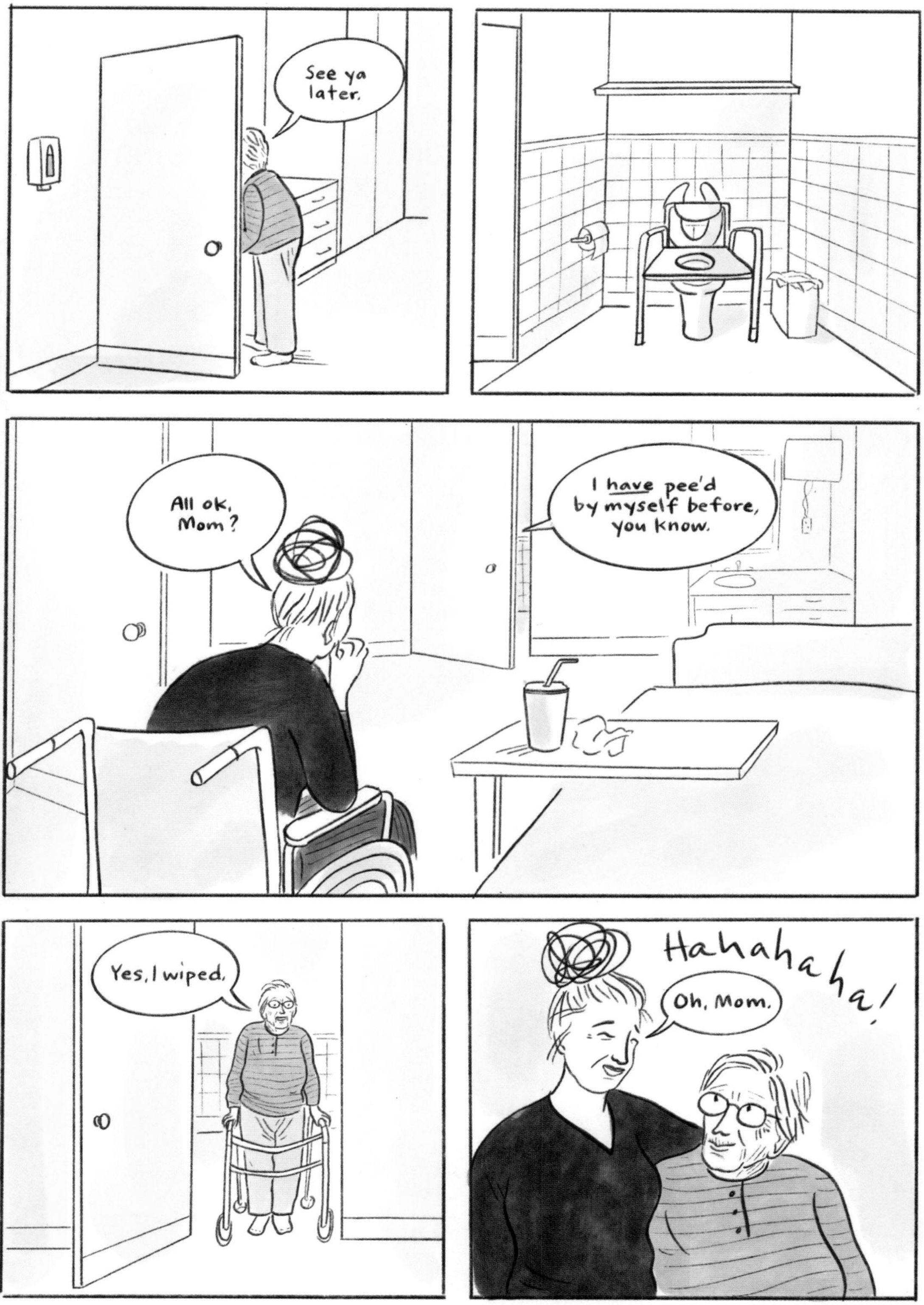
See ya later.
All ok, Mom?
I have pee'd by myself before, you know.
Yes, I wiped.
Hahahaha!
Oh, Mom.

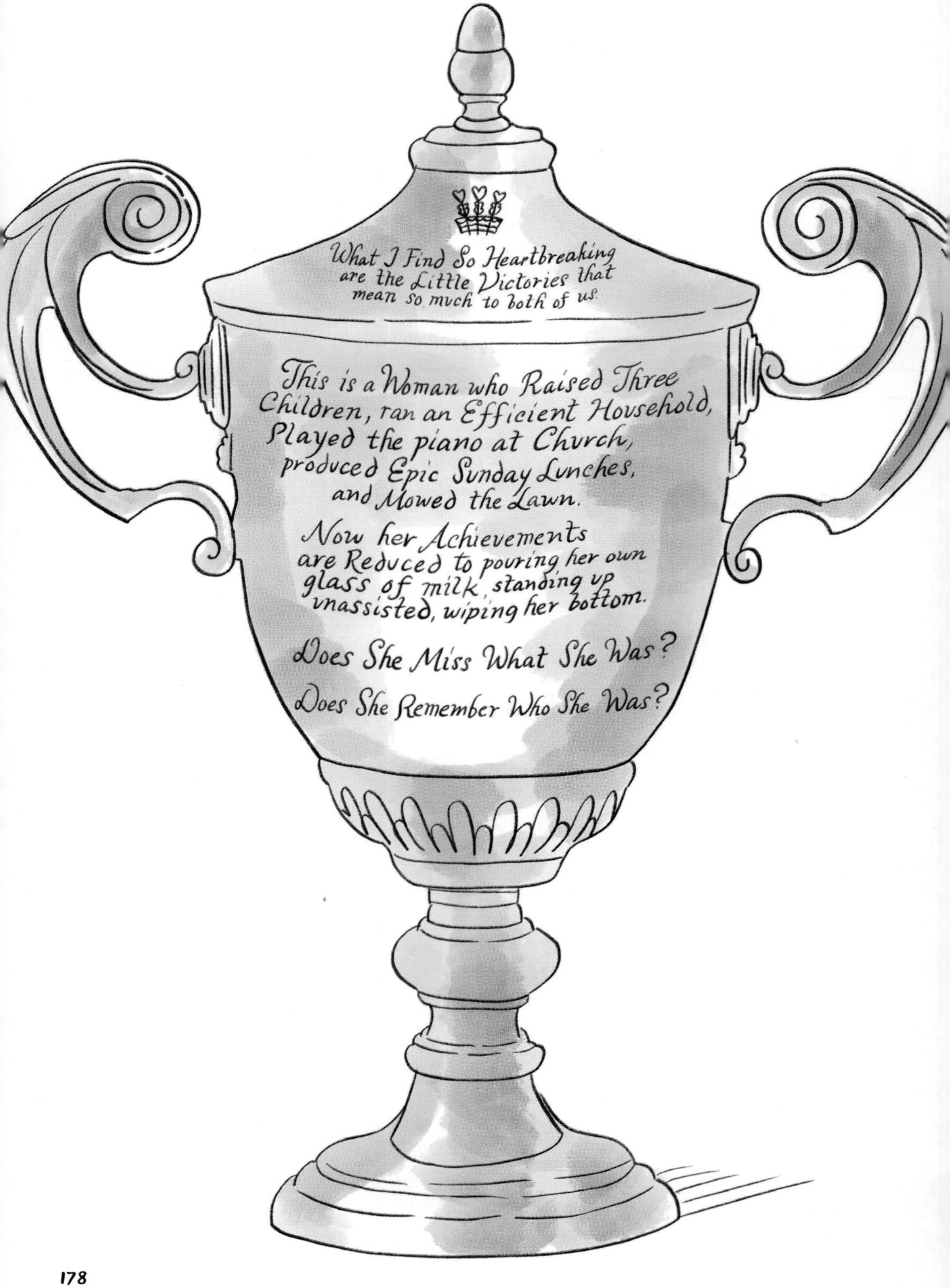

What I Find So Heartbreaking are the Little Victories that mean so much to both of us.
This is a Woman who Raised Three Children, ran an Efficient Household, Played the piano at Church, produced Epic Sunday Lunches, and Mowed the Lawn.
Now her Achievements are Reduced to pouring her own glass of milk, standing up unassisted, wiping her bottom.
Does She Miss What She Was?
Does She Remember Who She Was?

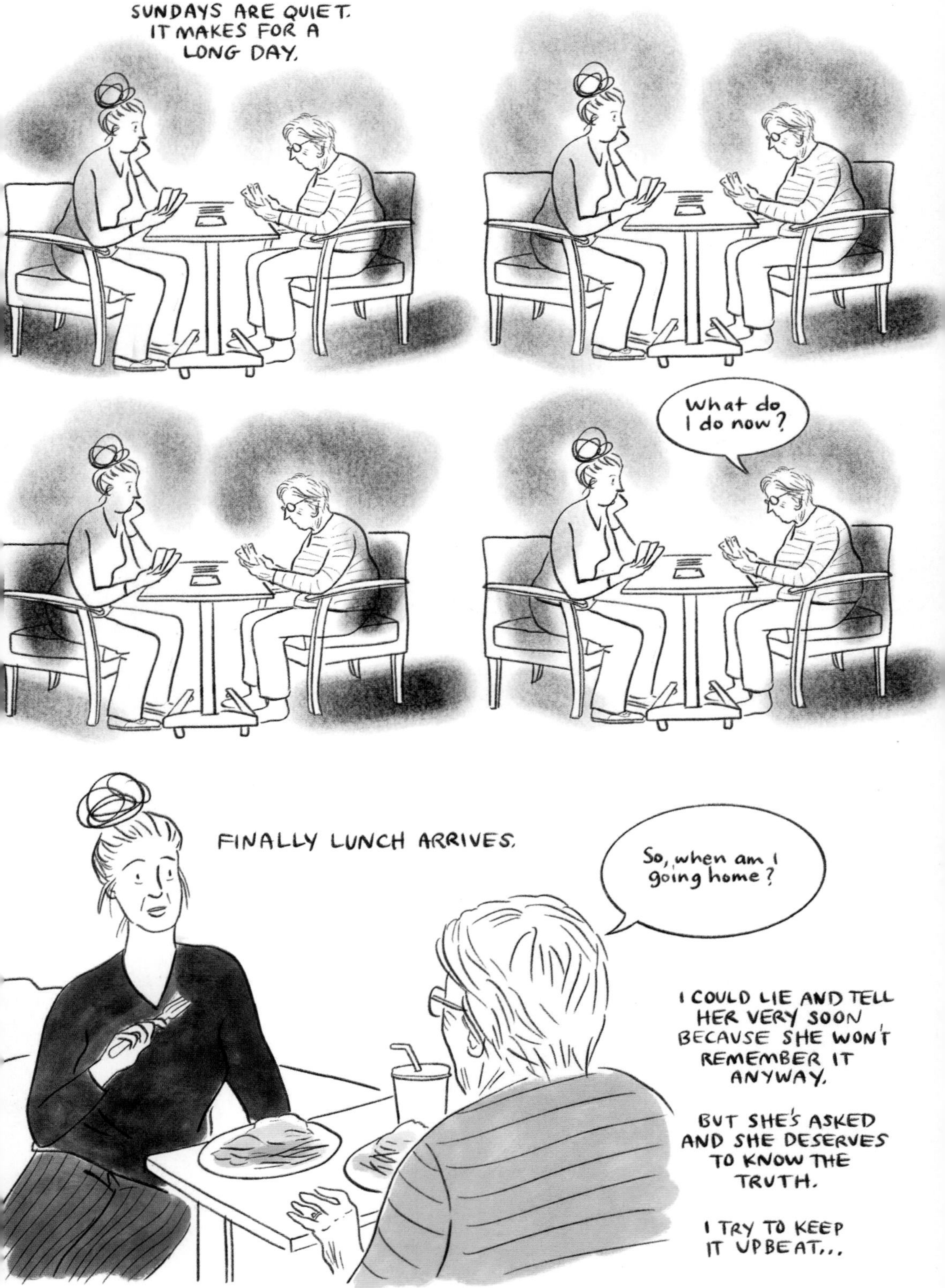
SUNDAYS ARE QUIET. IT MAKES FOR A LONG DAY.
What do I do now?
FINALLY LUNCH ARRIVES.
So, when am I going home?
I COULD LIE AND TELL HER VERY SOON BECAUSE SHE WON'T REMEMBER IT ANYWAY.
BUT SHE'S ASKED AND SHE DESERVES TO KNOW THE TRUTH.
I TRY TO KEEP IT UPBEAT...

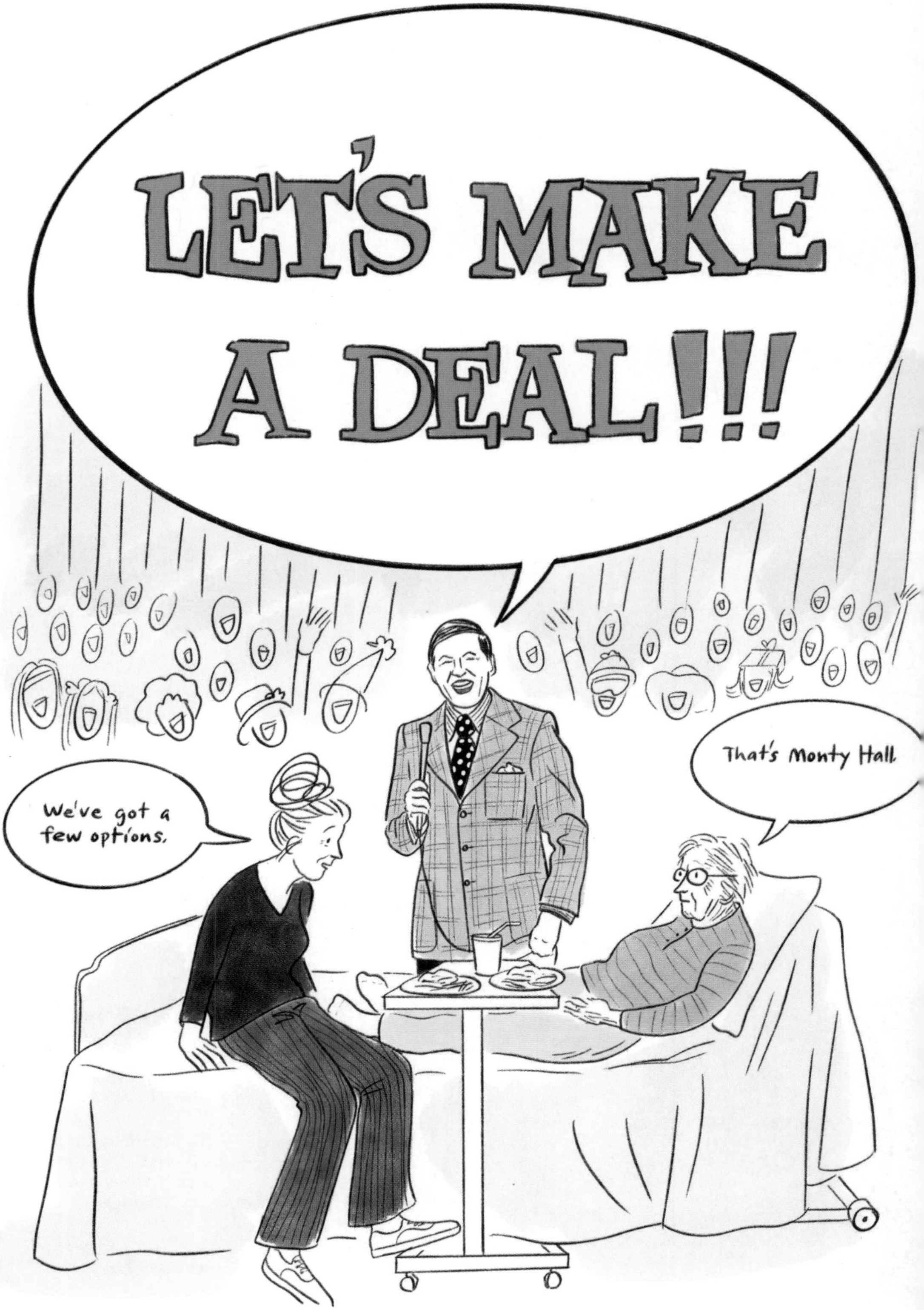
LET'S MAKE A DEAL!!!
We've got a few options.
That's Monty Hall.

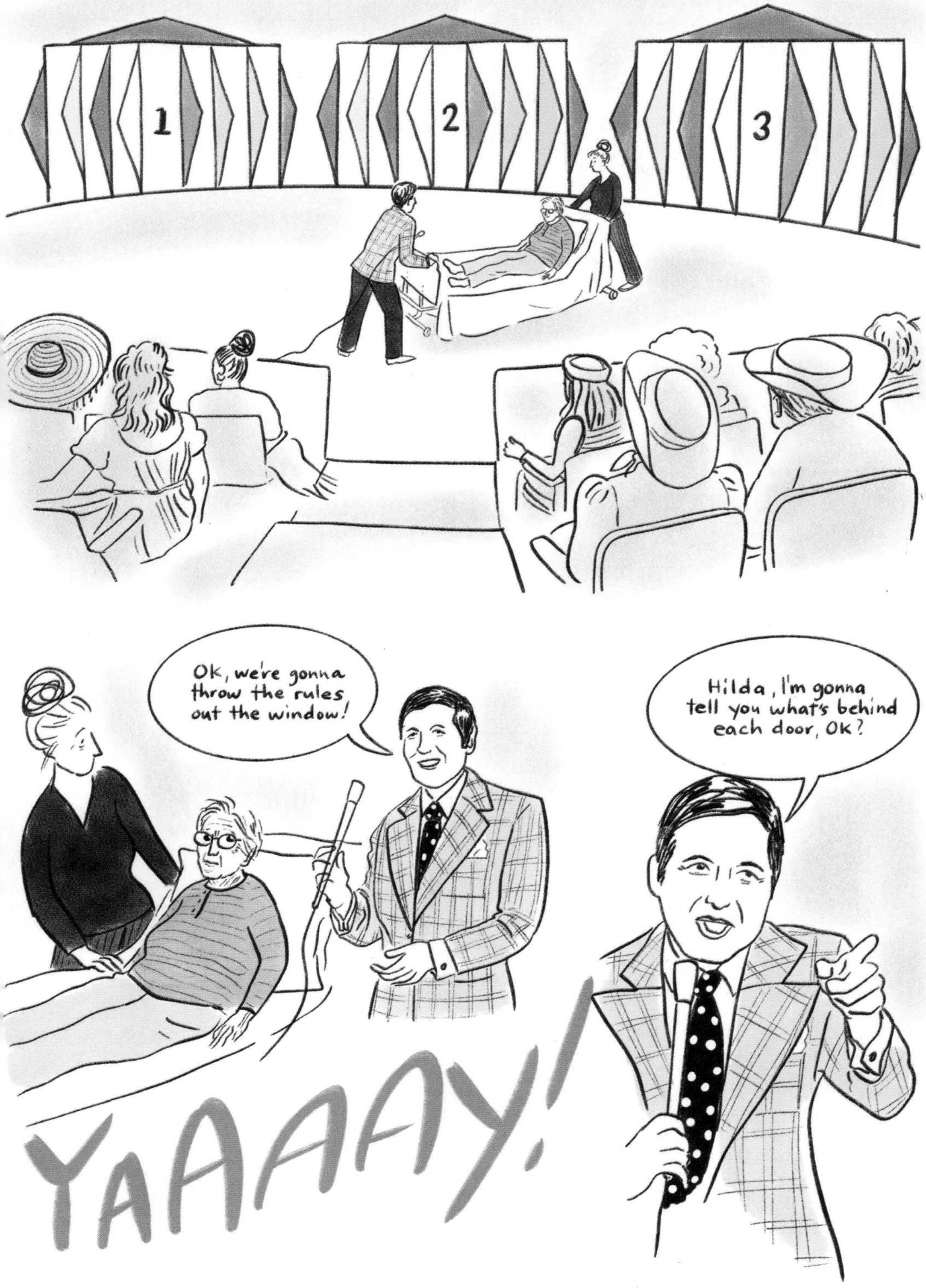
1
2
3
Ok, we're gonna throw the rules out the window!
Hilda, I'm gonna tell you what's behind each door, OK?
YAAAAY!

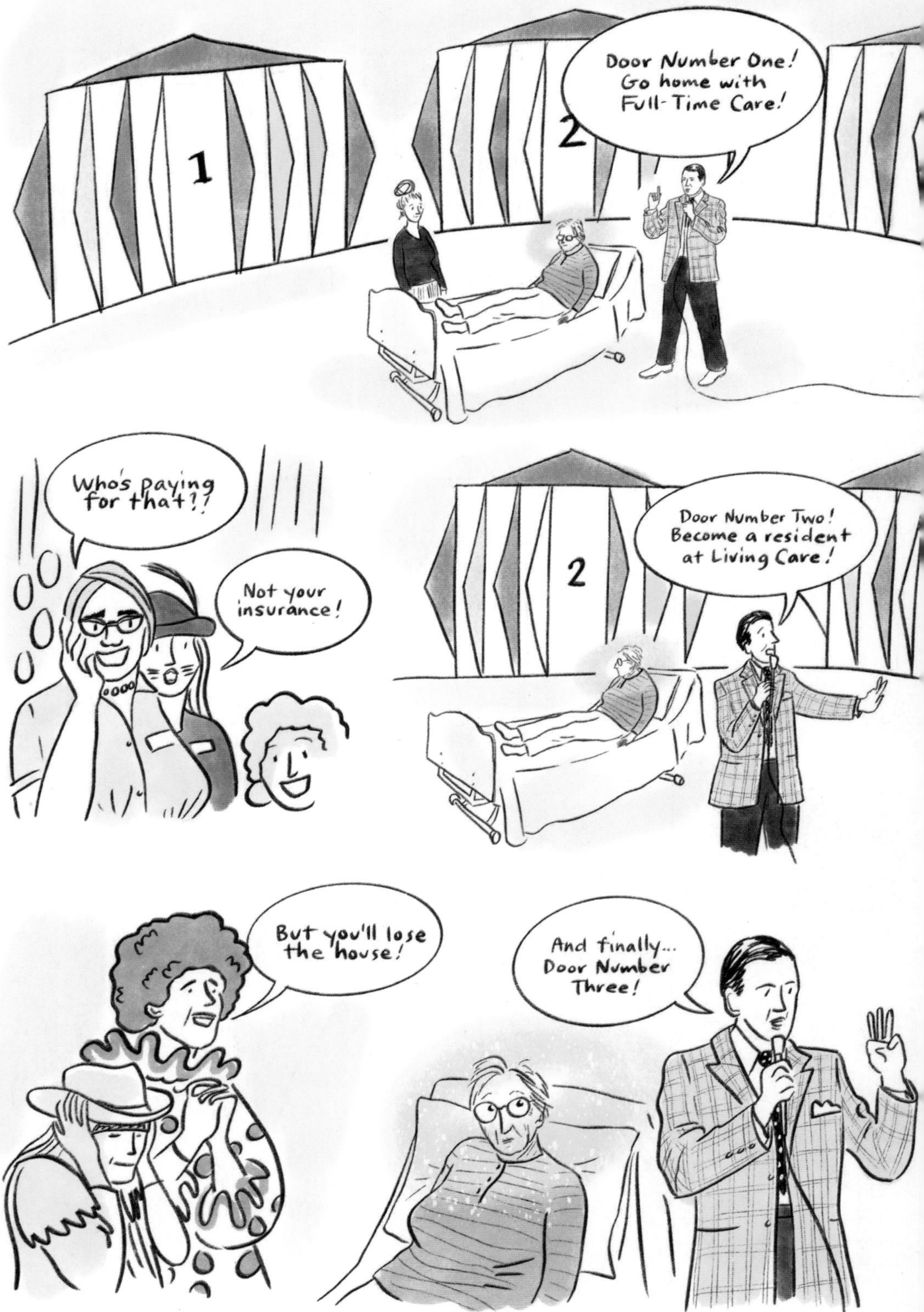
Door Number One! Go home with Full-Time Care!
Who's paying for that?!
Not your insurance!
Door Number Two! Become a resident at Living Care!
But you'll lose the house!
And finally... Door Number Three!

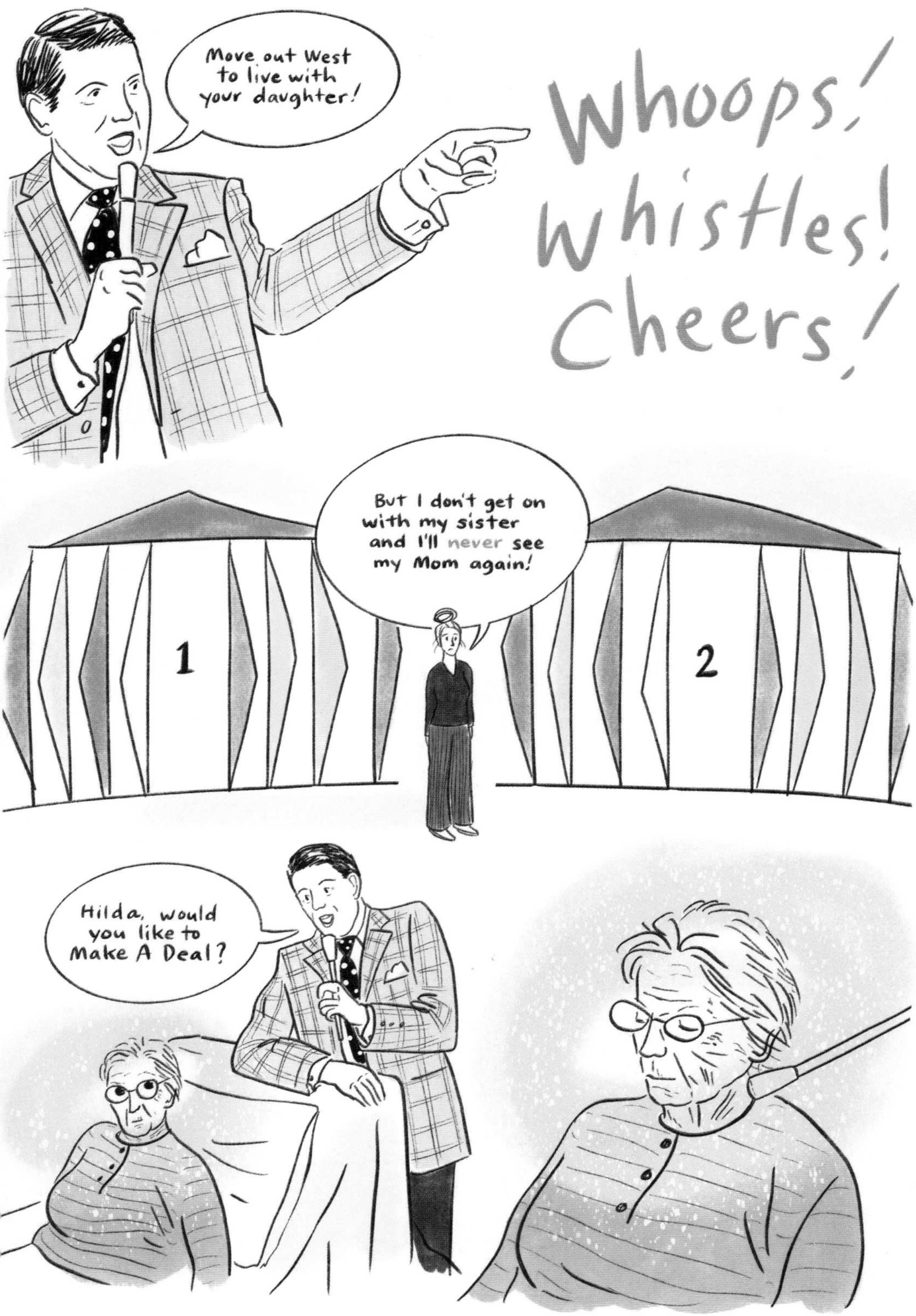
Move out West to live with your daughter!
Whoops! Whistles! Cheers!
But I don't get on with my sister and I'll never see my Mom again!
1
2
Hilda, would you like to Make A Deal?

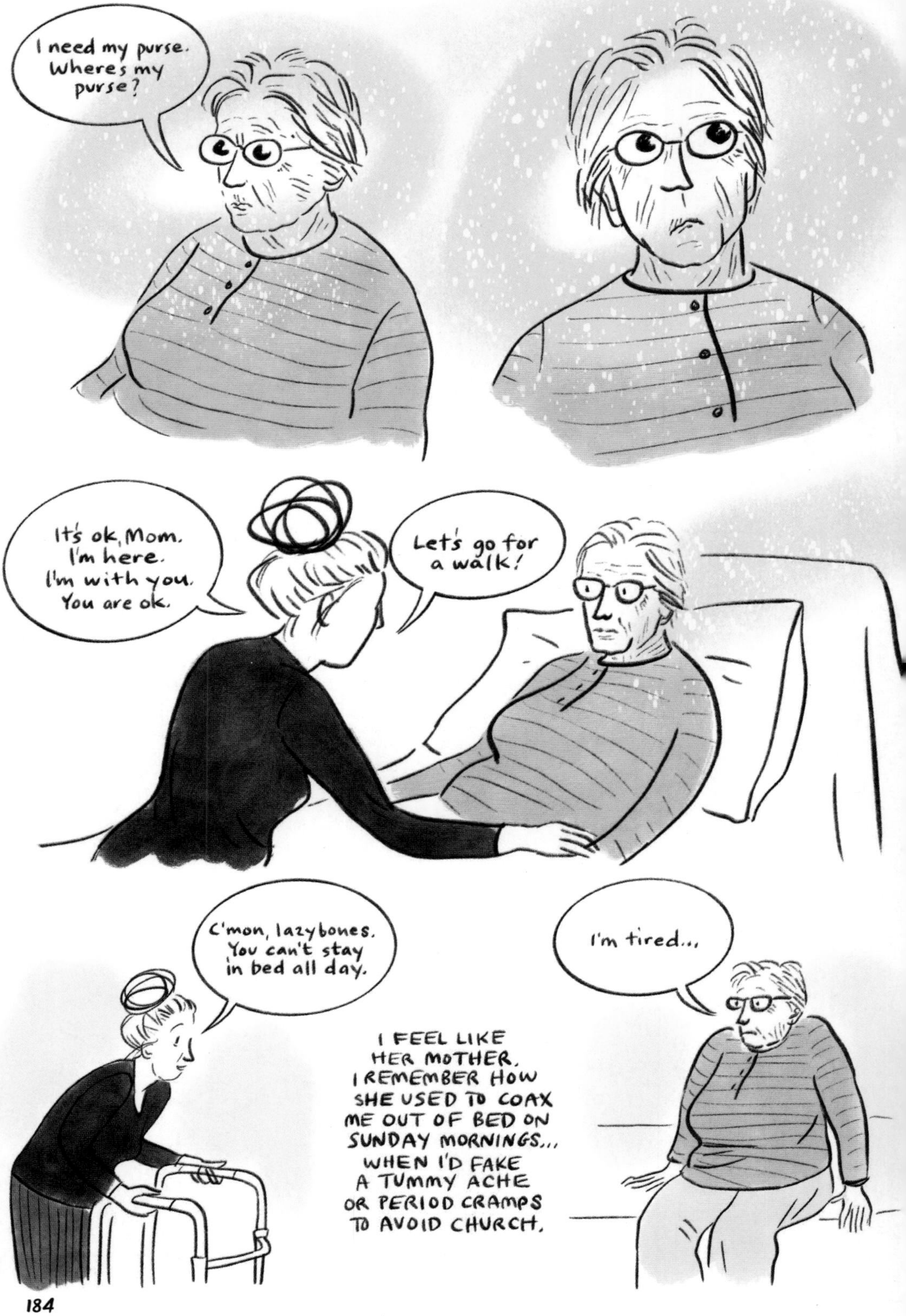
I need my purse. Where's my purse?
It's ok, Mom. I'm here. I'm with you. You are ok.
Let's go for a walk!
C'mon, lazybones. You can't stay in bed all day.
I'm tired...
I FEEL LIKE HER MOTHER. I REMEMBER HOW SHE USED TO COAX ME OUT OF BED ON SUNDAY MORNINGS... WHEN I'D FAKE A TUMMY ACHE OR PERIOD CRAMPS TO AVOID CHURCH.

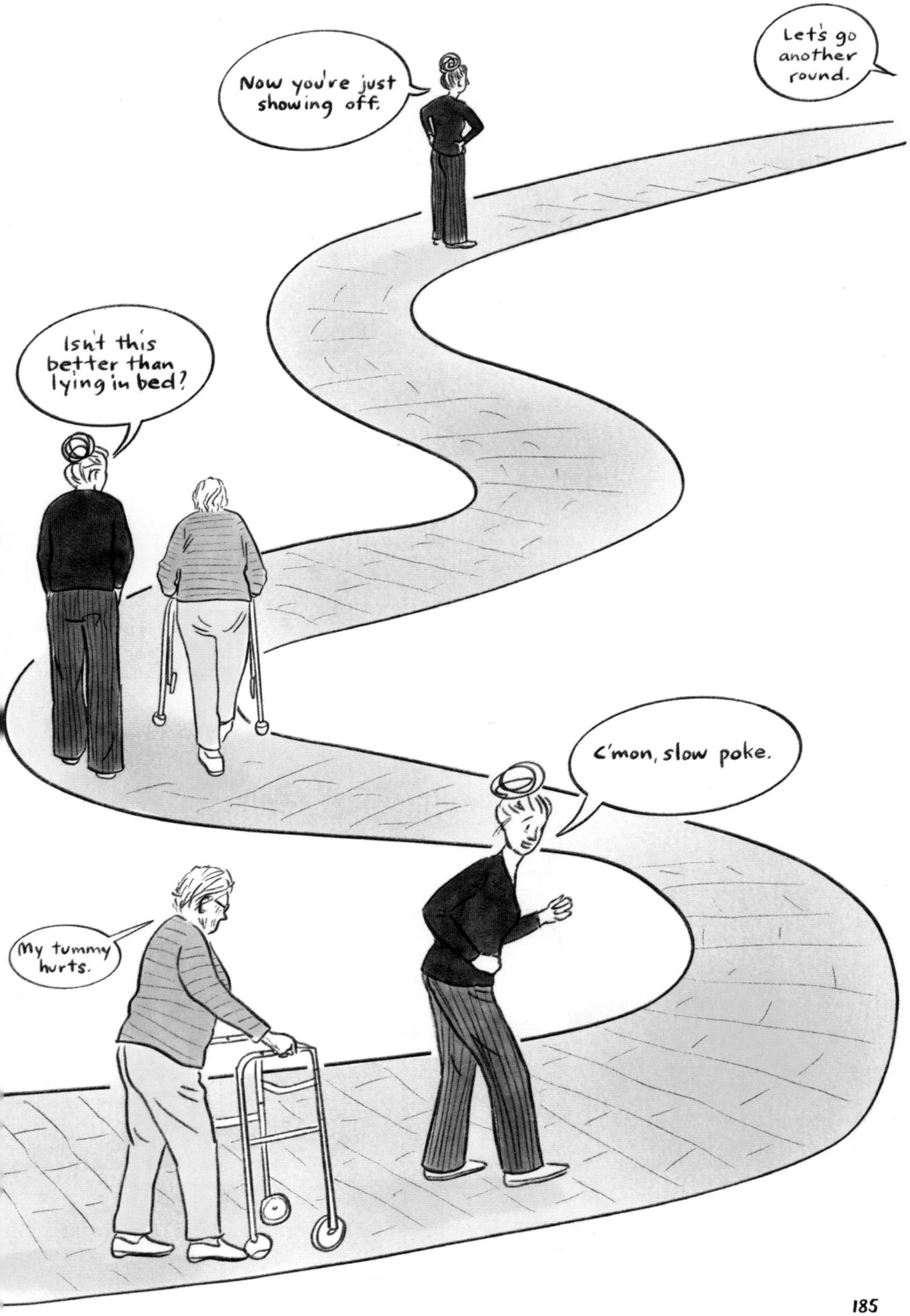
Now you're just showing off.
Let's go another round.
Isn't this better than lying in bed?
C'mon, slow poke.
My tummy hurts.

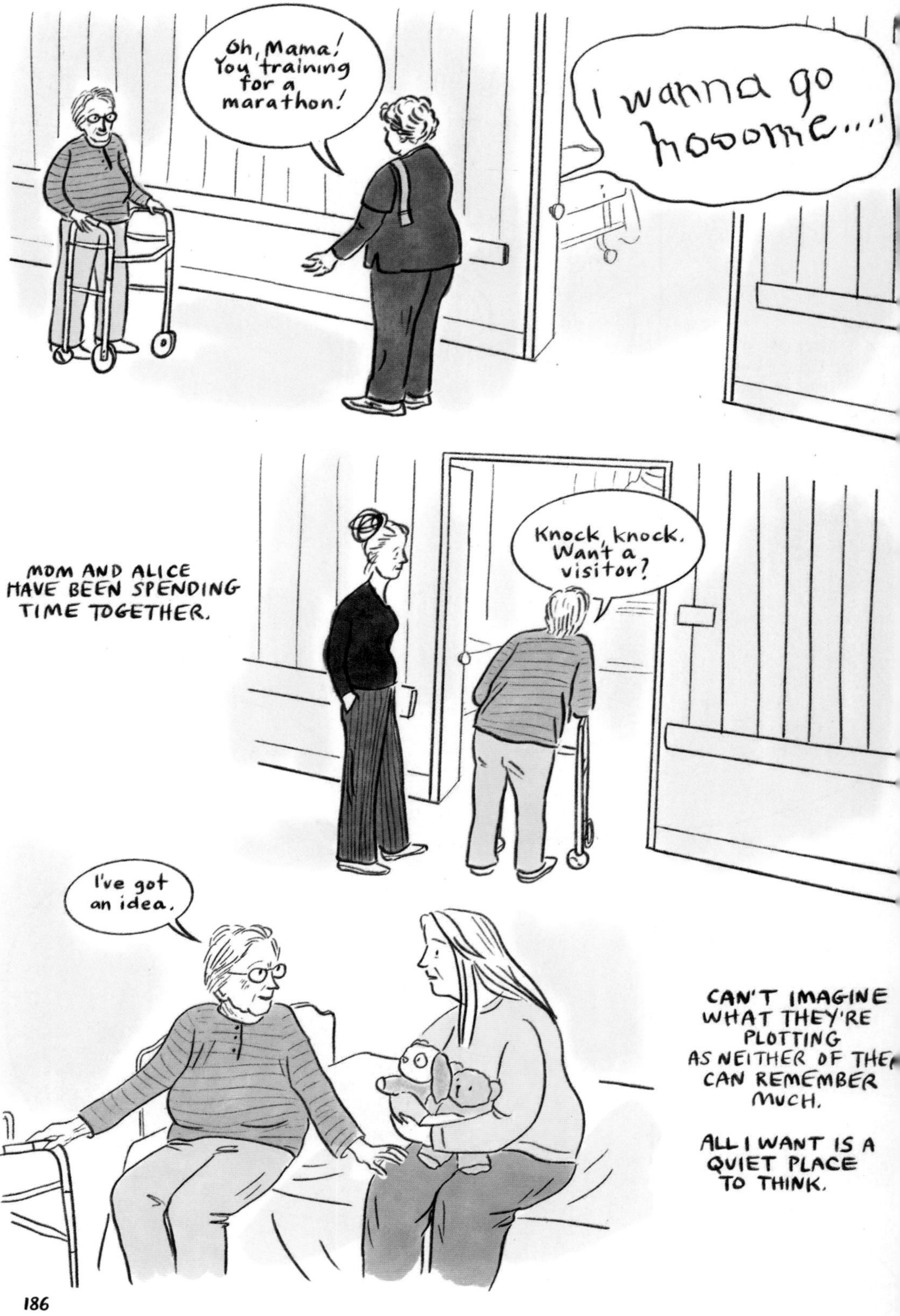
Oh, Mama! You training for a marathon!
I wanna go hooome....
MOM AND ALICE HAVE BEEN SPENDING TIME TOGETHER.
Knock, knock. Want a visitor?
I've got an idea.
CAN'T IMAGINE WHAT THEY'RE PLOTTING AS NEITHER OF THE CAN REMEMBER MUCH.
ALL I WANT IS A QUIET PLACE TO THINK.

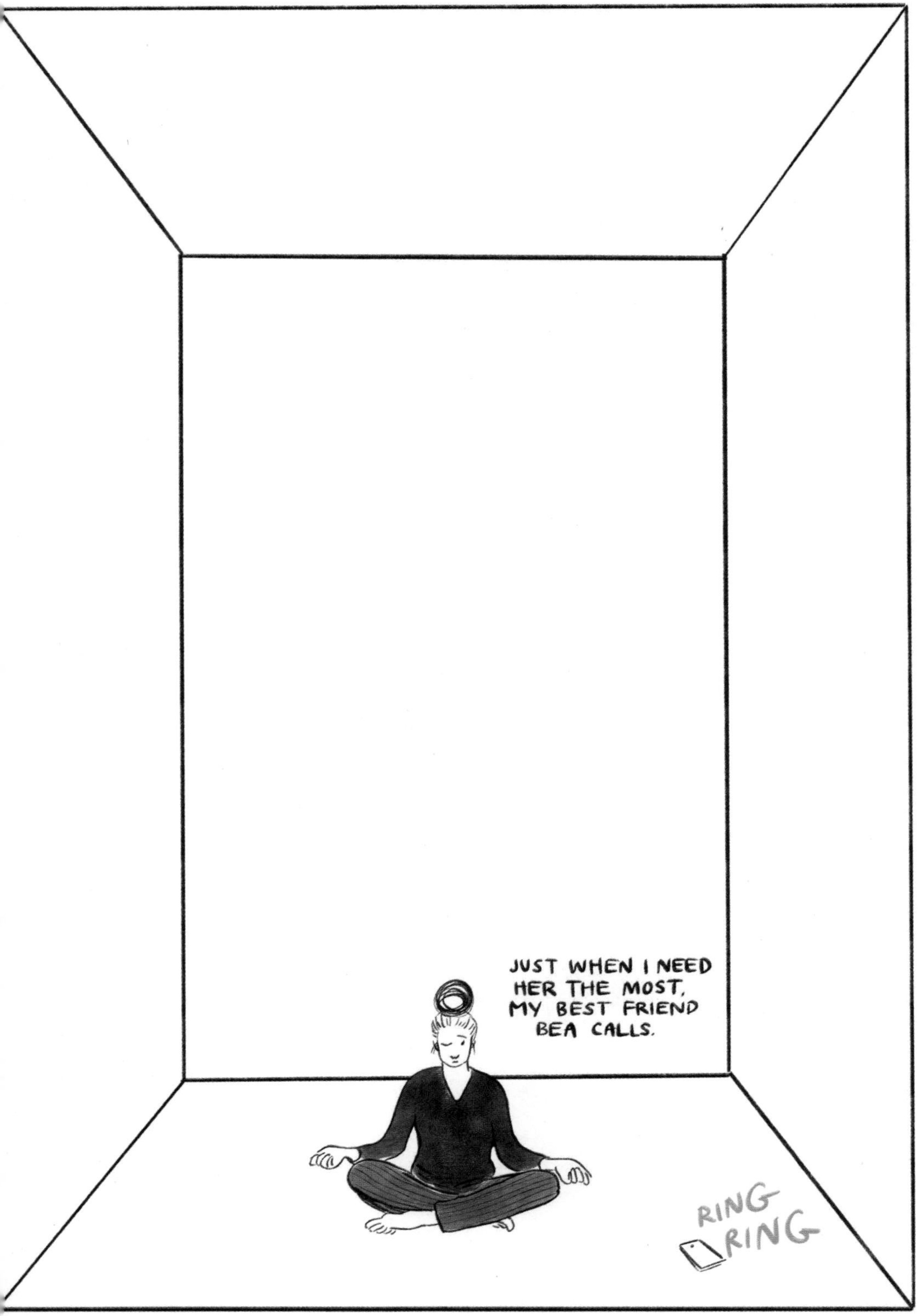
JUST WHEN I NEED HER THE MOST, MY BEST FRIEND BEA CALLS.
RING RING

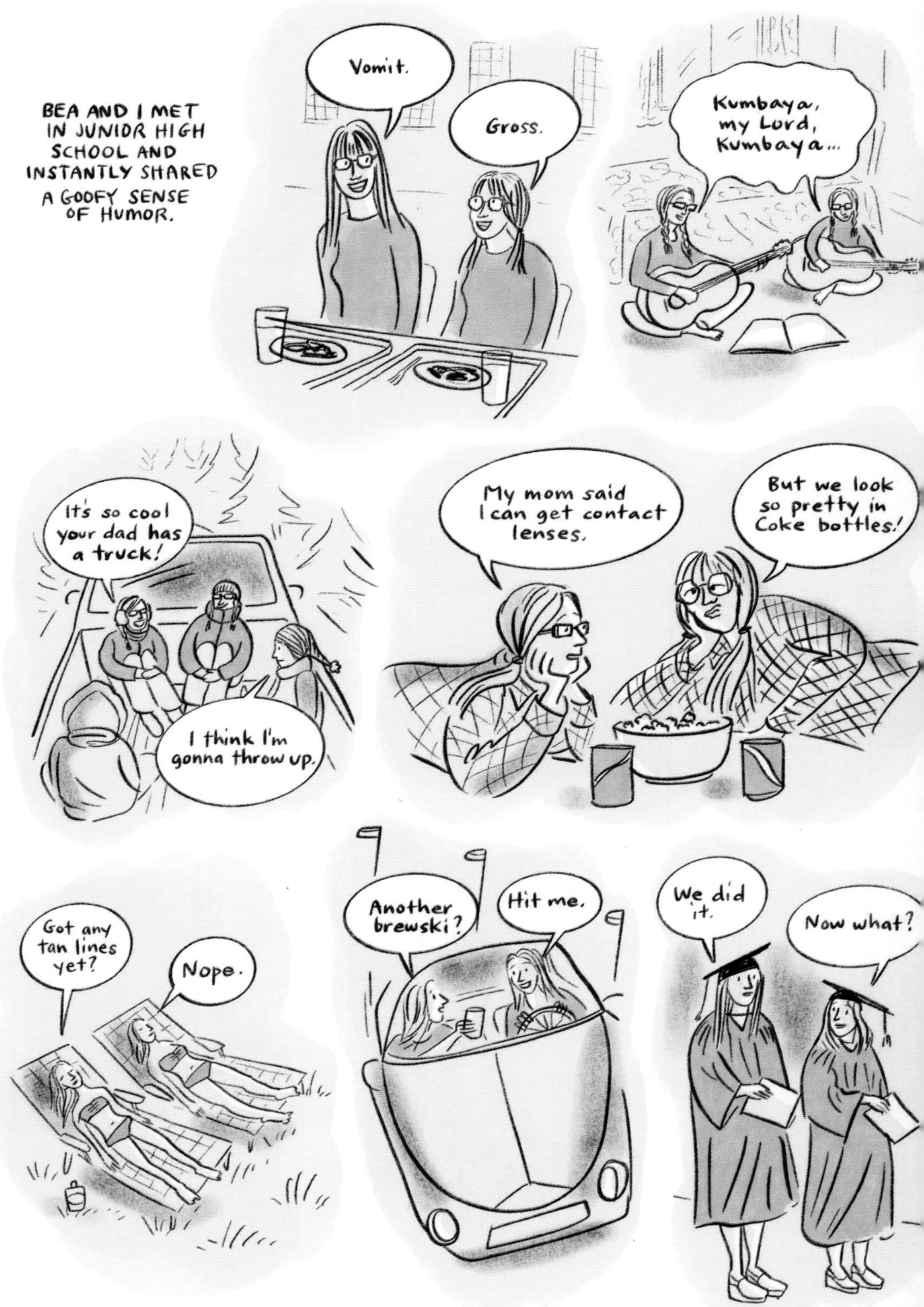
BEA AND I MET IN JUNIOR HIGH SCHOOL AND INSTANTLY SHARED A GOOFY SENSE OF HUMOR.
Vomit.
Gross.
Kumbaya, my Lord, Kumbaya...
It's so cool your dad has a truck!
I think I'm gonna throw up.
My mom said I can get contact lenses.
But we look so pretty in Coke bottles!
Got any tan lines yet?
Nope.
Another brewski?
Hit me.
We did it.
Now what?

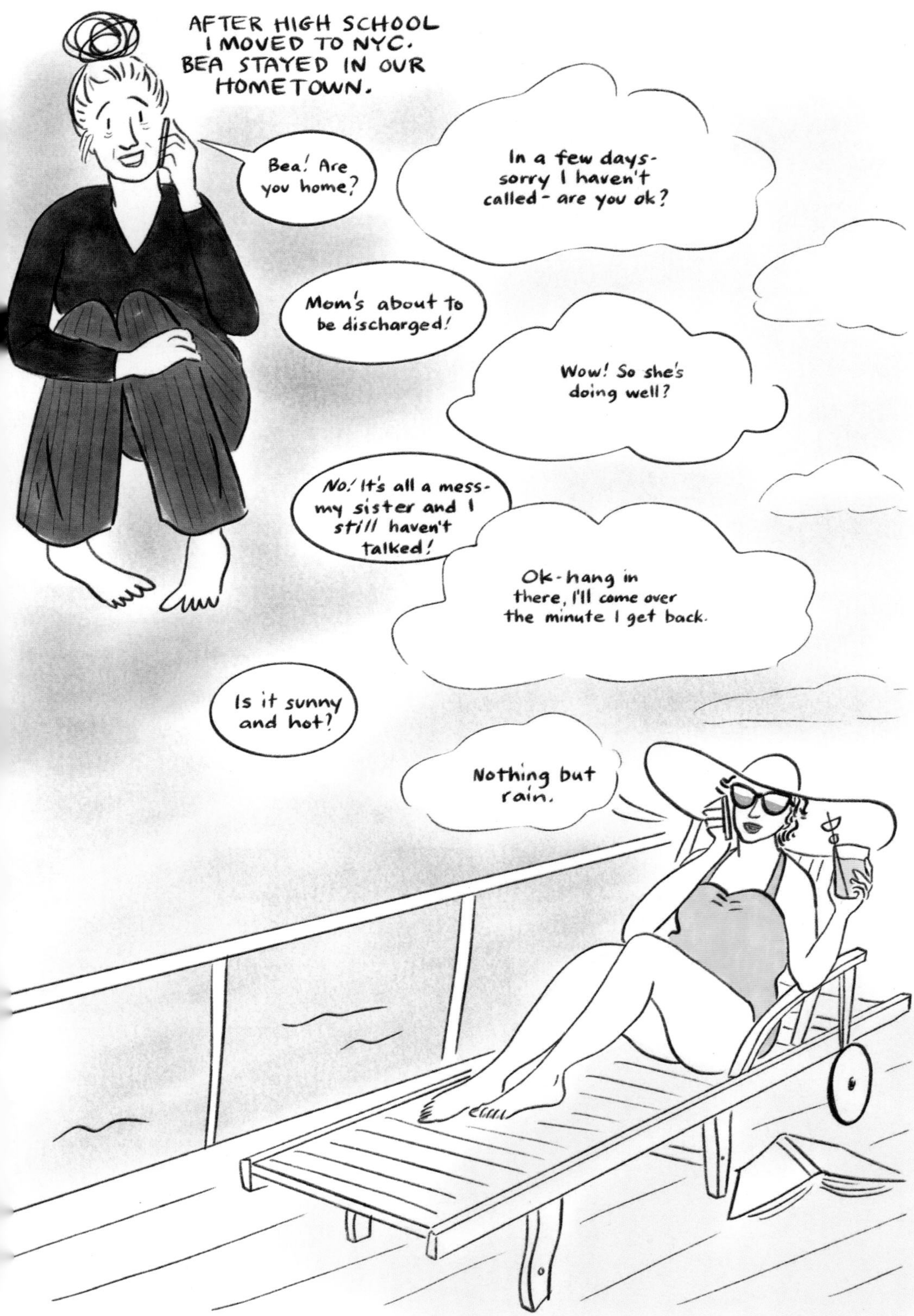
AFTER HIGH SCHOOL I MOVED TO NYC. BEA STAYED IN OUR HOMETOWN.
Bea! Are you home?
In a few days- sorry I haven't called - are you ok?
Mom's about to be discharged!
Wow! So she's doing well?
No! It's all a mess- my sister and I still haven't talked!
Ok-hang in there, I'll come over the minute I get back.
Is it sunny and hot?
Nothing but rain.

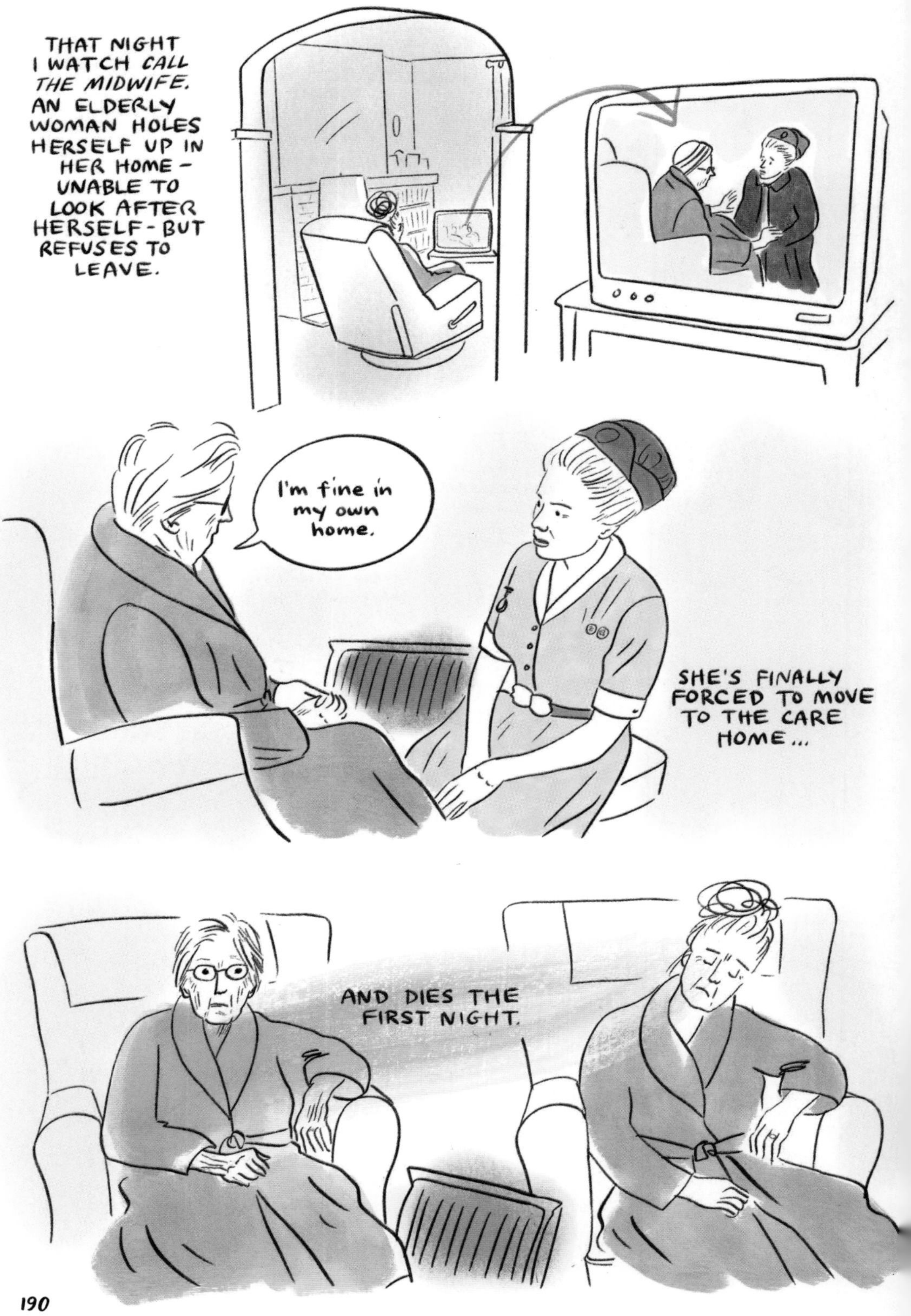
THAT NIGHT I WATCH CALL THE MIDWIFE. AN ELDERLY WOMAN HOLES HERSELF UP IN HER HOME - UNABLE TO LOOK AFTER HERSELF - BUT REFUSES TO LEAVE.
I'm fine in my own home.
SHE'S FINALLY FORCED TO MOVE TO THE CARE HOME...
AND DIES THE FIRST NIGHT.

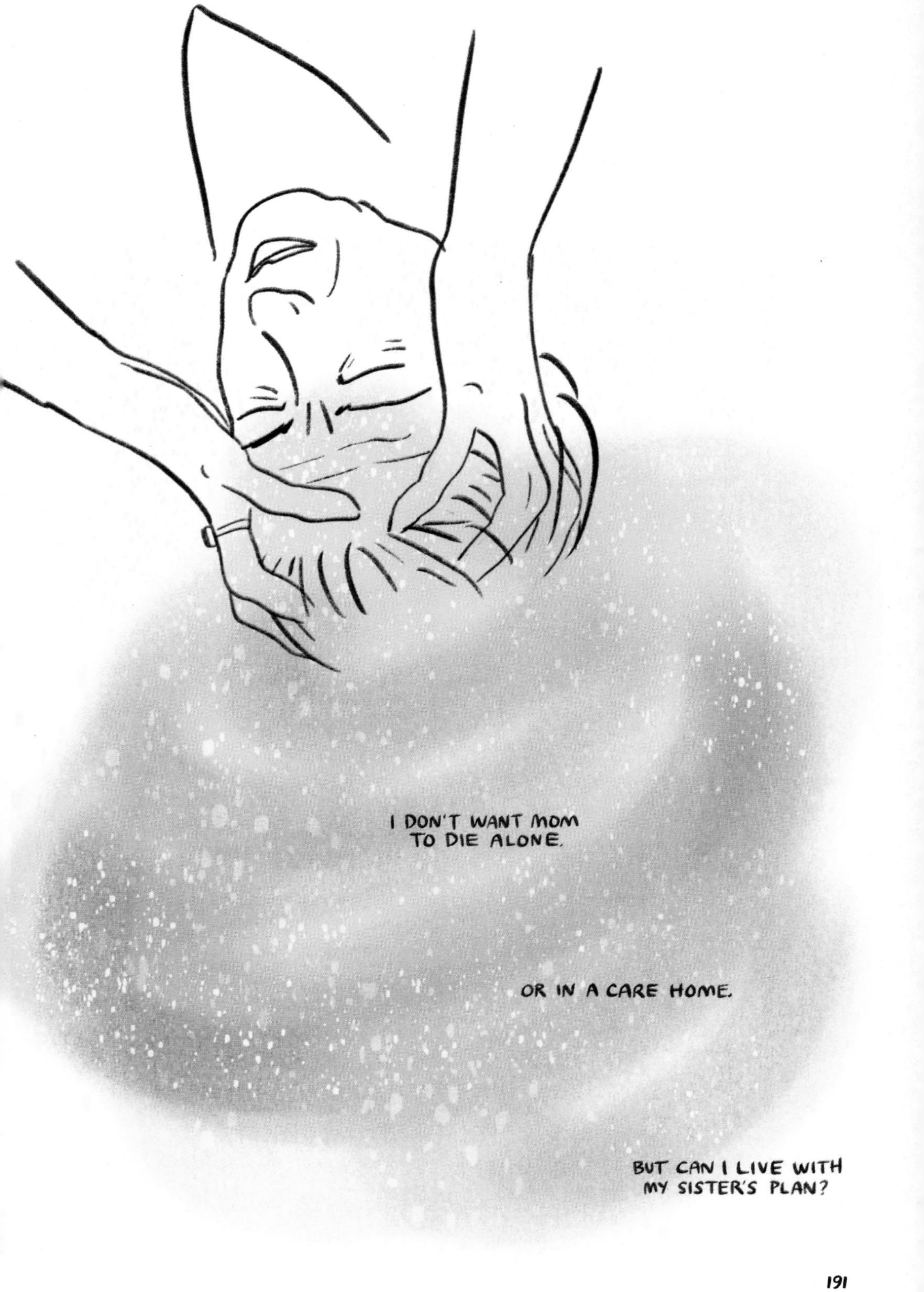
I DON'T WANT MOM TO DIE ALONE.
OR IN A CARE HOME.
BUT CAN I LIVE WITH MY SISTER'S PLAN?

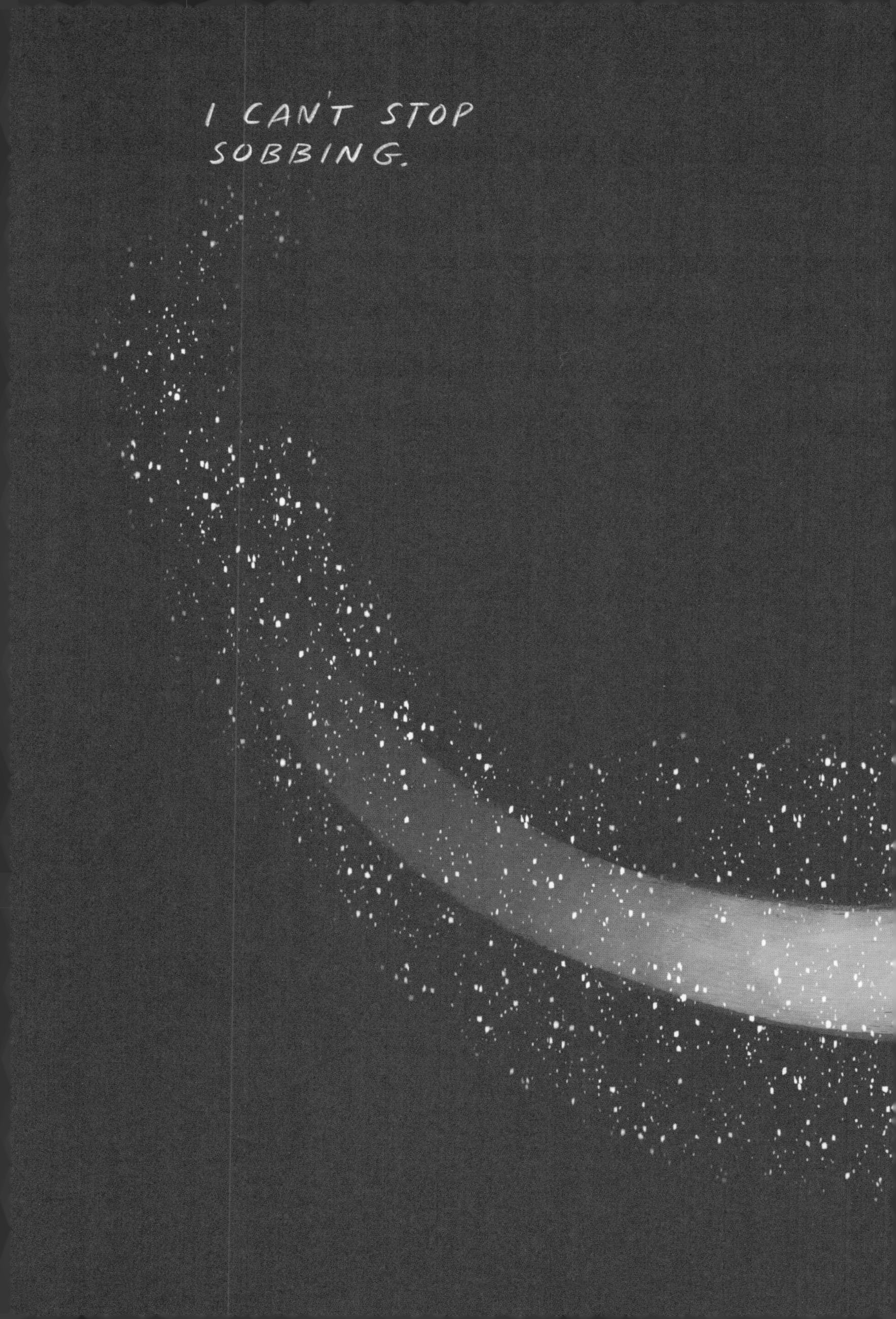
I CAN'T STOP SOBBING.

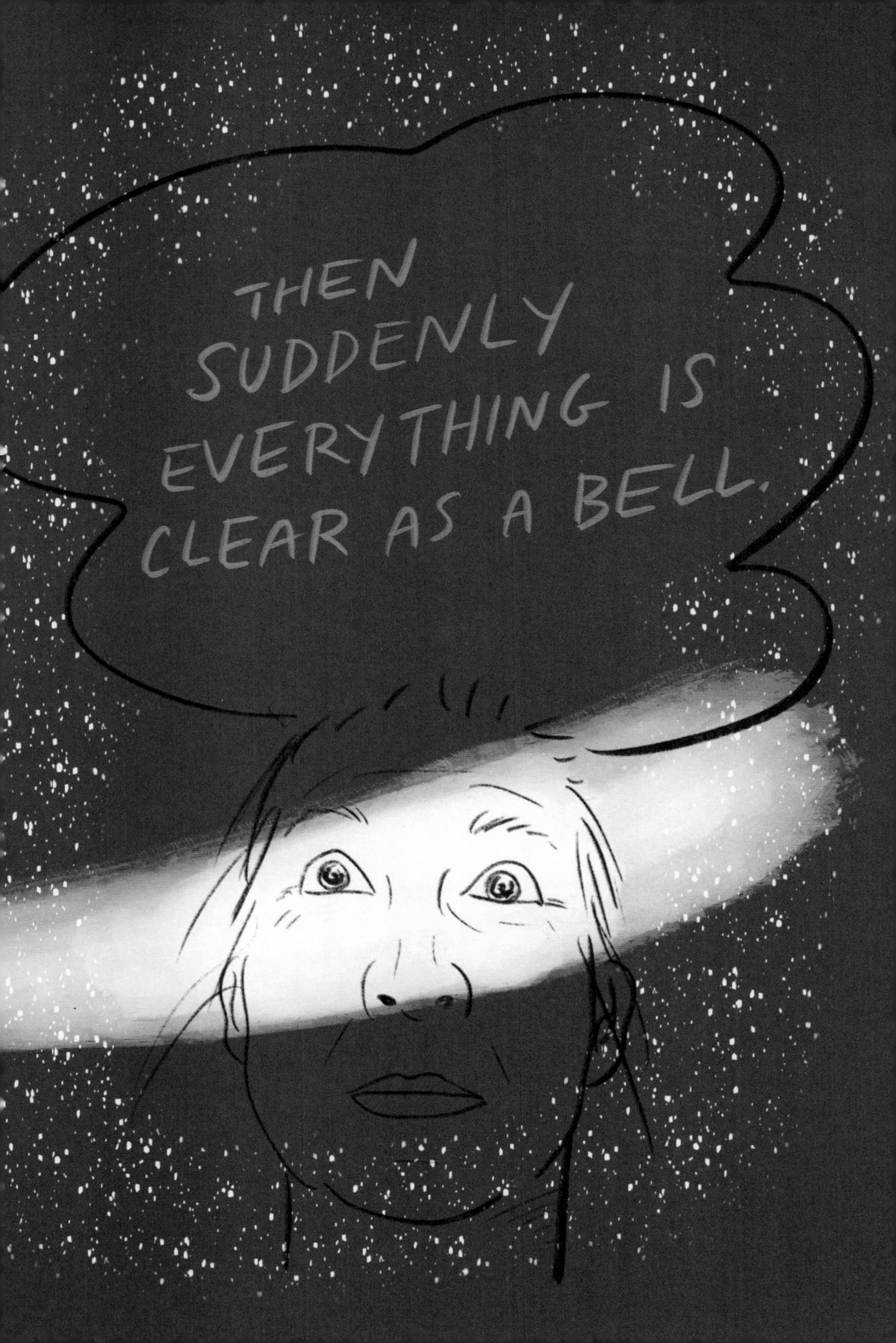
THEN SUDDENLY EVERYTHING IS CLEAR AS A BELL.

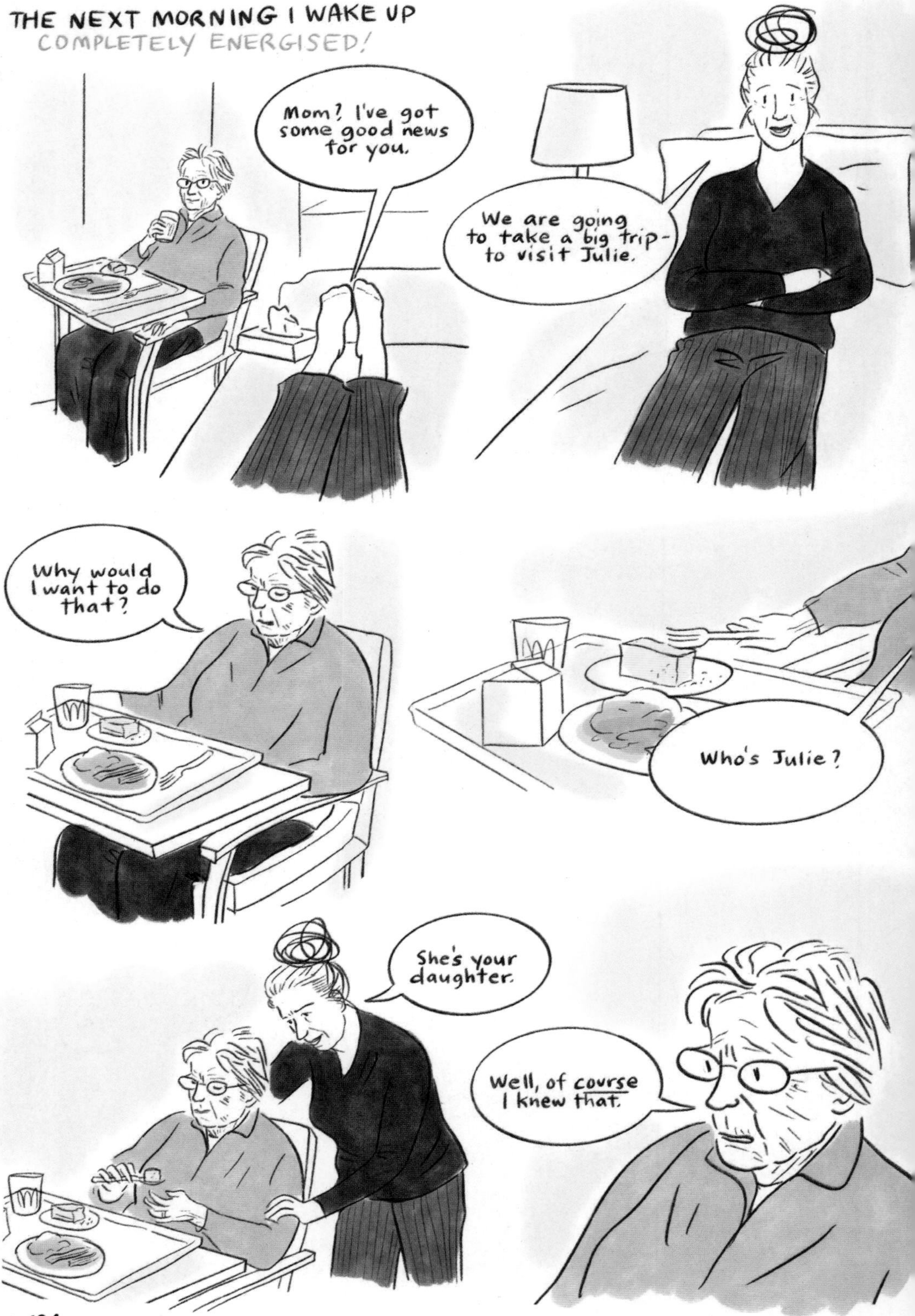
THE NEXT MORNING I WAKE UP
COMPLETELY ENERGISED!
Mom? I've got some good news for you.
We are going to take a big trip - to visit Julie.
Why would I want to do that?
Who's Julie?
She's your daughter.
Well, of course I knew that.

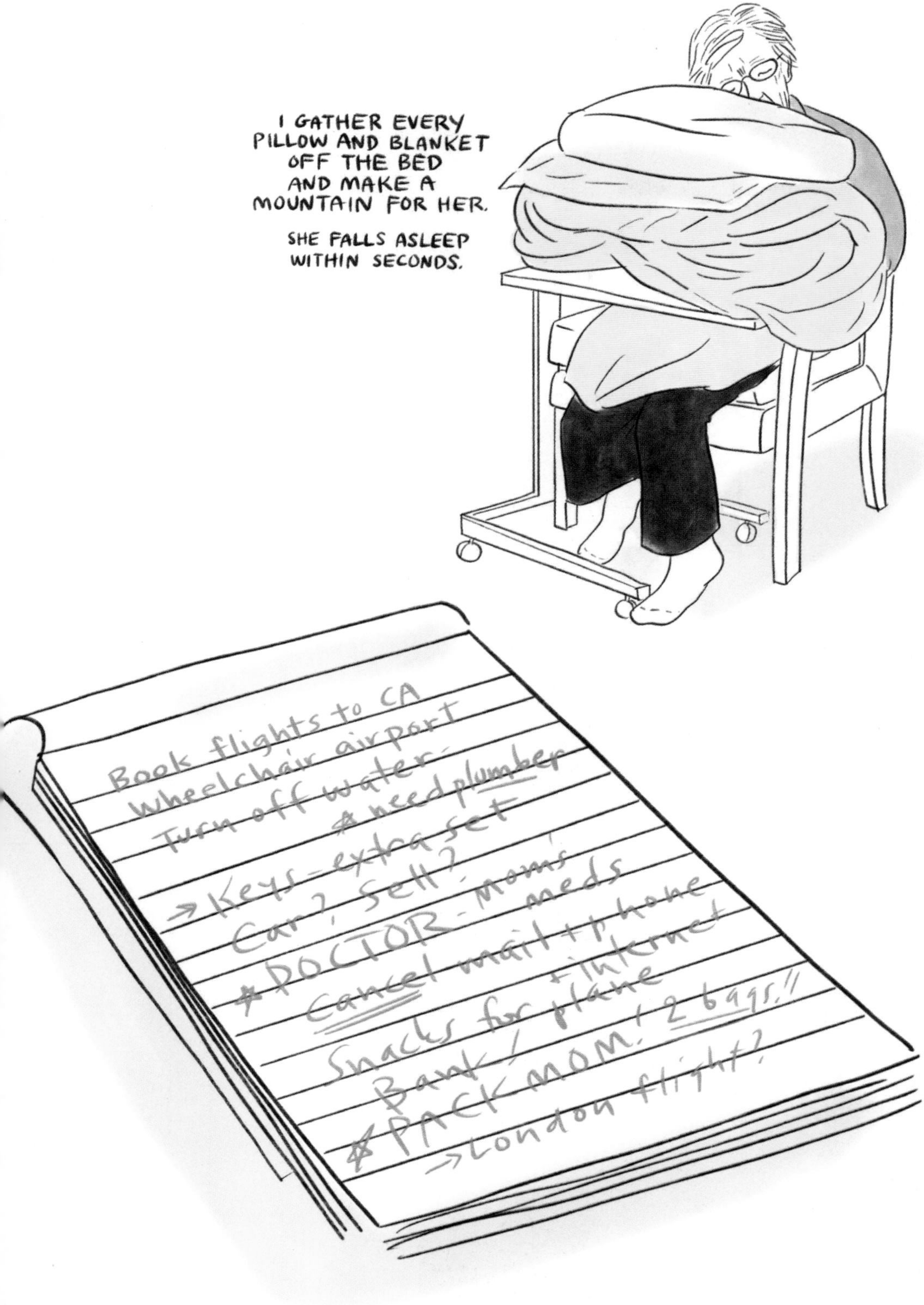
I GATHER EVERY PILLOW AND BLANKET OFF THE BED AND MAKE A MOUNTAIN FOR HER.
SHE FALLS ASLEEP WITHIN SECONDS.
Book flights to CA
Wheelchair airport
Turn off water
* need plumber
→ Keys - extra set
Car? Sell? mom's
* DOCTOR - meds
Cancel mail + phone
+ internet
Snacks for plane
Bank!
* PACK MOM! 2 bags!!
→ London flight?

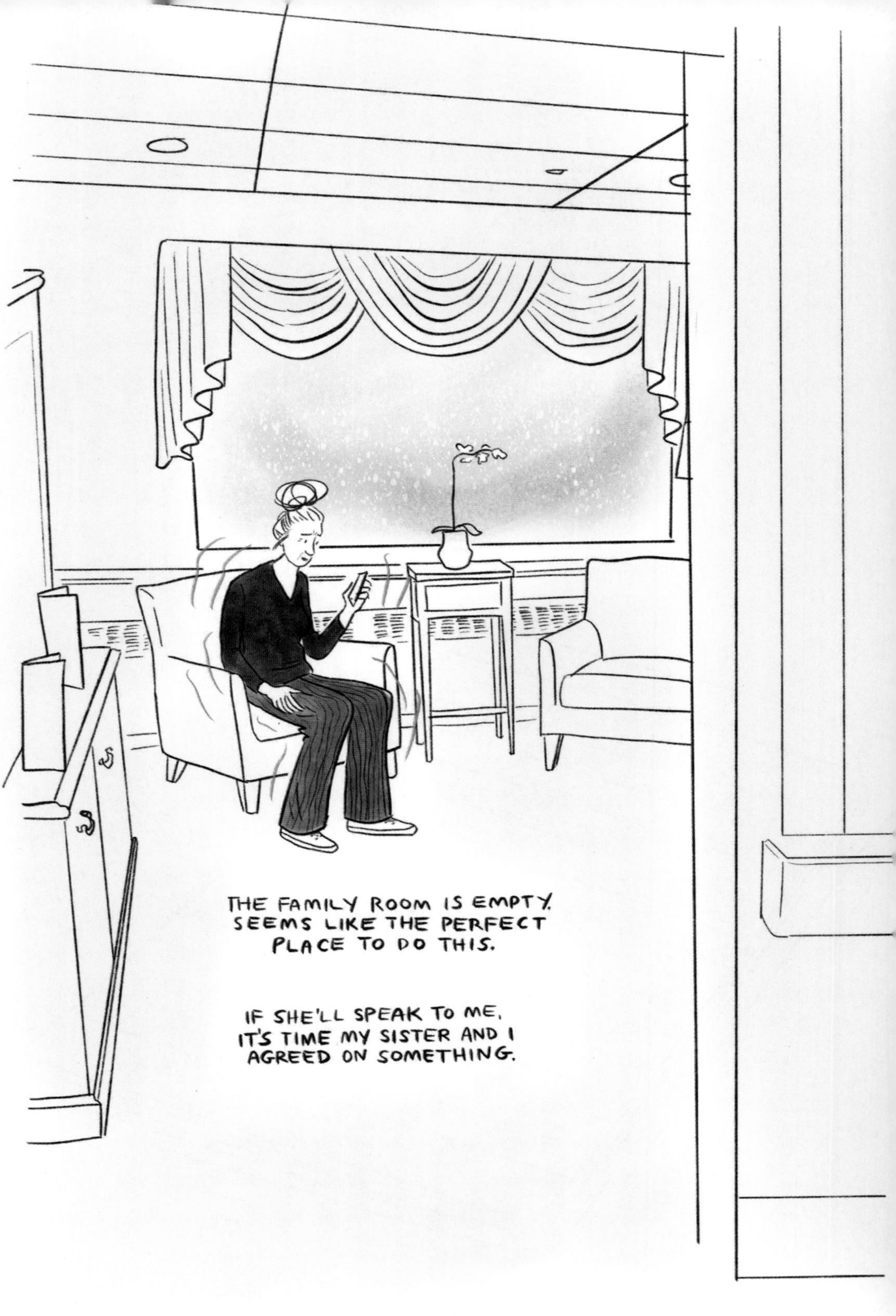
THE FAMILY ROOM IS EMPTY. SEEMS LIKE THE PERFECT PLACE TO DO THIS.
IF SHE'LL SPEAK TO ME, IT'S TIME MY SISTER AND I AGREED ON SOMETHING.

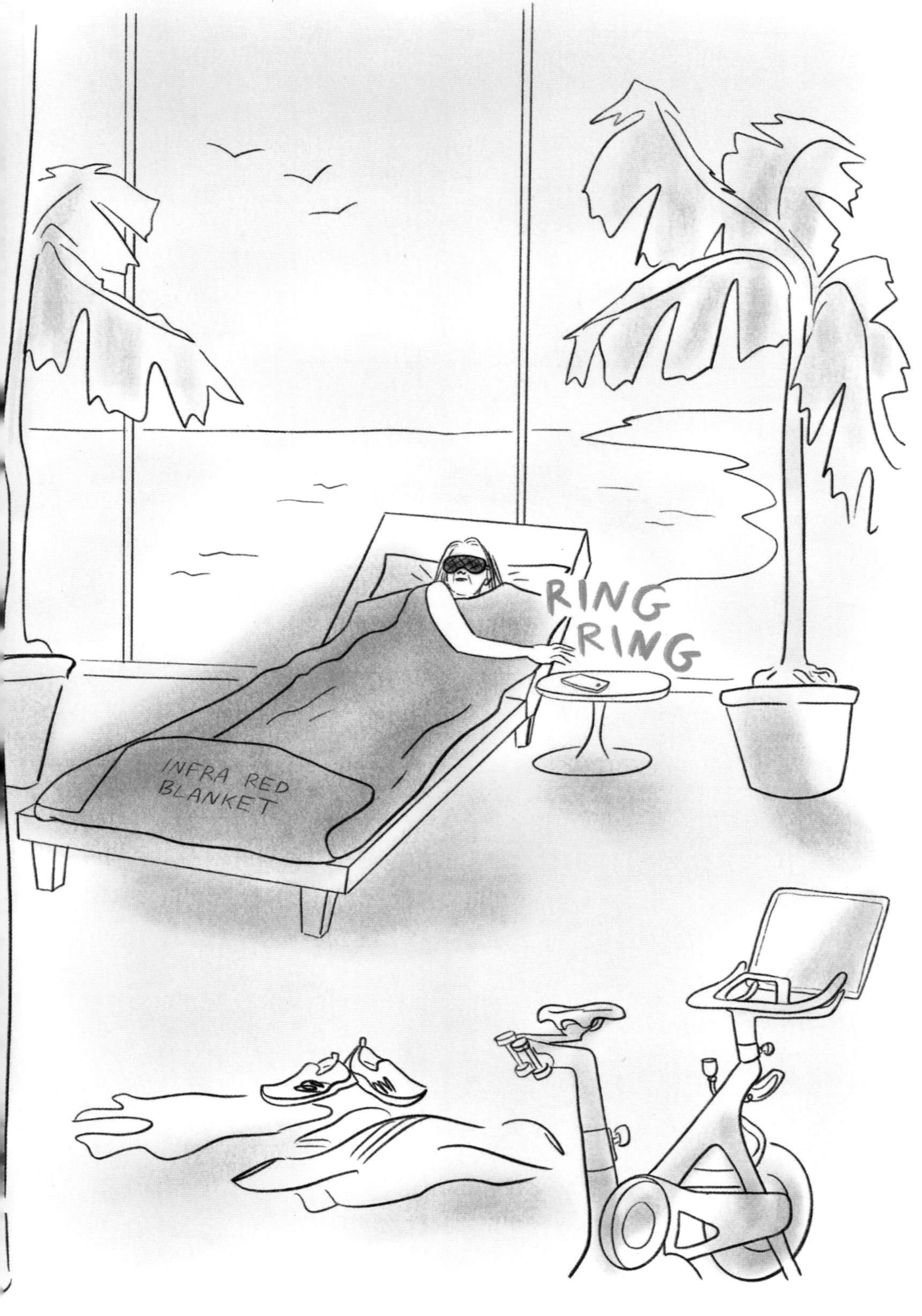
RING
RING
INFRA RED
BLANKET

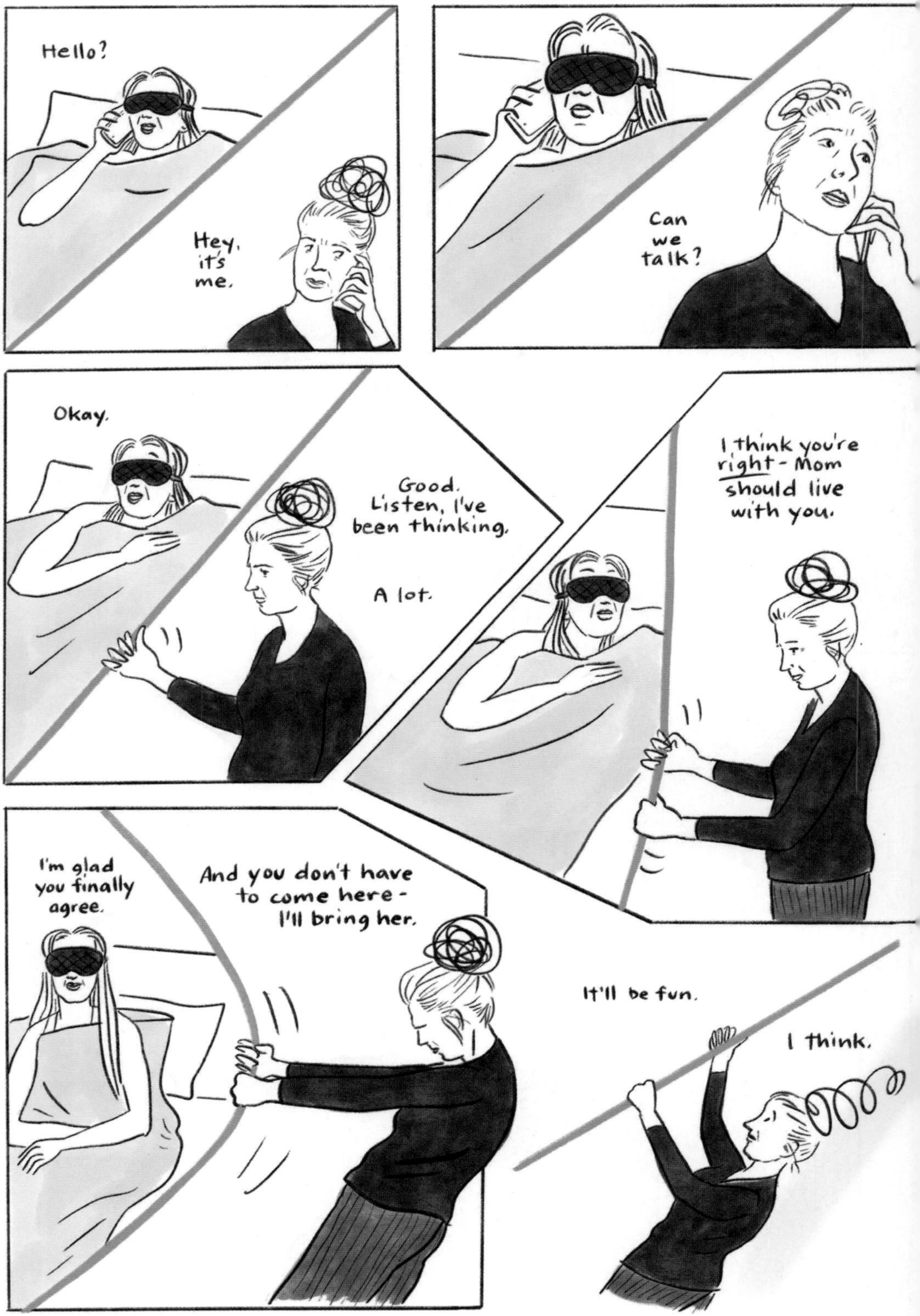

Hello?
Hey, it's me.
Can we talk?
Okay.
Good. Listen, I've been thinking.
A lot.
I think you're right - Mom should live with you.
I'm glad you finally agree.
And you don't have to come here - I'll bring her.
It'll be fun.
I think.

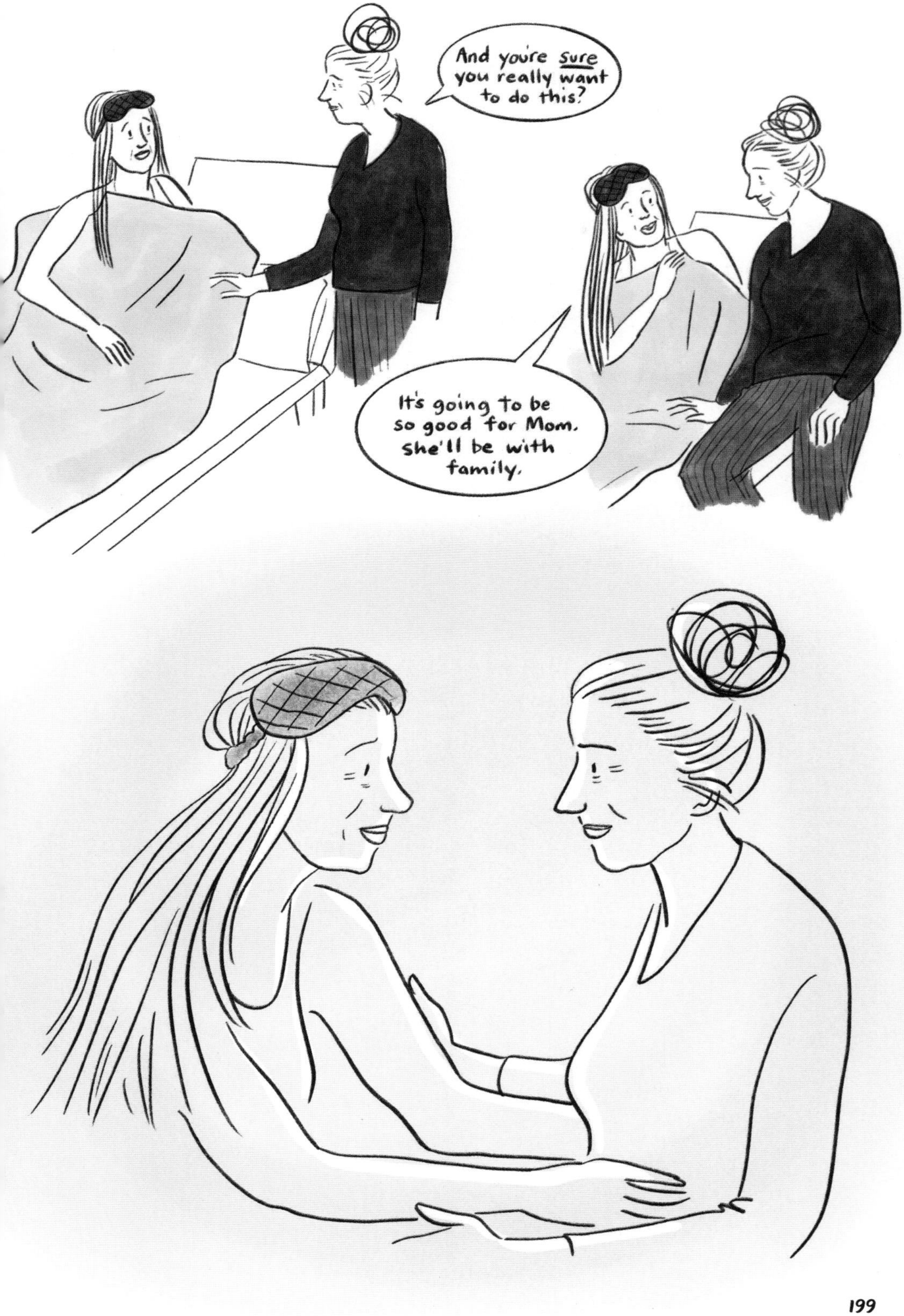
And you're sure you really want to do this?
It's going to be so good for Mom. She'll be with family.

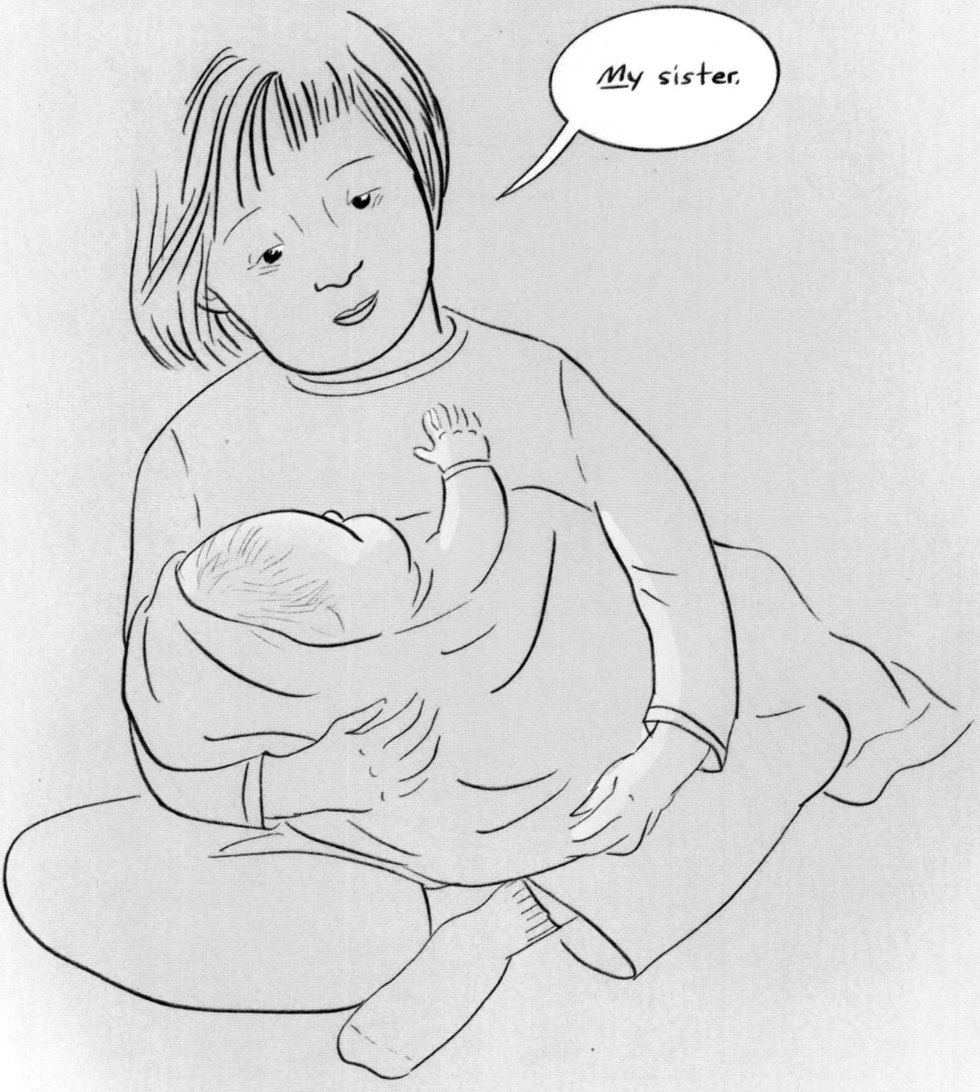
My sister.

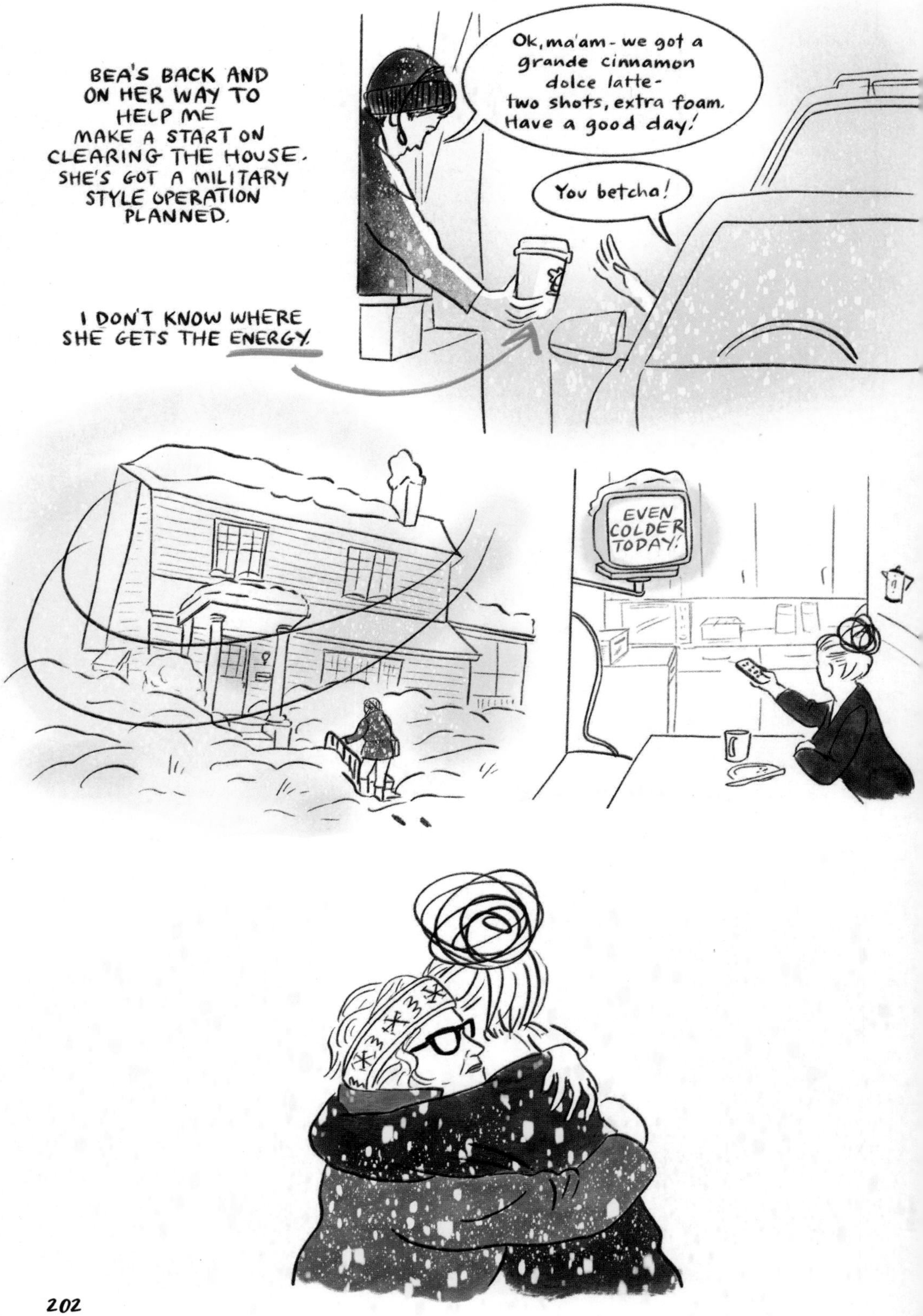
BEA'S BACK AND ON HER WAY TO HELP ME MAKE A START ON CLEARING THE HOUSE. SHE'S GOT A MILITARY STYLE OPERATION PLANNED.
Ok, ma'am - we got a grande cinnamon dolce latte - two shots, extra foam. Have a good day!
You betcha!
I DON'T KNOW WHERE SHE GETS THE ENERGY.
EVEN COLDER TODAY!

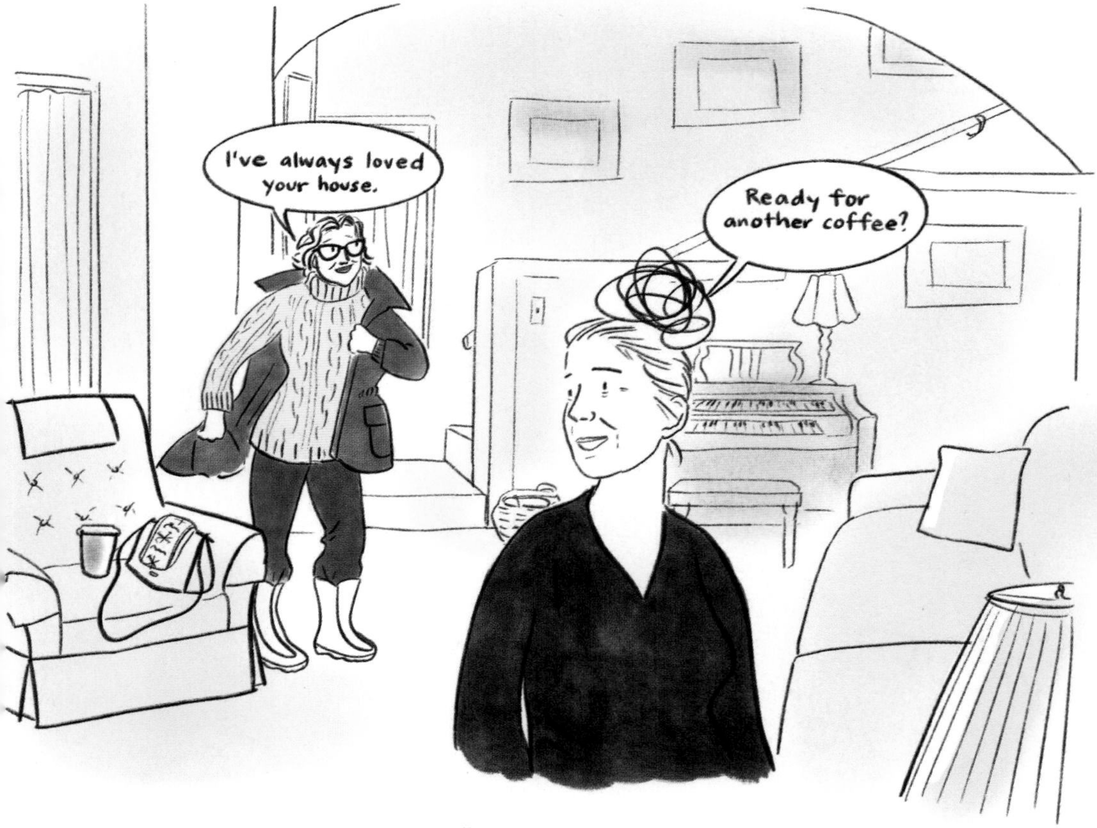
I've always loved your house.
Ready for another coffee?

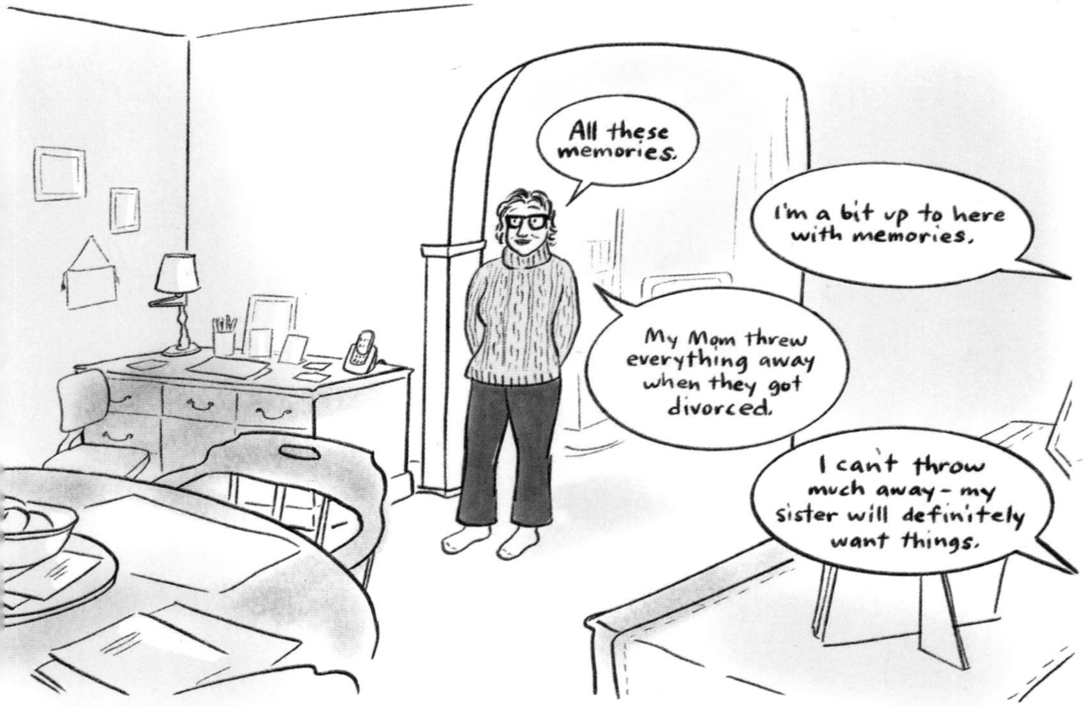
All these memories.
I'm a bit up to here with memories.
My Mom threw everything away when they got divorced.
I can't throw much away - my sister will definitely want things.

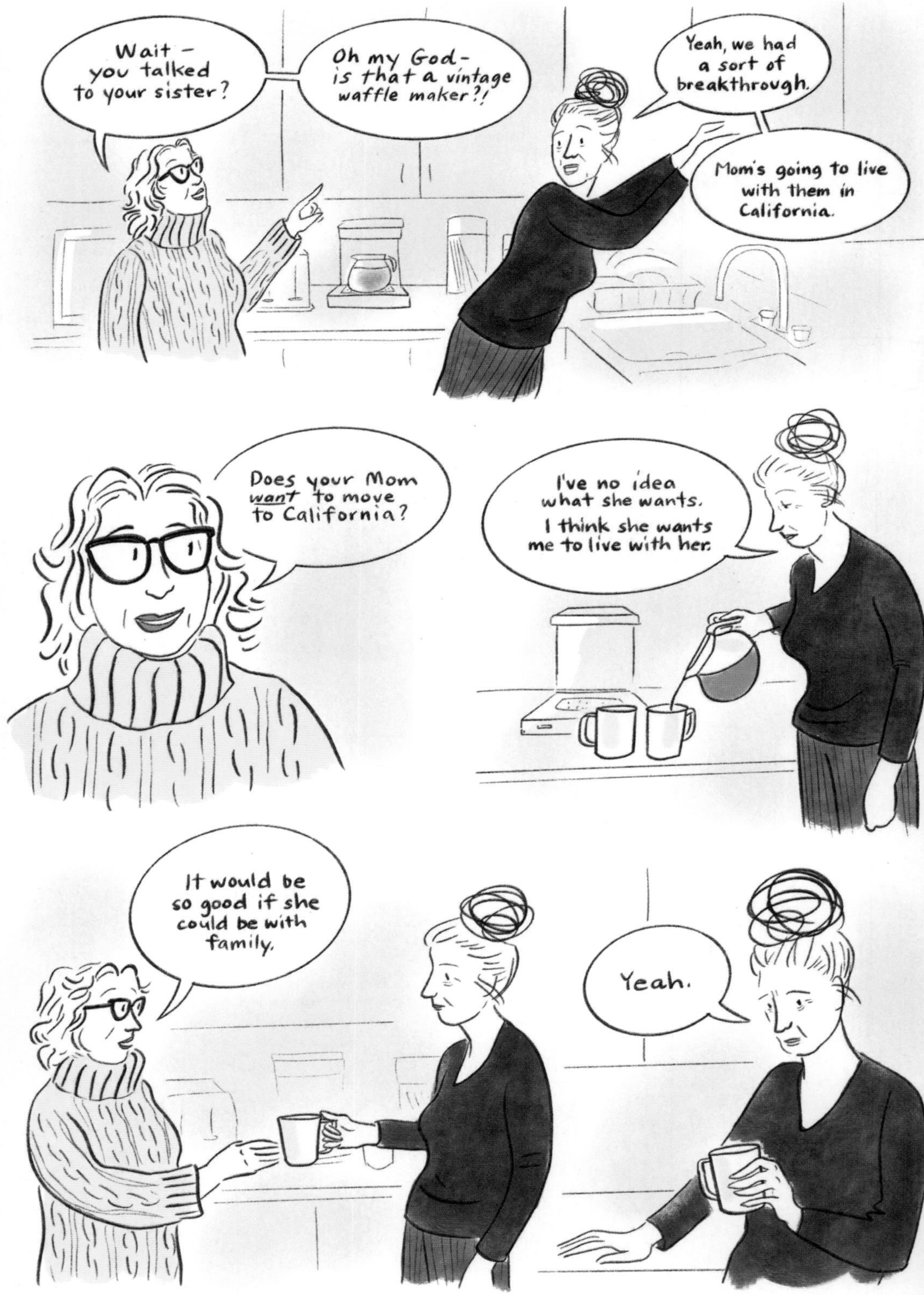
Wait - you talked to your sister?
Oh my God - is that a vintage waffle maker?!
Yeah, we had a sort of breakthrough.
Mom's going to live with them in California.
Does your Mom want to move to California?
I've no idea what she wants.
I think she wants me to live with her.
It would be so good if she could be with family.
Yeah.

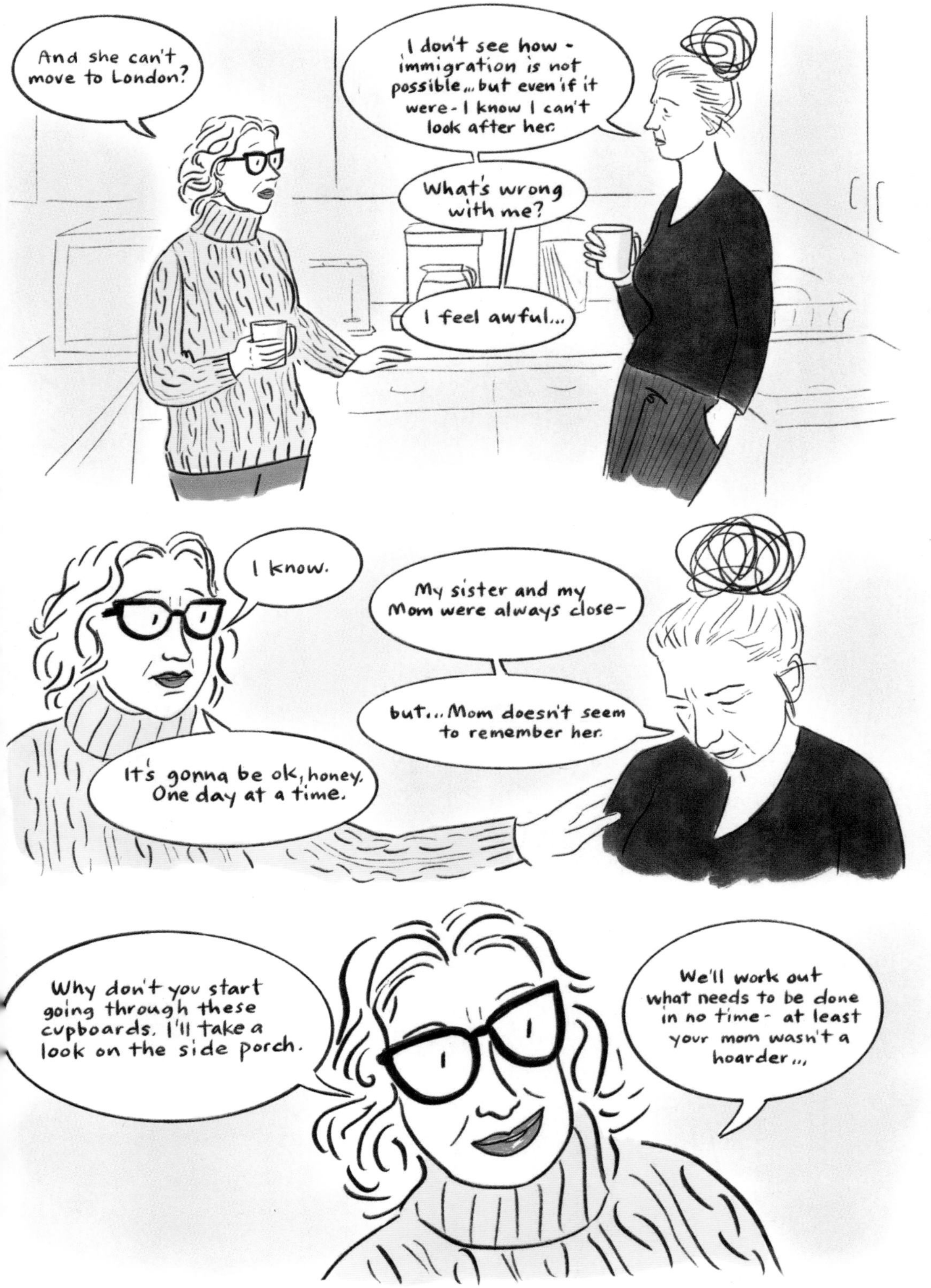

And she can't move to London?
I don't see how - immigration is not possible... but even if it were - I know I can't look after her.
What's wrong with me?
I feel awful...
I know.
My sister and my Mom were always close-
but... Mom doesn't seem to remember her.
It's gonna be ok, honey. One day at a time.
Why don't you start going through these cupboards. I'll take a look on the side porch.
We'll work out what needs to be done in no time - at least your mom wasn't a hoarder...

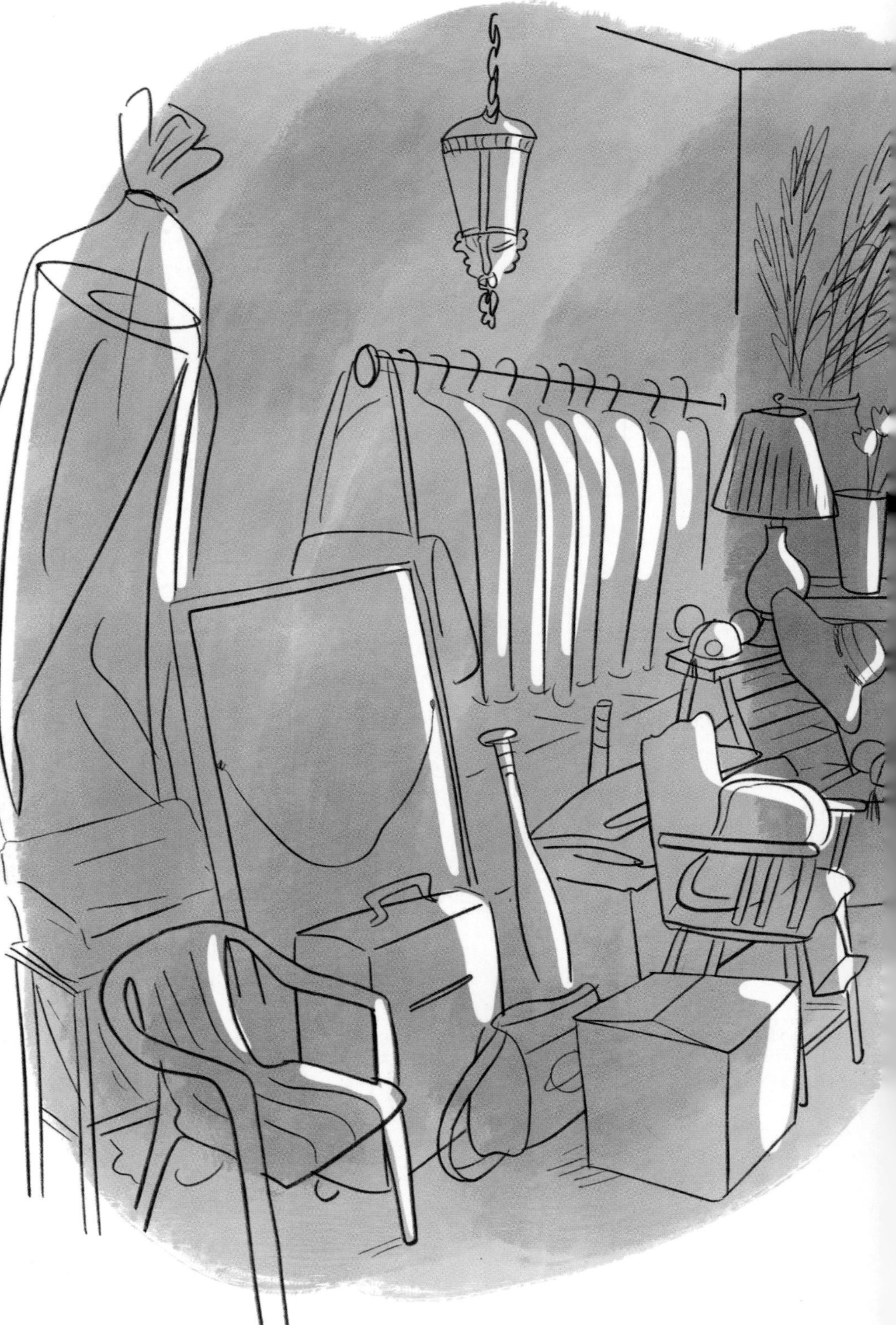

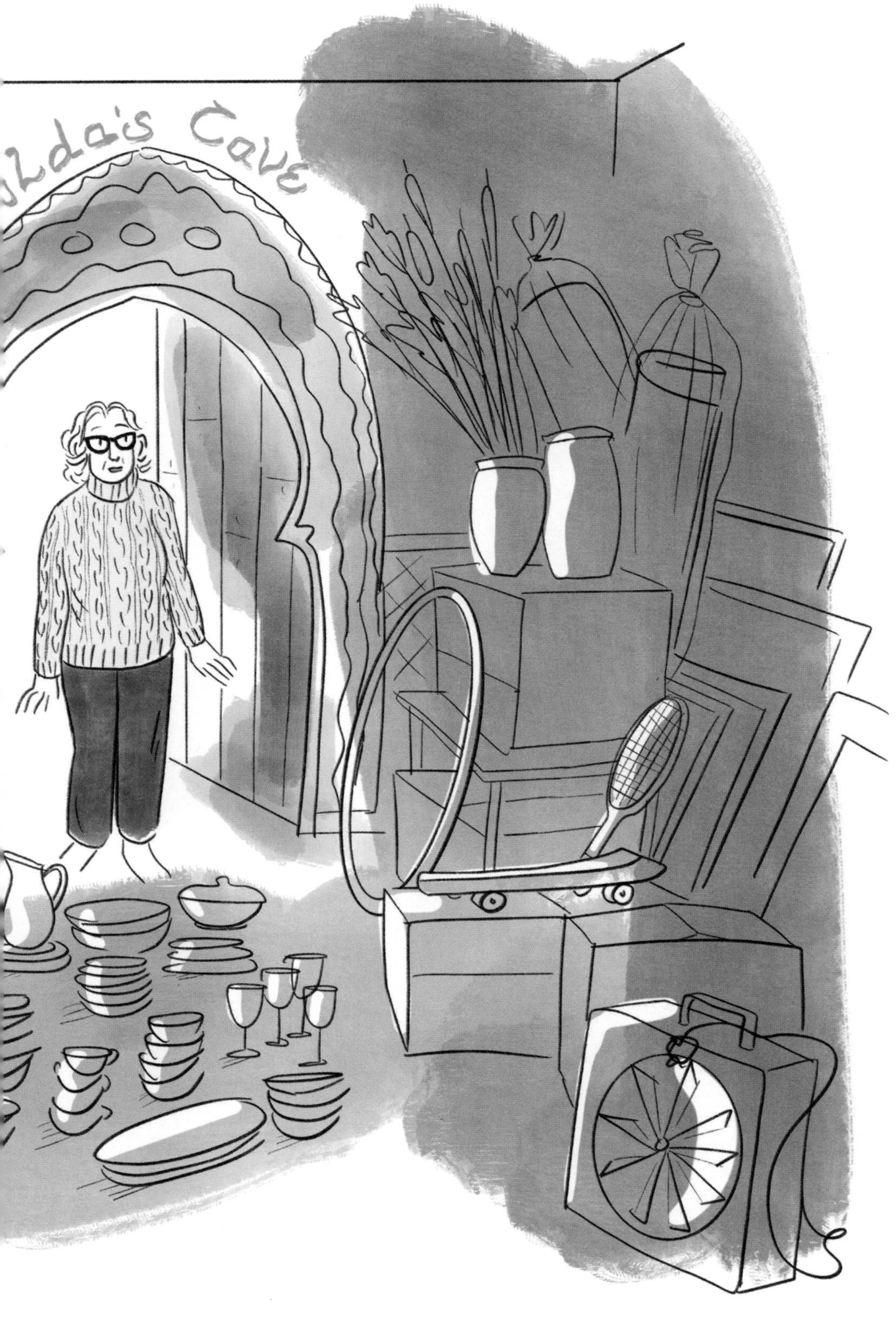
lda's Cave

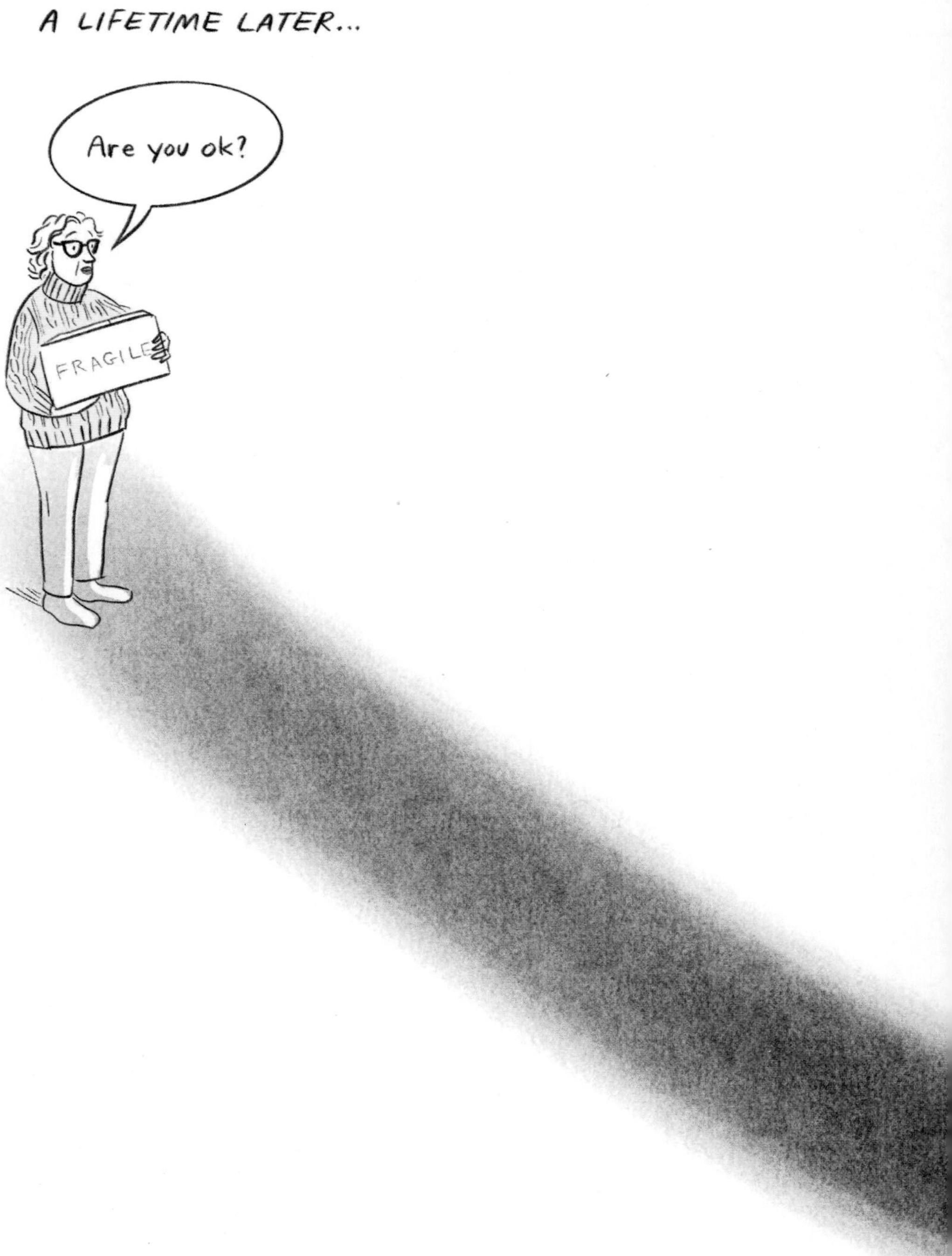
A LIFETIME LATER...
Are you ok?
FRAGILE

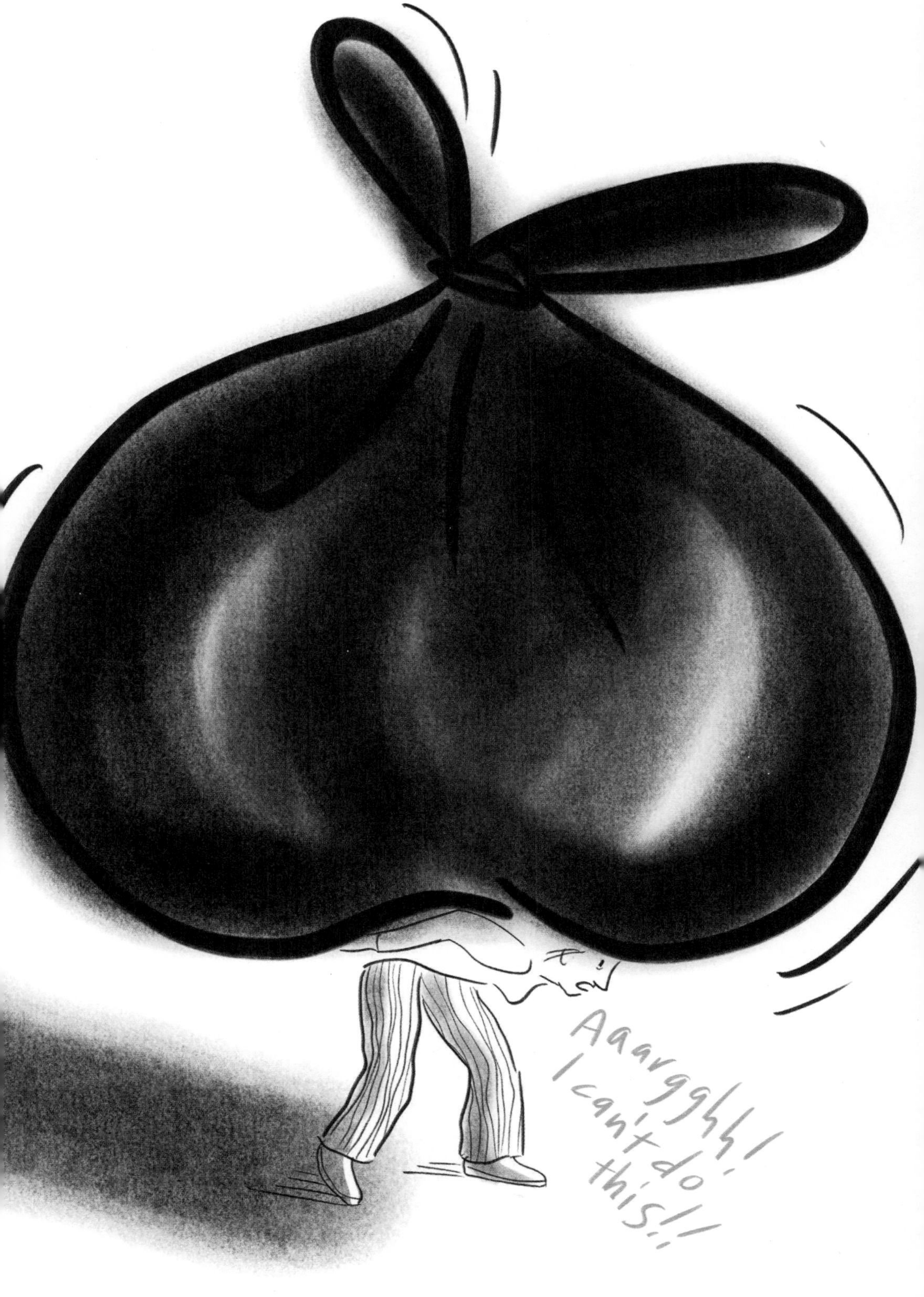
Aaarggh! I can't do this!!

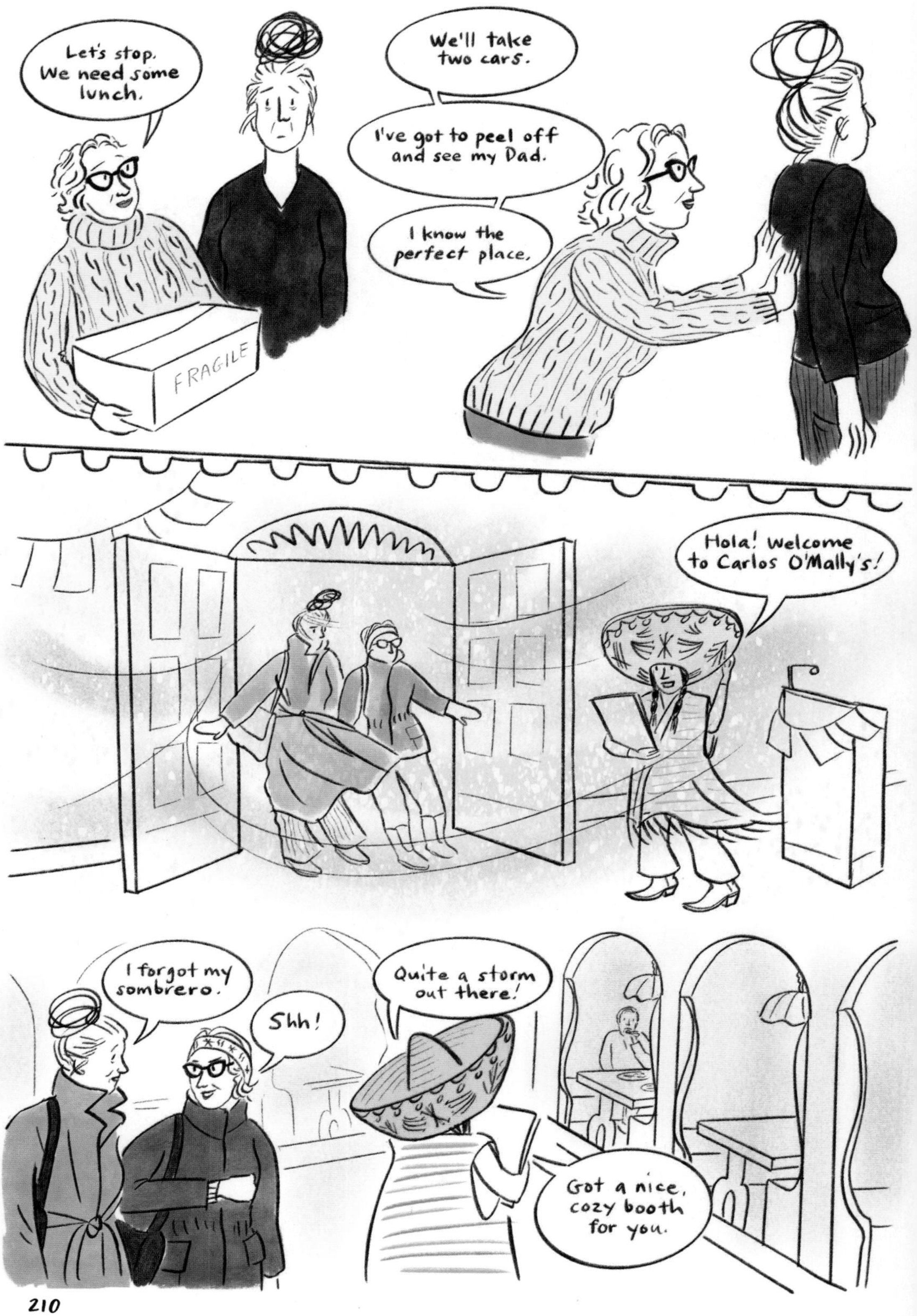
Let's stop. We need some lunch.
We'll take two cars.
I've got to peel off and see my Dad.
I know the perfect place.
FRAGILE
Hola! Welcome to Carlos O'Mally's!
I forgot my sombrero.
Shh!
Quite a storm out there!
Got a nice, cozy booth for you.

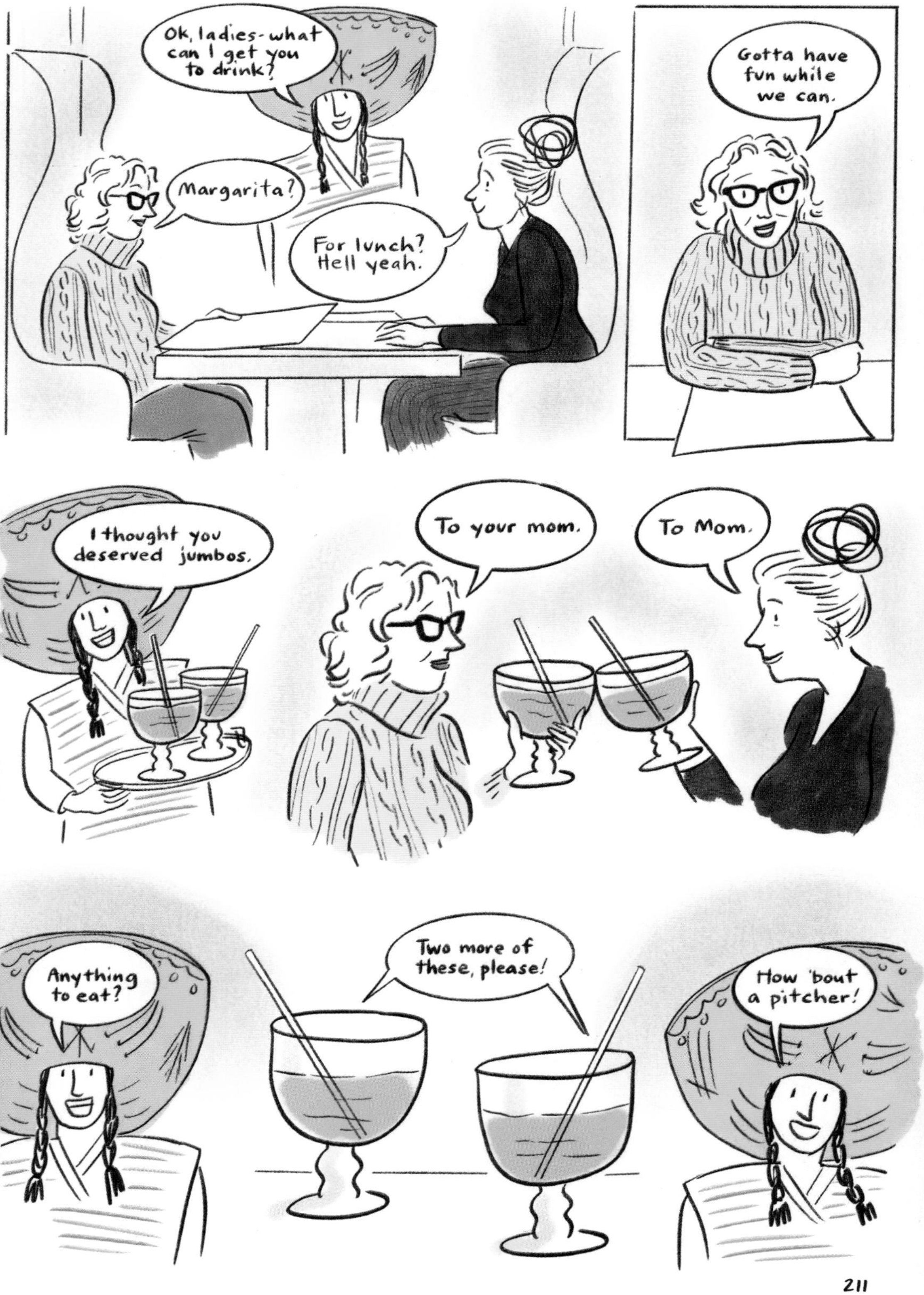

Ok, ladies- what can I get you to drink?
Margarita?
For lunch? Hell yeah.
Gotta have fun while we can.
I thought you deserved jumbos.
To your mom.
To Mom.
Anything to eat?
Two more of these, please!
How 'bout a pitcher!

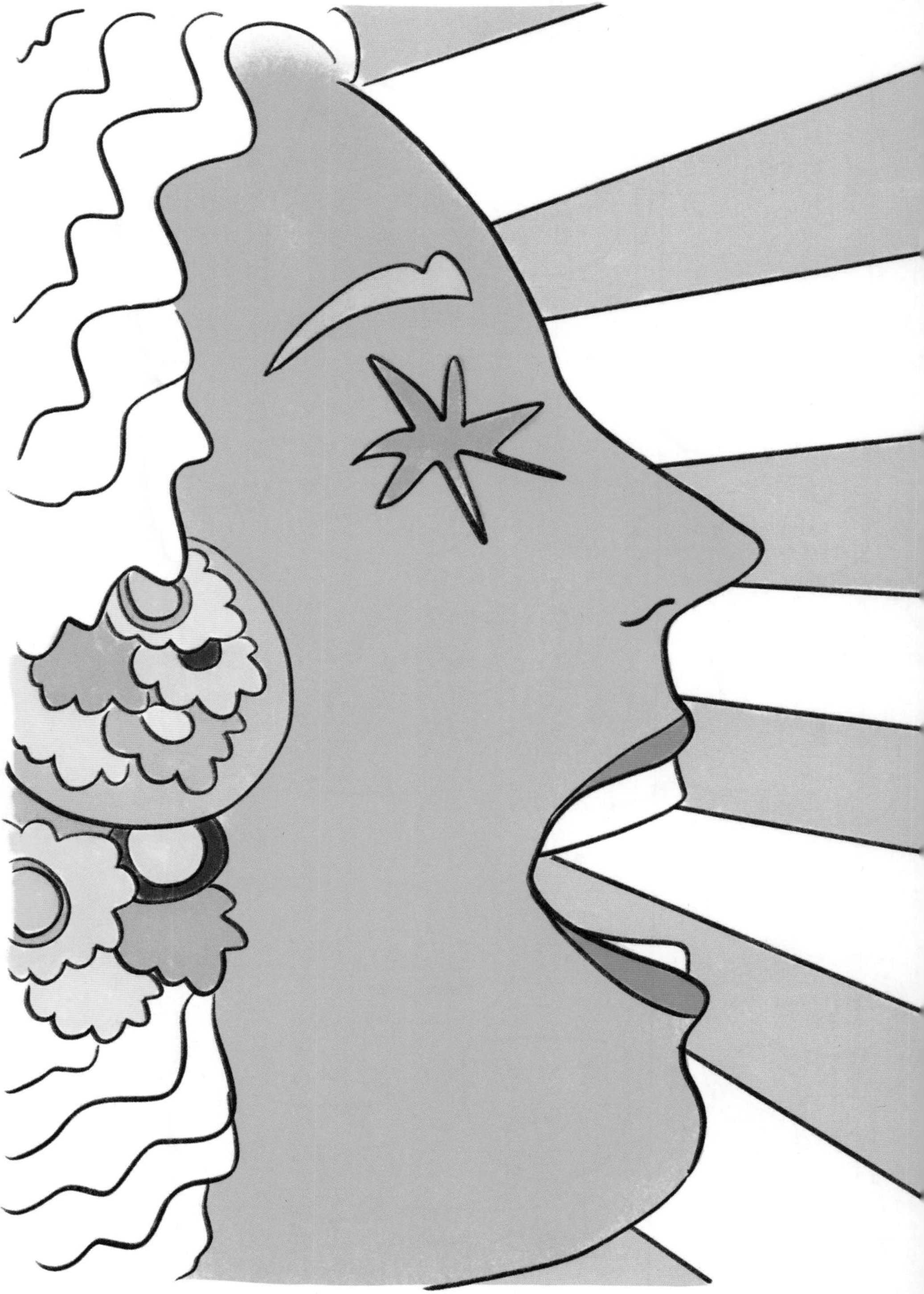

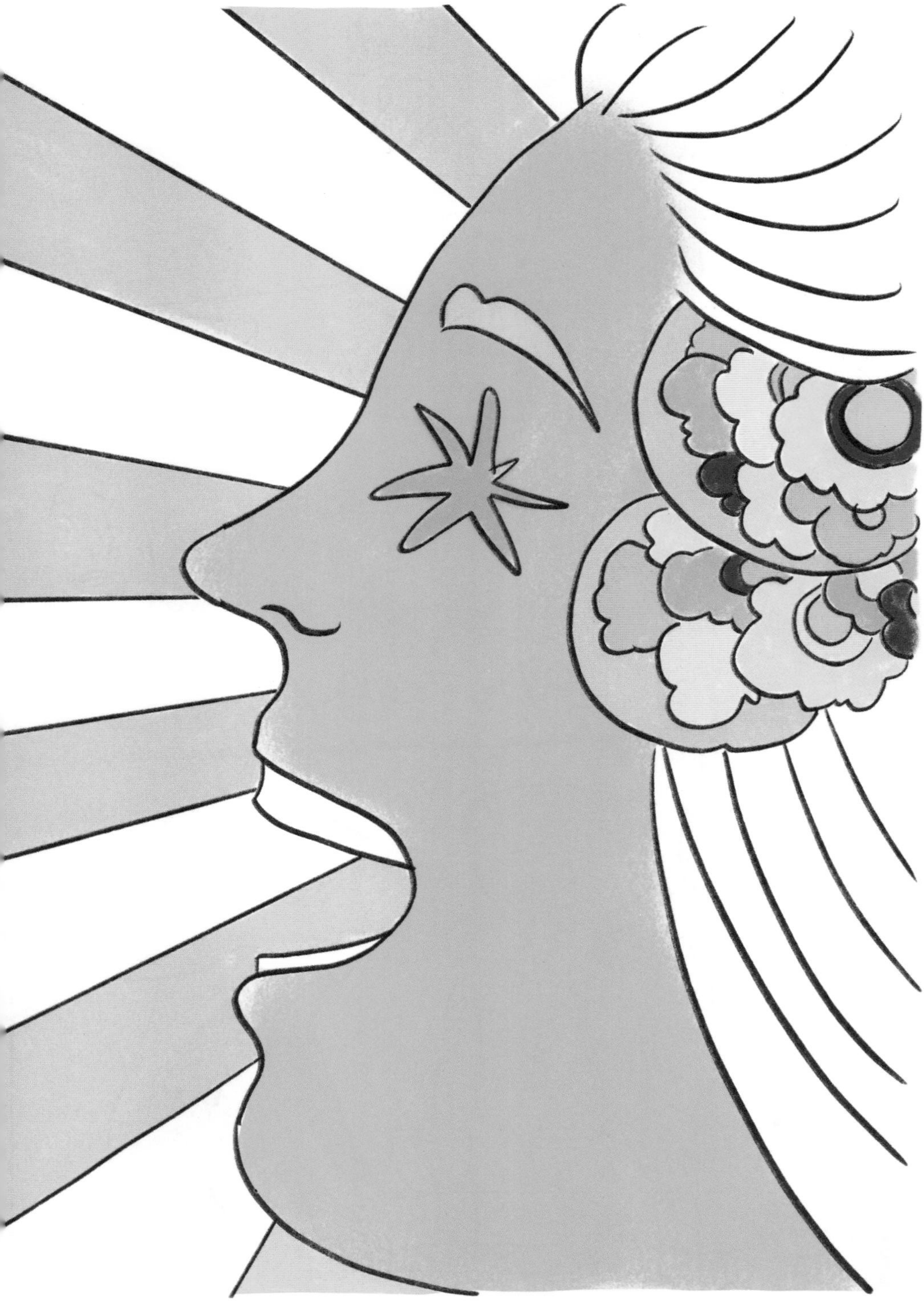

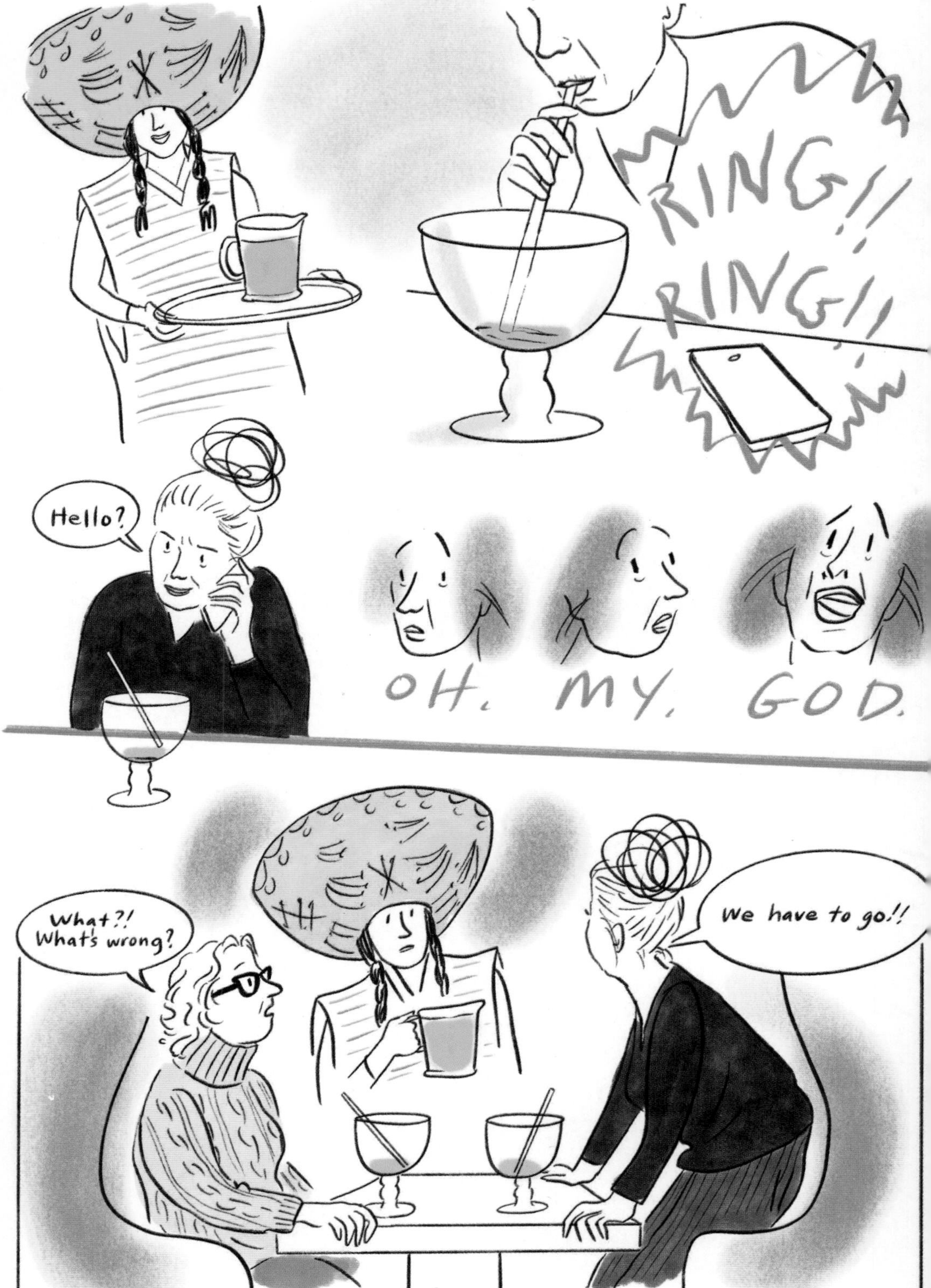
RING!!
RING!!
Hello?
OH. MY. GOD.
What?!
What's wrong?
We have to go!!

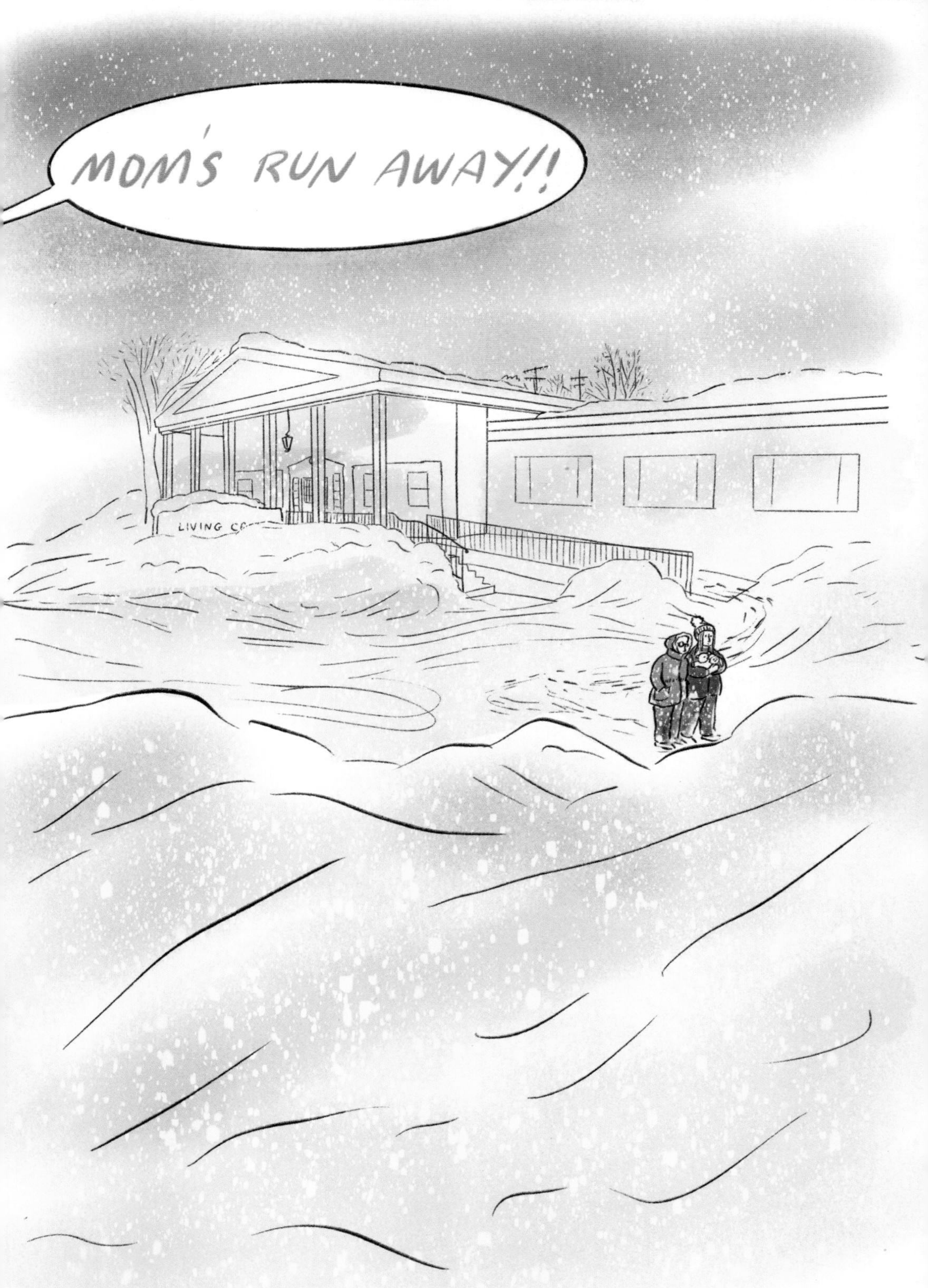
MOM'S RUN AWAY!!

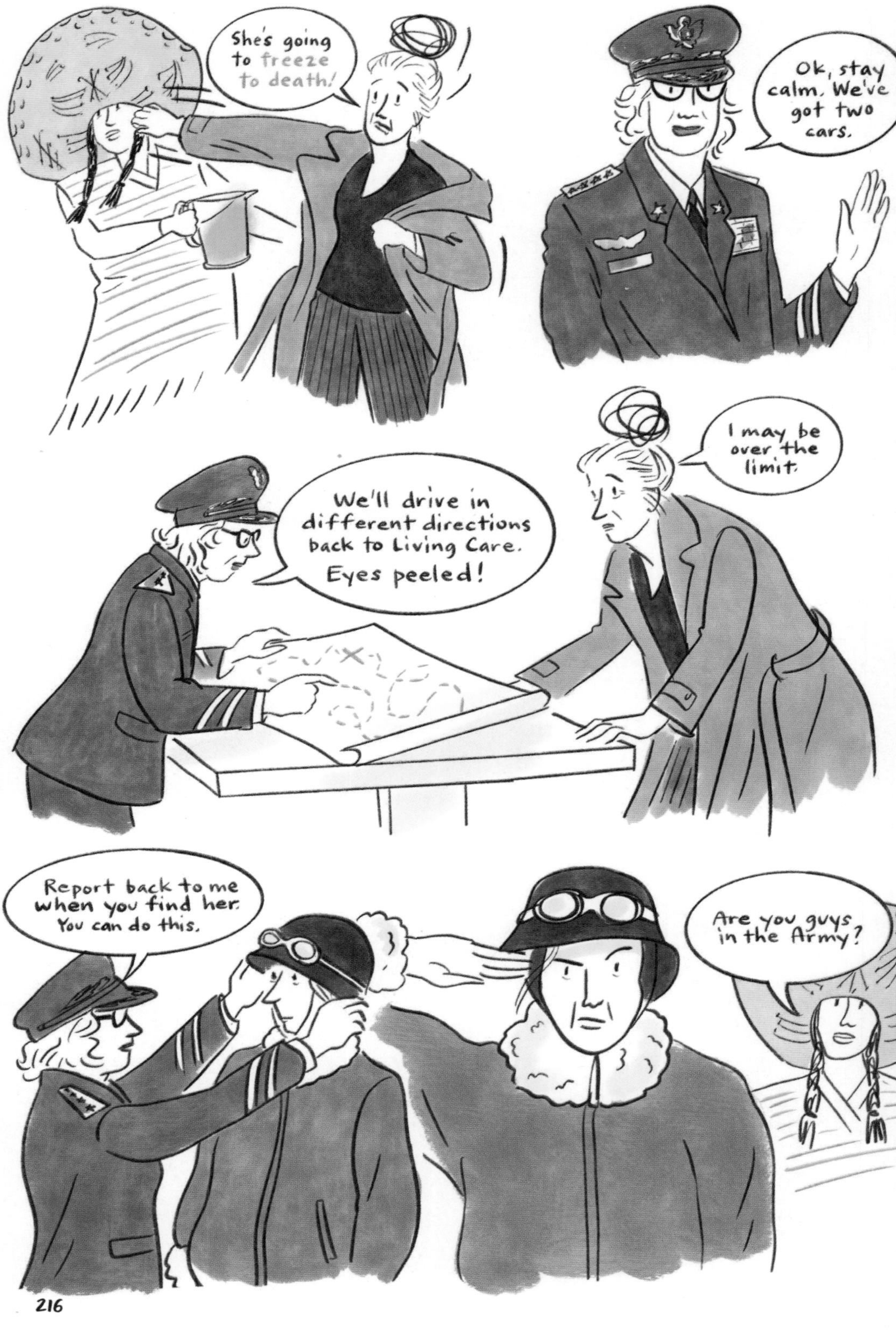
She's going to freeze to death!
Ok, stay calm. We've got two cars.
We'll drive in different directions back to Living Care. Eyes peeled!
I may be over the limit.
Report back to me when you find her. You can do this.
Are you guys in the Army?

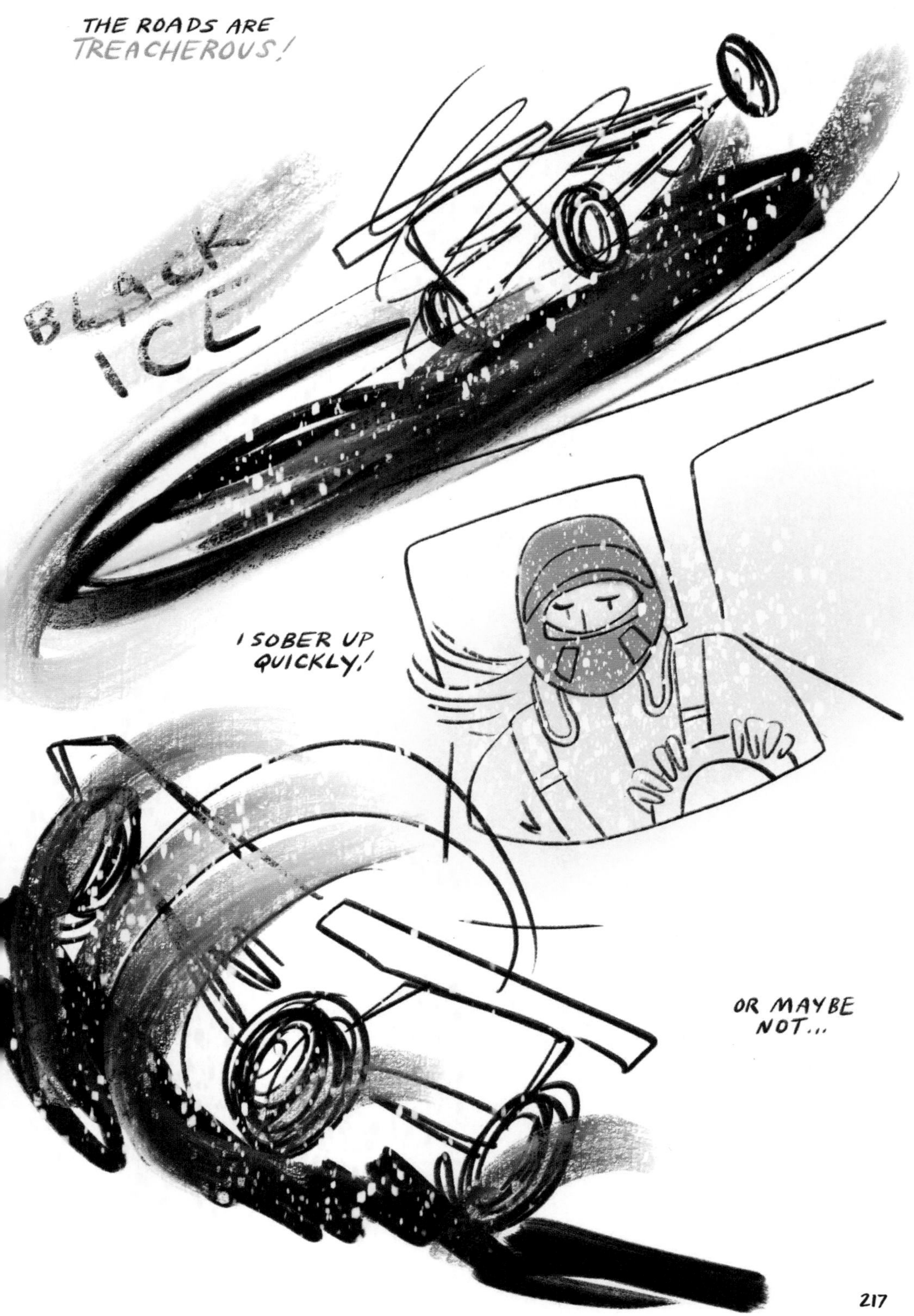
THE ROADS ARE TREACHEROUS!
BLACK ICE
I SOBER UP QUICKLY!
OR MAYBE NOT...

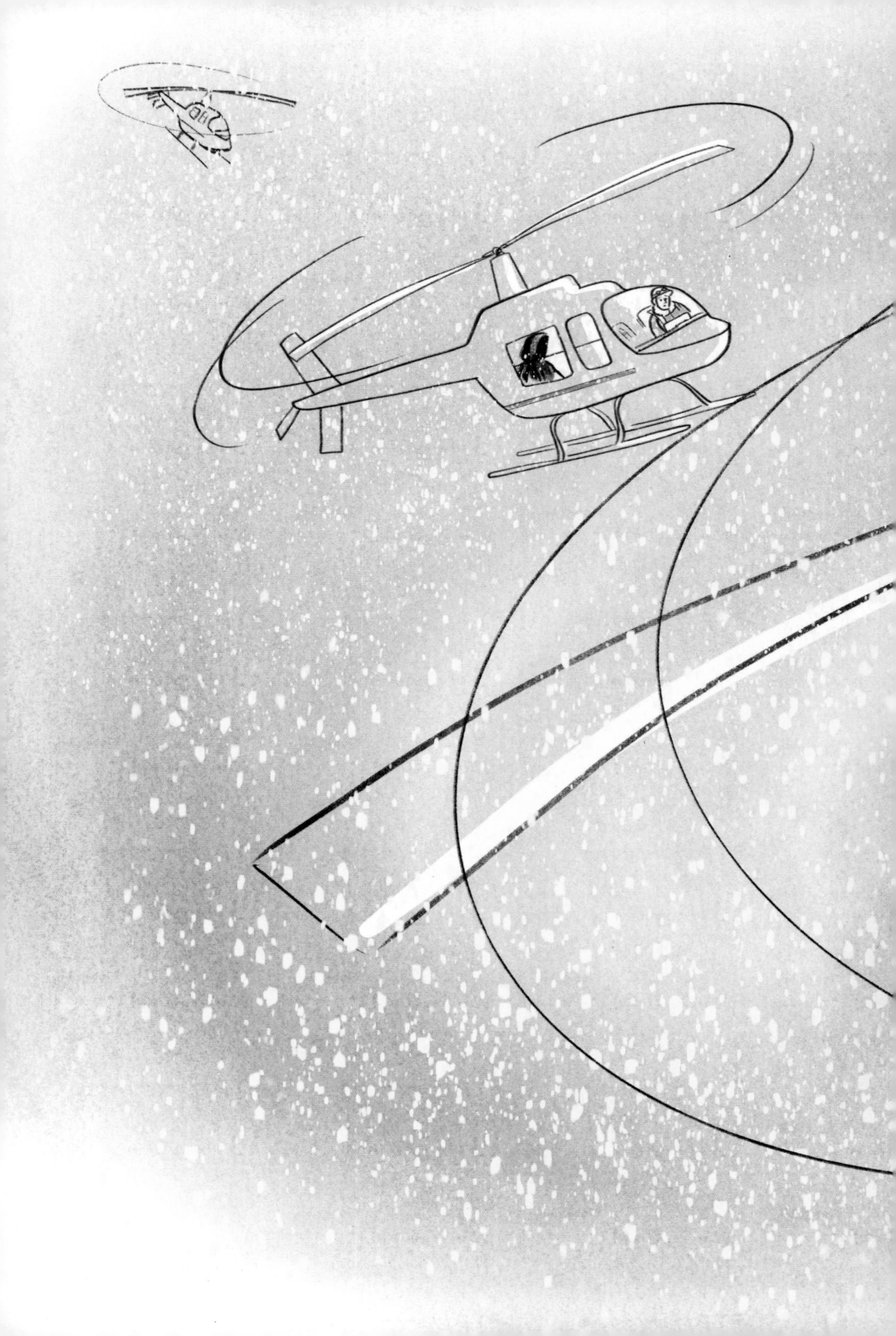

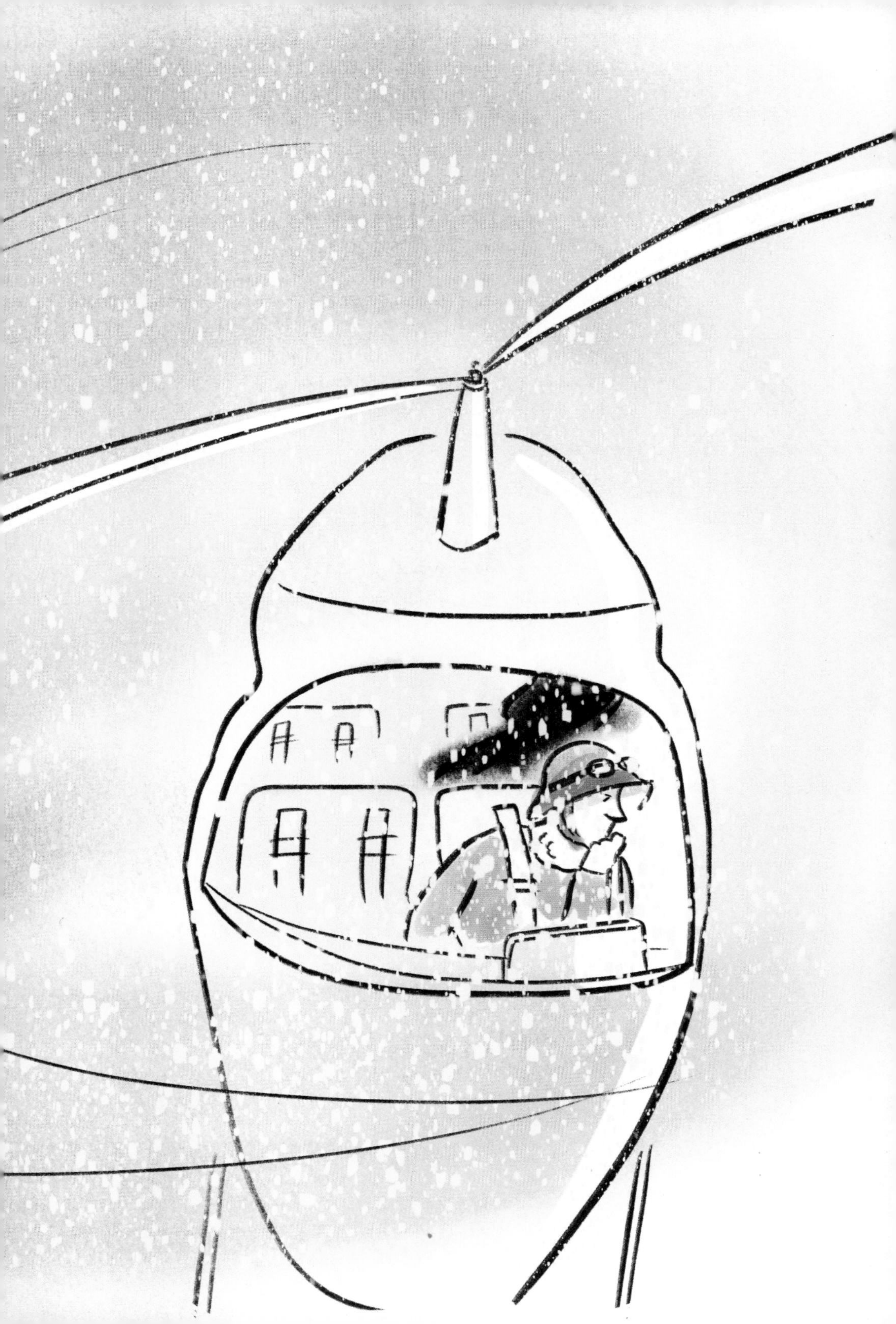

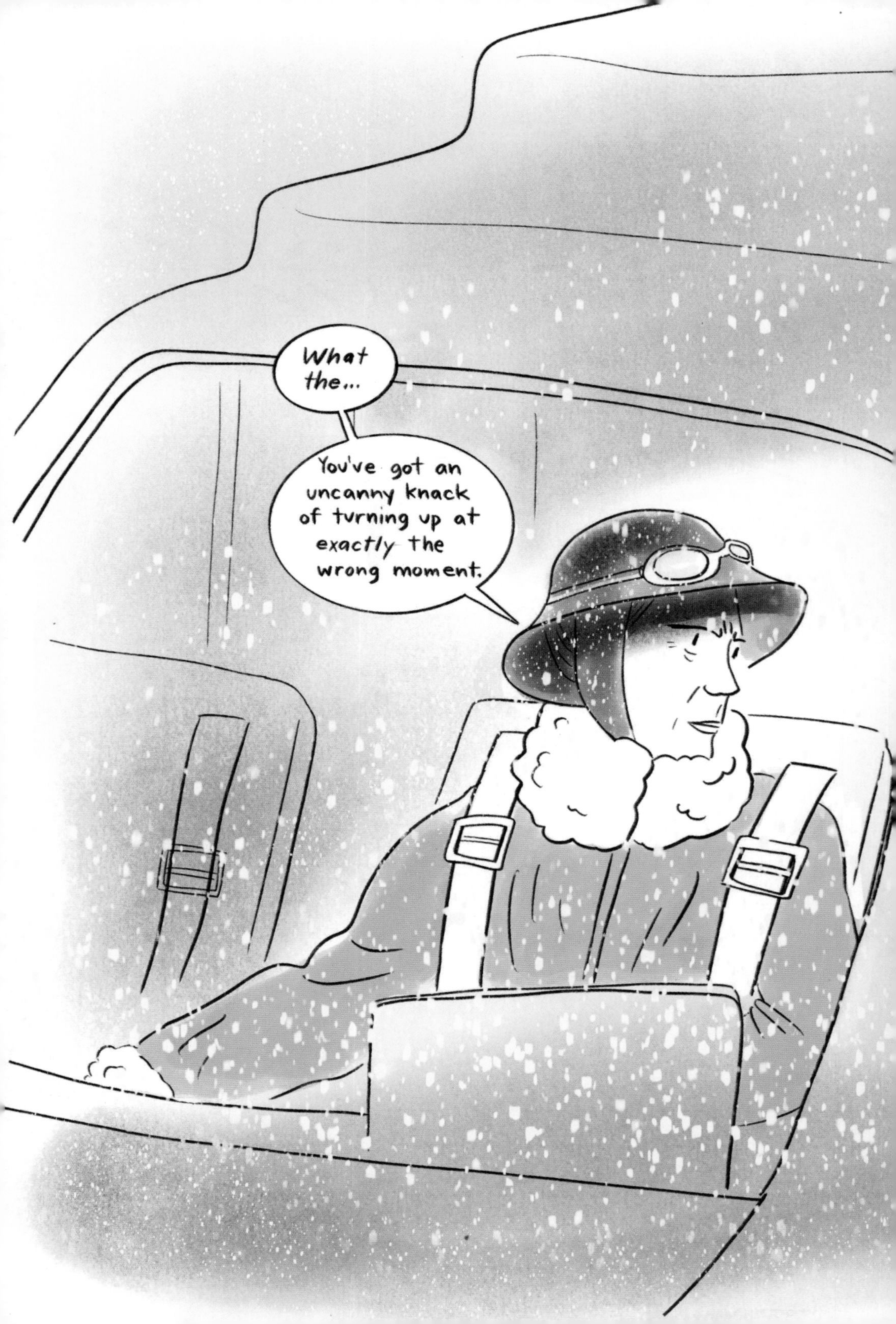
What the...
You've got an uncanny knack of turning up at exactly the wrong moment.

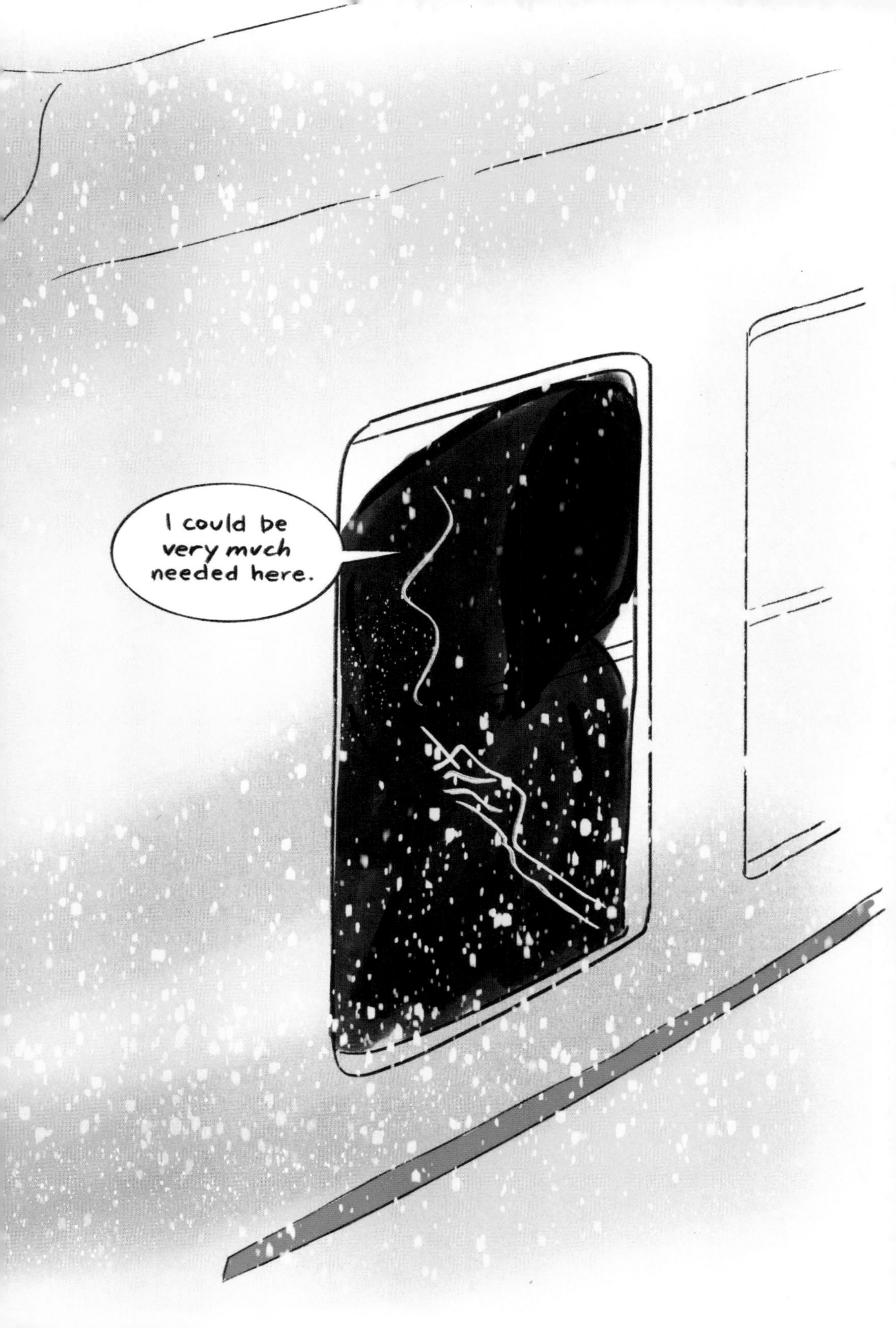
I could be very much needed here.

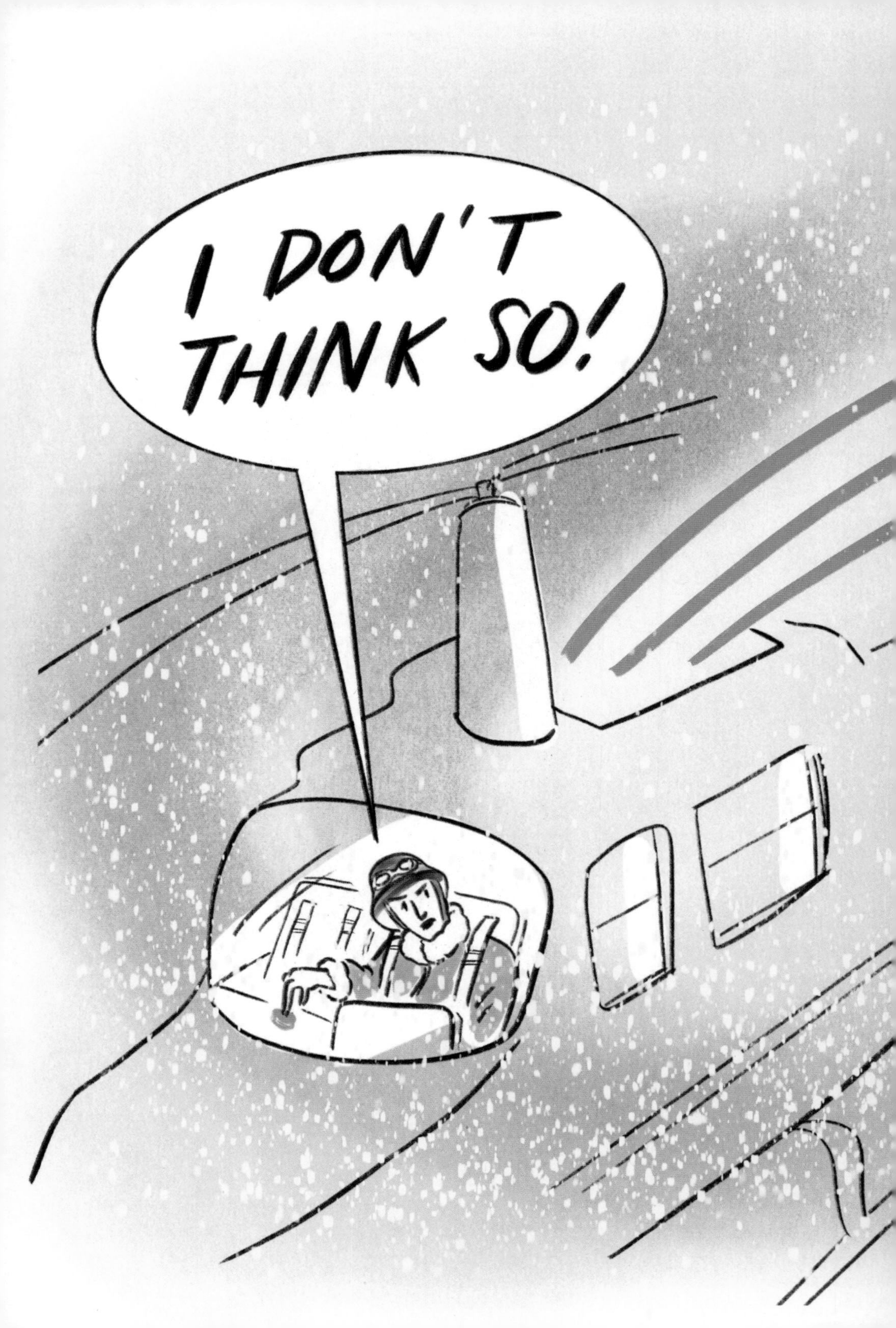
I DON'T THINK SO!

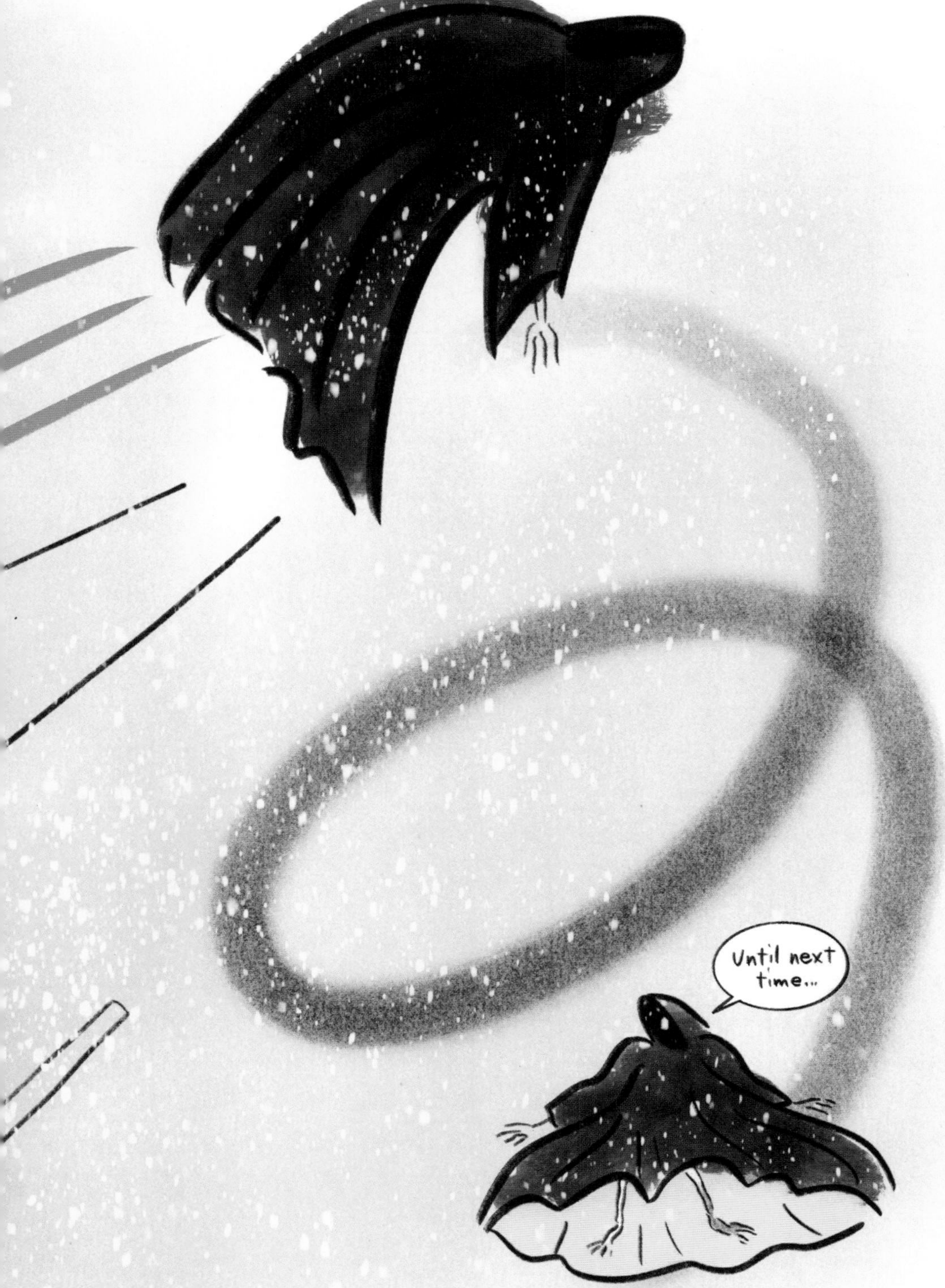
Until next time...

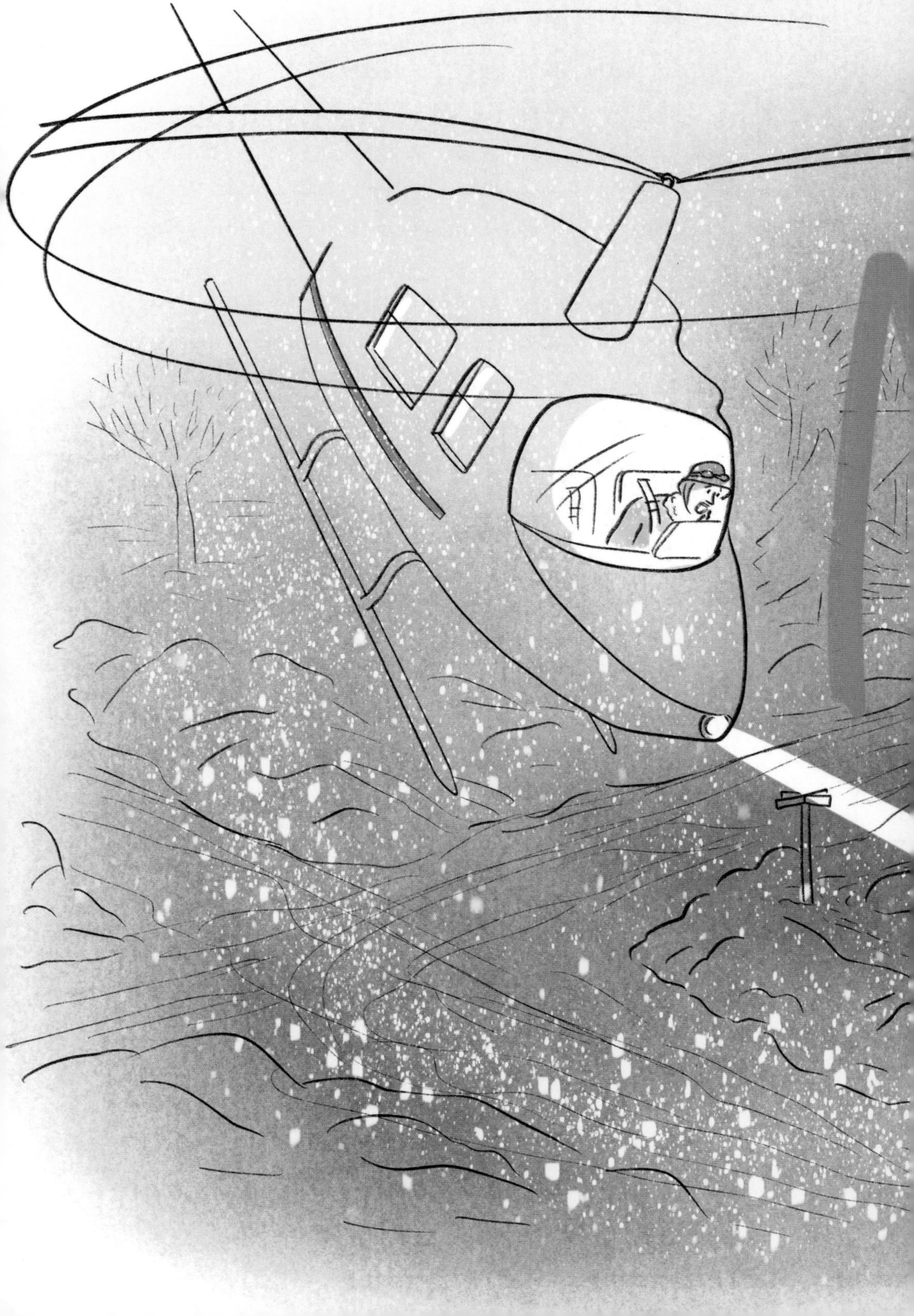

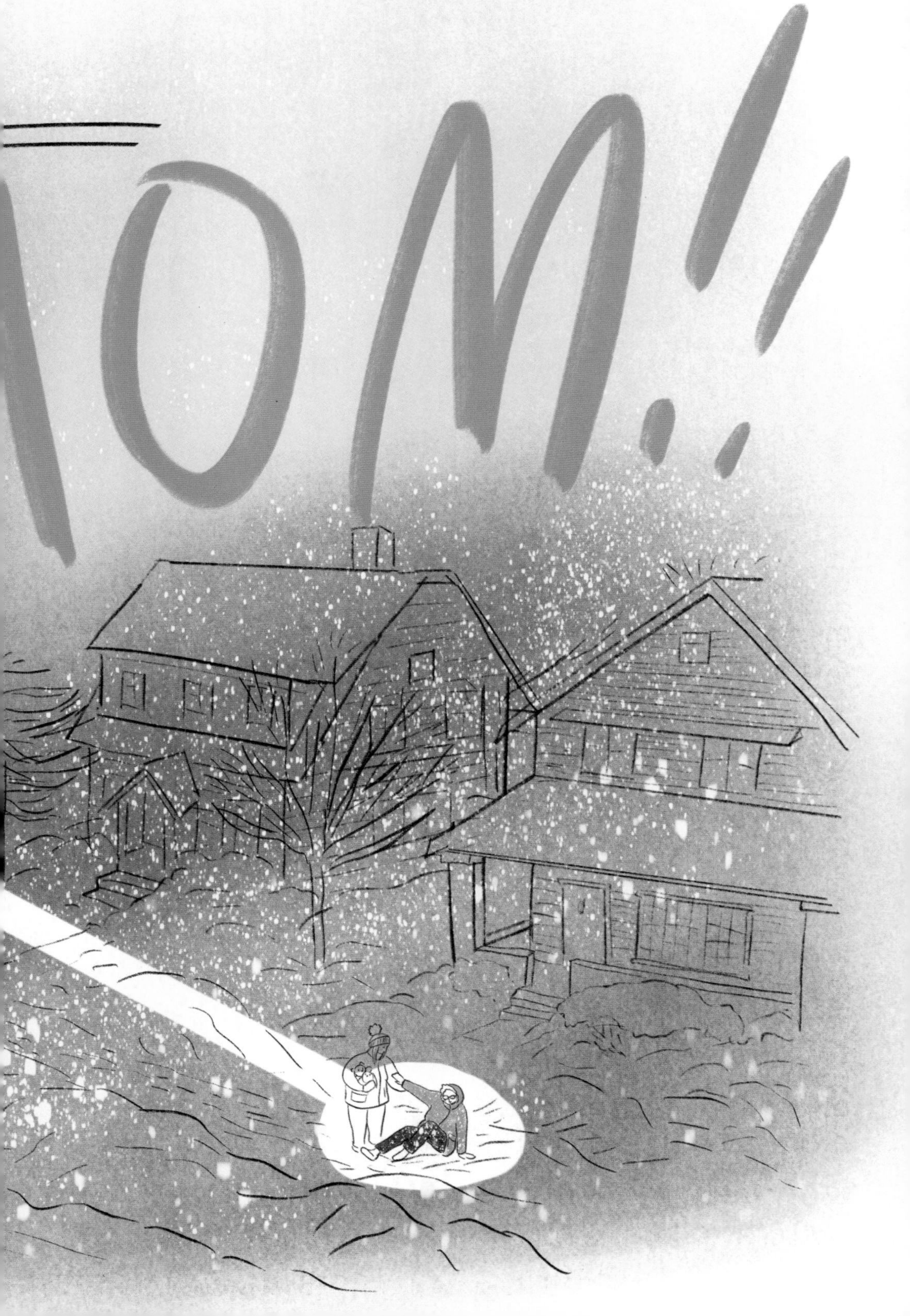
OM!!

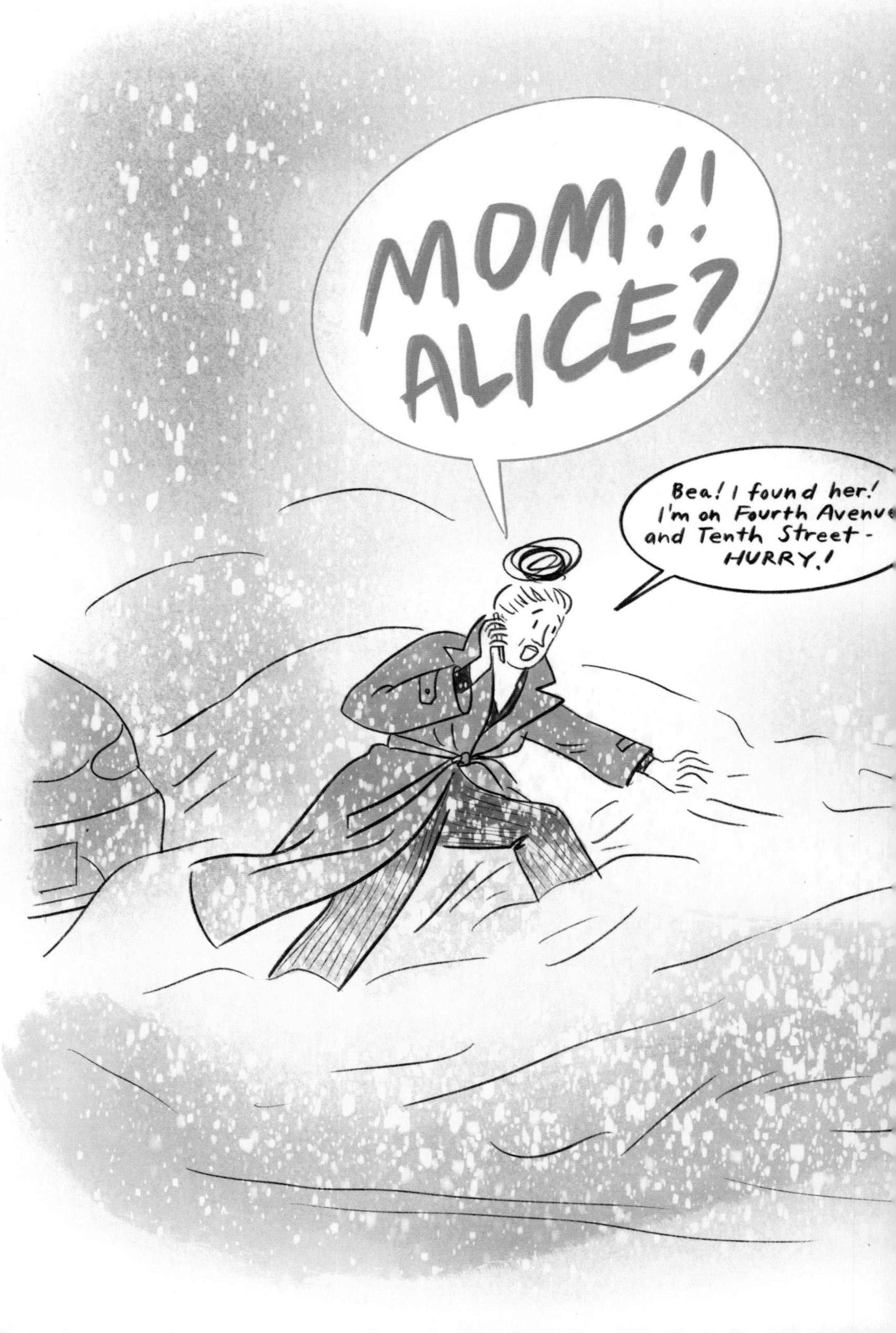
MOM!! ALICE?
Bea! I found her! I'm on Fourth Avenue and Tenth Street - HURRY!

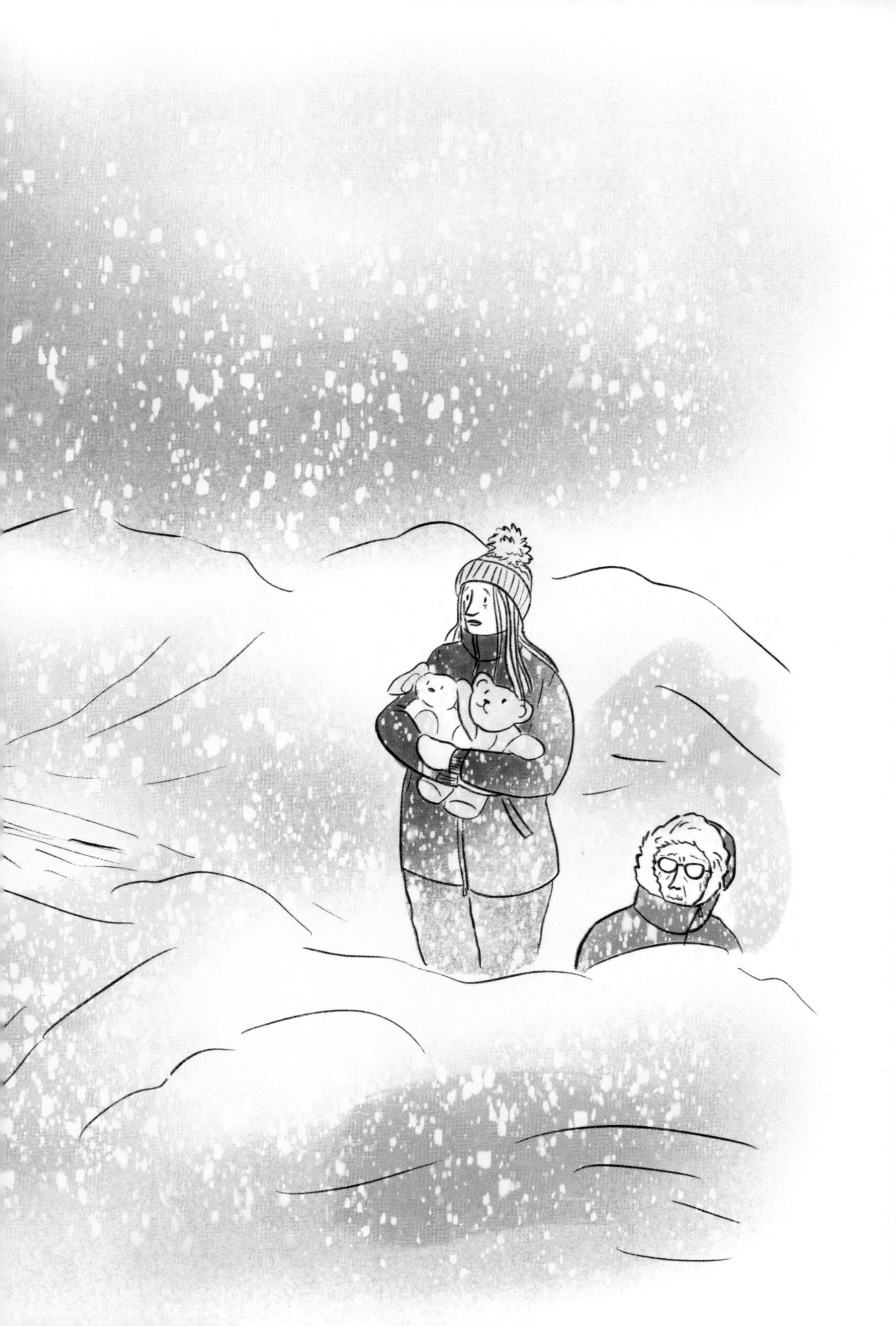

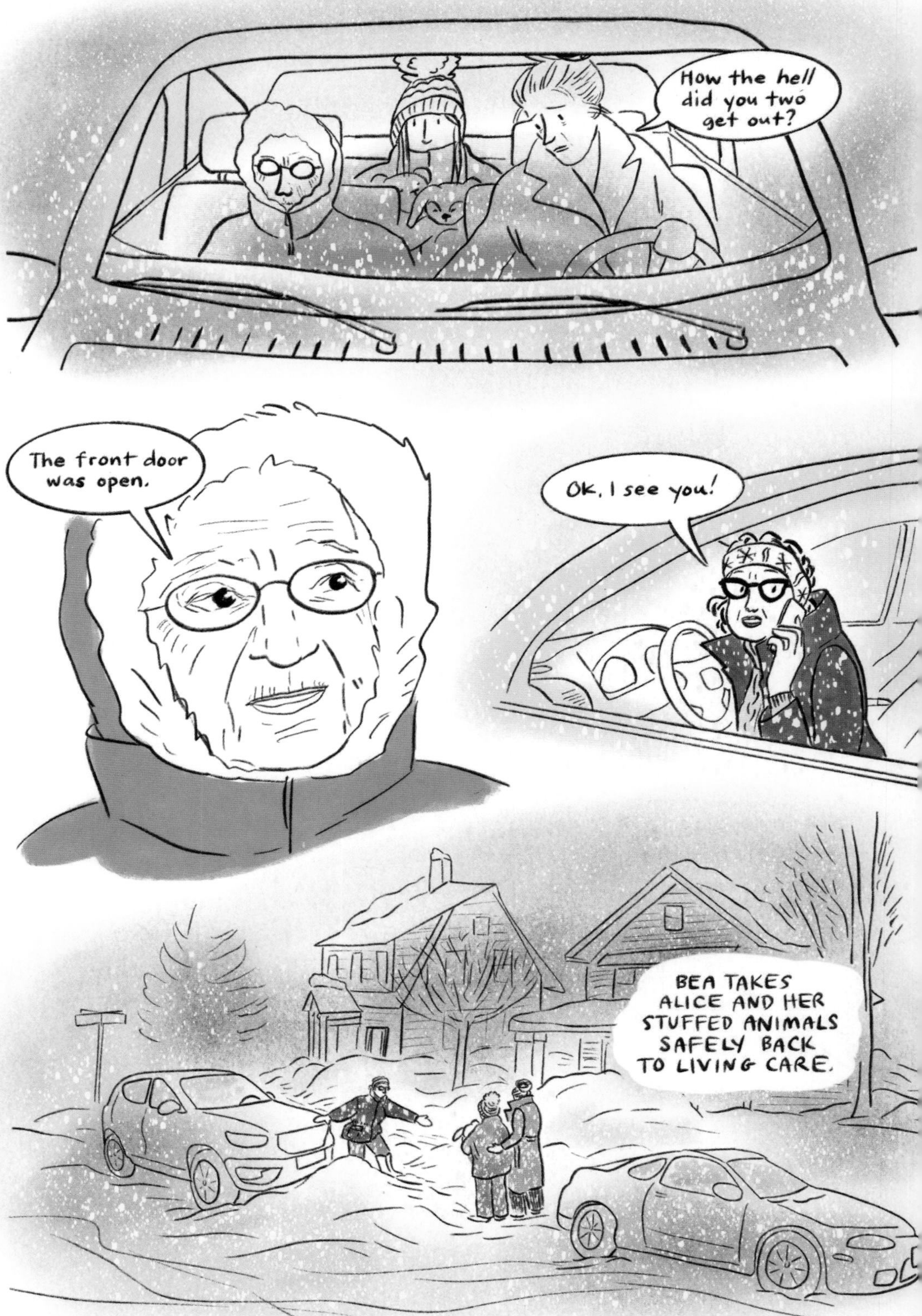
How the hell did you two get out?
The front door was open.
Ok, I see you!
BEA TAKES ALICE AND HER STUFFED ANIMALS SAFELY BACK TO LIVING CARE.

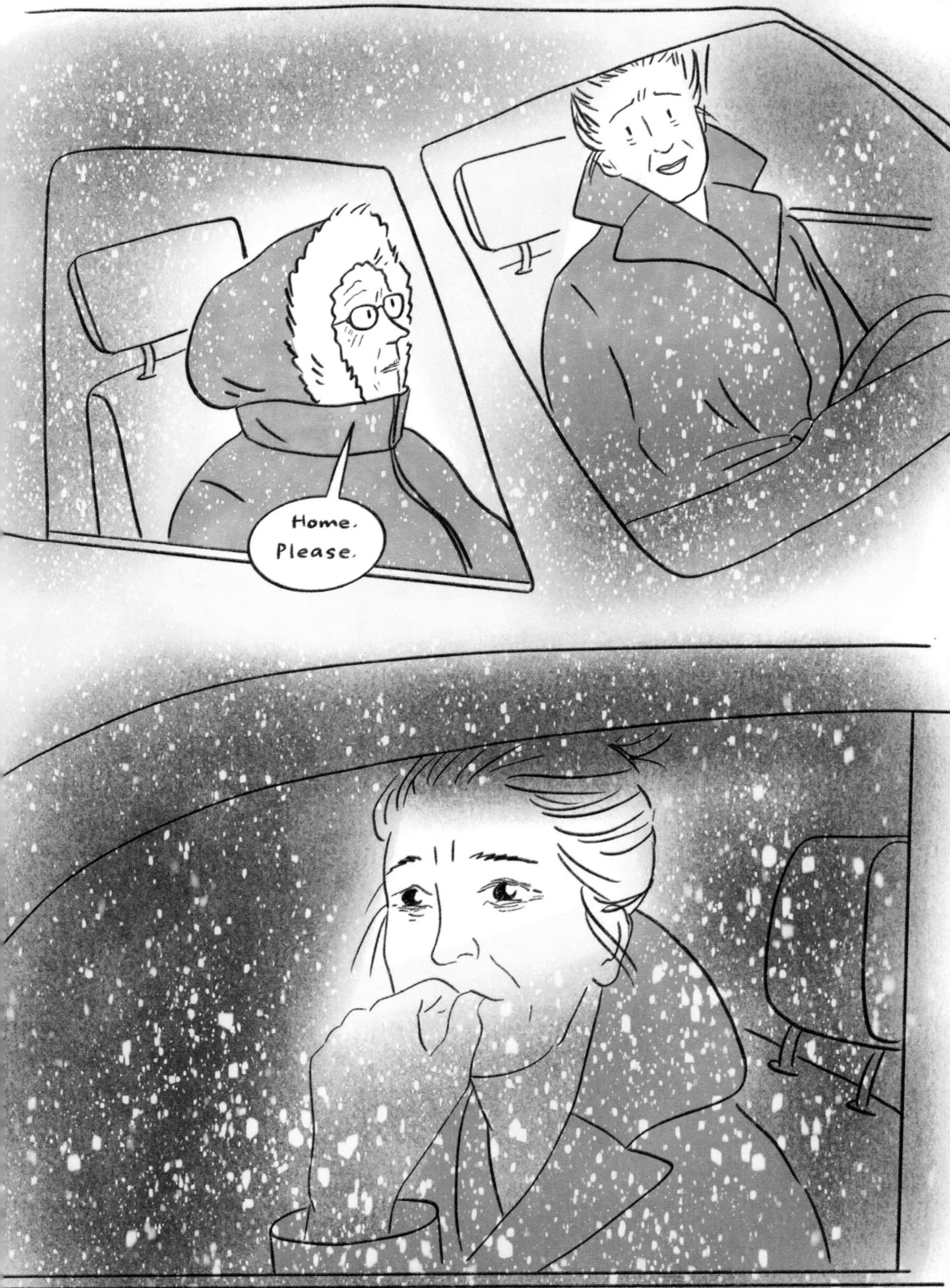
Home. Please.

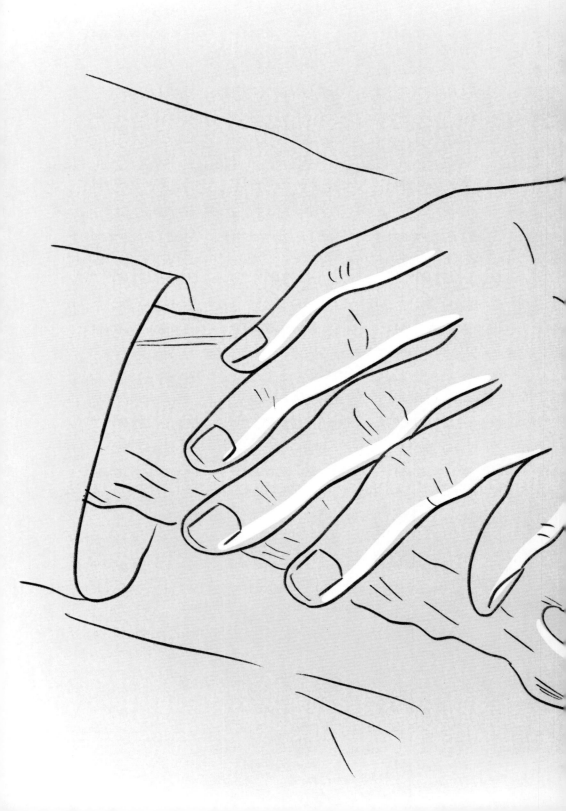

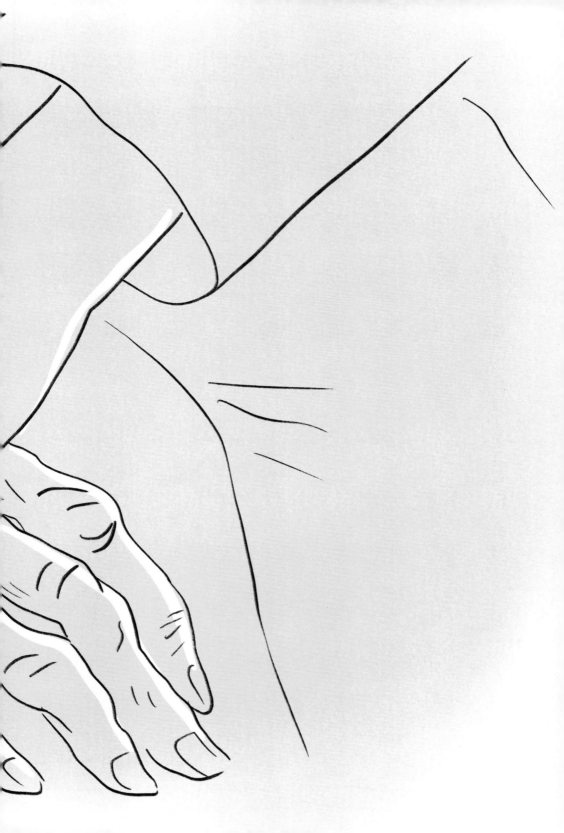

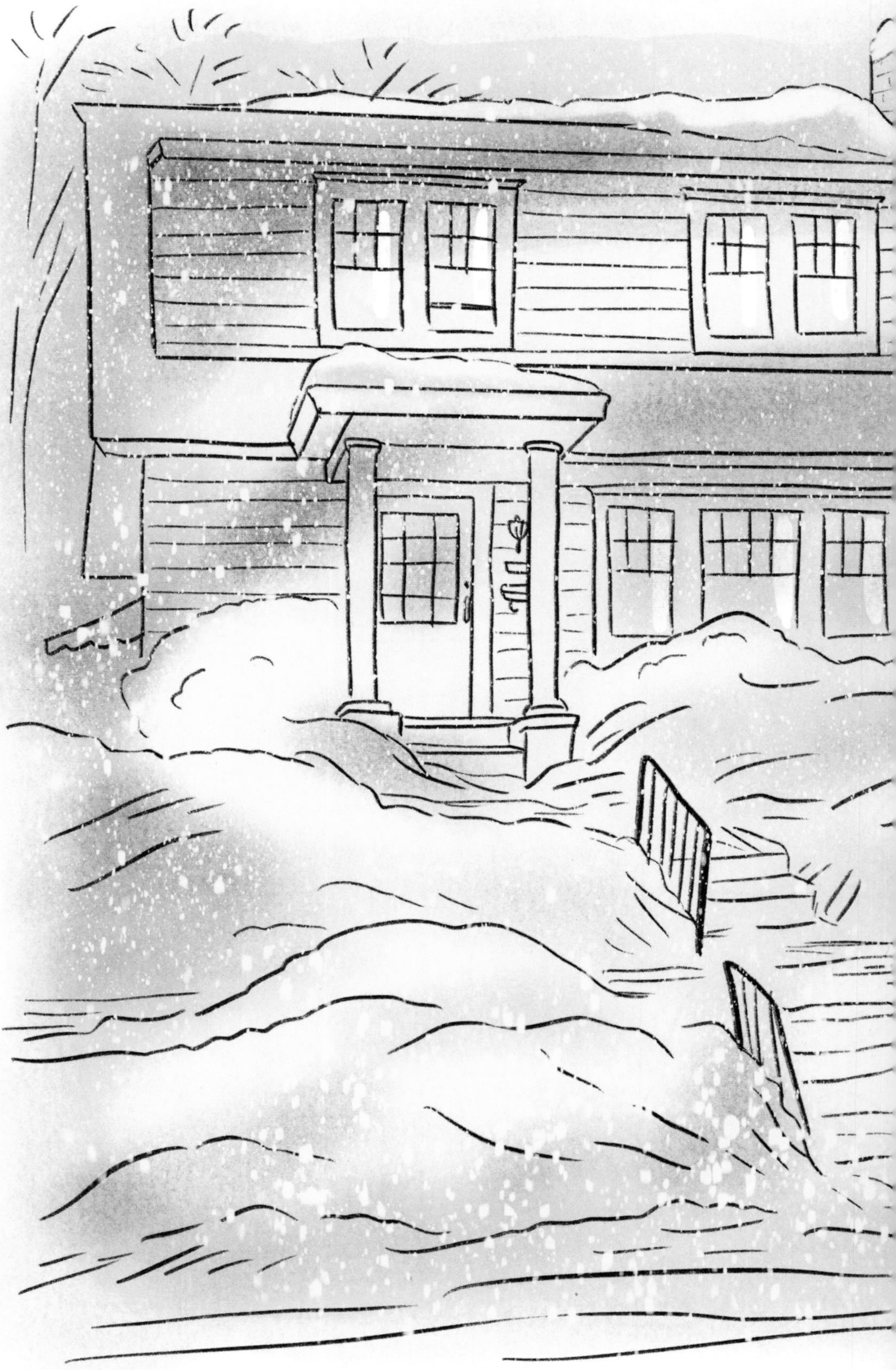

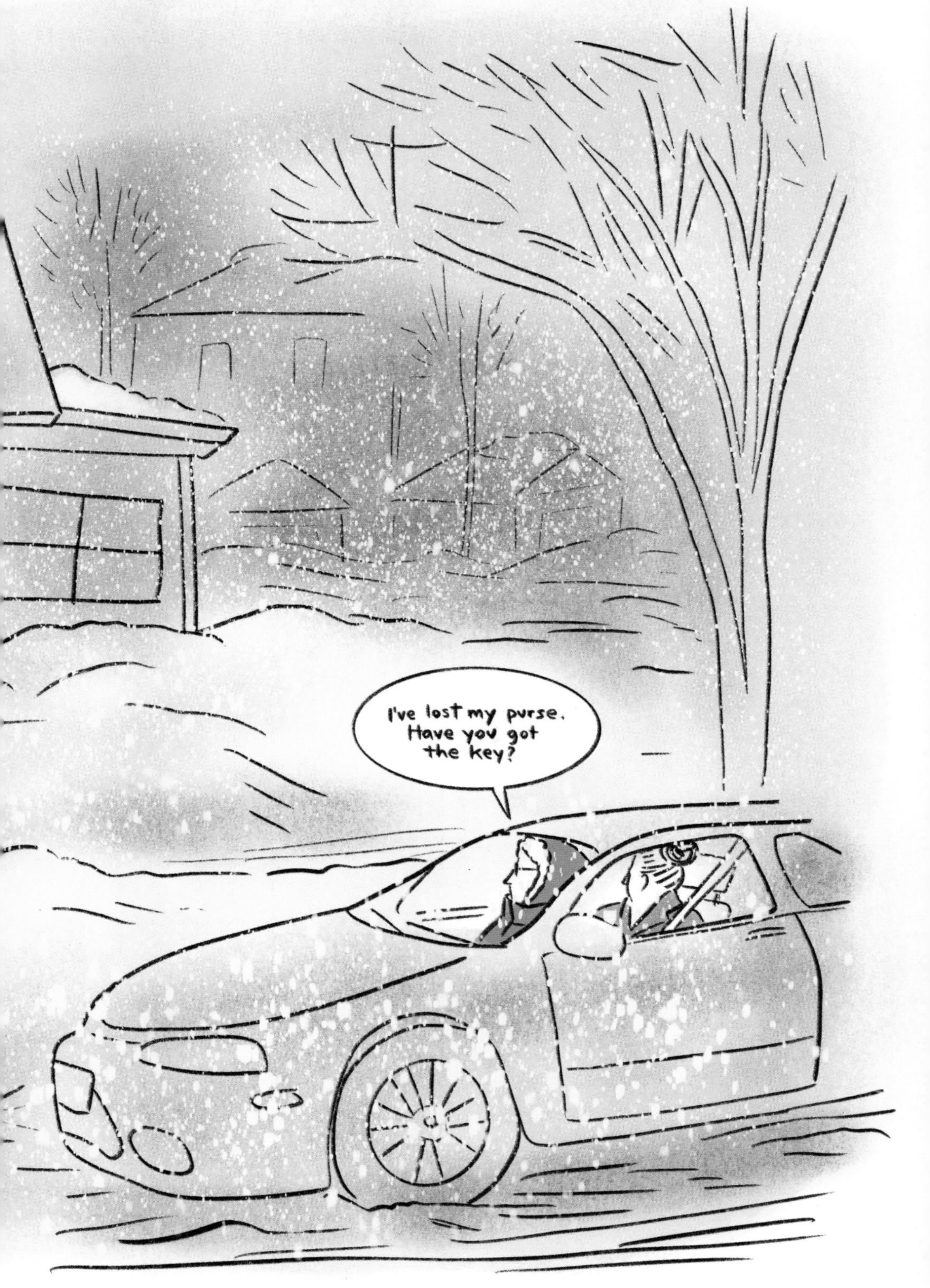
I've lost my purse. Have you got the key?

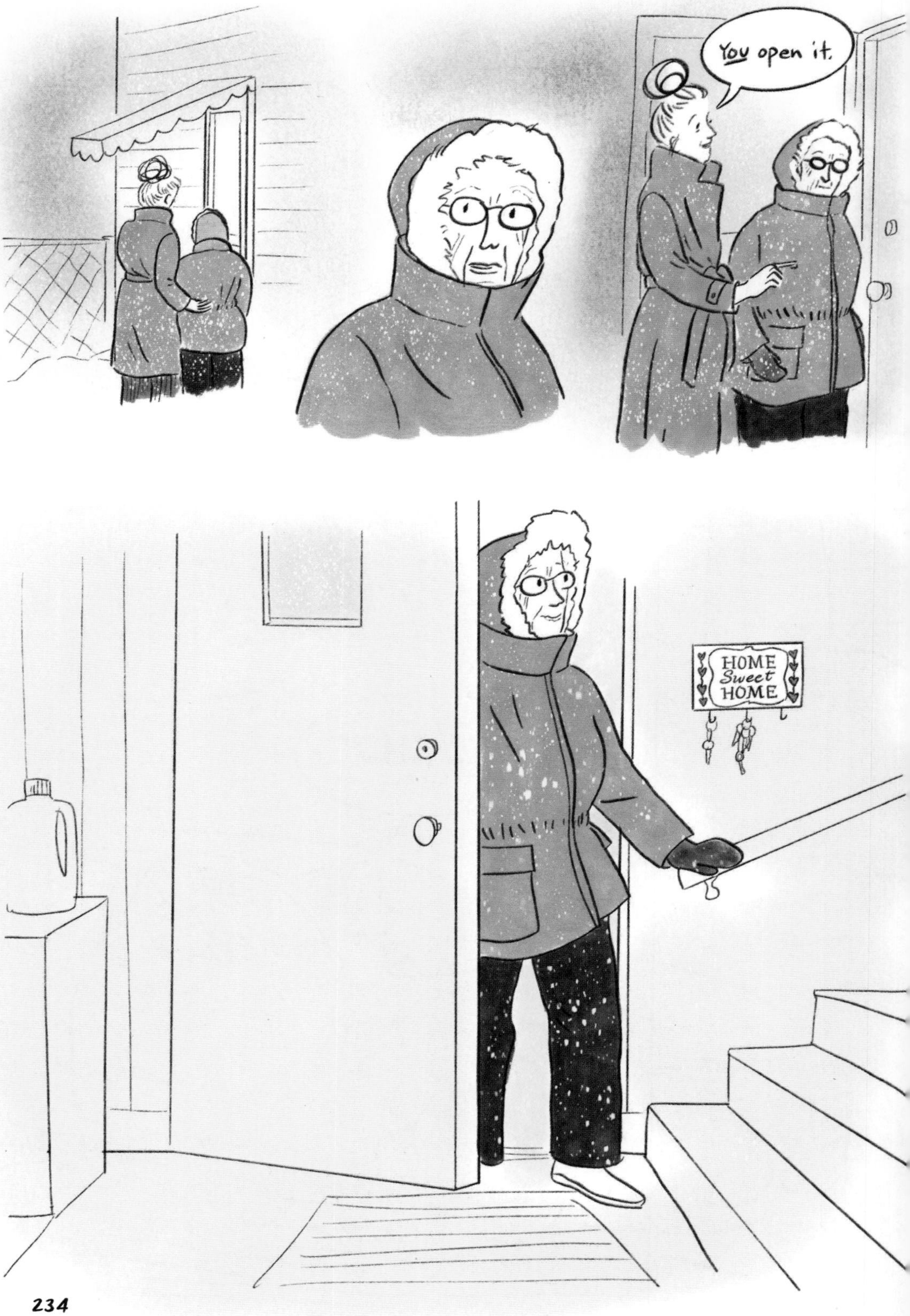
You open it.
HOME Sweet HOME

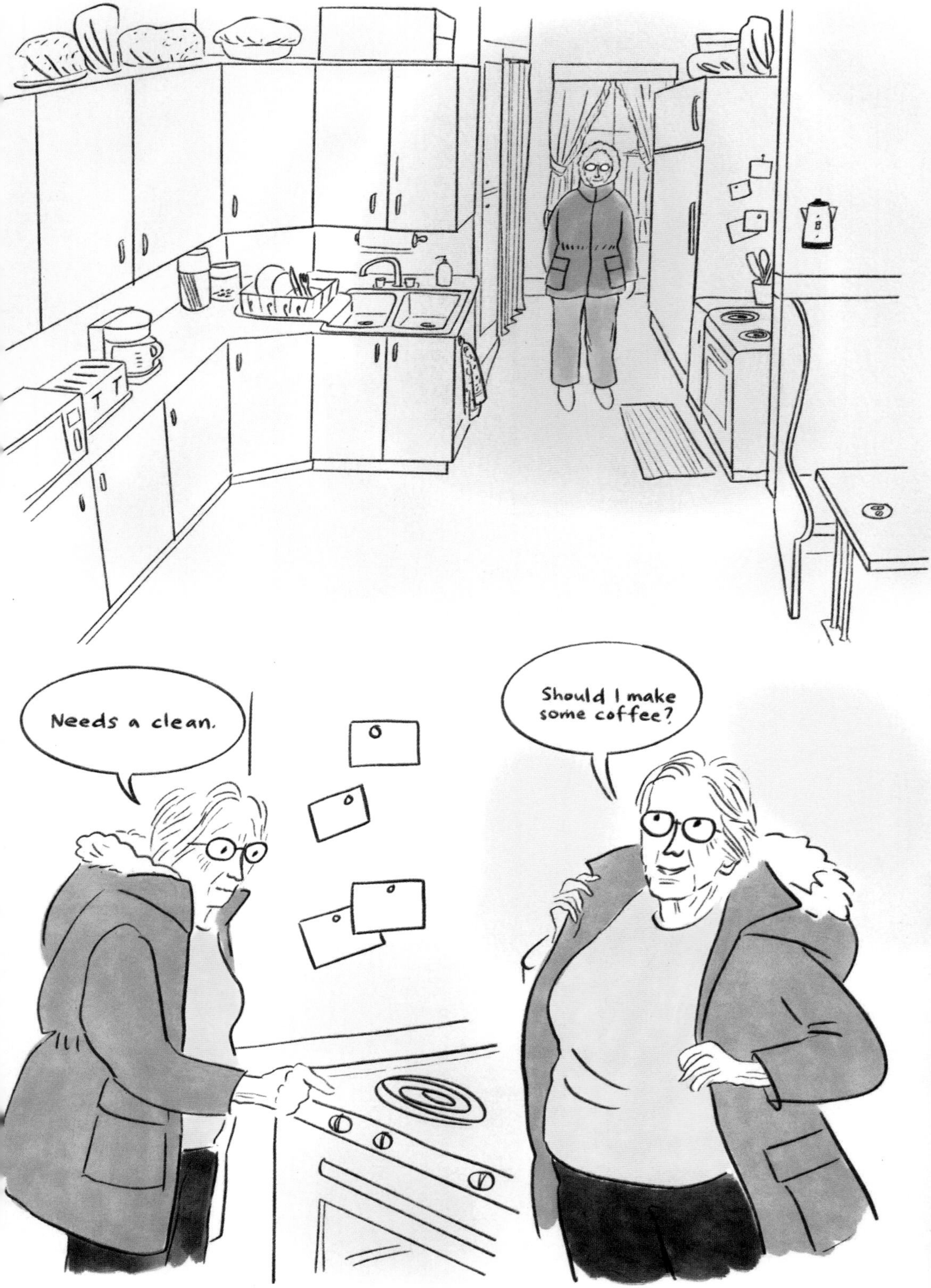
Needs a clean.
Should I make some coffee?

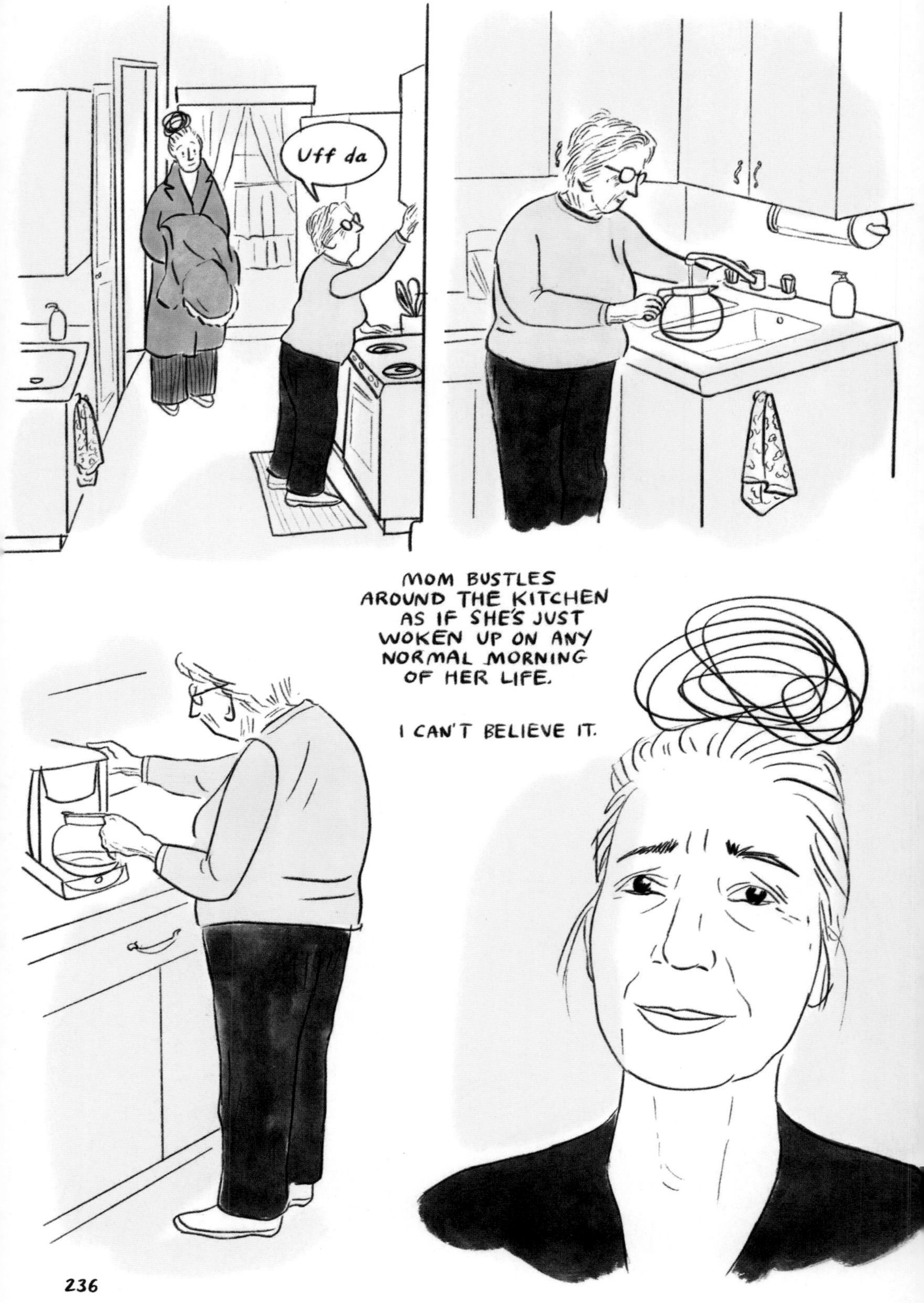
Uff da
MOM BUSTLES AROUND THE KITCHEN AS IF SHE'S JUST WOKEN UP ON ANY NORMAL MORNING OF HER LIFE.
I CAN'T BELIEVE IT.

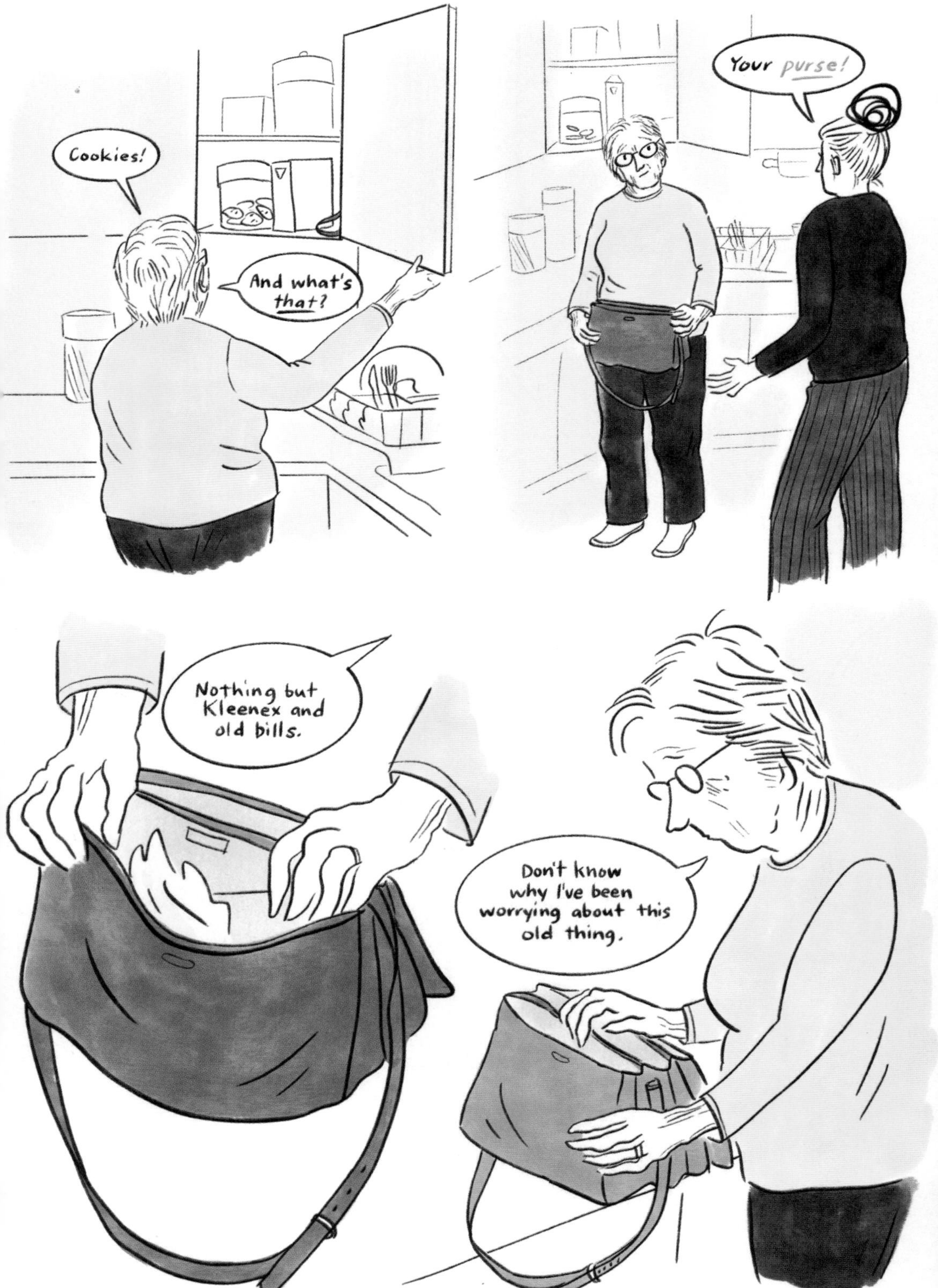
Cookies!
And what's that?
Your purse!
Nothing but Kleenex and old bills.
Don't know why I've been worrying about this old thing.

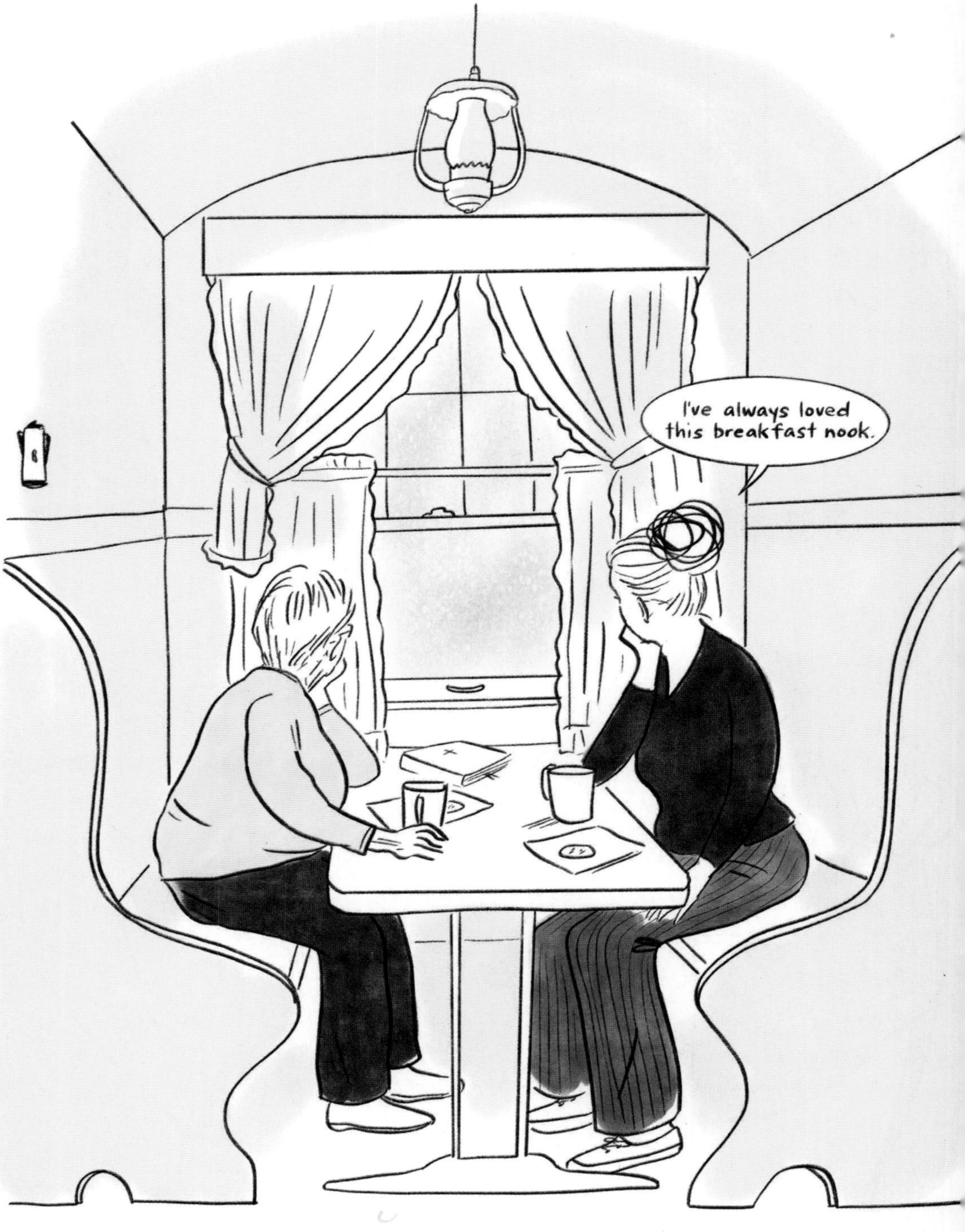
I've always loved this breakfast nook.

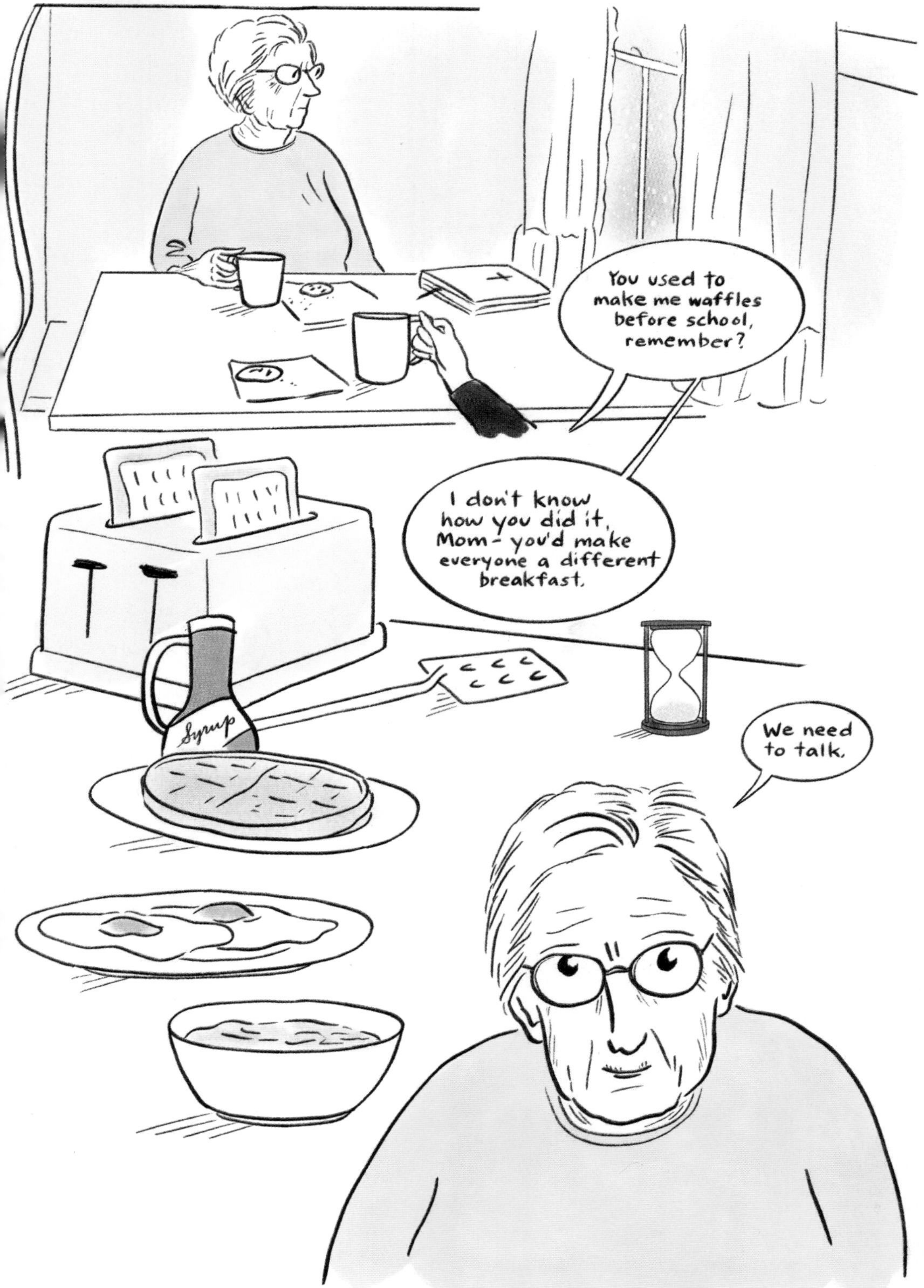
You used to make me waffles before school, remember?
I don't know how you did it, Mom- you'd make everyone a different breakfast.
Syrup
We need to talk.

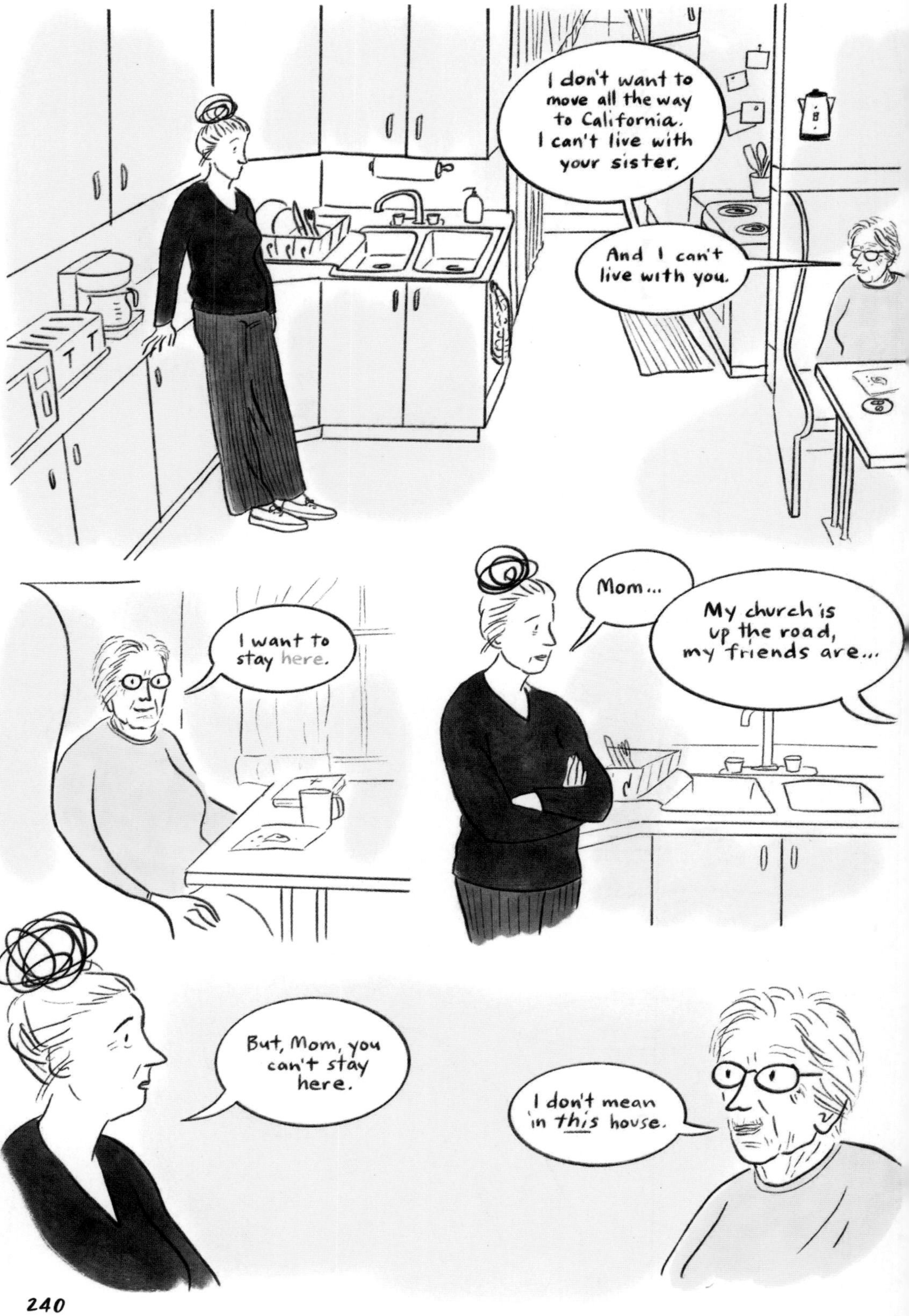
I don't want to move all the way to California. I can't live with your sister.
And I can't live with you.
I want to stay here.
Mom...
My church is up the road, my friends are...
But, Mom, you can't stay here.
I don't mean in this house.

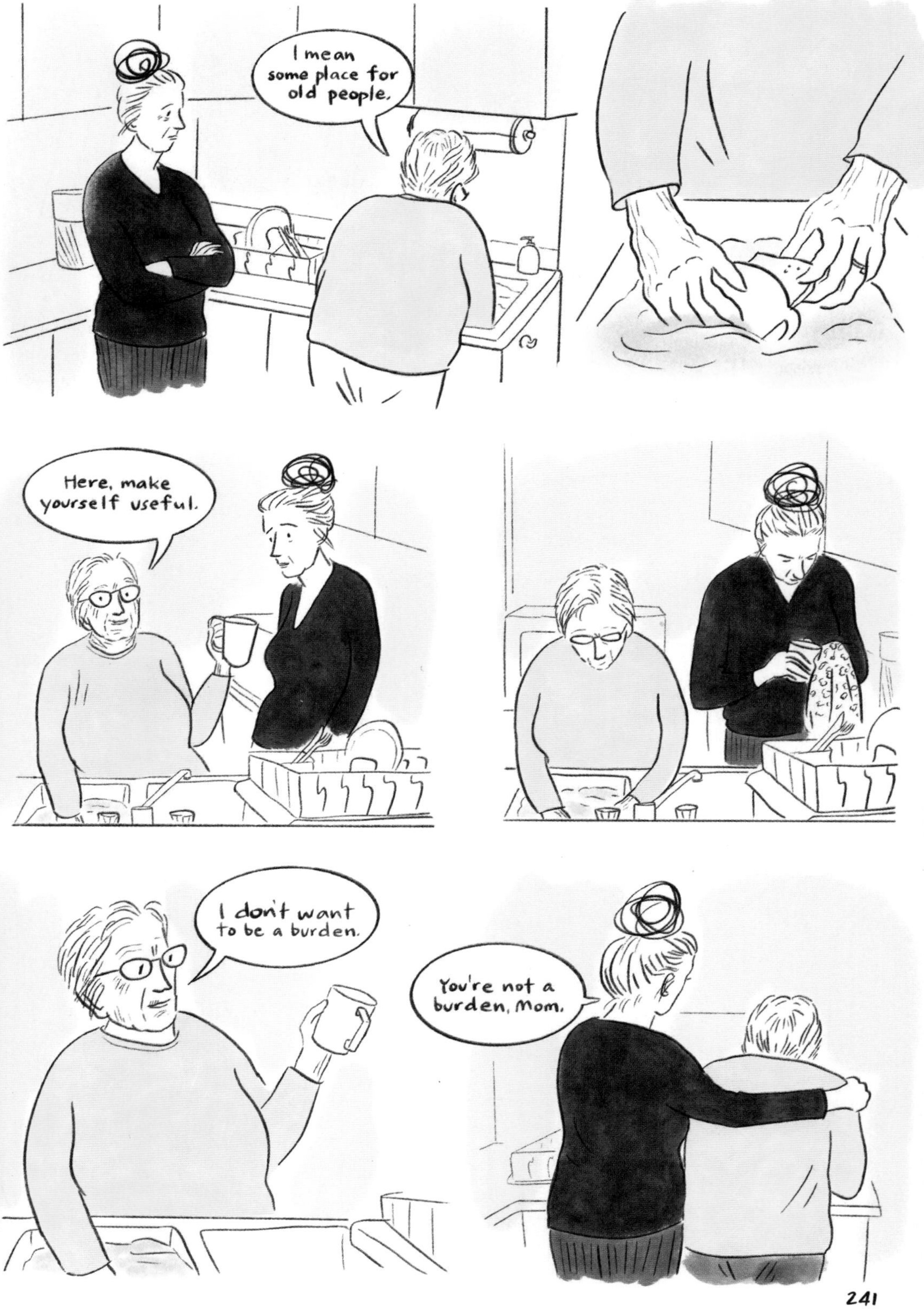
I mean some place for old people.
Here, make yourself useful.
I don't want to be a burden.
You're not a burden, Mom.

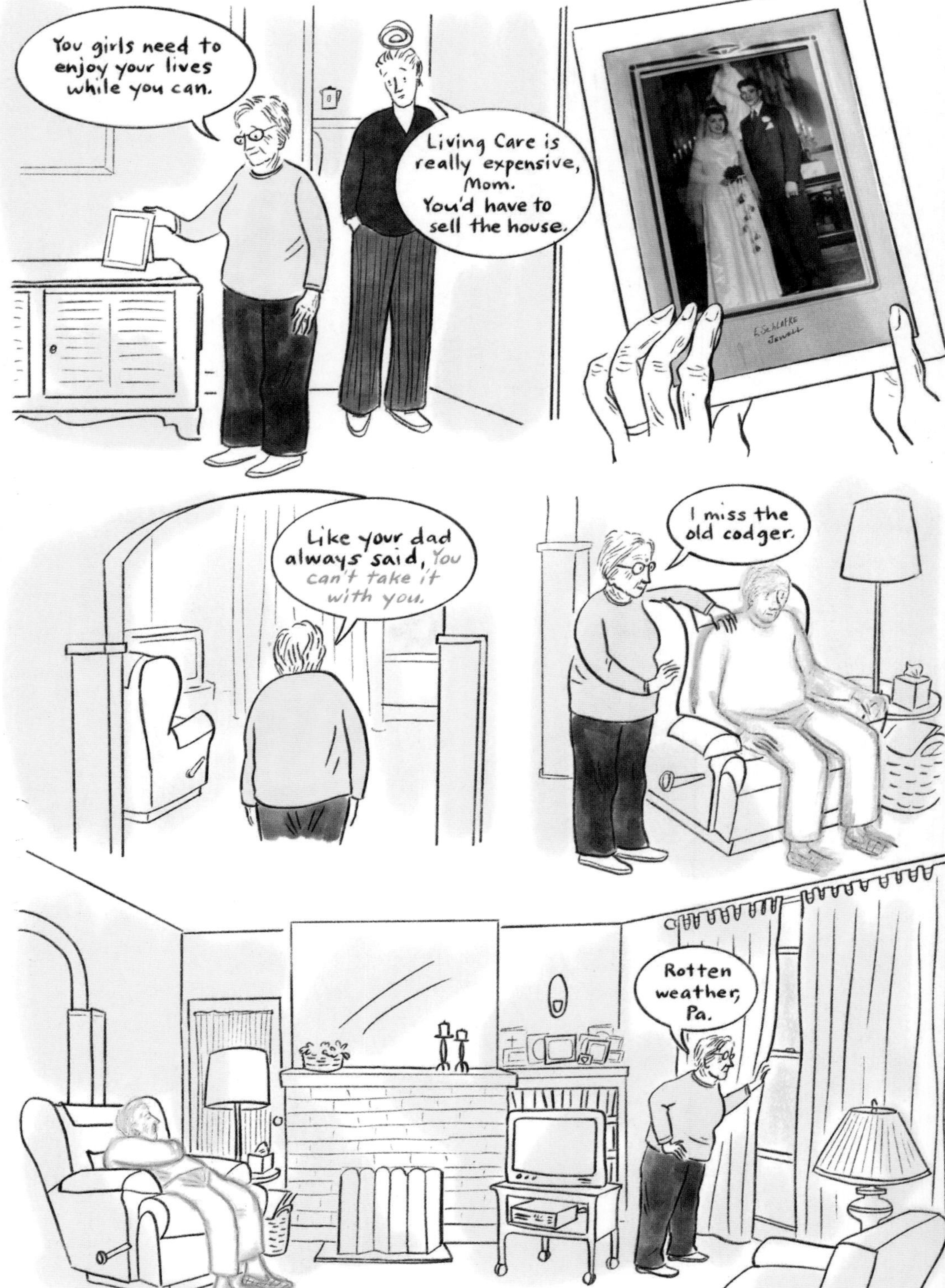
You girls need to enjoy your lives while you can.
Living Care is really expensive, Mom. You'd have to sell the house.
Like your dad always said, You can't take it with you.
I miss the old codger.
Rotten weather, Pa.

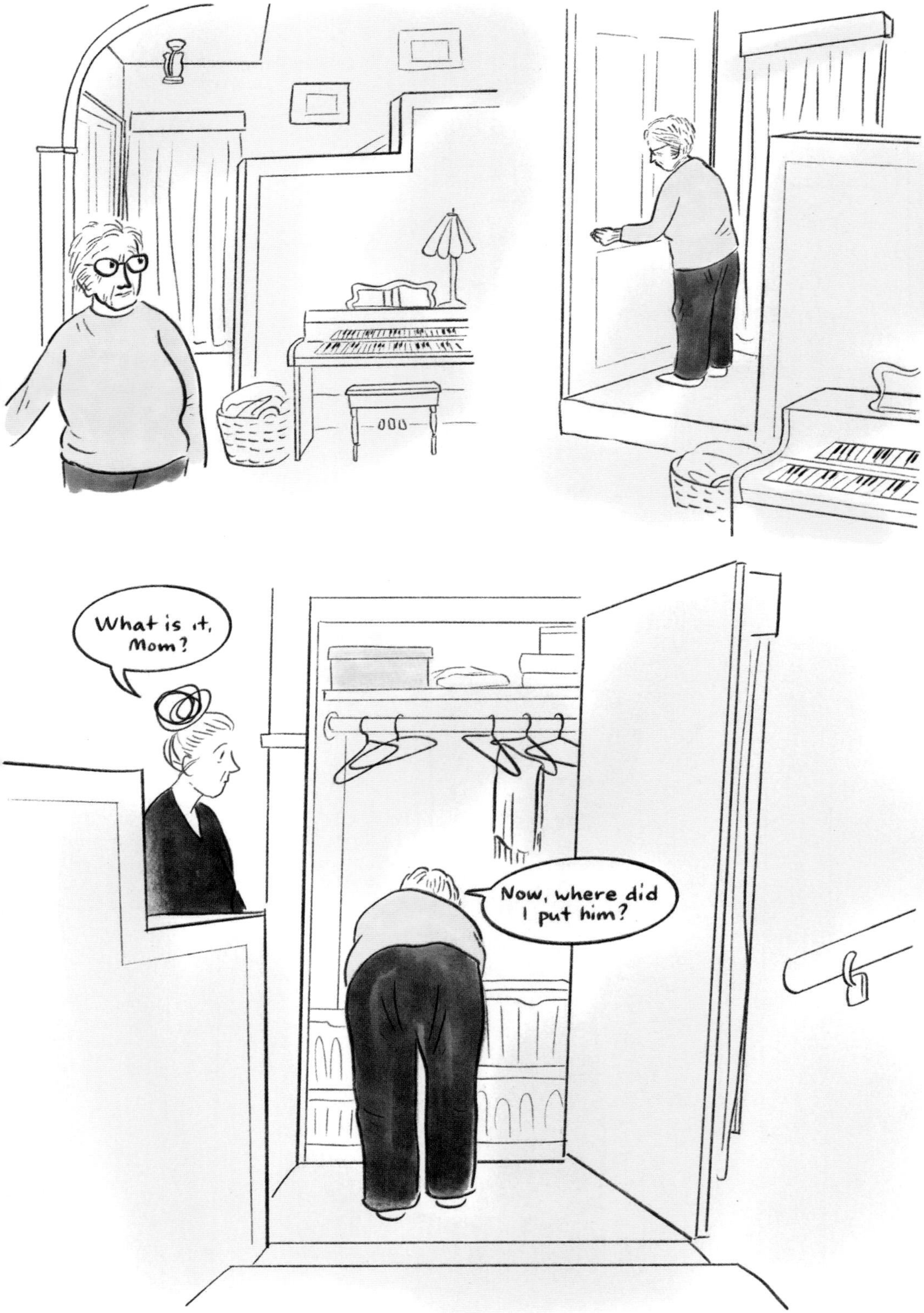
What is it, Mom?
Now, where did I put him?

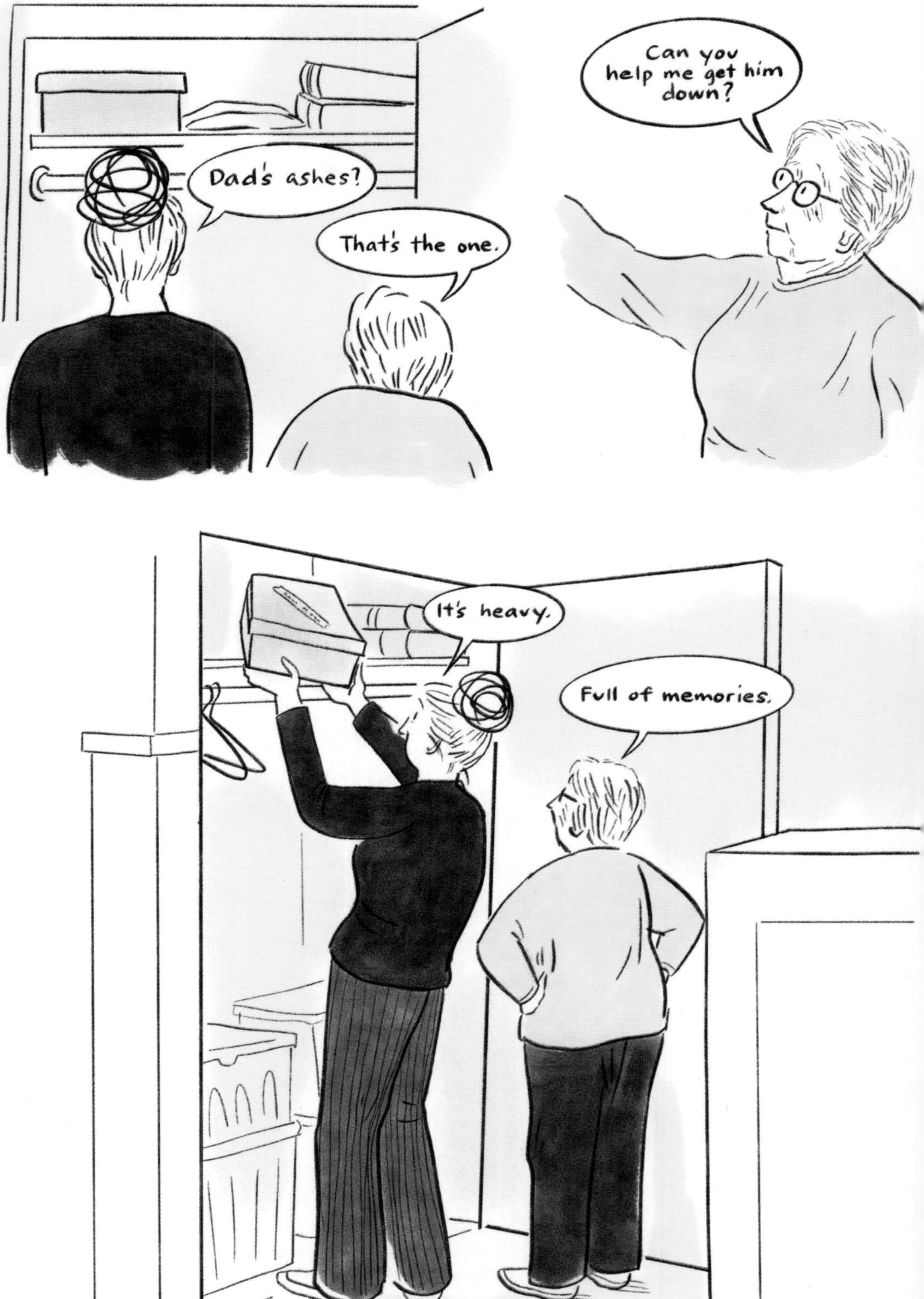
Dad's ashes?
That's the one.
Can you help me get him down?
It's heavy.
Full of memories.

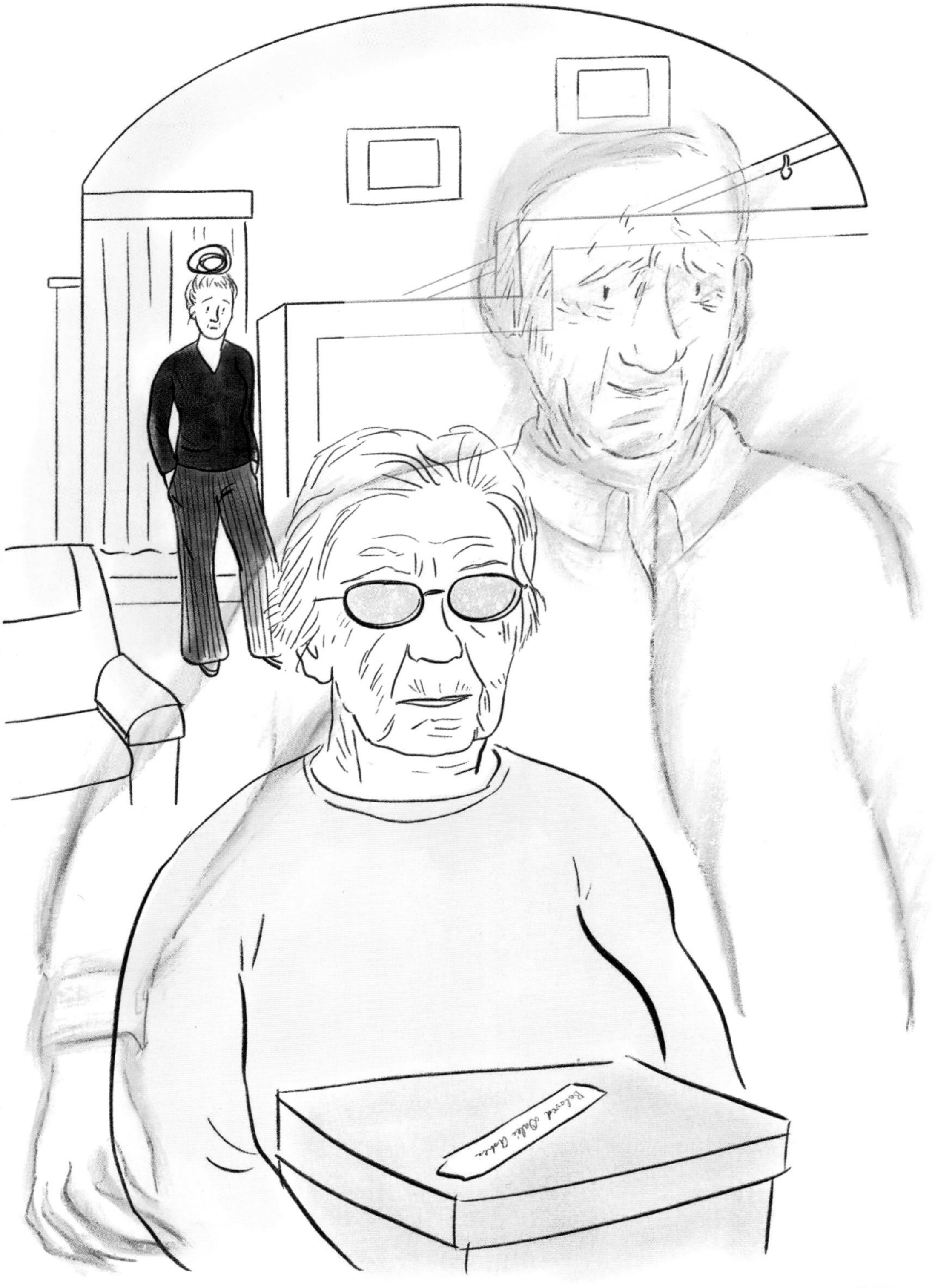

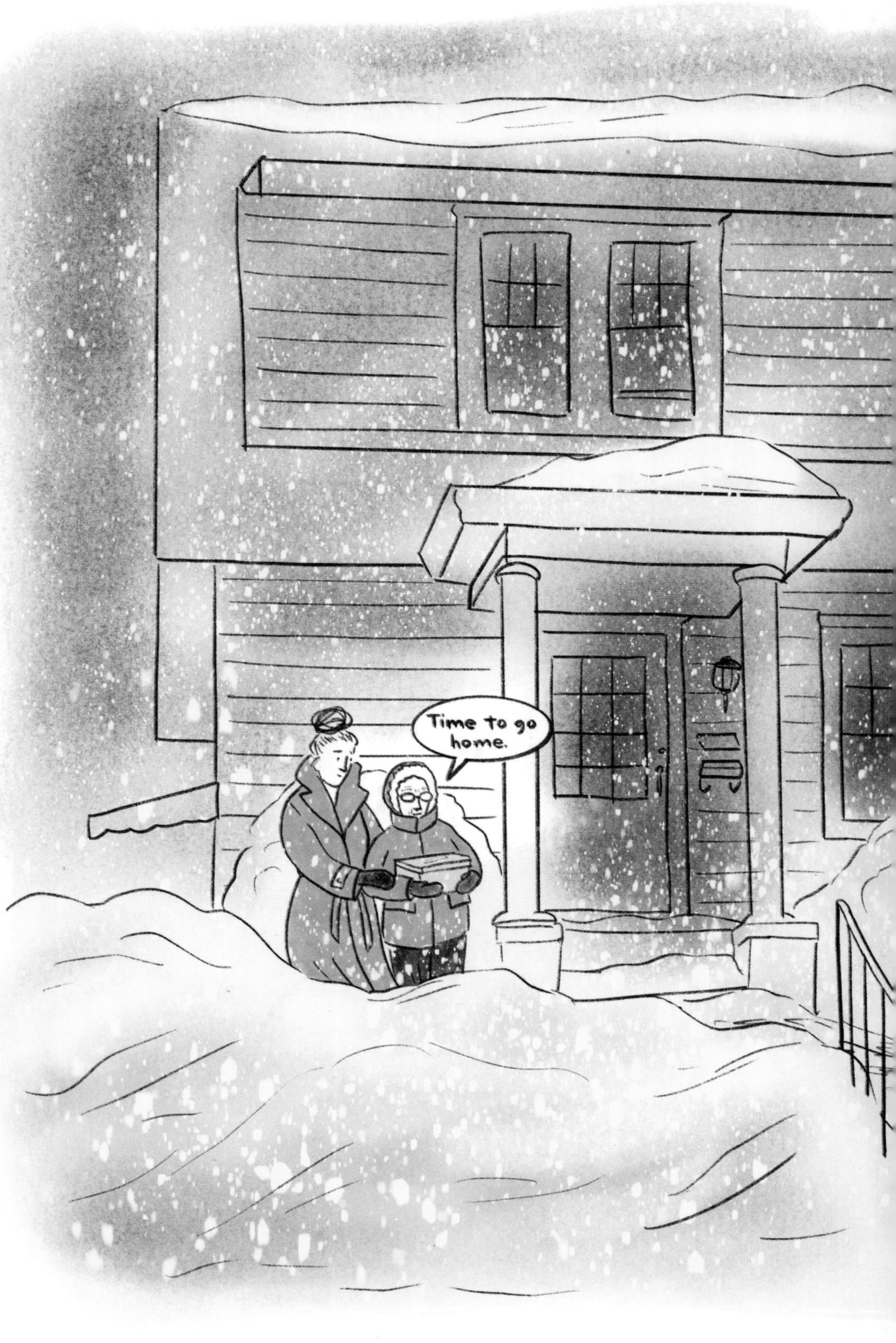
Time to go home.

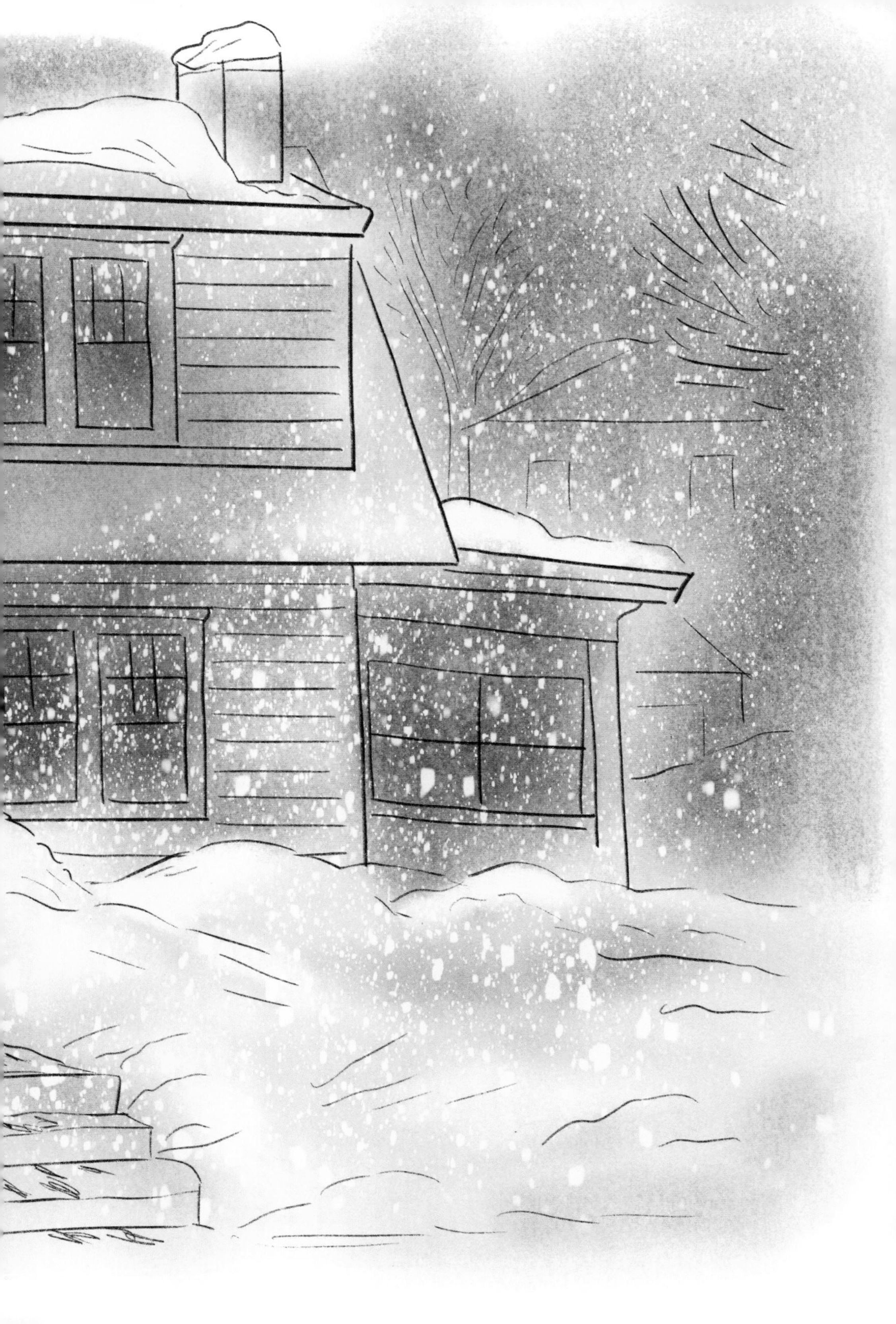

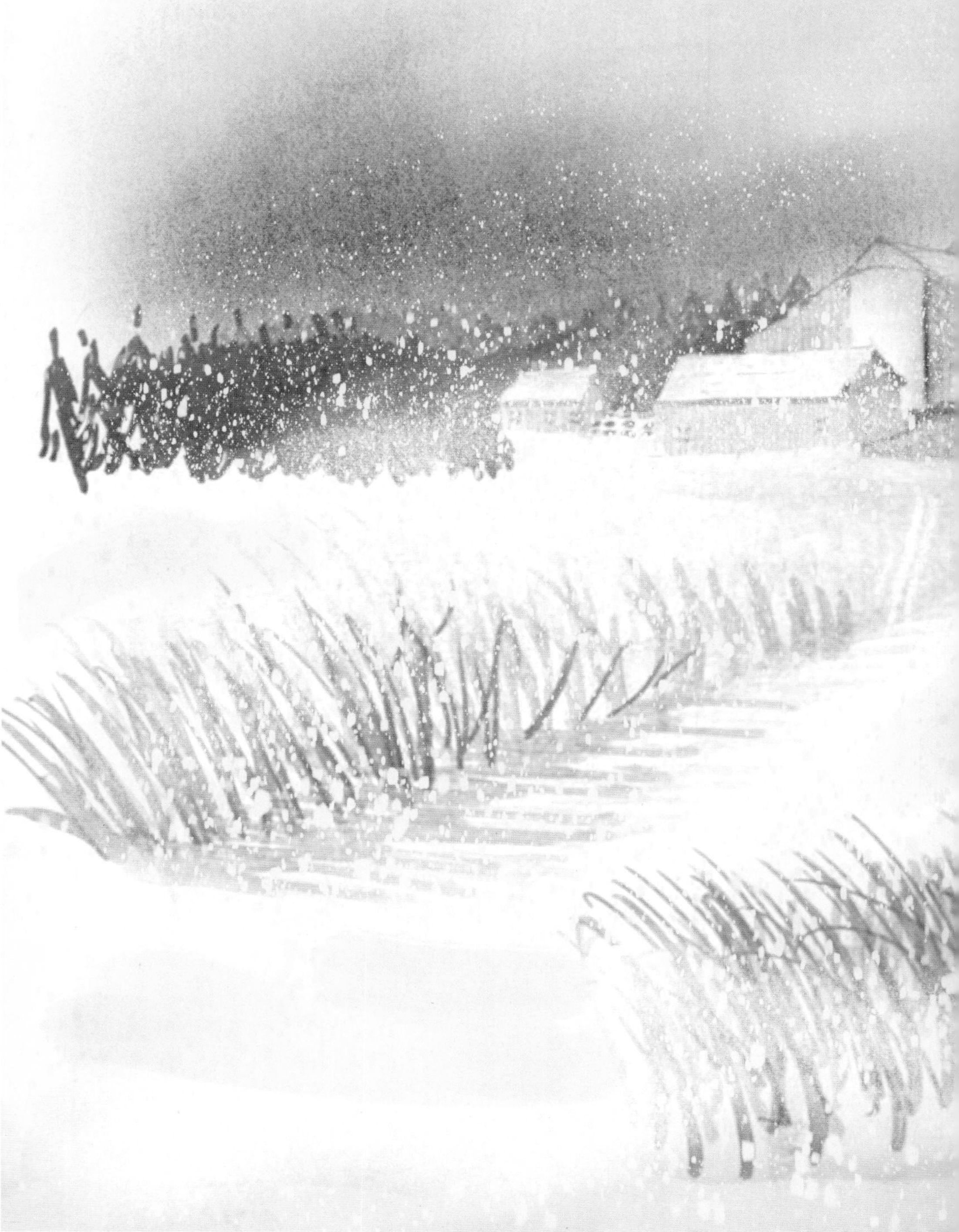

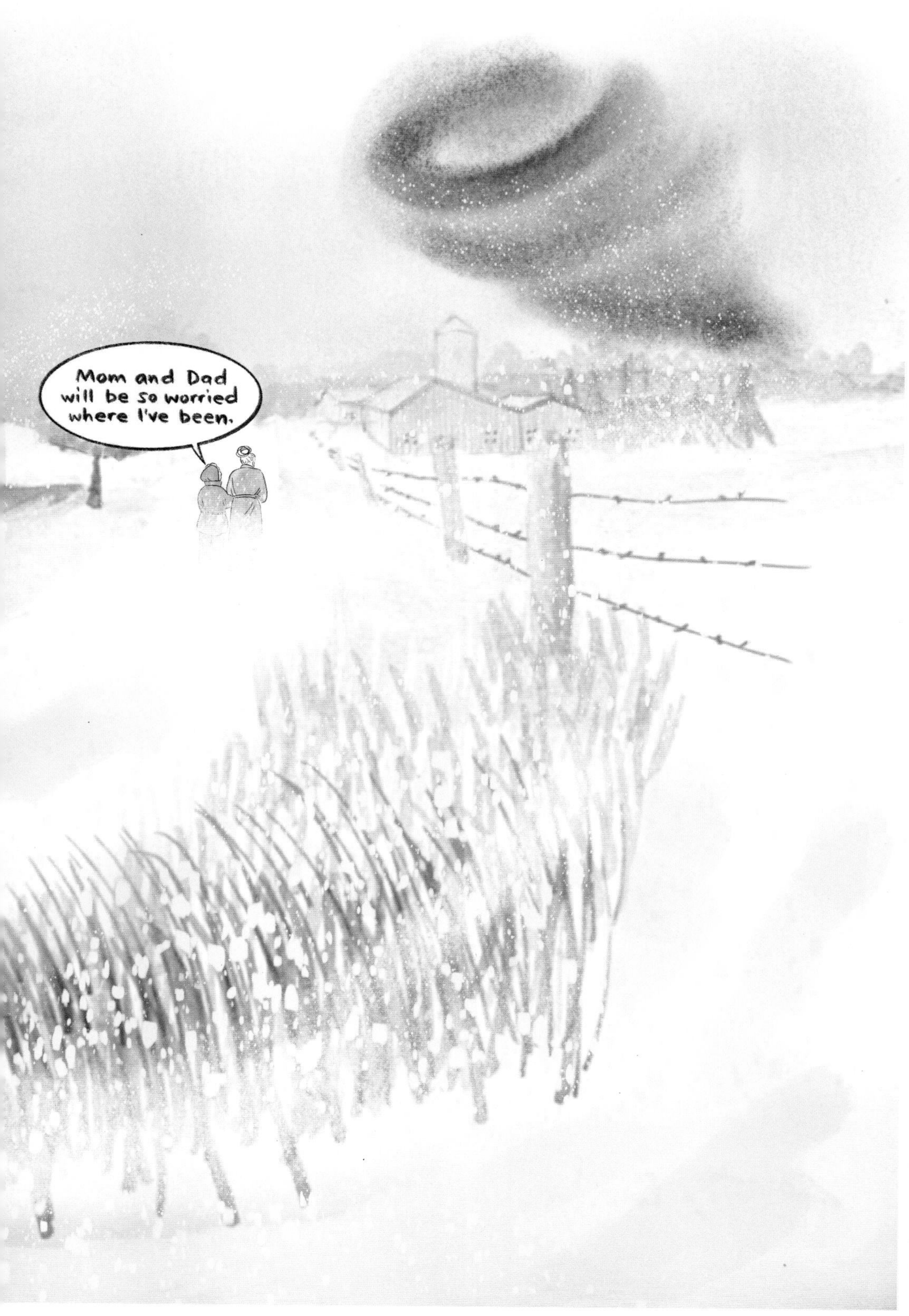
Mom and Dad will be so worried where I've been.

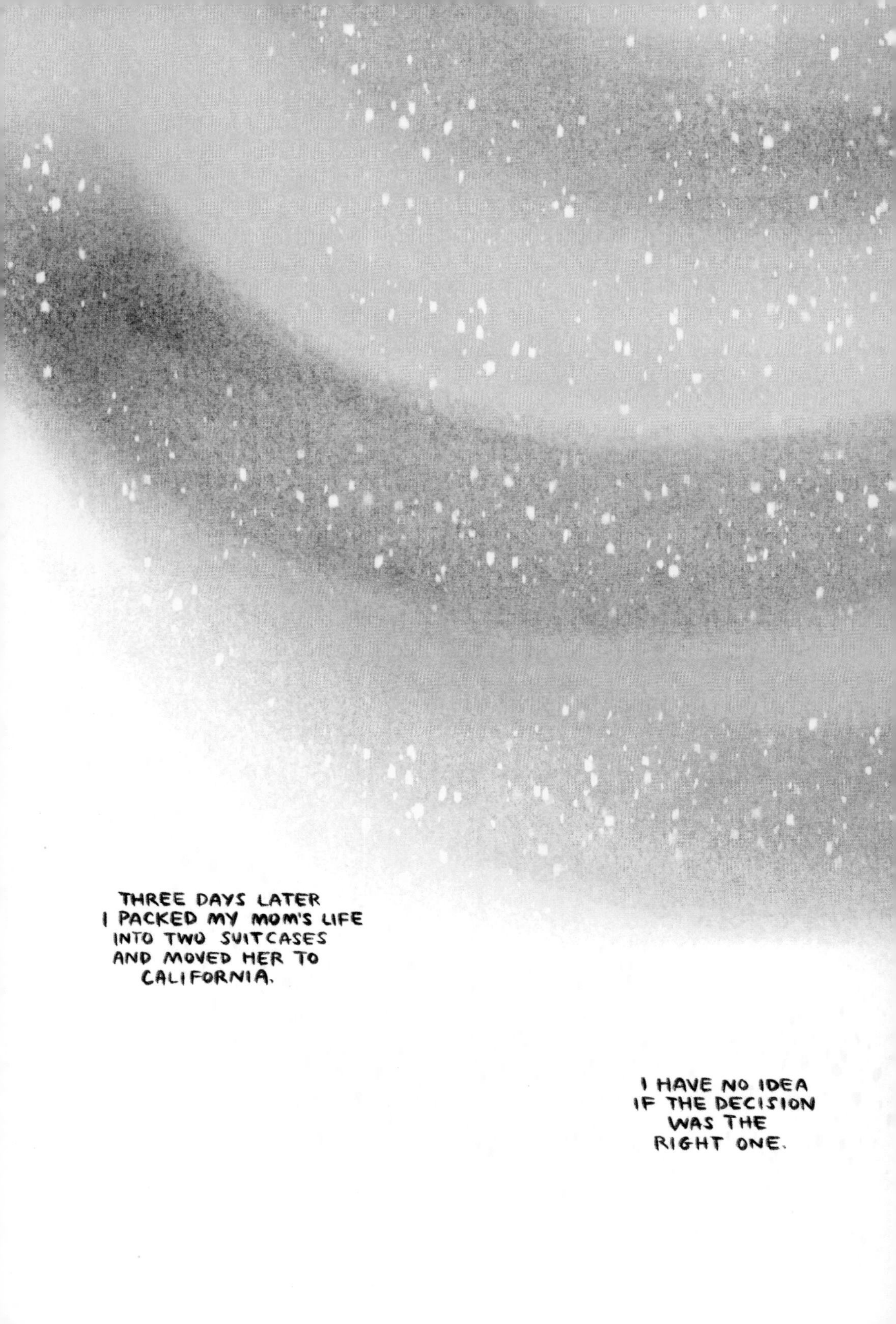
THREE DAYS LATER I PACKED MY MOM'S LIFE INTO TWO SUITCASES AND MOVED HER TO CALIFORNIA.
I HAVE NO IDEA IF THE DECISION WAS THE RIGHT ONE.

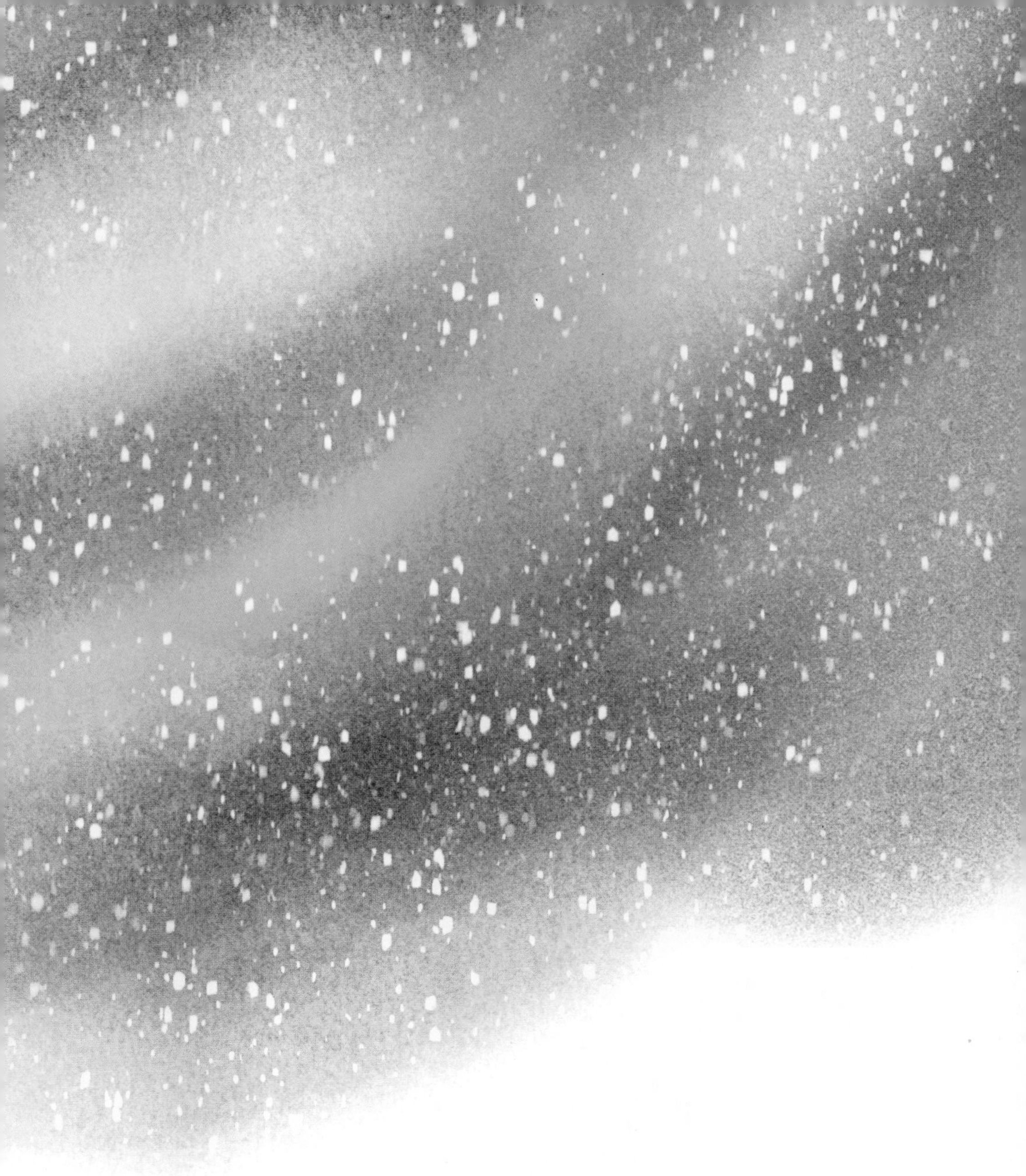

SHE NEVER WENT
HOME AGAIN.

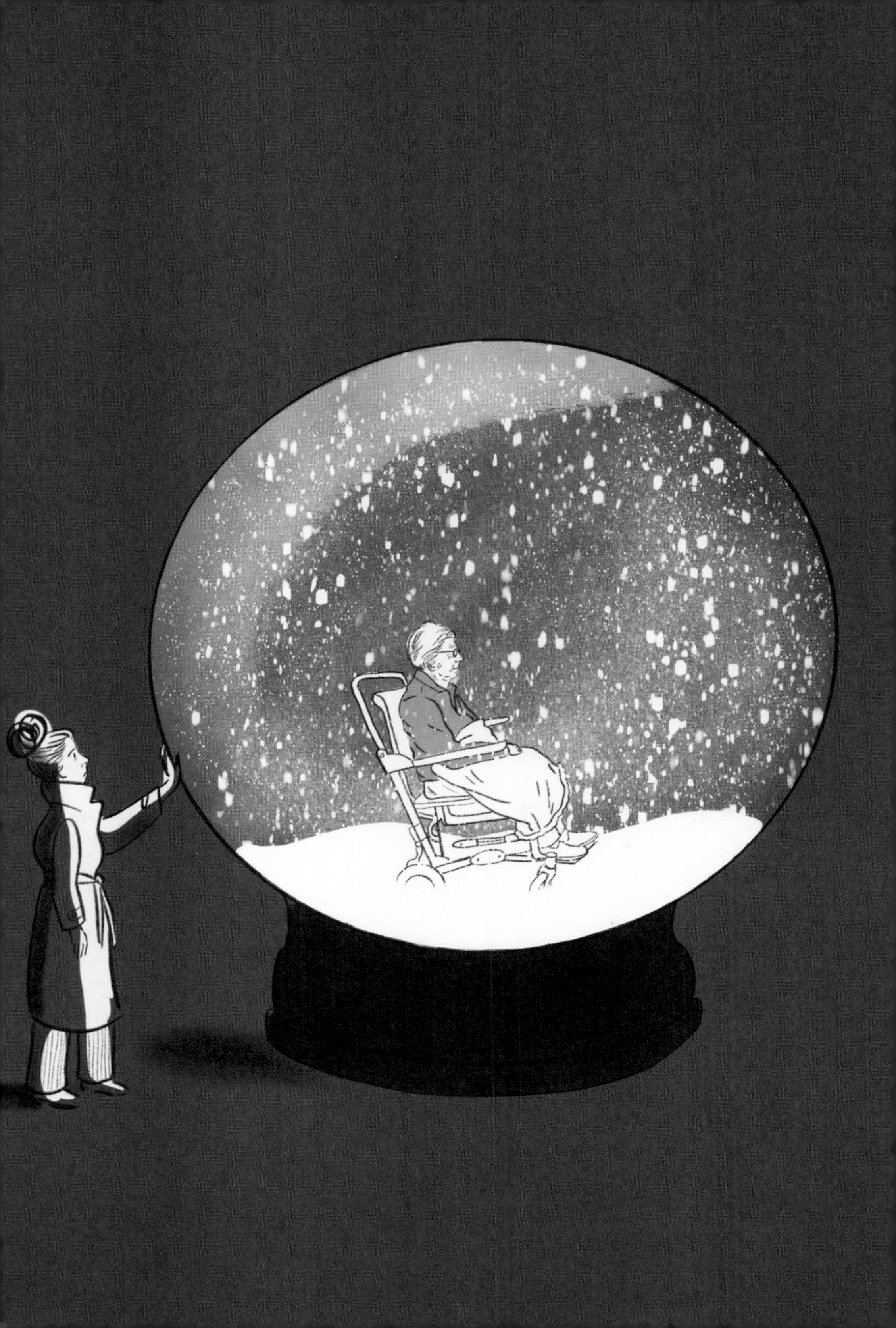

American-born cartoonist and illustrator **Denise Dorrance** worked in magazines in New York for twelve years (including at *Cosmopolitan* under Helen Gurley Brown) before moving to London in 1993. Her cartoons have run for decades in many publications, including the *Mail on Sunday (UK)*. *Polar Vortex* is her first graphic memoir. In the UK, it was short-listed for the Myriad First Graphic Novel competition and the winner of the LDComics Rosalind B. Penfold Prize.

Much love and huge thanks to
these dear people for their
notable contributions —

Aurea Carpenter + Rebecca Nicolson
at New River — your enthusiasm
and generous spirit made this possible.
And thanks to Charlotte Thompson
for introducing us.

Also, thanks to Stephanie Cabot at
Susannah Lea — and to Sarah Blake
for connecting us.

Winning the Rosalind B. Penfold Prize
from LDComics, when the book was in
development, was a huge injection
of confidence. Thank you Corinne
Pearlman + Nicola Streeten.

The book is designed by Alex Smith,
you made my scribbles beautiful.

I'm grateful to family + friends
who cheered me on, but
Miranda Cowley Heller, Dan Franklin,
Gillian Johnson, Rebecca Frayn,
Kim Evans, Yasmina Keynes and
Simon Crocker were helpful
beyond words.

But my heart is filled with
gratitude to my husband Paul
and son Louis, whose ideas,
edits + inexhaustible support
crucially helped shape this
book. their names really
should appear alongside
mine on the cover.

ORIGINALLY PUBLISHED IN THE UNITED KINGDOM BY NEW RIVER BOOKS. FIRST PUBLISHED IN NORTH AMERICA IN REVISED FORM BY THE EXPERIMENT, LLC.

THE EXPERIMENT, LLC
220 EAST 23RD STREET, SUITE 600
NEW YORK, NY 10010-4658
THEEXPERIMENTPUBLISHING.COM

LIBRARY OF CONGRESS CATALOGING-IN-PUBLICATION DATA AVAILABLE UPON REQUEST

ISBN 978-1-61519-905-1
EBOOK ISBN 978-1-61519-946-4

COVER DESIGN BY BETH BUGLER
TEXT DESIGN BY SMITH & GILMOUR
AUTHOR PHOTOGRAPH BY PAUL YULE

MANUFACTURED IN CHINA

FIRST PRINTING MARCH 2024
10 9 8 7 6 5 4 3 2 1

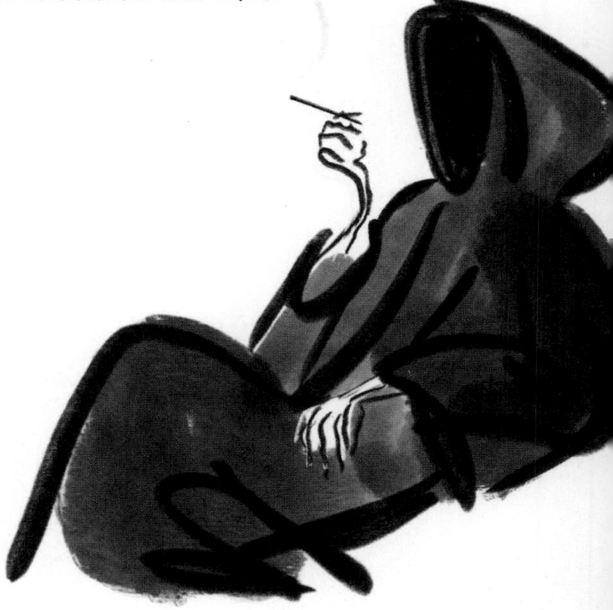